The Gigantic Book
of
Pirate Stories

Edited and Introduced by

Steve Brennan

Skyhorse Publishing

Library of Congress Cataloging-in-Publication Data

The gigantic book of pirate stories / edited and Introduced by Stephen
Vincent Brennan.
    p. cm.
 ISBN-13: 978-1-60239-156-7 (hardcover : alk. paper)
 ISBN-10: 1-60239-156-4 (hardcover : alk. paper)
 1. Pirates—History. 2. Pirates—Fiction. I. Brennan, Stephen Vincent.

G535.G49 2007
910.4'5—dc22

                              2007031822

10 9 8 7 6 5 4 3 2 1

Printed in the United States of America

In many cases the decks, by reason of the fancied security afforded by the harbor, would be deserted, and, taking advantage of this opportunity, the attacking party quickly leap over the sides and, under the noiselessly given commands of their captain, creep stealthily to the hatchways, cautiously taking their positions so that no miscalculations might frustrate their designs. And so, invading below decks, with weapons poised and every fibre on the alert, the concerted attack upon the sleeping victims would be given. With one fell swoop, and with the savagery born of their nefarious undertaking, the crew would be ruthlessly butchered, some few, perhaps, escaping in the general skirmish and fleeing up the gangway, only to be struck down by the villain on guard. For the present we will close our eyes to the awful picture of torture and murder here enacted, to revert to it upon a subsequent occasion.

With the crew slain, gagged or in chains, with all possible resistance overcome, the coming of the day was awaited. And as the first faint streaks of gray broke in upon the darkness of the night and the harbingers of the dawn sent their shafts athwart the horizon, the ship rode proudly at her anchor, silently and stately, giving no indication of the carnage of the night. The creaking of the chain around the capstan was but the mariners' music to sing the glory of the voyage to be begun, and so, without creating the least suspicion in the vessels lying round about, the captors brought their prize abreast their old vessel, transferred their stock of provisions and merchandise, if any, to the newly captured vessel, and, thus prepared, sailed grandly out of the harbor. When once again the breath of the ocean bellied their sails and sped them on to the unknown argosy, the dead, vanquished crew was rudely cast into the sea, without the semblance of respect for the dead, the decks thoroughly scrubbed, the scuppers flushed, the inventory prepared, and so, once again, the course was set for a port in which to dispose of their cargo. The argus-eyed lookout stationed far up in the foremast scanned every point of the far-reaching horizon, signalling to his mates the appearance of a spar against the heavens. Then, with course changed and wheel set, and sped on by conspiring winds, they bore down upon the unfortunate vessel, displaying at the proper moment the ominous and fateful black flag and its ghastly emblem of skull and cross-bones.

Thus, for months perhaps, the fitful winds and steady currents carried them hither and thither, ever alert, ever ready for combat and plunder. With guns primed and powder-horn stocked, these plunderers roamed the trackless sea, at times with impatience and drooping hopes, until the sight of a large, heavily riding merchantmen sent their blood a-leaping and transformed the deck into a scene of feverish activity. If we recall the peaceful errand of the merchantmen and reflect that their armature was little calculated to cope with the war-waging outlaws, it is quite apparent how gross the inequality of the struggle must necessarily be. While most of the merchantmen carried defensive armament, the unpractised, unskilled crew made the guns in their hands little more than ineffective. As the pirate ship approached, she displayed the same flag flying from the stern of the merchantman; and with the crew hidden below decks, in order not to betray their purpose, the vessels approached sufficiently close to enable the pirates to fire a broadside into the unsuspecting vessel and demand immediate surrender. At times a vessel, by reason of its superiority, would succeed in outsailing the pirates, but frequently the result was most disastrous. Often a stout-hearted merchantman, seeing that capture was inevitable, would offer battle in desperation, firing volley after volley of stone shot, the pirates, stubborn, furious, tenacious, fighting with all the ferocity their natures were capable of, resulting, after a decisive contest, in the lowering of the merchantman flag in disgrace and humiliation. With the lowering of the sails as an indication of surrender, the pirates sent out several boats with armed men, under the command of a chosen leader, who at once placed the captain under arrest and demanded the ship's papers under pain of death. This request was usually, though unwillingly, acceded to. The old vessel was thereupon dismantled, the captured boat refitted, and, burning the hull of the forsaken vessel, the pirates once more set sail, with the imprisoned captain and crew in chains cast into the dark, foul hold of the ship. Immunity was sometimes granted the captives upon their taking the oath of allegiance to the piratical horde. Can we not imagine how the intense anguish and unendurable torture finally forced from the unwilling lips the fearful avowal of allegiance?

We can plainly observe the purpose of the pirates in endeavoring to capture a large, powerful, and speedy vessel, for that was the only safeguard of their barbarous trade. They readily recognized that success and security depended solely upon speed to overtake a fleeing ship or to escape a powerful adversary. Their motto, "He who fights and runs away may live to fight another day," was in reality the only literature the bold and adventurous pirate would comprehend or accept. Therefore, well equipped in a stanch, trim vessel, with the lockers filled, the magazines stocked, the guns aimed and ready for action, they were brave enough to combat even a man-of-war. The books are replete with the thrilling accounts of engagements and set battles waged between pirates and resisting armed merchantmen, resulting completely in victory for the black flag which so defiantly floated from the mizzenmast. The gradual progress and growth of the energetic sea-robbers, from the looting of vessels riding peacefully at anchor in the harbors to the management of large and seaworthy craft, permitted them to undertake long and seemingly endless cruises, the most daring of which being undertaken, no doubt, by that notorious chieftain, Captain Nathaniel North, who cruised from Newfoundland to the West Indies, then across the Southern Atlantic to the Cape of Good Hope, thence via Mozambique to the Indian Ocean, and northward to the Red Sea, traversing the same track to the Arabian Sea and East Indies—a voyage of 28,670 miles, the toy of the monsoon, the victim of the typhoon, and the sport of the trade-winds in the many latitudes. History has reserved a rather infamous niche for such freebooters as Thomas Howard, Captain Misson, Captain Fly, and Captain Kidd, whose voyages and exploits have given themes to the historian, the narrator, and the novelist. It was during these long cruises that the coast towns suffered through the depredations, plundering, and pillage, and the inhabitants put in constant fear of these sudden and vicious onslaughts.

Not infrequently the pirates selected some desolate locality in which to bury their treasures and store their stolen goods, generally building a "village" inland, well hidden in the foliage of the forests or tropical shrubbery, and perhaps inaccessible save through the devious paths cunningly planned to secure immunity from attack. These natural defences were supplemented with a series of forts as a further protection from the incursions of the natives. The internecine wars so fiercely waged by the inhabitants of the African East Coast frequently brought the vanquished to these "villages" to secure protection—a safety usually given in exchange for practical slavery in tilling the ground and cultivating crops.

From time almost immemorial the word *pirate* has been synonymous with all that is villainous, bloodthirsty, and cruel, and capture by a gang of these assassins meant indescribable torture and suffering, and we will devote a few moments to a consideration of these awful scenes; the sudden attacks, the vain attempts at flight, the desperate hand-to-hand struggles for life, mingled with the brutal yells, interspersed with the piteous cries for mercy, followed by the horrible silence which finally settles over the slippery decks, and the gruesome spectacle of the dreadful vandalism as the murderers proceed to strip their victims.

Generally, after a successful attack, the captain of the unfortunate vessel would be placed in chains and questioned as to the cargo and treasures of his ship. A cutlass held menacingly over him indicated the danger of untruth, and frequently a savage gash brought a stubborn and silent captain to submission. Inquisitorial tortures, unrelieved by any mock civility, were continued to extract further confessions from the pain-racked prisoners. Devices born only of a devilish instinct and fiendish delight suggested all forms of suffering, and so the captain was frequently tied to the ship's pump and surrounded with burning combustibles; or, fastened to the deck, surrounded with gunpowder, which they ignited; or his limbs were severed from his body and his flesh prodded with the points of the cutlass, the fiendish pirates forming a circle around him for this inhuman "sport."

Despite these awful tortures, confessions were often suppressed, in the hope that the pirates would allow the vessel to proceed on its way (as was sometimes the case), and thus a part of the treasures be saved. But all hope of succor or consideration at the hands of these murderers was idle. Unsatisfied with the mere acquisition of booty, these human devils, devoid of the last spark of compassion, would mete out to each member of the crew and the passengers the most unheard-of tortures which human depravity could invent, for the amusement of the captors. Some were tied to a windlass and pelted into insensibility, or perhaps more charitable death. Others were lashed with ropes and cast, almost dead, into the sea; or, spiked hand and foot to the deck, were exposed mercilessly to the hot rays of the sun until the features were distorted into unrecognizability; some were placed before a gun and thus decapitated, while others were tied back to back and thrown into the waters. In fact, so low were these villainous wretches in their degradation that only the most cruel and cunningly devised torture could satiate their blood-thirsty cravings—human hyenas, who found rest only in the pains and shrieks of other mortals. By far the most favorite pastime was to make the victim "walk the plank" or hang him to the yardarm—a suggestion of the retribution suffered by the pirates when captured. No word picture can present the awful orgies indulged in by these social outcasts, who continued their carnage, assault, and abuse until the last victim had succumbed. Then, directing their attention to the ship, it was quietly dismantled, set adrift, or frequently burned to the water's edge, allowing the hull to float about, a rudderless derelict.

One must not form the impression, however, that this reckless lawlessness was attended with insubordination or lack of discipline. On the contrary, they were rigorously governed by an iron hand and by the unwritten "code of honor." A pirate entered upon "the account" (a term meaning piracy) by taking the oath of fealty to the cause, abjuring all social ties, pledging himself never to desert his ship or defraud his comrades or steal anything belonging to his fellows. Having thus bound him by an oath firm and dreadful in its malediction upon any violation of its terms, the organization is completed by the selection of a captain, who, usually, is the strongest, bravest, and most desperate of them all, well calculated to keep the crew in subjection. Mutiny and the spirit of insubordination frequently raised its ominous growl, to be quelled only by the fearlessness of the captain and his ability to keep his men in abject fear of his commands. It held the men in the thralls of hypnotism, and in its efficaciousness depended the safety of the captain and his "loyal" adherents. With some crews the title *Captain* did not convey autocratic power nor dictatorial prerogatives, his power to command absolutely being confined only to times of combat. A usurpation of power frequently brought death as a deterrent to any aspiring successor. In those cases where the captain was not recognized as the sole ruler, each man had a vote in affairs of moment, and had an undivided interest and title in all booty.

It can readily be understood how valueless the cast-iron oath of the pirate must be when occasion makes its rejection convenient, and thus apparent dissatisfaction with the captain or with his commands have frequently caused those secret plottings below decks, resulting in open revolt or mutiny:—pirate against pirate, brute force matched against brute force for power and supremacy. The severest punishment to a member of the crew for thieving from a fellow-pirate was marooning—slitting the ears and nose and depositing the offender upon some desolate island or lonely shore with but few provisions and limited ammunition. Life was little prized, for death had no terrors, and life beyond this world entered not into their calculations. Their fearlessness and courage was splendidly exampled when Captain Teach, alias Black Beard, appeared off Charleston in the year 1717 and sent word to the Governor of the colony to send out to him at once a certain number of medicine chests, in failure of which the port would be blockaded by his single vessel, and all persons on board in-going and out-going ships killed and their heads sent to the Governor as proof of the execution of the threat. He also threatened to set all ships on fire. It illustrates clearly in what dread these sea marauders were held in those times, when we learn that the Governor immediately complied with the demands and the embargo was raised. It is recorded that in moments of defeat pirates voluntarily have set fire to their powder magazines and thus were blown to destruction rather than plead for mercy. During long cruises, when no ships upon the horizon line varied the monotony of the daily routine, pastimes were invented, each one out-rivalling the other in sheer wickedness Captain Teach considered it rare sport to lock his men in the ship's hold and then set sulphur afire to ascertain how long they could withstand asphyxiation. Yet his greatest "bravery" was displayed (and herein he developed commendable Spartan fortitude) when he married fourteen times with a fearlessness highly worthy of a better purpose! His wickedness was as great as his fearlessness was unbounded, but wickedness was voted manly in a pirate and assured the esteem and admiration of his comrades.

With the progression of events and the growth of commerce, piracy waned, and gradually the black flag which had so long swept the Spanish Main was furled and drooped into the sea over which it had so long defiantly floated. The European governments made many futile attempts to check the rapid development of the unlawful enterprise, and many expeditions were successful, resulting in the trial, condemnation, and execution of the outlaws on land.

In England a proclamation of amnesty was issued, insuring freedom and rights of citizenship to all who renounced their calling—a privilege which many accepted, only to find their blood fire and yearn for the wild, aimless, and adventurous roaming on the seas, which gradually drew them back to their calling and away from the restraints of civilization. The capture of a pirate meant death, and, as no practicable defence was available, the prisoners usually entrenched themselves behind the plea that they were kidnapped or shanghaied and were compelled to enter into piracy for the preservation of their lives. But piracy, with its harrowing gruesomeness, its boldness and daring, its romance and adventure, its plunder and murder, its conflicts and reprisals, is a spectre of the past, and now is chiefly confined to the rivers and harbors of the Far East and Northern Africa. It has lost the glamor and enchanting, romantic atmosphere which pervaded the career of Captain Kidd and made him the worshipped hero of every school-boy, or which inspired the pen of a Scott, of an Edgar Allan Poe or Frank R. Stockton, or put the charm to the tales of W. Clark Russell, for pirates and piracy are now dead, and live ingloriously only in the pages of chronicling history.

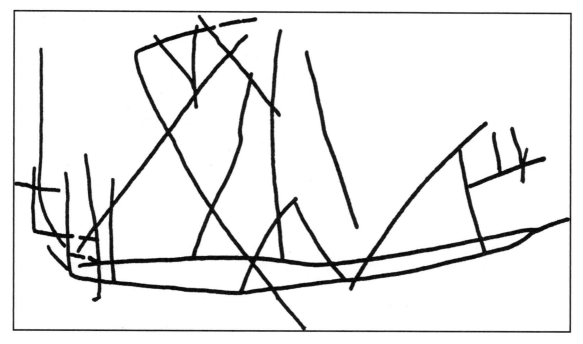

Piracy in the Ancient World

HENRY ORMEROD

Throughout its history the Mediterranean has witnessed a constant struggle between the civilised peoples dwelling on its coasts and the barbarians, between the peaceful trader using its highways and the pirate who infested the routes that he must follow. At different stages of their history most of the maritime peoples have belonged now to one class and now to the other. From the time when men first went down to the sea in ships, piracy and robbery have been regarded only as one of the means of livelihood that the sea offered. The earliest literature of Greece shows us the Homeric pirate pursuing a mode of life at sea almost identical with that of the Frankish corsairs; in our records of early Crete we can see the first attempts of a civilised state to cope with the evils of piracy and protect its sea-borne commerce. Only at rare intervals has a complete suppression been achieved. Perhaps the only times when the whole Mediterranean area has been free have been during the early centuries of the Roman empire and in our own day. The Romans succeeded by the disarmament of the barbarian communities, and still more by the spread of civilisation. In our own times an organised sea-police and the introduction of steam, for the time at any rate, have proved too strong for the Mediterranean pirate. But it is worth remembering that as late as the Crimean war, British ships were patrolling the Cyclades on the look-out for pirate-craft, one of which had contrived to rob a boat in sight of the harbour of Syra. If we remember that piracy was for centuries a normal feature of Mediterranean life, it will be realised how great has been the influence which it exercised on the life of the ancient world.

The coasts of the Mediterranean are peculiarly favourable to the development of piracy. Much of the shore line is rocky and barren, and unable to support a large population. We shall from time to time have to refer to particular localities, such as the Cilician, Ligurian and Illyrian coasts, where piracy was endemic. When the inhabitants took to the sea, navigation came easily to them on the land-locked bays and creeks of their native shore. By land, the poverty of the soil had forced them to become hunters and brigands rather than agriculturalists; the same pursuits were followed on the sea.

In addition to the natural allurements which drew the robber tribes to the sea, the features of Mediterranean lands are such as to make the pirate's business a particularly profitable one. We may leave aside for the moment the economic conditions which promoted piracy, and consider only the geographical. The structure of most Mediterranean countries has decreed that the principal lines of communication should be by sea, and that the bulk of commerce should be carried by the same routes. The interposition of mountain barriers renders the land routes difficult and dangerous; navigable rivers are few. But the place of roads and rivers as a means of internal communication is largely taken in Greece and western Asia Minor by deep arms of the sea running far inland, while islands lying off the coast provide a natural breakwater and shelter for small coasting vessels. But if the sea invites, it also imposes certain limitations. In early days of navigation the shipper is forced to hug the shores, creeping round the coasts, often becalmed or driven back by contrary winds, and lying-to for the night. If he endeavours to cross the sea, he is compelled to follow fixed routes, by which alone he can keep in sight of land, threading his way between islands and following well-known channels. There can be little concealment of his movements; the prevailing winds at certain seasons of the year tend to drive commerce in definite directions. The corsair knows this and like the Cretan in Homer will make use of the favourable five days' passage from Crete to raid the Egyptian coast, or way-lay the merchantmen who are following the same route. The French traveller D'Arvieux, in 1658, watched a corsair lying in wait for the merchantmen on their return journey from Egypt. One of the most illuminating descriptions of the corsair's routine that I know is the account given by the Englishman Roberts, who was wrecked at Nio (Ios) in 1692, captured by a "crusal," and compelled to serve as gunner on board. He tells us that the corsairs usually wintered at Paros, Antiparos, Melos and Ios from the middle of December to the beginning of March:

And then they go for the Furnoes, and lie there under the high Land hid, having a watch on the Hill with a little Flag, whereby they make a Signal, if they see any Sail: they slip out and lie athwart the Boak of Samos, and take their Prize; They lie in the same nature under Necaria, and Gadronise, and Leppiso in the Spring, and forepart of the Summer; Then for the middle of the Summer, they ply on the Coast of Cyprus; and if they hear the least noise of any Algerines and Grand Turks ships at Rhodes, away they scour for the Coast of Alexandria and Damiata, being shole Water, well knowing the Turks will not follow them thither. The latter part of the Summer they come stealing on the Coast of Syria, where they do most mischief with their Feleucca, which commonly Rows with 12 Oars, and carries 6 Sitters: For at Night they leave the Ship, and get under the shoar before Day, and go ashoar, where they way-lay the Turks ... From hence towards the Autumn they come lurking in about the Islands, to and fro about the Boakes again, until they put in also to lie up in the Winter.

During the winter, navigation was practically at an end; with it the pirate's business was suspended and the opportunity taken to refit. It is only rarely that we hear of them keeping the sea during the winter. The seamanship of the Cilician pirates allowed it, and the Governor of Zante, in 1603, complains of the British pirates, who were seriously molesting Venetian commerce, that "they keep the sea even in midwinter and in the roughest weather thanks to the handiness of their ships and the skill of their mariners." But the ordinary practice was a return to harbour or to a hidden base among the islands, where the pirate could be free from molestation. When the sailing season begins, there are many sheltered creeks among the islands, where a pirate vessel can lie hid and pounce upon an unsuspecting merchantman labouring up the channel.

The particular hunting-ground which Roberts' friends patronised was chosen in order to catch coasting vessels coming from the south of Asia Minor, or those working through the Cyclades from the mainland of Greece, and sheltering from the north wind under the lee of Icaria and Samos on their voyage to the Ionian coast. This, it will be remembered, was the route followed by the Peloponnesian squadron in 427 B.C. Strabo describes the neighbouring Tragia, the Gadronise of Roberts, as infested with pirates. A little to the south-east Julius Caesar was caught at Pharmacussa. Further to the north, a passage of Arrian describes how Memnon, in the war with Alexander, posted a part of his fleet at the Sigrium promontory in Lesbos to catch the merchant vessels coming from Chios, Geraestos, and Malea. On the more direct route to the Hellespont the islands of Scyros and Halonnesos had a bad reputation and, according to tradition, the "Pelasgian" natives of Lemnos carried their cruises as far as the coast of Attica.

The Gallipoli peninsula itself was full of pirates after the Persian wars, and was a constant source of danger in the fourth century.

One of the most dangerous passages was the Cythera channel. It was a favourite hunting-ground of submarines during the late war, and at all times has had a bad reputation. Thévenot describes the passage between Cerigo (Cythera) and the mainland as very much quicker than between Cerigo and Cerigotto. For this reason a Venetian *galeace* was stationed near Cerigo to guard the channel. His compatriot and contemporary, D'Arvieux, was chased by a suspicious vessel when making the passage. A storm of wind nearly carried him on to the point of Cerigo. Here the dangers of shipwreck were increased by the nearness of the Mainotes. Small mercy was shown to their captives, Christians being sold to the Turks and Turks to Christians. Dr. Covell describes the capture of some of the crew of his ship who had landed on the island of Elaphonisi, and were sold to the Turkish galleys. "These miscreant wretches lye constantly watching upon the rocks and mountains, not so much to secure themselves from the injuries of the pirates as themselves to thieve and rob whom they catch." It is in accord with the general principles of Mediterranean piracy to find that the Mainotes soon advanced from the stage of kidnappers and wreckers to that of genuine pirates. Beaufort, among others, states that there was a "regularly organised system of absolute and general piracy among them."

It was therefore not only the risks of storm that gave rise to the proverb "Round Malea and forget your home"; the risks from pirates in the Cythera channel were not less in antiquity than in the seventeenth and eighteenth centuries. At the time of the Peloponnesian war, the Spartans maintained a garrison in the island to prevent its occupation by pirates, and to give security to merchantmen coming from Libya and Egypt. At an earlier date, Chilon the wise had said that it would be better for Sparta that Cythera should be sunk in the sea. We shall find Malea haunted by Cretan, Illyrian, and Laconian pirates in the days of Nabis.

The small islands and rocks with which the Mediterranean is studded have always been a favourite haunt of the pirate, whether as a lurking-ground to catch merchantmen, or as a base for plundering the opposite mainland. In the West the Massaliotes were driven to occupy the Stoichades, to the East of their town. With these in pirate hands the land-route from Marseilles to Antipolis could be rendered as unsafe as a voyage along the coast. In the Black Sea an inscription of imperial date records the occupation of the island of Leuce at the mouth of the Danube by pirates. Their object, no doubt, was to catch the traffic as it issued from the Danube. The corresponding station in the Mediterranean would be at the mouth of a gulf. Such islands were Myonnesos at the entrance to the Malian Gulf, and Sciathos among the northern Sporades, through which ships northward bound from the Euripos and from the Malian and Pagasaean gulfs would pass, and a rich booty be taken from the traffic coming southward from Thessalonica and the Thermaic gulf. The Sporades are thus described by a traveller at the beginning of the last century:

> The group of isles at the entrance of the gulph of Salonica has been a principal resort of pirates, partly from the number of vessels passing this way; partly from the facility with which they can recruit their numbers among the Albanians who come down upon the coast ... In this unlawful vocation large row boats are chiefly employed; they are crowded with men, armed with pistols and cutlasses, who usually attempt to board the vessels on which their attack is made. On this coast the great number of the pirates are said to be native Albanians ... It must be remarked that on this side the Grecian continent every desperado is currently called an Albanian. In the Archipelago the pirates derive peculiar advantages from the isles which crowd its surface, some of them uninhabited, others having a population easily made subservient to schemes of illegal plunder.

The same writer alludes to the pirates of Meganisi on the western shore of Greece and to the protection given to them by the authorities of Santa Maura before the British occupation. They were largely recruited from the brigands expelled from the mainland by Ali Pasha of Janina. Dodwell also says that the canal of Santa Maura was looked upon as one of the most dangerous places for pirates, who "conceal themselves among the rocks and islands with which the canal is studded, and if they find themselves in danger, escape in a few minutes either to Leucadia or to the coast of Acarnania." The predecessors of these rascals in heroic days were the Taphians, the typical pirates of the *Odyssey*, who are located by later writers in these islands. They acted as carriers and slave-merchants to the inhabitants of the Ionian islands, with the authorities of which they cultivated good relations, the raids of which we hear being directed elsewhere—against Epiros, Sidon, and Mycenae. For the last exploit they and the Teleboans, who are perhaps identical with the Taphians, were punished by Amphitryon. Mentes' followers in the *Odyssey* were doubtless as mixed as the Meganisi pirates at the beginning of the last century, and made as good a thing out of the traffic which followed this coast.

When sailing vessels hugged the shore, an equal danger was presented by promontories. The cowardly man in Theophrastus is ridiculed for thinking every promontory at sea a pirate galley, but it was always possible that one was lurking there, to catch the merchantman endeavouring to round it. The emperor Julian compares the Cynics to brigands and those who occupy promontories to damage voyagers. D'Arvieux speaks with satisfaction of doubling Cape Spartivento without seeing any of the corsairs who usually haunted it. Cockerell had pointed out to him from Aegina the pirate boats lying off Sunium, one of their favourite haunts. We have already examined Memnon's ambush at Cape Sigrium. One of the best examples from antiquity is the advice given by the Milesians to the Peloponnesian privateers to lie off the Triopian promontory in order to catch the Athenian merchantmen on the voyage from Egypt.

From many of the illustrations which have been given it will have been realised that much of the work in more recent times was done close in shore and with small craft. The same was undoubtedly the case in antiquity. Frequently the pirate-boats were quite small, only large enough to hold the number of ruffians required to surprise the crew of a merchantman lying-to for the night, or off their guard. The boats used by the Megarian privateers for this purpose in the Peloponnesian war were small enough to be placed on a wagon. In the Black Sea we hear of a special kind of boat, the *camara* of the Caucasian coasts, capable of holding twenty-five or thirty men, which was so light that it could easily be lifted from the water and hidden in the scrub. In these craft the pirates would attack merchantmen at sea, or sail to raid the neighbouring coasts, where the boats were left in the marshes, while the men wandered through the district in search of prey. The sea-going ships of the Ligurian pirates are spoken of as wretched affairs, cheaper than rafts. The inhabitants of the Baleares kept watch from the rocks for the approach of foreign vessels, and then assailed them with a crowd of rafts. The ease with which such craft could be removed from the water and hidden made the task of suppression a peculiarly difficult one in certain localities. The authorities in the East Indies were faced with a similar difficulty in dealing with the Dyaks of Borneo. On an alarm, the pirates would sink or hide their boats in creeks and rivers, and it was only by intercepting the whole fleet on its return from a plundering expedition that Rajah Brooke was able to deal with them.

A shallow draught was, as we saw from Roberts' account, a necessity in the pirate boat. The warships, which the Cilicians are said to have built towards the end of their career, were unusual, and date from the time when the pirates were organised by Mithradates almost as a part of his regular navy. Normally, a light build was preferred, as it gave the speed necessary both in attack and in flight. When pursued by the heavier warships of the maritime powers, the pirate could easily escape by entering shoal waters, or if forced ashore could often save his ship by means of a portage. Spratt recounts the loss of the British frigate *Cambrian* in 1829, while operating against pirate shipping inside Grabusa harbour off Crete, on a reef running across the harbour like a mole.

The pirate boat is nearly always distinguished from the warship. As a rule, however, we do not find that the pirates made use of any particular rig or build. Probably, in most cases, the would-be pirate was content with the first boat that came to hand by theft or purchase. Some types of craft are native to, or named after particular communities, such as the *samaina* of Samos; the *lembus*, *pristis* and *liburna* were originated or developed among the tribes of the Illyrian coasts. But the latter designs were widely imitated by the shipbuilders of the naval powers, and were much employed in the regular navies from the third century onwards. Even the two vessels which in Hellenistic and Roman times are most closely associated with the pirates, the *hemiolia* and *myoparo*, were widely used by others. The *hemiolia* was employed by Alexander for river work, by Philip V of Macedon, and in the Roman fleets. As no ancient representation of it has survived we are uncertain as to its exact design and rig; it is usually held that it possessed one complete and one half-bank of rowers, the upper bank being reduced to give room for the fighting men. It is clear, however, that both the *hemioliae* and the *myoparones* used by the Cilicians were smaller than the two-banked vessels and triremes with which they were beginning to replace them. The *myoparo* was broader than the regular warship in proportion to its length, and, we may assume, more suitable for stowing loot. Both vessels were sea-going ships, the *myoparo*, at any rate, possessing a mast and sails, as well as oars.

For their in-shore work at Pylos the Messenian privateers were using a thirty-oared vessel and a *celes*, a small vessel built for speed, and used as a despatch-boat with the Greek navies. Although the *celes* is not often mentioned in connection with pirates, it is probable that its speed and size made it a convenient craft for this kind of work.

It goes without saying that the seamanship of the pirates was of the highest order. Their safety, as well as their success, depended on it as well as on a thorough knowledge of the coasts where they operated. When inexperienced landsmen took to piracy, their end was swift. In the Jewish wars with Rome a number of refugees seized Joppa, and building ships, endeavoured to plunder the trade route from Syria and Phoenicia to Egypt. When Vespasian sent to attack them, they fled on board their boats, but were soon caught by a squall (the *Melamboreion*), driven ashore, and destroyed.

So far, we have considered only one aspect of the pirate's activity, his attacks on ships, at sea or sheltering. There is a still more sinister side to his work, the plundering raids on shore and constant kidnappings of individuals. It was this that made him most feared and has had the greatest effect on Mediterranean life. When piracy was active, there could be little or no security for inhabitants of the coast; if ransom was not forthcoming for the victim, his inevitable lot was slavery.

The passage from Roberts has already indicated in what way this kidnapping was carried on. A small party would put into the shore at night and carry off anyone whom they met.

Certain localities were particularly dangerous. The difficult road along the coast from Megara to Corinth by the Scironian rocks bore in the seventeenth century the name of *Kake Skala*, from the frequency of the corsairs' visits. The Turks, in consequence, were afraid to use it. Though the robber Sciron in the Greek legend is a brigand rather than a pirate, the story may nevertheless have arisen from similar descents from the sea on travellers using this path. The lonely traveller carried off by pirates was a familiar figure in Greek story. "I was carried off by Taphian pirates as I was returning from the fields." "Did hostile men take you with their ships, as you were alone with the sheep or kine?" Normally a ransom would be accepted by the pirates. Julius Caesar was ransomed for the sum of fifty talents; Clodius on the other hand nursed a hatred against Ptolemy Auletes, because he had considered a subscription of two talents sufficient.

We have, unfortunately, little information as to how these matters were arranged in antiquity, and how the pirates were approached, but the transaction probably differed little from the scene attending the redemption of Stackelberg by his friend Haller. Stackelberg had been caught while crossing the gulf of Volo, and it fell to Haller to arrange the matter with the help of the Armenian Acob, who acted as intermediary. A sum of 60,000 piastres had been demanded: "The conference was opened by Acob with singular address: he represented himself as the captain of a privateer in those seas, assured the pirates that they were mistaken in supposing their prisoner was a man of fortune since he was merely an artist labouring for his bread, whose prospects they had injured by the destruction of his drawings; that if they rejected the offers he now made he should depart satisfied with having done his duty, and finally he represented to them that a Turkish man of war was on the coast, as really was the case, to the commander of which, if they continued obstinate, he should leave their punishment." Acob then offered 10,000 piastres, which the pirates refused. After an offer by Haller to take Stackelberg's place they retire, but are roused in the night by one of the pirates, offering to come down to 20,000 and finally 15,000 piastres. "Acob, however, conjecturing that they were in some alarm, remained steady to his former determination, which in the course of an hour brought the chief himself to their lodging, where the bargain was at last concluded for 10,000 piastres with an additional present of 1,000. A shake by the hand was the seal of this negotiation, as sacred and valid as the firman of the sultan." The ransom was paid next day by Haller in person. "Baron Stackelberg was then shaved by one of the gang, a ceremony which they never omit on these occasions, and handed over to his friends. They were all pressed very much to stay and partake of a roasted lamb and an entertainment about to be prepared. ... The robbers then wished them a good journey and expressed their hopes of capturing them again at some future time."

Dodwell, speaking of the pirates of Santa Maura, says that "one of the thieves takes a letter to the prisoner's friends demanding a certain sum for his liberty. If the sum demanded can be paid, a person accompanies the thief to the place appointed; and on his depositing the money, the prisoner is set at liberty. They never fail in their engagement when the sum is delivered; and the person who takes it risks nothing, as a deficiency of mutual confidence would ruin the trade."

In antiquity, the Black Sea pirates, according to Strabo, used to send word of their captures to the victim's friends and then took a ransom; the inhabitants of Bosporus not only provided them with an anchorage but also with the means of disposing of their plunder. The same was often the case in the Mediterranean, when control was lax. The Cilicians openly frequented the slave-market of Delos, and the people of Side in Pamphylia were in league with them, as were also the Phaselites in Lycia. The complicity of local authorities has, of course, been one of the pirate's chief advantages. The well-known inscription of Teos contains imprecations against magistrates who harbour pirates. The Venetian despatches are full of complaints against the Turkish authorities for abetting the English pirates. Frankish corsairs disposed of most of their booty through the so-called consuls. Doubtless a handsome profit was made both by consul and Turkish official, but frequently the authorities were compelled to come to terms in order to recover stolen goods.

In his kidnapping raids the pirate was quick to make use of the opportunities which chance might offer; one of the most favourable would be the celebration of a festival in the country or near the seashore, attended only by women or unarmed men. In Crete, Spratt heard the story of an event which was supposed to have happened some centuries earlier at the Chapel of St. Nikolas. When it was crowded with pilgrims on the eve of a *festa*, the fires lighted by the visitors were seen by a cruising corsair, who landed his crew, and stealing up to the sacred cave locked the door on the Christians. But the Saint showed a miraculous way of escape through the rock. Similar attempts were common in antiquity. Herodotus describes how the Pelasgians of Lemnos, "knowing well the festivals of the Athenians," lay in wait for the women celebrating the feast of Artemis at Brauron. An inscription of the second century B.C. tells of a descent made by pirates on the territory of the Ephesians and the capture of a number of persons from the shrine of Artemis Munychia. The Chian refugees after the battle of Lade were similarly thought by the Ephesians to be pirates come to carry off women on the occasion of the Thesmophoria, and were at once attacked and killed by the population.

Mistakes of this character were always liable to happen. In a story preserved by Apollodorus, Catreus, landing in Rhodes in search of his son, was mistaken for a pirate and killed, because his explanations could not be heard owing to the barking of the dogs. At sea, honest men were often mistaken for pirates. Peter Mundy, off Cape St. Vincent in 1608, nearly got into trouble through mistaking the King of Spain's fleet for "Turkish Pyrats," "there being notice of twenty-six saile lyeinge about the Straights mouth ... but God bee praised we parted friends." Conversely, the pirate would pose as an ordinary trader. In the seventeenth century, the Turkish authorities did not allow Christians to come up the gulf of Corinth, through fear that the corsairs of Malta would get in under the guise of merchant-ships loading currants at Corinth, and the Venetians in 1491 were compelled to increase the duty on the export of wines from Candia, because the pirates were in the habit of going there to load wines, and on their way back captured and plundered merchant-ships. The pirate posing as trader is as old as Homer; Strabo's account of the Corycian trick shows that when admitted to harbour the pirate could acquire much information that was useful to him.

Frequently, however, the pirate would boldly enter port without disguise and attack the shipping lying there. An inscription of Aegiale in Amorgos gives an account of an episode of this character. When he was strong enough for this, there was no need for petty subterfuges, nor were his attacks limited to the kidnapping of women or single travellers. The shores of the Mediterranean still bear traces of the effect which the continued descents of the pirates have wrought.

In his account of early conditions in Greece, Thucydides lays stress on the fact that the oldest inhabited sites, both on the mainland and in the islands, lay at a distance from the sea owing to the prevalence of piracy. It was only with the development of the Greek marine and increased wealth from trade, that more recent foundations could be planted on the shore and fortified by walls. Outside Greece the difference, which Thucydides notes between the ancient and more recent sites, has an important bearing on the history of Greek colonisation. The colonists found the best sites round the Mediterranean coast for the most part unoccupied at a time when they themselves had grown strong enough to occupy and fortify them. What Thucydides observes of primitive Greece has been the case all over the Mediterranean. Until the middle of the last century it was normal to find the principal towns or villages at some distance from the sea, and often hidden from it. The town was served by a *skala* on the shore, consisting only of one or two houses. In the Cornice, and also on the coast of Calabria, villages and ruined castles may be seen built high up on the cliffs to give protection against the Barbary pirates. Even on the Mainote coast of the Peloponnese the villages were built inland. The practice may best be illustrated from the Aegean islands. Thus in Leros, Nisyros and Telos, the principal villages are hidden from the sea and lie about half-a-mile from it. In Cos, the village of Antimachia was situated inside the circuit of an old castle of the Knights of Rhodes, on a hill some forty minutes from the sea. It was inhabited until the Crimean War, but the inhabitants have now dispersed to form villages round. In contrast to this modern dispersion, it is interesting to notice that the motive for the unification of Attica was said by an ancient writer to have been the "Carian" descents from the sea and Boeotian raids by land. The increased protection thereby offered was a strong motive for the inhabitants of a number of villages to combine and occupy a single fortified site. Thévenot records it of Scio, and says that all over the island groups of two or three villages had thus been united. In his day also there was only one village in Pholegandros, consisting of about 100 houses, three miles from the sea and approached by a rocky valley. There were no other houses in the island. The village, according to Tournefort, was of the usual semi-fortified type; there was no surrounding wall, but the houses on the outside of the town faced inwards and were joined to form a continuous blank wall at the exposed points. The more wealthy inhabitants might, in some cases, possess fortified houses of their own, but where no fortified refuges existed, the islands became uninhabitable. There was no fortress in Myconos in the seventeenth century and, consequently, no Turk would live there through fear of the Christian corsairs.

An interesting relic of one method of protection adopted by the Ancients survives in the numerous Towers, which are to be found in the Aegean islands. They are round, like the Naxian example, or square; some of them possessing a court-yard, others standing by themselves. The towers are placed for the most part in the more fertile parts of the islands at a distance from a town, and probably served as temporary refuges in the case of a raid, the towers sheltering the men and the courts the flocks. Some of them were perhaps intended to serve rather as forts to ward off attacks than as mere places of refuge.

Forts of this kind to serve as a protection against piratical descents were common in the Mediterranean at all times, when the dangers of piracy were great, and are frequently mentioned by later travellers. Thévenot, in the seventeenth century, says that in Scio, owing to the descents of corsairs, towers had been built round the island at intervals of two or three miles, each village sending two men as guards, who gave the signal when pirates approached. On the Syrian coast, D'Arvieux describes two towers, one square, the other round, connected by a curtain wall and mounted with small guns, which had been built to prevent the landing of the corsairs who infested this coast. In Crete, Spratt speaks of a small mediaeval fortress on a rocky eminence between Praesos and Rhokaka with the ruins of a large church in it, which was probably used by the inhabitants of villages on the slopes of Dicte when in danger from pirates.

Thévenot's description of the towers in Scio suggests that the ancient towers in the islands, in addition to being places of refuge, served also as signalling stations in the event of a raid. The signal would naturally be given by the smoke of beacons or by their flames at night. This was a common warning in later days. While Thévenot was sailing from Acre to Jaffa, his ship was suddenly fired on from a fort on shore, and flares were lit all along the coast. As he approached Jaffa, the ship was again fired on, and when admitted to harbour he found the inhabitants under arms and the women and children fled. The reason was that the boat had been mistaken for an Italian corsair operating off the coast, which had recently made a descent at Castel Pelegrino, between Acre and Jaffa. The flare was a recognised signal in antiquity in such emergencies. During Verres' government of Sicily, the news of the approach of the pirate squadron that had destroyed the guardships was flashed to Syracuse as much by the flames of the burning Sicilian vessels as by the fires of the regular beacons.

The fires which Odysseus saw burning in Ithaca were probably beacons of this kind. In this passage the explanation usually given is that the fires were the watchfires of the shepherds, or that it was a fire lighted to guide the ship in, or merely a fire on the farm "introduced into the picture to show how near they had come to their home." Spratt speaks of an Hellenic watch-tower called Palaeokastro, above Poro bay in Crete, on which the coast-guard in his day lit a signal fire at sunset, if any ship was in sight, as a warning against smugglers or pirates. This is obviously the case in the Homeric picture. Odysseus has been away for ten years, and his vessels are not recognised as Ithacan ships returning from Troy. As they draw near to the land, they are seen by the lookout men posted on the heights, and the warning beacons were fired.

To return to the towers—it is hardly to be expected that we should find much allusion to them in literature, but a series of inscriptions from the Southern Sporades contains interesting information regarding them, at a time when Rhodes was at war with certain of the Cretan states, and a Cretan attack on her allies and her dependants was expected.

The first inscription sums up the character of the war as waged by the Hierapytnians of Crete. The Cretans were noted corsairs, and their raids on this occasion differed little from those of the ordinary pirate. Information was received regarding an impending attack, which was met by the Rhodian admiral off the promontory Laceter in Cos (Antimachia Point), a Calymniote especially distinguishing himself in the action.

The second inscription records that a certain Diocles, having made arrangements with the commander of a Rhodian ship (or squadron) to land light-armed troops, held up the enemy at the *peripolion* and prevented them from doing damage to the countryside.

The third gives an account of the measures taken by Theucles, for the defence of the countryside. Realising that the most exposed districts of the island lacked protection, he arranged for the hurried fortification of the *peripolion*, so as to ensure the safety of the inhabitants of Halasarna with their wives and children; foreseeing also the enemy's attacks and the extent of the danger, he provided sufficient money for the walls to be put into a state of defence, but with an eye to the future arranged that the capital sum devoted to the *peripolia* should remain untouched. When the enemy attack was made on the city and countryside, he caused the country-folk to be released from service in the town garrison of Cos, thinking that they ought to remain in their own district to guard the forts. Without failing to make adequate provision for the defence of the capital, he displayed the greatest care for the *peripolion*, increasing the number of guards and their pay. When the country was overrun, he arranged for a covering force of cavalry and infantry, giving special instructions regarding the Halasarna district. As the weapons of the country-folk were inadequate or wanting, he also provided money for the proper arming of those entrusted with the duty of guarding the *peripolion*.

The fourth inscription narrates that Pamphilidas so encouraged his men that the enemies' attacks were beaten off, and "We in danger with our wives and children found safety," while the *peripolion* was held for the people.

This last inscription clearly deals with an attack on the *peripolion* itself, in which the natives of Potidaea had taken refuge with their families. The valour of Pamphilidas (or possibly his timely arrival with a relieving force) had driven off the enemy and saved the spot. In the second and third, it is not clear whether a *peripolion* already existed but had fallen into disrepair, or whether Theucles caused a new one to be built to meet the emergency. In any case, it was ready to receive the country-folk when the danger arrived. If the published reading of the second text can be trusted, it was not actually assaulted, the enemy attack being stopped at or below the *peripolion* with the help of troops landed from the fleet. It is clear that the *peripolia* on occasions of this kind, when the islands were attacked by enemies or marauders, served not only as refuges, but as strong-points, from which troops could operate to protect the countryside.

In the *peripolia* of these inscriptions we have something that exactly answers the purpose for which the towers in the islands were intended. The word is rightly explained by the editor as meaning not a "suburb" (a later use of the word) but a station for *peripoloi*, a guard-house. This exactly suits the character of the towers which we find in the Greek islands, the single towers being more in the nature of a fort, where only a few persons could take refuge, the towers with a surrounding or adjacent courtyard offering protection to a greater number. In some of the surviving Greek towers the courtyard does not surround the tower, but is adjacent to it. It cannot in such cases have been an outer line of defence to the tower itself, but only an additional place of refuge.

As the result of this general insecurity and continued harrying of the coasts, wide tracts of country passed out of cultivation. At the same time, the existence of fortified villages and strong-points inland gave a peculiar character to the pirates' descents, which may best be illustrated by a passage in the *Odyssey*:

> The wind bearing me from Ilios brought me to the Cicones, to Ismaros; there I sacked
> a city and slew the men, and taking from the city their wives and many possessions

we divided them, that no man for me might depart deprived of an equal share. Then, indeed, I ordered that we should fly with nimble foot, but they, fools that they were, obeyed not. But much wine was drunk, and many sheep they slew by the shore and shambling, crook-horned kine. Meantime Cicones going called unto Cicones, who were their neighbours, far more numerous and warlike, dwelling inland, knowing well to fight with men from chariots and on foot when need be. They came then, in number like the leaves and flowers in their season, in the morning. Then did an evil doom come upon us ill-fated.

The whole passage has been carefully examined by Bérard and illustrated with a wealth of quotation from the journals of travellers of the seventeenth century. He notes that the wide coastal plains of Thrace, equally with the lands of the Egyptian Delta, have always been the most exposed to the corsairs' raids. To his illustrations may be added what Polybius says about the exposed character of Elis and Messenia at the time of the Illyrian piracies: "The expedition began by making a descent on Elis and Messenia, lands which the Illyrians had always been in the habit of pillaging, because, owing to the extent of their seaboard and owing to the principal cities being in the interior, help against their raids was distant and slow in arriving; so that they could always overrun and plunder those countries unmolested."

The "city" which Odysseus and his companions sacked was therefore a small and unprotected site on the coast, which the captain was anxious to leave before the Cicones of the interior, "far more numerous and war like," could rally to the assault. To "flee with nimble foot" was the corsair's regular practice, as soon as the spoils lying ready to his hand had been collected. Muntaner thus describes a raid by Roger di Luria in Provence: "The pursuit lasted to within a league of Beziers, but it was vesper-time and the admiral feared that they would not be able to return to the galleys by daylight, and they were on the worst beach that there is, East or West." But Odysseus' men disobeyed the order to embark before night, and fell to carousing on the shore. The miseries of the corsair's life at sea, of which Roberts and Thévenot, who also was captured, give ample illustrations, were sufficient inducement to run the risk; much wine was drunk and cattle devoured, and in the morning the inhabitants, rallying from the interior, came down on them.

There are a few minor points in the description of this raid which Bérard remarks. He notes that here, as on other occasions, the spoils are equally divided among the crew, but contrasts the practice of the Franks, among whom the ordinary members of the crew got nothing. The difference, however, is only superficial; the crew of the Frankish corsair was divided into fighting men and those who worked the ship. The latter, in some cases, were actually slaves, or more usually men enticed or pressed on board at Italian ports. There was little chance of escape; if any succeeded in leaving the boat, Greek priests were captured on shore and forced to raise the natives to search. The fighting men on Roberts' ship consisted of about forty "Voluntiers," all ruffians guilty of crimes at home and without motive to return; they spy on the crew, and if a mutiny takes place, on board, it is "for want of Compliment of these Hell-hounds." They get all the plunder that there is but there are fixed perquisites belonging to the senior officers. The same principle prevailed among the British pirates of the Western seas, whose "articles," if we can trust the account given by Captain Chas. Johnson, contained a fixed system for the disposal of loot.

The priest figures also in the epilogue to the Ismaros raid. The wine with which Odysseus drugged the Cyclops is said to have been given to him by Maron, the priest of Apollo at Ismaros. It is possible that the priest Maron, as Bérard hints, was in league with the corsairs, or was utilised by them, in much the same way as Roberts' men employed the *papadhes* of the islands, to guide them to what they wanted. Hughes was warned against the *papas* at Delphi, who was reported to be in league with the *Clephts*, and quotes an earlier traveller's statement that a gang of robbers or boat of pirates was seldom without its chaplain. The case of Maron, however, is somewhat different. His life is spared, but his "gifts" to Odysseus, in addition to the twelve jars of wine, consisted of seven talents of gold and a silver bowl. The pirates' "reverence" for the priest did not prevent them from acquiring most of his substance, although no personal violence was offered to him or his family.

It is never easy to comprehend the part which superstition played in the pirate's life. Stackelberg gave an amusing description of the religious views of his captors, which is of considerable interest: They were mostly Turks, "but with the most imperfect knowledge of the Mussulman faith: in the hours of danger they had recourse to all kinds of superstition, but when secure they indulged in the most horrid blasphemies. In their bark a light was always kept burning before a picture of the Virgin, and in storms they vowed the dedication of wax tapers to St. Nicholas ... in a church dedicated to that saint upon an island which they sometimes visited; these vows they religiously performed."

Plutarch alludes to the strange sacrifices and secret rites practised by the pirates of Cilicia; but it would be obviously unwise to build much on his statement that the worship of Mithras was first disseminated by them.

Methods of dealing with these miscreants, when captured, have varied little in different parts of the world, the object in most cases being to ensure that the punishment should, so far as possible, fit the crime, and by its publicity act as a deterrent to others. In sixteenth century England it is said that "the punishment for corsairs is to hang them in such a way that their toes well night touch the water; so they are generally hanged on the banks of rivers and on the sea-shore." The later performances at Execution Dock were of a similar character, and Roman law provided that the punishment of brigands and pirates should be carried out as openly as possible. A public execution was no doubt a gratifying spectacle to those who had to fear the corsair's crimes. Cicero, at any rate, is insistent on the disappointment felt by the Syracusans, when deprived by Verres of the *iucundissimum spectaculum* of seeing the arch-pirate executed. Little mercy was shown to the pirate when he fell into his victims' hands. Miller quotes the case of a Turkish corsair who was driven ashore at Melos and slowly roasted for three hours by the populace about the year 1500, and burning seems to have been the usual penalty inflicted by the Turkish and Syrian peasantry. The official punishments of the Romans, however, were beheading, crucifixion and exposure to the beasts. Since pirates were regarded in Roman law as *the general enemies of mankind*, it was the duty of every provincial governor to proceed against them. The individual also was empowered to take the necessary measures of self-defence against pirates and brigands, but how far Julius Caesar was justified in ordering the crucifixion of his captors, in defiance of the governor of Asia, is doubtful.

We have little information regarding Greek law on the subject of piracy. It is probable enough that full provisions were made in the Rhodian code, if we may argue from one of the few fragments of it that have survived. An inscription from Ephesos tells us that captured pirates were dealt with in a "manner that befitted their villainy"; but having examined some of the methods favoured in the Mediterranean, we may perhaps refrain from further inquiries. There is, however, one interesting monument, which shows us that the practice of keel-hauling, beloved of the pirates of the Western seas, was known also to the ancients. But there is, unfortunately, nothing to show whether the patient on this occasion is the pirate or his captive.

Caesar and the Pirates

PLUTARCH, TRANS. JOHN DRYDEN

After Sylla became master of Rome, he wished to make Cæsar put away his wife Cornelia, daughter of Cinna, the late sole ruler of the commonwealth, but was unable to effect it either by promises or intimidation, and so contented himself with confiscating her dowry. The ground of Sylla's hostility to Cæsar was the relationship between him and Marius; for Marius, the elder, married Julia, the sister of Cæsar's father, and had by her the younger Marius, who consequently was Cæsar's first cousin. And though at the beginning, while so many were to be put to death, and there was so much to do, Cæsar was overlooked by Sylla, yet he would not keep quiet, but presented himself to the people as a candidate for the priesthood, though he was yet a mere boy. Sylla, without any open opposition took measures to have him rejected, and in consultation whether he should be put to death, when it was urged by some that it was not worth his while to contrive the death of a boy, he answered, that they knew little who did not see more than one Marius in that boy. Cæsar, on being informed of this saying, concealed himself, and for a considerable time kept out of the way in the country of the Sabines, often changing his quarters, till one night, as he was removing from one house to another on account of his health, he fell into the hands of Sylla's soldiers, who were searching those parts in order to apprehend any who had absconded. Cæsar, by a bribe of two talents, prevailed with Cornelius, their captain, to let him go and was no sooner dismissed but he put to sea and made for Bithynia. After a short stay there with Nicomedes, the king, in his passage back he was taken near the island of Pharmacusa by some of the pirates, who, at that time, with large fleets of ships and innumerable smaller vessels, infested the seas everywhere.

When these men at first demanded of him twenty talents for his ransom, he laughed at them for not understanding the value of their prisoner, and voluntarily engaged to give them fifty. He presently despatched those about him to several places to raise the money, till at last he was left among a set of the most bloodthirsty people in the world, the Cilicians, only with one friend and two attendants. Yet he made so little of them, that when he had a mind to sleep, he would send to them, and order them to make no noise. For thirty-eight days, with all the freedom in the world, he amused himself with joining in their exercises and games, as if they had not been his keepers, but his guards. He wrote verses and speeches, and made them his auditors, and those who did not admire them, he called to their faces illiterate and barbarous, and would often, in raillery, threaten to hang them. They were greatly taken with this, and attributed his free talking to a kind of simplicity and boyish playfulness. As soon as his ransom was come from Miletus, he paid it, and was discharged, and proceeded at once to man some ships at the port of Miletus, and went in pursuit of the pirates, whom he surprised with their ships still stationed at the island, and took most of them. Their money he made his prize, and the men he secured in prison at Pergamus, and he made application to Junius, who was then governor of Asia, to whose office it belonged, as prætor, to determine their punishment. Junius, having his eye upon the money, for the sum was considerable, said he would think at his leisure what to do with the prisoners, upon which Cæsar took his leave of him and went off to Pergamus, where he ordered the pirates to be brought forth and crucified; the punishment he had often threatened them with whilst he was in their hands, and they little dreamt he was in earnest.

The Danish and Norman Pirates

CHARLES ELLM

The Saxons, a people supposed to be derived from the Cimbri, uniting the occupations of fishing and piracy, commenced at an early period their ravages in the German Ocean; and the shores of Gaul and Britain were for ages open to their depredations. About the middle of the fifth century, the unwarlike Vortigern, then king of Britain, embraced the fatal resolution of requesting these hardy warriors to deliver him from the harassing inroads of the Picts and Scots; and the expedition of Hengist and Horsa was the consequence. Our mention of this memorable epoch is not for its political importance, great as that is, but for its effects on piracy; for the success attending such enterprises seems to have turned the whole of the northern nations towards sea warfare. The Danes, Norwegians, and Swedes, from their superior knowledge of navigation, gave into it most; and on whatever coast the winds carried them, they made free with all that came in their way. Canute the Fourth endeavored in vain to repress these lawless disorders among his subjects; but they felt so galled by his restrictions, that they assassinated him. On the king of Sweden being taken by the Danes, permission was given to such of his subjects as chose, to arm themselves against the enemy, pillage his possessions, and sell their prizes at Ribnitz and Golnitz. This proved a fertile nursery of pirates, who became so formidable under the name of "Victalien Broders," that several princes were obliged to arm against them, and hang some of their chiefs.

Even the females of the North caught the epidemic spirit, and proudly betook themselves to the dangers of sea-life. Saxo-Grammaticus relates an interesting story of one of them. Alwilda, the daughter of Synardus, a Gothic king, to deliver herself from the violence imposed on her inclination, by a marriage with Alf, the son of Sygarus, king of Denmark, embraced the life of a rover; and attired as a man, she embarked in a vessel of which the crew was composed of other young women of tried courage, dressed in the same manner. Among the first of her cruises, she landed at a place where a company of pirates were bewailing the loss of their commander; and the strangers were so captivated with the air and agreeable manners of Alwilda, that they unanimously chose her for their leader. By this reinforcement she became so formidable, that Prince Alf was despatched to engage her. She sustained his attacks with great courage and talent; but during a severe action in the gulf of Finland, Alf boarded her vessel, and having killed the greatest part of her crew, seized the captain, namely herself; whom nevertheless he knew not, because she had a casque which covered her visage. The prince was agreeably surprised, on removing the helmet, to recognize his beloved Alwilda; and it seems that his valor had now recommended him to the fair princess, for he persuaded her to accept his hand, married her on board, and then led her to partake of his wealth, and share his throne.

Charlemagne, though represented as naturally generous and humane, had been induced, in his extravagant zeal for the propagation of those tenets which he had himself adopted, to enforce them throughout Germany at the point of the sword; and his murders and decimations on that account disgrace humanity. The more warlike of the Pagans flying into Jutland, from whence the Saxons had issued forth, were received with kindness, and furnished with the means of punishing their persecutor, by harassing his coasts. The maritime towns of France were especially ravaged by those pirates called "Normands," or men of the North; and it was owing to their being joined by many malcontents, in the provinces since called Normandy, that that district acquired its name. Charlemagne, roused by this effrontery, besides fortifying the mouths of the great rivers, determined on building himself a fleet, which he did, consisting of 400 of the largest galleys then known, some having five or six benches of oars. His people were, however, extremely ignorant of maritime affairs, and in the progress of having them taught, he was suddenly called to the south, by the invasion of the Saracens.

Another division of Normans, some years afterwards, in the same spirit of emigration, and thirsting, perhaps, to avenge their injured ancestors, burst into the provinces of France, which the degeneracy of Charlemagne's posterity, and the dissensions which prevailed there, rendered an affair of no great difficulty. Louis le Debonnaire had taken every means of keeping on good terms with them; annually persuading some to become Christians, and then sending them home so loaded with presents, that it was discovered they came to be baptized over and over again, merely for the sake of the gifts, as Du Chesne tells us. But on the subsequent division of the empire among the undutiful sons of Louis, the pirates did not fail to take advantage of the general confusion; braving the sea almost every summer in their light coracles, sailing up the Seine, the Somme, or the Loire, and devastating the best parts of France, almost without resistance. In 845, they went up to Paris, pillaged it, and were on the point of attacking the royal camp at St. Dennis; but receiving a large sum of money from Charles the Bald, they retreated from thence, and with the new means thus supplied them, ravaged Bordeaux, and were there joined by Pepin, king of Aquitaine. A few years afterwards, they returned in great numbers. Paris was again sacked, and the magnificent abbey of St. Germain des Prés burnt. In 861, Wailand, a famous Norman pirate, returning from England, took up his winter quarters on the banks of the Loire, devastated the country as high as Tourraine, shared the women and girls among his crews, and even carried off the male children, to be brought up in his own profession. Charles the Bald, not having the power to expel him, engaged the freebooter, for 500 pounds of silver, to dislodge his countrymen, who were harassing the vicinity of Paris. In consequence of this subsidy, Wailand, with a fleet of 260 sail, went up the Seine, and attacked the Normans in the isle of Oiselle: after a long and obstinate resistance, they were obliged to capitulate; and having paid 6000 pounds of gold and silver, by way of ransom, had leave to join their victors. The riches thus acquired rendered a predatory life so popular, that the pirates were continually increasing in number, so that under a "sea-king" called Eric, they made a descent in the Elbe and the Weser, pillaged Hamburg, penetrated far into Germany, and after gaining two battles, retreated with immense booty. The pirates, thus reinforced on all sides, long continued to devastate Germany, France, and England; some penetrated into Andalusia and Hetruria, where they destroyed the flourishing town of Luni; whilst others, descending the Dnieper, penetrated even into Russia.

Meanwhile the Danes had been making several attempts to effect a *lodgment* in England; and allured by its fertility, were induced to try their fortune in various expeditions, which were occasionally completely successful, and at other times most fatally disastrous. At length, after a struggle of several years, their success was so decided, that king Alfred was obliged for a time to abandon his kingdom, as we all know, to their ravages. They immediately passed over to Ireland, and divided it into three sovereignties; that of Dublin fell to the share of Olauf; that of Waterford to Sitrih; and that of Limerick to Yivar. These arrangements dispersed the forces of the enemy, and watching his opportunity, Alfred issued from his retreat, fell on them like a thunderbolt, and made a great carnage of them. This prince, too wise to exterminate the pirates after he had conquered them, sent them to settle Northumberland, which had been wasted by their countrymen, and by this humane policy gained their attachment and services. He then retook London, embellished it, equipped fleets, restrained the Danes in England, and prevented others from landing. In the twelve years of peace which followed his fifty-six battles, this great man composed his body of laws; divided England into counties, hundreds, and tithings, and founded the University of Oxford. But after Alfred's death, fresh swarms of pirates visited the shores, among the most formidable of whom were the Danes, who spread desolation and misery along the banks of the Thames, the Medway, the Severn, the Tamar, and the Avon, for more than a century, though repeatedly tempted to desist by weighty bribes, raised by an oppressive and humiliating tax called *Danegelt*, from its object; and which, like most others, were continued long after it had answered its intent.

About the end of the 9th century, one of the sons of Rognwald, count of the Orcades, named Horolf, or Rollo, having infested the coasts of Norway with piratical descents, was at length defeated and banished by Harold, king of Denmark. He fled for safety to the Scandinavian island of Soderoe, where finding many outlaws and discontented fugitives, he addressed their passions, and succeeded in placing himself at their head. Instead of measuring his sword with his sovereign again, he adopted the wiser policy of imitating his countrymen, in making his fortune by plundering the more opulent places of southern Europe. The first attempt of this powerful gang was upon England, where, finding Alfred too powerful to be coped with, he stood over to the mouth of the Seine, and availed himself of the state to which France was reduced. Horolf, however, did not limit his ambition to the acquisition of booty; he wished permanently to enjoy some of the fine countries he was ravaging, and after many treaties made and broken, received the dutchy of Normandy from the lands of Charles the Simple, as a fief, together with Gisla, the daughter of the French monarch, in marriage. Thus did a mere pirate found the family which in a few years gave sovereigns to England, Naples, and Sicily, and spread the fame of their talents and prowess throughout the world.

Nor was Europe open to the depredations of the northern pirates only. Some Asiatic moslems, having seized on Syria, immediately invaded Africa, and their subsequent conquests in Spain faciliated their irruption into France, where they pillaged the devoted country, with but few substantial checks. Masters of all the islands in the Mediterranean, their corsairs insulted the coasts of Italy, and even threatened the destruction of the Eastern empire, While Alexis was occupied in a war with Patzinaces, on the banks of the Danube, Zachas, a Saracen pirate, scoured the Archipelago, having, with the assistance of an able Smyrniote, constructed a flotilla of forty brigantines, and some light fast-rowing boats, manned by adventurers like himself. After taking several of the surrounding islands, he established himself sovereign of Smyrna, that place being about the centre of his newly-acquired dominions. Here his fortunes prospered for a time, and Soliman, sultan of Nicea, son of the grand Soliman, sought his alliance, and married his daughter, about A. D. 1093. But in the following year, young Soliman being persuaded that his father-in-law had an eye to his possessions, with his own hand stabbed Zachas to the heart. The success of this freebooter shows that the Eastern emperors could no longer protect, or even assist, their islands.

Maritime pursuits had now revived, the improvement of nautical science was progressing rapidly, and the advantages of predatory expeditions, especially when assisted and masked by commerce, led people of family and acquirements to embrace the profession. The foremost of these were the Venetians and Genoese, among whom the private adventurers, stimulated by an enterprising spirit, fitted out armaments, and volunteered themselves into the service of those nations who thought proper to retain them; or they engaged in such schemes of plunder as were likely to repay their pains and expense. About the same time, the Roxolani or Russians, became known in history, making their debut in the character of pirates, ravenous for booty, and hungry for the pillage of Constantinople—a longing which 900 years have not yet satisfied. Pouring hundreds of boats down the Borysthenes, the Russian marauders made four desperate attempts to plunder the city of the Cæsars, in less than two centuries, and appear only to have been repulsed by the dreadful effects of the celebrated Greek fire.

England, in the mean time, had little to do with piracy: nor had she any thing worthy the name of a navy; yet Cœur de Lion had given maritime laws to Europe; her seamen, in point of skill, were esteemed superior to their cotemporaries; and King John enacted that those foreign ships which refused to lower their flags to that of Britain should, if taken, be deemed lawful prizes. Under Henry III, though Hugh de Burgh, the governor of Dover Castle, had defeated a French fleet by casting lime into the eyes of his antagonists, the naval force was impaired to such a degree that the Normans and Bretons were too powerful for the Cinque Ports, and compelled them to seek relief from the other ports of the kingdom. The taste for depredation had become so general and contagious, that privateers were now allowed to be fitted out, which equipments quickly degenerated to the most cruel of pirates. Nay more: on the disputes which took place between Henry and his Barons, in 1244, the Cinque Ports, who had shown much indifference to the royal requisitions, openly espoused the cause of the revolted nobles; and, under the orders of Simon de Montfort, burnt Portsmouth. From this, forgetful of their motives for arming, they proceeded to commit various acts of piracy, and considering nothing but their private interests, extended their violence not only against the shipping of all countries unfortunate enough to fall in their way, but even to perpetrate the most unwarrantable ravages on the property of their own countrymen. Nor was this confined to the Cinque Port vessels only; the example and the profits were too stimulating to the restless; and one daring association on the coast of Lincolnshire seized the Isle of Ely, and made it their receptacle for the plunder of all the adjacent countries. One William Marshall fortified the little island of Lundy, in the mouth of the Severn, and did so much mischief by his piracies, that at length it became necessary to fit out a squadron to reduce him, which was accordingly done, and he was executed in London; yet the example did not deter other persons from similar practices. The sovereign, however, did not possess sufficient naval means to suppress the enormities of the great predatory squadrons, and their ravages continued to disgrace the English name for upwards of twenty years, when the valor and conciliation of the gallant Prince Edward brought them to that submission which his royal parent had failed in procuring.

Those "harum-scarum" expeditions, the Crusades, were perhaps influential in checking piracy, although the rabble that composed the majority of them had as little principle as the worst of the freebooters. From the time that Peter the Hermit set Europe in a blaze, all ranks, and all nations, streamed to the East, so that few vessels were otherwise employed than in conveying the motly groups who sought the shores of Palestine; some from religious zeal; some from frantic fanaticism; some from desire of distinction; some for the numberless privileges which the crusaders acquired; and the rest and greater portion, for the spoil and plunder of which they had a prospect. The armaments, fitted in no fewer than nine successive efforts, were mostly equipped with such haste and ignorance, and with so little choice, that ruinous delays, shipwrecks, and final discomfiture, were naturally to be expected. Still, the effect of such incredible numbers of people betaking themselves to foreign countries, advanced civilization, although vast means of forwarding its cause were buried in the East; and those who assert that no benefit actually resulted, cannot deny that at least some evils were thereby removed. Montesquieu says, that Europe then required a general shock, to teach her, but the sight of contrasts, the theorems of public economy most conducive to happiness. And it is evident, that notwithstanding these follies wasted the population of Europe, squandered its treasures, and infected us with new vices and diseases, still the crusades diminished the bondage of the feudal system, by augmenting the power of the King, and the strength of the Commons; while they also occasioned a very increased activity in commerce: thus taming the ferocity of men's spirits, increasing agriculture in value from the safety it enjoyed, and establishing a base for permanent prosperity.

Narrative of the Capture of the Ship *Derby*, 1735

CAPTAIN ANSELM

I fell in with the Land of *Madagascar*, the Latitude of about 24 Degrees, 13 Minutes North: And some time before I had made it, I met with nothing but light Airs of Winds, and Calms, and continued so long. My People dropping down with the Scurvy, I took a small Still that I had, and distill'd Salt Water into Fresh. I allow'd them as much Pease and Flower as they could eat, that they might not eat any Salt Provision, tho' I boil'd it in fresh Water. I had been very liberal with my fresh Provision in my Passage, to my People, and the Passage so long, that I had hardly any left, and that only a few Fowls; and myself and Officers too had been much out of Order. At last, being got to the Northward of *Augustin* Bay, seeing my poor People fall down so very fast, it gave me very great Concern for them, but still was willing, in Hopes of Change of Wind, for *Johanna.* But the small Airs trifled with me, and what there were Northerly, a Current setting to the Southward, that what to do I could not well tell. To go into *Augustin* Bay I was very unwilling: I had two Boats came off to me, the People talking tolerable good *English.* At last, my Doctor, *Sharp,* told me there were above Thirty People down with the Scurvy, and all the rest, even some of the Petty Officers, were touch'd with the same. If I did not soon put into Port, I plainly found I should have been in a bad Condition, for Men; I consulted with my Officers, to go into *Augustin* Bay, and we agreed, and bore away for it. Soon after, the Wind came Southerly, and I bore away for *Johanna.* A fine Passage I had, and anchor'd the next Day about Four in the Afternoon, being *Sept.* 13. I thank God I brought all my People in alive, and that is as much I can say of a good many of them. I had a Tent made ashore for them, and supplied them all that ever I could, and the Doctors assisting with every thing in their Way for their speedy Recovery. After I had been here a Fortnight, the Winds in the Day-time set in very fresh from the N. N. W. to the N. N. E. Finding the People recover so very slowly, what to do I could not tell. To go out with my People as bad as when they came in, I was not willing, but resolv'd to have Patience one Week more. I consulted with Mr. *Rogers,* my Chief-Mate, and told him that we must consider the Condition of the People, and how we met the Winds and Currents before we came in. The People of the Island told me, that this was about the time of Year for the Northerly Winds and Southerly Currents, and I told him I thought it better to trim all our Casks, and fill what Water we could, fearing of a long Passage, if our Stay was a little longer. Mr. *Rogers* was of my Opinion. This I must say, I found the Cask not so well used in the Hold, as they ought to have been, which caus'd the Coopers more Work; neither did I make a little Noise about it, because I had more Words with my Chief and Second Mate, about my Third and Fourth Mate, than any thing else.

Having all my Water aboard, about 80 Tun, 25 Head of Oxen, *&c.,* I sail'd the 13th of *October,* with several of my Men not recover'd; some I buried at *Johanna,* and some after, to the Number of Ten, or thereabouts. Having a fine Gale, I made all the Sail I could, except Studding-sails, which I thought needless. The Wind veer'd to the Northward, and I was resolved to make the *Mallabar* Course as soon as possible, for the Advantage of the Land and Sea Winds. I had one Passenger aboard, a sad troublesome wicked Fellow, whose Behaviour was so bad, that I could hardly forbear using him ill. I forbid my Officers keeping Company with him; but Mr. *B——s* would do it at all Events. I turn'd him once off the Quarter-Deck for being with him there, yet that did not avail. I came out one Night about half an Hour past Ten, my second Mate's Watch, and this *B——s's* Turn to sleep; and seeing a Light in his Cabin, I sent Mr. *Cuddon,* the second Mate, to him, to know how he would be able to sit up one Watch, and keep his own. Upon this *B——s* came up half way the Steerage-Ladder, with his Pipe in his Hand, and talk'd to me very pertly; and that was not the first time. This put me into a Passion, to be so talk'd to by a Boy, that I did dismiss him for two or three Days, and then re-stated him, which was more than he deserv'd, for keeping Company with him for whom the the worst of Names is good enough, and those who recommended him to his Commission. *B——s* was told of this by Mr. *Rogers,* by my Orders, and I told him of it on the Quarter-Deck, and told him at the same time I was resolv'd to tell the Gentlemen at Home of——; and ask'd him what he imagin'd they would think of him for keeping such swearing drunken Company. This was before I dismiss'd him.

Before I came in with the Land, hearing much talk of *Angria,* by Capt. *Scarlet,* and Mr. *Rogers,* and of his great Force (for I had very little Notion of him before) I took care to put the Ship in a proper Posture of Defence: Powder-Chests on the Quarter-Deck, Poop, and Forecastle, a Puncheon fill'd with Water in the Main-top, a Hogshead in the Fore-top, and a Barrel in the Mizen-top, all fill'd with Water: Chests with good Coverings in the Tops for Grenado-Shells; all the small Arms, with 50 new ones in Readiness. My Ship being too deep to get the Gun-room Ports open, as the Gunner inform'd me, the Ship *sending,* and the Sea washing above the Tops of the Ports; I got those Guns into the Great Cabin; Quarter-Bills over the Guns; the Rewards and Close-quarters, *&c.* at the Mizen-mast, Shot-lockers and Shot in their proper Station; Pluggs for Shot-holes; and every thing that I could think of: and gave particular Orders to my Gunner, Carpenter, and Boatswain, to have every thing in their way, in Readiness, the two lower Yards flung with the Top-chains. Not being easy in my Mind about these Gun-room Stern-Ports, I sent Mr. *Rogers,* it being smooth Water, to open one of the Gun-room Stern-Ports, to see, if we could, on Occasion, get Guns out there, but he brought me Word it could not be done with Safety, the Ship being so deep. A few Days before I made the Land, the Winds used to vere and haul, that Offing in an Hour I could hardly up from E. N. E. to S. E. but the Winds chiefly kept to the Northward. I was very desirous to make the Land, not knowing how far the Southwest Currents might set me to the Westward. At noon, being *Dec.* 12. I made the Land of *Goa,* in the Latitude of 15 Degrees North. My Chief Mate wanted me to go into *Goa,* but I was resolved not, but to make the best of my Way for *Bombay.* The next Morning, having a fine Six-Knot-Gale, about Nine o' Clock Mr. *Rogers* told me, he saw *Gereah,* and desired me to haul further off Shore, and said, if *Angria* and his Grabbs should see us in his River, he would send them out after us. I asked him, if his Grabbs came out of Sight of Land. He told me they were afraid to do that, fearing the *Bombay* Vessels should get between them and the Shore, and keep them out of their Ports. To prevent running into Danger, I kept out of Sight of Land: I thought it better to do so, since it would make but a few Days Difference in getting at *Bombay;* making no Doubt I should get there the last of the Month, as doubtless we should, if we had not met with our sad Misfortune.

When it was too late, I was acquainted by those taken in the *Severn,* that Mr. *Rogers* inform'd me wrong; for *Angria* sometimes keeps the Shore aboard, and sometimes goes directly out to Sea 60 Leagues off. It was too late to reflect; neither could I blame myself, knowing I had done every thing to the best of my Judgment: But had I been better inform'd, it is my Opinion we might have escaped those cursed Dogs, by keeping in Shore, and taken the Advantage of the Land and Sea Winds.

I have since repented that we did not go into *Goa;* but God knows whether a Man goes too fast or too slow; for I had certainly a very suitable Cargo for that Place; But my earnest Desire was to get to *Bombay,* the Season of the Year being far advanc'd.

December 26. being my second Mate's Morning Watch, about Five o'Clock he came to me, and told me he saw Nine Sail of Gallivats. I got up, and found them to be Five Top-mast Vessels, and Four Gallivats, not above two Miles from us. I order'd all Hands to be call'd, and down with the Cabins in the Steerage, which was done in an Instant, and every body to their respective Quarters. They came up with us apace, having but light Airs of Winds, and found them to be *Angria's* Fleet. I had the Transome in the great Cabin, and the Balcony in the Round-house cut away, for traversing the Stern-Chase Guns. They came up with me very boldly within Pistol-shot. Before Six, they began firing upon us, throwing their Shot in at our Stern, raking us afore and aft. I order'd everything to be got ready for going about, to give them my Broad-side, when my Chief-Mate Mr. *Rogers,* and my Third Mate Mr. *Burroughs* came to me, and begg'd that I would not put about, for if I did, they would certainly board us. As to my Part, being a Stranger to this Coast and *Angria,* knowing my Chief Mate had been often this Way, and my Third Mate had sail'd in the Gallies, I was over prevail'd upon not to tack about. As the Enemy kept under my Stern, playing their Shot in very hot upon us, and destroying my Rigging so fast, I soon after endeavour'd to wear the Ship upon the Enemy; but the Wind dying away to a Calm, she would not regard her Helm, but lay like a Log in the Water. By Eight o'Clock most of my Rigging was destroy'd, and the Longboat taking Fire a-stern, was forc'd to cut her away. The Yaul being stove by their shot, we launch'd her overboard. By Nine, the Top-chain that flung the Main-yard, was shot away, with Geer and Geer-Blocks. The Main-yard came next down, with the Sails almost torn to Pieces with the Shot. As fast as our People knotted and spliced the Rigging, it was shot away in their Hands. The Water-Tubs in the Tops were shot to pieces, and the Boatswain's Mate's Leg shot off in the Main-top. One of the Foremast-Mens Leg was shot off in the Foretop, and one wounded. By Ten, the Mizen-mast was shot by the Board. Wanting People to cut the Mast-Rigging, *&c.* from her Side, found them appear very thin upon Deck, and desired my younger Mates to drive them out of their Holes. Word was then brought me, that my Chief Mate's Leg was shot off, but that he was in good Heart. All this time it was a Calm, and our Guns of the Broadside of no Service, not being able, during the Engagement, to bring one Gun to bear upon them. They kept throwing their shot so thick in at our Stern, with a continual Fire, and we return'd it as fast as we could load and fire. About One, my Main-mast was shot by the Board, and the Fall of that stove the Pinnace on the Booms. The Loss of my Main-mast gave me a very great Concern, and seeing the Condition of the Fore-mast, the Fore-yard half way down, and the Top-sail Yard-arm sprung in several Places, the Head of the Top-gallant-Mast shot away, render'd that Mast quite useless. I could not see which way it was in the Power of Men to save us from these Dogs. However, I made myself as easy as could be expected, and kept my Thoughts to myself. Tho' the Shot were like Hail about my Ears, I thank God I escaped them, neither did they give me much Uneasiness as to my Person. The Grabbs perceiving their great Advantage by the Fall of our Main-mast, *&c.* tho' all the time before within Musket-Shot, come up boldly within Call, throwing in at our Stern Double-round and Patridge as fast as they could load and fire; we doing the same with Bolts, *&c.* We saw a great many Holes in their Sails. Soon after this, they lodg'd two Double-head-Shot, and a large Stone in the Fore-mast, the Shrouds of which were mostly gone. I often sent Capt. *Scarlet* to Mr. *Cudden,* to encourage the People, and to take care to cool his Guns, and not fire in Haste, but take good Aim. We received two Double-headed-Shot in the Bread-room, which were soon plugg'd up, and one Shot under the Larboard Chesstree, but so low in the Water, that could not get at it, and the Ship prov'd leaky. I had a Pack of sad cowardly, ignorant Dogs as ever came into a Ship. As to my common Sailors, who were not above Twelve Seamen, with the Officers, they stood by me. It was all owing to my Misfortune on the *Mouse,* that I was so poorly Mann'd. As to my Third Mate, B———s, he did not seem to stomach what he was about; he was sometimes on the Quarter-Deck (not being able to use any Guns but the Stern-Chase) and every Shot the Enemy fir'd, he cowardly trembled, with his Head almost down to the Deck. This Captain *Scarlet* has often declared to the Gentlemen at *Bombay,* and before those that are now coming Home. I had six Men kill'd, and six their Legs shot off, with several others wounded by their Partridge-Shot, *&c.* Had our People kept the Deck like Men, there must have been several more kill'd and wounded. About Three,

I heard a great Call for Shot, and desired Capt. *Scarlet* to go to Mr. *Cuddon,* and tell him not to fire in Waste.

We lay now just like a Wreck in the Sea, and at our Wits Ends. Our Shot being almost spent, we had a Hole cut in the Well to try to come at the Company's. We continued on with Double-round and Partridge, and Bolts, &c. with a Double Allowance of Powder to each Gun, doing the utmost we could to save the Ship. The Tiller-rope was now shot away, tho' of no Service before. The Carpenter told me the Ship made a great deal of Water, and had above two Foot in her Hold. The Caulker afterwards told me she had three Foot. I saw nothing we could do more than firing our Stern-Chase. There was a sad Complaint for Shot; however we fir'd Bolts. I call'd out to the People to have good Hearts, and went into the Round-house to encourage them there. It was very hard we could stand no Chance for a Mast of theirs, nor no lucky Shot to disable some of them, in all the Number that we fir'd. As to our small Arms, they were of little Service, they keeping their Men so close. The Rigging of the Foremast being gone, and that fetching so much way, I expected it to go every Minute; and about Seven in the Evening, the Ship falling off into the Trough of the Sea, the Foremast came by the Board. It was now about Four o' Clock, when Mr. *Thomas Rogers,* my Chief Mate, sent my Steward to desire to speak with me. When I went to him, he spoke to me to this Purpose. "Sir, says he, I am inform'd what Condition the Ship is in; as her Masts are gone, you had better not be obstinate, in standing out longer; it will only be the Means of making more Objects, of murdering more Men, and all to no Purpose, but to be used worse by the Enemy, for it is impossible to get away. Therefore you had better surrender." To the best of my Knowledge, I hardly made him any Answer; nor had I, before he sent to me, the least Thoughts of surrendering, which I declare before God and Man; tho' I was well convine'd within myself, that it was impossible to save the Ship. I went up to my old Station the Quarter-Deck, and took several Turns, as usual, and proceeded in the Engagement. I begun to consider what Mr. *Rogers* told me, and the Condition of the Ship, and argue within myself the Impossibility of doing any more (for if a Gale had sprung up, it could be of no Service) and all the time from the Fall of our Main-mast, the Enemy were got so near, that I could hear them talk, and my Second Mate did the same. As to our Masts, they had gain'd their Ends, and their only Business now was to fire at the Hull. There was no Hopes of their leaving us, considering the condition they had brought us to, and it could not be long before we sunk: for as they lay so near us, and so low in Water, our Shot must doubtless fly over them. At last I was of Mr. *Rogers's* Opinion, that it was only sacrificing the Men to no Purpose; for they had so large a Mark of us, they could not miss us; and during all the Engagement, as they play'd their Shot so hot at our Stern, it is surprizing there were not many more Men Kill'd. I then sent for my Second and Third Mate, and told them

Mr. *Rogers's* Opinion and my own. They both agreed to it, and consented to the surrendering of the Ship. So we submitted to the Enemy, finding it in vain to proceed. By my Watch it was Five o' Clock. My Second and Third Mate went in to the Steerage to forbid firing, and myself in the Round-House, did the same. Every Body seem'd to be very well satisfied as to the surrendering Part, and no Objection was made. Colours we had none to strike; those and the Ensign-Staff were shot to Pieces; and what was left of the Ensign being made fast to the Main-Shrowds, went with the Mast. Capt. *Scarlet* went into the Round-House, and call'd the Enemy on board, and told them we had no Boats. They sent their Dingey aboard with Four Men for me and my chief Officers. They left Two of the Four aboard the *Derby.* Myself and my Second Mate went in the Dingey aboard the Grabb. We were gone an Hour and a half good, if not more; then we return'd in a Gallivat with 50 or 60 Men, but not a Soul went aboard the *Derby,* till we return'd. Then came aboard more Gallivats and more Men, and secured the Arms, &c. and drove our People up, some to the Pumps, and some to clear the Rigging off the Ship's Side. They transkipt to their Grabbs what Treasure could be got at, and the next Day turn'd out the Remainder, with myself, *Scarlet, Cuddon,* the two Ladies, and my Servants, into one of the Grabbs.

The Fight Between the *Dorrill* and the *Moca*

THE INDIAN ANTIQUARY

These truly representeth a scheem of what misfortune has befell us as we were going through the streights of Malacca, in the persuance to our pretended voyage, *vizt.,* Wednesday the 7th July, 5 o'clock morning we espied a ship to windward; as soon as was well light perceived her to bare down upon us. Wee thought at first she had been a Dutchman bound for Atcheen or Bengall, when perceived she had no Gallerys, did then suppose her to be what after, to our dreadful sorrow, found her. Wee gott our ship in the best posture of defence that suddain emergent necessity would permitt. Wee kept good looking out, expecting to see an Island called Pullo Verello [Pulo Barahla], but as then saw it not.

About 8 of the clock the ship came up fairely within shott. Saw in room of our Gallerys there was large sally ports, in each of which was a large gunn, seemed to be brass. Her tafferill was likewise taken downe. Wee having done what possibly could to prepare ourselves, fearing might be suddenly sett on, ordered our people to their respective stations for action. Wee now hoisted our colours.

The Captain commanded to naile our Ensigne to the staff in sight of the enimie, which was immediately done. As they perceived wee hoisted our colours they hoisted theirs, with the Union Jack, and let fly a broad red Pendant at their maintopmast head.

The Pirate being now in little more than half Pistoll shott from us, wee could discerne abundance of men who went aft to the Quarter Deck, which as wee suppose was to consult. They stood as we stood, but wee spoke neither to other. Att noone it fell calme, so that [wee] were affraid should by the sea have been hove on one another. Att I a clock sprang up a gale. The Pirate kept as wee kept. Att 3 a clock the villain backt her sailes and they went from us. Wee kept close hailed, having a contrary wind for Mallacca. When the Pirate was about 7 miles distant tackt and stood after us. Att 6 that evening saw the lookt for island, and the Pirate came up with us on our starboard side within shott. Wee see he kept a man at each topmast head, looking out till it was darke, then he halled a little from us, but kept us company all night.

At 8 in the morning he drew near us, but wee had time to mount our other four guns that were in hold, and now wee were in the best posture of defence could desire. He drawing near us and seeing that if [wee] would, [wee] could not gett from him, he far outsailing us by or large [in one direction or another], the Captain resolved to see what the rogue would doe, soe ordered to hand [furl] all our small sailes and furled our mainesaile. He, seeing this, did the like, and as [he] drew near us beat a drum and sounded trumpets, and then hailed us four times before we answered him.

At last it was thought fitt to know what he would say, soe the Boatswaine spoke to him as was ordered, which was that wee came from London. Then he enquired whether peace or war with France. Our answer, there was an universall peace through Europe, att which they paused and then said, "That's well." He further enquired if had touched at Attcheen. Wee said a boat came off to us, but [wee] came not near itt by several leagues. Further he enquired our Captain's name and whither wee were bound. Wee answered to Mallacca. They too and [would have] had the Captain gone aboard to drink a glass of wine. Wee said that would see one another at Mallacca. Then he called to lye by and he would come aboard us. Our answer was as before, saying it was late. He said, true, it was for China, and enquired whether should touch at the Water Islands [Pulo Ondan, off Malacca]. Wee said should. Then said he, So shall wee. After he had asked us all these questions wee desired to know from whence he was. He said from London, their Captain name Collyford, the ship named the *Resolution,* bound for China. This Collyford had been Gunners Mate at Bombay, and after run away with the Ketch.

Thus past the 8th July. Friday the 9th do., he being some distance from us, About 1/2 an hour after 10 came up with us. Then it grew calme. Wee could discerne a fellow on the Quarter Deck wearing a sword. As he drew near, this Hellish Imp cried, Strike you doggs, which [wee] perceived was not by a general consent for he was called away. Our Boatswaine in a fury run upon the poop, unknown to the Captain, and answered that wee would strike to noe such doggs as he, telling him the rogue Every and his accomplices were all hanged. The Captain was angry that he spake without order, then ordered to haile him and askt what was his reason to dogg us. One stept forward on the forecastle, beckoned with his hand and said, Gentlemen, wee want not your ship nor men, but money. Wee told them had none for them but bid them come up alongside and take it as could gett it. Then a parcell of bloodhound rogues clasht their cutlashes and said they would have itt or our hearts blood, saying, "What doe you not know us to be the *Moca?*" Our answer was Yes, Yes. Thereon they gave a great shout and so they all went out of sight and wee to our quarters. They were going to hoist colours but the ensigne halliards broke, which our people perceiving gave a great shout, so they lett them alone.

As soon as they could bring their chase gunns to bear, fired upon us and soe kept on our quarter. Our gunns would not bear in a small space, but as soon as did hap, gave them better than [the pirates] did like. His second shott carried away our spritt saile yard. About half on hour after or more he came up alongside and soe wee powered in upon him and continued, some time broadsides and sometimes three or four gunns as opportunity presented and could bring them to doe best service. He was going to lay us athwart the hawse, but by God's providence Captain Hide frustrated his intent by pouring a broadside into him, which made him give back and goe asterne, where he lay and paused without fireing, then in a small space fired one gunn. The shott come in at our round house window without damage to any person, after which he filled and bore away, and when was about 1/4 mile off fired a gunn to leeward, which wee answered by another to windward. About an hour after he tackt and came up with us againe. Wee made noe saile, but lay by to receive him, but he kept aloof off. The distance att most in all our fireing was never more than two ships length; the time of our engagement was from 1/2 an hour after 11 till about 3 afternoon.

When [wee] came to see what damage [wee] had sustained, found our Cheife Mate, Mr. Smith, wounded in the legg, close by the knee, with a splinter or piece of chaine, which cannot well be told, our Barber had two of his fingers shott off as was spunging one of our gunns, the Gunner's boy had his legg shott off in the waste, John Amos, Quartermaster, had his leg shott off [while] at the helme, the Boatswaine's boy (a lad of 13 years old) was shott in the thigh, which went through and splintered his bone, the Armorer Jos. Osborne in the round house wounded by a splinter just in the temple, the Captain's boy on the Quarter Deck a small shott raised his scull through his cap and was the first person wounded and att the first onsett. Wm. Reynolds's boy had the brim of his hatt 1/2 shott off and his forefinger splintered very sorely. John Blake, turner, the flesh of his legg and calfe a great part shott away.

Our ships damage is the Mizentopmast shott close by the cap and it was a miracle stood soe long and did not fall in the rogues sight. Our rigging shott that had but one running rope left clear, our mainshrouds three on one side, two on the other cutt in two. Our mainyard ten feet from the mast by a shott cutt 8 inches deep, our foretopmast backstays shott away, a great shott in the roundhouse, one on the Quarter Deck and two of the roundhouse shott came on the said deck, severall in the stearidge betwixt decks and in the forecastle, two in the bread room which caused us to make much water and damaged the greatest part of our bread. They dismounted one of our gunns in the roundhouse, two in the stearidge, two in the waste, one in the forecastle, with abundance more damage which may seem tedious to rehearse.

Their small shott were most Tinn and Tuthenage [*tutenaga,* spelter]. They fired pieces of glass-bottles, do. teapots, chains, stones and what not, which were found on our decks. We could observe abundance of great shott to have passed through the rogues foresaile, and our hope is have done that to him which [will] make him shunn having to do with any Europe ship againe. Att night wee perceived kept close their lights. Wee did the like and lay by. In the morning they were as far off as [wee] could discerne upon deck. Wee sent up to see how they stood, which was right with us. In the night wee knotted our rigging and in the morning made all haist to repare our carriages.

Our men, seeing they stood after us, [wee] could perceive their countinances to be dejected. Wee cheared them what wee could, and, for their encouragement, the Captain and wee of our proper money did give them, to every man and boy, three dollars each, which animated them, and promised to give them as much more if engaged againe, and that if [wee] took the ship, for every prisoner five pounds and besides a gratuity from the Gentlemen Employers. Wee read the King's Proclamation about Every, &c., and the Right Honble. Company's.

About 9 o'clock the 10th July wee perceived the rogue made from us, soe wee gave the Almighty our most condigne thanks for his mercy that delivered us not to the worst of our enimies, for truly he [the pirate] was very strong, having at least an hundred Europeans on board, 34 gunns mounted, besides 10 pattererers and 2 small mortars in the head; his lower tier, some of them, as wee judged, sixteen and eighteen pounders. We lay as near our course as could, and next day saw land on our starboard side which was the Maine [Land]. Kept on our way.

The 12th July dyed the Boatswaine's boy, George Mopp, in the morning. Friday the 16th do. in the evening dyed the Gunner's boy, Thomas Matthews. Sunday the 18th at anchor two leagues from the Pillo Sumbelong [Pulo Sembîlan] Islands dyed the Barber, Andrew Miller. Do. the 31st dyed the Cheife Mate, Mr. John Smith. The other two are yet in a very deplorable condition and wee are ashore here to refresh them. ... The Chinese further report ... the *Mocco* was at the Maldives and creaned [careened]; there they gave an end to the life of their commanding rogue Stout, who they murdered for attempting to run away.

The Wonderful Fight of the *Exchange* of Bristol with the Pirates of Algiers

SAMUEL PURCHAS

In the yeere 1621, the first of November, there was one *Iohn Rawlins*, borne in *Rochester*, and dwelling three and twenty yeere in *Plimmoth*, imployed to the Strait of *Gibraltar*, by Master *Richard*, and *Steven Treviles*, Merchants of Plimmoth, and fraighted in a Barke, called the *Nicholas* of *Plimmoth*, of the burden of forty Tun, which had also in her company another ship of *Plimmoth*, called the *George Benaventure* of seventy Tun burthen, or thereabouts; which by reason of her greatnesse beyond the other, I will name the *Admirall*; and *Iohn Rawlins* Barke shall, if you please, be the *Vice-admirall*. These two according to the time of the yeere, had a faire passage, and by the eighteenth of the same moneth came to a place at the entring of the straits, named *Trafflegar:* but the next morning, being in the sight of *Gibraltar*, at the very mouth of the straits, the watch descried five saile of ships, who as it seemed, used all the means they could to come neere us, and we as we had cause, used the same means to go as farre from them: yet did their *Admirall* take in both his top sailes, that either we might not suspect them, or that his owne company might come up the closer together. At last perceiving us *Christians,* they fell from devices to apparent discovery of hostility, and making out against us: we againe suspecting them Pirats, tooke our course to escape from them, and made all the sailes we possibly could for *Tirriff,* or *Gibraltar:* but all we could doe, could not prevent their approach. For suddenly one of them came right over against us to wind-ward, and so fell upon our quarter: another came upon our luffe, and so threatened us there, and at last all five chased us, making great speed to surprise us.

Their *Admirall* was called *Callfater,* having upon her maine top-saile, two top-gallant sailes, one above another. But whereas we thought them all five to be *Turkish* ships of war, we afterwards understood, that two of them were their prizes, the one a smal ship of *London,* the other of the West-countrey, that came out of the *Quactath* laden with figges, and other Merchandise, but now subiect to the fortune of the Sea, and the captivity of Pirats. But to our businesse. Three of these ships got much upon us, and so much that ere halfe the day was spent, the *Admirall* who was the best sailer, fetcht up the *George Bonaventure,* and made booty of it. The *Vice-Admirall* againe being neerest unto the lesser Barke, whereof *Iohn Rawlins* was Master, shewed him the force of a stronger arme, and by his *Turkish* name, called *Villa-Rise,* commanded him in like sort to strike his sailes, and submit to his mercy, which not to be gaine-saied nor prevented, was quickly done: and so *Rawlins* with his Barke was quickly taken, although the *Reare-Admirall* being the worst sayler of the three, called *Reggiprise,* came not in, till all was done.

The same day before night, the *Admirall* either loth to pester himselfe with too much company, or ignorant of the commodity that was to be made by the sale of *English* prisoners, or daring not to trust them in his company, for feare of mutinies, and exciting others to rebellion; set twelve persons who were in the *George Bonaventure* on the land, and divers other *English,* whom he had taken before, to trie their fortunes in an unknowne Countrey. But *Villa-Rise,* the *Vice-Admirall* that had taken. *Iohn Rawlins,* would not so dispence with his men, but commanded him and five more of his company to be brought aboord his ship, leaving in his Barke three men and his boy, with thirteene *Turkes* and *Moores,* who were questionlesse sufficient to over-master the other, and direct the Barke to Harbour. Thus they sailed directly for *Algier;* but the night following, followed them with great tempest and foule weather, which ended not without some effect of a storme: for they lost the sight of *Rawlins* Barke, called the *Nicholas,* and in a manner lost themselves, though they seemed safe a shipboord, by fearefull coniecturing what should become of us: at last, by the two and twentieth of the same moneth, they, or we (chuse you whether) arrived at *Algier,* and came in safety within the Mould, but found not our other Barke there; nay, though we earnestly inquired after the same, yet heard we nothing to our satisfaction; but much matter was ministred to our discomfort and amazement. For although the Captaine and our over-seers, were loth we should have any conference with our Country-men; yet did we adventure to informe ourselves of the present affaires, both of the Towne, and the shipping: so that finding many *English* at worke in other ships, they spared not to tell us the danger we were in, and the mischiefes we must needs incurre, as being sure if we were not used like slaves, to be sold as slaves; for there had beene five hundred brought into the market for the same purpose, and above a hundred hansome youths compelled to turne *Turkes,* or made subiect to more viler prostitution, and all *English:* yet like good *Christians,* they bade us be of good cheere, and comfort ourselves in this, that Gods trials were gentle purgations, and these crosses were but to cleanse the drosse from the gold, and bring us out of the fire againe more cleare and lovely. Yet I must needs confesse, that they afforded us reason for this cruelty, as if they determined to be revenged of our last attempt to fire their ships in the Mould, and therefore protested to spare none whom they could surprise and take alive; but either to sell them for money, or torment them to serve their owne turnes. Now their customes and usages in both these was in this manner.

First, concerning the first. The *Bashaw* had the over-seeing of all prisoners, who were presented unto him at their first comming into the harbour, and to choose one out of every eight for a present or fee to himselfe: the rest were rated by the Captaines, and so sent to the Market to be sold; whereat if either there were repining, or any drawing backe, then certaine *Moores* and Officers attended either to beate you forward, or thrust you into the sides with Goades; and this was the manner of the selling of Slaves.

Secondly, concerning their enforcing them, either to turne *Turke,* or to attend their filthines and impieties, although it would make a Christians heart bleed to heare of the same, yet must the truth not be hid, nor the terror left untold. They commonly lay them on their naked backs or bellies, beating them so long, till they bleed at the nose and mouth; and if yet they continue constant, then they strike the teeth out of their heads, pinch them by their tongues, and use many other sorts of tortures to convert them; nay, many times they lay them their whole length in the ground like a grave, and so cover them with boords, threatening to starve them, if they will not turne; and so many even for feare of torment and death, make their tongues betray their hearts to a most fearefull wickednesse, and so are circumcised with new names, and brought to confesse a new Religion. Others againe, I must confesse, who never knew any God, but their own sensuall lusts and pleasures, thought that any religion would serve their turnes, and so for preferment or wealth very voluntarily renounced their faith, and became *Renegadoes* in despight of any counsell which seemed to intercept them: and this was the first newes wee encountred with at our comming first to *Algier*.

The 26. of the same moneth, *Iohn Rawlins* his Barke, with his other three men and a boy, came safe into the Mould, and so were put all together to be carried before the *Bashaw*, but that they tooke the Owners servant, and *Rawlins* Boy, and by force and torment compelled them to turne *Turkes:* then were they in all seven *English*, besides *Iohn Rawlins*, of whom the *Bashaw* tooke one, and sent the rest to their Captaines, who set a valuation upon them, and so the Sould-iers hurried us like dogs into the Market, whereas men sell Hacknies in *England*. We were tossed up and downe to see who would give most for us; and although we had heavy hearts, and looked with sad countenances, yet many came to behold us, sometimes taking us by the hand, sometimes turning us round about, sometimes feeling our brawnes and naked armes, and so beholding our prices written on our breasts, they bargained for us accordingly, and at last we were all sold, and the Souldiers returned with the money to their Captaines.

Iohn Rawlins was the last who was sold, by reason of his lame hand, and bought by the Captaine that tooke him, even that dog *Villa Rise*, who better informing himselfe of his skill fit to be a Pilot, and his experience to bee an over-seer, bought him and his Carpenter at very easie rates. For as we afterwards understood by divers *English Renegadoes*, he paid for *Rawlins* but one hundred and fiftie Dooblets, which make of *English* money seven pound ten shilling. Thus was he and his Carpenter with divers other slaves sent into his ship to worke, and imployed about such affaires, as belonged to the well rigging and preparing the same. But the villanous *Turkes* perceiving his lame hand, and that he could not performe so much as other Slaves, quickly com-plained to their Patron, who as quickly apprehended the inconvenience; whereupon hee sent for him the next day, and told him he was unserviceable for his present purpose, and therefore unlesse he could procure fifteene pound of the *English* there for his ransome, he would send him up into the Countrey, where he should never see *Christendome* againe, and endure the extremity of a miserable banishment.

But see how God worketh all for the best for his servants, and confounded the presumption of Tyrants, frustrating their purposes, to make his wonders knowne to the sonnes of men, and releeves his people, when they least thinke of succour and releasement. Whilest *Iohn Rawlins* was thus ter-rified with the dogged answere of *Villa Rise*, the *Exchange of Bristow*, a ship formerly surprised by the Pirats, lay all unrigged in the Harbour, till at last one *Iohn Goodale*, an *English Turke*, with his confederates, understanding shee was a good sailer, and might be made a proper Man of Warre, bought her from the *Turkes* that tooke her, and prepared her for their owne purpose. Now the *Captaine* that set them at worke, was also an *English Renegado*, by the name of *Rammetham Rise*, but by his Christian name *Henrie Chandler*, who resolved to make *Goodale* Master over her; and because they were both *English Turkes*, having the command notwithstanding of many *Turkes* and *Moores*, they concluded to have all *English* slaves to goe in her, and for their Gunners, *English* and *Dutch Renegadoes*, and so they agreed with the Patrons of nine *English* and one *French* Slave for their ransoms, who were presently imployed to rig and furnish the ship for a Man of Warre, and while they were thus busied, two of *Iohn Rawlins* men, who were taken with him, were also taken up to serve in this Man of Warre, their names, *Iames Roe*, and *Iohn Davies*, the one dwelling in *Plimmoth*, and the other in *Foy*, where the Commander of this ship was also borne, by which occasion they came acquainted, so that both the Captaine, and the Master promised them good usage, upon the good service they should performe in the voyage, and withall demanded of them, if they knew of any *Englishman* to be bought, that could serve as a Pilot, both to direct them out of Harbour, and conduct them in their voyage. For in truth neither was the Captaine a Mariner, nor any *Turke* in her of sufficiency to dispose of her through the Straites in securitie, nor oppose any enemie, that should hold it out bravely against them. *Davies* quickly replied, that as farre as he understood, *Villa Rise* would sell *Iohn Rawlins* his Master, and Commander of the Barke which was taken, a man every way sufficient for Sea affaires, being of great resolution and good experience; and for all he had a lame hand, yet had he a sound heart and noble courage for any attempt or adventure.

When the Captaine understood thus much, he imployed *Davies* to search for Rawlins, who at last lighting upon him, asked him if the *Turke* would sell him: *Rawlins* suddenly answered, that by reason of his lame hand he was willing to part with him; but because he had disbursed money for him, he would gaine something by him, and so prized him at three hundred Dooblets, which amounteth to fifteene pound *English;* which he must procure, or incurre sorer indurances. When *Davies* had certified this much, the *Turkes* a ship-boord conferred about the matter, and the Master whose Christen name was *Iohn Goodale* joyned with two *Turkes*, who were consorted with him, and disbursed one hundred Dooblets a piece, and so bought him of *Villa Rise,* sending him into the said ship, called the *Exchange of Bristow,* as well to supervise what had been done, as to order what was left undone, but especially to fit the sailes, and to accommodate the ship, all which *Rawlins* was very carefull and dilligent in, not yet thinking of any peculiar plot of deliverance, more than a generall desire to be freed from this *Turkish* slaverie, and inhumane abuses.

By the seventh of Januarie, the ship was prepared with twelve good cast Pieces, and all manner of munition and provision, which belonged to such a purpose, and the same day haled out of the Mould of *Algier,* with this company, and in this manner.

There were in her sixtie three *Turkes* and *Moores*, nine *English* slaves, and one *French*, foure *Hollanders* that were free men, to whom the *Turkes* promised one prise or other, and so to returne to Holland; or if they were disposed to goe backe againe for *Algier,* they should have great reward and no enforcement offered, but continue as they would, both their religion and their customes: and for their Gunners they had two of our Souldiers, one *English* and one *Dutch* Renegado; and thus much for the companie. For the manner of setting out, it was as usuall as in other ships, but that the *Turkes* delighted in the ostentous braverie of their Streamers, Banners, and Top-sayles; the ship being a handsome ship, and well built for any purpose. The Slaves and *English* were imployed under Hatches about the Ordnance, and other workes of order, and accommodating themselves: all which *Iohn Rawlins* marked, as supposing it an intolerable slaverie to take such paines, and be subiect to such dangers, and still to enrich other men and maintaine their voluptuous filthinesse and lives, returning *themselves* as Slaves, and living worse than their Dogs amongst them. Whereupon hee burst out into these, or the like abrupt speeches: "Oh Hellish slaverie to be thus subiect to Dogs! Oh, God strengthen my heart and hand, that something shall be done to ease us of these mischiefs, and deliver us from these cruell *Mahumetan* Dogs. The other Slaves pittying his distraction (as they thought) bad him speake softly, lest they should all fare the worse for his distemperature. The worse (quoth *Rawlins*) what can be worse? I will either attempt my deliverance at one time, or another, or perish in the enterprise: but if you would be contented to hearken after a release, and joyne with me in the action, I would not doubt of facilitating the same, and shew you a way to make your credits thrive by some worke of amazement, and augment your glorie in purchasing your libertie." "I prethee be quiet (said they againe) and think not of impossibilities: yet if you can but open such a doore of reason and probabilite, that we be not condemned for desperate and distracted persons, in pulling the Sunne as it were out of the Firmament, wee can but sacrifice our lives, and you may be sure of secrecie and faithfulnesse."

The fifteenth of *Ianuarie*, the morning water brought us neere *Cape de Gatt,* hard by the shoare, we having in our companie a smal *Turkish* ship of Warre, that followed us out of *Algier* the next day, and now ioyning with us, gave us notice of seven small vessels, sixe of them being *Sallees,* and one *Pollack,* who very quickly appeared in sight, and so we made toward them: but having more advantage of the *Pollack,* then the rest, and loth to lose all, we both fetcht her up, and brought her past hope of recoverie, which when she perceived, rather then she would voluntarily come into the slaverie of these *Mahumetans,* she ran her selfe a shoare, and so all the men forsooke her. We still followed as neere as we durst, and for feare of splitting, let fall our anchors, sending out both our boates, wherein were many Musketeers, and some *English* and *Dutch* Renegadoes, who came aboord home at their *Conge,* and found three pieces of Ordnance, and foure Murtherers: but they straightway threw them all over-boord to lighten the ship, and so they got her off, being laden with Hides, and Logwood for dying, and presently sent her to *Algier*, taking nine *Turkes*, and one *English* Slave, out of one ship, and six out of the lesse, which we thought sufficient to man her.

In the rifling of this *Catelaynia*, our *Turkes* fell at variance one with another, and in such a manner, that we divided our selves, the lesser ship returned to *Algier*, and our *Exchange* tooke the opportunitie of the wind, and plyed out of the Streights, which reioyced *Iohn Rawlins* very much, as resolving on some Stratageme, when opportunities should serve. In the meane-while, the *Turkes* began to murmurre, and would not willingly goe into the *Marr Granada*, as the phrase is amongst them: notwithstanding the *Moores* being very *superstitious*, were contented to be directed by their *Hoshea*, who with us, signifieth a Witch, and is of great account and reputation amongst them, as not going in any great Vessell to Sea without one, and observing whatsoever he concludeth out of his Divination. The Ceremonies they use are many, and when they come into the Ocean, every second or third night they make their Conjuration; it beginneth and endeth with Prayer, using many Characters, and calling upon God by divers names: yet at this time, all that they did consisted in these particulars.

Upon the sight of two great ships, and as wee were afraid of their chasing us, they beeing supposed to bee *Spanish* men of Warre, a great silence is commanded in the ship, and when all is done, the company giveth as great a skreech; the Captaine comming to *John Rawlins*, and sometimes making him take in all his sayles, and sometimes causing him to hoyst them all out, as the Witch findeth by his Booke, and presages; then have they two Arrowes, and a Curtleaxe, lying upon a Pillow naked; the Arrowes are one for the Turkes, and the other for the Christians; then the Witch readeth, and the Captaine or some other taketh the Arrowes in their hand by the heads, and if the Arrow for the Christians commeth over the head of the Arrow for the *Turkes*, then doe they advance their sayles, and will not endure the fight, whatsoever they see: but if the Arrow of the *Turkes* is found in the opening of the hand upon the Arrow of the Christians, then will they stay and encounter with any shippe whatsoever. The Curtleaxe is taken up by some Childe, that is innocent, or rather ignorant of the Ceremonie, and so layd downe againe; then doe they observe, whether the same side is uppermost, which lay before, and so proceed accordingly.

They also observe Lunatickes and Changelings, and the Coniurer writeth downe their Sayings in a Booke, groveling on the ground, as if he whispered to the Devil to tell him the truth, and so expoundeth the Letter, as it were by inspiration. Many other foolish Rites they have, whereupon they doe dote as foolishly.

Whilest he was busied, and made demonstration that all was finished, the people in the ship gave a great shout, and cryed out, "a sayle, a sayle," which at last was discovered to bee another man of Warre of *Turkes*. For he made toward us, and sent his Boat aboord us, to whom our Captain complained, that being becalmed by the Southerne Cape, and having made no Voyage, the *Turkes* denyed to goe any further Northward: but the Captaine resolved not to returne to *Algier,* except he could obtayne some Prize worthy his endurances, but rather to goe to *Salle,* and tell his Christians to victuall his ship; which the other Captaine apprehended for his honour, and so perswaded the *Turkes* to be obedient unto him; whereupon followed a pacification amongst us, and so that *Turke* tooke his course for the Streights, and wee put up Northward, expecting the good houre of some beneficiall bootie.

All this while our slavery continued, and the *Turkes* with insulting tyrannie set us still on worke in all base and servile actions, adding stripes and inhumane revilings, even in our greatest labour, whereupon *Iohn Rawlins* resolved to obtane his libertie, and surprize the ship; providing Ropes with broad spikes of Iron, and all the Iron Crowes, with which hee knew a way, upon consent of the rest, to ramme up or tye fast their Scuttels, Gratings, and Cabbins, yea, to shut up the Captaine himselfe with all his consorts, and so to handle the matter, that upon the watch-word given, the *English* being Masters of the Gunner roome, Ordnance, and Powder, they would eyther blow them into the Ayre, or kill them as they adventured to come downe one by one, if they should by any chance open their Cabbins. But because hee would proceed the better in his enterprise, as he had somewhat abruptly discovered himselfe to the nine *English* slaves, so he kept the same distance with the foure *Hollanders,* that were free men, till finding them comming somewhat toward them, he acquainted them with the whole Conspiracie, and they affecting the Plot, offered the adventure of their lives in the businesse. Then very warily he undermined the *English* Renegado, which was the Gunner, and three more his Associats, who at first seemed to retract. Last of all were brought in the *Dutch* Renegadoes, who were also in the Gunner roome, for alwayes there lay twelve there, five Christians, and seven *English,* and *Dutch Turkes:* so that when another motion had settled their resolutions, and *Iohn Rawlins* his constancie had put new life as it were in the matter, the foure *Hollanders* very honestly, according to their promise, sounded the *Dutch* Renegadoes, who with easie perswasion gave their consent to so brave an Enterprize; whereupon *Iohn Rawlins,* not caring whether the *English* Gunners would yeeld or no, resolved in the Captaines morning watch, to make the attempt. But you must understand that where the *English* slaves lay, there hung up alwayes foure or five Crowes of Iron, being still under the carriages of the Peeces, and when the time approached being very darke, because *Iohn Rawlins* would have his Crow of Iron ready as other things were, and other men prepared in their severall places, in taking it out of the carriage, by chance, it hit on the side of the Peece, making such a noyse, that the Souldiers hearing it awaked the *Turkes,* and bade them come downe: whereupon the Botesane of the *Turkes* descended with a Candle, and presently searched all the slaves places, making much adoe of the matter, but finding neyther Hatchet nor Hammer, nor any thing else to move suspicion of the Enterprize, more then the Crow of Iron, which lay slipped downe under the carriages of the Peeces, they went quietly up againe, and certified the Captaine what had chanced, who satisfied himselfe, that it was a common thing to have a Crow of Iron slip from its place. But by this occasion wee made stay of our attempt, yet were resolved to take another or a better oportunitie.

For we sayled still more North-ward, and *Rawlins* had more time to tamper with his Gunners, and the rest of the *English* Renegadoes, who very willingly, when they considered the matter, and perpended the reasons, gave way unto the Proiect, and with a kind of joy seemed to entertayne the motives: only they made a stop at the first on-set, who should begin the enterprize, which was no way fit for them to doe, because they were no slaves, but Renegadoes, and so had always beneficiall entertaynment amongst them. But when it is once put in practice, they would be sure not to faile them, but venture their lives for God and their Countrey. But once againe he is disappointed, and a suspitious accident brought him to recollect his spirits anew, and studie on the danger of the enterprize, and thus it was. After the Renegado Gunner, had protested secrecie by all that might induce a man to bestow some beliefe upon him, he presently went up the Scottle, but stayed not aloft a quarter of an houre; nay he came sooner down, & in the Gunner roome sate by *Rawlins*, who tarryed for him where he left him: he was no sooner placed, and entred into some conference, but there entred into the place a furious *Turke*, with his Knife drawne, and presented it to *Rawlins* his body, who verily supposed, he intended to kill him, as suspitious that the Gunner had discovered something, whereat *Rawlins* was much moved, and hastily asked what the matter meant, and whether he would kill him, observing his companion's countenance to change colour, whereby his suspitious heart, condemned him for a Traytor: but at more leisure he sware the contrary, and afterward proved faithfull and industrious in the enterprize. For the present, he answered *Rawlins* in this manner, "no Master, be not afraid, I thinke hee doth but *iest.*" With that *John Rawlins* gave backe a little and drew out his Knife, stepping also to the Gunners sheath and taking out his, whereby he had two Knives to one, which when the *Turke* perceived, he threw downe his Knife, saying, hee did but iest with him. But when the Gunner perceived, *Rawlins* tooke it so ill, hee whispered something in his eare, that at last satisfied him, calling Heaven to witnesse, that he never spake word of the Enterprize, nor ever would, either to the preiudice of the businesse, or danger of his person. Notwithstanding, *Rawlins* kept the Knives in his sleeve all night, and was somewhat troubled, for that hee had made so many acquainted with an action of such importance; but the next day, when hee perceived the Coast cleere, and that there was no cause of further feare, hee somewhat comforted himselfe.

All this while, *Rawlins* drew the Captaine to lye for the Northerne Cape, assuring him, that thereby he should not misse a prize, which accordingly fell out, as a wish would have it: but his drift was in truth to draw him from any supply, or help of *Turkes,* if God should give way to their Enterprize, or successe to the victorie: yet for the present the sixth of February, being twelve leagues from the Cape, wee descryed a sayle, and presently took the advantage of the wind in chasing her, and at last fetched her up, making her strike all her sayles, whereby wee knew her to be a Barke belonging to *Tor Bay,* neere *Dartmouth,* that came from *Auerure* laden with Salt. Ere we had fully dispatched, it chanced to be foule weather, so that we could not, or at least *would not* make out our Boat, but caused the Master of the Barke to let downe his, and come aboord with his Company, being in the Barke but nine men, and one Boy; and so the Master leaving his Mate with two men in the ship, came himselfe with five men, and the boy unto us, whereupon our *Turkish* Captain sent ten *Turkes* to man her, amongst whom were two *Dutch,* and one English Renegado, who were of our confederacie, and acquainted with the businesse.

But when *Rawlins* saw this partition of his friends; before they could hoyst out their Boat for the Barke, he made meanes to speake with them, and told them plainly, that he would prosecute the matter eyther that night, or the next and therefore whatsoever came of it they should acquaint the *English* with his resolution, and make toward *England,* bearing up the helme, whiles the *Turkes* slept, and suspected no such matter: for by Gods grace in his first watch about mid-night, he would shew them a light, by which they might understand, that the Enterprize was begunne, or at least in a good forwardnesse for the execution: and so the Boat was let downe, and they came to the Barke of *Tor Bay,* where the Masters Mate beeing left (as before you have heard) apprehended quickly the matter, and heard the Discourse with amazement. But time was precious, and not to be spent in disputing, or casting of doubts, whether the *Turkes* that were with them were able to master them, or no, beeing seven to sixe, considering they had the helme of the ship, and the *Turkes* being Souldiers, and ignorant of Sea Affaires, could not discover, whether they went to *Algier* or no; or if they did, they resolved by *Rawlins* example to cut their throats, or cast them over-boord: and so I leave them to make use of the Renegadoes instructions, and returne to *Rawlins* againe.

The Master of the Barke of *Tor Bay,* and his Company were quickly searched, and as quickly pillaged, and dismissed to the libertie of the shippe, whereby *Rawlins* had leisure to entertayne him with the lamentable newes of their extremities, and in a word, of every particular which was befitting to the purpose: yea, he told him, that that night he should lose the sight of them, for they would make the helme for *England* and hee would that night and evermore pray for their good successe, and safe deliverance.

When the Master of the Barke of *Tor Bay* had heard him out, and that his company were partakers of his Storie, they became all silent, not eyther diffident of his Discourse, or afraid of the attempt, but resolved to assist him. Yet to shew himselfe an understanding man, hee demanded of *Rawlins,* what weapons he had, and in what manner he would execute the businesse: to which he answered, that he had Ropes, and Iron Hookes to make fast the Scottels, Gratings, and Cabbines, he had also in the Gunner roome two Curtleaxes, and the slaves had five Crowes of Iron before them: Besides, in the scuffling they made no question of some of the Souldiers weapons. Then for the manner, hee told them, they were sure of the Ordnance, the Gunner roome, and the Powder, and so blocking them up, would eyther kill them as they came downe, or turne the Ordnance against their Cabbins, or blow them into the Ayre by one Strategeme or other; and thus were they contented on all sides, and resolved to the Enterprize.

The next morning, being the seventh of February, the Prize of *Tor Bay* was not to bee seene or found, whereat the Captaine began to storme and sweare, commanding *Rawlins* to search the Seas up and downe for her, who bestowed all that day in the businesse, but to little purpose: whereupon when the humour was spent, the Captaine pacified himselfe, as conceiting he should sure find her at *Algier:* but by the permission of the Ruler of all actions, that *Algier* was England, and all his wickednesse frustrated: for *Rawlins* beeing now startled, lest hee should returne in this humour for the Streights, on the eight of February went downe into the hold, and finding a great deale of water below, told the Captaine of the same, adding, that it did not come to the Pumpe, which he said very politickly, that he might remove the Ordnance. For when the Captaine askt him the reason, he told him the ship was too farre after the head: then hee commanded to use the best meanes he could to bring her in order: "sure then," quoth *Rawlins,* "wee must quit our Cables, and bring foure Peeces of Ordnance after, and that would bring the water to the Pumpe;" which was presently put in practice, so the Peeces beeing usually made fast thwart the ship, we brought two of them with their mouthes right before the Binnacle, and because the Renegadoe *Flemmings* would not begin, it was thus concluded: that the ship having three Deckes, wee that did belong to the Gunner roome should bee all there, and breake up the lower Decke. The *English* slaves, who always lay in the middle Decks, should doe the like, and watch the Scuttels: *Rawlins* himselfe prevayled with the Gunner, for so much Powder, as should prime the Peeces, and so told them all there was no better watch-word, nor meanes to begin, then upon the report of the Peece to make a cry and shout, for God, and King *Iames,* and Saint *George* for *England!*

When all things were prepared, and every man resolved, as knowing what hee had to doe, and the houre when it should happen, to be two in the afternoone, *Rawlins* advised the Master Gunner to speake to the Captaine, that the Souldiers might attend on the Poope, which would bring the ship after: to which the Captaine was very willing, and upon the Gunners information, the Souldiers gat themselves to the Poope, to the number of twentie, and five or sixe went into the Captaines Cabbin, where always lay divers Curtleaxes, and some Targets, and so wee fell to worke to pumpe the water, and carryed the matter fairely till the next day, which was spent as the former, being the ninth of February, and as God must have the prayse, the triumph of our victorie.

For by that time all things were prepared, and the Souldiers got upon the Poope as the day before: to avoid suspition, all that did belong to the Gunner-roome went downe, and the slaves in the middle decke attended their business, so that we could cast up our account in this manner. First, nine *English* slaves, besides *Iohn Rawlins:* five of the *Tor Bay* men, and one boy, foure *English* Renegadoes, and two *French,* foure *Hollanders:* in all four and twenty and a boy: so that lifting up our hearts and hands to God for the successe of the businesse, we were wonderfully incouraged; and setled our selves, till the report of the peece gave us warning of the enterprise. Now, you must consider, that in this company were two of *Rawlins* men, *Iames Roe,* and *Iohn Davies,* whom he brought out of *England,* and whom the fortune of the Sea brought into the same predicament with their Master. These were imployed about noone (being as I said, the ninth of February) to prepare their matches, while all the *Turkes* or at least most of them stood on the Poope, to weigh down the ship as it were, to bring the water forward to the Pumpe: the one brought his match lighted betweene two spoons, the other brought his in a little peece of a Can: and so in the name of God, the *Turkes* and *Moores* being placed as you have heard, and five and forty in number, and *Rawlins* having proined the Tuch-holes, *Iames Roe* gave fire to one of the peeces, about two of the clocke in the afternoone, and the confederates upon the warning, shouted most cheerefully: the report of the peece did teare and breake down all the Binnacle, and compasses, and the noise of the slaves made all the Souldiers amased at the matter, till seeing the quarter of the ship rent, and feeling the whole body to shake under them: understanding the ship was surprised, and the attempt tended to their utter destruction, never Beare robbed of her whelpes was so fell and mad: For they not onely cald us dogs, and cried out, *Usance de Lamair,* which is as much to say, the Fortune of the wars: but attempted to teare up the planckes, setting a worke hammers, hatchets, knives, the oares of the Boate, the Boat-hooke, their curtleaxes, and what else came to hand, besides stones and brickes in the Cooke-roome, all which they threw amongst us, attempting still and still to breake and rip up the hatches, and boords of the steering, not desisting from their former execrations, and horrible blasphemies and revilings.

When *Iohn Rawlins* perceived them so violent, and understood how the slaves had cleared the deckes of all the *Turkes* and *Moores* beneath, he set a guard upon the Powder, and charged their owne Muskets against them, killing them from divers scout-holes, both before and behind, and so lessened their number, to the ioy of all our hearts, whereupon they cried out, and called for the Pilot, and so *Rawlins,* with some to guard him, went to them, and understood them by their kneeling, that they cried for mercy, and to have their lives saved, and they would come downe, which he bade them doe, and so they were taken one by one, and bound, yea killed with their owne Curtleaxes; which when the rest perceived, they called us *English* dogs, and reviled us with many opprobrious termes, some leaping over-boord, crying, it was the chance of war; some were manacled, and so throwne over-boord, and some were slaine and mangled with the Curtleaxes, till the ship was well cleared, and our selves assured of the victory.

At the first report of our Peece, and hurliburly in the decks, the Captaine was a writing in his Cabbin, and hearing the noyse, thought it some strange accident, and so came out with his Curtleaxe in his hand, presuming by his authority to pacifie the mischiefe: But when hee cast his eyes upon us, and saw that we were like to surprise the ship, he threw downe his Curtleaxe, and begged us to save his life, intimating unto *Rawlins,* how he had redeemed him from *Villa-Rise,* and ever since admitted him to place of command in the ship, besides honest usage in the whole course of the Voyage. All which *Rawlins* confessed, and at last condescended to mercy, and brought the Captaine and five more into *England.* The Captain was called *Ramtham-Rise,* but his Christen name, *Henry Chandler,* and as they say, was a Chandler's sonne in Southwarke. *Iohn Goodale,* was also an *English Turke. Richard Clarke,* in *Turkish, Iafar; George Cooke, Ramdam; Iohn Browne, Mamme; William Winter, Mustapha;* besides all the slaves and *Hollanders,* with other Renegadoes, who were willing to be reconciled to their true Saviour, as being formerly seduced with the hopes of riches, honour, preferment, and such like devillish baits, to catch the soules of mortall men, and entangle frailty in the fetters of horrible abuses, and imposturing deceit.

When all was done, and the ship cleared of the dead bodies, *Iohn Rawlins* assembled his men together, and with one consent gave the praise unto God, using the accustomed service on ship-boord, and for want of bookes lifted up their voyces to God, as he put into their hearts, or renewed their memories: then did they sing a Psalme, and last of all, embraced one another for playing the men in such a Deliverance, whereby our feare was turned into joy, and trembling hearts exhillirated, that we had escaped such inevitable dangers, and especially the slavery and terror of bondage, worse than death it selfe. The same night we washed our ship, put every thing in as good order as we could, repaired the broken quarter, set up the Binnacle, and bore up the Helme for *England,* where by Gods grace and good guiding, we arrived at *Plimmoth,* the thirteenth of February, and were welcommed like the recovery of the lost sheepe, or as you read of a loving mother, that runneth with embraces to entertaine her sonne from a long Voyage and escape of many dangers.

Not long after we understood of our confederats, that returned home in the Barke of *Torbay,* that they arrived in *Pensance* in *Corne-wall* the eleventh of February: and if any aske after their deliverance, considering there were ten *Turkes* sent to man her, I will tell you that too: the next day after they lost us, as you have heard and that the three Renegadoes had acquainted the Masters Mate, and the two *English* in her with *Rawlins* determination, and that they themselves would be true to them, and assist them in any enterprise: then if the worst came, there were but seven to sixe: but as it fell out, they had a more easie passage, then turmoile, or man-slaughter. For they made the *Turkes* beleeve, the wind was come faire, and that they were sayling to *Algier,* till they came within sight of *England,* which one of them amongst the rest discovered, saying plainely, that that land was not like *Cape Vincent;* "yes faith," said he, that was at the Helme, "and you will be contented, and goe downe into the hold, and trim the salt over to windward, whereby the ship may beare full saile, you shall know and see more to morrow": Whereupon five of them went downe very orderly, the Renegadoes faining themselves asleep, who presently start up, and with the helpe of the two *English,* nailed downe the hatches, whereat the principall amongst them much repined, and began to grow into choller and rage, had it not quickly beene suppressed. For one of them stepped to him, and dasht out his braines, and threw him over-boord: the rest were brought to *Excester,* and either to be arraigned, according to the punishment of delinquents in such a kind, or disposed of, as the King and Counsell shall thinke meet and this is the story of this deliverance, and end of *Iohn Rawlins* Voyage. The Actors in this Comick Tragedie are most of them alive; The *Turkes* are in prison; the ship is to be seene, and *Rawlins* himselfe dare justifie the matter.

The Remarkable History of the Joassamee Pirates of the Persian Gulf

CHARLES ELLMS

The line of coast from Cape Mussenndom to Bahrain, on the Arabian side of the Persian Gulf, had been from time immemorial occupied by a tribe of Arabs called Joassamees. These, from local position, were all engaged in maritime pursuits. Some traded in their own small vessels to Bussorah, Bushire, Muscat, and even India; others annually fished in their own boats on the pearl banks of Bahrain; and a still greater number hired themselves out as sailors to navigate the coasting small craft of the Persian Gulf.

The Joassamees at length perceiving that their local position enabled them to reap a rich harvest by plundering vessels in passing this great highway of nations, commenced their piratical career. The small coasting vessels of the gulf, from their defenceless state, were the first object of their pursuit, and these soon fell an easy prey; until, emboldened by success, they directed their views to more arduous enterprises, and having tasted the sweets of plunder in the increase of their wealth, had determined to attempt more promising victories.

About the year 1797, one of the East India Company's vessels of war, the Viper, of ten guns, was lying at anchor in the inner roads of Bushire. Some dows of the Joassamees were at the same moment anchored in the harbor; but as their warfare had hitherto been waged only against what are called native vessels, and they had either feared or respected the British flag, no hostile measures were ever pursued against them by the British ships. The commanders of these dows had applied to the Persian agent of the East India Company there, for a supply of gunpowder and cannon shot for their cruise: and as this man had no suspicions of their intentions, he furnished them with an order to the commanding officer on board for the quantity required. The captain of the Viper was on shore at the time, in the agent's house, but the order being produced to the officer on board, the powder and shot were delivered, and the dows weighed and made sail. The crew of the Viper were at this moment taking their breakfast on deck, and the officers below; when on a sudden, a cannonading was opened on them by two of the dows, who attempted also to board.

The officers, leaping on deck, called the crew to quarters, and cutting their cable, got sail upon the ship, so as to have the advantage of manoeuvring. A regular engagement now took place between this small cruiser and four dows, all armed with great guns, and full of men. In the contest Lieut. Carruthers, the commanding officer, was once wounded by a ball in the loins; but after girding a handkerchief round his waist, he still kept the deck, till a ball entering his forehead, he fell. Mr. Salter, the midshipman on whom the command devolved, continued the fight with determined bravery, and after a stout resistance, beat them off, chased them some distance out to sea, and subsequently regained the anchorage in safety.

Several years elapsed before the wounds of the first defeat were sufficiently healed to induce a second attempt on vessels under the British flag, though a constant state of warfare was still kept up against the small craft of the gulf. In 1804, the East India Company's cruiser, Fly, was taken by a French privateer, off the Island of Kenn, in the Persian Gulf; but before the enemy boarded her, she ran into shoal water, near that island, and sunk the government dispatches, and some treasure with which they were charged, in about two and a half fathoms of water, taking marks for the recovery of them, if possible, at some future period. The passengers and crew were taken to

Bushire where they were set at liberty, and having purchased a country dow by subscription, they fitted her out and commenced their voyage down the gulf, bound for Bombay.

On their passage down, as they thought it would be practicable to recover the government packet and treasure sunk off Kenn, they repaired to that island, and were successful, after much exertion, in recovering the former, which being in their estimation of the first importance, as the dispatches were from England to Bombay, they sailed with them on their way thither, without loss of time.

Near the mouth of the gulf, they were captured by a fleet of Joassamee boats, after some resistance, in which several were wounded and taken into their chief port at Ras-el-Khyma. Here they were detained in hope of ransome, and during their stay were shown to the people of the town as curiosities, no similar beings having been before seen there within the memory of man. The Joassamee ladies were so minute in their enquiries, indeed, that they were not satisfied without determining in what respect an uncircumcised infidel differed from a true believer.

When these unfortunate Englishmen had remained for several months in the possession of the Arabs, and no hope of their ransom appeared, it was determined to put them to death, and thus rid themselves of unprofitable enemies. An anxiety to preserve life, however, induced the suggestion, on their parts, of a plan for the temporary prolongation of it, at least. With this view they communicated to the chief of the pirates the fact of their having sunk a quantity of treasure near the island of Kenn, and of their knowing the marks of the spot, by the bearings of objects on shore, with sufficient accuracy to recover it, if furnished with good divers. They offered, therefore, to purchase their own liberty, by a recovery of this money for their captors; and on the fulfillment of their engagement it was solemnly promised to be granted to them.

They soon sailed for the spot, accompanied by divers accustomed to that occupation on the pearl banks of Bahrain; and, on their anchoring at the precise points of bearing taken, they commenced their labors. The first divers who went down were so successful, that all the crew followed in their turns, so that the vessel was at one time almost entirely abandoned at anchor. As the men, too, were all so busily occupied in their golden harvest, the moment appeared favorable for escape; and the still captive Englishmen were already at their stations to overpower the few on board, cut the cable, and make sail. Their motions were either seen or suspected, as the divers repaired on board in haste, and the scheme was thus frustrated. They were now given their liberty as promised, by being landed on the island of Kenn, where, however, no means offered for their immediate escape. The pirates, having at the same time landed themselves on the island, commenced a general massacre of the inhabitants, in which their released prisoners, fearing they might be included, fled for shelter to clefts and hiding places in the rocks. During their refuge here, they lived on such food as chance threw in their way; going out under cover of the night to steal a goat and drag it to their haunts. When the pirates had at length completed their work of blood, and either murdered or driven off every former inhabitant of the island, they quitted it themselves, with the treasure which they had thus collected from the sea and shore. The Englishmen now ventured to come out from their hiding places, and to think of devising some means of escape. Their good fortune in a moment of despair, threw them on the wreck of a boat, near the beach, which was still capable of repair. In searching about the now deserted town, other materials were found, which were of use to them, and sufficient plank and logs of wood for the construction of a raft. These were both completed in a few days, and the party embarked on them in two divisions, to effect a passage to the Persian shore. One of these rafts was lost in the attempt, and all on board her perished; while the raft, with the remainder of the party reached land.

Having gained the main land they now set out on foot towards Bushire, following the line of the coast for the sake of the villages and water. In this they are said to have suffered incredible hardships and privations of every kind. No one knew the language of the country perfectly, and the roads and places of refreshment still less; they were in general destitute of clothes and money, and constantly subject to plunder and imposition, poor as they were. Their food was therefore often scanty, and always of the worst kind; and they had neither shelter from the burning sun of the day, nor from the chilling dews of night.

The Indian sailors, sipakees, and servants, of whom a few were still remaining when they set out, had all dropped off by turns; and even Europeans had been abandoned on the road, in the most affecting way, taking a last adieu of their comrades, who had little else to expect but soon to follow their fate. One instance is mentioned of their having left one who could march no further, at the distance of only a mile from a village; and on returning to the spot on the morrow, to bring him in, nothing was found but his mangled bones, as he had been devoured in the night by jackalls. The packet being light was still, however, carried by turns, and preserved through all obstacles and difficulties; and with it they reached at length the island of Busheap, to which they crossed over in a boat from the main. Here they were detained by the Sheik, but at length he provided them with a boat for the conveyance of themselves and dispatches to Bushire. From this place they proceeded to Bombay, but of all the company only two survived. A Mr. Jowl, an officer of a merchant ship, and an English sailor named Penmel together with the bag of letters and dispatches.

In the following year, two English brigs, the Shannon, Capt. Babcock, and the Trimmer, Capt. Cummings, were on their voyage from Bombay to Bussorah. These were both attacked, near the Islands of Polior and Kenn, by several boats, and after a slight resistance on the part of the Shannon only, were taken possession of, and a part of the crew of each, cruelly put to the sword. Capt. Babcock, having been seen by one of the Arabs to discharge a musket during the contest, was taken by them on shore; and after a consultation on his fate, it was determined that he should forfeit the arm by which this act of resistance was committed. It was accordingly severed from his body by one stroke of a sabre, and no steps were taken either to bind up the wound, or to prevent his bleeding to death. The captain, himself, had yet sufficient presence of mind left, however, to think of his own safety, and there being near him some clarified butter, he procured this to be heated, and while yet warm, thrust the bleeding stump of his arm into it. It had the effect of lessening the effusion of blood, and ultimately of saving a life that would otherwise most probably have been lost. The crew were then all made prisoners, and taken to a port of Arabia, from whence they gradually dispersed and escaped. The vessels themselves were additionally armed, one of them mounting twenty guns, manned with Arab crews, and sent from Ras-el-Khyma to cruise in the gulf, where they committed many piracies.

In the year 1808, the force of the Jossamees having gradually increased, and becoming flushed with the pride of victory, their insulting attacks on the British flag were more numerous and more desperate than ever. The first of these was on the ship Minerva, of Bombay, on her voyage to Bussorah. The attack was commenced by several boats, (for they never cruize singly,) and a spirited resistance in a running fight was kept up at intervals for several days in succession. A favorable moment offered, however, for boarding; the ship was overpowered by numbers, and carried amidst a general massacre. The captain was said to have been cut up into separate pieces, and thrown overboard by fragments; the second mate and carpenter alone were spared, probably to make use of their services; and an Armenian lady, the wife of Lieut. Taylor, then at Bushire, was reserved perhaps for still greater sufferings. But was subsequently ransomed for a large sum.

A few weeks after this, the Sylph, one of the East India Company's cruisers, of sixty tons and mounting eight guns, was accompanying the mission under Sir Hartford Jones, from Bombay, to Persia; when being separated from the rest of the squadron, she was attacked in the gulf by a fleet of dows. These bore down with all the menacing attitude of hostility; but as the commander, Lieut. Graham had received orders from the Bombay government, not to open his fire on any of these vessels until he had been first fired on himself, the ship was hardly prepared for battle, and the colors were not even hoisted to apprise them to what nation she belonged. The dows approached, threw their long overhanging prows across the Sylph's beam, and pouring in a shower of stones on her deck, beat down and wounded almost every one who stood on it. They then boarded, and made the ship an easy prize, before more than a single shot had been fired, and in their usual way, put every one whom they found alive to the sword. Lieut. Graham fell, covered with wounds, down the fore hatchway of his own vessel, where he was dragged by some of the crew into a store room, in which they had secreted themselves, and barricaded the door with a crow-bar from within. The cruiser was thus completely in the possession of the enemy, who made sail on her, and were bearing her off in triumph to their own port, in company with their boats. Soon after, however, the commodore of the squadron in the Neried frigate hove in sight, and perceiving this vessel in company with the dows, judged her to be a prize to the pirates. She accordingly gave them all chase, and coming up with the brig, the Arabs took to their boats and abandoned her. The chase was continued after the dows, but without success.

These repeated aggressions at length opened the eyes of the East India Government, and an expedition was accordingly assembled at Bombay. The naval force consisted of La Chiffone, frigate, Capt. Wainwright, as commodore. The Caroline of thirty-eight guns; and eight of the East India Company's cruisers, namely, the Mornington, Ternate, Aurora, Prince of Wales, Ariel, Nautilus, Vestal and Fury, with four large transports, and the Stromboli bomb-ketch. The fleet sailed from Bombay in September, and after a long passage they reached Muscat, where it remained for many days to refresh and arrange their future plans; they sailed and soon reached Ras-el-Khyma, the chief port of the pirates within the gulf. Here the squadron anchored abreast of the town, and the troops were landed under cover of the ships and boats. The inhabitants of the town assembled in crowds to repel the invaders; but the firm line, the regular volleys, and the steady charge of the troops at the point of the bayonet, overcame every obstacle, and multiplied the heaps of the slain. A general conflagration was then ordered, and a general plunder to the troops was permitted. The town was set on fire in all parts, and about sixty sail of boats and dows, with the Minerva, a ship which they had taken, then lying in the roads were all burnt and destroyed.

The complete conquest of the place was thus effected with very trifling loss on the part of the besiegers, and some plunder collected; though it was thought that most of the treasure and valuables had been removed into the interior. This career of victory was suddenly damped by the report of the approach of a large body of troops from the interior, and although none of these were seen, this ideal reinforcement induced the besiegers to withdraw. The embarkation took place at daylight in the morning; and while the fleet remained at anchor during the whole of the day, parties were still seen assembling on the shore, displaying their colors, brandishing their spears, and firing muskets from all points; so that the conquest was scarcely as complete as could be wished, since no formal act of submission had yet been shown. The expedition now sailed to Linga, a small port of the Joassamees, and burnt it to the ground. The force had now become separated, the greater portion of the troops being sent to Muscat for supplies, or being deemed unnecessary, and some of the vessels sent on separate services of blockading passages, &c. The remaining portion of the blockading squadron consisting of La Chiffone, frigate, and four of the cruisers, the Mornington, Ternate, Nautilus, and Fury, and two transports, with five hundred troops from Linga, then proceeded to Luft, another port of the Joassamees. As the channel here was narrow and difficult of approach, the ships were warped into their stations of anchorage, and a summons sent on shore, as the people had not here abandoned their town, but were found at their posts of defence, in a large and strong castle with many batteries, redoubts, &c. The summons being treated with disdain, the troops were landed with Col. Smith at their head; and while forming on the beach a slight skirmish took place with such of the inhabitants of the town, as fled for shelter to the castle. The troops then advanced towards the fortress, which is described to have had walls fourteen feet thick, pierced with loop holes, and only one entrance through a small gate, well cased with iron bars and bolts, in the strongest manner. With a howitzer taken for the occasion, it was intended to have blown this gate open, and to have taken the place by storm; but on reaching it while the ranks opened, and the men sought to surround the castle to seek for some other entrance at the same time, they were picked off so rapidly and unexpectedly from the loop holes above, that a general flight took place, the howitzer was abandoned, even before it had been fired, and both the officers and the troops sought shelter by lying down behind the ridges of sand and little hillocks immediately underneath the castle walls. An Irish officer, jumping up from his hiding place, and calling on some of his comrades to follow him in an attempt to rescue the howitzer, was killed in the enterprise. Such others as even raised their heads to look around them, were picked off by the musketry from above; and the whole of the troops lay therefore hidden in this way, until the darkness of the night favored their escape to the beach, where they, embarked after sunset, the enemy having made no sally on them from the fort. A second summons was sent to the chief in the castle, threatening to bombard the town from a nearer anchorage if he did not submit, and no quarter afterwards shown. With the dawn of morning, all eyes were directed to the fortress, when, to the surprise of the whole squadron, a man was seen waving the British Union flag on the summit of its walls. It was lieutenant Hall, who commanded the Fury which was one of the vessels nearest the shore. During the night he had gone on shore alone, taking an union-jack in his hand, and advanced singly to the castle gate. The fortress had already been abandoned by the greater number of the inhabitants, but some few still remained there. These fled at the approach of an individual supposing him to be the herald of those who were to follow. Be this as it may, the castle was entirely abandoned, and the

British flag waived on its walls by this daring officer, to the surprise and admiration of all the fleet. The town and fortifications were then taken possession of. After sweeping round the bottom of the gulf, the expedition returned to Muscat.

On the sailing of the fleet from hence, the forces were augmented by a body of troops belonging to the Imaun of Muscat, destined to assist in the recovery of a place called Shenaz, on the coast, taken by the Joassamees. On their arrival at this place, a summons was sent, commanding the fort to surrender, which being refused, a bombardment was opened from the shins and boats, but without producing much effect. On the following morning, the whole of the troops were landed, and a regular encampment formed on the shore, with sand batteries, and other necessary works for a siege. After several days bombardment, in which about four thousand shot and shells were discharged against the fortress, to which the people had fled for refuge after burning down the town, a breach was reported to be practicable, and the castle was accordingly stormed. The resistance still made was desperate; the Arabs fighting as long as they could wield the sword, and even thrusting their spears up through the fragments of towers, in whose ruins they remained irrevocably buried. The loss in killed and wounded was upwards of a thousand men. Notwithstanding that the object of this expedition might be said to be incomplete, inasmuch as nothing less than a *total* extirpation of their race could secure the tranquility of these seas, yet the effect produced by this expedition was such, as to make them reverence or dread the British flag for several years afterwards.

At length in 1815, their boats began to infest the entrance to the Red Sea; and in 1816, their numbers had so increased on that coast, that a squadron of them commanded by a chief called Ameer Ibrahim, captured within sight of Mocha, four vessels bound from Surat to that port, richly laden and navigating under the British flag, and the crews were massacred.

A squadron consisting of His Majesty's ship Challenger, Captain Brydges, and the East India Company's cruisers, Mercury, Ariel, and Vestal, were despatched to the chief port of the Joassamees, Ras-el-Khyma. Mr. Buckingham the Great Oriental traveller, accompanied the expedition from Bushire. Upon their arrival at Ras-el-Khyma, a demand was made for the restoration of the four Surat vessels and their cargoes; or in lieu thereof twelve lacks of rupees. Also that the commander of the piratical squadron, Ameer Ibrahim, should be delivered up for punishment. The demand was made by letter, and answer being received, Captain Brydges determined to go on shore and have an interview with the Pirate Chieftain. Mr. Buckingham (says,) He requested me to accompany him on shore as an interpreter. I readily assented. We quitted the ship together about 9 o'clock, and pulled straight to the shore, sounding all the way as we went, and gradually shoaling our water from six to two fathoms, within a quarter of a mile of the beach, where four large dows lay at anchor, ranged in a line, with their heads seward, each of them mounting several pieces of cannon, and being full of men. On landing on the beach, we found its whole length guarded by a line of armed men, some bearing muskets, but the greater part armed with swords, shields, and spears; most of them were negroes, whom the Joassamees spare in their wars, looking on them rather as property and merchandise, than in the light of enemies. We were permitted to pass this line, and upon our communicating our wish to see the chief, we were conducted to the gate of the principal building, nearly in the centre of the town, and were met by the Pirate Chieftain attended by fifty armed men. I offered him the Mahommedan salutation of peace, which he returned without hesitation.

The chief, Hassan ben Rahma, whom we had seen, was a small man, apparently about forty years of age, with an expression of cunning in his looks, and something particularly sarcastic in his smile. He was dressed in the usual Arab garments, with a cashmeer shawl, turban, and a scarlet benish, of the Persian form, to distinguish him from his followers. There were habited in the plainest garments. One of his eyes had been wounded, but his other features were good, his teeth beautifully white and regular, and his complexion very dark.

The town of Ras-el-Khyma stands on a narrow tongue of sandy land, pointing to the northeastward, presenting its northwest edge to the open sea, and its southeast one to a creek, which runs up within it to the southwestward, and affords a safe harbor for boats. There appeared to be no continued wall of defence around it, though round towers and portions of walls were seen in several parts, probably once connected in line, but not yet repaired since their destruction. The strongest points of defence appear to be in a fortress at the northeast angle, and a double round tower, near the centre of the town; in each of which, guns are mounted; but all the other towers appear to afford only shelter for musketeers. The rest of the town is composed of ordinary buildings of unhewn stone, and huts of rushes and long grass, with narrow avenues winding between them. The present number of inhabitants may be computed at ten thousand at least. They are thought to have at present (1816), sixty large boats out from their own port, manned with crews of from eighty, to three hundred men each, and forty other boats that belong to other ports. Their force concentrated, would probably amount to at least one hundred boats and eight thousand fighting men. After several fruitless negociations, the signal was now made to weigh, and stand closer in towards the town. It was then followed by the signal to engage the enemy. The squadron bore down nearly in line, under easy sail, and with the wind right aft, or on shore; the Mercury being on the starboard bow, the Challenger next in order, in the centre, the Vestal following in the same line, and the Ariel completing the division.

A large fleet of small boats were seen standing in from Cape Mussundum, at the same time; but these escaped by keeping closer along shore, and at length passing over the bar and getting into the back water behind the town. The squadron continued to stand on in a direct line towards the four anchored dows, gradually shoaling from the depth of our anchorage to two and a half fathoms, where stream anchors were dropped under foot, with springs on the cables, so that each vessel lay with her broadside to the shore. A fire was now opened by the whole squadron, directed to the four dows. These boats were full of men, brandishing their weapons in the air, their whole number exceeding, probably, six hundred. Some of the shot from the few long guns of the squadron reached the shore, and were buried in the sand; others fell across the bows and near the hulls of the dows to which they were directed; but the cannonades all fell short, as we were then fully a mile from the beach.

The Arab colors were displayed on all the forts; crowds of armed men were assembled on the beach, bearing large banners on poles, and dancing around them with their arms, as if rallying around a sacred standard, so that no sign of submission or conquest was witnessed throughout. The Ariel continued to discharge about fifty shot after all the others had desisted, but with as little avail as before, and thus ended this wordy negociation, and the bloodless battle to which it eventually led.

In 1818, these pirates grew so daring that they made an irruption into the Indian Ocean, and plundered vessels and towns on the islands and coasts. A fleet was sent against them, and intercepted them off Ashlola Island, proceeding to the westward in three divisions; and drove them back into the gulf. The Eden and Psyche fell in with two trankies, and these were so closely pursued that they were obliged to drop a small captured boat they had in tow. The Thetes one day kept in close chase of seventeen vessels, but they were enabled to get away owing to their superior sailing. The cruisers met with the Joassamees seventeen times and were constantly employed in hunting them from place to place.

At length, in 1819, they became such a scourge to commerce that a formidable expedition under the command of Major General Sir W. Grant Keir, sailed against them. It arrived before the chief town in December, and commenced operations. In his despatches Gen. Keir says—I have the satisfaction to report the town of Ras-el Khyma, after a resistance of six days, was taken possession of this morning by the force under my command.

On the 18th, after completing my arrangements at Muscat, the Liverpool sailed for the rendezvous at Kishme; on the 21st, we fell in with the fleet of the Persian Gulf and anchored off the island of Larrack on the 24th November.

As it appeared probable that a considerable period would elapse before the junction of the ships which were detained at Bombay, I conceived it would prove highly advantageous to avail myself of all the information that could be procured respecting the strength and resources of the pirates we had to deal with.

No time was lost in making the necessary preparations for landing, which was effected the following morning without opposition, at a spot which had been previously selected for that purpose, about two miles to the westward of the town. The troops were formed across the isthmus connecting the peninsula on which the town is situated with the neighboring country, and the whole of the day was occupied in getting the tents on shore, to shelter the men from rain, landing engineers, tools, sand bags, &c., and making arrangements preparatory to commencing our approaches the next day. On the morning of the 4th, our light troops were ordered in advance, supported by the the pickets, to dislodge the enemy from a bank within nine hundred yards of the outer fort, which was expected to afford good cover for the men. The whole of the light companies of the force under Capt. Backhouse, moved forward, and drove the Arabs with great gallantry from a date grove, and over the bank close under the walls of the fort, followed by the pickets under Major Molesworth, who took post at the sand banks, whilst the European light troops were skirmishing in front. The enemy kept up a sharp fire of musketry and cannon; during these movements, Major Molesworth, a gallant officer was here killed. The troops kept their position during the day, and in the night effected a lodgment within three hundred yards of the southernmost tower, and erected a battery of four guns, together with a mortar battery.

The weather having become rather unfavorable for the disembarkation of the stores required for the siege, but this important object being effected on the morning of the 6th, we were enabled to open three eighteen pounders on the fort, a couple of howitzers, and six pounders were also placed in the battery on the right, which played on the defences of the towers and nearly silenced the enemy's fire, who, during the whole of our progress exhibited a considerable degree of resolution in withstanding, and ingenuity in counteracting our attacks, sallied out at 8 o'clock this evening along the whole front of our entrenchments, crept close up to the mortar battery without being perceived, and entered it over the parapet, after spearing the advance sentries. The party which occupied it were obliged to retire, but being immediately reinforced charged the assailants, who were driven out of the battery with great loss. The enemy repeated his attacks towards morning but was vigorously repulsed. During the seventh every exertion was made to land and bring up the remaining guns and mortars, which was accomplished during the night. They were immediately placed in the battery, together with two twenty-four pounders which were landed from the Liverpool, and in the morning the whole of the ordnance opened on the fort and fired with scarcely any intermission till sunset, when the breach on the curtain was reported nearly practicable and the towers almost untenable. Immediate arrangements were made for the assault, and the troops ordered to move down to the entrenchments by daylight the next morning. The party moved forward about 8 o'clock, and entered the fort through the breaches without firing a shot, and it soon appeared the enemy had evacuated the place. The town was taken possession of and found almost entirely deserted, only eighteen or twenty men, and a few women remaining in their houses.

The expedition next proceeded against Rumps, a piratical town, eight miles north of Ras-el-Khyma, but the inhabitants abandoned the town and took refuge in the hill fort of Zyah, which is situated at the head of a navigable creek nearly two miles from the sea coast. This place was the residence of Hussein Bin Alley, a sheikh of considerable importance among the Joassamee tribes, and a person who from his talents and lawless habits, as well as from the strength and advantageous situation of the fort, was likely to attempt the revival of the piratical system upon the first occasion. It became a desirable object to reduce the power of this chieftain.

On the 18th December, the troops embarked at Ras-el-Khyma, at day break in the boats of the fleet under command of Major Warren, with the 65th regiment and the flank companies of the first and second regiment, and at noon arrived within four miles of their destination. This operation was attended with considerable difficulty and risk, owing to the heavy surf that beat on the shore; and which was the occasion of some loss of ammunition, and of a few boats being upset and stove in.

At half past three, P. M., having refreshed the men, (says Major Warren) we commenced our march, and fording the creek or back water, took up our position at sunset, to the northeastward of the fort, the enemy firing at us as we passed, notwithstanding that our messenger, whom we had previously sent in to summon the Sheikh, was still in the place; and I lost no time in pushing our riflemen and pickets as far forward as I could without exposing them too much to the firing of the enemy, whom I found strongly posted under secure cover in the date tree groves in front of the town. Captain Cocke, with the light company of his battalion, was at the same time sent to the westward, to cut off the retreat of the enemy on that side.

At day break the next morning, finding it necessary to drive the enemy still further in, to get a nearer view of his defences, I moved forward the rifle company of the 65th regiment, and after a considerable opposition from the enemy, I succeeded in forcing him to retire some distance; but not without disputing every inch of ground, which was well calculated for resistance, being intersected at every few yards, by banks and water courses raised for the purpose of irrigation, and covered with date trees. The next morning the riflemen, supported by the pickets, were again called into play, and soon established their position within three and four hundred yards of the town, which with the base of the hill, was so completely surrounded, as to render the escape of any of the garrison now almost impossible. This advantage was gained by a severe loss. Two twenty-four pounders and the two twelves, the landing of which had been retarded by the difficulty of communication with the fleet from which we derived all our supplies, having been now brought on shore, we broke ground in the evening, and notwithstanding the rocky soil, had them to play next morning at daylight.

Aware, however, that the families of the enemy were still in the town, and humanity dictating that some effort should be made to save the innocent from the fate that awaited the guilty; an opportunity was afforded for that purpose by an offer to the garrison of security to their women and children, should they be sent out within the hour; but the infatuated chief, either from an idea that his fort on the hill was not to be reached by our shot, or with the vain hope to gain time by procrastination, returning no answer to our communication, while he detained our messenger; we opened our fire at half past eight in the morning, and such was the precision of the practice, that in two hours we perceived the breach would soon be practicable. I was in the act of ordering the assault, when a white flag was displayed; and the enemy, after some little delay in assembling from the different quarters of the place, marched out without their arms, with Hussein Bin Alley at their head, to the number of three hundred and ninety-eight; and at half past one, P. M., the British flags were hoisted on the hill fort and at the Sheikh's house. The women and children to the number of four hundred, were at the same time collected together in a place of security, and sent on board the fleet, together with the men. The service has been short but arduous; the enemy defended themselves with great obstinacy and ability worthy of a better cause.

From two prisoners retaken from the Joassamees, they learnt that the plunder is made a general stock, and distributed by the chief, but in what proportions the deponents cannot say; water is generally very scarce. There is a quantity of fish caught on the bank, upon which and dates they live. There were a few horses, camels, cows, sheep, and goats; the greatest part of which they took with them; they were in general lean, as the sandy plain produces little or no vegetation, except a few dates and cocoanut trees. The pirates who abandoned Ras-el-Khyma, encamped about three miles in the interior, ready to retreat into the desert at a moment's warning. The Sheikh of Rumps is an old man, but looks intelligent, and is said to be the man who advises upon all occasions the movements of the different tribes of pirates on the coast, and when he was told that it was the wish of the Company to put a stop to their piracy, and make an honest people of them by encouraging them to trade, seemed to regret much that those intentions were not made known, as they would have been most readily embraced. Rumps is the key to Ras-el-Khyma, and by its strength is defended from a strong banditti infesting the mountains, as also the Bedouin Arabs who are their enemies. A British garrison of twelve hundred men was stationed at Ras-el-Khyma, and a guardship. The other places sent in tokens of submission, as driven out of their fortresses on the margin of the sea, they had to contend within with the interior hostile tribes.

Pirates at Panama

JOHN ESQUEMELING

The next morning, which was on April 23rd, 1680, that day being dedicated to St. George, our Patron of England, we came before sunrise within view of the city of Panama, which makes a pleasant show to the vessels that are at sea from off the shore. Soon after we saw also the ships belonging to the said city which lay at anchor at an island called Perico, distant only two leagues from Panama. On the aforesaid island are to be seen several storehouses which are built there, to receive the goods delivered out of the ships. At that present there rode at anchor at Perico five great ships and three pretty big barks, called Barcos de la Armadilla, or little men-of-war; the word *Armadilla* signifying a *Little Fleet*. These had been suddenly manned with design to fight us, and prevent any further attempts we should make upon the city or coasts of those seas. As soon as they spied us, they instantly weighed anchor and got under sail, coming directly to meet us whom they expected very shortly, according to the intelligence they had received of our coming. Our two *periaguas* being heavy could not row so fast as we that were in the canoes, and hence we were got pretty far before them. In our five canoes (for so many we were now in company) we had only 36 men, in a very unfit condition to fight, being tired with so much rowing, and so few in number in comparison with the enemy that came against us. They sailed towards us directly before the wind, insomuch that we feared lest they should run us down before it. Hereupon we rowed up into the wind's eye, as the seamen term it, and got close to windward of them. While we were doing this, our lesser *periaguas*, in which were 32 or more of our company, came up with us. So that we were in all 68 men that were engaged in the fight of that day, the King himself, who was in the *periagua* aforementioned, being one of our number. In the vessel that was admiral of these three small men-of-war were fourscore and six Biscayners, who have the repute of being the best mariners and also the best soldiers amongst the Spaniards. These were all volunteers, who came designedly to show their valour, under the command of Don Jacinto de Barahona, who was High Admiral of those seas. In the second were 77 negroes, who were commanded by an old and stout Spaniard, a native of Andalusia in Spain, named Don Francisco de Peralta. In the third and last were 65 *mestizos* or mulattos or tawnymores, commanded by Don Diego de Carabaxal. So that in all they made the number of 228 men. The Commanders had strict orders given them, and their resolution was to give quarter to none of the Pirates or Buccaneers. But such bloody commands as these seldom or never do happen to prosper.

The canoe of Captain Sawkins, and also that wherein I was, were much to leeward of the rest; so that the ship of Don Diego de Carabaxal came between us two, and fired presently on me to windward, and on him to leeward, wounding with these broadsides four men in his canoe and one in that I was in; but he paid so dear for his passage between us that he was not very quick in coming about again and making the same way. For we killed with our first volley of shot several of his men upon the decks. Thus we also got to windward, as the rest were before. At this time the Admiral of the *Armadilla*, or *Little Fleet*, came up with us suddenly, scarce giving us time to charge, and thinking to pass by us all with as little or less damage as the first of his ships had done. But, as it happened, it fell out much worse with him, for we were so fortunate as to kill the man at the helm, so that his ship ran into the wind, and her sails lay a-back, as is usually said in marinery. By this means we had time to come all up under his stern, and, firing continually into his vessel, we killed as many as came to the helm, besides which slaughter we cut asunder his main sheet and brace with our shot. At this time the third vessel, in which Captain Peralta was, was coming up to the aid of their general. Hereupon Captain Sawkins, who had changed his canoe and was gone into the *periagua*, left the Admiral to us four canoes (for his own was quite disabled) and met the said Peralta. Between him and Captain Sawkins the dispute, or fight, was very hot, lying board on board together, and both giving and receiving death unto each other as fast as they could charge. While we were thus engaged, the first ship tacked about, and came up to relieve the Admiral. But we, perceiving that and foreseeing how hard it would go with us if we should be beaten from the Admiral's stern, determined to prevent his design. Hereupon two of our canoes, to wit Captain Springer's and my own, stood off to meet him. He made up directly towards the Admiral, who stood upon the quarterdeck waving to him with a handkerchief so to do. But we engaged him so closely in the middle of his way, that had he not given us the helm and made away from us, we had certainly been on board him. We killed so many of them that the vessel had scarce men enough left alive or unwounded to carry her off. Yet, the wind now blowing fresh, they made shift to get away from us, and hereby saved their lives.

The vessel which was to relieve the Admiral being thus put to flight, we came about again upon the Admiral, and all together gave a loud halloo, which was answered by our men in the *periagua*, though at a distance from us. At that time we came so close under the stern of the Admiral that we wedged up the rudder; and withal killed both the Admiral himself and the chief pilot of his ship, so that now they were almost quite disabled and disheartened likewise, seeing what a bloody massacre we had made among them with our shot. Hereupon, two-thirds of their men being killed and many others wounded, they cried for quarter, which had several times been offered unto them and as stoutly denied until then. Captain Coxon entered on board the Admiral, and took with him Captain Harris, who had been shot through both his legs, as he boldly adventured up along the side of the ship. This vessel being thus taken, we put on board her also all the rest of our wounded men, and instantly manned two of our canoes to go and aid Captain Sawkins, who now had been three times beaten from on board by Peralta, such valiant defence had he made. And indeed, to give our enemies their due, no men in the world did ever act more bravely than these Spaniards.

Thus coming up close under Peralta's side, we gave him a full volley of shot, and expected to have the like return from him again, but on a sudden we saw his men blown up that were abaft the mast—some of them falling on the deck, and others into the sea. This disaster was no sooner perceived by their valiant Captain Peralta than he leaped overboard, and, in spite of all our shot, got several of them into the ship again, though he was much burnt in both his hands himself. But, as one misfortune seldom comes alone, whilst he was recovering these men to reinforce his ship withal and renew the fight, another jar of powder took fire forward, and blew up several others upon the forecastle. Among this smoke, and under cover thereof, Captain Sawkins laid them on board and took the ship. Soon after they were taken, I went on board Captain Peralta, to see what condition they were in, and indeed such a miserable sight I never saw in my life, for not one man there was found but was either killed, desperately wounded, or horribly burnt with powder, insomuch that their black skins were turned white in several places, the powder having torn it from their flesh and bones. Having compassionated their misery, I went afterwards on board the Admiral, to observe likewise the condition of his ship and men. Here I saw what did much astonish me, and will scarcely be believed by others than ourselves who saw it. There were found on board this ship but 25 men alive, whose number before the fight had been four-score-and-six, as was said above. So that three-score-and-one, out of so small a number, were destroyed in the battle. But, what is more, of these 25 men only eight were able to bear arms, all the rest being desperately wounded, and by their wounds totally disabled to make any resistance or defend themselves. Their blood ran down the decks in whole streams, and scarce one place in the ship was found that was free from blood.

Having possessed ourselves of these two *Armadilla* vessels, or *little men-of-war*, Captain Sawkins asked the prisoners how many men there might be on board the greatest ship that we could see, lying in the harbour of the island of Perico above-mentioned, as also in the others that were something smaller. Captain Peralta, hearing these questions, dissuaded him as much as he could from attempting them, saying that in the biggest alone there were 350 men, and that he would find the rest too well provided for defence against his small number. But one of his men, who lay a-dying upon the deck, contradicted him as he was speaking, and told Captain Sawkins there was not one man on board any of those ships that were in view; for they had all been taken out of them to fight us in these three vessels called the *Armadilla*, or *Little Fleet*. Unto this relation we gave credit, as proceeding from a dying man; and, steering our course to the island, we went on board them, and found, as he had said, not one person there. The biggest ship of these, which was called *La Santissima Trinidad*, or *The Blessed Trinity*, they had set on fire, made a hole in her, and loosened her foresail; but we quenched the fire with all speed, and stopped the leak. This being done, we put our wounded men on board her, and thus constituted her for the time being our hospital.

Having surveyed our own loss and damages, we found that 18 of our men had been killed in the fight, and 22 were wounded. These three Captains against whom we fought were esteemed by the Spaniards to be the valiantest in all the South Seas. Neither was this reputation undeservedly conferred upon them, as may easily be inferred from the relation we have given of this bloody engagement. As the third ship was running away from the fight, she met with two more that were coming out to their assistance, but gave them so little encouragement that they returned back and dared not engage us. We began the fight about half-an-hour after sunrise, and by noon had finished the battle and quite overcome them. Captain Peralta, while he was our prisoner, would often break out in admiration of our valour, and say: *Surely we Englishmen were the valiantest men in the whole world, who designed always to fight open, whilst all other nations invented all the ways imaginable to barricade themselves, and fight as close as they could.* And yet, notwithstanding, we killed more of our enemies than they of us.

Two days after our engagement, we buried Captain Peter Harris, a brave and stout soldier and a valiant Englishman, born in the county of Kent; whose death we very much lamented. He died of the wounds he received in the battle, and besides him only one man more: all the rest of our wounded men recovered. Being now come before Panama, I here inquired of Don Francisco de Peralta, our prisoner, many things concerning the state and condition of this city and the neighbouring country, and he satisfied me in manner following.

Description of the state and condition of Panama, and the parts adjacent. What vessels they took while they blocked up the said Port. Captain Coxon with seventy more return home. Sawkins is chosen in chief.

The famous city of Panama is situated in the latitude of 9 degrees North. It stands in a deep bay, belonging to the South Sea. It is in form round, excepting only that part where it runs along the sea-side. Formerly it stood four miles more to the East, when it was taken by Sir Henry Morgan, as is related in the *History of the Buccaneers*. But then, being burnt, and three times more since that time by casualty, they removed it to the place where it now stands. Yet, notwithstanding, there are some poor people still inhabiting the old town, and the cathedral church is still kept there, the beautiful building whereof makes a fair show at a distance, like that of St. Paul's in London. This new city of which I now speak is much bigger than the old one, and is built for the most part of brick, the rest being of stone, and tiled. As for the churches belonging thereto, they are not as yet finished. These are eight in number, whereof the chief is called Santa Maria. The extent of the city comprehends better than a mile and a half in length, and above a mile in breadth. The houses for the most part are three stories in height. It is well walled round about, with two gates belonging thereto, excepting only where a creek comes into the city, the which at high water lets in barks, to furnish the inhabitants with all sorts of provisions and other necessaries. Here are always 300 of the King's soldiers to garrison the city; besides which number, their militia, of all colours, are 1,100. But, at the time that we arrived there, most of their soldiers were out of town, insomuch that our coming put the rest into great consternation, they having had but one night's notice of our being in those seas. Hence we were induced to believe that, had we gone ashore instead of fighting their ships, we had certainly rendered ourselves masters of the place; especially considering that all their chief men were on board the Admiral—I mean such as were undoubtedly the best soldiers. Round about the city, for the space of seven leagues, more or less, all the adjacent country is Savanna, as they call it in the Spanish language, that is to say, plain and level ground, as smooth as a sheet, for this is the signification of the word Savanna. Only here and there is to be seen a small spot of woody land, and everywhere this level ground is full of *vacadas* or *beef stantions*, where whole droves of cows and oxen are kept, which serve as well as so many look-outs, or watch-towers, to descry if an enemy is approaching by land. The ground whereon the city stands is very damp and moist, which renders the place of bad repute for the concern of health. The water is also very full of worms, and these are much prejudicial to shipping; which is the cause that the King's ships lie always at Lima, the capital city of Peru, unless when they come down to Panama to bring the King's plate, which is only at such times as the fleet of *galleons* comes from Old Spain to fetch and convey it thither. Here, in one night after our arrival, we found worms of three-quarters of an inch in length, both in our bedclothes and other apparel.

At the island of Perico above-mentioned we seized in all five ships; of these, the first and biggest was named, as was said before, the *Trinidad*, and was a great ship, of the burden of 400 tons. Her lading consisted of wine, sugar, sweetmeats (whereof the Spaniards in those hot countries make infinite use), skins, and soap. The second ship was of about 300 tons burden, and not above half laden with bars of iron, which is one of the richest commodities that are brought into the South Sea. This vessel we burnt with the lading in her, because the Spaniards pretended not to want that commodity, and therefore would not redeem it. The third was laden with sugar, being of the burden of one hundred and four score tons, more or less. This vessel was given to be under the command of Captain Cook. The fourth was an old ship of sixty tons burden, which was laden with flour of meal. This ship we likewise burnt with her lading, esteeming both bottom and cargo at that time to be useless to us. The fifth was a ship of fifty tons, which, with a *periagua*, Captain Coxon took along with him when he left us.

Within two or three days after our arrival at Panama, Captain Coxon being much dissatisfied with some reflections which had been made upon him by our company, determined to leave us and return back to our ships in the Northern Seas by the same way he came thither. Unto this effect he persuaded several of our company, who sided most with him and had had the chief hand in his election, to fall off from us, and bear him company in his journey or march overland. The main cause of those reflections was his backwardness in the last engagement with the *Armadilla*, concerning which point some sticked not to defame, or brand, him with the note of cowardice. He drew off with him three score and ten of our men, who all returned back with him in the ship and *periagua* above-mentioned towards the mouth of the river of Santa Maria. In his company also went back the Indian King, Captain Antonio, and Don Andræas, who, being old, desired to be excused from staying any longer with us. However, the King desired we would not be less vigorous in annoying their enemy and ours, the Spaniards, than if he were personally present with us. And, to the intent we might see how faithfully he intended to deal with us, he at the same time recommended both his son and nephew to the care of Captain Sawkins, who was now our newly chosen General or Commander-in-Chief in the absence of Captain Sharp. The two *Armadilla* ships which we took in the engagement we burnt also, saving no other thing of them both but their rigging and sails. With them also we burnt a small bark which came into the port laden with fowls and poultry.

On Sunday, which was April 25th, Captain Sharp with his bark and company came in and joined us again. His absence was occasioned by want of water, which forced him to bear up to the King's Islands. Being there, he found a new bark, which he at once took, and burnt his old one. This vessel did sail excellently well. Within a day or two after the arrival of Captain Sharp came in likewise the people of Captain Harris who were still absent. These had also taken another bark, and cut down the masts of their old one by the board, and thus without masts or sails turned away the prisoners they had taken in her. The next day we took in like manner another bark which arrived from Nata, being laden with fowls, as before. In this bark we turned away all the meanest of the prisoners we had on board us.

Having continued before Panama for the space of ten days, being employed in the affairs aforementioned, on May 2nd we weighed from the island of Perico, and stood off to another island, distant two leagues farther from thence, called Tavoga. On this island stands a town which bears the same name, and consists of a hundred houses, more or less. The people of the town had all fled on seeing our vessels arrive. While we were here, some of our men being drunk on shore happened to set fire to one of the houses; which consumed twelve houses more before any could get ashore to quench it. To this island came several Spanish merchants from Panama, and sold us what commodities we needed, buying also of us much of the goods we had taken in their own vessels. They gave us likewise 200 pieces-of-eight for each negro we could spare them of such as were our prisoners. From this island we could easily see all the vessels that went out or came into the Port of Panama; and here we took likewise several barks that were laden with fowls.

Eight days after our arrival at Tavoga we took a ship that was coming from Truxillo and bound for Panama. In this vessel we found 2,000 jars of wine, fifty jars of gunpowder, and 51,000 pieces-of-eight. This money had been sent from that city to pay the soldiers belonging to the garrison of Panama. From the said prize we had information given us that there was another ship coming from Lima with 100,000 pieces-of-eight more; which ship was to sail ten or twelve days after them, and which they said could not be long before she arrived at Panama. Within two days after this intelligence we took also another ship laden with flour from Truxillo, belonging to certain Indians, inhabitants of the same place or thereabouts. This prize confirmed what the first told us of that rich ship, and said, as the others had done before, that she would be there in the space of eight or ten days.

Whilst we lay at Tavoga, the President, that is to say the Governor, of Panama, sent a message by some merchants to us to know what we came for into those parts. To this message Captain Sawkins made answer: *That we came to assist the King of Darien, who was the true Lord of Panama and all the country thereabouts. And that since we were come so far, there was no reason but that we should have some satisfaction. So that if he pleased to send us 500 pieces-of-eight for each man, and 1,000 for each Commander, and not any farther to annoy the Indians but suffer them to use their own power and liberty as became the true and natural lords of the country, that then we would desist from all further hostilities and go away peaceably; otherwise, that we should stay there, and get what we could, causing to them what damage was possible.* By the merchants also that went and came to Panama we understood there lived then as Bishop of Panama one who had been formerly Bishop of Santa Matha, and who was prisoner to Captain Sawkins when he took the said place about four or five years past. The Captain having received this intelligence, sent two loaves of sugar to the Bishop as a present. On the next day the merchant who carried them, returning to Tavoga, brought to the Captain a gold ring for a retaliation of said present. And withal he brought a message to Captain Sawkins from the President above-mentioned, to know farther of him, since we were Englishmen, *from whom we had our commission, and to whom he ought to complain for the damages we had already done them.* To this message Captain Sawkins sent back for answer: *That as yet all his company were not come together; but that when they were come up we would come and visit him at Panama, and bring our commissions on the muzzles of our guns, at which time he should read them as plain as the flame of gunpowder could make them.*

At this island of Tavoga Captain Sawkins would fain have stayed longer, to wait for the rich ship above-mentioned that was coming from Peru; but our men were so importunate for fresh victuals that no reason could rule them, nor their own interest persuade them to anything that might conduce to this purpose. Hereupon, on May 15th, we weighed anchor, and sailed thence to the island of Otoque. Being arrived there, we lay by it while our boat went ashore and fetched off fowls and hogs and other things necessary for sustenance. Here at Otoque I finished a draft from point Garachine to the bay of Panama, etc. Of this I may dare to affirm that it is in general more correct and true than any the Spaniards have themselves, for which cause I have here inserted it, for the satisfaction of those that are curious in such things.

From Otoque we sailed to the island of Cayboa, which is a place very famous for the pearl-fishery thereabouts, and is at the distance of eight leagues from another place called Puebla Nueva, on the mainland. In our way to this island we lost two of our barks, the one whereof had fifteen men in her, and the other seven. Being arrived, we cast anchor at the said island.

Captain Sawkins, Chief Commander of the Buccaneers, is killed before Puebla Nueva. They are repulsed from the said place. Captain Sharp chosen to be their leader. Many more of their company leave them and return home overland.

While we lay at anchor before Cayboa our two Chief Commanders, Captain Sawkins and Captain Sharp, taking with them threescore men, more or less, went in the ship of Captain Cook to the mouth of the river where Puebla Nueva is situated. The day of this action, as I find it quoted in my Journal, was May 22nd, 1679. When they came to the river's mouth, they put themselves into canoes, and were piloted up the river towards the town by a negro who was one of our prisoners. I was chosen to be concerned in this action, but happened not to land, being commanded to remain in Captain Cook's ship while they went up to assault the town. But here at Puebla Nueva the inhabitants were too well prepared for the reception of our party. For a distance of a mile below the town they had cut down great trees and laid them across the river, with design to hinder the ascent of any boats. In like manner on shore before the town itself they had raised three strong breastworks, and made other things for their defence. Here, therefore, Captain Sawkins, running up to the breastworks at the head of a few men, was killed: a man who was as valiant and courageous as any could be, and likewise, next to Captain Sharp, the best beloved of all our company or the most part thereof. Neither was this love undeserved by him, for we ought justly to attribute to him the greatest honour we gained in our engagement before Panama with the Spanish *Armadilla*, or *Little Fleet*, especially, considering that, as has been said above, Captain Sharp was by accident absent at the time of that great and bloody fight.

We that remained behind on board the ship of Captain Cook carried her within the mouth of the river of Puebla Nueva, and entered close by the East shore, which here is crowned with a round hill. Here within two stones' cast of shore we had four fathom water. Within the point opens a very large and fine river, which falls from a sandy bay at a small distance thence. But, as we were getting in, being strangers to the place we unwittingly ran our ship aground, nigh to a rock which lies on the Westward shore: for the true channel of the said river is nearer to the East than the West shore. With Captain Sawkins, in the unfortunate assault of this place, there died two men more, and three were wounded in the retreat, which they performed to the canoes in pretty good order. On their way down the river Captain Sharp took a ship, whose lading consisted of indigo, otto, manteca, or butter, and pitch, and likewise burnt two vessels more, as being of no value. With this he returned on board our ships, much troubled in his mind, and grieved for the loss of so bold and brave a partner in his adventures as Sawkins had constantly shown himself to be. His death was much lamented, and occasioned another party of our men to mutiny and leave us, returning overland as Captain Coxon and his company had done before.

Three days after the death of Captain Sawkins, Captain Sharp, who was now Commander-in-Chief, gave the ship which he had taken in the river of Puebla Nueva, which was of the burden of one hundred tons, more or less, to Captain Cook, to command and sail in—ordering withal that the old vessel which he had should go with those men that designed to leave us, their mutiny and our distraction being now grown very high. Hereupon Captain Sharp coming on board *La Trinidad*, the greatest of our ships, asked our men in full council who of them were willing to go or stay, and prosecute the design Captain Sawkins had undertaken, which was to remain in the South Sea and there to make a complete voyage; after which, he intended to go home round about America, through the Strait of Magellan. He added withal that he did not as yet fear, or doubt in the least, but to make each man who should stay with him worth one thousand pounds by the fruits he hoped to reap of that voyage. All those who had remained after the departure of Captain Coxon, for love of Captain Sawkins and only to be in his company and under his conduct, thinking thereby to make their fortunes, would stay no longer, but pressed to depart. Among this number I acknowledge myself to have been one, being totally desirous in my mind to quit those hazardous adventures, and return homewards with those who were now going to leave us. Yet, being much afraid and averse to trust myself among wild Indians any farther, I chose rather to stay, though unwilling, and venture on that long and dangerous voyage. Besides which danger of the Indians, I considered that the rains were now already up, and it would be hard passing so many gullies which of necessity would then be full of water and consequently create more than one single peril to the undertakers of that journey. Yet, notwithstanding, sixty-three men of our company were resolved to encounter all these hardships, and to depart from us. Hereunto they took their leave of us, and returned homewards, taking with them the Indian King's son and the rest of the Indians for their guides overland. They had, as was said above, the ship wherein Captain Cook sailed to carry them, and out of our provisions as much as would serve for treble their number.

Thus on the last day of May they departed, leaving us employed about taking in water and cutting down wood at the island of Cayboa aforementioned, where this mutiny happened. Here we caught very good tortoises and red-deer. We killed also alligators of a very large size, some of them being above twenty feet in length. But we could not find but that they were very fearful of a man, and would fly from us very hastily when we hunted them. This island lies S.S.E. from the mouth of the river above-mentioned. On the South-east side of the island is a shoal, or spit, of sand, which stretches itself the space of a quarter of a league into the sea. Here, therefore, just within this shoal, we anchored in fourteen fathom water. The island on this side thereof makes two great bays, in the first of which we watered at a certain pond not distant above the cast of a stone from the bay. In this pond, as I was washing myself and standing under a mançanilla tree, a small shower of rain happened to fall on the tree, and thence dropped on my skin. These drops caused me to break out all over my body into red spots, of which I was not well for the space of a week after. Here I ate very large oysters, the biggest that ever I ate in my life, insomuch that I was forced to cut them into four pieces, each quarter of them being a good mouthful.

Three days after the departure of the mutineers Captain Sharp ordered us to burn the ship that they hitherto had sailed in, only out of design to make use of the ironwork belonging to the said vessel. Withal, we put all the flour that was her lading into the last prize, taken in the river of Puebla Nueva, and Captain Cook, as was said before, was ordered to command her. But the men belonging to his company would not sail any longer under his command. Hereupon he quitted his vessel and came on board our Admiral, the great ship above-mentioned, called *La Trinidad*, determining to rule over such unruly company no longer. In his place was put one whose name was John Cox, an inhabitant of New England, who forced kindred, as was thought, upon Captain Sharp, out of old acquaintance, in this conjuncture of time, only to advance himself. Thus he was made, as it were, Vice-Admiral to Captain Sharp. The next day three of our prisoners, viz., an Indian, who was Captain of a ship, and two mulattos ran away from us, and made their escape.

After this it was thought convenient to send Captain Peralta prisoner in the Admiral, on board the ship of Mr. Cox. This was done to the intent he might not hinder the endeavours of Captain Juan, who was Commander of the money-ship we took, as was mentioned, at the island of Tavoga. For this man had now promised to do great things for us, by piloting and conducting us to several places of great riches, but more especially to Guayaquil, where he said we might lay down our silver and lade our vessels with gold. This design was undertaken by Captain Sawkins, and had not the head-strongness of his men brought him to the island of Cayboa, where he lost his life, he had certainly effected it before now. That night we had such thunder and lightning as I never had heard before in all my life. Our prisoners told us that in these parts it very often causes great damages both by sea and land. And my opinion led me to believe that our mainmast received some damage on this occasion. The rainy season being now entered, the wind for the most part was at N.W., though not without some calms.

Autobiography

EDWARD JOHN TRELAWNY

Continually in chase of something, I fell in, among other coasting and country craft, with a Chinese junk, drifted out of her course, on her return from Borneo. She looked like a huge tea-chest afloat, and sailed about as well. She was flat-bottomed and flat-sided; decorations of green and yellow dragons were painted and gilded all over her; she had four or five masts, bamboo yards, mat sails and coir rigging, double galleries all round, with ornamented head and stern, high as my main top, and was six hundred tons burden. Her interior was a complete bazaar; swarms of people were on board, and every individual, having a portion of tonnage in measured space, had partitioned off his own, and converted it into a shop or warehouse; they were like the countless cells of a bee-hire, and must have amounted to some hundreds. All sorts of handicraft trades were going on, as if on shore, from iron forging to making paper of rice straw, and glass of rice, chasing ivory fans, embroidering gold on muslins, barbacuing fat pigs, and carrying them about on bamboos for sale. In one cabin a voluptuous Tartar and a tun-bellied Chinese had joined their dainties together; a fat dog, roasted entire, stuffed with turmeric, rice, suet, and garlic, and larded with hog's grease, the real, delectable, and celebrated sea-slug, or sea-swallow's nest, shark's fins stewed to a jelly, salted eggs, and yellow-dyed pilaff formed their repast. A mighty china bowl of hot arrack punch stood in the centre of the table, from which a boy was continually ladling out its contents. Such voracious feeders I never beheld, they wielded their chop-sticks with the rapidity and incessant motion of a juggler with his balls. The little, black, greedy twinkling eye of the Chinese, almost buried in mounds of fat, glistened like a fly flapping in a firkin of butter. The Tartar, with a mouth the size of the ship's hatchway, seemed to have a proportionate hold for stowage. Understanding these were the two principal merchants on board, I had come to speak to them; but like hogs, buried up to the eyes in a savoury waste of garbage, there was no moving them from the dainties they gloated on. A sailor, who had conducted me, whispered his Tartar owner who I was; he grunted out some reply, and with a greasy paw, placed several handfuls of boiled rice on a corner of the table, indented it with his fist, poured into the hollow of the hog's lardings out of the platter containing the roast dog, and then, adding five or six hard-boiled salt eggs, motioned me to sit down and eat.

Driven away by these unclean brutes, I went into the Tartar captain's cabin, built over the rudder. He was stretched on a mat, smoking opium through a small reed, watching the card of the compass, and chanting out, "Kie! Hooé!—Kie! Chee!" Finding I might as well ask questions of the rudder as of him, I hailed the schooner to send a strong party of men.

We then commenced a general search, forcing our way into every cabin, when such a scene of confusion, chattering, and noise followed, as I never had heard before. Added to this, there was the mowing and gibbering of monkeys, apes, parrots, parroquets, bories, mackaws, hundreds of ducks, fish-divers, pigs, and divers other beasts and birds, hundreds of which were in this Mackow ark. The consternation and panic among the motley ship's crew, and merchant-passengers, are neither to be imagined nor described. They never had dreamed that a ship, under the sacred flag of the emperor of the universe, the king of kings, the sun of God which enlightens the world, the father and mother of all mankind, could, and in his seas, be thus assailed and overhauled. They exclaimed, "Who are you?—Whence did you come?—What do you here?" Scarcely deigning to look at the little schooner, whose low, black hull, as she lay athwart the junk's stern, looked like a boat or a water-snake, they wondered at so many armed and ferocious fellows, not believing that they could be stowed in so insignificant a vessel whose hull scarcely emerged from the water. A Hong silk merchant, while his bales were handed into one of our boats, offered us a handkerchief apiece, but protested against our taking his great bales, when we could not possibly have room for them.

A few grew refractory, and called out for aid to defend their property. Some Tartar soldiers got together with their arms; and the big-mouthed Tartar and his comrade, swollen out with their feed of roast dog and sea-slug, armed themselves, and came blowing and spluttering towards me. I caught the Tartar by his mustachios, which hung down to his knees; in return he snapped a musket in my face; it missed fire; his jaw was expanded, and I stopped it for ever with my pistol. The ball entered his mouth, (how could it miss it?) and he fell, not so gracefully as Caesar, but like a fat ox knocked on the head by a sledge-hammer. The Chinese have as much antipathy to villainous saltpetre, except in fire-works, as Hotspur's neat and trimly dressed lord; and their emperor, the light of the universe, is as unforgiving and revengeful towards those who kill his subjects, as our landed proprietors are towards those who slaughter their birds. An English earl told me the other day he could see no difference between the crime of killing a hare on his property, and a man on his property, arguing that the punishment should be the same for both. However, I have killed many of the earl's hares, and a leash or two of Chinese in my time, instigated to commit these heinous crimes by the same excitement—that of their being forbidden and guarded against by vindictive threats of pains and penalties.

But to return to the junk. We had a skirmish on the deck for a minute or two, a few shots were fired, and a life or two more lost in the fray. The schooner sent us more men, and no further opposition was made. Then, instead of gleaning a few of the most valuable articles, and permitting them to redeem the remainder of the cargo by paying a sum of money, as the rogues had resisted, I condemned her as lawful prize. We therefore began a regular pillage, and almost turned her inside out. Every nook, hole, and corner were searched; every bale cut, and every chest broken open. The bulky part of her cargo, which consisted of camphor, woods for dyeing, drugs, spices, and pigs of iron and tin, we left; but silks, copper, selected drugs, a considerable quantity of gold dust, a few diamonds and tiger-skins were ours; and, not forgetting Louis, who had entreated me to look out for sea-slug, I found some bags of it in the cabin of my late friend, the defunct merchant. Neither did I neglect the salted eggs, which with rice and jars of melted fat, victualled the ship. I took some thousands of these eggs, a new and excellent sort of provision for my ship's company. The Chinese preserve them by merely boiling them in salt and water till they are hard; the salt penetrates the shell, and thus they will keep for years.

The philosophic captain, whose business it was to attend to the navigation and pilotage of the junk, having nothing to do with the men or cargo, continued to inhale the narcotic drug. His heavy eye was still fixed on the compass, and his drowsy voice called out, "Kie! Hooé!—Kie! Chee!" Though I repeatedly asked him whither he was bound, his invariable answer was "Kie! Hooé!—Kie! Chee!" I pointed my cutlass to his breast, but his eyes remained fixed on the compass. I cut the bowl from the stem of his pipe, but he continued drawing at the reed, and repeating, "Kie! Hooé!—Kie! Chee!" On shoving off, as I passed under the stern, I cut the tiller ropes, and the junk broached up in the wind, but I still heard the fellow singing out, from time to time, "Kie! Hooé!—Kie! Chee!"

We had altogether a glorious haul out of the Chinaman. Every part of our little vessel was crammed with merchandise. Our men exchanged their tarred rags for shirts and trowsers of various coloured silks, and looked more like horse-jockeys than sailors. Nay, a few days after I roused a lazy and luxurious old Chinese sow from the midst of a bale of purple silk, where she was reclining; perhaps she thought she had the best right to it, as it might have belonged to her master, or because she was one of the junk's crew, or probably she was the owner herself transmigrated into this shape,—there needed little alteration. I also got some curious arms, particularly the musket, or fowling-piece, which, had it obeyed its master's intention, would have finished my career. The barrel, lock, and stock, are deeply chased all over with roses and figures of solid gold worked in. I preserve it now, and it has recalled the circumstance by which it came into my possession; otherwise, it might have been driven, like any others of greater moment, from my memory by the lapse of time, and by more recent events.

The Terrible Ladrones

RICHARD GLASSPOOLE

On the 17th of September, 1809, the Honorable Company's ship *Marquis of Ely* anchored under the Island of *Sam Chow*, in China, about twelve English miles from Macao, where I was ordered to proceed in one of our cutters to procure a pilot, and also to land the purser with the packet. I left the ship at 5 P.M. with seven men under my command, well armed. It blew a fresh gale from the N. E. We arrived at Macao at 9 P.M., where I delivered the packet to Mr. Roberts, and sent the men with the boat's sails to sleep under the Company's Factory, and left the boat in charge of one of the Compradore's men; during the night the gale increased. At half-past three in the morning I went to the beach, and found the boat on shore half-filled with water, in consequence of the man having left her. I called the people, and baled her out; found she was considerably damaged, and very leaky. At half-past 5 A.M., the ebb-tide making, we left Macao with vegetables for the ship.

One of the Compradore's men who spoke English went with us for the purpose of piloting the ship to Lintin, as the Mandarines, in consequence of a late disturbance at Macao, would not grant permission for regular pilots. I had every reason to expect the ship in the roads, as she was preparing to get under weigh when we left her; but on our rounding Cabaretta-Point, we saw her five or six miles to leeward, under weigh, standing on the starboard tack: it was then blowing fresh at N. E. Bore up, and stood towards her; when about a cable's length to windward of her, she tacked; we hauled our wind and stood after her. A hard squall then coming on, with a strong tide and heavy swell against us, we drifted fast to leeward, and the weather being hazy, we soon lost sight of the ship. Struck our masts, and endeavored to pull; finding our efforts useless, set a reefed foresail and mizzen, and stood towards a country-ship at anchor under the land to leeward of Cabaretta-Point. When within a quarter of a mile of her she weighed and made sail, leaving us in a very critical situation, having no anchor, and drifting bodily on the rocks to leeward. Struck the masts: after four or five hours hard pulling, succeeded in clearing them.

At this time not a ship in sight; the weather clearing up, we saw a ship to leeward, hull down, shipped our masts, and made sail towards her; she proved to be the Honourable Company's ship *Glatton*. We made signals to her with our handkerchiefs at the mast-head, she unfortunately took no notice of them, but tacked and stood from us. Our situation was now truly distressing, night closing fast, with a threatening appearance, blowing fresh, with hard rain and a heavy sea; our boat very leaky, without a compass, anchor or provisions, and drifting fast on a lee-shore, surrounded with dangerous rocks, and inhabited by the most barbarous pirates. I close-reefed my sails, and kept tack and tack 'till daylight, when we were happy to find we had drifted very little to leeward of our situation in the evening. The night was very dark, with constant hard squalls and heavy rain.

Tuesday, the 19th, no ships in sight. About ten o'clock in the morning it fell calm, with very hard rain and a heavy swell;—struck our masts and pulled, not being able to see the land, steered by the swell. When the weather broke up, found we had drifted several miles to leeward. During the calm a fresh breeze springing up, made sail, and endeavored to reach the weather-shore, and anchor with six muskets we had lashed together for that purpose. Finding the boat made no way against the swell and tide, bore up for a bay to leeward, and anchored about one A.M. close under the land in five or six fathoms water, blowing fresh, with hard rain.

Wednesday, the 20th, at daylight, supposing the flood-tide making, weighed and stood over to the weather-land, but found we were drifting fast to leeward. About ten o'clock perceived two Chinese boats steering for us. Bore up, and stood towards them, and made signals to induce them to come within hail; on nearing them, they bore up, and passed to leeward of the islands. The Chinese we had in the boat advised me to follow them, and he would take us to Macao by the leeward passage. I expressed my fears of being taken by the Ladrones. Our ammunition being wet, and the muskets rendered useless, we had nothing to defend ourselves with but cutlasses, and in too distressed a situation to make much resistance with them, having been constantly wet, and eaten nothing but a few green oranges for three days.

As our present situation was a hopeless one, and the man assured me there was no fear of encountering any Ladrones, I complied with his request, and stood in to leeward of the islands, where we found the water much smoother, and apparently a direct passage to Macao. We continued pulling and sailing all day. At six o'clock in the evening I discovered three large boats at anchor in a bay to leeward. On seeing us they weighed and made sail towards us. The Chinese said they were Ladrones, and that if they captured us they would most certainly put us all to death! Finding they gained fast on us, struck the masts, and pulled head to wind for five or six hours. The tide turning against us, anchored close under the land to avoid being seen. Soon after we saw the boats pass us to leeward.

Thursday, the 21st, at daylight, the flood making, weighed and pulled along shore in great spirits, expecting to be at Macao in two or three hours, as by the Chinese account it was not above six or seven miles distant. After pulling a mile or two perceived several people on shore, standing close to the beach; they were armed with pikes and lances. I ordered the interpreter to hail them, and ask the most direct passage to Macao. They said if we came on shore they would inform us; not liking their hostile appearance, I did not think proper to comply with the request. Saw a large fleet of boats at anchor close under the opposite shore. Our interpreter said they were fishing-boats, and that by going there we should not only get provisions, but a pilot also to take us to Macao.

I bore up, and on nearing them perceived there were some large vessels, very full of men, and mounted with several guns. I hesitated to approach nearer; but the Chinese assuring me they were Mandarine junks and salt-boats, we stood close to one of them, and asked the way to Macao. They gave no answer, but made some signs to us to go in shore. We passed on, and a large rowboat pulled after us; she soon came alongside, when about twenty savage-looking villains, who were stowed at the bottom of the boat, leaped on board us. They were armed with a short sword in each hand, one of which they laid on our necks, and the other pointed to our breasts, keeping their eyes fixed on their officer, waiting his signal to cut or desist. Seeing we were incapable of making any resistance, he sheathed his sword, and the others immediately followed his example. They then dragged us into their boat, and carried us on board one of their junks, with the most savage demonstrations of joy, and as we supposed, to torture and put us to a cruel death. When on board the junk, they searched all our pockets, took the handkerchiefs from our necks, and brought heavy chains to chain us to the guns.

At this time a boat came, and took me, with one of my men and the interpreter, on board the chief's vessel. I was then taken before the chief. He was seated on deck, in a large chair, dressed in purple silk, with a black turban on. He appeared to be about thirty years of age, a stout commanding-looking man. He took me by the coat, and drew me close to him; then questioned the interpreter very strictly, asking who we were, and what was our business in that part of the country. I told him to say we were Englishmen in distress, having been four days at sea without provisions. This he would not credit, but said we were bad men, and that he would put us all to death; and then ordered some men to put the interpreter to the torture until he confessed the truth.

Upon this occasion, a Ladrone, who had been once to England and spoke a few words of English, came to the chief, and told him we were really Englishmen, and that we had plenty of money, adding, that the buttons on my coat were gold. The chief then ordered us some coarse brown rice, of which we made a tolerable meal, having eat nothing for nearly four days, except a few green oranges. During our repast, a number of Ladrones crowded round us, examining our clothes and hair, and giving us every possible annoyance. Several of them brought swords, and laid them on our necks, making signs that they would soon take us on shore, and cut us in pieces, which I am sorry to say was the fate of some hundreds during my captivity.

I was now summoned before the chief, who had been conversing with the interpreter; he said I must write to my captain, and tell him, if he did not send a hundred thousand dollars for our ransom, in ten days he would put us all to death. In vain did I assure him it was useless writing unless he would agree to take a much smaller sum; saying we were all poor men, and the most we could possibly raise would not exceed two thousand dollars. Finding that he was much exasperated at my expostulations, I embraced the offer of writing to inform my commander of our unfortunate situation, though there appeared not the least probability of relieving us. They said the letter should be conveyed to Macao in a fishing-boat, which would bring an answer in the morning. A small boat accordingly came alongside, and took the letter.

About six o'clock in the evening they gave us some rice and a little salt fish, which we ate, and they made signs for us to lay down on the deck to sleep; but such numbers of Ladrones were constantly coming from different vessels to see us, and examine our clothes and hair, they would not allow us a moment's quiet. They were particularly anxious for the buttons of my coat, which were new, and as they supposed gold. I took it off, and laid it on the deck to avoid being disturbed by them; it was taken away in the night, and I saw it on the next day stripped of its buttons.

About nine o'clock a boat came and hailed the chief's vessel; he immediately hoisted his mainsail, and the fleet weighed apparently in great confusion. They worked to windward all night and part of the next day, and anchored about one o'clock in a bay under the island of Lantow, where the head admiral of Ladrones was lying at anchor, with about two hundred vessels and a Portuguese brig they had captured a few days before, and murdered the captain and part of the crew.

Saturday, the 23rd, early in the morning, a fishing-boat came to the fleet to inquire if they had captured an European boat; being answered in the affirmative, they came to the vessel I was in. One of them spoke a few words of English, and told me he had a Ladrone-pass, and was sent by Captain Kay in search of us; I was rather surprised to find he had no letter. He appeared to be well acquainted with the chief, and remained in his cabin smoking opium, and playing cards all the day.

In the evening I was summoned with the interpreter before the chief. He questioned us in a much milder tone, saying, he now believed we were Englishmen, a people he wished to be friendly with; and that if our captain would lend him seventy thousand dollars 'till he returned from his cruise up the river, he would repay him, and send us all to Macao. I assured him it was useless writing on those terms, and unless our ransom was speedily settled, the English fleet would sail, and render our enlargement altogether ineffectual. He remained determined, and said if it were not sent, he would keep us, and make us fight, or put us to death. I accordingly wrote, and gave my letter to the man belonging to the boat before mentioned. He said he could not return with an answer in less than five days.

The chief now gave me the leter I wrote when first taken. I have never been able to ascertain his reasons for detaining it, but suppose he dare not negotiate for our ransom without orders from the head admiral, who I understood was sorry at our being captured. He said the English ships would join the mandarines and attack them. He told the chief that captured us, to dispose of us as he pleased.

Monday, the 24th, it blew a strong gale, with constant hard rain; we suffered much from the cold and wet, being obliged to remain on deck with no covering but an old mat, which was frequently taken from us in the night by the Ladrones who were on watch. During the night the Portuguese who were left in the brig murdered the Ladrones that were on board of her, cut the cables, and fortunately escaped through the darkness of the night. I have since been informed they ran her on shore near Macao.

Tuesday, the 25th, at daylight in the morning, the fleet, amounting to about five hundred sail of different sizes, weighed, to proceed on their intended cruise up the rivers, to levy contributions on the towns and villages. It is impossible to describe what were my feelings at this critical time, having received no answers to my letters, and the fleet under-way to sail,—hundreds of miles up a country never visited by Europeans, there to remain probably for many months, which would render all opportunities of negotiating for our enlargement totally ineffectual; as the only method of communication is by boats, that have a pass from the Ladrones, and they dare not venture above twenty miles from Macao, being obliged to come and go in the night, to avoid the Mandarines; and if these boats should be detected in having any intercourse with the Ladrones, they are immediately put to death, and all their relations, though they had not joined in the crime, share in the punishment, in order that not a single person of their families should be left to imitate their crimes or revenge their death. This severity renders communication both dangerous and expensive; no boat would venture out for less than a hundred Spanish dollars.

Wednesday, the 26th, at daylight, we passed in sight of our ships at anchor under the island of Chun Po. The chief then called me, pointed to the ships, and told the interpreter to tell us to look at them, for we should never see them again. About noon we entered a river to the westward of the Bogue, three or four miles from the entrance. We passed a large town situated on the side of a beautiful hill, which is tributary to the Ladrones; the inhabitants saluted them with songs as they passed.

The fleet now divided into two squadrons (the red and the black) and sailed up different branches of the river. At midnight the division we were in anchored close to an immense hill, on the top of which a number of fires were burning, which at daylight I perceived proceeded from a Chinese camp. At the back of the hill was a most beautiful town, surrounded by water, and embellished with groves of orange trees. The chop-house (custom-house) and a few cottages were immediately plundered, and burned down; most of the inhabitants, however, escaped to the camp.

The Ladrones now prepared to attack the town with a formidable force, collected in row-boats from the different vessels. They sent a messenger to the town, demanding a tribute of ten thousand dollars annually, saying, if these terms were not complied with, they would land, destroy the town, and murder all the inhabitants; which they would certainly have done, had the town laid in a more advantageous situation for their purpose; but being placed out of the reach of their shot, they allowed them to come to terms. The inhabitants agreed to pay six thousand dollars, which they were to collect by the time of our return down the river. This finesse had the desired effect, for during our absence they mounted a few guns on a hill, which commanded the passage, and gave us in lieu of the dollars a warm salute on our return.

October the 1st, the fleet weighed in the night, dropped by the tide up the river, and anchored very quietly before a town surrounded by a thick wood. Early in the morning the Ladrones assembled in rowboats and landed; then gave a shout, and rushed into the town, sword in hand. The inhabitants fled to the adjacent hills, in numbers apparently superior to the Ladrones. We may easily imagine to ourselves the horror with which these miserable people must be seized, on being obliged to leave their homes, and everything dear to them. It was a most melancholy sight to see women in tears, clasping their infants in their arms, and imploring mercy for them from those brutal robbers! The old and the sick, who were unable to fly, or to make resistance, were either made prisoners or most inhumanly butchered! The boats continued passing and repassing from the junks to the shore, in quick succession, laden with booty, and the men besmeared with blood! Two hundred and fifty women, and several children, were made prisoners, and sent on board different vessels. They were unable to escape with the men, owing to that abominable practice of cramping their feet: several of them were not able to move without assistance, in fact, they might all be said to totter, rather than walk. Twenty of these poor women were sent on board the vessel I was in; they were hauled on board by the hair, and treated in a most savage manner.

When the chief came on board, he questioned them respecting the circumstances of their friends, and demanded ransoms accordingly, from six thousand to six hundred dollars each. He ordered them a berth on deck, at the after part of the vessel, where they had nothing to shelter them from the weather, which at this time was very variable,—the days excessively hot, and the nights cold, with heavy rains. The town being plundered of every thing valuable, it was set on fire, and reduced to ashes by the morning. The fleet remained here three days, negotiating for the ransom of the prisoners, and plundering the fish-tanks and gardens. During all this time, the Chinese never ventured from the hills, though there were frequently not more than a hundred Ladrones on shore at a time, and I am sure the people on the hills exceeded ten times that number.

October 5th, the fleet proceeded up another branch of the river, stopping at several small villages to receive tribute, which was generally paid in dollars, sugar and rice, with a few large pigs roasted whole, as presents for their joss (the idol they worship). Every person on being ransomed, is obliged to present him with a pig, or some fowls, which the priest offers him with prayers;

it remains before him a few hours, and is then divided amongst the crew. Nothing particular occurred 'till the 10th, except frequent skirmishes on shore between small parties of Ladrones and Chinese soldiers. They frequently obliged my men to go on shore, and fight with the muskets we had when taken, which did great execution, the Chinese principally using bows and arrows. They have match-locks, but use them very unskillfully.

On the 10th, we formed a junction with the black squadron, and proceeded many miles up a wide and beautiful river, passing several ruins of villages that had been destroyed by the black squadron. On the 17th, the fleet anchored abreast four mud batteries, which defended a town, so entirely surrounded with wood that it was impossible to form any idea of its size. The weather was very hazy, with hard squalls of rain. The Ladrones remained perfectly quiet for two days. On the third day the forts commenced a brisk fire for several hours: the Ladrones did not return a single shot, but weighed in the night and dropped down the river.

The reasons they gave for not attacking the town, or returning the fire, were that Joss had not promised them success. They are very superstitious, and consult their idol on all occasions. If his omens are good, they will undertake the most daring enterprizes.

The fleet now anchored opposite the ruins of the town where the women had been made prisoners. Here we remained five or six days, during which time about a hundred of the women were ransomed; the remainder were offered for sale amongst the Ladrones, for forty dollars each. The woman is considered the lawful wife of the purchaser, who would be put to death if he discarded her. Several of them leaped overboard and drowned themselves, rather than submit to such infamous degradation.

The fleet then weighed and made sail down the river, to receive the ransom from the town before mentioned. As we passed the hill, they fired several shots at us, but without effect. The Ladrones were much exasperated, and determined to revenge themselves; they dropped out of reach of their shot, and anchored. Every junk sent about a hundred men each on shore, to cut paddy, and destroy their orange-groves, which was most effectually performed for several miles down the river. During our stay here, they received information of nine boats lying up a creek, laden with paddy; boats were immediately dispatched after them.

Next morning these boats were brought to the fleet; ten or twelve men were taken in them. As these had made no resistance, the chief said he would allow them to become Ladrones, if they agreed to take the usual oaths before Joss. Three or four of them refused to comply, for which they were punished in the following cruel manner: their hands were tied behind their back, a rope from the mast-head rove through their arms, and hoisted three or four feet from the deck, and five or six men flogged them with three rattans twisted together 'till they were apparently dead;

then hoisted them up to the mast-head, and left them hanging nearly an hour, then lowered them down, and repeated the punishment, 'till they died or complied with the oath.

October the 20th, in the night, an express-boat came with the information that a large mandarine fleet was proceeding up the river to attack us. The chief immediately weighed, with fifty of the largest vessels, and sailed down the river to meet them. About one in the morning they commenced a heavy fire till daylight, when an express was sent for the remainder of the fleet to join them: about an hour after a counter-order to anchor came, the mandarine fleet having run. Two or three hours afterwards the chief returned with three captured vessels in tow, having sunk two, and eighty-three sail made their escape. The admiral of the mandarines blew his vessel up, by throwing a lighted match into the magazine as the Ladrones were boarding her; she ran on shore, and they succeeded in getting twenty of her guns.

In this action very few prisoners were taken: the men belonging to the captured vessels drowned themselves, as they were sure of suffering a lingering and cruel death if taken after making resistance. The admiral left the fleet in charge of his brother, the second in command, and proceeded with his own vessel towards Lantow. The fleet remained in this river, cutting paddy, and getting the necessary supplies.

On the 28th of October, I received a letter from Captain Kay, brought by a fisherman, who had told him he would get us all back for three thousand dollars. He advised me to offer three thousand, and if not accepted, extend it to four; but not farther, as it was bad policy to offer much at first: at the same time assuring me we should be liberated, let the ransom be what it would. I offered the chief the three thousand, which he disdainfully refused, saying he was not to be played with; and unless they sent ten thousand dollars, and two large guns, with several casks of gunpowder, he would soon put us all to death. I wrote to Captain Kay, and informed him of the chief's determination, requesting if an opportunity offered, to send us a shift of clothes, for which it may be easily imagined we were much distressed, having been seven weeks without a shift; although constantly exposed to the weather, and of course frequently wet.

On the first of November, the fleet sailed up a narrow river, and anchored at night within two miles of a town called Little Whampoa. In front of it was a small fort, and several mandarine vessels lying in the harbor. The chief sent the interpreter to me, saying I must order my men to make cartridges and clean their muskets, ready to go on shore in the morning. I assured the interpreter I should give the men no such orders, that they must please themselves. Soon after the chief came on board, threatening to put us all to a cruel death if we refused to obey his orders. For my own part I remained determined, and advised the men not to comply, as I thought by making ourselves useful we should be accounted too valuable.

A few hours afterwards he sent to me again, saying, that if myself and the quartermaster would assist them at the great guns, that if also the rest of the men went on shore and succeeded in taking the place, he would then take the money offered for our ransom, and give them twenty dollars for every Chinaman's head they cut off. To these proposals we cheerfully acceded, in hopes of facilitating our deliverance.

Early in the morning the forces intended for landing were assembled in rowboats, amounting in the whole to three or four thousand men. The largest vessels weighed, and hauled in shore, to cover the landing of the forces, and attack the fort and mandarine vessels. About nine o'clock the action commenced, and continued with great spirit for nearly an hour, when the walls of the fort gave way, and the men retreated in the greatest confusion.

The mandarine vessels still continued firing, having blocked up the entrance of the harbor to prevent the Ladrone boats entering. At this the Ladrones were much exasperated, and about three hundred of them swam on shore, with a short sword lashed close under each arm; they then ran along the banks of the river 'till they came abreast of the vessels, and then swam off again and boarded them. The Chinese thus attacked, leaped overboard, and endeavored to reach the opposite shore; the Ladrones followed, and cut the greater number of them to pieces in the water. They next towed the vessels out of the harbor, and attacked the town with increased fury. The inhabitants fought about a quarter of an hour, and then retreated to an adjacent hill, from which they were soon driven with great slaughter.

After this the Ladrones returned, and plundered the town, every boat leaving it when laden. The Chinese on the hills perceiving most of the boats were off, rallied, and retook the town, after killing near two hundred Ladrones. One of my men was unfortunately lost in this dreadful massacre! The Ladrones landed a second time, drove the Chinese out of the town, then reduced it to ashes, and put all their prisoners to death, without regarding either age or sex!

I must not omit to mention a most horrid (though ludicrous) circumstance which happened at this place. The Ladrones were paid by their chief ten dollars for every Chinaman's head they produced. One of my men turning the corner of a street was met by a Ladrone running furiously after a Chinese; he had a drawn sword in his hand, and two Chinaman's heads which he had cut off, tied by their tails, and slung round his neck. I was witness myself to some of them producing five or six to obtain payment!

On the 4th of November an order arrived from the admiral for the fleet to proceed immediately to Lantow, where he was lying with only two vessels, and three Portuguese ships and a brig constantly annoying him; several sail of mandarine vessels were daily expected. The fleet weighed and proceeded towards Lantow. On passing the island of Lintin, three ships and a brig gave chase to us. The Ladrones prepared to board; but night closing we lost sight of them: I am convinced they altered their course and stood from us. These vessels were in the pay of the Chinese government, and style themselves the Invincible Squadron, cruising in the river Tigris to annihilate the Ladrones!

On the fifth, in the morning, the red squadron anchored in a bay under Lantow; the black squadron stood to the eastward. In this bay they hauled several of their vessels on shore to bream their bottoms and repair them.

In the afternoon of the 8th of November, four ships, a brig and a schooner came off the mouth of the bay. At first the pirates were much alarmed, supposing them to be English vessels come to rescue us. Some of them threatened to hang us to the mast-head for them to fire at; and with much difficulty we persuaded them that they were Portuguese. The Ladrones had only seven junks in a fit state for action; these they hauled outside, and moored them head and stern across the bay; and manned all the boats belonging to the repairing vessels ready for boarding.

The Portuguese observing these maneuvers hove to, and communicated by boats. Soon afterwards they made sail, each ship firing her broadside as she passed, but without effect, the shot falling far short. The Ladrones did not return a single shot, but waved their colors, and threw up rockets, to induce them to come further in, which they might easily have done, the outside junks lying in four fathoms water which I sounded myself: though the Portuguese in their letters to Macao lamented there was not sufficient water for them to engage closer, but that they would certainly prevent their escaping before the mandarine fleet arrived!

On the 20th of November, early in the morning, I perceived an immense fleet of mandarine vessels standing for the bay. On nearing us, they formed a line, and stood close in; each vessel as she discharged her guns tacked to join the rear and reload. They kept up a constant fire for about two hours, when one of their largest vessels was blown up by a firebrand thrown from a Ladrone junk; after which they kept at a more respectful distance, but continued firing without intermission 'till the 21st at night, when it fell calm.

The Ladrones towed out seven large vessels, with about two hundred rowboats to board them; but a breeze springing up, they made sail and escaped. The Ladrones returned into the bay, and anchored. The Portuguese and mandarines followed, and continued a heavy cannonading during that night and the next day. The vessel I was in had her foremast shot away, which they supplied very expeditiously by taking a mainmast from a smaller vessel.

On the 23rd, in the evening, it again fell calm; the Ladrones towed out fifteen junks in two divisions, with the intention of surrounding them, which was nearly effected, having come up with and boarded one, when a breeze suddenly sprung up. The captured vessel mounted twenty-two guns. Most of her crew leaped overboard; sixty or seventy were taken immediately, cut to pieces and thrown into the river. Early in the morning the Ladrones returned into the bay, and anchored in the same situation as before. The Portuguese and mandarines followed, keeping up a constant fire. The Ladrones never returned a single shot, but always kept in readiness to board, and the Portuguese were careful never to allow them an opportunity.

On the 28th, at night, they sent in eight fire-vessels, which if properly constructed must have done great execution, having every advantage they could wish for to effect their purpose; a strong breeze and tide directly into the bay, and the vessels lying so close together that it was impossible to miss them. On their first appearance the Ladrones gave a general shout, supposing them to be mandarine vessels on fire, but were very soon convinced of their mistake. They came very regularly into the center of the fleet, two and two, burning furiously; one of them came alongside of the vessel I was in, but they succeeded in booming her off. She appeared to be a vessel of about thirty tons; her hold was filled with straw and wood, and there were a few small boxes of combustibles on her deck, which exploded alongside of us without doing any damage. The Ladrones, however, towed them all on shore, extinguished the fire, and broke them up for fire-wood. The Portuguese claim the credit of constructing these destructive machines, and actually sent a dispatch to the Governor of Macao, saying they had destroyed at least one-third of the Ladrones' fleet, and hoped soon to effect their purpose by totally annihilating them!

On the 29th of November, the Ladrones being all ready for sea, they weighed and stood boldly out, bidding defiance to the invincible squadron and imperial fleet, consisting of ninety-three war-junks, six Portuguese ships, a brig, and a schooner. Immediately the Ladrones weighed, they made all sail. The Ladrones chased them two or three hours, keeping up a constant fire; finding they did not come up with them, they hauled their wind and stood to the eastward.

Thus terminated the boasted blockade, which lasted nine days, during which time the Ladrones completed all their repairs. In this action not a single Ladrone vessel was destroyed, and their loss about thirty or forty men. An American was also killed, one of three that remained out of eight taken in a schooner. I had two very narrow escapes: the first, a twelve-pounder shot fell within three or four feet of me; another took a piece out of a small brass-swivel on which I was standing. The chief's wife frequently sprinkled me with garlic-water, which they consider an effectual charm against shot. The fleet continued under sail all night, steering towards the eastward. In the morning they anchored in a large bay surrounded by lofty and barren mountains.

On the 2nd of December I received a letter from Lieutenant Maughn, commander of the Honorable Company's cruiser *Antelope,* saying that he had the ransom on board, and had been three days cruising after us, and wished me to settle with the chief on the securest method of delivering it. The chief agreed to send us in a small gunboat, 'till we came within sight of the *Antelope;* then the Compradore's boat was to bring the ransom and receive us.

I was so agitated at receiving this joyful news, that it was with considerable difficulty I could scrawl about two or three lines to inform Lieutenant Maughn of the arrangements I had made. We were all so deeply affected by the gratifying tidings, that we seldom closed our eyes, but continued watching day and night for the boat. On the 6th she returned with Lieutenant Maughn's answer, saying he would respect any single boat; but would not allow the fleet to approach him. The chief then, according to his first proposal, ordered a gunboat to take us, and with no small degree of pleasure we left the Ladrone fleet about four o'clock in the morning.

At one P.M. saw the *Antelope* under all sail, standing toward us. The Ladrone boat immediately anchored, and dispatched the Compradore's boat for the ransom, saying, that if she approached nearer, they would return to the fleet; and they were just weighing when she shortened sail, and anchored about two miles from us. The boat did not reach her 'till late in the afternoon, owing to the tide's being strong against her. She received the ransom and left the *Antelope* just before dark. A mandarine boat that had been lying concealed under the land, and watching their maneuvers, gave chase to her, and was within a few fathoms of taking her, when she saw a light, which the Ladrones answered, and the Mandarine hauled off.

Our situation was now a most critical one; the ransom was in the hands of the Ladrones, and the Compradore dare not return with us for fear of a second attack from the mandarine boat. The Ladrones would not remain 'till morning, so we were obliged to return with them to the fleet.

In the morning the chief inspected the ransom, which consisted of the following articles: two bales of superfine scarlet cloth; two chests of opium; two casks of gunpowder; and a telescope; the rest in dollars. He objected to the telescope not being new; and said he should detain one of us 'till another was sent, or a hundred dollars in lieu of it. The Compradore however agreed with him for the hundred dollars.

Every thing being at length settled, the chief ordered two gunboats to convey us near the *Antelope;* we saw her just before dusk, when the Ladrone boats left us. We had the inexpressible pleasure of arriving on board the *Antelope* at 7 P.M., where we were most cordially received, and heartily congratulated on our safe and happy deliverance from a miserable captivity, which we had endured for eleven weeks and three days.

A few Remarks on the Origin, Progress, Manners, and Customs of the Ladrones

The Ladrones are a disaffected race of Chinese, that revolted against the oppressions of the mandarins. They first commenced their depredations on the Western coast (Cochin-China), by attacking small trading vessels in rowboats, carrying from thirty to forty men each. They continued this system of piracy several years; at length their successes, and the oppressive state of the Chinese, had the effect of rapidly increasing their numbers. Hundreds of fishermen and others flocked to their standard; and as their number increased they consequently became more desperate. They blockaded all the principal rivers, and captured several large junks, mounting from ten to fifteen guns each.

With these junks they formed a very formidable fleet, and no small vessels could trade on the coast with safety. They plundered several small villages, and exercised such wanton barbarity as struck horror into the breasts of the Chinese. To check these enormities the government equipped a fleet of forty imperial war-junks, mounting from eighteen to twenty guns each. On the very first rencontre, twenty-eight of the imperial junks struck to the pirates; the rest saved themselves by a precipitate retreat.

These junks, fully equipped for war, were a great acquisition to them. Their numbers augmented so rapidly, that at the period of my captivity they were supposed to amount to near seventy thousand men, eight hundred large vessels, and nearly a thousand small ones, including rowboats. They were divided into five squadrons, distinguished by different colored flags: each squadron commanded by an admiral, or chief; but all under the orders of A-juo-Chay (Ching Yih Saou), their premier chief, a most daring and enterprising man, who went so far as to declare his intention of displacing the present Tartar family from the throne of China, and to restore the ancient Chinese dynasty.

This extraordinary character would have certainly shaken the foundation of the government, had he not been thwarted by the jealousy of the second in command, who declared his independence, and soon after surrendered to the mandarines with five hundred vessels, on promise of a pardon. Most of the inferior chiefs followed his example. A-juo-Chay (Ching Yih Saou) held out a few months longer, and at length surrendered with sixteen thousand men, on condition of a general pardon, and himself to be made a mandarine of distinction.

The Ladrones have no settled residence on shore, but live constantly in their vessels. The after-part is appropriated to the captain and his wives; he generally has five or six. With respect to conjugal rights they are religiously strict; no person is allowed to have a woman on board, unless married to her according to their laws. Every man is allowed a small berth, about four feet square, where he stows with his wife and family.

From the number of souls crowded in so small a space, it must naturally be supposed they are horridly dirty, which is evidently the case, and their vessels swarm with all kinds of vermin. Rats in particular, which they encourage to breed, and eat them as great delicacies; in fact, there are very few creatures they will not eat. During our captivity we lived three weeks on caterpillars boiled with rice. They are much addicted to gambling, and spend all their leisure hours at cards and smoking opium.

Authentic History of the Malay Pirates
of the Indian Ocean

CHARLES ELLMS

A glance at the map of the East India Islands will convince us that this region of the globe must, from its natural configuration and locality; be peculiarly liable to become the seat of piracy. These islands form an immense cluster, lying as if it were in the high road which connects the commercial nations of Europe and Asia with each other, affording a hundred fastnesses from which to waylay the traveller. A large proportion of the population is at the same time confined to the coasts or the estuaries of rivers; they are fishermen and mariners; they are barbarous and poor, therefore rapacious, faithless and sanguinary. These are circumstances, it must be confessed, which militate strongly to beget a piratical character. It is not surprising, then, that the Malays should have been notorious for their depredations from our first acquaintance with them.

Among the tribes of the Indian Islands, the most noted for their piracies are, of course, the most idle, and the least industrious, and particularly such as are unaccustomed to follow agriculture or trade as regular pursuits. The agricultural tribes of Java, and many of Sumatra, never commit piracy at all; and the most civilized inhabitants of Celebes are very little addicted to this vice.

Among the most confirmed pirates are the true Malays, inhabiting the small islands about the eastern extremity of the straits of Malacca, and those lying between Sumatra and Borneo, down to Billitin and Cavimattir. Still more noted than these, are the inhabitants of certain islands situated between Borneo and the Phillipines, of whom the most desperate and enterprising are the Soolos and Illanoons, the former inhabiting a well known group of islands of the same name, and the latter being one of the most numerous nations of the great island of Magindando. The depredations of the proper Malays extend from Junkceylon to Java, through its whole coast, as far as Grip to Papir and Kritti, in Borneo and the western coast of Celebes. In another direction they infest the coasting trade of the Cochin Chinese and Siamese nations in the Gulf of Siam, finding sale for their booty, and shelter for themselves in the ports of Tringham, Calantan and Sahang. The most noted piratical stations of these people are the small islands about Lingin and Rhio, particularly Galang, Tamiang and Maphar. The chief of this last has seventy or eighty proas fit to undertake piratical expeditions.

The Soolo pirates chiefly confine their depredations to the Phillipine Islands, which they have continued to infest, with little interruption, for near three centuries, in open defiance of the Spanish authorities, and the numerous establishments maintained to check them. The piracies of the Illanoons, on the contrary, are widely extended, being carried on all the way from their native country to the Spice Islands, on one side, and to the Straits of Malacca on the other. In these last, indeed, they have formed, for the last few years, two permanent establishments; one of these situated on Sumatra, near Indragiri, is called Ritti, and the other a small island on the coast of Linga, is named Salangut. Besides those who are avowed pirates, it ought to be particularly noticed that a great number of the Malayan princes must be considered as accessories to their crimes, for they afford them protection, contribute to their outfit, and often share in their booty; so that a piratical proa is too commonly more welcome in their harbours than a fair trader.

The Malay piratical proas are from six to eight tons burden, and run from six to eight fathoms in length. They carry from one to two small guns, with commonly four swivels or rantakas to each side, and a crew of from twenty to thirty men. When they engage, they put up a strong bulwark of thick plank; the Illanoon proas are much larger and more formidable, and commonly carry from four to six guns, and a proportionable number of swivels, and have not unfrequently a double bulwark covered with buffalo hides; their crews consist of from forty to eighty men. Both, of course, are provided with spears, krisses, and as many fire arms as they can procure. Their modes of attack are cautious and cowardly, for plunder and not fame is their object. They lie concealed under the land, until they find a fit object and opportunity. The time chosen is when a vessel runs aground, or is becalmed, in the interval between the land and sea breezes. A vessel underway is seldom or never attacked. Several of the marauders attack together, and station themselves under the bows and quarters of a ship when she has no longer steerage way, and is incapable of pointing her guns. The action continues often for several hours, doing very little mischief; but when the crew are exhausted with the defence, or have expended their ammunition, the pirates take this opportunity of boarding in a mass. This may suggest the best means of defence. A ship, when attacked during a calm, ought, perhaps, rather to stand on the defensive, and wait if possible the setting in of the sea breeze, than attempt any active operations, which would only fatigue the crew, and disable them from making the necessary defence when boarding is attempted. Boarding netting, pikes and pistols, appear to afford effectual security; and, indeed, we conceive that a vessel thus defended by resolute crews of Europeans or Americans stand but little danger from any open attack of pirates whatsoever; for their guns are so ill served, that neither the hull or the rigging of a vessel can receive much damage from them, however much protracted the contest. The pirates are upon the whole extremely impartial in the selection of their prey, making little choice between natives and strangers, giving always, however, a natural preference to the most timid, and the most easily overcome.

When an expedition is undertaken by the Malay pirates, they range themselves under the banner of some piratical chief noted for his courage and conduct. The native prince of the place where it is prepared, supplies the adventurers with arms, ammunition and opium, and claims as his share of the plunder, the female captives, the cannon, and one third of all the rest of the booty.

In Nov. 1827, a principal chief of pirates, named Sindana, made a descent upon Mamoodgoo with forty-five proas, burnt three-fourths of the campong, driving the rajah with his family among the mountains. Some scores of men were killed, and 300 made prisoners, besides women and children to half that amount. In December following, when I was there, the people were slowly returning from the hills, but had not yet attempted to rebuild the campong, which lay in ashes. During my stay here (ten weeks) the place was visited by two other piratical chiefs, one of which was from Kylie, the other from Mandhaar Point under Bem Bowan, who appeared to have charge of the whole; between them they had 134 proas of all sizes.

Among the most desperate and successful pirates of the present day, Raga is most distinguished. He is dreaded by people of all denominations, and universally known as the "prince of pirates." For more than seventeen years this man has carried on a system of piracy to an extent never before known; his expeditions and enterprizes would fill a large volume. They have invariably been marked with singular cunning and intelligence, barbarity, and reckless inattention to the shedding of human blood. He has emissaries every where, and has intelligence of the best description. It was about the year 1813 Raga commenced operations on a large scale. In that year he cut off three English vessels, killing the captains with his own hands. So extensive were his depredations about that time that a proclamation was issued from Batavia, declaring the east coast of Borneo to be under strict blockade. Two British sloops of war scoured the coast. One of which, the Elk, Capt. Reynolds, was attacked during the night by Raga's own proa, who unfortunately was not on board at the time. This proa which Raga personally commanded, and the loss of which he frequently laments, carried eight guns and was full of his best men.

An European vessel was faintly descried about three o'clock one foggy morning; the rain fell in torrents; the time and weather were favorable circumstances for a surprise, and the commander determined to distinguish himself in the absence of the Rajah Raga, gave directions to close, fire the guns and board. He was the more confident of success, as the European vessel was observed to keep away out of the proper course on approaching her. On getting within about an hundred fathoms of the Elk they fired their broadside, gave a loud shout, and with their long oars pulled towards their prey. The sound of a drum beating to quarters no sooner struck the ear of the astonished Malays than they endeavoured to get away: it was too late; the ports were opened, and a broadside, accompanied with three British cheers, gave sure indications of their fate. The captain hailed the Elk, and would fain persuade him it was a mistake. It was indeed a mistake, and one not to be rectified by the Malayan explanation. The proa was sunk by repeated broadsides, and the commanding officer refused to pick up any of the people, who, with the exception of five were drowned; these, after floating four days on some spars, were picked up by a Pergottan proa, and told the story to Raga, who swore anew destruction to every European he should henceforth take. This desperado has for upwards of seventeen years been the terror of the Straits of Macassar, during which period he has committed the most extensive and dreadful excesses sparing no one. Few respectable families along the coast of Borneo and Celebes but have to complain of the loss of a proa, or of some number of their race; he is not more universally dreaded than detested; it is well known that he has cut off and murdered the crews of more than forty European vessels, which have either been wrecked on the coasts, or entrusted themselves in native ports. It is his boast that twenty of the commanders have fallen by his hands. The western coast of Celebes, for about 250 miles, is absolutely lined with proas belonging principally to three considerable rajahs, who act in conjunction with Raga and other pirates. Their proas may be seen in clusters of from 50, 80, and 100 (at Sediano I counted 147 laying on the sand at high water mark in parallel rows,) and kept in a horizontal position by poles, completely ready for the sea. Immediately behind them are the campongs, in which are the crews; here likewise are kept the sails, gunpowder, &c. necessary for their equipment. On the very summits of the mountains, which in many parts rise abruptly from the sea, may be distinguished innumerable huts; here reside people who are constantly on the look-out. A vessel within ten miles of the shore will not probably perceive a single proa, yet in less than two hours, if the tide be high, she may be surrounded by some hundreds. Should the water be low they will push off during the night. Signals are made from mountain to mountain along the coast with the utmost rapidity; during the day time by flags attached to long bamboos; at night, by fires. Each chief sends forth his proas, the crews of which, in hazardous cases, are infuriated with opium, when they will most assuredly take the vessel if she be not better provided than most merchantmen.

Mr. Dalton, who went to the Pergottan river in 1830 says, "whilst I remained here, there were 71 proas of considerable sizes, 39 of which were professed pirates. They were anchored off the point of a small promontory, on which the rajah has an establishment and bazaar. The largest of these proas belonged to Raga, who received by the fleet of proas, in which I came, his regular supplies of arms and ammunition from Singapore. Here nestle the principal pirates, and Raga holds his head quarters; his grand depot was a few miles farther up. Rajah Agi Bota himself generally resides some distance up a small river which runs eastward of the point; near his habitation stands the principal bazaar, which would be a great curiosity for an European to visit if he could only manage to return, which very few have. The Raga gave me a pressing invitation to spend a couple of days at his country house, but all the Bugis' nacodahs strongly dissuaded me from such an attempt. I soon discovered the cause of their apprehension; they were jealous of Agi Botta, well knowing he would plunder me, and considered every article taken by him was so much lost to the Sultan of Coti, who naturally would expect the people to reserve me for his own particular plucking. When the fact was known of an European having arrived in the Pergottan river, this amiable prince and friend of Europeans, impatient to seize his prey, came immediately to the point from his country house, and sending for the nacodah of the proa, ordered him to land me and all my goods instantly. An invitation now came for me to go on shore and amuse myself with shooting, and look at some rare birds of beautiful plumage which the rajah would give me if I would accept of them; but knowing what were his intentions, and being well aware that I should be supported by all the Bugis' proas from Coti, I feigned sickness, and requested that the birds might be sent on board. Upon this Agi Bota, who could no longer restrain himself, sent off two boats of armed men, who robbed me of many articles, and would certainly have forced me on shore, or murdered me in the proa had not a signal been made to the Bugis' nacodahs, who immediately came with their people, and with spears and krisses, drove the rajah's people overboard. The nacodahs, nine in number, now went on shore, when a scene of contention took place showing clearly the character of this chief. The Bugis from Coti explained, that with regard to me it was necessary to be particularly circumspect, as I was not only well known at Singapore, but the authorities in that settlement knew that I was on board the Sultan's proa, and they themselves were responsible for my safety. To this circumstance alone I owe my life on several occasions, as in the event of any thing happening to me, every nacodah was apprehensive of his proa being seized on his return to Singapore; I was therefore more peculiarly cared for by this class of men, and they are powerful. The rajah answered the nacodahs by saying, I might be disposed of as many others had been, and no further notice taken of the circumstance; he himself would write to Singapore that I had been taken by an alligator, or bitten by a snake whilst out shooting; and as for what property I might have in the proa he would divide it with the Sultan of Coti. The Bugis, however, refused to listen to any terms, knowing the Sultan of Coti would call him to an account for the property, and the authorities of Singapore for my life. Our proa, with others, therefore dropped about four miles down the river, where we took in fresh water. Here we remained six days, every argument being in vain to entice me on shore. At length the Bugis' nacodahs came to the determination to sail without passes, which brought the rajah to terms. The proas returned to the point, and I was given to understand I might go on shore in safety. I did so, and was introduced to the rajah whom I found under a shed, with about 150 of his people; they were busy gambling, and had the appearance of what they really are, a ferocious set of banditti. Agi Bota is a good looking man, about forty years of age, of no education whatever; he divides his time between gaming, opium and cockfighting; that is in the interval of his more serious and profitable employment, piracy and rapine. He asked me to produce what money I had about me; on seeing only ten rupees, he remarked that it was not worth while to win so small a sum, but that if I would fight cocks with him he would lend me as much money as I wanted, and added it was beneath his dignity to fight under fifty reals a battle. On my saying it was contrary to an Englishman's religion to bet wagers, he dismissed me; immediately after the two rajahs produced their cocks and commenced fighting for one rupee a side. I was now obliged to give the old Baudarre five rupees to take some care of me, as whilst walking about, the people not only thrust their hands into my pockets, but pulled the buttons from my clothes. Whilst sauntering behind the rajah's campong I caught sight of an European woman, who on perceiving herself observed, instantly ran into one of the houses, no doubt dreading the consequences of being recognized. There are now in the house of Agi Bota two European women; up the country there are others, besides several men. The Bugis, inimical to the rajah, made no secret of the fact; I had heard of it on board the proa, and some person in the bazaar confirmed the statement. On my arrival, strict orders had been given to the inhabitants to put all European articles out of sight. One of my servants going into the bazaar, brought me such accounts as induced me to visit it. In one house were the following articles: four Bibles, one in English, one in Dutch, and two in the Portuguese languages; many articles of wearing apparel, such as jackets and trowsers, with the buttons altered to suit the natives; pieces of shirts tagged to other parts of dress; several broken instruments, such as quadrants, rants, spy glasses (two,) binnacles, with pieces of ship's sails, bolts and hoops; a considerable variety of gunner's and carpenter's tools, stores, &c. In another shop were two pelisses of faded lilac colour; these were of modern cut and fashionably made. On enquiring how they became possessed of these articles, I was told they were some wrecks of European vessels on which no people were found, whilst others made no scruple of averring that they were formerly the property of people who had died in the country. All the goods in the bazaar belonged to the rajah, and were sold on his account; large quantities were said to be in his house up the river; but on all hands it was admitted Raga and his followers had by far the largest part of what was taken. A Mandoor, or head of one of the campongs, showed me some women's stockings, several of which were marked with the letters S. W.; also two chemises, one with the letters S. W.; two flannel petticoats, a miniature portrait frame (the picture was in the rajah's house,) with many articles of dress of both sexes. In consequence of the strict orders given on the subject I could see no more; indeed there were both difficulty and danger attending these inquiries. I particularly wanted to obtain the miniature picture, and offered the Mandoor fifty rupees if he could procure it; he laughed at me, and pointing significantly to his kris, drew one hand across my throat, and then across his own, giving me to understand such would be the result to us both on such an application to the rajah. It is the universal custom of the pirates, on this coast, to sell the people for slaves immediately on their arrival, the rajah taking for himself a few of the most useful, and receiving a percentage upon the purchase money of the remainder, with a moiety of the vessel and every article on board. European vessels are taken up the river, where they are immediately broken up. The situation of European prisoners is indeed dreadful in a climate like this, where even the labor of natives is intolerable; they are compelled to bear all the drudgery, and allowed a bare sufficiency of rice and salt to eat.

It is utterly impossible for Europeans who have seen these pirates at such places as Singapore and Batavia, to form any conception of their true character. There they are under immediate control, and every part of their behaviour is a tissue of falsehood and deception. They constantly carry about with them a smooth tongue, cringing demeanor, a complying disposition, which always asserts, and never contradicts; a countenance which appears to anticipate the very wish of the Europeans, and which so generally imposes upon his understanding, that he at once concludes them to be the best and gentlest of human beings; but let the European meet them in any of their own campongs, and a very different character they will appear. The character and treacherous proceeding narrated above, and the manner of cutting off vessels and butchering their crews, apply equally to all the pirates of the East India Islands, by which many hundred European and American vessels have been surprised and their crews butchered.

On the 7th of February, 1831, the ship Friendship, Capt. Endicott, of Salem (Mass.,) was captured by the Malays while lying at Qualla Battoo, on the coast of Sumatra. In the forenoon of the fatal day, Capt. Endicott, Mr. Barry, second mate, and four of the crew, it seems went on shore as usual, for the purpose of weighing pepper, expecting to obtain that day two boat loads, which had been promised them by the Malays. After the first boat was loaded, they observed that she delayed some time in passing down the river, and her crew being composed of Malays, was supposed by the officers to be stealing pepper from her, and secreting it in the bushes. In consequence of this conjecture, two men were sent off to watch them, who on approaching the boat, saw five or six Malays leap from the jungle, and hurry on board of her. The former, however, supposed them to be the boat's crew, as they had seen an equal number quit her previous to their own approach. In this they were mistaken, as will subsequently appear. At this time a brig hove in sight, and was seen standing towards Soo Soo, another pepper port, distant about five miles. Capt. Endicott, on going to the beach to ascertain whether the brig had hoisted any colors, discovered that the boat with pepper had approached within a few yards of the Friendship, manned with an unusual number of natives.

It appears that when the pepper boats came alongside of the Friendship, as but few of the hands could work at a time, numbers of the Malays came on board, and on being questioned by Mr. Knight, the first officer, who was in the gangway, taking an account of the pepper, as to their business, their reply was, that they had come to see the vessel. Mr. Knight ordered them into their boat again, and some of them obeyed, but only to return immediately to assist in the work of death, which was now commenced by attacking Mr. Knight and the rest of the crew on board. The crew of the vessel being so scattered, it was impossible to concentrate their force so as to make a successful resistance. Some fell on the forecastle, one in the gangway, and Mr. Knight fell upon the quarter deck, severely wounded by a stab in the back while in the act of snatching from the bulwarks a boarding pike with which to defend himself.

The two men who were taking the pepper on a stage, having vainly attempted to get on board to the assistance of their comrades, were compelled to leap into the sea. One of them, Charles Converse, of Salem, being severely wounded, succeeded in swimming to the bobstays, to which he clung until taken on board by the natives, and from some cause he was not afterwards molested. His companion, John Davis, being unable to swim, drifted with the tide near the *boat tackle*, or *davit falls*, the blocks being over-hauled down near the water; one of these he laid hold of, which the Malays perceiving, dropped their boat astern and despatched him! the cook sprang into a canoe along side, and in attempting to push off she was capsized; and being unable to swim, he got on the bottom, and paddled ashore with his hands, where he was made prisoner.

Gregory, an Italian, sought shelter in the foretop-gallant cross-trees, where he was fired at several times by the Malays with the muskets of the Friendship, which were always kept loaded and ready for use while on the coast.

Three of the crew leaped into the sea, and swam to a point of land near a mile distant, to the northward of the town; and, unperceived by the Malays on shore, pursued their course to the northward towards Cape Felix, intending to go to the port of Annalaboo, about forty-five miles distant. Having walked all night, they found themselves, on the following morning, near the promontory, and still twenty-five miles distant from Annalaboo.

When Mr. Endicott, Mr. Barry, and the four seamen arrived at the beach, they saw the crew jumping into the sea; the truth now, with all its horrors, flashed upon his mind, that the vessel was attacked, and in an instant they jumped on board the boat and pushed off; at the same time a friendly rajah named Po Adam, sprang into the boat; he was the proprietor of a port and considerable property at a place called Pulo Kio, but three miles distant from the mouth of the river Quallah Battoo. More business had been done by the rajah during the eight years past than by any other on the pepper coast; he had uniformly professed himself friendly to the Americans, and he has generally received the character of their being honest. Speaking a little English as he sprang into the boat, he exclaimed, "Captain, you got trouble; Malay kill you, he kill Po Adam too!" Crowds of Malays assembled on both sides of the river, brandishing their weapons in a menacing manner, while a ferry boat, manned with eight or ten of the natives, armed with spears and krisses, pushed off to prevent the officers' regaining their ship. The latter exhibited no fear, and flourished the cutlass of Po Adam in a menacing manner from the bows of the boat; it so intimidated the Malays that they fled to the shore, leaving a free passage to the ship; but as they got near her they found that the Malays had got entire possession of her; some of them were promenading the deck, others were making signals of success to the people on shore, while, with the exception of one man aloft, not an individual of the crew could be seen. Three Malay boats, with about fifty men, now issued from the river in the direction of the ship, while the captain and his men, concluding that their only hope of recovering their vessel was to obtain assistance from some other ships, directed their course towards Muchie, where they knew that several American vessels were lying at anchor. Three American captains, upon hearing the misfortunes of their countrymen, weighed anchor immediately for Quallah Battoo, determined, if possible, to recover the ship. By four o'clock on the same day they gained an anchorage off that place; the Malays, in the meantime, had removed on shore every moveable article belonging to the ship, including specie, besides several cases of opium, amounting in all to upwards of thirty thousand dollars. This was done on the night of the 9th, and on the morning of the 10th, they contrived to heave in the chain cable, and get the anchor up to the bows; and the ship was drifting finely towards the beach, when the cable, not being stopped abaft the bitts, began suddenly to run out with great velocity; but a bight having by accident been thrown forward of the windlass, a riding turn was the consequence, and the anchor, in its descent, was suddenly checked about fifteen fathoms from the hawse. A squall soon after coming on, the vessel drifted obliquely towards the shore, and grounded upon a coral reef near half a mile to the southward of the town. The next day, having obtained a convenient anchorage, a message was sent by a friendly Malay who came on board at Soo Soo, demanding the restoration of the ship. The rajah replied that he would not give her up, but that they were welcome to take her if they could; a fire was now opened upon the Friendship by the vessels, her decks were crowded with Malays, who promptly returned the fire, as did also the forts on shore. This mode of warfare appeared undecisive, and it was determined to decide the contest by a close action. A number of boats being manned and armed with about thirty officers and men, a movement was made to carry the ship by boarding. The Malays did not wait the approach of this determined attack, but all deserted the vessel to her lawful owners, when she was taken possession of and warped out into deep water. The appearance of the ship, at the time she was boarded, beggars all description; every part of her bore ample testimony of the scene of violence and destruction with which she had been visited. The objects of the voyage were abandoned, and the Friendship returned to the United States. The public were unanimous in calling for a redress of the unparalleled outrage on the lives and property of citizens of the United States. The government immediately adopted measures to punish so outrageous an act of piracy by despatching the frigate Potomac, Commodore Downs, Commander. The Potomac sailed from New York the 24th of August, 1831, after touching at Rio Janeiro and the Cape of Good Hope. She anchored off Quallah Battoo in February 1832, disguised as a Danish ship, and came to in merchantman style, a few men being sent aloft, dressed in red and blue flannel shirts, and one sail being clewed up and furled at a time. A reconnoitering party were sent on shore disguised as pepper dealers, but they returned without being able to ascertain the situations of the forts. The ship now presented a busy scene; it was determined to commence an attack upon the town the next morning, and every necessary preparation was accordingly made, muskets were cleaned, cartridge-boxes buckled on, cutlasses examined and put in order, &c.

At twelve o'clock at night, all hands were called, those assigned to take part in the expedition were mustered, when Lieut. Shubrick, the commander of the detachment, gave them special orders; when they entered the boats and proceeded to the shore, where they effected a landing near the dawn of day, amid a heavy surf, about a mile and a half to the north of the town, undiscovered by the enemy, and without any serious accident having befallen them, though several of the party were thoroughly drenched by the beating of the surf, and some of their ammunition was injured.

The troops then formed and took up their line of march against the enemy, over a beach of deep and heavy sand. They had not proceeded far before they were discovered by a native at a distance, who ran at full speed to give the alarm. A rapid march soon brought them up with the first fort, when a division of men, under the command of Lieut. Hoff, was detached from the main body, and ordered to surround it. The first fort was found difficult of access, in consequence of a deep hedge of thorn-bushes and brambles with which it was environed. The assault was commenced by the pioneers, with their crows and axes, breaking down the gates and forcing a passage. This was attended with some difficulty, and gave the enemy time for preparation. They raised their warwhoop, and resisted most manfully, fighting with spears, sabres, and muskets. They had also a few brass pieces in the fort, but they managed them with so little skill as to produce no effect, for the balls uniformly whizzed over the heads of our men. The resistance of the Malays was in vain, the fort was stormed, and soon carried; not, however, till almost every individual in it was slain. Po Mahomet, a chief of much distinction, and who was one of the principal persons concerned in the outrage on the Friendship was here slain; the mother of Chadoolah, another rajah, was also slain here; another woman fell at this port, but her rank was not ascertained; she fought with the spirit of a desperado. A seaman had just scaled one of the ramparts, when he was severely wounded by a blow received from a weapon in her hands, but her life paid the forfeit of her daring, for she was immediately transfixed by a bayonet in the hands of the person whom she had so severely injured. His head was wounded by a javelin, his thumb nearly cut off by a sabre, and a ball was shot through his hat.

Lieutenants Edson and Ferret proceeded to the rear of the town, and made a bold attack upon that fort, which, after a spirited resistance on the part of the Malays, surrendered. Both officers and marines here narrowly escaped with their lives. One of the natives in the fort had trained his piece in such a manner as to rake their whole body, when he was shot down by a marine while in the very act of applying a match to it. The cannon was afterwards found to have been filled with bullets. This fort, like the former, was environed with thick jungle, and great difficulty had been experienced in entering it. The engagement had now become general, and the alarm universal. Men, women and children were seen flying in every direction, carrying the few articles they were able to seize in the moments of peril, and some of the men were cut down in the flight. Several of the enemy's proas, filled with people, were severely raked by a brisk fire from the six pounder, as they were sailing up the river to the south of the town, and numbers of the natives were killed. The third and most formidable fort was now attacked, and it proved the most formidable, and the co-operation of the several divisions was required for its reduction; but so spirited was the fire poured into it that it was soon obliged to yield, and the next moment the American colors were seen triumphantly waving over its battlements. The greater part of the town was reduced to ashes. The bazaar, the principal place of merchandize, and most of the private dwellings were consumed by fire. The triumph had now been completed over the Malays; ample satisfaction had been taken for their outrages committed upon our own countrymen, and the bugle sounded the return of the ship's forces; and the embarkation was soon after effected. The action had continued about two hours and a half, and was gallantly sustained both by officers and men, from its commencement to its close. The loss on the part of the Malays was near a hundred killed, while of the Americans only two lost their lives. Among the spoils were a Chinese gong, a Koran, taken at Mahomet's fort, and several pieces of rich gold cloth. Many of the men came off richly laden with spoils which they had taken from the enemy, such as rajah's scarfs, gold and silver chunam boxes, chains, ear rings and finger rings, anklets and bracelets, and a variety of shawls, krisses richly hilted and with gold scabbards, and a variety of other ornaments. Money to a considerable amount was brought off. That nothing should be left undone to have an indelible impression on the minds of these people, of the power of the United States to inflict punishment for aggressions committed on her commerce, in seas however distant, the ship was got underway the following morning, and brought to, with a spring on her cable, within less than a mile of the shore, when the larboard side was brought to bear nearly upon the site of the town. The object of the Commodore, in this movement, was not to open an indiscriminate or destructive fire upon the town and inhabitants of Quallah Battoo, but to show them the irresistible power of thirty-two pound shot, and to reduce the fort of Tuca de Lama, which could not be reached on account of the jungle and stream of water, on the morning before, and from which a fire had been opened and continued during the embarcation of the troops on their return to the ship. The fort was very soon deserted, while the shot was cutting it to pieces, and tearing up whole cocoa-trees by the roots. In the afternoon a boat came off from the shore, bearing a flag of truce to the Commodore, beseeching him, in all the practised forms of submission of the east, that he would grant them peace, and cease to fire his big guns. Hostilities now ceased, and the Commodore informed them that the objects of his government in sending him to their shores had now been consummated in the punishment of the guilty, who had committed their piracies on the Friendship. Thus ended the intercourse with Quallah Battoo. The Potomac proceeded from this place to China, and from thence to the Pacific Ocean; after looking to the interests of the American commerce in those parts she arrived at Boston in 1834, after a three years' absence.

The Pirates of Malabar

COLONEL JOHN BIDDULPH

Rise of European Piracy in the East

From the first days of European enterprise in the East, the coasts of India were regarded as a favourable field for filibusters, the earliest we hear of being Vincente Sodre, a companion of Vascoda Gama in his second voyage. Intercourse with heathens and idolaters was regulated according to a different code of ethics from that applied to intercourse with Christians. The authority of the Old Testament upheld slavery, and Africans were regarded more as cattle than human beings; while Asiatics were classed higher, but still as immeasurably inferior to Europeans. To prey upon Mahommedan ships was simply to pursue in other waters the chronic warfare carried on against Moors and Turks in the Mediterranean. The same feelings that led the Spaniards to adopt the standard of the Cross in their conquest of Mexico and Peru were present, though less openly avowed, in the minds of the merchants and adventurers of all classes and nationalities who flocked into the Indian seas in the sixteenth and seventeenth centuries. With the decadence of buccaneering and the growth of Indian trade, there was a corresponding increase of piracy, and European traders ceased to enjoy immunity.

In 1623 the depredations of the Dutch brought the English into disgrace. Their warehouses at Surat were seized, and the president and factors were placed in irons, in which condition they remained seven months. This grievance was the greater, as it happened at the time that the cruel torture and execution of Captain Towerson and his crew by the Dutch took place at Amboyna. It was bad enough to be made responsible for the doings of their own countrymen, but to be punished for the misdeeds of their enemies was a bitter pill to swallow. In 1630, just as peace was being concluded with France and Spain, Charles I., who was beginning his experiment of absolute government, despatched the *Seahorse*, Captain Quail, to the Red Sea to capture the ships and goods of Spanish subjects, as well as of any other nations not in league and amity with England. There were no Spaniards in the Red Sea or the Indian Ocean, but international arrangements in Europe were not regarded when the equator had been crossed. Quail captured a Malabar vessel, for which the Company's servants at Surat were forced to pay full compensation. The *Seahorse* returned to England in 1633, but in view of the new field of enterprise opened up, Endymion Porter, Gentleman of the King's bedchamber, embarked on a piratical speculation, in partnership with two London merchants, Bonnell and Kynaston, with a licence under the privy seal to visit any part of the world and capture ships and goods of any state not in league and amity with England. Two ships, the *Samaritan* and *Roebuck*, were fitted out with such secrecy that the East India Company were kept in ignorance, and sailed in April, 1635, for the Red Sea, under Captain Cobb.

The *Samaritan* was wrecked in the Comoro Islands; but Cobb, continuing his cruise with the *Roebuck*, captured two Mogul vessels at the mouth of the Red Sea, from one of which he took a large sum of money and a quantity of goods, though the vessel had a pass from the Surat factory. Again the Company's servants at Surat were imprisoned, and not released till they had paid full compensation. Some small satisfaction was experienced when it became known that John Proud, master of the *Swan*, one of the Company's ships, had encountered the *Roebuck* in the Comoro Islands, and had attacked the freebooter. He was unable to capture it, but succeeded in procuring restitution of the captured goods; the treasure, however, was carried off to London, where it must have seemed as if the days of Drake and Hawkins had come again.

The Company laid their grievance before the King, who expressed much concern, promising to write to the Great Mogul and explain matters; so the Company commenced an action against

Bonnell and Kynaston in the Admiralty Court. Porter was too highly placed to be struck at. Bonnell evaded arrest and escaped to France, but Kynaston was arrested and lodged in gaol; upon which Charles ordered his release on bail, saying he would try the case himself at his leisure.

But Porter's views went beyond a single piratical voyage. Hardly had Cobb started on his cruise, when he entered into partnership with Sir William Courten for an association to establish a separate trade to the East Indies. A royal grant was obtained, and the King himself was credited with a share to the nominal extent of £10,000. The grant was a flagrant breach of faith, and was the inauguration of the system of interlopers that in after years caused so much loss and trouble to the Company. Four ships were equipped and sent out, and before long it became known that two vessels from Surat and Diu had been plundered by Courten's ships, and their crews tortured. Again the Company's servants at Surat were seized and thrown into prison, where they were kept for two months, being only released on payment of Rs. 1,70,000, and on solemnly swearing to respect Mogul ships.

The Civil War brought these courtly piracies to an end, and the decay of the Spanish power drew the more turbulent spirits of Europe and America to the Spanish main, so that for a time there was a diminution of European piracy in Indian waters. As buccaneering became more dangerous, or less lucrative, adventurers of all nations again appeared in Eastern waters, and the old trouble reappeared in an aggravated form. The Indian Red Sea fleet offered an especially tempting booty to the rovers. Lobo, a Jesuit priest, writing in the seventeenth century, tells us that so vast was the commerce of Jeddah, and so great the value of the ships trading to that place, that when, in India, it was wished to describe a thing of inestimable price, it was customary to say, 'It is of more value than a Jeddah ship.' Every year during the winter months, Indian traders, and pilgrims for Mecca, found their way in single ships to the Red Sea. On the setting in of the monsoon, they collected at Mocha, and made their way back in a single body. All Indian trade with the Red Sea was paid for in gold and silver, so that the returning ships offered many tempting prizes to freebooters.

In 1683 John Hand, master of the *Bristol*, interloper, cleared his ship with papers made out for Lisbon and Brazil, and sailed for Madeira. There he called his crew together, and told them he intended to take his ship to the East Indies. Those who were unwilling were overawed, Hand being a mighty 'pastionate' man. He appears to have been half pirate and half trader; equally ready to attack other traders, or to trade himself in spices and drugs. On the Sumatra coast, finding the natives unwilling to do business with him, he went ashore with a pistol in his pocket to bring the 'black dogs' to reason. The pistol went off in his pocket and shattered his thigh, and that was the end of John Hand.

In the same year, six men, of whom four were English and two Dutch, while on passage in a native merchant's ship from the Persian Gulf to Surat, seized the ship, killing the owner and his two wives. The lascars were thrown overboard, six being retained to work the ship. Their cruise did not last long. Making for Honore, they threw the six lascars overboard when nearing the port. The men managed to get to land, and reaching Honore, gave information of the would-be pirates to the local authorities, who seized the ship, and soon disposed of the rogues.

Three years later, two ships under English colours, mounting respectively forty-four and twenty guns, were reported to have captured vessels in the Red Sea, to the value of Rs.600,000. The Seedee of Jinjeera, who styled himself the Mogul's Admiral, received a yearly subsidy of four lakhs for convoying the fleet, a duty that he was quite unable to perform against European desperadoes. Public opinion at Surat was at once excited against the English, and further inflamed by the Dutch and French, who were only too anxious to see a rival excluded from the trade. Sir John Child, to pacify the Governor, offered to send a man-of-war to look for the pirates; but the Dutch and French factors continued to 'spitt their venom' till the Governor laughed in their faces and asked why they did not join in sending vessels to look for the rogues, since the matter seemed to them so serious.

In the same season a gallant engagement was fought against pirates, though not in Indian waters. The Company's ship *Cæsar*, Captain Wright, bound from England for Bombay, was chased off the coast of Gambia by five ships, carrying each from twenty to thirty guns, under French colours. Wright had no intention of yielding without a struggle, so put his ship before the wind, to gain time for getting into fighting trim. The *Cæsar* was carrying soldiers, and there were plenty of men to fight the ship. The boats were cut away, the decks cleared, ammunition and arms served out, three thousand pounds of bread which cumbered the gun-room were thrown overboard, and the tops were filled with marksmen. As soon as all was ready, the mainsail was furled, and the ship kept under easy sail. Before long the two smaller ships came up, hoisted the red flag, and began firing, one on the *Cæsar's* quarter and one astern. Soon the three other ships, two of which Wright styled the Admiral and Vice-Admiral, came up. The Admiral ranged up on the quarter and tried to board, but was obliged to sheer off, with the loss of many men and a bowsprit shot away. The Vice-Admiral tried to board at the bow, but with no better success, losing a foreyard and mizzen-mast. For five hours the engagement lasted, but the small-arm men in the *Cæsar's* tops fired so well that the pirates could hardly serve their guns. The crew showed a wonderful spirit, cheering loudly at every successful shot, till the discomfited pirates bore up, leaving the *Cæsar* to pursue her way to Bombay, much knocked about as to hull, but having lost only one man killed and eight wounded.

In the following year came news to Surat of two vessels, under Danish colours, that had stopped English ships and seized native ones between Surat and Bombay. The *Phœnix*, a British man-of-war, was at Surat at the time, so, together with the *Kent*, East Indiaman, it was despatched to look after the marauders, taking with them also two small hoys, sent to represent the French and the Dutch. In due time Captain Tyrrell returned, and reported that he had found a squadron of four vessels; that after a two days' chase he had brought them to, when they turned out to be two Danish ships, with two prizes they had taken. They showed him their commission, authorizing them to make reprisals on the Mogul's subjects for affronts offered to Danish traders; so he left them alone. A few months later the Portuguese factory at Cong, in the Persian Gulf, was plundered by an English pirate; another was heard of in the Red Sea, while Philip Babington, an Irish pirate, was cruising off Tellichery in the *Charming Mary*.

By 1689 a number of sea rovers from the West Indies had made their appearance, and the factory at Fort St. George reported that the sea trade was 'pestered with pirates.' The first comers had contented themselves with plundering native ships. Now their operations were extended to European vessels not of their own nationality. In time this restriction ceased to be observed; they hoisted the red or black flag, with or without the colours of the nationality they affected, and spared no vessel they were strong enough to capture.

The Armenian merchants were loud in their complaints. An Armenian ship, bound from Goa to Madras, with twenty thousand pagodas on board, was taken by a pirate ship of two hundred tons, carrying twenty-two guns and a crew of sixty men. Another Armenian ship, with fifty thousand xeraphims, was taken near Bombay, on its voyage from Goa to Surat. Besides those that beset the Malabar coast, there were pirates in the Persian Gulf, at the mouth of the Red Sea, and in the Mozambique Channel, while five pirate vessels were cruising off Acheen. During the next ten years the losses caused by the pirates were prodigious.

Ovington mentions that at St. Helena (1689) they were told, by a slaver, of three pirates, two English and the other Dutch, so richly laden with booty that they could hardly navigate their ships, which had become weather-beaten and unseaworthy from their long cruises off the Red Sea mouth. Their worn-out canvas sails were replaced with double silk.

> "They were prodigal in the expences of their unjust gain, and quenched their thirst with Europe liquor at any rate this Commander (the slaver) would put upon it; and were so frank both in distributing their goods, and guzzling down the noble wine, as if they were both wearied with the possession of their rapine, and willing to stifle all the melancholy reflections concerning it."

Such an account was bound to fire the imagination of every seaman who heard it.

The number of pirates was increased by the interlopers, merchant adventurers trading without a licence, who, like John Hand, when they failed to get cargoes, plundered native ships. Their proceedings were imitated by the permission ships, vessels that held the Company's licence for a single voyage. Not seldom the crews of interlopers and permission ships rose and seized the vessel against the will of their owners and commanders and hoisted the Jolly Roger. Commissions were granted to the East India Company's commanders to seize interlopers; but the interlopers, as a rule, were remarkably well able to take care of themselves. As pirates and interlopers alike sailed under English colours, the whole odium fell on the English. In August, 1691, a ship belonging to the wealthy merchant, Abdul Guffoor, was taken at the mouth of the Surat river, with nine lakhs in hard cash on board. A guard was placed on the factory at Surat, and an embargo laid on English trade. As the pirate had shown the colours of several nationalities, the authorities were loth to proceed to extremities. Fortunately for the English Company, a member of the pirate crew was captured, and proved to be a Dane; so the embargo on English trade was taken off.

Though they plied their calling at sea, almost with impunity, the pirates occasionally fell victims to Oriental treachery on shore. Thus, James Gilliam, a rover, having put into Mungrole, on the Kattiawar coast, was made welcome and much praised for the noble lavishness with which he paid for supplies. Soon there came an invitation to a banquet, and Gilliam, with some of his officers and crew, twenty in all, were received by the representative of the Nawab of Junaghur with excessive ceremony. Much polite curiosity was evinced about the noble strangers. "Why did they always go armed? Were their muskets loaded? Would they discharge them to show their host the European method?" The muskets were discharged, and immediately the banquet was announced. "Delay to reload the muskets was inexpedient. It would be time to recharge their weapons after the feast." And then, when seated and defenceless, there was an irruption of armed men, and Gilliam, with his followers, were seized and fettered. For a year they lay at Junaghur, where two of them died. In vain Gilliam contrived to send a letter to the Surat factory, asking that they might be claimed as British subjects. President Harris knew that the least interest shown in the fate of the rovers would be fatal to the interests of the Company, and was relieved when he heard that they had been sent to Aurungzeeb's camp; after which they are heard of no more.

In the beginning of 1692, authority was given to the Company's commanders to seize pirates and hold them till the King's pleasure was known, but the measure was of small effect. The pirates were prime seamen, who outsailed and outfought the Company's ships; while among the Company's crews they had numerous sympathizers. The prizes to be gained were so great and the risks so small, that the Company could hardly restrain their own men from joining the sea rovers. Thus, in 1694, John Steel ran away with the long boat of the *Ruby* frigate. Sixteen others who had plotted to join him were detected in time, and clapped in irons. The French and Dutch gave passes to all who applied for them, so Steel placed himself under French protection, and for two years 'that rogue Steel' finds frequent mention in the coast letters. Four years later Steel was arrested in England. But though the directors had been supplied with many accounts of his misdeeds, no sworn evidence could be produced against him, so Steel escaped scot-free.

All other pirates, however, were destined to be eclipsed in fame by Henry Every, *alias* Bridgman, who now made his appearance in the Indian seas. His exploits, the great wealth he amassed by piracy, and his reputed marriage with a Mogul princess, continued to excite the public mind long after he had disappeared from the scene. Several biographies of him were written, one of them attributed to Defoe, all of them containing great exaggerations; and a play, *The Successful Pirate*, was written in his honour. His biographers generally give his name as John Avery, but it was as is here given. According to the account of Van Broeck, a Dutchman, who was detained on board his ship for a time, and was on good terms with him, he was born at Plymouth, the son of a trading captain who had served in the navy under Blake. Every himself served in the navy, in the *Resolution* and *Edgar*, before he got the command of a merchant ship, in which he made several voyages to the West Indies. In May, 1694, he was first mate of the *Charles the Second*, one of the small squadron of English ships hired from Sir James Houblon, by the Spanish Government, to act against French smugglers who were troubling their Peruvian traded. The Spaniards were bad paymasters, and Houblon's squadron was detained at Corunna three or four months, while the crews became more and more discontented as their wages remained unpaid. As their sense of grievance increased, a plot was formed among the most turbulent spirits to seize a ship and turn rovers, under Every's command. On the night of the 30th May, the captain of the *Charles the Second* was made prisoner while in bed. A boat-load of men sent from the *James* to prevent the capture, joined the mutineers; the cables were cut, and the ship ran out of harbour. The captain and all who were unwilling to join were put into a boat, and the *Charles*, renamed the *Fancy*, was headed south for the coast of Africa. The only man detained against his will was the doctor, as he was a useful man.

Some months were spent on the Guinea coast, where some negroes were captured, and five ships—three English and two Danish—were plundered and burnt. Before the end of the year Every was east of the Cape, intent on the Red Sea traders. The first intelligence of him that reached Bombay was in May, 1695, when three outward-bound merchantmen reported that they had seen him at Johanna.

"Your Honor's ships going into that island gave him chase, but he was too nimble for them by much, having taken down a great deale of his upper works and made her exceeding snugg, which advantage being added to her well sailing before, causes her to sail so hard now, that she fears not who follows her. This ship will undoubtedly (go) into the Red Sea, which will procure infinite clamours at Surat."

Accompanying this report came the following characteristic letter from Every:—

"February yᵉ 28th, 1695/4.

"To all English Commanders lett this Satisfye that I was Riding here att this Instant in yᵉ Ship fancy man of Warr formerly the Charles of yᵉ Spanish Expedition who departed from Croniæ yᵉ 7th of May. 94: Being and am now in A Ship of 46 guns 150 Men & bound to Seek our fortunes I have Never as Yett Wronged any English or Dutch nor never Intend whilst I am Commander. Wherefore as I Commonly Speake wᵗʰ all Ships I Desire who ever Comes to yᵉ perusal of this to take this Signall that if you or aney whome you may informe are desirous to know wᵗ wee are att a Distance then make your Antient Vp in a Ball or Bundle and hoyst him att yᵉ Mizon Peek yᵉ Mizon Being furled I shall answere wᵗʰ yᵉ same & Never Molest you: for my men are hungry Stout and Resolute: & should they Exceed my Desire I cannott help my selfe.

"as Yett
"An Englishman's freind
"HENRY EVERY.

"Here is 160 od french Armed men now att Mohilla who waits for Opportunity of getting aney ship, take Care of your Selves."

According to Van Broeck, he was a man of good natural disposition, who had been soured by the bad treatment he received at the hands of his relations. The letter shows him to have been a man of some education, and during his short but active career in the Indian seas he appears to have attacked native ships only. The Company's records do not mention the loss of a single English ship at Every's hands, a circumstance that no doubt told heavily against the English in native opinion at Surat.

The same ships that brought Every's letter to Sir John Gayer brought intelligence of a wellknown French pirate having got aground at Mohilla. The three Company's ships watering at Johanna, heard of the occurrence, and proceeded to the spot, burnt the French ship after taking out what treasure was on board, and captured six of the Frenchmen, who were brought to Bombay. Every's friendly warning about the '160 od French armed men' evidently referred to the wrecked crew.

The value of Perim, or Bab's Key, as it was then called by mariners, to command the trade of the Red Sea, was at once perceived by Every, who attempted to make a settlement there.

After some unprofitable digging for water, he abandoned the project, and established himself in Madagascar, which had before this become known as a pirate resort. During the next thirty years the only traders who dared show themselves on the Madagascar coast were those who did business with the pirates, owing to the number of pirate settlements that sprang up at different points; the best known being at St. Mary's Island, St. Augustine's, Port Dauphin, and Charnock's Point. They built themselves forts and established a reign of terror over the surrounding country, sometimes taking a part in native quarrels, and sometimes fighting among themselves; dubbing themselves kings, and living in squalid dignity with large seraglios of native women. Captain Woodes Rogers, who touched at Madagascar for slaves, sixteen years after Every's time, described those he met as having been on the islands above twenty-five years, with a motley crowd of children and grandchildren.

> "Having been so many years upon this Island, it may be imagined their Cloaths had long been worn out, so that their Majesties were extremely out at the Elbows: I cannot say they were ragged, since they had no Cloaths, they had nothing to cover them but the Skins of Beasts without any tanning, but with all the Hair on, nor a Shoe nor Stocking, so they looked like the Pictures of Hercules in the Lion's Skin; and being overgrown with Beard, and Hair upon their Bodies, they appeared the most savage Figures that a Man's Imagination can frame."

One remarkable settlement was founded in the north, near Diego Suarez, by Misson, a Frenchman, and the most humane of pirates, with whom was allied Tew, the English pirate. Misson's aim was to build a fortified town "that they might have some place to call their own; and a receptacle, when age and wounds had rendered them incapable of hardship, where they might enjoy the fruits of their labour and go to their graves in peace." The settlement was named Libertatia. Slavery was not permitted, and freed slaves were encouraged to settle there. The harbour was strongly fortified, as a Portuguese squadron that attacked them found to its cost. A dock was made; crops were sown; a Lord Conservator was appointed for three years, with a Parliament to make laws. The colony was still in its infancy when it was surprised and destroyed by the natives, while Misson was away on a cruise; and so Libertatia came to an end. Tew succeeded in escaping to his sloop with a quantity of diamonds and gold in bars. On Misson rejoining him, they determined to go to America. Misson's ship foundered in a storm, while Tew made his way to Rhode Islands, and lived there for a time unquestioned. But the fascinations of a rover's life were too much for him. He fitted out a sloop and made again for the Red Sea, and was killed in action there with a Mogul ship.

From their Madagascar settlements the pirates scoured the east coast of Africa, the Indian Ocean as far as Sumatra, the mouth of the Red Sea, where the Mocha ships offered many rich prizes, the Malabar coast, and the Gulf of Oman. From time to time, ships from New England and the West Indies brought supplies and recruits, taking back those who were tired of the life, and who wished to enjoy their booty. European prisoners were seldom treated barbarously when there was no resistance, and the pirate crews found many recruits among captured merchantmen. Their worst cruelties were reserved for the native merchants of India who fell into their hands. They believed all native traders to be possessed of jewels, as was indeed often the case, and the cruellest tortures were inflicted on them to make them surrender their valuables. One unhappy Englishman we hear of, Captain Sawbridge, who was taken by pirates, while on a voyage to Surat with a ship-load of Arab horses from Bombay. His complaints and expostulations were so annoying to his captors that, after repeatedly telling him to hold his tongue, they took a sail needle and twine and sewed his lips together. They kept him thus several hours, with his hands tied behind him, while they plundered his ship, which they afterwards set on fire, burning her and the horses in her. Sawbridge and his people were carried to Aden and set on shore, where he died soon after.

Before long, Every made some notable captures. Off Aden he found five pirate ships of English nationality, three of them from America, commanded by May, Farrell, and Wake. In the Gulf of Aden he burned the town of Mahet on the Somali coast because the people refused to trade with him. In September, while cruising off Socotra with the *Fancy*, two sloops, and a galley, he took the *Futteh Mahmood* with a valuable cargo, belonging to Abdool Guffoor, the wealthiest and most influential merchant in Surat. A few days later he took off Sanjan, north of Bombay, a ship belonging to the Emperor, called the *Gunj Suwaie* (Exceeding Treasure). This was the great capture that made Every famous. According to the legend, there was a grand-daughter of Aurungzeeb on board, whom Every wedded by the help of a moollah, and carried off to Madagascar. But the story is only the most sensational of the many romantic inventions that have accumulated round Every's name. The native historian who relates the capture of the *Gunj Suwaie*, and who had friends on board, would certainly not have refrained from mentioning such an event if it had occurred; nor would the Mogul Emperor have failed to wreak vengeance on the English for such an insult to his family.

The *Gunj Suwaie* was the largest ship belonging to the port of Surat. It carried eighty guns and four hundred matchlocks, besides other warlike implements, and was deemed so strong that it disdained the help of a convoy. On this occasion it was returning from the Red Sea with the result of the season's trading, amounting to fifty-two lakhs of rupees in silver and gold, and having on board a number of Mahommedan ladies returning from pilgrimage to Mecca. In spite of the disparity of force, Every bore down and engaged. The first gun fired by the *Gunj Suwaie* burst, killing three or four men and wounding others. The main mast was badly damaged by Every's broadsides, and the *Fancy* ran alongside and boarded. This was the moment when a decent defence should have been made. The sailor's cutlass was a poor match for the curved sword and shield, so much so that the English were notorious in the East for their want of boldness in sword-play. But Ibrahim Khan, the captain, was a coward, and ran below at the sight of the white faces. His crew followed his example, and the vessel was taken almost without resistance.

So rich a prize was not to be relinquished without a very complete search. For a whole week the *Gunj Suwaie* was rummaged from stem to stern, while the crew of the *Fancy* indulged in a horrible orgy, excited beyond measure by the immense booty that had fallen into their hands. Several of the women threw themselves into the sea or slew themselves with daggers; the last piece of silver was sought out and carried on board the *Fancy*, the last jewel torn from the passengers and crew, and then the *Gunj Suwaie* was left to find its way to Surat as it best could.

The vials of long-accumulated wrath were poured out on the English. Instigated by Abdul Guffoor, the populace of Surat flew to arms to wreak vengeance on the factory. The Governor, Itimad Khan, was well disposed to the English, but popular excitement ran so high that he found it difficult to protect them. Guards were placed on the factory to save it from plunder. A mufti urged that the English should be put to death in revenge for the death of so many true believers, and quoted an appropriate text from the Koran. Soon came an order from Aurungzeeb directing the Seedee to march on Bombay, and for all the English in Surat and Broach to be made prisoners. President Annesley and the rest, sixty-three in all, were placed in irons, and so remained eleven months. To make matters worse, news arrived of Every having captured the *Rampura*, a Cambay ship with a cargo valued at Rs. 1,70,000.

> "It is strange," wrote Sir John Gayer, "to see how almost all the merchants are incensed against our nation, reproaching the Governor extremely for taking our part, and as strange to see that notwithstanding all, he stems the stream against them more than well could be imagined, considering his extreme timorous nature."

The strangeness of the merchants' hostility is hardly apparent, but it is not too much to say that Itimad Khan's friendly behaviour alone saved English trade from extinction. The Dutch, always hostile in the East, whatever might be the relations between Holland and England in

Europe, strove to improve the occasion by fomenting popular excitement, and tried to get the English permanently excluded from the Indian trade. In the words of Sir John Gayer, "they retained their Edomitish principles, and rejoice to see Jacob laid low." But Itimad Khan knew that the pirates were of all nationalities, and refused to hold the English alone responsible. To propitiate the Governor, Sir John Gayer made over to him the six French pirates taken at Mohilla, not without qualms at handing over Christians to Mahommedan mercies. He fully expected that the treasure taken out of the wreck would also be demanded of him; but Itimad Khan was not an avaricious man, and no such demand was made. "His contempt of money is not to be paralleled by any of the King's Umbraws or Governors," Sir John wrote, a year later, when Itimad Khan was dead. To forestall the Dutch with the Emperor, Gayer sent an agent offering to convoy the Red Sea fleet for the future, in return for a yearly payment of four lakhs a year. The offer was refused, but it served to place the English in a more favourable light, and to procure the cancelling of orders that had been given for attacking Bombay and Madras. Had it been accepted, the Seedee would have been added to the number of the Company's enemies. The Dutch, not to be outdone, offered to perform the same service in return for a monopoly of trade in the Emperor's dominions. This brought all other Europeans into line against the Dutch proposal, and the intrigue was defeated. The embargo on all European trade at Surat was maintained, while the Dutch, French, and English were directed to scour the seas and destroy the pirates. It was further ordered that Europeans on shore were not to carry arms or use palanquins, and their ships were forbidden to hoist their national flags. The Dutch and French hung back. They would not send a ship to sea without payment, except for their own affairs. Sir John Gayer, more wisely, sent armed ships to convoy the Mocha fleet, at the Company's charge, and so the storm passed off.

Meanwhile, Every, glutted with booty, made up his mind to retire with his enormous gains. According to Johnson, he gave the slip, at night, to his consorts, sailed for Providence in the Bahamas, where his crew dispersed, and thence made his way to England, just at the time a royal proclamation offering £500 for his apprehension was published. The reward was doubled by an offer of four thousand rupees from the Company; eight rupees being the equivalent of a pound at that time. Several of his crew also straggled home and were captured, but before he left the Indian coast, twenty-five Frenchmen, fourteen Danes, and some English were put ashore, fearing to show themselves in Europe or America. This fact would seem to throw some doubt on the account of his having left his consorts by stealth.

On the 19th October, 1696, six of his crew were tried and sentenced at the Old Bailey, and a true bill was found and an indictment framed against Every himself, though he had not been apprehended. According to Johnson, Every changed his name and lived unostentatiously, while trying to sell the jewels he had amassed. The merchant in whose hands he had placed them, suspecting how they had been come by, threatened him. Every fled to Ireland, leaving his jewels in the merchant's hands, and finally died in Devonshire in extreme poverty. But the authority for this, as for most of the popular accounts of Every, is extremely doubtful. That he was cheated out of some of his ill-gotten gains is probable enough, but it is in the highest degree improbable that he was known to be living in poverty, and yet that the large reward offered for his apprehension was not earned. What is alone certain is that he was never apprehended, and that in a few months he carried off an amount of plunder such as never before was taken out of the Indian seas by a single rover. For long he was the hero of every seaport town in England and North America; innumerable legends gathered round his name, and an immense impulse was given to piracy.

A few months after his departure, there were five pirate ships in the Red Sea, under English colours; two more, each mounting fourteen guns, were in the Persian Gulf, and another was cruising off Tellicherry. At Madagascar others were coming in fast. The news of Every's great booty had spread from port to port, and every restless spirit was intent on seeking his fortune in this new Eldorado, as men nowadays flock to a new goldfield. The Company's sailors were not proof against the temptation. While on the way from Bombay to China the crew of the *Mocha* frigate mutinied, off the coast of Acheen, killed their captain, Edgecombe, and set afloat in the pinnace twenty-seven officers and men who refused to join them. The *Mocha* was then renamed the *Defence*, and for the next three years did an infinity of damage in the Indian Ocean. At the same time, the crew of the *Josiah* ketch from Bombay, while at anchor in the Madras roads, took advantage of the commander being on shore to run away with the ship. The whole thing had been planned between the two crews before leaving Bombay; their intention being to meet off the coast of Sumatra, and cruise in company. The piratical career of the *Josiah* did not last long. Making first for the Nicobars, the crew flocked on shore, and were soon involved in quarrels with the natives; leaving on board only two men, one of whom was James Cruffe, the armourer, who had been forced to join them against his will. The other man was but a lukewarm pirate, and Cruffe prevailed on him to join in an attempt to carry off the ship. They cut the cable, and by great good fortune, without any knowledge of navigation, succeeded in carrying the ship into Acheen.

Stout's command of the *Defence*, once *Mocha*, quickly came to an end. According to one account, he was put to death by his comrades, at the Laccadives, for trying to desert them; according to another account, he was slain by some Malays. His place was taken by Culliford, who had been the leader of the mutineers of the *Josiah*. He changed the ship's name to the *Resolution*, and proved himself one of the most daring rovers of his day.

The untrustworthiness of his crews placed Sir John Gayer in an awkward dilemma. He had to report to the Directors that he dared not send ships to convoy pilgrims lest the crews should mutiny; that a boat could not be manned in Bombay harbour for fear of desertion, while, on shore, he had not a soldier fit to be made a corporal. A powerful French squadron had appeared on the coast, and the Surat President calculated that the Company's recent losses on captured ships sailing from Surat amounted to a million sterling. The losses of the native merchants were even more serious; trade was almost at a standstill, while three more pirate ships from New York appeared in the Gulf of Cambay, and captured country ships to the value of four lakhs of rupees. Every letter along the coast at this date speaks of the doings of the rovers: every ship coming into harbour told of pirates, of chases and narrow escapes, and of reported captures.

> "These pirates spare none but take all they meet, and take the Europe men into
> their own ships, with such goods as they like, and sink the ships, sending the lascars
> on rafts to find the shore."

So bold were the marauders that they cruised in sight of Bombay harbour, and careened their ships in sight of factories along the coast.

To avenge their losses, the Muscat Arabs, in April, 1697, seized the *London*, belonging to Mr. Affleck, a private merchant. The Arabs were engaged in hostilities with the Portuguese at the time, and forced the crew of the *London* to fight for them. Those who were unwilling were lashed to masts exposed to Portuguese fire, from which they did not escape scatheless. In vain the commanders of two of the Company's vessels assured the Imaum that the *London* was not a pirate.

> "You have sent me a letter," he wrote, "about my people taking one of your ships. It
> is true that I have done so, in return for one you English took from me, so now we are
> even and have ship for ship; for this one I will not surrender. If you wish to be friends,
> I am willing to be so; if not, I will fight you and take all the ships I can."

One pirate ship was reported to have chased two Cong ships, capturing one and forcing the other ashore, where it became a total wreck. "What influence this may have on the Rt. Hon. Company's affairs, God alone knows," wrote the Surat President, mournfully. Soon he was in better spirits. The same pirates had landed and plundered Cong; but, allowing themselves to be surprised, fifty-six of the crew had been set upon and killed.

With few exceptions, the English pirates came from the American colonies. Every year, from New York, Boston, Jamaica, and the Bahamas, ships were fitted out, nominally for the slave trade, though it was no secret that they were intended for piracy in the Eastern seas. Whatever compunction might be felt at attacking European ships, there was none about plundering Asiatic merchants, where great booty was to be gained with little risk. Sometimes the Governors were in league with the pirates, who paid them to wink at their doings. Those who were more honest had insufficient power to check the evil practices that were leniently, if not favourably, regarded by the colonial community, while their time was fully occupied in combating the factious opposition of the colonial legislatures, and in protective measures against the French and Indians. The English Government, absorbed in the French war, had no ships in the Indian seas; but the straits to which English trade in the East had been reduced, and the enormous losses caused by the pirates, at last forced some measures to be adopted for coping with the evil that had assumed such gigantic proportions.

The Rise of Conajee Angria

Europeans were not the only offenders. The Delhi Emperor, who claimed universal dominion on land, made no pretension to authority at sea. So long as the Mocha fleet did not suffer, merchants were left to take care of themselves. There was no policing of the sea, and every trader had to rely on his own efforts for protection. The people of the Malabar coast were left to pursue their hereditary vocation of piracy unmolested. The Greek author of the "Periplus of the Erythræan Sea," who wrote in the first century of our era, mentions the pirates infesting the coast between Bombay and Goa. Two hundred years before Vasco da Gama had shown the way to India by sea, Marco Polo had told Europe of the Malabar pirates.

> "And you must know that from this Kingdom of Melibar, and from another near it called Gozurat, there go forth every year more than a hundred corsair vessels on cruize. These pirates take with them their wives and children, and stay out the whole summer. Their method is to join in fleets of 20 or 30 of these pirate vessels together, and then they form what they call a sea cordon, that is, they drop off till there is an interval of 5 or 6 miles between ship and ship, so that they cover something like a hundred miles of sea, and no merchant ship can escape them. For when any one corsair sights a vessel a signal is made by fire or smoke, and then the whole of them make for this, and seize the merchants and plunder them. After they have plundered they let them go, saying, 'Go along with you

and get more gain, and that mayhap will fall to us also!' But now the merchants are aware of this, and go so well manned and armed, and with such great ships, that they don't fear the corsairs. Still mishaps do befal them at times."

From the Persian Gulf to Cape Comorin the whole coast was beset by native pirates, and, with the rise of the Mahratta power, the evil increased. Petty chiefs sometimes levied blackmail by giving passports to those who would pay for them, claiming the right to plunder all ships that did not carry their passes; but often the formality was dispensed with. Owing to the paucity of records of the early days, and the more serious hostility of the Portuguese and Dutch, we hear little of the losses sustained from native pirates, except when some ship with a more valuable cargo than usual was captured. Fryer tells us how, in his day, a rock off Mangalore was known as Sacrifice Island, "in remembrance of a bloody butchery on some English by the pirate Mala-bars." He further tells us how, in 1674, between Goa and Vingorla, he took part in an attack on a pirate ship that they came on as it was plundering a prize it had just taken, while the Dutch watched the engagement from the shore.

> "We soon made him yield his prize to engage with us, which they did briskly for two hours, striving to board us, casting stink-pots among us, which broke without any execution, but so frightened our rowers, that we were forced to be severe to restrain them. They plied their chambers and small shot, and slung stones, flourishing their targets and darting long lances. They were well manned in a boat ten times as big as our barge, and at least sixty fighting men besides rowers. We had none to manage our small gun," the gunner having deserted at Goa.

However, the pirates were beaten off, and Fryer and his companions were mightily praised by the Dutch. These pirates hailed probably from Vingorla, where the Sawunt Waree chief, known in those days as the 'Kempsant,' carried on a brisk piratical trade. The name was a corruption of Khem Sawunt, a common name of the Vingorla chiefs; the Portuguese changed it into Quemar Santo, 'the saint burner,' on account of his sacrilegious treatment of their churches.

There were no more determined pirates than the Arabs of Muscat and the Sanganians of Beyt and Dwarka, who, between them, intercepted the trade of the Persian Gulf, while the Coolee rovers of Guzarat took their toll of the plunder. In 1683 the Company's ship *President* was attacked by the Muscat Arabs with two ships and four grabs, and fought a gallant action. The grabs were generally two-masted ships, from one hundred and fifty to three hundred tons burden, built to draw very little water, and excellent sailers, especially in the light winds prevalent on the Western coast. They had no bowsprit, but the main-deck was continued into a long overhanging prow. The favourite mode of using them was for two or three of them to run aboard their victim at the same time, and attack, sword in hand, along the prow. Being built for fighting, and not for trade, they could sail round the clumsy merchantmen that hailed from the Thames, and, if pressed, could find safety in the shallow bays and mouths of rivers along the coast. Three grabs grappled the *President* at once, but the boarders were beaten back, and all three were blown up and sunk, on which the rest of the squadron made off. The *President* was set on fire in sixteen places, and lost eleven men killed and thirty-three wounded.

In the following year the *Josiah* ketch was attacked by the Sanganians while at anchor, and in the heat of the engagement blew up. A few of the crew saved themselves in a skiff, but the greater number perished, among them the commander, Lieutenant Pitts, whose father was known in Bombay as 'the drunken lieutenant.'

In September, 1685, the *Phœnix*, a British man-of-war that had been sent for a two-years' cruise in Indian waters, was attacked by a Sanganian vessel that mistook her for a merchantman. It was almost a calm, and Captain Tyrrell hoisted out his boats to capture the Sanganian ship, but they were beaten off, so he sunk her with a couple of broadsides. Forty-one of the pirates were picked up, but many of them refused quarter, and one hundred and seven were killed or drowned. The *Phœnix* had three men killed, one wounded, and two drowned. According to Hamilton, Sir George Byng, the first lieutenant, was dangerously wounded; but the log of the *Phœnix* is silent on that point, though it gives the names of the casualties.

Three years later, the *Thomas*, Captain Lavender, was less fortunate. Attacked by four Beyt ships, after a brave resistance, the *Thomas* took fire, and all on board perished.

Their depredations were not confined to the sea. In 1697 some Beyt pirates landed and plundered a village within sight of Broach.

But the losses occasioned by native pirates were at first nearly lost sight of in the more serious losses occasioned by European corsairs.

"As for those Sanganians and those Mallabars and professed pirates," wrote the Directors in 1699, "we see no cause why you should not wage an offensive as well as a defensive war against them when they fall in your way: but it is hardly worth the while to keep small vessels to look after them, for they are poor rogues and nothing to be got of them to answer any charge."

In 1707, the year of Aurungzeeb's death, the pirates of the Persian Gulf made a great haul of plunder. A squadron of them made their way to the Red Sea, waylaid the Mocha fleet, and returned home laden with booty. In the following year, a squadron of fourteen Arab ships from the Gulf, carrying from thirty to fifty guns, and with seven thousand men on board, appeared on the Malabar coast and surprised Honore, Mangalore, and Balasore (?); but the people, having lately been plundered by the Seedee, were ready with their arms, and beat them off with the loss of four or five hundred men.

> "The Arab insolencies are often in the thought of the Court," wrote the London directors, "but the Court fears they shall not be able to do anything effectually to check their growing strength during the present war, which finds employment for all our naval force. Further the Court sympathizes with Madras on their severe losses by the pirates, which puts a damp on the Company's trade, and affects their revenues."

Annoying as were the losses that were suffered from the chronic depredations of the Arabs and Sanganians, they sank into insignificance when compared with the troubles experienced on the rise to power of Conajee (Kanhojee) Angria. The growth of the Mahratta power under Sivajee had been accompanied by the formation of a formidable fleet which harried the coast of the Concan, and against which the Seedee chief, the Emperor's representative afloat, could hardly maintain himself. In 1698 Conajee Angria succeeded to the command of the Mahratta navy, with the title of Darya-Sáranga. In the name of the Satara chief he was master of the whole coast from Bombay to Vingorla, with the exception of the Seedee's territory. Defenceless towns as far south as Travancore were attacked and plundered, while, at sea, vessels of native merchants were preyed upon. For a time he seems not to have meddled with the Company's vessels; as the size of his ships increased, he grew bolder, and, in 1702, his doings began to excite apprehension. In that year he was addressed to release a small trading vessel from Calicut with six Englishmen on board that had been seized and carried into one of his harbours. What had roused his anger against the English does not appear, but a month later we find him sending word to Bombay that he would give the English cause to remember the name of Conajee Angria, a threat that he carried out only too well. Two years later we find him described as a 'Rebel Independent of the Rajah Sivajee,' and Mr. Reynolds was deputed to find him and tell him that he could not be permitted searching, molesting, or seizing vessels in Bombay waters: to which he returned a defiant answer, that he had done many benefits to the English, who had broken faith with him, and henceforth he would seize their vessels wherever he could find them. In 1707 his ships attacked the *Bombay* frigate, which was blown up after a brief engagement, and for the next half-century Angrian piracy was a scourge to the European trade of the West coast. In 1710 Conajee Angria seized and fortified Kennery, and his ships fought the *Godolphin* for two days, within sight of Bombay, but were finally beaten off. He had now grown so powerful that, in 1711, the Directors were told he could take any ship except the largest Europe ones "along the coast from Surat to Dabul he takes all private merchant vessels he meets."

Owing to the minority and imprisonment of Sivajee's grandson, Sahoojee, the Mahrattas were torn by internal divisions, in which Conajee Angria played his part. On the death of Aurung zeeb, Sahoojee regained his liberty, and was seated on the guddee of Satara. Owing to his want of hardihood, and weakness of character, the dissensions continued, and Sivajee's kingdom seemed to be on the point of breaking up into a number of independent chiefships. Among those aiming at independence was Conajee Angria. In 1713, an army sent against him under the Peishwa, Bhyroo Punt, was defeated, and Bhyroo Punt taken prisoner. It was reported that Conajee was preparing to march on Satara. Ballajee Rao, who afterwards became Peishwa, was placed at the head of such troops as could hastily be collected together, and opened negotiations with Conajee. An accommodation was arrived at, by which Conajee agreed to acknowledge allegiance to Satara, in return for which he was confirmed in command of the fleet, with the title of Surkheil, and granted twenty-six forts and fortified places with their dependent villages. The first result of this treaty was a war with the Seedee, who had enjoyed some of the places in question for a number of years. Conajee was supported by the Satara arms, and the Seedee was forced to submit to the loss. To all intents and purposes, Conajee was now an independent chief. He was the recognized master of a strip of territory between the sea and the western ghauts, extending from Bombay harbour to Vingorla, excluding the Seedee's territories, a tract, roughly speaking, about two hundred and forty miles in length by forty miles in breadth. With his harbours strongly fortified, while the western ghauts made his territories difficult of access by land, he was in a position to bid defiance to all enemies. Moreover, he was the recognized chief of the hardy coast population of hereditary seamen, who to this day furnish the best lascars to our Indian marine.

Angria's exploits on land had not interfered with his interests at sea. In November, 1712, he captured the Governor of Bombay's armed yacht together with the *Anne* ketch from Carwar. In the engagement, Mr. Chown, chief of the Carwar factory, was killed, and his young wife, a widow for the second time at the age of eighteen, became Angria's prisoner. A month later, the *Somers* and *Grantham*, East Indiamen, on their voyage from England to Bombay, were attacked by a grab and a gallivat belonging to Angria, off the coast north of Goa. Owing to there being a calm at the time, the East Indiamen were unable to bring their guns to bear: "for which reason and by ye earnest intercession of ye whole ship's company to ye captain" the boats of the *Somers* and *Grantham* were hoisted out, and an attempt was made to board the pirates. The attack was beaten off with the loss of four men killed and seventeen wounded; but the pirates found the entertainment so little to their liking that they made off.

On hearing of the capture of the Governor's yacht, the Portuguese wrote to propose a joint attack on Angria. A few months before, he had captured the greater part of a Portuguese 'armado,' and disabled a thirty-gun man-of-war that was convoying it. Governor Aislabie declined the Portuguese offer, but it had the effect of bringing Angria to terms. Thinking it politic to make peace with the English, while his affairs with the Rajah of Satara were still unsettled, he sent a messenger to Bombay, offering to deliver up all vessels, goods, and captives taken from the Company, if an Englishman of credit was sent to him to settle on terms of peace for the future. Aislabie demanded that in future English ships should be free from molestation; that no ships of any nation coming into Bombay should be interfered with between Mahim and Kennery; that English merchants should have liberty of trade in Angria's ports, on payment of the usual dues; and that Angria should be responsible for any damage done in future by the ships belonging to his Mahratta superiors. In return, the Governor engaged to give passes only to ships belonging to merchants recognized by the Company, and to allow Angria's people full trading facilities in Bombay, on the usual dues being paid. To these terms Angria agreed, but failed to get the Governor's consent to additional terms of an egregious nature; that he should be supplied by the Company with powder and shot on payment; that a place should be assigned to him to make powder in; that if pressed by his enemies, he should be assisted by the Company; that merchant ships should not be convoyed in or out of Bombay harbour.

There remained the duty of sending him 'an Englishman of credit' to 'deliver him the articles.' The Council, 'knowing him to be a man of ill principles,' thought it improper to order any man on such a risky service, but Lieutenant Mackintosh, in consideration of a gratuity of one thousand rupees, undertook to go, and departed for Colaba, with Rs.30,000 as ransom for the European prisoners, the convention sealed with the Council's seal, and ships to bring back the restored goods.

And so for a time there was security from Angria's attacks, but, with his hands free on the Satara side, and in a more secure position than ever, it was not likely that the peace would be of long continuance. With a fleet of armed vessels carrying thirty and forty guns apiece, with Kennery island in his possession within sight of Bombay harbour, Angria and his successors continued to be a menace to the existence of Bombay, while the Angrian territory became the Alsatia of the Indian seas, where desperadoes of all nationalities were made welcome.

The next few years saw an enormous increase of piracy in the Indian seas. Angria was practically secure in his fastnesses along the coast, and plundered every ship not strong enough to defend itself. His finest vessels were commanded by Europeans, generally Dutch. The signing of the Peace of Utrecht brought a fresh swarm of European adventurers to reap the harvest of the seas. The privateersmen, disregarding the peace, under pretence of making war on France and Spain, plundered ships of all nations. Conden, White, England, Taylor, and many others, made Madagascar their headquarters, and emulate the feats of Every and Kidd. The Beyt pirate were as mischievous as ever, while the Muscat Arabs could muster, in 1715, a ship of seventy-four guns, two of sixty, one of fifty, eighteen carrying thirty-two to twelve guns each, and host of smaller vessels carrying never less than four guns. The Company was forced to rely on its own exertions, as there was not a single King's ship in Indian waters. The few armed vessels belonging to Bombay convoyed the more valuable vessels along the coast. The larger ships that made the ocean voyage between India and Europe, sailed in company for mutual protection.

The Ways of the Buccaneers

JOHN MASEFIELD

Throughout the years of buccaneering, the buccaneers often put to sea in canoas and periaguas, just as Drake put to sea in his three pinnaces. Life in an open boat is far from pleasant, but men who passed their leisure cutting logwood at Campeachy, or hoeing tobacco in Jamaica, or toiling over gramma grass under a hot sun after cattle, were not disposed to make the worst of things. They would sit contentedly upon the oar bench, rowing with a long, slow stroke for hours together without showing signs of fatigue. Nearly all of them were men of more than ordinary strength, and all of them were well accustomed to the climate. When they had rowed their canoa to the Main they were able to take it easy till a ship came by from one of the Spanish ports.

If she seemed a reasonable prey, without too many guns, and not too high charged, or high built, the privateers would load their muskets, and row down to engage her. The best shots were sent into the bows, and excused from rowing, lest the exercise should cause their hands to tremble. A clever man was put to the steering oar, and the musketeers were bidden to sing out whenever the enemy yawed, so as to fire her guns. It was in action, and in action only, that the captain had command over his men. The steersman endeavored to keep the masts of the quarry in a line, and to approach her from astern. The marksmen from the bows kept up a continual fire at the vessel's helmsmen, if they could be seen, and at any gun-ports which happened to be open. If the helmsmen could not be seen from the sea, the canoas aimed to row in upon the vessel's quarters, where they could wedge up the rudder with wooden chocks or wedges. They then laid her aboard over the quarter, or by the after chains, and carried her with their knives and pistols. The first man to get aboard received some gift of money at the division of the spoil.

When the prize was taken, the prisoners were questioned, and despoiled. Often, indeed, they were stripped stark naked, and granted the privilege of seeing their finery on a pirate's back. Each buccaneer had the right to take a shift of clothes out of each prize captured. The cargo was then rummaged, and the state of the ship looked to, with an eye to using her as a cruiser. As a rule, the prisoners were put ashore on the first opportunity, but some buccaneers had a way of selling their captives into slavery. If the ship were old, leaky, valueless, in ballast, or with a cargo useless to the rovers, she was either robbed of her guns, and turned adrift with her crew, or run ashore in some snug cove, where she could be burnt for the sake of the iron-work. If the cargo were of value, and, as a rule, the ships they took had some rich thing aboard them, they sailed her to one of the Dutch, French or English settlements, where they sold her freight for what they could get—some tenth or twentieth of its value. If the ship were a good one, in good condition, well found, swift, and not of too great draught (for they preferred to sail in small ships), they took her for their cruiser as soon as they had emptied out her freight. They sponged and loaded her guns, brought their stores aboard her, laid their mats upon her deck, secured the boats astern, and sailed away in search of other plunder. They kept little discipline aboard their ships. What work had to be done they did, but works of supererogation they despised and rejected as a shade unholy. The night watches were partly orgies. While some slept, the others fired guns and drank to the health of their fellows. By the light of the binnacle, or by the light of the slush lamps in the cabin, the rovers played a hand at cards, or diced each other at "seven and eleven," using a pannikin as dice-box. While the gamblers cut and shuffled, and the dice rattled in the tin, the musical sang songs, the fiddlers set their music chuckling, and the sea-boots stamped approval. The cunning dancers showed their science in the moonlight, avoiding the sleepers if they could. In this jolly fashion were the nights made short. In the daytime, the gambling continued with little intermission; nor had the captain any authority to stop it. One captain, in the histories, was so bold as to throw the dice and cards overboard, but, as a rule, the captain of a buccaneer cruiser was chosen as an artist, or navigator, or as a lucky fighter. He was not expected to spoil sport. The continual gambling nearly always led to fights and quarrels. The lucky dicers often won so much that the unlucky had to part with all their booty. Sometimes a few men would win all the plunder of the cruise, much to the disgust of the majority, who clamored for a redivision of the spoil. If two buccaneers got into a quarrel they fought it out on shore at the first opportunity, using knives, swords, or pistols, according to taste. The usual way of fighting was with pistols, the combatants standing back to back, at a distance of ten or twelve paces, and turning round to fire at the word of command. If both shots missed, the question was decided with cutlasses, the man who drew first blood being declared the winner. If a man were proved to be a coward he was either tied to the mast, and shot, or mutilated, and sent ashore. No cruise came to an end until the company declared themselves satisfied with the amount of plunder taken. The question, like all other important questions, was debated round the mast, and decided by vote.

At the conclusion of a successful cruise, they sailed for Port Royal, with the ship full of treasure, such as vicuna wool, packets of pearls from the Hatch, jars of civet or of ambergris, boxes of "marmalett" and spices, casks of strong drink, bales of silk, sacks of chocolate and vanilla, and rolls of green cloth and pale blue cotton which the Indians had woven in Peru, in some sandy village near the sea, in sight of the pelicans and the penguins. In addition to all these things, they usually had a number of the personal possessions of those they had taken on the seas. Lying in the chests for subsequent division were swords, silver-mounted pistols, daggers chased and inlaid, watches from Spain, necklaces of uncut jewels, rings and bangles, heavy carved furniture, "cases of bottles" of delicately cut green glass, containing cordials distilled of precious mints, with packets of emeralds from Brazil, bezoar stones from Patagonia, paintings from Spain, and medicinal gums from Nicaragua. All these things were divided by lot at the main-mast as soon as the anchor held. As the ship, or ships, neared port, her men hung colors out—any colors they could find—to make their vessel gay. A cup of drink was taken as they sailed slowly home to moorings, and as they drank they fired off the cannon, "bullets and all," again and yet again, rejoicing as the bullets struck the water. Up in the bay, the ships in the harbor answered with salutes of cannon; flags were dipped and hoisted in salute; and so the anchor dropped in some safe reach, and the division of the spoil began.

After the division of the spoil in the beautiful Port Royal harbor, in sight of the palm-trees and the fort with the colors flying, the buccaneers packed their gear, and dropped over the side into a boat. They were pulled ashore by some grinning black man with a scarlet scarf about his head and the brand of a hot iron on his shoulders. At the jetty end, where the Indians lounged at their tobacco and the fishermen's canoas rocked, the sunburnt pirates put ashore. Among the noisy company which always gathers on a pier they met with their companions. A sort of Roman triumph followed, as the "happily returned' lounged swaggeringly towards the taverns. Eager hands helped them to carry in their plunder. In a few minutes the gang was entering the tavern, the long, cool room with barrels round the walls, where there were benches and a table and an old blind fiddler jerking his elbow at a jig. Noisily the party ranged about the table, and sat themselves upon the benches, while the drawers, or potboys, in their shirts, drew near to take the orders. I wonder if the reader has ever heard a sailor in the like circumstance, five minutes after he has touched his pay, address a company of parasites in an inn with the question: "What's it going to be?"

The Female Captive

LUCRETIA PARKER

The event which is here related is the capture by the Pirates of the English sloop *Eliza Ann*, bound from St. Johns to Antigua, and the massacre of the whole crew (ten in number) with the exception of one female passenger, whose life, by the interposition of Divine Providence, was miraculously preserved. The particulars are copied from a letter written by the unfortunate Miss Parker (the female passenger above alluded to) to her brother in New York.

"St. Johns, April 3, 1825.

"Dear Brother,

"You have undoubtedly heard of my adverse fortune, and the shocking incident that has attended me since I had the pleasure of seeing you in November last. Anticipating your impatience to be made acquainted with a more circumstantial detail of my extraordinary adventures, I shall not on account of the interest which I know you must feel in my welfare, hesitate to oblige you; yet, I must declare to you that it is that consideration alone that prompts me to do it, as even the recollection of the scenes which I have witnessed you must be sensible must ever be attended with pain: and that I cannot reflect on what I have endured, and the scenes of horror that I have been witness to, without the severest shock. I shall now, brother, proceed to furnish you with a detail of my misfortunes as they occurred, without exaggeration, and if it should be your wish to communicate them to the public, through the medium of a public print, or in any other way, you are at liberty to do it, and I shall consider myself amply rewarded if in a single instance it proves beneficial in removing a doubt in the minds of such, who, although they dare not deny the existence of a Supreme Being, yet disbelieve that he ever in any way revealed Himself to his creatures. Let Philosophy (as it is termed) smile with pity or contempt on my weakness or credulity, yet the superintendence of a particular PROVIDENCE, interfering by second causes, is so apparent to me, and was so conspicuously displayed in the course of my afflictions, that I shall not banish it from my mind from the beginning to the end of my narration.

On the 28th February I took passage on board the sloop *Eliza Ann*, captain Charles Smith, for Antigua, in compliance with the earnest request of brother Thomas and family, who had advised me that they had concluded to make that island the place of their permanent residence, having a few months previous purchased there a valuable Plantation. We set sail with a favorable wind, and with every appearance of a short and pleasant voyage, and met with no incident to destroy or diminish those flattering prospects, until about noon of the 14th day from that of our departure, when a small schooner was discovered standing toward us, with her deck full of men, and as she approached us from her suspicious appearance there was not a doubt in the minds of any on board, but that she was a Pirate. When within a few yards of us, they gave a shout and our decks were instantly crowded with the motley crew of desperadoes, armed with weapons of almost every description that can be mentioned, and with which they commenced their barbarous work by unmercifully beating and maiming all on board except myself. As a retreat was impossible, and finding myself surrounded by wretches, whose yells, oaths, and imprecations, made them more resemble demons than human-beings, I fell on my knees, and from one who appeared to have the command, I begged for mercy, and for permission to retire to the cabin, that I might not be either the subject or a witness of the murderous scene that I had but little doubt was about to ensue. The privilege was not refused me. The monster in human shape (for such was then his appearance) conducted me by the hand himself to the companionway, and pointing to the cabin said to me, "Descend and remain there and you will be perfectly safe, for although Pirates, we are not barbarians to destroy the lives of innocent females!" Saying this he closed the companion doors and left me alone, to reflect on my helpless and deplorable situation. It is indeed impossible for me, brother, to paint to your imagination what were my feelings at this moment; being the only female on board, my terror it cannot be expected was much less than that of the poor devoted mariners! I resigned my life to the Being who had lent it, and did not fail to improve the opportunity (which I thought it not improbable might be my last, to call on Him for that protection, which my situation so much at this moment required—and never shall I be persuaded but that my prayers were heard.

While I remained in this situation, by the sound of the clashing of swords, attended by shrieks and dismal groans, I could easily imagine what was going on on deck, and anticipated nothing better than the total destruction by the Pirates of the lives of all on board. After I had remained about one hour and a half alone in the cabin, and all had become silent on deck, the cabin doors were suddenly thrown open, and eight or ten of the Piratical crew entered, preceded by him whom I had suspected to be their leader, and from whom I had received assurances that I should not be injured. By him I was again addressed and requested to banish all fears of personal injury—that they sought only for the money which they suspected to be secreted somewhere on board the vessel, and which they were determined to have, although unable to extort a disclosure of the place of its concealment by threats and violence from the crew. The Pirates now commenced a thorough search throughout the cabin, the trunks and chests belonging to the captain and mate were broken open, and rifled of their most valuable contents—nor did my baggage and stores meet with any better fate, indeed this was a loss which at this moment caused me but little uneasiness. I felt that my life was in too much jeopardy to lament in any degree the loss of my worldly goods, surrounded as I was by a gang of the most ferocious looking villains that my eyes ever before beheld, of different complexions, and each with a drawn weapon in his hand, some of them fresh crimsoned with the blood (as I then supposed) of my murdered countrymen and whose horrid imprecations and oaths were enough to appal the bravest heart!

Their search for money proving unsuccessful (with the exception of a few dollars which they found in the captain's chest) they returned to the deck, and setting sail on the sloop, steered her for the place of their rendezvous, a small island or key not far distant I imagine from the island of Cuba, where we arrived the day after our capture. The island was nearly barren, producing nothing but a few scattered mangroves and shrubs, interspersed with the miserable huts of these outlaws of civilization, among whom power formed the only law, and every species of iniquity was here carried to an extent of which no person who had not witnessed a similar degree of pollution, could form the most distant idea.

As soon as the sloop was brought to an anchor, the hatches were thrown off and the unfortunate crew ordered on deck—a command which to my surprise was instantly obeyed, as I had harboured strong suspicions that they had been all murdered by the Pirates the day previous. The poor devoted victims, although alive, exhibited shocking proofs of the barbarity with which they had been treated by the unmerciful Pirates; their bodies exhibiting deep wounds and bruises too horrible for me to attempt to describe! Yet, however great had been their sufferings, their lives had been spared only to endure still greater torments. Being strongly pinioned they were forced into a small leaky boat and rowed on shore, which we having reached and a division of the plunder having been made by the Pirates, a scene of the most bloody and wanton barbarity ensued, the bare recollection of which still chills my blood. Having first divested them of every article of clothing but their shirts and trousers, with swords, knives, axes, etc., they fell on the unfortunate crew of the *Eliza Ann* with the ferocity of cannibals. In vain did they beg for mercy and intreat of their murderers to spare their lives. In vain did poor capt. S. attempt to touch their feelings and to move them to pity by representing to them the situation of his innocent family; that he had a wife and three small children at home wholly dependent on him for support. But, alas, the poor man intreated in vain. His appeal was to monsters possessing hearts callous to the feelings of humanity. Having received a heavy blow from one with an ax, he snapped the cords with which he was bound, and attempted an escape by flight, but was met by another of the ruffians, who plunged a knife or dirk to his heart. I stood near him at this moment and was covered with his blood. On receiving the fatal wound he gave a single groan and fell lifeless at my feet. Nor were the remainder of the crew more fortunate. The mate while on his knees imploring mercy, and promising to accede to anything that the vile assassins should require of him, on condition of his life being spared, received a blow from a club, which instantaneously put a period to his existence! Dear brother, need I attempt to paint to your imagination my feelings at this awful moment? Will it not suffice for me to say that I have described to you a scene of horror which I was compelled to witness! and with the expectation too of being the next victim selected by these ferocious monsters, whose thirst for blood appeared to be insatiable. There appeared now but one alternative left me, which was to offer up a prayer to Heaven for the protection of that Being who has power to stay the assassin's hand, and "who is able to do exceeding abundantly above what we can ask or think,"—sincerely in the language of scripture I can say, "I found trouble and sorrow, then called I upon the name of the Lord."

I remained on my knees until the inhuman wretches had completed their murderous work, and left none but myself to lament the fate of those who but twenty-four hours before, were animated with the pleasing prospects of a quick passage, and a speedy return to the bosoms of their families! The wretch by whom I had been thrice promised protection, and who seemed to reign chief among them, again approached me with hands crimsoned with the blood of my murdered countrymen, and, with a savage smile, once more repeated his assurances that if I would but become reconciled to my situation, I had nothing to fear. There was indeed something truly terrific in the appearance of this man, or rather monster as he ought to be termed. He was of a swarthy complexion, near six feet in height, his eyes were large, black and penetrating; his expression was remarkable, and when silent, his looks were sufficient to declare his meaning. He wore around his waist a leathern belt, to which was suspended a sword, a brace of pistols and a dirk. He was as I was afterward informed the acknowledged chief among the Pirates, all appeared to stand in awe of him, and no one dared to disobey his commands. Such, dear brother, was the character who had promised me protection if I would become reconciled to my situation, in other words, subservient to his will. But, whatever might have been his intentions, although now in his power, without a visible friend to protect me, yet such full reliance did I place in the Supreme Being, who sees and knows all things, and who has promised his protection to the faithful in the hour of tribulation, that I felt myself in a less degree of danger than you or any one would probably imagine.

As the day drew near to a close, I was conducted to a small temporary hut or cabin, where I was informed I might repose peaceably for the night, which I did without being disturbed by any one. This was another opportunity that I did not suffer to pass unimproved to pour out my soul to that Being, who had already given me reasons to believe that he did not say to the house of Jacob, seek you me in vain. Oh! that all sincere Christians would in every difficulty make Him their refuge; He is a hopeful stay.

Early in the morning ensuing I was visited by the wretch alone whom I had viewed as chief of the murderous band. As he entered and cast his eyes upon me, his countenance relaxed from its usual ferocity to a feigned smile. Without speaking a word, he seated himself on a bench that the cabin contained, and drawing a table toward him, leaned upon it resting his cheek upon his hand. His eyes for some moments were fixed in stedfast gaze upon the ground, while his whole soul appeared to be devoured by the most diabolical thoughts. In a few moments he arose from his seat and hastily traversed the hut, apparently in extreme agitation, and not unfrequently fixing his eyes stedfastly upon me. But, that Providence, which while it protects the innocent, never suffers the wicked to go unpunished, interposed to save me and to deliver me from the hands of this remorseless villain, at the very instant when in all probability he intended to have destroyed my happiness forever.

On a sudden the Pirate's bugle was sounded, which (as I was afterward informed) was the usual signal of a sail in sight. The ruffian monster there-upon without uttering a word left my apartment, and hastened with all speed to the place of their general rendezvous on such occasions. Flattered by the pleasing hope that Providence might be about to complete her work of mercy, and was conducting to the dreary island some friendly aid, to rescue me from my perilous situation, I mustered courage to ascend to the roof of my hovel, to discover if possible the cause of the alarm, and what might be the issue.

A short distance from the island I espied a sail which appeared to be lying to, and a few miles therefrom to the windward, another, which appeared to be bearing down under a press of sail for the former—in a moment the whole gang of Pirates, with the exception of four, were in their boats, and with their oars, etc., were making every possible exertion to reach the vessel nearest to their island; but by the time they had effected their object the more distant vessel (which proved to be a British sloop of war disguised) had approached them within fair gunshot, and probably knowing or suspecting their characters, opened their ports and commenced a destructive fire upon them. The Pirates were now, as nearly as I could judge with the naked eye, thrown into great confusion. Every possible exertion appeared to have been made by them to reach the island, and escape from their pursuers. Some jumped from their boats and attempted to gain the shore by swimming, but these were shot in the water, and the remainder who remained in their boats were very soon after overtaken and captured by two well manned boats dispatched from the sloop of war for that purpose; and, soon had I the satisfaction to see them all on board of the sloop, and in the power of those from whom I was fully satisfied that they would meet with the punishment due to their crimes.

In describing the characters of this Piratical band of robbers, I have, dear brother, represented them as wretches of the most frightful and ferocious appearance—blood-thirsty monsters, who, in acts of barbarity ought only to be ranked with cannibals, who delight to feast on human flesh. Rendered desperate by their crimes and aware that they should find no mercy if so unfortunate as to fall into the hands of those to whom they show no mercy, to prevent a possibility of detection, and the just execution of the laws wantonly destroy the lives of every one, however innocent, who may be so unfortunate as to fall into their power—such, indeed, brother, is the true character of the band of Pirates (to the number of 30 or 40) by whom it was my misfortune to be captured, with the exception of a single one, who possessed a countenance less savage, and had the appearance of possessing a heart less callous to the feelings of humanity. Fortunately for me, as Divine Providence ordered, this person was one of the four who remained on the island, and on whom the command involved after the unexpected disaster which had deprived them forever of so great a portion of their comrades. From this man (after the capture of the murderous tyrant to whose commands he had been compelled to yield) I received the kindest treatment, and assurances that I should be restored to liberty and to my friends when an opportunity should present, or when it could be consistently done with the safety of their lives and liberty.

This unhappy man (for such he declared himself to be) took an opportunity to indulge me with a partial relation of a few of the most extraordinary incidents of his life. He declared himself an Englishman by birth, but his real name and place of nativity was he said a secret he would never disclose! "although I must (said he) acknowledge myself by profession a Pirate, yet I can boast of respectable parentage, and the time once was when I myself sustained an unimpeachable character. Loss of property, through the treachery of those whom I considered friends, and in whom I had placed implicit confidence, was what first led me to and induced me to prefer this mode of life, to any of a less criminal nature—but, although I voluntarily became the associate of a band of wretches the most wicked and unprincipled perhaps on earth, yet I solemnly declare that I have not in any one instance personally deprived an innocent fellow creature of life. It was an act of barbarity at which my heart ever recoiled, and against which I always protested. With the property I always insisted we ought to be satisfied, without the destruction of the lives of such who were probably the fathers of families, and who had never offended us. But our gang was as you may suppose chiefly composed of and governed by men without principle, who appeared to delight in the shedding of blood, and whose only excuse has been that by acting with too much humanity in sparing life, they might thereby be exposed and themselves arraigned to answer for their crimes at an earthly tribunal. You can have no conception, madam (continued he), of the immense property that has been piratically captured, and of the number of lives that have been destroyed by this gang alone, and all without the loss of a single one on our part until yesterday, when by an unexpected circumstance our number has been reduced as you see from thirty-five to four! This island has not been our constant abiding place, but the bodies of such as have suffered here have always been conveyed a considerable distance from the shore, and thrown into the sea, where they were probably devoured by the sharks, as not a single one has ever been known afterward to drift on our shores. The property captured has not been long retained on this island, but shipped to a neighboring port, where we have an agent to dispose of it.

"Of the great number of vessels captured by us (continued he) you are the first and only female that has been so unfortunate as to fall into our hands—and from the moment that I first saw you in our power (well knowing the brutal disposition of him whom we acknowledged our chief) I trembled for your safety, and viewed you as one deprived perhaps of the protection of a husband or brother, to become the victim of an unpitying wretch, whose pretended regard for your sex, and his repeated promises of protection, were hypocritical—a mere mask to lull your fears until he could effect your ruin. His hellish designs, agreeable to his own declarations, would have been carried into effect the very morning that he last visited you, had not an all-wise Providence interfered to save you—and so sensible am I that the unexpected circumstance of his capture, as well as that of the most of our gang, as desperate and unprincipled as himself, must have been by order of Him, from whose all-seeing eye no evil transaction can be hidden, that were I so disposed I should be deterred from doing you any injury through fear of meeting with a similar fate. Nor do my three remaining companions differ with me in opinion, and we all now most solemnly pledge ourselves, that so long as you remain in our power, you shall have nothing to complain of but the deprivation of the society of those whose company no doubt would be more agreeable to you; and as soon as it can be done consistently with our own safety, you shall be conveyed to a place from which you may obtain a passage to your friends. We have now become too few in number to hazard a repetition of our Piratical robberies, and not only this, but some of our captured companions to save their own lives, may prove treacherous enough to betray us; we are therefore making preparation to leave this island for a place of more safety, when you, madam, shall be conveyed and set at liberty as I have promised you."

Dear brother, if you before doubted, is not the declaration of this man (which I have recorded as correctly as my recollection will admit of) sufficient to satisfy you that I owe my life and safety to the interposition of a Divine Providence! Oh, yes! surely it is—and I feel my insufficiency to thank and praise my Heavenly Protector as I ought, for his loving kindness in preserving me from the evil designs of wicked men, and for finally restoring me to liberty and to my friends!

I cannot praise Him as I would,
But He is merciful and good.

From this moment every preparation was made by the Pirates to remove from the island. The small quantity of stores and goods which remained on hand (principally of the *Ann Eliza's* cargo) was either buried on the island, or conveyed away in their boats in the night to some place unknown to me. The last thing done was to demolish their temporary dwellings, which was done so effectually as not to suffer a vestige of any thing to remain that could have led to a discovery that the island had ever been inhabited by such a set of beings. Eleven days from that of the capture of the *Ann Eliza* (the Pirates having previously put on board several bags of dollars, which from the appearance of the former, I judged had been concealed in the earth) I was ordered to embark with them, but for what place I then knew not.

About midnight I was landed on the rocky shores of an island which they informed me was Cuba, they furnished me with a few hard biscuit and a bottle of water, and directed me to proceed early in the morning in a northeast direction, to a house about a mile distant, where I was told I would be well treated and be furnished with a guide that would conduct me to Mantansies. With these directions they left me, and I never saw them more.

At daybreak I set out in search of the house to which I had been directed by the Pirates, and which I had the good fortune to reach in safety in about an hour and a half. It was a humble tenement thatched with canes, without any flooring but the ground, and was tenanted by a man and his wife only, from whom I met with a welcome reception, and by whom I was treated with much hospitality. Although Spaniards, the man could speak and understand enough English to converse with me, and to learn by what means I had been brought so unexpectedly alone and unprotected to his house. Though it was the same to which I had been directed by the Pirates, yet he declared that so far from being in any way connected with them in their Piratical robberies, or enjoying any portion of their ill-gotten gain, no one could hold them in greater abhorrence. Whether he was sincere in these declarations or not, is well known to Him whom the lying tongue cannot deceive—it is but justice to them to say that by both the man and his wife I was treated with kindness, and it was with apparent emotions of pity that they listened to the tale of my sufferings. By their earnest request I remained with them until the morning ensuing, when I set out on foot for Mantansies, accompanied by the Spaniard who had kindly offered to conduct me to that place, which we reached about seven in the evening of the same day.

At Mantansies I found many Americans and Europeans, by whom I was kindly treated, and who proffered their services to restore me to my friends, but as there were no vessels bound direct from thence to Antigua or St. Johns, I was persuaded to take passage for Jamaica, where it was the opinion of my friends I might obtain a passage more speedily for one or the other place, and where I safely arrived after a pleasant passage of four days.

The most remarkable and unexpected circumstance of my extraordinary adventures, I have yet, dear brother, to relate. Soon after my arrival at Jamaica, the Authority having been made acquainted with the circumstance of my recent capture by the Pirates, and the extraordinary circumstance which produced my liberation, requested that I might be conducted to the Prison, to see if I could among a number of Pirates recently committed, recognize any of those by whom I had been captured. I was accordingly attended by two or three gentlemen, and two young ladies (who had politely offered to accompany me) to the prison apartment, on entering which, I not only instantly recognized among a number therein confined, the identical savage monster of whom I have had so much occasion to speak (the Pirates' Chief) but the most of those who had composed his gang, and who were captured with him!

The sudden and unexpected introduction into their apartment of one, whom they had probably in their minds numbered with the victims of their wanton barbarity, produced unquestionably on their minds not an inconsiderable degree of horror as well as surprise! and, considering their condemnation now certain, they no doubt heaped curses upon their more fortunate companions, for sparing the life and setting at liberty one whom an all-wise Providence had conducted to and placed in a situation to bear witness to their unprecedented barbarity.

Government having through me obtained the necessary proof of the guilt of these merciless wretches, after a fair and impartial trial they were all condemned to suffer the punishment due to their crimes, and seven ordered for immediate execution, one of whom was the barbarian their chief. After the conviction and condemnation of this wretch, in hopes of eluding the course of justice, he made (as I was informed) an attempt upon his own life, by inflicting upon himself deep wounds with a knife which he had concealed for that purpose; but in this he was disappointed, the wounds not proving so fatal as he probably anticipated.

I never saw this hardened villain or any of his equally criminal companions after their condemnation, although strongly urged to witness their execution, and am therefore indebted to one who daily visited them, for the information of their behavior from that period until that of their execution; which, as regarded the former, I was informed was extremely impenitent—that while proceeding to the place of ignominy and death, he talked with shocking unconcern, hinting that by being instrumental in the destruction of so many lives, he had become too hardened and familiar with death to feel much intimidated at its approach! He was attended to the place of execution by a Roman Catholic Priest, who it was said labored to convince him of the atrociousness of his crimes, but he seemed deaf to all admonition or exhortation, and appeared insensible to the hope of happiness or fear of torment in a future state—and so far from exhibiting a single symptom of penitence, declared that he knew of but one thing for which he had cause to reproach himself, which was in sparing my life and not ordering me to be butchered as the others had been! How awful was the end of the life of this miserable criminal! He looked not with harmony, regard, or a single penitent feeling toward one human being in the last agonies of an ignominious death.

After remaining nine days at Jamaica, I was so fortunate as to obtain a passage with Capt. Ellsmore, direct for St. Johns—the thoughts of once more returning home and of so soon joining my anxious friends, when I could have an opportunity to communicate to my aged parents, to a beloved sister and a large circle of acquaintances, the sad tale of the misfortunes which had attended me since I bid them adieu, would have been productive of the most pleasing sensations, had they not been interrupted by the melancholy reflection that I was the bearer of tidings of the most heart-rending nature, to the bereaved families of those unfortunate husbands and parents who had in my presence fallen victims to Piratical barbarity. Thankful should I have been had the distressing duty fell to the lot of some one of less sensibility—but, unerring Providence had ordered otherwise. We arrived safe at our port of destination after a somewhat boisterous passage of 18 days. I found my friends all well, but the effects produced on their minds by the relation of the distressing incidents and adverse fortune that had attended me since my departure, I shall not attempt to describe—and much less can you expect, brother, that I should attempt a description of the feelings of the afflicted widow and fatherless child, who first received from me the melancholy tidings that they were so!

Thus, brother, have I furnished you with as minute a detail of the sad misfortunes that have attended me, in my intended passage to Antigua, in February and March last, as circumstances will admit of—and here permit me once more to repeat the enquiry—is it not sufficient to satisfy you and every reasonable person, that I owe my life and liberty to the interposition of a Divine Providence?—so fully persuaded am I of this, dear brother, and of my great obligations to that Supreme Being who turned not away my prayer nor his mercy from me, that I am determined to engage with my whole heart to serve Him the residue of my days on earth, by the aid of his heavenly grace—and invite all who profess to fear Him (should a single doubt remain on their minds) to come and hear what he hath done for me!

I am, dear brother, affectionately yours,

Lucretia Parker."

The Passing of Mogul Mackenzie:
The Last of the North Atlantic Pirates

ARTHUR HUNT CHUTE

In the farther end of the Bay of Fundy, about a mile off from the Nova Scotian coast, is the Isle of Haut. It is a strange rocky island that rises several hundred feet sheer out of the sea, without any bay or inlets. A landing can only be effected there in the calmest weather; and on account of the tremendous ebb of the Fundy tides, which rise and fall sixty feet every twelve hours, the venturesome explorer cannot long keep his boat moored against the precipitous cliffs.

Because of this inaccessibility little is known of the solitary island. Within its rampart walls of rock they say there is a green valley, and in its center is a fathomless lake, where the Micmac Indians used to bury their dead, and hence its dread appellation of the "Island of the Dead." Beyond these bare facts nothing more is certain about the secret valley and the haunted lake. Many wild and fabulous descriptions are current, but they are merely the weavings of fancy.

Sometimes on a stormy night the unhappy navigators of the North Channel miss the coast lights in the fog, and out from the Isle of Haut a gentle undertow flirts with their bewildered craft. Then little by little they are gathered into a mighty current against which all striving is in vain, and in the white foam among the iron cliffs their ship is pounded into splinters. The quarry which she gathers in so softly at first and so fiercely at last, however, is soon snatched away from the siren shore. The ebb-tide bears every sign of wreckage far out into the deeps of the Atlantic, and not a trace remains of the ill-starred vessel or her crew. But one of the boats in the fishing fleet never comes home, and from lonely huts on the coast reproachful eyes are cast upon the "Island of the Dead."

On the long winter nights, when the "boys" gather about the fire in Old Steele's General Stores at Hall's Harbor, their hard gray life becomes bright for a spell. When a keg of hard cider is flowing freely the grim fishermen forget their taciturnity, the ice is melted from their speech, and the floodgates of their souls pour forth. But ever in the background of their talk, unforgotten, like a haunting shadow, is the "Island of the Dead." Of their weirdest and most blood-curdling yarns it is always the center; and when at last, with uncertain steps, they leave the empty keg and the dying fire to turn homeward through the drifting snow, fearful and furtive glances are cast to where the island looms up like a ghostly sentinel from the sea. Across its high promontory the Northern Lights scintillate and blaze, and out of its moving brightness the terrified fishermen behold the war-canoes of dead Indians freighted with their redskin braves; the forms of *cœur de bois* and desperate Frenchmen swinging down the sky-line in a ghastly snake-dance; the shapes and spars of ships long since forgotten from the "Missing List"; and always, most dread-inspiring of them all, the distress signals from the sinking ship of Mogul Mackenzie and his pirate crew.

Captain Mogul Mackenzie was the last of the pirates to scourge the North Atlantic seaboard. He came from that school of freebooters that was let loose by the American Civil War. With a letter of marque from the Confederate States, he sailed the seas to prey on Yankee shipping. He and his fellow-privateers were so thorough in their work of destruction, that the Mercantile Marine of the United States was ruined for a generation to come. When the war was over the defeated South called off her few remaining bloodhounds on the sea. But Mackenzie, who was still at large, had drunk too deeply of the wine of a wild, free life. He did not return to lay down his arms, but began on a course of shameless piracy. He lived only a few months under the black flag, until he went down on the Isle of Haut. The events of that brief and thrilling period are unfortunately obscure, with only a ray of light here and there. But the story of his passing is the most weird of all the strange yarns that are spun about the "Island of the Dead."

In May, 1865, a gruesome discovery was made off the coast of Maine, which sent a chill of fear through all the seaport towns of New England. A whaler bound for New Bedford was coming up Cape Cod one night long after dark. There was no fog, and the lights of approaching vessels could easily be discerned. The man on the lookout felt no uneasiness at his post, when, without any warning of bells or lights, the sharp bow of a brigantine suddenly loomed up, hardly a ship's length in front.

"What the blazes are you trying to do?" roared the mate from the bridge, enraged at this unheard-of violation of the right of way. But no voice answered his challenge, and the brigantine went swinging by, with all her sails set to a spanking breeze. She bore directly across the bow of the whaler, which just grazed her stern in passing.

"There's something rotten on board there," said the mate.

"Ay," said the captain, who had come on the bridge, "there's something rotten there right enough. Swing your helm to port, and get after the devils," he ordered.

"Ay, ay, sir!" came the ready response, and nothing loth the helmsman changed his course to follow the eccentric craft. She was evidently bound on some secret mission, for not otherwise would she thus tear through the darkness before the wind without the flicker of a light.

The whaler was the swifter of the two ships, and she could soon have overhauled the other; but fearing some treachery, the captain refrained from running her down until daylight. All night long she seemed to be veering her course, attempting to escape from her pursuer. In the morning, off the coast of Maine, she turned her nose directly out to sea. Then a boat was lowered from the whaler, and rowed out to intercept the oncoming vessel. When they were directly in her course, they lay on their oars and waited. The brigantine did not veer again, but came steadily on, and soon the whalemen were alongside, and made themselves fast to a dinghy which she had in tow. A few minutes of apprehensive waiting followed, and as nothing happened, one of the boldest swung himself up over the tow-rope on to the deck. He was followed by the others, and they advanced cautiously with drawn knives and pistols.

Not a soul was to be seen, and the men, who were brave enough before a charging whale, trembled with fear. The wheel and the lookout were alike deserted, and no sign of life could be discovered anywhere below. In the galley were the embers of a dead fire, and the table in the captain's cabin was spread out ready for a meal which had never been eaten. On deck everything was spick and span, and not the slightest evidence of a storm or any other disturbance could be found. The theory of a derelict was impossible. Apparently all had been well on board, and they had been sailing with good weather, when, without any warning, her crew had been suddenly snatched away by some dread power.

The sailors with one accord agreed that it was the work of a sea-serpent. But the mate had no place for the ordinary superstitions of the sea, and he still scoured the hold, expecting at any minute to encounter a dead body or some other evil evidence of foul play. Nothing more, however, was found, and the mate at length had to end his search with the unsatisfactory conclusion that the *St. Clare*, a brigantine registered from Hartpool, with cargo of lime, had been abandoned on the high seas for no apparent reason. Her skipper had taken with him the ship's papers, and had not left a single clue behind.

A crew was told off to stand by the *St. Clare* to bring her into port, and the others climbed into the long-boat to row back to the whaler.

"Just see if there is a name on that there dinghy, before we go," said the mate.

An exclamation of horror broke from one of the men as he read on the bow of the dinghy the name, *Kanawha*.

The faces of all went white with a dire alarm as the facts of the mystery suddenly flashed before them. The *Kanawha* was the ship in which Captain Mogul Mackenzie had made himself notorious as a privateersman. Every one had heard her awe-inspiring name, and every Yankee seafaring man prayed that he might never meet her on the seas. After the *Alabama* was sunk, and the *Tallahassee* was withdrawn, the *Kanawha* still remained to threaten the shipping of the North. For a long time her whereabouts had been unknown, and then she was discovered by a Federal gunboat, which gave chase and fired upon her. Without returning fire, she raced in for shelter amongst the dangerous islands off Cape Sable, and was lost in the fog. Rumor had it that she ran on the rocks off that perilous coast, and sank with all on board. As time went by, and there was no more sign of the corsair, the rumor was accepted as proven. Men began to spin yarns in the forecastle about Mogul Mackenzie, with an interest that was tinged with its former fear. Skippers were beginning to feel at ease again on the grim waters, when suddenly, like a bolt from the blue, came the awful news of the discovery of the *St. Clare*.

Gunboats put off to scour the coast-line; and again with fear and trembling the look-out began to eye suspiciously every new sail coming up on the horizon.

One afternoon, toward the end of May, a schooner came tearing into Portland harbor, with all her canvas crowded on, and flying distress signals. Her skipper said that off the island of Campabello he had seen a long gray sailing-ship with auxiliary power sweeping down upon him.

As the wind was blowing strong inshore, he had taken to his heels and made for Portland. He was chased all the way, and his pursuer did not drop him until he was just off the harbor bar.

Many doubted his story, however, saying that no one would dare to chase a peaceful craft so near to a great port in broad daylight. And, again, it was urged that an auxiliary vessel could easily have overhauled the schooner between Campabello and Portland. The fact that the captain of the schooner was as often drunk as sober, and that when he was under the influence of drink he was given to seeing visions, was pointed to as conclusive proof that his yarn was a lie. After the New Bedford whaler came into port with the abandoned *St. Clare*, it was known beyond doubt that the *Kanawha* was still a real menace. But nobody cared to admit that Mogul Mackenzie was as bold as the schooner's report would imply, and hence countless arguments were put forward to allay such fears.

But a few days later the fact that the pirates were still haunting their coast was absolutely corroborated. A coastal packet from Boston arrived at Yarmouth with the news that she had not only sighted *Kanawha* in the distance, but they had crossed each other's paths so near that the name could be discerned beyond question with a spyglass. She was heading up the Bay of Fundy, and did not pause or pay any heed to the other ship.

This news brought with it consternation, and every town and village along the Fundy was a-hum with stories and theories about the pirate ship. The interest, instead of being abated, was augmented as the days went by with no further report. In the public-houses and along the quays it was almost the only topic of conversation. The excitement became almost feverish when it was known that several captains, outward bound, had taken with them a supply of rifles and ammunition. The prospect of a fight seemed imminent.

About a week after the adventure of the Boston packet Her Majesty's ship *Buzzard* appeared off Yarmouth harbor. The news of the *Kanawha* had come to the Admiral at Halifax, and he had dispatched the warship to cruise about the troubled coast.

"That'll be the end of old Mogul Mackenzie, now that he's got an English ship on his trail," averred a Canadian as he sat drinking in the "Yarmouth Light" with a group of seafaring men of various nationalities. "It takes the British jack-tar to put the kibosh on this pirate game. One of them is worth a shipload of Yankees at the business."

"Well, don't you crow too loud now," replied a Boston skipper. "I reckon that that Nova Scotian booze-artist, who ran into Portland the other day scared of his shadow, would not do you fellows much credit."

"Yes; but what about your gunboats that have had the job of fixing the *Kanawha* for the last three years, and haven't done it yet?" The feelings between Canada and the United States were none too good just after the Civil War, and the Canadian was bound not to lose this opportunity for horseplay. "You're a fine crowd of sea-dogs, you are, you fellows from the Boston Tea-Party. Three years after one little half-drowned rat, and haven't got him yet. Wouldn't Sir Francis Drake or Lord Nelson be proud of the record that you long-legged, slab-sided Yankees have made on the sea!"

"Shut your mouth! you blue-nosed, down-East herring-choker!" roared the Yankee skipper. "I reckon we've given you traitors that tried to stab us in the back a good enough licking; and if any more of your dirty dogs ever come nosing about down south of Mason and Dixon's Line, I bet they'll soon find out what our record is."

"Well, you fools can waste your tongue and wind," said a third man, raising his glass, "but for me here's good luck to the *Buzzard*."

"So say we all of us," chimed in the others, and the Yankee and the Canadian drank together to the success of the British ship, forgetting their petty jealousies before a common foe.

Everywhere the news of the arrival of the British warship was hailed with delight. All seemed to agree that her presence assured the speedy extermination of the pirate crew. But after several days of futile cruising about the coast, her commander, to escape from a coming storm, had to put into St. Mary's Bay, with the object of his search still eluding his vigilance. He only arrived in time to hear the last chapter of the *Kanawha's* tale of horrors.

The night before, Dominic Lefountain, a farmer living alone at Meteighan, a little village on the French shore, had been awakened from his sleep by the moaning and wailing of a human voice. For days the imminent peril of an assault from the pirates had filled the people of the French coast with forebodings. And now, awakened thus in the dead of night, the lonely Frenchman was wellnigh paralyzed with terror. With his flesh creeping, and his eyes wide, he groped for his rifle, and waited in the darkness, while ever and anon came those unearthly cries from the beach. Nearly an hour passed before he could gather himself together sufficiently to investigate the cause of the alarm. At last, when the piteous wailing had grown weak and intermittent, the instinct of humanity mastered his fears, and he went forth to give a possible succor to the one in need.

On the beach, lying prostrate, with the water lapping about his feet, he found a man in the last stage of exhaustion. The blood was flowing from his mouth, and as Dominic turned him over to stanch its flow, he found that his tongue had been cut out, and hence the unearthly wailing which had roused him from his sleep. The beach was deserted by this time, and it was too dark to see far out into the bay.

Dominic carried the unfortunate man to his house, and nursed him there for many weeks. He survived his frightful experiences, and lived on for twenty years, a pathetic and helpless figure, supported by the big-hearted farmers and fishermen of the French shore. Evidently he had known too much for his enemies, and they had sealed his mouth forever. He became known as the "Mysterious Man of Meteighan," and his deplorable condition was always pointed to as a mute witness of the last villainy of Mogul Mackenzie.

On the night following the episode of the "Mysterious Man of Meteighan," a wild and untoward storm swept down the North Atlantic and over the seaboard far and near. In the Bay of Fundy that night the elements met in their grandest extremes. Tide-rips and mountain waves opposed each other with titanic force. All along the bleak and rock-ribbed coast the boiling waters lay churned into foam. Over the breakwaters the giant combers crashed and soared far up into the troubled sky; while out under the black clouds of the night the whirlpools and the tempests met. Was ever a night like this before? Those on shore thanked God; and those with fathers on the sea gazed out upon a darkness where no star of hope could shine.

Now and again through the Stygian gloom a torrent of sheet-lightning rolled down across the heavens, bringing in its wake a moment of terrible light. It was in one of these brief moments of illumination that the wan watchers at Hall's Harbor discerned a long gray ship being swept like a specter before the winds towards the Isle of Haut. Until the flash of lightning the doomed seamen appeared to have been unconscious of their fast approaching fate; and then, as if suddenly awakened, they sent a long thin trail of light, to wind itself far up into the darkness. Again and again the rockets shot upward from her bow, while above the noises of the tempest came the roar of a gun.

The people on the shore looked at each other with blanched faces, speechless, helpless. A lifetime by that shore had taught them the utter puniness of the sons of men. Others would have tried to do something with what they thought was their strong arm. But the fishermen knew too well that the Fundy's arm was stronger. In silence they waited with bated breath while the awful moments passed. Imperturbable they stood there, with their feet in the white foam and their faces in the salt spray, and gazed at the curtain of the night, behind which a tragedy was passing, as dark and dire as any in the annals of the sea.

Another flash of lightning, and there, dashing upon the iron rocks, was a great ship, with all her sails set, and a cloud of lurid smoke trailing from her funnel. She was gray-colored, with auxiliary power, and as her lines dawned upon those who saw her in the moment of light, they burst out with one accord, "It's the *Kanawha!* It's the *Kanawha!*" As if an answer to their sudden cry another gun roared, and another shower of rockets shot up into the sky; and then all was lost again in the darkness and the voices of the tempest.

Next morning the winds had gone out with the tide, and when in the afternoon the calm waters had risen, a boat put off from Hall's Harbor and rowed to the Isle of Haut. For several hours the rocky shores were searched for some traces of the wreck, but not a spar or splinter could be found. All about the bright waters laughed, with naught but the sunbeams on their bosom, and not a shadow remained from last night's sorrow on the sea.

So Mogul Mackenzie, who had lived a life of stress, passed out on the wings of storm. In his end, as always, he baffled pursuit, and was sought but could not be found. His sailings on the sea were in secret, and his last port in death was a mystery. But, as has been already related, when the Northern Lights come down across the haunted island, the distress signals of his pirate crew are still seen shooting up into the night.

The Barbarous Conduct and Romantic Death
of the Joassamee Chief Rahmah-ben-Jabir

CHARLES ELLMS

The town of Bushire, on the Persian Gulf is seated in a low peninsula of sand, extending out of the general line of the coast, so as to form a bay on both sides. One of these bays was in 1816, occupied by the fleet of a certain Arab, named Rahmah-ben-Jabir, who has been for more than twenty years the terror of the gulf, and who was the most successful and the most generally tolerated pirate, perhaps, that ever infested any sea. This man by birth was a native of Grain, on the opposite coast, and nephey of the governor of that place. His fellow citizens had all the honesty, however, to declare him an outlaw, from abhorrence of his profession; but he found that aid and protection at Bushire, which his own townsmen denied him. With five or six vessels, most of which were very large, and manned with crews of from two to three hundred each, he sallied forth, and captured whatever he thought himself strong enough to carry off as a prize. His followers, to the number of two thousand, were maintained by the plunder of his prizes; and as the most of these were his own bought African slaves, and the remainder equally subject to his authority, he was sometimes as prodigal of their lives in a fit of anger as he was of his enemies, whom he was not content to slay in battle only, but basely murdered in cold blood, after they had submitted. An instance is related of his having put a great number of his own crew, who used mutinous expressions, into a tank on board, in which they usually kept their water, and this being shut close at the top, the poor wretches were all suffocated, and afterwards thrown overboard. This butcher chief, like the celebrated Djezzar of Acre, affecting great simplicity of dress, manners, and living; and whenever he went out, could not be distinguished by a stranger from the crowd of his attendants. He carried this simplicity to a degree of filthiness, which was disgusting, as his usual dress was a shirt, which was never taken off to be washed, from the time it was first put on till worn out; no drawers or coverings for the legs of any kind, and a large black goat's hair cloak, wrapped over all with a greasy and dirty handkerchief, called the keffeea, thrown loosely over his head. Infamous as was this man's life and character, he was not only cherished and courted by the people of Bushire, who dreaded him, but was courteously received and respectfully entertained whenever he visited the British Factory. On one occasion (says Mr. Buckingham), at which I was present, he was sent for to give some medical gentlemen of the navy and company's cruisers an opportunity of inspecting his arm, which had been severely wounded. The wound was at first made by grape-shot and splinters, and the arm was one mass of blood about the part for several days, while the man himself was with difficulty known to be alive. He gradually recovered, however, without surgical aid, and the bone of the arm between the shoulder and elbow being completely shivered to pieces, the fragments progressively worked out, and the singular appearance was left of the fore arm and elbow connected to the shoulder by flesh and skin, and tendons, without the least vestige of bone. This man when invited to the factory for the purpose of making an exhibition of his arm, was himself admitted to sit at the table and take some tea, as it was breakfast time, and some of his followers took chairs around him. They were all as disgustingly filthy in appearance as could well be imagined; and some of them did not scruple to hunt for vermin on their skins, of which there was an abundance, and throw them on the floor. Rahmah-ben-Jabir's figure presented a meagre trunk, with four lank members, all of them cut and hacked, and pierced with wounds of sabres, spears and bullets, in every part, to the number, perhaps of more than twenty different wounds. He had, besides, a face naturally ferocious and ugly, and now rendered still more so by several scars there, and by the loss of one eye. When asked by one of the English gentlemen present, with a tone of encouragement and familiarity, whether he could not still dispatch an enemy with his boneless arm, he drew a crooked dagger, or yambeah, from the girdle round his shirt, and placing his left hand, which was sound, to support the elbow of the right, which was the one that was wounded, he grasped the dagger firmly with his clenched fist, and drew it back ward and forward, twirling it at the same time, and saying that he desired nothing better than to have the cutting of as many throats as he could effectually open with his lame hand. Instead of being shocked at the uttering of such a brutal wish, and such a savage triumph at still possessing the power to murder unoffending victims, I knew not how to describe my feelings of shame and sorrow when a loud roar of laughter burst from the whole assembly, when I ventured to express my dissent from the general feeling of admiration for such a man.

This barbarous pirate in the year 1827, at last experienced a fate characteristic of the whole course of his life. His violent aggressions having united the Arabs of Bahrene and Ratiffe against him they blockaded his port of Daman from which Rahmah-ben-Jabir, having left a garrison in the fort under his son, had sailed in a well appointed bungalow, for the purpose of endeavoring to raise a confederacy of his friends in his support. Having failed in this object he returned to Daman, and in spite of the boats blockading the port, succeeded in visiting his garrison, and immediately re-embarked, taking with him his youngest son. On arriving on board his bungalow, he was received by his followers with a salute, which decisive indication of his presence immediately attracted the attention of his opponents, one of whose boats, commanded by the nephew of the Sheikh of Bahrene, proceeded to attack him. A desperate struggle ensued, and the Sheikh finding after some time that he had lost nearly the whole of his crew by the firing of Hahmah's boat, retired for reinforcements. These being obtained, he immediately returned singly to the contest. The fight was renewed with redoubled fury; when at last, Rahmah, being informed (for he had been long blind) that his men were falling fast around him, mustered the remainder of the crew, and issued orders to close and grapple with his opponent. When this was effected, and after embracing his son, he was led with a lighted torch to the magazine, which instantly exploded, blowing his own boat to atoms and setting fire to the Sheikh's, which immediately afterwards shared the same fate. Sheikh Ahmed and few of his followers escaped to the other boats; but only one of Hahmah's brave crew was saved; and it is supposed that upwards of three hundred men were killed in this heroic contest.

A Correct Account of the Late Piracies Committed in the West Indies

CAPTAIN CHARLES JOHNSON

The public mind has been much agitated by the depredations of these enemies of all laws, human and divine. It is strange, that in this enlightened age, when the principles of civil liberty are so well understood, and when the doctrines of the rights of man are gaining so many adherents both in this country and in Europe, that there should be found men so lost to every good principle, as to pursue such a predatory warfare against defenceless people; and with the slightest pretext, butcher those unfortunate fellow creatures who may fall in their way. And it is no less astonishing, as piracy does exist, that all civilized governments have not combined to suppress this horrid practice, and teach these refractory and deluded men, that the arm of justice is not shortened, nor the rulers of the earth asleep.

Our government has taken a forward step to arrest these free-botters in their blood-thirsty projects, and no doubt the expedition which was under the command of that gallant officer,

Commodore PORTER, has done much towards putting down this nefarious practice in the West-India seas.

Piracies, &c.
Mutiny on Board the British Ship Kate

The crew, 8 in number, of the ship Kate, Captain Purdy, landed in the island of Guadaloupe, on the 24th of January, 1821. They slept on the beach that night, and next morning a planter in the neighbourhood came to them, and brought them to his house. Their story was uniform, all said they belonged to the American ship Retrieve, Capt. Jacob Hawes, belonging to Messrs. Suydam & Wyckoff, merchants, of New-York; that after 6 weeks boisterous weather, not being able to keep the ship free, she being very leaky, the Captain had given orders to get the boat in readiness, and that they were doing it, and getting into the boat about 10 o'clock at night, when the Captain's son, about 10 years old, fell overboard in trying to get into the boat, and that the Captain threw himself into the sea to save him, but both perished, and the ship went down; that after one night and two days in the boat, they reached the beach near the Mole, with great hazard of their lives.

They were afterwards escorted to Point Petre, where they were examined by the Judge, and persisted in the same story; except one French lad, who privately disclosed the truth to the attorney general.

They had with them all their baggage, and considerable money. Among the baggage was a Bible, with the label, "Presented by the Merchants' Seamen Auxiliary Bible Society, to the ship Kate, of London—Gravesend, 11th May, 1818." This, the mate, Thomas Murdock, said was given to him by a fellow lodger in New-York. The Judge, however, availed himself of this circumstance to interrogate them a second time. Calling on Murdock, he said—"There is the Bible belonging to the ship Kate, of London, Capt. George Purdy, and upon that very same Bible you swear to tell the truth, and nothing but the truth." Murdock, much embarrassed, said in broken words, that he was not accustomed to swear on the Bible, and resisted some time, when the Judge observed to him, that if he would not answer to the questions, he would pronounce him guilty immediately; for to refuse answering the questions of the Court was declaring himself guilty. Murdock then kissed the Bible. "Since I have taken an oath, (said he,) on the Bible, I will speak the truth," and related the real story, in substance—

"That they belonged to the ship Kate, of London, Capt. George Purdy, which ship had been chartered in August last, at Halifax, for a voyage to Berbice and back to Halifax. The ship took a cargo of fish, beef, and some lumber. They reached Berbice, where the cargo was sold for cash. The proceeds were put on board in two boxes iron hooped, containing 5600 dollars. The ship sailed for Halifax in ballast. The mate had been discharged at Berbice, after some quarrel with the Captain. Six weeks after sailing, finding constant head winds, and in want of provisions, the water nearly consumed, the crew asked the Captain what he intended to do—the Captain told them, he had still some coffee which he would give them for their support, and that he would try to get to Bermuda; but after 24 hours, the winds against them, they tried for New-York, but without success. On the morning of the 8th of January, three of the crew went and seized the Captain, as he was walking on the deck, and tied him. They said that he and those that lived in the cabin, must either jump overboard, or go into the jolly boat along side. They then embarked the Captain, who wished and asked to go into the cabin for his cloak and boots, but he was not allowed. They begged earnestly for a compass; his lady also went on her knees and begged for a compass, but this was refused also. His lady with their two children, one a boy two years old, the other a girl four years old, Mr. Robert Meredith, a passenger, and a mulatto boy named William, steward in the cabin, were then forced into the boat, with 20 lbs. of bread, two trunks of the Captain's and Mr. Meredith's trunks and two oars, were sent adrift. The crew were ignorant of their then latitude. After ten days sailing for the West-Indies, Deseada was the first land he made. They had rigged the long boat as a sloop, put in their baggage and money, which had been equally divided among them, excepting the two lads, who had a share between them, when two of the crew went below and scuttled the ship."

Afterwards the rest of the crew confessed their crime. About 1400 dollars were found and lodged at the Register's office—Murdock said he buried in the yard of the tavern at the Mole 450 dollars, but the money could not be found. He had an American protection, said he was born in New-Brunswick (N. J.) and had papers from the grand and private lodges of New-York. The cook was a negro, from Philadelphia, from whence he went in a schooner to Halifax; his name was Philip Fisher; he stuttered. One was a French lad; one a London boy, one Welshman, an Irishman, and two Scotchmen.

List of Atrocious Piracies and Barbarities

Boston, Nov. 6, 1821.

The brig Cobbessecontee, Capt. Jackson, arrived yesterday from the Havana, sailed thence on the morning of the 8th ult and on the evening of the same day, about four miles from the Moro, was brought to by a piratical sloop, containing about 30 men. A boat from her, with ten men, came along side, and soon after they got on board commenced plundering. They took nearly all the clothing from the Captain and mate—all the cooking utensils and spare rigging—unrove part of the running rigging—cut the small cable—broke the compasses—cut the mast's coats to pieces—took from the Captain his watch and four boxes cigars—and from the cargo three bales of cochineal and six boxes cigars. They beat the mate unmercifully, and hung him up by the neck under the maintop. They also beat the Captain severely—broke a large broad sword across his back, and ran a long knife through his thigh, so that he almost bled to death. Capt. Jackson saw the sloop at Regla the day before.

Capt. Jackson informs us, and we have also been informed by other persons from the Havana, that this system of Piracy is openly countenanced by some of the inhabitants of that place—who say that it is a retaliation on the Americans for interfering against the Slave Trade, and for allowing Patriot privateers to refit in their ports. The pirates, therefore, receiving such countenance, grow more daring—and increase in number from the success which has attended this new mode of filling their pockets.

Capt. Bugnon, who arrived yesterday from Charleston, spoke on the 2nd inst. off the S. Shoal of Nantucket, the brig Three Partners, from Jamaica for St. John—had been robbed, off Cape Antonio, by a piratical vessel, of about 35 tons, and 17 men, of clothing, watches, &c. and the captain was hung up by the neck to the fore-yard arm, till he was almost dead.

Capt. Bourn, who arrived yesterday, from Cape Haytien, spoke on the 26th ult. lat. 33, lon. 78, brig Sea Lion, 36 days from Cape Haytien for Belfast, Ireland, which had been plundered by a pirate in the Gulf.

The brig Harriet, Capt. Dimond, from St. Jago de Cuba for Baltimore, arrived at Havana on the 16th ult. having been robbed of all her cargo of sugar, and $4000 in specie, off Cape Antonio, by a boat with 15 men, having two schooners in co. Capt. D was hung up by the neck, and remained senseless for some time after he was taken down.

The Dutch brig Mercury, 77 days from Marseilles, arrived at Havana on the 16th ult. after having been robbed of $10,000 worth of her cargo, by a piratical schooner and boat, off Cape Antonio.

Fortunately a U. S. vessel has arrived at the scene of these daring robberies, and has already protected two fleets. It is to be hoped some of the villains who have so long preyed with impunity on mercantile property, and been guilty of the most savage acts, will speedily be caught and brought to justice.

U. S. Brig Spark

A letter from a gentleman belonging to this vessel, dated St. Barts, Nov. 3, 1821, says—

"We arrived here, after a rather rough passage, in eighteen days from Boston, all well. We expect to sail again in two or three days. We found here the piratical ship which robbed the Orleans Packet. She is now in possession of the Swedish government. She came into their possession in the following manner:—The crew landed her cargo on a small island near this, from whence it was taken by a schooner to St. Thomas;—they then run the ship into Five Island Harbour, where all the crew, except two men, deserted her.—The government hearing of her being there, sent a guard and took possession of her, brought her into this harbour, and confined the two men found in her as pirates.—It is said, Capt. Elton has requested the Governor to allow him to take them to the United States for trial. This piratical ship was originally the U. S. brig Prometheus, which was condemned two years since, and was then sold."

A letter from on board the Hornet, dated at Cape Maise, 31st, October, says, "The pirate which we took yesterday mounted two long four pounders, and her crew consisted of twenty gallows-looking scoundrels."—After the capture of the Hornet, spoke three merchant brigs, which probably would have fallen into the hands of the pirates;—and were very happy at their escape.

Piratical Forts.—Captain Sisson, from Havana, reports that seventy of the Pirates belonging to the vessels captured and destroyed by the Enterprize, have erected two forts on Cape Antonio, for their defence.

From the American Monthly Magazine, of Feb. 1824.

Piracy

In the early part of June I sailed from Philadelphia in the schooner Mary, on a voyage to New-Orleans. My principal object in going round by sea was the restoration of my health, which had been for many months declining. Having some friends in New-Orleans whose commercial operations were conducted on an extensive scale, I was charged with the care of several sums of money in gold and silver, amounting altogether to nearly eighteen thousand dollars. This I communicated to the captain, and we concluded to secure it in the best manner our circumstances would admit. A plank was accordingly taken off the ribs of the schooner in my own cabin, and the money being deposited in the vacancy, the plank was nailed down in its original place, and the seams filled and tarred over. Being thus relieved from any apprehension that the money would be found upon us in case of an attack from pirates, my mind was somewhat easier. What other articles of value I could conveniently carry about with me, I did so. I had also brought a quantity of bank notes to the amount of fifteen thousand dollars. Part of these I caused to be carefully sewed in the left lappel of my coat, supposing that in case of my being lost at sea, my coat, should my body be found, would still contain the most valuable of my effects. The balance was carefully quilted into my black silk cravat.

Our crew consisted of the Captain and four men, with a supply of live stock for the voyage, and a Newfoundland dog, valuable for his fidelity and sagacity. He had once saved his master from a watery grave, when he had been stunned and knocked overboard by the sudden shifting of the boom. I was the only passenger on board. Our voyage at first was prosperous, and time went on rapidly. I felt my strength increase the longer I was at sea, and when we arrived off the southern coast of Florida, my feelings were like those of another man.

It was towards the evening of the fourteenth day, two hours before sun-set, that we espied a sail astern of us. As twilight came, it neared us with astonishing rapidity. Night closed, and all around was impenetrable darkness. Now and then a gentle wave would break against our bow and sparkle for a moment, and at a distance behind us, we could see the uneven glow of light, occasioned by the foaming of the strange vessel. The breeze that filled our canvass was gentle, though it was fresh.

We coursed our way steadily through the night; though once or twice the roaring of the waves increased so suddenly, as to make us believe we had passed a breaker. At the time it was unaccountable to me, but I now believe it to be occasioned by the bark behind us, coming rather near in the darkness of the night.—At midnight I went on deck. Nothing but an occasional sparkle was to be seen, and the ocean was undisturbed. Still it was a fearful and appalling darkness, and in spite of my endeavours I could not compose myself. At the windlass, on the forecastle, three of the sailors, like myself, unable to sleep had collected for conversation. On joining them, I found our fears were mutual. They all kept their eyes steadily fixed upon the unknown vessel, as if anticipating some dreadful event. They informed me that they had put their arms in order and were determined to stand or die.

At this moment a flash of light, perhaps a musket burning priming, proceeded from the vessel in pursuit, and we saw distinctly that her deck was covered with men. My heart almost failed me. I had never been in battle, and I knew not what it was. Day at length dawned, and setting all her canvass, our pursuer gained alarmingly upon us. It was evident that she had followed us the whole night, being unwilling to attack us in the dark.—In a few minutes, she fired a swivel and came along side. She was a pirate. Her boat was lowered, and about a dozen hideous looking objects jumped in, with a commander at their head. The boat pushed off, and was nearing us fast, as we arranged ourselves for giving her a broadside. Our whole stock of arms consisted of six muskets and an old swivel used as a signal gun, belonging to the Mary, and a pair of pistols of my own, which I carried in my belt. The pirate boat's crew were armed with muskets, pistols, swords, cutlasses, and knives; and when she came within her own length of us, we fired five of our muskets and the swivel into her. Her fire was scarcely half given, when she filled and went down with all her crew. At this success we were inclined to rejoice, but looking over the pirate schooner, we observed her deck still swarming with the same description of horrid looking wretches. A second boat's crew pushed off, with their muskets pointed directly at us the whole time. When they came within the same distance as the other, we fired, but with little, if any effect. The pirate immediately returned the fire, and with horrid cries jumped aboard of us. Two of our brave crew were lying dead upon the deck, and the rest of us expected nothing better. French, Spanish, and English, were spoken indiscriminately, and all at once. The most horrid imprecations were uttered against us, and threats that fancy cannot imagine.

A wretch whose black, shaggy whiskers covered nearly his whole face, whose eyes were only seen at intervals from beneath his bushy eye-brows, and whose whole appearance was more that of a hell-hound than of a human being, approached me with a drawn cutlass in his hand. I drew one of my pistols and snapped it in his face; but it flashed in the pan, and before I could draw the other, the pirate, with a brutality that would have disgraced a cannibal, struck me over the face with his cutlass, and knocked me down. I was too much wounded by the blow to resist, and the blood ran in torrents from my forehead. In this situation the wretch seized me by the scalp, and thrusting his cutlass in my cravat, cut it through completely. I felt the cold iron glide along my throat, and even now the very thought makes me shudder. The worst idea I had ever formed of human cruelty seemed now realized, and I could see death stare me in the face. Without stopping to examine the cravat, he put it in his pocket, and in a voice of thunder exclaimed *"levez vous?"* I accordingly rose on my feet, and he pinioned my hands behind my back, led me to the gunwale of the vessel, and asked another of the gang, in French, whether he should throw me overboard. At the recollection of that scene I am still staggered. I endeavoured to call the prospects of eternity before me, but could think of nothing except the cold and quiverless apathy of the tomb. His infamous companion replied, *"Il est trop bonne hetire l'envoyer au diable,"* and led me to the foremast, where he tied me with my face to the stern of the vessel. The cords were drawn so tight around my arms and legs, that my agony was excruciating. In this situation he left me.

On looking round, I found them all employed in plundering and ransacking every thing we had. Over my left shoulder one of our sailors was strung up to the yard arm, and apparently in the last agonies of death; while before me our gallant Captain was on his knees and begging for his life. The wretches were endeavouring to extort from him the secret of our money; but for a while he was firm and dauntless. Provoked at his obstinacy, they extended his arms and cut them off at the elbows. At this, human nature gave way, and the injured man confessed the spot where we had concealed our specie.—In a few moments it was aboard their own vessel. To revenge themselves on our unhappy captain, when they had satisfied themselves that nothing else was hidden, they spread a bed of oakum on the deck before, and after soaking it through with turpentine, tied the captain on it, filled his mouth with the same combustibles, and set the whole on fire. The cries of the unfortunate man were heart-rending, and his agonies must have been unutterable; but they were soon over. All this I was compelled to witness. Heart-sick with the sight, I once shut my eyes, but a musket discharged close to my ear, was a warning sufficient to keep them open.

On casting my eyes to the stern of the vessel I discovered that the boatswain had been nailed to the deck through his feet, and the body spiked through to the tiller. He was writhing in the last agonies of crucifixion.—Our fifth comrade was out of sight during all this tragedy; in a few minutes, however, he was brought upon the deck blindfolded. He was then conducted to the muzzle of the swivel, and commanded to kneel. The swivel was then fired off, and his head was dreadfully wounded by the discharge. In a moment after, it was agonizing to behold his torments and convulsions—language is too feeble to describe them. I have seen men hung upon the gibbet, but their death is like sinking in slumber when compared with his.

Excited with the scene of human butchery, one of those wretches fired his pistol to the captain's dog. The ball struck his shoulder and disabled him; he finished him by shooting him again, and at last by cutting out his tongue! At this last hell-engendered act, my blood boiled with indignation at such savage brutality on a helpless, inoffensive dog! But I was unable to give utterance or action to my feelings.

Seeing that the crew had been every one despatched, I began to think more of myself. My old enemy, who seemed to forget me, once more approached me; but shockingly besmeared with blood and brains. He had stood by the side of the unfortunate sailor who suffered before the swivel, and supported him with the point of his bayonet. He drew a stiletto from his side, placed its point upon my heart and gave it a heavy thrust. I felt its point touch my skin; but the quilting of my bank bills prevented its further entrance. This savage monster then ran it up my breast, as if intending to divide my lungs, and in doing so, the bank bills fell upon the deck. He snatched them up greedily, and exclaimed, "Ah! laissez mois voir ce que reste." My dress in a few moments, was ripped to pieces at the peril of my life. He frequently came so near as to tear my skin and deluge me with blood; but by the mercy of Providence, I escaped from every danger.—At this moment a heavy flaw struck the schooner, and I heard one of the pirates say, "Voila un vaisseau!" They all retreated precipitately, and gaining their own vessel, was soon out of sight.

Helpless as I now was, I had the satisfaction of knowing that the pirates had been frightened by the appearance of a sail, but it was impossible for me to see it. Still tied to the foremast, I knew not what was my prospect of release.—An hour or two had elapsed after they left me; and it was now noon. The sun played violently upon my head, and I felt a languor and debility that indicated approaching fever. My head gradually sunk upon my breast, when I was shocked by hearing the water pouring into the cabin windows. The wretches had scuttled the vessel, and left me pinioned to go down with her. I commended my Spirit to my Maker, and gave myself up for lost. I felt myself gradually dying away, and the last thing I remembered was the foaming noise of the waves. This was occasioned by a ship passing by me. I was taken in, restored to health, and am now a poor, ruined, helpless man.

The ship Liverpool Packet, Ricker, of Portsmouth, N. H. was boarded on the 16th off Cape St. Antonio, Cuba, by two piratical schooners; two barges containing thirty or forty men, robbed the vessel of everything moveable, even to her *flags*, rigging, one boat which happened to be afloat, and having a boy in it which belonged to the ship. They held a consultation whether they should murder the crew, as they had done before, or not—in the mean time taking the ship into anchoring ground. On bringing her to anchor, the crew saw a brig close along side, burnt to the water's edge, and three dead bodies floating near her.—The pirates said they had burnt the brig the day before, and *murdered all the crew!*—and intended doing the same with them. They said "look at the turtles, (meaning the dead bodies) you will soon be the same." They said the vessel was a Baltimore brig, which they had robbed and burnt, and murdered the crew as before stated, of which they had little doubt.—Capt. Ricker was most shockingly bruised by them. The mate was hung till he was supposed to be dead, but came to, and is now alive. They told the captain that they belonged in Regla, and should kill them all to prevent discovery.

Brig Dover

Extract from the Log-Book of the brig Dover, Capt. Sabins, from Matanzas for Charleston.

Jan. 16, 1822, sea account, at 1 P. M.—Pan of Matanzas bearing S. saw a boat coming to us from a small drogher, which came out of Matanzas the night before us, with five Spaniards, armed with long knives, pistols, cutlasses, &c. When they got within hail, they fired a musket at us, cheered, and came on board. They were the most villanous looking rascals that any one had probably ever beheld. They immediately drew their weapons, and after beating us severely with their cutlasses, drove us below. They then robbed us of all our clothes except what we had on, our watches, and every thing of value. We were afterwards called up singly. Four men with drawn knives stood over the captain, and threatened him if he did not give up his money, they would kill all hands and burn the vessel. After robbing the people they commenced plundering the brig. They broke open the hatches, made us get out our boat and carry their plunder to their vessel. They took from us one compass, five bags coffee, one barrel sugar, nearly all our provisions, our colours, rigging, and cooking utensils. They then ordered us to stand to the north, or they would overhaul us, murder the crew and burn the vessel. We made sail, and shortly after were brought to by another boat of the same character, which fired into us, but left us upon being informed that we had been already robbed.

The Porpoise, Capt. Ramage, arrived at Charleston from his successful cruise against the Pirates, having recaptured a Baltimore schooner which had been in their possession three days, destroyed three of their establishments on shore, 12 of their vessels, besides two on the stocks, and brought in four prisoners, against whom it is supposed there is strong evidence.

It is stated, that a Pirate Captain and his mate quarrelled on the question of putting to death all captives,—they fought a duel with muskets, the Captain was killed, and the Mate (who was the advocate of mercy) succeeded to the command.

The schooner Jane, of Boston, was taken the 24th Jan. by a pirate schooner.—They were carried into a place where were three more of the same trade.—The captain and crew were threatened, beat, and the vessel plundered of much property; after which they were released.

If the Spanish Government is unable to drive the Pirates from their strong holds in Cuba, the Baltimore Chronicle suggests the necessity of occupying the island with American forces for that purpose, as robbers and pirates have a right to enjoy no protection whatever; and in this case all civilized powers are warranted in carrying the war into the enemy's territory.

Pirates Captured

Charleston, Feb. 12.—The four pirates brought into this port by the United States Porpoise, were landed yesterday from that vessel, and committed to prison. Three of them are Spaniards, the other a Portuguese; two of the former father and son, the son being only about 18 years of age.

Charleston, Feb. 14, 1824.—The United States schooner Grampus, Lieut. Gregory, from a cruise of 4 months in the West-Indies and along the Spanish Main, arrived at our port yesterday morning, last from Santa Martha. She has brought in three Pirates, viz. James Maxfield, one of the crew that robbed the Orleans, of Philadelphia, and Charles Owens and James Ross, who robbed a Portsmouth schooner of $2600 in the Bite of Leogane. One of these daring freebooters was delivered up to Lieut. G. by the Governor of St. Barts, and the other two by the President of Hayti, for trial by the United States. The G. has boarded several privateers during her cruise, and traversed a space of 9000 miles, spreading terror among those wretches whose impotence is equal to their atrocity, and who only require active pursuit to frighten them out of visible existence.

Mobile, June 1, 1822.—Capt. Carter of the schr. Swan, arrived yesterday from Havana, reports that on his outward passage from this port, on the 27th ult. at 8 o'clock, A. M. being then within 30 miles from Havana, he was boarded by an open boat from the shore, manned with nine men, who all appeared to be Spanish, armed with muskets, pistols, cutlasses, and knives, who plundered the vessel of every thing they could carry off. They also robbed the captain and crew of their clothing, even stripping the jackets from their backs, and the shoes from their feet.

The villains would not even spare the property of a Spanish Priest, passenger on board, but they robbed him also of his clothes, money, and plate, the value of 800 dollars; they however afterwards returned his gown.

A sail heaving in sight, they left the schooner with orders to steer E. N. E. and not go over three leagues from shore, under pain of death. From their conversation while on board, it appeared that they intended to board the schooner again in the evening, run her ashore and burn her, but she escaped by the darkness of the night.

Lieut. Allen's Victory and Death

Extract of a letter from Matanzas, dated November 11, 1822.

"The gallant ALLEN is no more!—You witnessed the promptitude with which he hastened to relieve the vessels which I informed him had been captured off this port. He arrived just in time to save five sail of vessels which he found in possession of a gang of pirates, 300 strong, established in the Bay of Lejuapo, about 15 leagues east of this. He fell, pierced by two musket balls, in the van of a division of boats, attacking their principal vessel, a fine schooner of about eighty tons, with a long eighteen pounder on a pivot, and four smaller guns, *with the bloody flag nailed to the mast.* Himself, Capt. Freeman of Marines, and twelve men, were in the boat, much in advance of his other boats, and even took possession of the schooner, after a desperate resistance, which nothing but a bravery almost too daring could have overcome. The pirates, all but one, escaped by taking to their boats and jumping overboard, before the Alligator's boats reached them. Two other schooners escaped by the use of their oars, the wind being light.

Capt. Allen survived about four hours, during which his conversation evinced a composure and firmness of mind, and correctness of feeling, as honourable to his character, and more consoling to his friends than even the dauntless bravery he before exhibited."

The Surgeon of the Alligator in a letter to a friend, says, "He continued giving orders and conversing with Mr. Dale and the rest of us, until a few minutes before his death, with a degree of cheerfulness that was little to be expected from a man in his condition. He said he wished his relatives and his country to know that he had fought well, and added that he died in peace and good will towards all the world, and hoped for his reward in the next."

Lieut. Allen had but few equals in the service. He was ardently devoted to the interest of his country, was brave, intelligent, and accomplished in his profession. He displayed, living and dying, a magnanimity that sheds lustre on his relatives, his friends, and his country.

Pirates Entrapped

The British schooner Speedwell arrived at Nassau N. P. in November, bringing in 18 pirates, who had been captured by the Speedwell and her consort. The schooner had been disguised as a merchantman, and the pirates, taking her to be an easy prize, came carelessly along side of her, for the purpose of boarding, when she gave them a hot fire, and threw them into confusion. Many jumped overboard and were drowned; and with these and the killed, the loss of the pirates was about 15 or 16. The remainder of them, 18 in number, were taken prisoners and carried into Nassau.

Sailing of Commodore Porter

BALTIMORE, JAN. 17, 1823.

Yesterday Commodore PORTER left this port in the steam galley Enterprize, to join the squadron fitted out at Norfolk, for the purpose of suppressing piracy on the coast of Cuba. Every friend of humanity must wish that the efforts of the distinguished officer who has been selected to this command will be crowned with success. The means adopted are certainly the best calculated to effect the object. Frigates and sloops of war are totally inadequate, by means of their great draft of water; but the vessels which have been selected by Commodore PORTER, are precisely calculated to ferret the banditti from their lurking places. The aid of steam we think a most valuable addition to the squadron, and from the manner in which the Enterprize has been fitted out, we have every reason to believe she will completely answer the expectations formed. Commodore PORTER has been indefatigable since he came here, and several of our citizens conversant in steam affairs, volunteered their services to aid him in the necessary equipments for that department. We learn that she is provided with duplicates of every piece of machinery which might be carried away in action, and that able and experienced engineers were also procured for her.

In a very short time we hope to hear of the Commodore's arrival at his cruising ground, and we doubt not he will soon put an end to the ravages of those lawless barbarians.

Execution of the Pirates

Ten of the pirates captured by the British sloop of War Tyne, were executed at Kingston, Jamaica, on Friday, the 7th of February, 1823.

About a quarter of an hour before day dawn, the wretched culprits were taken from the jail, under a guard of soldiers from the 50th regiment, and the City Guard. On their arrival at the wherry wharf, the military retired, and the prisoners, with the Town Guard were put on board two wherries, in which they proceeded to Port Royal Point, the usual place of execution in similar cases. They were there met by a strong party of military, consisting of 50 men, under command of an officer. They formed themselves into a square round the place of execution, with the Sheriff and his officers with the prisoners in the centre. The gallows was of considerable length, and contrived with a drop so as to prevent the unpleasant circumstances which frequently occur.

The unfortunate men had been in continual prayer from the time they were awakened out of a deep sleep till they arrived at that place, where they were to close their existence.

They all expressed their gratitude for the attention they had met with from the Sheriff and the inferior officers. Many pressed the hands of the turnkey to their lips, others to their hearts, and, on their knees, prayed that God, Jesus Christ, and the Virgin Mary, would bless him and the other jailers for their goodness. They all then fervently joined in prayer. To the astonishment of all, no clerical character, of any persuasion, was present. They repeatedly called out, "Adonde esta et padre," (Where is the holy father.)

Juan Hernandez called on all persons present to hear him—he was innocent; what they had said about his confessing himself guilty was untrue. He had admitted himself guilty, because he hoped for pardon; but that now he was to die, he called God, Jesus Christ, the Holy Ghost, the Virgin Mary, and the Saints, to witness that he spoke truth—that he was no pirate, no murderer —he had been forced. The Lieutenant of the pirates was a wretch, who did not fear God, and had compelled him to act.

Juan Gutterez and Francisco de Sayas were loud in their protestations of innocence.

Manuel Lima said, for himself, he did not care; he felt for the old man (Miguel Jose). How could he be a pirate who could not help himself? If it were a Christian country, they would have pardoned him for his gray hairs. He was innocent—they had both been forced. Let none of his friends and relations ever venture to sea—he hoped his death would be a warning to them, that the innocent might suffer for the guilty. The language of this young man marked him a superior to the generality of his companions in misfortune. The seamen of the Whim stated that he was very kind to them when prisoners on board the piratical vessel. Just before he was turned off, he addressed the old man—"Adios viejo, para siempre adios."—(Farewell, old man, for ever farewell.)

Several of the prisoners cried out for mercy, pardon, pardon.

Domingo Eucalla, the black man, then addressed them. "Do not look for mercy here, but pray to God; we are all brought here to die. This is not built for nothing; here we must end our lives. You know I am innocent, but I must die the same as you all. There is not any body here who can do us any good, so let us think only of God Almighty. We are not children but men, you know that all must die; and in a few years those who kill us must die, too. When I was born, God set the way of my death; I do not blame any body. I was taken by the pirates, and they made me help them; they would not let me be idle. I could not show that this was the truth, and therefore they have judged me by the people they have found me with. I am put to death unjustly, but I blame nobody. It was my misfortune. Come, let us pray. If we are innocent, so much the less we have to repent. I do not come here to accuse any one. Death must come one day or other; better to the innocent than guilty." He then joined in prayer with the others. He seemed to be much reverenced by his fellow prisoners. He chose those prayers he thought most adapted to the occasion. Hundreds were witnesses to the manly firmness of this negro. Observing a bystander listening attentively to the complaints of one of his fellow wretches, he translated what had been said into English. With a steady pace, and a resolute and resigned countenance, he ascended the fatal scaffold. Observing the executioner unable to untie a knot on the collar of one of the prisoners, he with his teeth undid it. He then prayed most fervently till the drop fell.

Miguel Jose protested his innocence.—"No he robado, no he matado ningune, muero innocente."—(I have robbed no one, I have killed no one, I die innocent. I am an old man, but my family will feel my disgraceful death.)

Francisco Miguel prayed devoutly, but inaudibly. His soul seemed to have quitted the body before he was executed.

Breti Gullimillit called on all to witness his innocence; it was of no use for him to say an untruth for he was going before the face of God.

Augustus Hernandez repeatedly declared his innocence, requested that no one would say he had made a confession; he had none to make.

Juan Hernandez was rather obstinate when the executioner pulled the cap over his eyes. He said, rather passionately—"Quita is de mis ojos."—(Remove it from my eyes.) He then rubbed it up against one of the posts of the gallows.

Miguel Jose made the same complaint, and drew the covering from his eyes by rubbing his head against a fellow sufferer.

Pedro Nondre was loud in his ejaculations for mercy. He wept bitterly. He was covered with the marks of deep wounds.

The whole of the ten, included in the death warrant, having been placed on the scaffold, and the ropes suspended, the drop was let down. Nondre being an immense heavy man, broke the rope, and fell to the ground alive. Juan Hernandez struggled long. Lima was much convulsed. The old man Gullimillit, and Miguel, were apparently dead before the drop fell. Eucalla (the black man) gave one convulsion, and all was over.

When Nondre recovered from the fall and saw his nine lifeless companions stretched in death, he gave an agonizing shriek; he wrung his hands, screamed "Favor, favor, me matan sin causa. O! buenos Christianos, me amparen, ampara me, ampara me, no hay Christiano en asta, tiara?" (Mercy, mercy, they kill me without cause—Oh, good Christians, protect me, protect me, Oh, protect me. Is there no Christian in this land.)

He then lifted his eyes to Heaven, and prayed long and loud. Upon being again suspended, he was for a long period convulsed. He was an immense powerful man, and died hard.

Pirates Captured

The famous pirate, La Cata, was captured, off the Isle of Pines, about the 1st of March, 1823, by the British cutter, Grecian, after a smart action. The cutter had 50 men—the pirate 100, and 8 guns; it was believed that about 30 of the crew of the latter were killed, but only three prisoners were made, the rest making their escape on shore. Considerable quantities of goods were found on board the prize.

The Grecian conveyed the prisoners to Jamaica, where, it seems, there is more law to reach cases of piracy than in the United States.

Lafitte, the Noted Pirate, Killed

A British sloop of war fell in with and captured a piratical vessel with a crew of sixty men, under command of the famous LAFITTE. He hoisted the bloody flag and refused quarter, and fought until nearly every man was killed or wounded—LAFITTE being among the former.

The schooner Pilot, of Norfolk, was captured by the pirates off Matanzas, and her crew much abused; but they were put ashore, and the wretches went on a cruise in the prize, and captured and robbed two vessels *within two miles of the Moro castle,* Havana. A few days after, the U. S. schooner Jackall fell in with her and made a re-capture, securing, however, only one of the pirates; but several of them were killed in the action, fighting desperately. Several captures were made about the same time by Com. Porter's squadron, which was actively employed.

Battle with the Pirates

Almost every day furnished accounts evincing the activity of Commodore Porter, and the officers and men under his command; but for a long time their industry and zeal was rather shown in the *suppression* of piracy than the *punishment* of it. At length, however, an opportunity offered for inflicting the latter, as detailed in the following letter, dated Matanzas, July 10, 1823.

"I have the pleasure of informing you of a brilliant achievement, obtained against the pirates on the 5th inst. by two barges attached to Commodore PORTER's squadron, the Gallinipper, Lieut. Watson, 18 men, and the Musquito, Lieut. Inman, 10 men. The barges were returning from a cruise to windward; when they were near Jiguapa Bay, 13 leagues to windward of Matanzas, they entered it—it being a rendezvous for pirates. They immediately discovered a large schooner under way, which they supposed to be a Patriot privateer; and as their stores were nearly exhausted, they hoped to obtain some supplies from her. They therefore made sail in pursuit. When they were within cannon shot distance, she rounded to and fired her long gun, at the same time run up the bloody flag, directing her course towards the shore, continuing to fire without effect. When she had got within a short distance of the shore, she came to, with springs on her cable, continuing to fire; and when the barges were within 30 yards, they fired their muskets without touching boat or man; our men gave three cheers, and prepared to board; the pirates, discovering their intention, jumped into the water, when the bargemen, calling on the name of "ALLEN," commenced a destructive slaughter, killing them in the water and as they landed. So exasperated were our men, that it was impossible for their officers to restrain them, and many were killed after orders were given to grant quarter. Twenty-seven dead were counted, some sunk, five taken prisoners by the bargemen, and eight taken by a party of Spaniards on shore. The officers calculated that from 30 to 35 were killed. The schooner mounted a long nine pounder on a pivot, and 4 four pounders, with every other necessary armament, and a crew of 50 to 60 men, and ought to have blown the barges to atoms. She was commanded by the notorious Diableto or Little Devil. This statement I have from Lieut. Watson himself, and it is certainly the most decisive operation that has been effected against these murderers, either by the English or American force.

"This affair occurred on the same spot where the brave ALLEN fell about one year since. The prize was sent to Thompson's Island."

A British sloop of war, about the same time, captured a pirate schooner off St. Domingo, with a crew of 60 men. She had 200,000 dollars in specie, and other valuable articles on board. The brig Vestal sent another pirate schooner to New-Providence.

Capture of a Piratical Station in CUBA

The U. S. schooners of war Greyhound and Beagle left. Thompson's Island, June 7, 1823, under the command of Lieuts. Kearney and Newton, and cruised within the Keys, on the south side of Cuba, as far as Cape Cruz, touching at all the intermediate ports on the island, to intercept pirates. On the 21st July, they came to anchor off Cape Cruz, and Lieut. Kearney went in his boat to reconnoitre the shore, when he was fired on by a party of pirates who were concealed among the bushes. A fire was also opened from several pieces of cannon erected on a hill, a short distance off. The boat returned, and five or six others were manned from the vessels, and pushed off for the shore, but a very heavy cannonade being kept up by the pirates on the heights, as well as from the boats were compelled to retreat. The two schooners were then warped in, when they discharged several broadsides, and covered the landing of the boats. After a short time the pirates retreated to a hill that was well fortified. A small hamlet, in which the pirates resided was set fire to and destroyed. Three guns, one a four pounder, and two large swivels, with several pistols, cutlasses, and eight large boats, were captured. A cave, about 150 feet deep, was discovered, near where the houses were, and after considerable difficulty, a party of seamen got to the bottom, where was found an immense quantity of plunder, consisting of broadcloths, dry goods, female dresses, saddlery, &c. Many human bones were also in the cave, supposed to have been unfortunate persons who were taken and put to death. A great deal of the articles were brought away, and the rest destroyed. About forty pirates escaped to the heights, but many were supposed to have been killed, from the fire of the schooners, as well as from the men who landed. The bushes were so thick that it was impossible to go after them. Several other caves are in the neighborhood, in which it was conjectured they occasionally take shelter.

Pirates Taken and Executed

A piratical vessel, and her crew of thirty-eight men were captured off Matanzas on the 16th May, 1825, by a British cutter and a steamboat fitted out at that place. Several of the pirates were killed, and the rest sent to Havana for trial. It was ascertained that some of them had assisted in capturing more than twenty American vessels, whose crews were MURDERED!!

An additional gang of pirates was hung at the same period, at Porto Rico—eleven at once.

Charles Gibbs, otherwise James D. Jeffers, and Thomas I. Wansley

This atrocious villain was a native of Providence in Rhode Island. His true name was James D. Jeffers, but as he was more generally known as Charles Gibbs we shall give him that appellation. His adventures, excepting the crime for which he was finally hanged, are only known from his own admissions while under sentence of death, and our readers must judge for themselves how far they are to be credited.

It appears from evidence legally taken, that the brig Vineyard sailed from New Orleans about the first of November, eighteen hundred and thirty, for Philadelphia. William Thornby was the master of the vessel, and William Roberts the mate. The crew consisted of seven persons, viz. Charles Gibbs, John Brownrigg, Robert Dawes, Henry Atwell, James Talbot, A. Church, and Thomas I. Wansley, a young negro native of Delaware, who acted as cook.

When the Vineyard had been five days at sea, Wansley made it known to the crew that there were fifty thousand dollars in specie on board. This information excited their cupidity, and induced them to consult on the means of getting the money into their own hands. Many conversations took place on the subject, and while these were going on, Dawes, who was a mere boy, was sent to converse with the officers, in order to divert their attention from what was passing. Finally it was *resolved*, that as the master and mate were old men, it was time they should die and make room for the rising generation. Moreover, they were of opinion that as the mate was of a peevish disposition, he deserved death. Yet, to do no man injustice, it does not appear that Brownrigg or Talbot had any part in these deliberations, or in the foul deed that resulted from them.

The conspirators agreed to commit the greatest earthly crimes, murder and piracy, on the night of the twenty-third. The murder of the master was assigned to Gibbs and Wansley; that of the mate to Atwell and Church.

The vessel was off Cape Hatteras, when the time fixed for the murder arrived. The master was standing on the quarter deck, Dawes had the helm, and Brownrigg was aloft. Dawes called Wansley aft to trim the light in the binnacle. The black moved as if to obey, but coming behind Mr. Thornby, struck him on the back of the neck with the pump brake, so that he fell forward, crying "murder!" Wansley repeated his blows till the master was dead, and then, with the assistance of Gibbs, threw the body overboard. While this deed of darkness was being done, the mate, aroused by the noise, came up the companion ladder from the cabin. Atwell and Church were waiting for him at the top of the ladder, and one of them struck him down with a club; but the blow did not kill him. Gibbs followed to complete the work, but not being able to find the mate in the dark, returned to the deck for the binnacle light. With this he descended and laid hands on the victim, but was not able to overcome him, even with the aid of Atwell; but finally, with the assistance of Church, he was dragged on deck, beaten and thrown overboard. He was not yet dead, and swam after the vessel four or five minutes, crying for help, before he sank. All these transactions were witnessed by the boy Dawes, who had a passive, if not an active part in them.

The pirates then took possession of the vessel, and Wansley busied himself in wiping up the blood that had been spilled on deck, declaring, with an oath, that though he had heard that the stains of blood of a murdered person could not be effaced, he would wipe away these. Then, after drinking all round, they got up the money. It was distributed in equal portions to all on board; Brownrigg and Talbot being assured that if they would keep the secret, and share the plunder, they should receive no injury.

They then steered a northeasterly course toward Long Island, till they came within fifteen or twenty miles of South-Hampton Light, where they resolved to leave the vessel, in the boats, though the wind was blowing hard. Atwell scuttled the brig and got into the jolly boat with Church and Talbot, while Gibbs, Wansley, Dawes and Brownrigg, put off in the long boat. The jolly boat swamped on a bar two miles from the shore, and all on board were drowned. The long boat was in great danger also, and was only saved from a like fate by throwing over several bags of specie. Nevertheless, the crew at last got on shore on Pelican Island, where they buried their money, and found a sportsman who told them where they were. They then crossed to Great Barn Island, and went to the house of a Mr. Johnson, to whom Brownrigg gave the proper information. Thence they went to the house of a Mr. Leonard, where they procured a wagon to carry them farther. As they were about to get in, Brownrigg cried aloud that they might go whither they pleased, but he would not accompany them, for they were murderers. On hearing this Mr. Leonard sent for, a magistrate, and Gibbs and Dawes were apprehended. Wansley escaped into the woods, but was followed and soon taken.

The evidence of the guilt of the prisoners was full and conclusive. Their own confessions of the crime gratuitously made to Messrs. Meritt and Stevenson, who had the custody of them from Flatbush to New-York, could have left not the shadow of a doubt on the mind of any person who heard the testimony of those officers. Wansley told the whole story, occasionally prompted by Gibbs, and both admitted that Brownrigg was innocent of any participation in their crimes. Their confession was not, however, so favorable to Dawes.

Gibbs was arraigned for the murder of William Roberts, and Wansley for that of William Thornby. They were both found guilty, and the district attorney moved for judgment on the verdict. There was nothing peculiar in their deportment during the trial. The iron visage of Gibbs was occasionally darkened with a transient emotion, but he had evidently abandoned all hope of escape, and sat the greater part of the time with his hands between his knees, calmly surveying the scene before him. Wansley was more agitated, and trembled visibly when he rose to hear the verdict of the jury.

The judge proceeded to pass sentence on them severally, that each should be taken from the place where they then were, and thence to the place of confinement, and should be hanged by the neck till dead; and that the marshal of the Southern District of New York should see this sentence carried into execution on the twenty-second day of April following, between the hours of ten and four o'clock.

The first account which Gibbs gave of himself is, that his father obtained a situation for him in the United States sloop of war Hornet, Captain Lawrence, during the last war with England, in which vessel he made two cruises; in the last of which she captured and sunk the enemy's sloop of war Peacock off the coast of Pernambuco, after an engagement of twenty minutes. On the arrival of the Hornet in the United States, Captain Lawrence was assigned by the government to the command of the frigate Chesapeake, then lying in Boston harbor, and Gibbs accompanied him to that ill-fated vessel in the month of April, eighteen hundred and thirteen.

This statement of his services was proved to be false, and acknowledged as such by himself. His motive for the falsehood was, to conceal his real adventures about this time, that his proper name might not be discovered. There is much to corroborate and nothing to disprove what follows.

After his exchange, he abandoned all idea of following the sea for a subsistence, went home to Rhode Island, and remained there a few months, but being unable to conquer his propensity to roving, he entered on board a ship bound to New Orleans, and thence to Stockholm. On the homeward passage they were compelled to put into Bristol, England, in distress, where the ship was condemned, and he proceeded to Liverpool. He returned to the United States in the ship Amity, Captain Maxwell.

After its arrival, he left the ship, and entered on board the Colombian privateer Maria, Captain Bell. They cruised for about two months in the Gulf of Mexico, around Cuba, but the crew becoming dissatisfied in consequence of the non-payment of their prize-money, a mutiny arose, the crew took possession of the schooner, and landed the officers near Pensacola. A number of days elapsed before it was finally decided by them what course to pursue. Some advised that they should cruise as before, under the Colombian commission; others proposed to hoist the black flag. They cruised for a short time without success, and it was then unanimously determined to hoist the black flag and declare war against all nations. At last one of the crew, named Antonio, suggested that an arrangement could be made with a man in Havana, that would be mutually beneficial; that he would receive all their goods, sell them, and divide the proceeds. This suggestion being favorably received, they ran up within two miles of Moro Castle, and sent Antonio on shore to see the merchant and make a contract with him, which was done.

The Maria now put to sea, with a crew of about fifty men. The first vessel she fell in with was the Indispensable, an English ship, bound to Havana, which was taken and carried to Cape Antonio. The crew were immediately destroyed: those who resisted were hewed to pieces: those who offered no resistance, were reserved to be shot and thrown overboard. Such was the manner in which they proceeded in all their subsequent captures. The unhappy being that cried for mercy, in the hope that something like humanity was to be found in the breasts even of the worst of men, shared the same fate with him who resolved to sell his life at the highest price. A French brig, with a valuable cargo of wine and silk, was taken shortly after: the vessel was burnt and the crew murdered.

The sanguinary scenes through which Gibbs had passed, now effectually wrought up his desperation to the highest pitch, and being as remarkable for his coolness and intrepidity as he was for his skill in navigation, he was unanimously chosen to be their leader in all future enterprises. To reap a golden harvest without the hazard of encountering living witnesses of their crimes, it was unanimously resolved to spare no lives, and to burn and plunder without mercy. They knew that the principle inculcated by the old maxim that "dead men tell no tales," was the safe one for them, and they scrupulously followed it. Gibbs states that he never had occasion to give orders to begin the work of death.

He now directed his course towards the Bahama Banks, where they captured a brig, believed to be the William of New York, from some port in Mexico, with a cargo of furniture, destroyed the crew, took her to Cape Antonio, and sent the furniture and other articles to their friend in Havana. Sometime during this cruise, the pirate was chased for nearly a whole day by a United States ship, supposed to be the John Adams; he hoisted Patriot colors, and finally escaped. In the early part of the summer of eighteen hundred and seventeen, they took the Earl of Moira, an English ship from London, with a cargo of dry goods. The crew were destroyed, the vessel burnt, and the goods carried to the Cape. There they had a settlement with their Havana friend, and the proceeds were divided according to agreement.

During the cruise which was made in the latter part of eighteen hundred and seventeen, and the beginning of eighteen hundred and eighteen, a Dutch ship from Curacoa was captured, with a cargo of West India goods, and a quantity of silver plate. The passengers and crew, to the number of thirty, were all destroyed, with the exception of a young female about seventeen, who fell upon her knees and implored Gibbs to save her life. The appeal was sucessful, and he promised to save her, though he knew it would lead to dangerous consequences among his crew. She was carried to Cape Antonio, and kept there about two months; but the dissatisfaction increased until it broke out at last into open mutiny, and one of the pirates was shot by Gibbs for daring to lay hold of her with a view of beating out her brains. Gibbs was compelled in the end to submit her fate to a council of war, at which it was decided that the preservation of their own lives made her sacrifice indispensable. He therefore acquiesced in the decision, and gave orders to have her destroyed by poison, which was immediately done.

The piratical schooner was shortly after driven ashore near the Cape, and so much damaged that it was found necessary to destroy her. A new sharp-built schooner was in consequence provided by their faithful friend in Havana, called the Picciana, and despatched to their rendezvous. In this vessel they cruised successfully for more than four years. Among the vessels taken and destroyed with their crews, were the Belvidere, Dido, a Dutch brig, the British barque Larch, the other vessels enumerated in the list furnished to Justice Hopson, and many others whose names are not recollected. They had a very narrow escape, at one time, from the English man-of-war brig Coronation. In the early part of October, eighteen hundred and twenty-one, they captured a ship from Charleston, took her to Cape Antonio, and were busily engaged in landing her cargo, when the United States brig Enterprise, Captain Kearney, hove in sight, and discovering their vessels at anchor, sent in her barges to attack them. A serious engagement followed; they defended themselves for some time behind a four gun battery, but in the end were defeated with a considerable loss, and compelled to abandon their vessels and booty, and fly to the mountains for safety.

They left hot poisoned coffee on the cabin table in hopes that some of the American officers would drink it. This statement is confirmed by Captain Kearney.

On Friday, April twenty-second, 1831, Gibbs and Wansley paid the penalty of their crimes. Both prisoners arrived at the gallows about twelve o'clock, accompanied by the marshal, his aids, and some twenty or thirty United States marines. Two clergymen attended them to the fatal spot, where every thing being in readiness, and the ropes adjusted about their necks, the throne of mercy was fervently addressed in their behalf. Wansley then prayed earnestly himself, and afterwards joined in singing a hymn.

The boy Dawes was not prosecuted, having been received as State's evidence against Gibbs and Wansley.

Piracies on the BRIG Mexican

On the 26th day of August, 1834, His Britannic Majesty's brig of war Savage, from Portsmouth, England, arrived at Salem, Massachusetts, having on board sixteen of the crew of the piratical schooner Panda, which robbed the brig Mexican, of Salem, on the high seas, nearly two years since.

The robbery committed upon the Mexican was one of the most audacious and cruel acts of piracy ever recorded. She was bound to Rio Janeiro from Salem, and was boarded by a piratical schooner under Brazilian colors, on the 20th of September, 1832, lat. 33 long. 34, 30, and robbed of twenty thousand dollars in specie, the officers and crew stripped of every thing valuable, and fastened below, and the vessel set on fire with the horrid intention of destroying her with all on board. Captain Butman and his men succeeded in getting on deck through the scuttle which the pirates had left unsecured, and extinguished the flames, and returned home. Our government ordered a vessel to cruise in pursuit, but she gave up the chase as hopeless. The piratical vessel was afterwards taken on the coast of Africa, by His Britannic Majesty's brig Curlew, and destroyed, under the following circumstances:

The Curlew arrived at St. Thomas, west coast of Africa, from India, with orders to cruise on that coast; and her commander having obtained information that a schooner, suspected to be a pirate, was lying in the river Nazareth, on the southern extremity of the coast, immediately sailed in pursuit, and found the schooner as described. The boats of the Curlew were manned to take possession of her, when the crew of the schooner fled to the shore, with the exception of four who were taken prisoners. They had kindled a fire to destroy the schooner, and she had been stripped of every thing valuable. The fire was extinguished without damage. She had no cargo on board, but her water casks were all filled, and she was apparently ready for another cruise. In her cabin were found a compass, marked Boston, the flags and ensigns of different nations, and customhouse papers made out at Havana. In taking her down the river, she accidentally blew up, and the Curlew's purser and one man were killed. The four men taken were shipped at St. Thomas after the robbery of the Mexican. The Curlew's crew pursued the fugitives in various directions, and succeeded in capturing an additional number of the pirates; and several natives' towns were burned by the Curlew's men. The pirates had an examination in England before the proper authorities, when five of them offered to turn king's evidence, two of whom were admitted to testify. They were fully committed, and the British government ordered them to this country for trial, and the affidavits and documents relative to their capture and subsequent confinement and examination were delivered to the authorities in this country.

The pirates were tried before the United States court at Boston, November 11th, 1834, which continued for fourteen days, and resulted in the conviction of seven of their number, five of whom were executed agreeably to their sentence, the other two received a reprieve from the President of the United States.

Execution of the Spanish Pirates.—[Thursday, June 11, 1835.]—Pursuant to previous arrangement, Captain Don Pedro Gibert, and Juan Montenegro, Manuel Castillo, Angel Garcia, and Manuel Boyga, were yesterday morning summoned to prepare for their immediate execution, agreeably to their sentnce, for having, while belonging to the schooner Panda, committed piracy, by robbing the brig Mexican, of Salem, of twenty thousand dollars, and afterwards attempting to destroy the crew and all evidence of their crime, by setting fire to the vessel. It is understood, that, when the prisoners became thoroughly convinced that there was no longer any grounds to hope for a further respite, they entered into a mutual agreement to commit suicide on Wednesday night. Angel Garcia made the first attempt, in the evening, by trying to open the veins in each arm, with a fragment of a bottle, but was discovered before he could effect his purpose, and a stricter guard was afterwards maintained upon all of them during the remainder of the night, and every thing removed with which they might be supposed to renew any attempt upon their own lives. Yesterday morning, however, about nine o'clock, while the avenues of the jail resounded with the heavy steps of a host of acting marshals, and the "busy note of preparation" struck solemnly upon the ears of the spectators within reach of its echo, Boyga succeeded in inflicting a deep gash on the left side of his neck with a piece of tin. The officer's eye had been withdrawn from him scarcely a minute, before he was discovered lying on his pallet, with a peculiar trembling of his knees, which induced the officers to examine if any thing had suddenly happened to him. They found him covered with blood, and nearly insensible; medical aid was at hand, and the wound was immediately sewed up, but Boyga, who had fainted from loss of blood, never revived again. Two Catholic clergymen, the Rev. Mr. Varella, a Spanish gentleman, and pastor of the Spanish congregation at New York, and the Rev. Mr. Curtin, of this city, were in close attendance upon the prisoners during the whole morning; and at a quarter past ten, under the escort of the Marshal and his deputies, accompanied them to the gallows, erected on an insulated angle of land in the rear of the jail.

When the procession arrived at the foot of the ladder leading up to the platform of the gallows, the Rev. Mr. Varella, looking directly at Captain Gibert, said—"Spaniards, ascend to heaven." Gibert mounted with a quick step, and was followed by his comrades at a more moderate pace, but without the least perceptible indication of hesitancy. Boyga, unconscious of his situation and destiny, was carried up in a chair, and seated beneath the rope prepared for him. Gibert, Montenegro, Garcia, and Castillo all smiled subduedly as they took their appointed stations on the platform. Judging only from Gibert's air, carriage, and unembarrassed eye, as he glanced at the surrounding multitude, and surveyed the mechanism of his shameful death, he might have well been mistaken for an officer in attendance, instead of one of the doomed. With the exception of repeating his prayers, after the clergyman, he spoke but little. Soon after he ascertained his position on the stage, he left it, and passing over to the spot where the apparently lifeless Boyga was seated on the chair, he bent over his shoulder and kissed him very affectionately. He then resumed his station, but occasionally turned round to Mr. Peyton the interpreter, and the clergymen. Addressing his followers, he said—"Boys, we are going to die; but let us be firm, for we are innocent." To Mr. Peyton, removing his linen collar, and handing it to him, he said—"This is all I have to part with—take it as a keepsake. I die innocent, but I'll die like a noble Spaniard. Good bye, brother, we die in the hope of meeting you in heaven. Montenegro and Garcia, though exhibiting no terror, vociferated their innocence, exclaiming—"Americans, we are not *culpable*—we are innocent; but we forgive all who have injured us." Castillo addressed himself to an individual, whom he recognised in the front rank of the officers below the stage, and said—"Adieu, my friend—I shall see you in heaven—I do not care so much about dying, as to have the Americans think I am guilty," [culpable]. All of them expressed great satisfaction at the intelligence of De Soto's reprieve.

The Marshal having read the warrant for their execution, and stated that De Soto was respited for sixty days, and Ruiz for thirty, the ropes were adjusted round the necks of the prisoners, and a slight hectic flush spread over the countenance of each; but not an eye quailed, not a limb trembled, nor a muscle quivered. As the cap was about to be drawn over Gibert's face, the Spanish Priest fervently embraced him, and during the operation of covering the faces of the others, the Rev. Mr. Curtin advanced to the railing of the stage, and read a brief declaration on behalf of the prisoners, addressed to the citizens of America assembled, setting forth, that as at the trial they had declared their innocence, so did they now continue to do so. Boyga's cap and rope were adjusted, as he sat, supported by an officer, in the chair, which was so placed as to fall with the drop. At a quarter before 11, after every preparation was completed, and while they were repeating to themselves, in scarcely audible tones, their prayers, Deputy Marshal Bass suddenly cut the small cord which restrained the spring, and the platform fell without even the creaking of a hinge. In falling, Boyga's chair struck against the bodies of the Captain and Garcia. Boyga struggled slightly once after his descent, and Montenegro and Castillo but little; Capt. Gibert did not die quite so easily, the rope being placed behind his neck. Garcia struggled most and longest—about 3 minutes. After being suspended 30 minutes, the physicians in attendance pronounced them dead, and they were cut down, and placed in black coffins, in readiness in the yard.

It is stated in many of the papers, that Captain Gibert attempted to cut his throat on Wednesday night, but this is not the fact. It is true that he pursued a line of conduct on that night which induced the officers to suspect that he intended to commit suicide. Mr. Tavers, one of the guards, who understands the Spanish language, overheard the signal agreed upon, by the whole party. The Captain proposed to write till one o'clock, when he was to bid "Good bye" to the rest, and they were then to despatch themselves with pieces of glass. Accordingly, at the appointed hour, the Captain, having terminated his writing, destroyed a part of his papers, retired to a corner of his cell, and appeared to be arranging his person to "die with dignity;" but being closely watched at the window, the officers, Messrs. Shute and Pierce, entered his cell before he had completed his toilet. They asked him what he intended to do; but he was irritated by their undesired intrusion, and, showing temper, declined answering. Upon searching, they found a piece of glass in his pocket. They then ironed him, with his hands behind his back. He remained dogged in his disposition, and blew the light out four times, which the officer as often relighted it, and threatened to put his legs in irons if he persisted in putting it out.

Montenegro, it was discovered, *after* his execution, had cut his throat in two places, and had bled very profusely, but had washed his shirt out in the morning to conceal the attempt. It was the irritation of the wounds, probably, that made him hold his head a little awry when the rope was first put round his neck. He was one of the most piratical looking of the crew, but one of the most innocent, and was always in pleasant humor. Garcia inflicted wounds upon his arms after he was ironed.

DYING DECLARATION OF THE PIRATES.—The Catholic Sentinel of Saturday contains the following declaration of innocence, written in Spanish by Capt. Gibert, and signed by his companions. The substance of it was delivered from the platform, a few minutes before their execution, by the Rev. Mr. Curtin, one of the Catholic clergymen in attendance:—

"Americans! we, the undersigned, were reduced to this sad and ignominious fate by misfortune, not by guilt. In this world we have nothing to hope; but in the next, we confidently expect salvation from the benign mercy of our heavenly Redeemer. Then, Americans, we declare to you with our dying breath, that we are innocent; and we now aver so in the hearing of that God before whom we must in a few moments appear;—but our souls will not, at that sacred tribunal, be charged with debasing the last act of our lives by the utterance of falsehood. We speak the solemn truth;—we are not culpable,—and we reiterate here, under the gallows, what we declared on our trial, *'that we die innocent men.'* May God forgive those who brought us to this fatal end, as we leave the world in peace with all men. Farewell, Americans.

Angel Garcia,
Juan Montenegro,
Pedro Gibert,

Manuel Boyga,
Manuel Castillo."

Capture, Sufferings, and Escape of Captain Barnabas Lincoln: A Narrative

CAPTAIN BARNABAS LINCOLN

I have reluctantly yielded to the urgent solicitation of friends, to give a short narrative of the capture, sufferings and escape of myself and crew, after having been taken by a piratical schooner, called the Mexican, December, 1821. The peculiar circumstances attending our situation, gave us ample opportunity for learning the character of those cruisers which have lately infested our southern coasts, destroying the lives and plundering the property of so many peaceable traders. If this narrative should effect any good, or urge our government to still more vigorous measures for the protection of our commerce, my object will be attained.

    I sailed from Boston bound for Trinidad, in the island of Cuba, on the 13th November, 1821, in the schooner Exertion, burthen 107 tons, owned by Messrs. Joseph Ballister and Henry Farnam, with a crew consisting of the following persons:—

| Joshua Bracket, | mate, | Bristol, |
| David Warren, | cook, | Saco, |

Thomas Goodall,	seaman,	Baltimore,
Thomas Young,	"	Orangetown,
Francis de Suze,	"	St. John's,
George Read,	"	Greenock, Scotland.

The cargo consisted of flour, beef; pork, lard, butter, fish, beans, onions, potatoes, apples, hams, furniture, sugar box shooks, &c. invoiced at about eight thousand dollars. Nothing remarkable occurred during the passage, except much bad weather, until my capture, which was as follows:—

Monday, December 17*th*, 1821, commenced with fine breezes from the eastward. At day break saw some of the islands northward of Cape Cruz, called Keys—stood along N. W. every thing now seemed favourable for a happy termination of our voyage. At 3 o'clock, P. M. saw a sail coming round one of the Keys, into a channel called Boca de Cavolone by the chart, nearly in lat. 20° 55' N. long. 79° 55' W. she made directly for us with all sail set, sweeps on both sides (the wind being light) and was soon near enough for us to discover about forty men on her deck, armed with muskets, blunderbusses, cutlasses, long knives, dirks, &c. two carronades, one a twelve, the other a six pounder; she was a schooner, wearing the Patriot flag, (blue, white and blue) of the Republic of Mexico. I thought it not prudent to resist them, should they be pirates, with a crew of seven men, and only five muskets; accordingly ordered the arms and ammunition to be immediately stowed away in as secret a place as possible, and suffer her to speak us, hoping and believing that a republican flag indicated both honour and friendship from those who wore it, and which we might expect even from Spaniards. But how great was my astonishment, when the schooner having approached very near us, hailed in English, and ordered me to heave my boat out immediately and come on board of her with my papers.—Accordingly my boat was hove out, but filled before I could get into her.—I was then ordered to tack ship and lay by for the pirates' boat to board me; which was done by Bolidar, their first lieutenant, with six or eight Spaniards armed with as many of the before mentioned weapons as they could well sling about their bodies. They drove me into the boat and two of them rowed me to their privateer, (as they called their vessel,) where I shook hands with her commander, capt. Jonnia, a Spaniard, who before looking at my papers, ordered Bolidar, his lieutenant, to follow the Mexican in, back of the Key they had left, which was done. At six o'clock, P. M. the Exertion was anchored in eleven feet water, near their vessel, and an island, which they called Twelve League Key, (called by the chart Key Largo,) about thirty or thirty-five leagues from Trinidad. After this strange conduct they began examining my papers by a Scotchman who went by the name of Nickola, their sailing master—He spoke good English, had a countenance rather pleasing, although his beard and mustachoes had a frightful appearance—his face, apparently full of anxiety, indicated something in my favour; he gave me my papers saying "take good care of them, for I am afraid that you have fallen into bad hands." The pirate's boat was then sent to the Exertion with more men and arms; a part of them left on board her; the rest returning with three of my crew to their vessel; viz. Thomas Young, Thomas Goodall, and George Reed—they treated them with something to drink, and offered them equal shares with themselves, and some money, if they would enlist, but they could not prevail on them. I then requested permission to go on board my vessel which was granted, and further requested Nickola should go with me, but was refused by the captain, who vociferated in a harsh manner, "*No, No, No,*" accompanied with a heavy stamp upon the deck. When I got on board, I was invited below by Bolidar, where I found they had emptied the case of liquors, and broken a cheese to pieces and crumbled it on the table and cabin floor; the pirates elated with their *prize,* (as they called it,) had drank so much as to make them desperately abusive. I was permitted to lie down in my birth; but reader, if you have ever been awakened by a gang of armed desperadoes, who have taken possession of your habitation in the midnight hour, you can imagine my feelings—Sleep was a stranger to me, and anxiety was my guest. Bolidar, however, pretended friendship, and flattered me with the prospect of being soon set at liberty. But I found him, as I suspected, a consummate hypocrite; indeed, his very looks indicated it. He was a stout and well built man, of a dark, swarthy complexion, with keep, ferocious eyes, huge whiskers and beard under his chin and on his lips four or five inches long; he was a Portuguese by birth, but had become a naturalized Frenchman—had a wife, if not children, (as I was told) in France, and was well known there as commander of a first rate privateer. His appearance was truly terrific; he could talk some in English, and had a most lion-like voice.

Tuesday, 18th.—Early this morning the captain of the pirates came on board the Exertion; took a look at the cabin-stores, and cargo in the state rooms, and then ordered me back with him to his vessel, where he, with his crew, held a consultation for some time, respecting the cargo. After which, the interpreter, Nickola, told me that "the captain had or *pretended to have* a commission under gen. Traspelascus, commander in chief of the republic of Mexico, authorizing him to take all cargoes whatever of provisions, bound to any Spanish royalist port—that my cargo being bound to an enemy's port, must be condemned; but that the vessel should be given up and be put into a fair channel for Trinidad where I was bound." I requested him to examine the papers thoroughly, and perhaps he would be convinced to the contrary, and told him my cargo was all American property taken in at Boston and consigned to an American gentleman, agent at Trinidad. But the captain would not take this trouble, but ordered both vessels under way immediately, and commenced beating up amongst the Keys through most of the day, the wind being very light. They now sent their boats on board the Exertion for stores, and commenced plundering her of bread, butter, lard, onions, potatoes, fish, beans, &c. took up some sugar box shooks that were on deck, and found the barrels of apples; selected the best of them, and threw the rest overboard. They inquired for spirits, wine, cider, &c. and were told "they had already taken all that was on board." But not satisfied they proceeded to search the state rooms and fore-castle, ripped up the floor of the latter and found some boxes of bottled cider, which they carried to their vessel, gave three cheers, in an exulting manner to me, and then began drinking it with such freedom, that a violent quarrel arose between officers and men, which came very near ending in bloodshed. I was accused of falsehood, for saying they had already got all the liquors that were on board, and I thought they had; the truth was, I never had any bill of lading of the cider, and consequently had no recollection of its being on board; yet it served them as an excuse for being insolent. In the evening peace was restored and they sung songs. I was suffered to go below for the night, and they placed a guard over me, stationed at the companion way.

Wednesday, 19th, commenced with moderate easterly winds, beating towards the N. E. the pirate's boats frequently going on board the Exertion for potatoes, fish, beans, butter, &c. which were used with great waste, and extravagance. They gave me food and drink, but of bad quality more particularly the victuals, which was wretchedly cooked. The place assigned me to eat was covered with dirt and vermin. It appeared that their great object was to hurt my feelings with threats and observations, and to make my situation as unpleasant as circumstances would admit. We came to anchor near a Key, called by them Brigantine, where myself and mate were permitted to go on shore, but were guarded by several armed pirates. I soon returned to the Mexican and my mate to the Exertion, with George Reed one of my crew; the other two being kept on board the Mexican. In the course of this day I had considerable conversation with Nickola, who appeared well disposed towards me. He lamented most deeply his own situation, for he was one of those men, whose early good impressions were not entirely effaced, although confederated with guilt. He told me "those who had taken me, were no better than pirates, and their end would be the halter," "but," he added, with peculiar emotion, "I will never be hung as a pirate," shewing me a bottle of laudanum which he had found in my medicine chest, saying. "If we are taken, *that* shall cheat the hangman, before we are condemned." I endeavored to get it from him, but did not succeed then asked him how he came to be in such a company as he appeared to be dissatisfied. He stated, "that he was at New Orleans last summer out of employment, and became acquainted with one capt. August Orgamar, a Frenchman, who had bought a small schooner of about fifteen tons, and was going down to the bay of Mexico to get a commission, under gen. Traspelascus, in order to go a privateering under the patriot flag. Capt. Orgamar made him liberal offers respecting shares, and promised him a sailing master's birth, which he accepted and embarked on board the schooner, without sufficiently reflecting on the danger of such an undertaking. Soon after she sailed for Mexico; where they got a commission, and the vessel was called Mexican. They made up a complement of twenty men, and after rendering the general some little service, in transporting his troops to a place called——proceeded on a cruise; took some small prizes off Campeachy; afterwards came on the south coast of Cuba, where they took other small prizes and the one which we were now on board of. By this time the crew were increased to about forty, nearly one half Spaniards, the others Frenchmen and Portuguese. Several of them had sailed out of ports in the United States, with American protections; but, I confidently believe none are natives, especially of the northern states. I was careful in examining the men, being desirous of knowing if any of my countrymen were among this wretched crew; but am satisfied there were none, and my Scotch friend concurred in the opinion. They had an excellent pilot named Baltizar, belonging to Spirito Santo, near Trinidad de Cuba, who was able to pilot them safely among all the small Keys or Islands, and find their hiding places.—They soon came to a conclusion to destroy the little old Mexican which they first had, and take the present one for a cruiser; and apply the old commission to her and call her by the same name. This shews their respect for the government from which they had obtained that commission. And now with a new vessel, which was the prize of these plunderers, they sailed up Manganeil Bay; previously, however, they fell in with an American schooner from which they bought four barrels of beef, and paid in tobacco. At the bay was an English brig belonging to Jamaica, owned by Mr. John Louden of that place. On board of this vessel the Spanish part of the crew commenced their depredations as pirates, although capt. Orgamar and Nickola protested against it, and refused any participation; but they persisted, and like so many ferocious blood-hounds, boarded the brig, plundered the cabin stores, furniture, captain's trunk, &c. took a hogshead of rum, one twelve pound carronade some rigging and sails. One of them plundered the chest of a sailor, who made some resistance, so that the Spaniard took his cutlass and beat and wounded him without mercy. Nickola asked him "why he did it?" the fellow answered. "I will let you know," and took up the cook's axe and gave him a cut on the head, which nearly deprived him of life. Then they ordered capt. Orgamar to leave his vessel, allowing him his trunk and turned him ashore, to seek for himself. Nickola begged them to dismiss him with his captain, but *no, no,* was the answer; for they had no complete navigator but him. After capt. Orgamar was gone, they put in his stead the present brave (or as I should call him cowardly) capt. Jonnia, who headed them in plundering the before mentioned brig, and made Bolidar their first lieutenant, and then proceeded down among those Keys or Islands, where I was captured. This is the amount of what my friend Nickola told me of their history.

Thursday, 20th, continued beating up, wind being light the pirates' boats were sent to the Exertion for more stores, such as bread, lard, &c. I this day discovered on board the Mexican three black girls, of whom it is well to say no more. It is impossible to give an account of the filthiness of this crew, and were it possible it would not be expedient. In their appearance they were terrific, wearing black whiskers and long beards, the receptacles of dirt and vermin. They used continually the most profane language; had frequent quarrels; and so great was their love of gambling that the captain would play cards with the meanest man on board. All these things rendered them to me objects of total disgust (with a few exceptions, as will hereafter appear.)—I was told they had a stabbing match, but a few days before I was taken, and one man came near being killed; they put him ashore at a fisherman's hut and there left him to perish. I saw the wound of another who had his nose split open.

Friday, 21st.—After laying at anchor through the night in ten fathoms water, made sail and stood to the eastward—by this time I was out of my reckoning, having no quadrant, charts or books. The pirates' boats were again sent for stores. The captain for the second time demanded of me where my wine, brandy, &c. were, I again told him, they had already got the whole. They took the deep sea line and some cordage from the Exertion and at night came to anchor.

Saturday, 22d.—Both vessels under way standing to the eastward, they ran the Exertion aground on a bar, but after throwing overboard most of her deck load of shooks, she floated off; a pilot was sent to her, and she was run into a narrow creek between two keys, where they moored her head and stern along side the mangrove trees, sent down her yards and topmasts, and covered her mast heads and shrouds with bushes to prevent her being seen by vessels which might pass that way. I was then suffered to go on board my own vessel, and found her in a very filthy condition; sails torn, rigging cut to pieces, and every thing in the cabin in waste and confusion. The swarms of moschetoes and sand-flies made it impossible to get any sleep or rest. The pirates' large boat was armed and manned under Bolidar, and sent off with letters to a merchant (as they called him) by the name of Dominico, residing in a town called Principe, on the main island of Cuba. I was told by one of them who could speak English, that Principe was a very large and populous town, situated at the head of St. Maria, which was about 20 miles N. E. from where we lay, and the Keys lying around us were called Cotton Keys.—The captain pressed into his service Francis de Suze, one of my crew, saying that he was one of his countrymen. Francis was very reluctant in going, and said me, with tears in his eyes, "I shall do nothing but what I am obliged to do and will not aid in the least to hurt you or the vessel; I am very sorry to leave you." He was immediately put on duty and Thomas Goodall sent back to the Exertion.

Sunday, 23d.—Early this morning a large number of the pirates came on board of the Exertion, threw out the long boat, broke open the hatches and took out considerable of the cargo, in search of rum, gin, &c. still telling me "I had some and that they would find it," uttering the most awful profaneness. In the afternoon their boat returned with a perough, having on board the captain, his first lieutenant and seven men of a patriot or piratical vessel that was chased ashore at Cape Cruz by a Spanish armed brig. These seven men made their escape in said boat and, after four days, found our pirates and joined them; the remainder of the crew being killed or taken prisoners.

Monday, 24th—Their boat was manned and sent to the before mentioned town.—I was informed by a line from Nickola, that the pirates had a man on board, a native of Principe, who in the garb of a sailor was a partner with Dominico, but I could not get sight of him. This lets us a little into the plans by which this atrocious system of piracy has been carried on. Merchants having partners on board of these pirates! thus pirates at sea and robbers on land are associated to destroy the peaceable trader. The willingness exhibited by the seven above mentioned men, to join our gang of pirates, seems to look like a general understanding among them; and from there being merchants on shore so base as to encourage the plunder and vend the goods, I am persuaded there has been a systematic confederacy on the part of these unprincipled desperadoes, under cover of the patriot flag; and those on land are no better than those on the sea. If the governments to whom they belong know of the atrocities committed (and I have but little doubt they do) they deserve the execration of all mankind.

Tuesday, 25th.—Still on board the Exertion—weather very calm and warm. The pirates' boat returned from St. Maria, and came for candles, cheese, potatoes, &c. they saying they must have them, and forbid my keeping any light on board at night—took a case of trunks for the captain's use and departed. Their irritating conduct at this time can hardly be imagined.

Wednesday, 26th.—I was told by Bolidar that three Spanish cruisers were in search of them, that they could fight two of them at once, (which by the way I believe was not true) and were disappointed at not finding them. Same evening they took both of my boats, and their own men, towed their vessel out of the creek, and anchored at its mouth, to get rid of sand-flies; while they obliged us to stay on deck under an awning, exposed to all the violence of these flies; we relieved ourselves in some measure by the burning of tobacco, which lasted but for a short time.

Thursday, 27th.—A gang of the pirates came and stripped our masts of the green bushes, saying, "she appeared more like a sail than trees"—took one barrel of bread and one of potatoes, using about one of each every day. I understood they were waiting for boats to take the cargo; for the principal merchant had gone to Trinidad.

Friday, 28th.—Nothing remarkable occurred this day—were frequently called upon for tar and butter, and junk to make oakum. Capt. Jonnia brought on board with him his new captain and officer before mentioned. Again they asked for wine, and were told as before, they had gotten the whole.

Saturday, 29th.—Same insulting conduct continued.—Took off a barrel of crackers.

Sunday, 30th.—The beginning of trouble! This day which peculiarly reminds Christians of the high duties of compassion and benevolence, was never observed by these pirates. This, of course, we might expect, as they did not often know when the day came, and if they knew it, it was spent in gambling. The old saying among seamen, "no Sunday off soundings," was not thought of; and even this poor plea was not theirs, for they were on soundings and often at anchor.—Early this morning the merchant, as they called him, came with a large boat for the cargo. I was immediately ordered into the boat with my crew, not allowed any breakfast, and carried about three miles to a small island out of sight of the Exertion and left there by the side of a little pond of thick, muddy water, which proved to be very brackish, with nothing to eat but a few biscuit. One of the boat's men told us the merchant was afraid of being recognized, and when he had gone the boat would return for us; but we had great reason to apprehend they would deceive us, and therefore passed the day in the utmost anxiety. At night, however, the boats came and took us again on board the Exertion; when, to our surprise and astonishment we found they had broken open the trunks and chests and taken all our wearing apparel, not even leaving a shirt or pair of pantaloons, nor sparing a small miniature of my wife which was in my trunk. The little money I and my mate had, with some belonging to the owners, my mate had previously distributed about the cabin in three or four parcels, while I was on board the pirate, for we dare not keep it about us; one parcel in a butter pot they did not discover—A midst the hurry with which I was obliged to leave my vessel to go to the before mentioned island, I fortunately snatched my vessel's papers and hid them in my bosom, which the reader will find was a happy circumstance for me. My writing desk, with papers, accounts, &c. all Mr. Lord's letters (the gentleman to whom my cargo was consigned) and several others were taken and maliciously destroyed. My medicine chest, which I so much wanted, was kept for their own use. What their motive could be to take my papers I could not imagine, except they had hopes of finding bills of lading for some Spaniards, to clear them from piracy. Mr. Bracket had some notes and papers of consequence to him, which shared the same fate. My quadrant, charts, books and some bedding were not yet taken, but I found it impossible to hide them, and they were soon gone from my sight.

Monday, 31st.—We complained to them, expressing the necessity of having clothes to cover us—but, as well might we have appealed to the winds, and rather better, for they would not have upbraided us in return. The captain, however, sent word he would see to it, and ordered their clothes bags to be searched, where he found some of our things, but took good care to put them in his own cabin. I urgently requested him to give me the miniature, but, *no* was all I could get.

Tuesday, January 1st, 1822.—A sad new year's day to me. Before breakfast orders came for me to cut down the Exertion's railing and bulwarks on one side, for their vessel to heave out by, and clean her bottom. On my hesitating a little they observed with anger, "very well captain, suppose you no do it quick, we do it for you."—Directly afterwards another boat full of armed men came along side; they jumped on deck with swords drawn and ordered all of us into her immediately; I stepped below, in hopes of getting something which would be of service to us; but the captain hallooed, "Go in the boat directly or I will fire upon you"—Thus compelled to obey, we were carried, together with four Spanish prisoners, to a small, low island or key of sand in the shape of a half moon and partly covered with mangrove trees; which was about one mile from and in sight of my vessel. There they left nine of us, with a little bread, flour, fish, lard, a little coffee and molasses; two or three kegs of water, which was brackish; an old sail for a covering, and a pot and some other small articles no way fit to cook in. Leaving us these, which were much less than they appear in the enumeration, they pushed off, saying, "we will come to see you in a day or two."—Selecting the best place, we spread the old sail for an awning; but no place was free from flies, moschetoes, snakes, the venemous stinged scorpion and the more venemous santipee. Sometimes they were found crawling inside of our pantaloons, but fortunately no injury was received. This afternoon the pirates hove their vessel out by the Exertion and cleaned one side, using her paints, oil, &c. for that purpose.—To see my vessel in that situation and to think of our prospects was a source of the deepest distress. At night we retired to our tent; but having nothing but the cold damp ground for a bed, and the heavy dew of night penetrating the old canvass—the situation of the island being fifty miles from the usual track of friendly vessels, and one hundred and thirty five from Trinidad—seeing my owner's property so unjustly and wantonly destroyed—considering my condition, the hands at whose mercy I was, and deprived of all hopes, rendered sleep or rest a stranger to me.

Wednesday, 2rd. The pirates hove out and cleaned the other side. She then commenced loading with the Exertion's cargo, which appeared to be flour and lard. In the afternoon their boat came and took two of the Spaniards with them to another island for water, and soon after returned with four kegs of poor, unwholesome water, and left us, saying they should not bring us provisions again for some time; as they were going away with goods from the prize, to be gone two or three days. Accordingly they brought a present supply of beef, pork, and a few potatoes, with some bedding for myself and mate. The mangrove wood afforded us a good fire, as one of the Spanish prisoners happened to have fire-works; and others had tobacco and paper with which we made cigars. About this time one of my men began to be unwell; his legs and body swelled considerably, but having no medicine I could not do much to relieve him.

Thursday, 3d. The pirates had dropped off from the Exertion; but kept their boats employed in bringing the cargo from her; I supposed it to be kegs of lard to make stowage. They then got under way with a perough in tow, both deeply laden, ran out of the harbour, hauled on the wind to the eastward till out of sight behind the Keys; leaving a guard on board the Exertion.—The following is description of their vessel, given in hopes that some American cruiser may fall in with her, and that they may not be deceived by her wearing the patriot flag. She is a schooner of about forty tons, pilot boat built, apparently in the Chesapeake bay; is not very straight, being hogged a little abaft her main chains; making a hollow between the fore and main mast; stem droops a little, and has a plank painted light yellow, about nine inches wide, round the waist, which leaves common open skuppers; canvass waist cloths, tarred and painted black, about eighteen inches wide; bottom, Spanish brown, but latterly has been white-boot topped; masts, dark coloured southern pine, rake a little aft; carries fore top sail, top gallant sail, lug fore sail, gaft top sail, main top mast stay sail, a ring tail and flying gib; sails well with a free wind, and middling upon the wind.

Friday, 4th.—Commenced with light winds and hot sun, saw a boat coming from the Exertion, apparently loaded; she passed between two small Keys to northward, supposed to be bound for Cuba. At sunset a boat came and inquired if we wanted any thing, but instead of adding to our provisions took away our molasses, and pushed off. We found one of the Exertion's water casks, and several pieces of plank, which we carefully laid up, in hopes of getting enough to make a raft.

Saturday, 5th.—Pirates again in sight coming from the eastward; they beat up along side their prize, and commenced loading. In the afternoon Nickola came to us, bringing with him two more prisoners, which they had taken in a small sail boat coming from Trinidad to Manganeil, one a Frenchman, the other a Scotchman, with two Spaniards, who remained on board the pirate, and who afterwards joined them. The back of one of these poor fellows was extremely sore, having just suffered a cruel beating from Bolidar, with the broad side of a cutlass. It appeared, that when the officer asked him "where their money was, and how much," he answered, "he was not certain but believed they had only two ounces of gold"—Bolidar furiously swore he said "ten," and not finding any more, gave him the beating. Nickola now related to me a singular fact; which was, that the Spanish part of their crew were determined to shoot him; that they tied him to the mast, and a man was appointed for the purpose; but Lyon, a Frenchman, his particular friend, stepped up and told them, if they shot him, they must shoot several more; some of the Spaniards sided with him, and he was released. Nichola told me, the reason for such treatment was, that he continually objected to their conduct towards me, and their opinion was if he should escape they would be discovered, as he declared he would take no prize money. While with us, he gave me a letter written in great haste, which contains some particulars respecting the cargo;—as follows:—

January 4, 1822.

SIR—We arrived here this morning, and before we came to anchor, had five canoes alongside ready to take your cargo, part of which we had in; and as I heard you express a wish, to know what they took out of her, to this moment, you may depend on this account of *Jamieson*, for quality and quantity; if I have the same opportunity you will have an account of the whole. The villain who bought your cargo is from the town of *Principe*, his name is Dominico, as to that it is all that I can learn; they have taken your charts on board the schooner Mexican and I suppose mean to keep them, as the other captain has agreed to act the same infamous part in the tragedy of his life. Your clothes are here on board, but do not let me flatter you, that you will get them back; it may be so, and it may not. Perhaps in your old age, when you recline with ease in a corner of your *cottage*, you will have the goodness to drop a tear of pleasure to the memory of him, whose highest ambition should have been to subscribe himself, though devoted to the gallows, your friend,

NICKOLA MONACRE.

Excuse haste.

P. S. Your answer in writing when I come again.

Sunday, 6th.—The pirates were under way at sunrise, with a full load of the Exertion's cargo, going to Principe again, to sell a second freight, which was done readily for cash. I afterwards heard that the flour brought only five dollars per barrel, when it was worth at Trinidad thirteen; so that the villain who bought my cargo at Principe, made very large profits by it.

Monday, 7th.—The pirates brought more water, but being very brackish, it was unfit for use. We were now greatly alarmed at Thomas' ill health, being suddenly attacked with a pain in the head, and swelling of the right eye, attended with derangement. He however soon became better; but his eye remained swollen several days without much pain. In the evening we had some heavy showers of rain, and having no secure cabin, no sheltered retreat, our exposure made us pass a very uncomfortable night.

Tuesday, 8th.—Early this morning the pirates in sight again, with fore top sail and top gallant sail set; beat up along side of the Exertion and commenced loading; having, as I supposed, sold and discharged her last freight among some of the inhabitants of Cuba. They appeared to load in great haste; and the song "O he oh," which echoed from one vessel to the other, was distinctly heard by us. How wounding was this to me! How different was this sound from what it would have been, had I been permitted to pass unmolested by these lawless plunderers, and been favoured with a safe arrival at the port of my destination, where my cargo would have found an excellent sale. Then would the "O he oh," on its discharging, have been a delightful sound to me. In the afternoon she sailed with the perough in tow, both with a full load; having chairs, which was part of the cargo, slung at her quarters.

Wednesday, 9th.—Very calm and warm. The swarms of moschetoes and flies made us pass a very uncomfortable day. We dug in the sand for water, but were disappointed at finding none so good as they left us. In walking round among the bushes, I accidently discovered a hole in the sand, and saw something run into it; curiosity led me to dig about it. With the help of Mr. Bracket I found at the distance of seven feet from its mouth, and one from the surface, a large solitary rat, apparently several years old; he had collected a large nest of grass and leaves; but there was not the least appearance of any other being, on the island.

Thursday, 10th.—No pirates in sight. The day was passed in anxious suspense; David Warren being quite sick.

Friday, 11th.—They came and hauled alongside of the Exertion, but I think took out none of her cargo; but had, as I supposed, a vendue on board, wherein was sold among themselves, all our clothing, books, quadrants, charts, spy-glasses, and every thing belonging to us and our fellow prisoners. I was afterwards told they brought a good price; but what they could want of the Bible, Prayer-Book and many other books in English, was matter of astonishment to me.

Saturday, 12th.—They remained along side the Exertion; took her paints, oil, brushes, &c. and gave their vessel a new coat of paint all round, and a white boot top—took the perough to another key and caulked her—there was no appearance of their taking any cargo out; the Exertion however appeared considerably high out of water. About sunset the pirates went out of the harbour on a cruise.—Here we had been staying day after day and exposed night after night —apprehensions for our safety were much increased; what was to become of us, seemed now to rush into every one's mind.

Sunday, 13th.—Deprived of our good books, deprived in fact of every thing, save life, and our ideas respecting our fate so gloomy, all tended to render time, especially the Lord's day, burthensome to us. In the afternoon a boat came for cargo, from, as I supposed, that villain Dominico.

Monday, 14th.—They again hove in sight, and beat up, as usual, along side their prize. While passing our solitary island, they laughed at our misery which was almost insupportable—looking upon us as though we had committed some heinous crime, and they had not sufficiently punished us; they hallooed to us, crying out "Captain, Captain," accompanied with obscene motions and words, with which I shall not blacken these pages—yet I heard no check upon such conduct, nor could I expect it among such a gang, who have no idea of subordination on board, except when in chase of vessels, and even then but very little. My resentment was excited at such a malicious outrage, and I felt a disposition to revenge myself, should fortune ever favor me with an opportunity. It was beyond human nature not to feel and express some indignation at such treatment.—Soon after, Bolidar, with five men, well armed, came to us; he having a blunderbuss, cutlass, a long knife and pair of pistols—but for what purpose did he come? He took me by the hand saying, "Captain, me speak with you, walk this way." I obeyed, and when we were at some distance from my fellow prisoners, (his men following) he said, "the captain send me for your *wash*." I pretended not to understand what he meant and replied "I have no clothes, nor any soap to wash with—you have taken them all"—for I had kept my watch about me, hoping they would not discover it. He demanded it again as before; and was answered, "I have nothing to wash;" this raised his anger, and lifting his blunderbuss he roared out, "what the d—l you call him that make clock? give it me"—I considered it imprudent to contend any longer and submitted to his unlawful demand.—As he was going off, he gave me a small bundle in which was a pair of linen drawers, sent to me by Nickola, and also the Rev. Mr. Brooks' "Family Prayer Book." This gave me great satisfaction.—Soon after, he returned with his captain who had one arm slung up, yet with as many implements of war, as his diminitive, wicked self could conveniently carry; he told me (through an interpreter who was a prisoner) "that on his cruise, he had fallen in with two Spanish privateers, and beat them off; but had three of his men killed and himself wounded in the arm"—Bolidar turned to me and said "it is a d—n lie"—which words proved to be correct; for his arm was not wounded, and when I saw him again, which was soon afterwards, he forgot to sling it up. He further told me, "after tomorrow you shall go with your vessel and we will accompany you towards Trinidad." This gave me some new hopes, and why I could not tell. They then left us without rendering any assistance.—This night we got some rest.

Tuesday, 15th.—The words "go after to-morrow," were used among our Spanish fellow prisoners, as though that happy to-morrow would never come—in what manner it came will soon be noticed.

Wednesday, 16th.—One of their boats came to inquire if we had seen a boat pass by last night, for their small sloop sail boat was gone and two men deserted: I told them "no"—at heart I could not but rejoice at the escape, and approve the deserters—I said nothing, however, of this kind to the pirates. On their return, they manned three of their boats and sent them in different directions to search, but at night came back without finding boat or men. They now took our old sail, which hitherto had somewhat sheltered us, to make, as I supposed, some small sail for their vessel. This rendered our night more uncomfortable than before, for in those islands the night dews are very heavy.

Thursday, 17th, was passed with great impatience.—The Exertion having been unmoored and swung to her anchor, gave some hopes of being restored to her; but was disappointed.

Friday, 18th, commenced with brighter prospects of liberty than ever—the pirates were employed in setting up our devoted schooner's shrouds, stays, &c. My condition now reminded me of the hungry man, chained in one corner of a room, while at another part was a table loaded with delicious food and fruits, the smell and sight of which he was continually to experience, but, alas! his chains were never to be loosed that he might go and partake—at almost the same moment they were thus employed, the axe was applied with the greatest dexterity to both her masts, and I saw them fall over the side! Here fell my hopes—I looked at my condition, and then thought of home.—Our Spanish fellow prisoners were so disappointed and alarmed, that they recommended hiding ourselves, if possible, among the mangrove trees, believing, as they said, we should now certainly be put to death; or, what was worse, compelled to serve on board the Mexican as pirates. Little else it is true seemed left for us; however, we kept a bright look out for them during the day, and at night "an anchor watch" as we called it, determined if we discovered their boats coming towards us, to adopt the plan of hiding, although starvation stared us in the face; yet preferred that to instant death. This night was passed in sufficient anxiety—I took the first watch.

Saturday, 19th.—The pirates large boat came for us—it being day light, and supposing they could see us, determined to stand our ground and wait the result. They ordered us all into the boat, but left every thing else; they rowed towards the Exertion—I noticed a dejection of spirits in one of the pirates, and inquired of him where they were going to carry us? He shook his head and replied "I do not know." I now had some hopes of visiting my vessel again—but the pirates made sail, run down, took us in tow and stood out of the harbour. Bolidar afterwards took me, my mate and two of my men on board and gave us some coffee. On examination I found they had several additional light sails, made of the Exertion's. Almost every man, a pair of canvass trowsers; and my colours cut up and made into belts to carry their money about them.—My jolly boat was on deck, and I was informed, all my rigging was disposed of. Several of the pirates had on some of my clothes, and the captain one of my best shirts, a cleaner one, than I had ever seen him have on before.—He kept at a good distance from me, and forbid my friend Nickola's speaking to me.—I saw from the companion way in the captain's cabin my quadrant, spy glass and other things which belonged to us, and observed by the compass, that the course steered was about W. by S.—distance nearly twenty miles, which brought them up with a cluster of islands called by some "Cayman Keys." Here they anchored and caught some fish, (one of which was named *guard fish*) of which we had a taste. I observed that my friend Mr. Bracket was somewhat dejected, and asked him in a low voice, what his opinion was with respect to our fate? He answered, "I cannot tell you, but it appears to me the worst is to come," I told him that I hoped not, but thought they would give us our small boat and liberate the prisoners. But mercy even in this shape was not left for us. Soon after, saw the captain and officers whispering for some time in private conference. When over, their boat was manned under the command of Bolidar, and went to one of those Islands or Keys before mentioned. On their return, another conference took place—whether it was a jury upon our lives we could not tell—I did not think conscience could be entirely extinguished in the human breast, or that men could become fiends. In the afternoon while we knew not the doom which had been fixed for us, the captain was engaged with several of his men in gambling, in hopes to get back some of the 500 dollars, they said, he lost but a few nights before; which had made him unusually fractious. A little before sunset he ordered all the prisoners into the large boat with a supply of provisions and water, and to be put on shore. While we were getting into her, one of my fellow prisoners, a Spaniard, attempted with tears in his eyes to speak to the captain, but was refused, with the answer—"I'll have nothing to say to any prisoner, go into the boat." In the mean time Nickola said to me, "My friend, I will give you your book," (being Mr. Colman's Sermons,) "it is the only thing of yours that is in my possession, I dare not attempt any thing more." But the captain forbid his giving it to me, and I stepped into the boat—at that moment Nickola said in a low voice, "never mind, I may see you again before I die." The small boat was well armed and manned, and both set off together for the island, where they had agreed to leave us to perish! The scene to us was a funeral scene. There were no arms in the prisoners' boat, and, of course, all attempts to relieve ourselves would have been throwing our lives away, as Bolidar was near us, well armed. We were rowed about two miles northeasterly from the pirates, to a small low island, lonely and desolate. We arrived about sunset; and for the support of us eleven prisoners, they only left a ten gallon keg of water, and perhaps a few quarts, in another small vessel, which was very poor; part of a barrel of flour, a small keg of lard, one ham and some salt fish; a small kettle and an old broken pot; an old sail for a covering, and a small mattress and blanket, which was thrown out as the boats hastened away. One of the prisoners happened to have a little coffee in his pocket, and these comprehended all our means of sustaining life, and for what length of time we knew not. We now felt the need of water, and our supply was comparatively nothing.—A man may live nearly twice as long without food, as without water.—Look at us now, my friends, left benighted on a little spot of sand in the midst of the ocean, far from the usual track of vessels, and every appearance of a violent thunder tempest, and a boisterous night. Judge of my feelings, and the circumstances which our band of sufferers now witnessed.—Perhaps you can and have pitied us—I assure you, we were very wretched; and to paint the scene, is not within my power. When the boats were moving from the shore, on recovering myself a little, I asked Bolidar, "If he was going to leave us so"?—he answered, "no, only two days—we go for water and wood, then come back, take you." I requested him to give us bread and other stores, for they had plenty in the boat, and at least one hundred barrels of flour in the Mexican "no, no, suppose to-morrow morning me come, me give you bread," and hurried off to their vessel. This was the last time I saw him. We then turned our attention upon finding a spot most convenient for our comfort, and soon discovered a little roof supported by stakes drove into the sand; it was thatched with leaves of the cocoanut tree, considerable part of which was torn or blown off. After spreading the old sail over this roof, we placed our little stock of provisions under it. Soon after came on a heavy shower of rain which penetrated the canvass, and made it nearly as uncomfortable inside, as it would have been out. We were not prepared to catch water, having nothing to put it in. Our next object was to get fire, and after gathering some of the driest fuel to be found, and having a small piece of cotton wick-yarn, with flint and steel, we kindled a fire, which was never afterwards suffered to be extinguished. The night was very dark, but we found a piece of old rope, which when well lighted served for a candle. On examining the ground under the roof, we found perhaps thousands of creeping insects, scorpions, lizards, crickets, &c. After scraping them out as well as we could, the most of us having nothing but the damp earth for a bed, laid ourselves down in hopes of some rest; but it being so wet, gave many of us severe colds, and one of the Spaniards was quite sick for several days.

Sunday, 20*th.*—As soon as daylight came on, we proceeded to take a view of our little island, and found it to measure only one acre, of coarse, white sand; about two feet, and in some spots perhaps three feet above the surface of the ocean. On the highest part were growing some bushes and small mangroves, (the dry part of which was our fuel) and the wild castor oil beans. We were greatly disappointed in not finding the latter suitable food; likewise some of the prickly pear bushes, which gave us only a few pears about the size of our small button pear; the outside has thorns, which if applied to the fingers or lips, will remain there, and cause a severe smarting similar to the nettle; the inside a spungy substance full of juice and seeds, which are red and a little tartish—had they been there in abundance, we should not have suffered so much for water—but a last even this substitute was not for us. On the northerly side of the island was a hollow, where the tide penetrated the sand, leaving stagnated water. We presumed in hurricanes the island was nearly overflowed. According to the best calculations I could make, we were about thirty five miles from any part of Cuba, one hundred from Trinidad and forty from the usual track of American vessels, or others which might pass that way. No vessel of any considerable size, can safely pass among those Keys or "Queen's Gardens," (as the Spaniards call them) being a large number extending from Cape Cruz to Trinidad, one hundred and fifty miles distance; and many more than the charts have laid down, most of them very low and some covered at high water, which makes it very dangerous for navigators without a skilful pilot. After taking this view of our condition, which was very gloomy, we began to suspect we were left on this desolate island by those merciless plunderers to perish. Of this I am now fully convinced; still we looked anxiously for the pirate's boat to come according to promise with more water and provisions, but looked in vain. We saw them soon after get under way with all sail set and run directly from us until out of our sight, and *we never saw them again!* one may partially imagine our feelings, but they cannot be put into words. Before they were entirely out of sight of us, we raised the white blanket upon a pole, waving it in the air, in hopes, that at two miles distance they would see it and be moved to pity. But pity in such monsters was not to be found. It was not their interest to save us from the lingering death, which we now saw before us. We tried to compose ourselves, trusting that God, who had witnessed our sufferings, would yet make use of some one, as the instrument of his mercy towards us. Our next care, now, was to try for water. We dug several holes in the sand and found it, but quite too salt for use. The tide penetrates probably through the island.—We now came on short allowance for water; having no means of securing what we had by lock and key, some one in the night would slyly drink, and it was soon gone. The next was to bake some bread, which we did by mixing flour with salt water and frying it in lard, allowing ourselves eight quite small pancakes to begin with. The ham was reserved for some more important occasions, and the salt fish was lost for want of fresh water. The remainder of this day was passed in the most serious conversation and reflection.—At night, I read prayers from the "Prayer Book," beforementioned, which I most carefully concealed while last on board the pirates. This plan was pursued morning and evening, during our stay there.—Then retired for rest and sleep, but realized little of either.

Monday, 21st.—In the morning we walked round the beach, in expectation of finding something useful. On our way picked up a paddle about three feet long, very similar to the Indian canoe paddle, except the handle, which was like that of a shovel; the top part being split off, we laid it by for the present. We likewise found some konchs and roasted them; they were a pretty good shell fish, though rather tough. We discovered at low water, a bar or spit of sand extending northeasterly from us about three miles distant, to a cluster of Keys, which were covered with mangrove trees, perhaps as high as our quince tree. My friend Mr. Bracket and George attempted to wade across, being at that time of tide only up to their armpits; but were pursued by a shark and returned without success. The tide rises about four feet.

Tuesday, 22nd.—We found several pieces of the palmetto or cabbage tree, and some pieces of boards, put them together in the form of a raft, and endeavoured to cross, but that proved ineffectual. Being disappointed, we set down to reflect upon other means of relief, intending to do all in our power for our safety while our strength continued. While setting here, the sun was so powerful and oppressive, reflecting its rays upon the sea, which was then calm, and the white sand which dazzled the eye, was so painful, that we retired under the awning; there the moschetoes and flies were so numerous, that good rest could not be found. We were, however, a little cheered, when, in scraping out the top of the ground to clear out, I may say thousands of crickets and buggs, we found a hatchet, which was to us peculiarly serviceable. At night the strong northeasterly wind, which prevails there at all seasons, was so cold as to make it equally uncomfortable with the day.—Thus day after day, our sufferings and apprehensions multiplying, we were very generally alarmed.

Wednesday, 23rd.—Early this morning one of our Spanish fellow prisoners crossed the bar, having taken with him a pole sharpened at one end; this he said "was to kill sharks"—but he saw none to trouble him. White he was gone, we tried for water in several places, but still it was very salt; but not having any other we drank of it, and found it had a similar effect, to that of glauber salts. We now concluded to reduce the allowance of bread or rather pancakes, being too sensible that our little stock of provisions could last but a few days longer; we had the faintest hope of any supplies, or escape before it would be too late to save life. Towards night the Spaniard returned, but almost famished for want of water and food. He reported that he found some plank on one of the islands, (but they proved to be sugar-box shooks) which revived us a little; but *no water.*—He said he had great difficulty to make his way through the mangrove trees, it being very swampy; so that we should not better ourselves by going there, although the key was rather larger than ours. This, I understood through Joseph, the English prisoner who could speak Spanish. After prayers laid ourselves down upon our bed of sand, and being nearly exhausted we obtained some sleep.

Thursday, 24th.—This morning, after taking a little coffee, made of the water which we thought least salt, and two or three of the little cakes, we felt somewhat refreshed, and concluded to make another visit to those Keys in hopes of finding something more, which might make a raft for us to escape the pirates and avoid perishing by thirst. Accordingly seven of us set off, waded across the bar and searched all the Keys thereabouts.—On one we found a number of sugar-box shooks, two lashing plank and some pieces of old spars, which were a part of the Exertion's deck load, that was thrown overboard when she grounded on the bar, spoken of in the first part of the narrative.—It seems they had drifted fifteen miles, and had accidentally lodged on these very Keys within our reach. Had the pirates known this, they would undoubtedly have placed us in another direction. They no doubt thought that they could not put us on a worse place. The wind at this time was blowing so strong on shore, as to prevent rafting our stuff round to our island, and were obliged to haul it upon the beach for the present, then dug for water in the highest place, but found it as salt as ever, and then returned to our habitation.—But hunger and thirst began to prey upon us, and our comforts were as few as our hopes.

Friday, 25th.—Again passed over to those Keys to windward in order to raft our stuff to our island, it being most convenient for building. But the surf on the beach was so very rough, that we were again compelled to postpone it. Our courage however did not fail where there was the slightest hopes of life—Returning without it, we found on our way an old top timber of some vessel; it had several spikes in it, which we afterwards found very serviceable. In the hollow of an old tree, we found two guarnas of small size, one male, the other female.—One only was caught. After taking off the skin, we judged it weighed a pound and a half; with some flour and lard, (the only things we had except salt water,) it made us a fine little mess. We thought it a rare dish though a small one for eleven half starved persons.—At the same time a small vessel hove in sight; we made a signal to her with the blanket tied to a pole and placed it on the highest tree—some took off their white clothes and waved them in the air, hoping they would come to us; should they be pirates, they could do no more than kill us, and perhaps would give us some water for which we began to suffer most excessively; but, notwithstanding all our efforts, she took no notice of us.

Saturday, 26th.—This day commenced with moderate weather and smooth sea; at low tide found some cockles, boiled and eat them, but they were very painful to the stomach. David Warren had a fit of strangling with swelling of the bowels; but soon recovered, and said, "something like salt, rose in his throat and choaked him." Most of us then set off for the Keys, where the plank and shooks were put together in a raft, which we with pieces of boards paddled over to our island; when we consulted the best plan, either to build a raft large enough for us all to go on, or a boat; but the shooks having three or four nails in each, and taking a piece of large reed or bamboo, previously found, of which we made pins, concluded to make a boat.

Sunday, 27th.—Commenced our labour, for which I know we need offer no apology. We took the two planks, which were about fourteen feet long, and two and a half wide, and fixed them together for the bottom of the boat; then with moulds made of palmetto bark, cut timber and knees from mangrove trees which spread so much as to make the boat 4 feet wide at the top, placed them exactly the distance apart of an Havanna sugar box.—Her stern was square and the bows tapered to a peak, making her form resemble a flat-iron. We proceeded thus far and retired to rest for the night—but Mr. Bracket was too unwell to get much sleep.

Monday, 28th.—Went on with the work as fast as possible.—Some of the Spaniards had long knives about them, which proved very useful in fitting timbers, and a gimblet of mine, accidently found on board the pirates, enabled us to use the wooden pins.—And now our spirits began to revive, though *water, water*, was continually in our minds. We now feared the pirates might possibly come, find out our plan and put us to death, (although before we had wished to see them, being so much in want of water.) Our labour was extremely burthensome, and the Spaniards considerably peevish—but they would often say to me "never mind capitan, by and by, Americana or Spanyola catch them, me go see 'um hung." We quitted work for the day, cooked some cakes but found it necessary to reduce the quantity again, however small before. We found some herbs on a windward Key, which the Spaniards called Spanish tea.—This when well boiled we found somewhat palatable, although the water was very salt. This herb resembles penny-royal in look and taste, though not so pungent. In the evening when we were setting round the fire to keep off the moschetoes, I observed David Warren's eyes shone like glass. The mate said to him—"David I think you will die before morning—I think you are struck with death now." I thought so too, and told him, "I thought it most likely we should all die here soon; but as some one of us may survive to carry the tidings to our friends, if you have any thing to say respecting your family, now is the time."—He then said, "I have a mother in Saco where I belong—she is a second time a widow—tomorrow if you can spare a scrap of paper and pencil I will write something." But no to-morrow came to him.—In the course of the night he had another spell of strangling, and soon after expired, without much pain and without a groan. He was about twenty six years old.—How solemn was this scene to us! Here we beheld the ravages of death commenced upon us. More than one of us considered death a happy release. For myself I thought of my wife and children; and wished to live if God should so order it, though extreme thirst, hunger and exhaustion had well nigh prostrated my fondest hopes.

Tuesday, 29th.—Part of us recommenced labour on the boat, while myself and Mr. Bracket went and selected the highest clear spot of sand on the northern side of the island, where we dug Warren's grave and boxed it up with shooks, thinking it would be the most suitable spot for the rest of us—whose turn would come next, we knew not. At about ten o'clock, A. M. conveyed the corpse to the grave, followed by us survivers—a scene, whose awful solemnity can never be painted. We stood around the grave, and there I read the funeral prayer from the Rev. Mr. Brooks's Family Prayer Book; and committed the body to the earth; covered it with some pieces of board and sand, and returned to our labour.—One of the Spaniards an old man, named Manuel, who was partial to me, and I to him, made a cross and placed at the head of the grave saying, "Jesus Christ hath him now." Although I did not believe in any mysterious influence of this cross, yet I was perfectly willing it should stand there. The middle part of the day being very warm, our mouths parched with thirst, and our spirits so depressed, that we made but little progress during the remainder of this day, but in the evening were employed in picking oakum out of the bolt rope taken from the old sail.

Wednesday, 30th.—Returned to labour on the boat with as much vigour as our weak and debilitated state would admit, but it was a day of trial to us all; for the Spaniards and we Americans could not well understand each other's plans, and they being naturally petulant would not work, nor listen with any patience for Joseph our English fellow prisoner to explain our views—they would sometimes undo what they had done and in a few minutes replace it again; however before night we began to calk her seams, by means of pieces of hard mangrove, made in form of a calking-iron, and had the satisfaction of seeing her in a form something like a boat.

Thursday, 31st.—Went on with the work, some at calking, others at battening the seams with strips of canvass, and pieces of pine nailed over, to keep the oakum in. Having found a suitable pole for a mast, the rest went about making a sail from the one we had used for a covering, also fitting oars of short pieces of boards, in form of a paddle, tied on a pole, we having a piece of fishing line brought by one of the prisoners. Thus, at 3 P. M. the boat was completed and put afloat.—We had all this time confidently hoped, that she would be sufficiently large and strong to carry us all—we made a trial and were disappointed! This was indeed a severe trial, and the emotions it called up were not easy to be suppressed. She proved leaky, for we had no carpenter's yard, or smith's shop to go to.—And now the question was, "who should go, and how many?" I found it necessary for six; four to row, one to steer and one to bale. Three of the Spaniards and the Frenchman claimed the right, as being best acquainted with the nearest inhabitants; likewise, they had when taken, two boats left at St. Maria (about 40 miles distant) which they were confident of finding. They promised to return within two or three days for the rest of us—I thought it best to consent—Mr. Bracket it was agreed should go in my stead, because my papers must accompany me as a necessary protection, and my men apprehended danger if they were lost. Joseph Baxter (I think was his name) they wished should go, because he could speak both languages—leaving Manuel, George, Thomas and myself, to wait their return. Having thus made all arrangements, and putting up a keg of the least salt water, with a few pancakes and salt fish, they set off a little before sunset with our best wishes and prayers for their safety and return to our relief.—To launch off into the wide ocean, with strength almost exhausted, and in such a frail boat as this, you will say was very hazardous, and in truth it was; but what else was left to us?—Their intention was to touch at the Key where the Exertion was, and if no boat was to be found there, to proceed on to St. Maria and if none there, to go to Trinidad and send us relief.—But alas! it was the last time I ever saw them!—Our suffering this day was most acute.

Tuesday, February 1st.—This day we rose early and traversed the beach in search of cockles, &c. but found very few—I struck my foot against something in the sand, which proved to be a curious shell, and soon found two others of a different kind; but they were to me like Crusoe's lump of gold, of no value. I could not drink them; so laid them by.—I returned to our tent and we made some skillygolee, or flour and salt water boiled together, which we found better than clear salt water. We passed the day very uncomfortably, and my people were dissatisfied at not having an equal chance, as they called it, with the others in the boat—but it is not always, that we know what is for our good.

Saturday, 2d.—Thomas and George made another visit to the windward Keys, where they found some more shooks and two pieces of spars; towed them round as before. We now had some hopes of finding enough to make us a raft, which would carry us to some place of relief, in case the boat should not return.

Sunday, 3d.—A calm warm day, but a very gloomy one to us, it being more difficult to support life—our provisions nearly expended, no appearance of rain since the night we first landed, our thirst increasing, our strength wasting, our few clothes hanging in rags, our beards of great length and almost turned white, nothing like relief before us, no boat in sight.—Think, compassionate reader, our situation. We had marked out for each one the place for his grave. I looked at mine, and thought of my wife and family.—Again we reduced the allowance of bread; but even the little which now fell to my share, I could scarcely swallow—I never seemed to feel the sensation of hunger, the extreme of thirst was so overpowering.—Perhaps never shall I be more reconciled to death, but my home made me want to live, although every breath seemed to increase thirst.

Monday, 4th.—Having seriously reflected on our situation, concluded to put all the shooks, &c. together and form a raft, and ascertain what weight it would carry; but here again we were disappointed, for we had not enough to carry two of us.

Tuesday, 5th.—About 10 o'clock, A. M. discovered a boat drifting by on the S. E. side of the island about a mile distant. I deemed it a providential thing to us, and urged Thomas and George trying the raft for her. They reluctantly consented and set off, but it was nearly three P. M. when they came up with her.—It was the same boat we had built! Where then was my friend Bracket and those who went with him? Every appearance was unfavourable.—I hoped that a good Providence had yet preserved him.—The two men who went for the boat, found it full of water, without oars, paddle, or sail; being in this condition, and about three miles to the leeward, the men found it impossible to tow her up, so left her, and were till eleven o'clock at night getting back with the raft. They were so exhausted, that had it not been nearly calm, they could never have returned.

Wednesday, 6th.—This morning was indeed the most gloomy I had ever experienced.—There appeared hardly a ray of hope that my friend Bracket could return, seeing the boat was lost.—Our provisions nearly gone; our mouths parched extremely with thirst; our strength wasted; our spirits broken, and our hopes imprisoned within the circumference of this desolate sland in the midst of an unfrequented ocean; all these things gave to the scenes around us the hue of death. In the midst of this dreadful despondence, a sail hove in sight, bearing the white flag. Our hopes were raised, of course—but no sooner raised than darkened, by hearing a gun fired. Here then was another gang of pirates.—She soon, however, came near enough to anchor, and her boat pushed off towards us with three men in her.—Thinking it no worse now to die by sword than famine I walked down immediately to meet them. I knew them not.—A moment before the boat touched the ground, a man leaped from her bows and caught me in his arms! *It was Nickola!!*—saying, "Do you now believe Nickola is your friend? yes, said he, *Jamieson* will yet prove himself so."—No words can express my emotions at this moment.—This was a friend indeed. The reason of my not recognising them before, was that they had cut off their beards and whiskers. Turning to my fellow-sufferers, Nickola asked—"Are these all that are left of you? where are the others?"—At this moment seeing David's grave—"Are they dead then? ah I suspected it, I know what you were put here for." As soon as I could recover myself, gave him an account of Mr. Bracket and the others.—"How unfortunate, he said, they must be lost or some pirates have taken them"—"but, he continued, we have no time to lose; you had better embark immediately with us, and go where you please, we are at your service." The other two in the boat with him were Frenchmen, one named Lyon, the other Parrikete. They affectionately embraced each of us; then holding to my mouth the nose of a tea-kettle, filled with wine, said "Drink plenty, no hurt you." I drank as much as I judged prudent. They then gave it to my fellow-sufferers.—I experienced almost immediate relief, not feeling it in my head; they had also brought in the boat for us, a dish of salt beef and potatoes, of which we took a little. Then sent the boat on board for the other two men, being five in all; who came ashore, and rejoiced enough was I to see among them Thomas Young, one of my crew, who was detained on board the Mexican, but had escaped through Nickola's means; the other a Frenchman, named John Cadedt. I now thought, again and again, with troubled emotion of my friend Bracket's fate.—I took the last piece of paper I had, and wrote with pencil a few lines, informing him (should he come there,) that "I and the rest were safe; that I was not mistaken in the friend in whom I had placed so much confidence, that he had accomplished my highest expectations; and that I should go immediately to Trinidad, and requested him to go there also, and apply to Mr. Isaac W. Lord, my consignee, for assistance." I put the paper into a junk bottle, previously found on the beach, put in a stopper, and left it, together with what little flour remained, a keg of water brought from Nickola's vessel, and a few other things which I thought might be of service to him. We then repaired with our friends on board, where we were kindly treated. She was a sloop from Jamaica, of about twelve tons, with a cargo of rum and wine, bound to Trinidad. I asked "which way they intended to go?" They said "to Jamaica if agreeable to me." As I preferred Trinidad, I told them, "if they would give me the Exertion's boat which was along side (beside their own) some water and provisions, we would take chance in her," "for perhaps, said I, you will fare better at Jamaica, than at Trinidad." After a few minutes consultation, they said "you are too much exhausted to row the distance of one hundred miles, therefore we will go and carry you—we consider ourselves at your service." I expressed a wish to take a look at the Exertion, possibly we might hear something of Mr. Bracket. Nickola said "very well," so got under way, and run for her, having a light westerly wind. He then related to me the manner of their desertion from the pirates; as nearly as I can recollect his own words, he said, "A few days since, the pirates took four small vessels. I believe Spaniards; they having but two officers for the two first, the third fell to me as prize master, and having an understanding with the three Frenchmen and Thomas, selected them for my crew, and went on board with orders to follow the Mexican; which I obeyed. The fourth, the pirates took out all but one man and bade him also follow their vessel. Now our schooner leaked so bad, that we left her and in her stead agreed to take this little sloop, (which we are now in) together with the one man. The night being very dark we all agreed to desert the pirates—altered our course and touched at St. Maria, where we landed the one man—saw no boats there, could hear nothing from you, and agreed one and all at the risk of our lives to come and liberate you if you were alive; knowing, as we did, that you were put on this Key to perish. On our way we boarded the Exertion, thinking possibly you might have been there. On board her we found a sail and paddle. We took one of the pirates' boats which they had left along side of her, which proves how we come by two boats. My friend, the circumstance I am now about to relate, will somewhat astonish you. When the pirates' boat with Bolidar was sent to the before mentioned Key, on the 19th of January, it was there intention to leave you prisoners there, where was nothing but salt water and mangroves, and no possibility of escape. This was the plan of Baltizar, their abandoned pilot; but Bolidar's heart failed him, and he objected to it; then, after a conference, capt. Jonnia ordered you to be put on the little island from whence we have now taken you. But after this was done, that night the French and Portuguese part of the Mexican's crew protested against it; so that capt. Jonnia to satisfy them, sent his large boat to take you and your fellow prisoners back again, taking care to select his confidential Spaniards for this errand. And will you believe me, they set off from the Mexican and after spending about as much time as would really have taken them to come to you, they returned, and reported they had been to your island, and landed, and that none of you were there; somebody having taking you off! This, all my companions here know to be true.—I knew it was impossible you could have been liberated, and therefore we determined among ourselves, that should an opportunity occur we would come and save your lives, as we now have." He then expressed, as he hitherto had done, (and I believe with sincerity) his disgust with the bad company which he had been in, and looked forward with anxiety to the day when he might return to his native country. I advised him to get on board an American vessel, whenever an opportunity offered, and come to the United States; and on his arrival direct a letter to me: repeating my earnest desire to make some return for the disinterested friendship which he had shewn toward me. With the Frenchmen I had but little conversation, being unacquainted with the language.

Here ended Nickola's account. "And now" said the Frenchmen, "our hearts be easy." Nickola observed he had left all and found us. I gave them my warmest tribute of gratitude, saying, I looked upon them under God as the preservers of our lives, and promised them all the assistance which my situation might ever enable me to afford.—This brings me to

Thursday evening, 7th, when, at eleven o'clock, we anchored at the creek's mouth, near the Exertion. I was anxious to board her; accordingly took with me Nickola, Thomas, George and two others, well armed, each with a musket and cutlass. I jumped on her deck, saw a fire in the camboose, but no person there: I called aloud Mr. Bracket's name several times, saying "it is capt. Lincoln, don't be afraid, but show yourself;" but no answer was given. She had no masts, spars, rigging, furniture, provisions or any thing left, except her bowsprit, and a few barrels of salt provisions of her cargo. Her sealing had holes cut in it, no doubt in their foolish search for money. I left her with peculiar emotions, such as I hope never again to experience; and returned to the little sloop where we remained till—

Friday, 8th—when I had a disposition to visit the island on which we were first imprisoned.—Found nothing there—saw a boat among the mangroves, near the Exertion. Returned, and got under way immediately for Trinidad. In the night, while under full sail, run aground on a sunken Key, having rocks above the water, resembling old stumps of trees; we, however, soon got off and anchored. Most of those Keys have similar rocks about them, which navigators must carefully guard against.

Saturday, 9th.—Got under way again, and stood along close in for the main island of Cuba, in order, that if we should see the pirates, to take our boats and go on shore.

Sunday, 10th.—Saw the highlands of Trinidad. At night came to anchor in sight of the town, near a small Key; next morning—

Monday, 11th—Got under way—saw a brig at anchor about five miles below the mouth of the harbour: we hoped to avoid her speaking us; but when we opened in sight of her, discovered a boat making towards us, with a number of armed men in her. This alarmed my friends, and as we did not see the brig's ensign hoisted, they declared the boat was a pirate, and looking through the spy-glass, thought they knew some of them to be the Mexican's men! This state of things was quite alarming. They said, "we will not be taken alive by them." Immediately the boat fired a musket; the ball passed through our main sail. My friends insisted on beating them off: I endeavoured to dissuade them, believing, as I did, that the brig was a Spanish man of war, who had sent her boat to ascertain who we were. I thought we had better heave too. Immediately another shot came. Then they insisted on fighting and said, "if I would not help them, I was no friend." I reluctantly acquiesced, and handed up the guns—commenced firing upon them and they upon us. We received several shot through the sails, but no one was hurt on either side. Our two boats had been cast adrift to make us go the faster, and we gained upon them—continued firing until they turned from us, and went for our boats, which they took in tow for the brig. Soon after this, it became calm: then I saw that the brig had us in her power.—She manned and armed two more boats for us. We now concluded, since we had scarcely any ammunition, to surrender; and were towed down along side the brig, taken on board, and was asked by the captain, who could speak English, "what for you fire on the boat?" I told him "we thought her a pirate, and did not like to be taken by them again, having already suffered too much;" showing my papers. He said, "capt. Americana, never mind, go and take some dinner—which are your men?" I pointed them out to him, and he ordered them the liberty of the decks; but my friend Nickola and three associates were immediately put in irons. They were however, afterwards taken out of irons and examined; and I understood the Frenchmen agreed to enlist as they judged it the surest way to better their condition. Whether Nickola enlisted, I do not know, but think that he did, as I understood that offer was made to him I however endeavoured to explain more distinctly to the captain, the benevolent efforts of these four men.

The Scourge of the Eastern Seas

JOHN S. SEWALL

If any part of the world might seem to have been originally designed for a pirates' paradise, the southern coast of China is the place. Fringed with capes, beaded with islands of every size and shape, pierced by estuaries made up of numberless winding channels, it opens to the sea-rover countless coves and pockets and watery labyrinths, for lying in ambush or hiding from pursuit. One of the wide-spread groups of islands through whose tortuous passages the Canton River finds its way to the sea has been the scene of so many of these tragedies that it has richly earned its sinister title: the Ladrones (Robbers). Ever since primeval commerce began to creep along the shores of the great empire, it has doubtless had its bloody parasites. The lonely trader and the clumsy fleet have had to reckon with this ever-present menace as one of the risks of the voyage. It was never certain from behind what headland or out of what lagoon might issue at any moment a pack of these ocean wolves. If departing voyagers never returned, it was sometimes the typhoons and sometimes the pirates. Dead men tell no tales.

It is easy to cover with facile phrase the long and painful evolution of the centuries, especially the slow-moving cycles of Cathay. It is not so easy to fill in the picture with the actual details; to imagine the growing commerce and the growing piracy that preyed upon it; to portray the long ages of sorrow on the sea—first the stealthy surprise, the sharp attack, the vain attempt to flee, the desperate stand at bay, the fight for life, the brutish yells, the cry for mercy, the ghastly silence that settles on the slippery decks as the butchers leisurely proceed to rifle their prey. What myriads of tragedies like this have been enacted far back in the dim primeval, while the Celestial Empire has been slowly emerging from savagery into national life, no chronicler has told. But at least it was a process of martial training. As Chinese commerce has run the gauntlet and fought its way into existence, it has developed in its own mariners, and in their assailants as well, those qualities of courage, hardihood, and grit which the Western world could but admire in the brave fellows of the Yalu fight in 1894. The handling of the *Ting Yuen* and the *Chen Yuen,* especially in the latter part of the action, affords ample proof of the pluck of the Chinese man-of-war's man when his blood is up.

The victory fell to Japan; but history will award to the Admiral Ting Ju Chang and his men the credit due to their daring and skill. They fought for their country against what they believed to be unjust usurpation; and, as one reads of their deeds of valor, it is easy to imagine that in the veins of some of those warriors ran the blood of generations of old-time buccaneers. The annals of Chinese piracy have not wholly faded into oblivion. Some epochs in its history are familiar to those students who have a fancy for mousing about in the unbeaten tracks of oriental life. A glimpse at the *modus operandi* will help to develop an intelligent appreciation of these gruesome records. A few modern samples will suffice.

The year before our futile quest for these various gentlemen of the high seas as narrated in the last chapter, Captain Massie of the steamship H. B. M. *Cleopatra* sent out a boat expedition among the islands, which, after a running fight of five hours, captured three eighteen-gun lorchas; and yet two months afterward, on about the same cruising ground, the *Brillante* was cut off by free-booters, plundered of a large amount of treasure, the crew massacred, and the ship scuttled and sunk. In March 1853, her majesty's steam-sloop *Hermes* came upon the scent of a whole squadron a little way up the coast. After a hot pursuit, the outlaws turned at bay and defended themselves with savage ferocity. But they were no match for British guns and steam. The *Hermes* avenged some of their villainies by sending four junks to the bottom and towing three more as prizes back to Hong Kong.

In the summer of 1835 there came limping into Hong Kong harbor a much-abused hulk whose misadventures inspired sympathy wherever her pitiful story came to be known. It was the English barque *Troughton* from Singapore. First of all, she encountered a typhoon that did not leave her until her masts were wrenched out of her and her bulwarks were torn off clean with the decks. Her exhausted crew managed to keep her afloat with the pumps and, rigging a sail on a jury-mast, were slowly wafted in toward the land. Here a new enemy awaited them. Surrounded by trading junks and fishing craft, whose crews would often come on board and lend a hand at the pumps, their crippled condition was speedily recognized. At sundown one afternoon, two piratical luggers laid her alongside and poured a swarm of Celestial cutthroats on board. The captain and mate dashed into the cabin for their firearms; but before a shot could be fired two hundred pirates had overpowered the crew and lashed them to the deck. The captain and mate fought from the cabin as long as their ammunition lasted and then did their best to blow up the ship. Exhausted from loss of blood, they were at last driven from their refuge and bound with the rest of the crew. The pirates looted their prize of everything the typhoon had spared and then vanished in the darkness.

Sometimes these amiable enterprises are conducted by amateurs, so to speak, by your own crew for example, if you happen to have shipped a gang of Chinamen. Things have changed somewhat even in the Central Flowery Kingdom, but time was when a little professional venture of this sort was not uncongenial to the average Chinese coolie, whether ashore or afloat. In 1828 a French merchantman, the *Navigateur*, was wrecked on the coast of Cochin China. The commander hired a junk to carry the remnants of his crew and cargo northward to Macao. As they neared their destination, the natives, five times their number, rose up, murdered all but one, and then made off with booty. That one, after fighting desperately for his life, leaped overboard and was picked up by a passing fisherman. It helps to bear the outrage to know that by his evidence in court, other miscreants were identified and paid for their crime.

There have been bloody epochs in the history of Chinese commerce when piracy was as much an organized system as the opium traffic is now. Whole fleets of sea-robbers prowled about the coasts, plundered villages, levied blackmail on native and foreigner alike, and generally silenced their victims by sending them to the bottom of the sea. Let us not be unreasonable. Those were days of the iron hand everywhere.

Why not give the Mongol his chance as well as the Roman, the Norseman, the Corsican, the Turk? Why not allow the Koshinga to play his drama along with Morgan, Hastings, Kidd, Lafitte, Duval, and all the other great actors of tragedy?

Chinese annals record two periods during which these marauding fleets became so powerful and insolent that the empire with all its resources could not yet destroy them nor even repel their attacks. There is plenty of romance in the story.

The most famous corsairs known to Chinese history, most famous perhaps because of their ferociousness, were a father and son, Ching Chelung and Ching Chingkung.

They flourished about the time of the Manchu conquest in 1644. The son was familiarly called Kwoshing, but is better known by his Portuguese Latinized name Koshinga. The father, after years of adventure, honest and dishonest, untold and untellable, found himself at the head of an immense nondescript fleet with which he harried the helpless coasts and laid waste the seas. Bribes of wealth and rank decoyed the redoubtable chieftain into the imperial service. He was made supreme commander of the Chinese navy. In his new position it became his duty to protect commerce and destroy piracy. He accordingly protected commerce and destroyed piracy. He knew how. No petty scruples of honor or generous memory stood in the way. It was as a sort of grim atonement for his own crimes that whole squadrons of his former comrades were, with unpitying impartiality, dispatched to their infernal shades.

He assumed the monopoly of all lucrative commerce and levied tribute on all manner of craft. He did what he liked, and no power in the empire dared question his right. The emperor even bestowed on his son in marriage a princess of the blood. In course of time his unchallenged supremacy made him careless. Detected in an intrigue against the government he was enticed to court and there found himself in a gilded cage beyond whose bars he was never again permitted to go. There he languished for many years where he finally died as a prisoner of state.

It would take lurid colors to paint the wrath of Koshinga when it became apparent that the old tiger, his sire, was held in hopeless captivity. No doubt the atmosphere reeked with Chinese rhetoric. Vowing eternal hate to the whole Tatar race, he summoned his fellow ruffians and betook himself to this home on the wave. This was in 1646. For more than thirty years his name was the terror of the seas. He preyed upon commerce until from sheer fright, commerce shut itself up in port and dared not come out. As a result the few prizes he caught were not enough to maintain and feed his vast squadron. Then he invaded the shores and plundered not only villages and towns but capital cities and provinces. He besieged Nanking. He captured and fortified Amoy. He finally stole and occupied the island of Formosa, seized the government, established arsenals and ports for his fleets, and thence hurled his filibustering raids upon the opposite coasts.

At last his bloody incursions became such an intolerable scourge to the empire, which could neither prevent nor resist them, that the extraordinary measure was adopted of abandoning for the time all trade on the seas and withdrawing the entire population from the coast. This was actually done, probably the only instance of its kind in history, and the Chinese were the only people who would ever have dreamed of tactics so absurd and so masterly. For hundreds of leagues up and down the shores of the great realm there stretched between the hungry vampires and their victims a strip of abandoned seacoast twelve miles broad, whose fields lay untilled, whose once populous cities and villages lay deserted and crumbling in decay, whose useless junks slumbered and foundered at their moorings in the harbors. Byron's "dream which was not all a dream" sounds almost like the work of a newspaper reporter writing up the details:

> "The rivers, lakes and ocean all stood still,
> And nothing stirred within their silent depths,
> Ships sailorless, lay rotting on the sea."

Macao was excepted, and that because the Portuguese colonists were presumed to be competent to protect themselves. It was seven years before the deserted sea-fringe of the empire was reoccupied and trade was allowed to flow into its wonted channels. The death of the dreaded Koshinga soon after closed the seventeenth-century piratical era.

Minor adventurers still carried on their more stealthy depredations, and have done so intermittently ever since. The growing value of an increasing commerce, along with the addition of several priceless argosies from Europe and from America, furnished ample temptation.

In December 1806, the mate of an English ship was captured and brought into the presence of the commandant of the fleet. He found himself in a squadron of some six hundred junks and lorchas, carrying batteries of from six to eighteen pounders, and classed in five divisions under five independent chiefs. During his captivity he became familiar with the entire system, its organization, its stringent regulations, the numbers and armament of the divisions, their plans and methods of attack. After some five months of captivity, he was finally ransomed. Three years later another Englishman fell into their hands. The fleet had grown. There were six divisions. The total force operating, though rarely all together, he estimated at eight hundred large vessels and a thousand smaller craft, carrying a complement of some seventy thousand men. The atrocities he witnessed are detailed with a sailor's frankness and do not make pleasant reading. It was the destruction wreaked by Koshinga *redivivus*, only this time it was worse.

The Englishman's story fully corroborates the chronicle written down by Yung-lun-yuen, a Chinese scholar who was a contemporary of the bloody actors and exploits he describes. The six squadrons sailed under six flags—red, yellow, black, blue, green, and white. It was the yellow fleet that has furnished this chapter with its label, for it was the admiral of the yellow, Woo-che-tsing, who assumed the winsome title "Scourge of the Eastern Seas." If actions speak louder than words, he more than made his title good. The red fleet is of still more thrilling interest, partly because it outnumbered all the rest put together, partly because it was for a time commanded by a woman. In 1807 the arch-outlaw Ching-yih, who had driven it into the smoke and flame of many a desperate conflict, perished in a violent storm. His widow at once took command, and in a hundred fights, demonstrated that she had inherited the temper and prowess of her bloody mate. The "new woman" had come. Men feared and obeyed. She maintained the discipline of a martinet and exacted implicit submission. Never was petticoat government more strenuous or more efficient. She was punctilious in her dealings with the folk on shore and, by honest and liberal payment for supplies, won their confidence and favor—a policy the other divisions of the fleet might have followed with advantage.

Some of the exploits of these red-rovers are curiously interesting. If any of my readers have sailed up the Canton River, you will recall the Chinese fortress of the Boca Tigris at its mouth, on the starboard side as you enter. Down by the waterside a long white parapet stretches along the shore; at each end a wall reaches up the hill and disappears over the crest. Whether there is a fourth wall out of sight, joining the two and completing the square, I do not remember; but certain British tars could tell you if they have lasted from 1841 to this present year of grace. During the Opium War the fortress was attacked. The storming party pulled quietly around the headland and, forming on the beach, clambered up over the hill; the first notice the Celestials had that they were being attacked was the sight of the foreign troops rushing down upon them from the rear within the walls. There was nothing for it but to surrender. They surrendered, therefore, but bristling with wrath at such a breach of military manners. "Hiyah! Why you no come front side! More better make fight where we make ready!"

It was an earlier commandant of this same fortress who met with equally bad luck. One of the fleets appeared in his neighborhood, and he sallied out to attack it. The pirates surrounded him, and after a furious action that lasted all day and with such havoc as may better be left to the imagination, captured him and such fragments of his fleet as were still afloat. This disaster was partly avenged the next year when the Chinese admiral with a hundred junks attacked another fleet on the same cruising ground. Great numbers of the pirates were destroyed and some two hundred taken prisoner. If you are familiar with Chinese methods, you can readily judge how long the two hundred were kept from joining their bloody shipmates in the shades below. In another encounter not far from the same place, before the combatants could close upon one another, it fell dead calm, whereupon crowds of the pirates leaped into the sea like savages, swam to the enemy with their knives in their teeth, and attacked with such fierceness that they could not be beaten off, and actually cut out several junks from the imperial fleet. The fortunes of war varied. With provoking impartiality and apparently showing no preference on the score of justice or ethics, victory would perch on the standard of the pirate as often as on the banners of the righteous defenders of their country. We read of whole squadrons engaged, fighting all day and all night, two days, even three days at a time, two hundred or three hundred junks on a side, and a drawn game at the end. No child's play this. At one time the admiral was lying quietly at anchor among the islands; suddenly two hundred pirate craft slip around the headland and pounce upon him with an onset so furious that twenty-five of his fleet are gone with their captors before he can get up his anchors and chase them.

These conflicts were not confined only to the sea. There were raids on the villages that lined the harbors and rivers. Spies made their way into the bazaars disguised as peddlers, barbers, traders; if they came out alive they brought news to the waiting fleet where were to be found the easiest conquests and the richest booty. Sometimes the villagers fled, and the women and cattle were scooped up by the invaders; sometimes they made a stand, and the bloody struggle proved the valor of the longshoreman as well as of the bandit. Large towns were sacked, and prisoners were gathered not by the score only or by the hundred but even by the thousand. Some unique exploits are recorded. When Mei-ying, the bonny wife of Kee-chu-yang, was captured, she railed at her captors with such stinging eloquence that one of the ruffians knocked her down; whereupon she leaped to her feet, seized him with her teeth, and sprang overboard, dragging the brute with her to a watery grave.

It more than once happened that when a commander found the brigands were too many for him and were closing in upon him for the *coup de grâce*, he retreated to the magazine and turned the tables on them by blowing himself and them out of the water. On one occasion, by a stroke of fortune, the pirate fleet was caught and penned in its own lair. Great preparations were made for a mighty stroke of destruction. Twenty-five fire junks were sent blazing in among the anchored craft. The imperial fleet followed, intending by a supreme blow to annihilate the whole bloody horde. With the corsairs it was a fight for life. Anyone who has witnessed a Chinese battle can imagine the uproar of such an encounter. Hundreds of the pirates paid the penalty of their crimes, but the mangled remnant of their fleet broke through the blockade and scuttled out to the open sea. The plucky admiral pursued them and sank a few more. After dark, they turned back on him and repaid him in kind.

Among such turbulent spirits, we need not wonder if the internal conditions were not always serene. In process of time, a violent feud broke out in the squadron under the petticoat chief. Words came to blows. The mutineers drew off their clientele and staked their destiny on a pitched battle. The vanquished party after an overwhelming defeat concluded to retire from business and submit to government. We get an inkling of the magnitude of these operations from the fact that this one capitulation included no less than some eight thousand men, about 126 vessels, some five hundred battery guns, and several thousand stand of miscellaneous arms. The commander of the defunct fleet was honored with a government position.

This appealed to the heart of the widow chieftain. Perhaps a life spent among scenes of carnage may have begun to pall upon her. She negotiated. And, after various diplomatic interchanges, assured at last of safety, she decided to capitulate, and, with the wives and children of some of her officers, the bloodstained tigress presented herself before the governor general at Canton. The pardon accorded by government put an end to what was left of the famous red squadron and cleaned out the middle and eastern channels of the Canton River. Many of her red-handed followers enlisted in the imperial fleets and were put at once to the work of "pacification." The other fleets were destroyed or saved themselves by submission. The "Scourge of the Eastern Seas" came in with the rest and so retained his worthless head. And the Chinese historian who is my authority for this *dénouement* adds with a cheerful optimism that is hardly sustained by the sequel, that now, (that is, in 1810) "ships pass and repass in tranquillity. All is quiet on the rivers, the four seas are tranquil, and people live in peace and plenty."

But an opulent commerce, growing richer every year, was very attractive and made piracy as tempting as ever. And so it came to pass that the great "pacification" of 1810 did not stay pacified. The China seas have never since been vexed by such enormous squadrons of buccaneers, nor have witnessed such tremendous battles; but local adventurers have been plentiful and, on occasion, have combined into very considerable fleets. The Chinese navy has now and then roused itself to a spurt of zeal, but has never accomplished much in the way of clearing the seas; apparently it has not had much stomach for the attempt. Most of the actual suppression of Chinese piracy has been due to the courage and skill of British tars.

Many officers of the Royal Navy, while serving in the East, have had a hand in the exciting task of ferreting out and destroying these highwaymen of the sea. Captain St. John, who was thus employed for several years, gives graphic details of his various expeditions, now chasing them into the winding channels that form so large a part of the intricate network of the Canton River, now surprising them in the snug harbors where they lay concealed behind the hills. His account of their attack on the mail steamer plying between Hong Kong and Canton gives a sample of their audacity. A fleet of forty-four junks pounced upon her from the reaches that open into the river; she had to run the gauntlet of them all and was badly hulled with shot before she managed to escape.

On another page he describes a large opium junk that lay at anchor close by his own berth. She was bound up the coast to Swatow, and with a crew of forty-five and a full battery of twelve and eighteen pounders seemed so absolutely secure that some forty passengers came on board to take advantage of a conveyance so safe. She got underway at nightfall but had scarcely cleared the Lymoon Pass before it fell calm and she was obliged to anchor. At midnight a large junk slipped quietly alongside, boarded her, and overpowered the watch on deck before they fairly knew they were attacked. The passengers and crew were driven below and secured under hatches and the vessel taken around to a secluded spot on the south side of the island, where every soul on board except a small boy was lashed hand and foot and flung overboard. The junk was then rifled and sunk.

It is an immense satisfaction to know that these miscreants occasionally fall into their own traps. The fate they prepare for their victims rebounds, and they get a taste of their own villainy. A thrilling adventure of this sort happened to Major Shore of the English army. Having occasion just after the Opium War to visit Ningpo, he was obliged to return at once and at night over a route swarming with pirates. He was in a Chinese passage boat, his own little boy the only other passenger, and his only weapons two double-barreled duck guns and a brace of heavy pistols. The night was still and he slept with his guns for company. Just before daybreak one of his boatmen, blanched with terror, roused him with the news that the pirates were coming. He seized his arms and leaped on deck. The silvery mist of the dawn obscured his vision, but presently he made out a dark object looming through the haze, a large and ugly-looking boat crowded with a gang of assassins stealthily creeping toward his defenseless craft. One can imagine his reflections in the brief interval before they would be alongside. His only chance lay in giving them such a sudden and hot reception that they would suppose his boat filled with men. He could see them now, a score of bronze villains with long knives in their hands, some of them stripped to the waist, some of them with dirks stuck through the coils of their pigtails. There they crouched like tigers ready to spring, as vicious a lot as ever murdered an honest crew. For just such game as this, if he should have the ill fortune to meet any, he had taken the safe precaution to load each barrel with a double charge, and, as it would not do to misfire, he re-primed his percussion locks with fresh caps. In the deathly stillness he even noticed the ticking of his watch and the beating of his heart, and "wondered how soon both would cease forever."

Crouching behind the rail and scarcely breathing until the boats were within ten yards of each other, he took careful aim and then let drive both barrels straight in the ruffians' faces. Shrieks of rage and pain and a crash of tumbling bodies bore witness to the execution. Those two shots cleared the forecastle. Not daring to lose any chances, he seized the other gun and blazed away at the crowd in the waist. Another yell, a panic, and a babel of confusion. He was swiftly reloading when a ball from a swivel gun on the pirates' bow whizzed by his head and shivered the mast. The savage who had thus missed his mark was apparently the leader of the gang, a muscular chief whose giant frame loomed dark against the gray dawn. Then the major instantly covered him with a pistol; a sharp explosion, and the miscreant with his fuse still burning pitched headlong into the black waters beneath.

At this final blow the pirates stood not on the order of their going but incontinently fled. The passage boat with sail and oars scuttled away from so dangerous a neighborhood at the top of her speed. The chastisement inflicted by the brave major taught the brigands a lesson not soon forgotten. It was a long time before they dared attack anything, native or foreign, until well assured that their victim was unarmed, or that they could dash upon him unawares.

While the southern coast seems to have been the favorite field of operation for these Celestial vikings, the northern seas have also suffered from the same dread scourge. None of the estuaries of the north are so admirably contrived for buccaneering purposes as the Canton River, with its countless branches, channels, and creeks; but there are plenty of islands and jutting capes and snug coves behind or within which any discreet pirate could conduct his business in safe seclusion. Whoever, therefore, has had the occasion to entrust himself to wind and wave on errands of commerce or science or travel has found it to his advantage to take account of the corsairs as one of the perils of the deep.

Mr. Fortune describes in his entertaining book a trip he once took on the steamer *Erin* from Ningpo to Shanghai. They had scarcely cleared the river Min below the city when they found themselves in the midst of a squadron of freebooters engaged in blockading the passage between Silver Island and the shore and capturing every sort of native craft that attempted to run the gauntlet in or out. Some of the prizes were plundered at once and turned adrift. The more valuable were taken to the pirates' den to be held until ransomed by their rich owners in Ningpo. Negotiations would be carried on sometimes for weeks and all the while a posse of Chinese men-of-war sleeping lazily at their anchors within half a dozen miles of the scene. The *Erin* threaded her way through the fleet unmolested, witnessing as she passed the capture of a big Shantung junk they had decoyed into their ambuscade. "During the time they were in sight," Mr. Fortune continues, "we observed several vessels from the north fall into their hands. They were in such numbers and their plans were so well laid that nothing that passed in daylight could possibly escape. Long after we had lost sight of their vessels we saw and pitied the unsuspecting northern junks running down with a fair wind and all sail into the trap which had been prepared for them."

In a short time, however, the avenging furies were on the track of the outlaws. On her way up the coast, the *Erin* met an English cruiser, which was called *Bittern*, and gave her the needed information. The rendezvous of the piratical fleet was found to be at She-poo, a landlocked harbor a few miles south of Chusan. The *Bittern* headed for She-poo with her ally the *Paoushan*, a steamer that had been recently purchased and equipped by a company of Chinese merchants for the protection of their commerce. The pirates had a well-organized system of sentries and spies and knew of their assailants long before they appeared off the narrow entrance to the harbor. Confident in their overwhelming numbers they welcomed the two vessels with derisive yells and the deafening clamor of guns and gongs.

The steamer towed the brig into position, where she leisurely anchored, so close to the pirate lines that the storm of shot from their batteries passed over her and splashed harmlessly into the water beyond. Her response was something terrific. The first broadside demolished or sank more than one of the braggart junks. Her guns were aimed by British gunners and every shot told. Junk after junk went to the bottom. The derisive yells were turned into shrieks of terror and pain. The harbor was strewn with mangled wreckage and floating bodies. Hundreds of the pirates were mowed down by shot and shell or were drowned as they dashed overboard and vainly struck out for land. Some two hundred or three hundred succeeded in scrambling on shore and, by throwing up a hasty redoubt, mounted some guns. A squad of British tars landed in pursuit and, by a swift flank movement, routed them to the four winds. The victory was supreme. The annihilation of the pirates and their fleet was as great a surprise and almost as complete as though a volcano had suddenly risen in their midst with a fiery eruption in full blast. The throngs of village and country folk who crowded the hillsides around the bay were lost in admiration at the bravery of the "foreign devils." How the plucky little brig and her consort dared venture into the tiger's dangerous lair and grapple such an enormously superior force was a miracle quite beyond the Celestial imagination.

But the centuries pass. Even China yields to the pressure of modern life. Railroads are beginning to run their lines of steel toward the heart of the empire. Telegraphs and telephones are spinning their web of wires over all the land. The government is minting its own coinage, developing its mines with Yankee machinery, establishing arsenals, steam-works, navy yards like the rest of the world. Chinese schools are teaching science developed in the West. Christian missions are disseminating a higher faith, a purer morality, and a more rational civilization. The same progressive spirit has laid hold of commerce. The sleepy junk cannot keep pace with the swift demands of business. Now along the vast waterfront of fifteen hundred miles, most of the carrying trade is handled by a fleet of jaunty steamers owned by the government and sailed by European officers. The inland waters are open to steam navigation, foreign as well as native, and that means not only an enormous increase of commerce but also the penetration of the Chinese world in every direction with Western ideas. It may indeed happen that an occasional paroxysm of reaction, like the Boxer massacres, may sweep over some section of the great empire and may for the time turn all progress and all hope into chaos. But the world moves fast. And no oriental barrier can long withstand the flood tide of modern civilization.

These forward movements are enough to make old Koshinga's bones rattle in his tomb. The modern bandit, too, looks out from his lair with consternation. His old lorchas and Mandarin boats are no match for steam. He can do little more than a small and stealthy retail business. A sudden dash upon a lonely trader and a stab in the dark may win an occasional prize; but let him come out into the open and dare anything on a larger scale, and the imperial steam navy would speedily hunt him down on his own blood-stained seas. And if the Yellow Dragon needs help in the operation, many another knight errant like Chinese Gordon would be eager to volunteer.

Cruising After Pirates

CAPTAIN H. C. ST. JOHN, RN

Although my first acquaintance with China was in 1855, I mean to relate a few piratical incidents of a later date, and afterwards, perhaps, return to that year, and the war which immediately followed.

In 1864 the coasts of China, and particularly the southern parts, were infested with pirates. I commanded a gunboat, whose particular duty was to keep them in check. The Gulf of Tonquin, the island of Hainan, and the coast from thence up to Macao was unknown and unvisited except by myself, or an occasional other gunboat. There was no commerce, neither port nor town existing of sufficient size to excite trade, excepting perhaps Hoihou, the chief town of Hainan. The anchorage there, however, is very bad, being merely a roadstead, and to get to it numerous dangerous shoals have to be passed. Islands and shoal water stretch a long way out from the main coast line, forming at all times innumerable safe retreats. Rough sketches of the coast have been taken at different times, but to this day it remains unsurveyed.

The island of Hainan is 300 miles round, and the length of the other coasts which I have mentioned would amount to, roundly, 400 miles. The whole of this considerable extent of coast was, in the days I am speaking of, entirely at the disposal of these lawless Chinamen.

I was lying at my anchorage in Hong-Kong harbour one day; a fine large opium junk, armed to the teeth with a dozen 12 to 18 pounder guns on board, and a crew of about forty-five men lay close to me.

In the afternoon a number of passengers went on board her. These people intended taking advantage of the security afforded by such a vessel—supposed security would perhaps be more applicable. At any rate, when an opium junk was about to proceed up the coast, owing to the strength of her crew and armament, applications for passages were sure to be made.

She was bound for Swatow, a port 180 miles to the northward, and towards dusk she got under weigh. As she reached the outer roads of Hong-Kong, or a few miles from the Lymoon Pass, it fell calm, and she anchored. This was about nine o'clock. A few hours afterwards, probably about midnight, a large junk quietly ran alongside, a number of men jumped on board, and before the passengers and crew could show any resistance, they were entirely in the power of a band of pirates. The crew and passengers were at once secured under hatches, and the junk got under weigh and steered for the back or south side of the island of Hong-Kong.

Soon after daylight, one by one of these unfortunate beings, men and women, as they came up from below, had their hands tied behind them, their feet tied together, and were then flung overboard, a single exception being made of the eighty-three on board. This was a boy about twelve years old. He was spared, being small enough to make their tea and prepare their opium pipes, etc. The pirates then took the junk, which had a most valuable cargo of opium, a description of plunder these gentlemen particularly appreciate, being easily turned into money, and made for a favourite harbour a little to the north of Macao. Here they divided their spoil, burnt the junk, and dispersed. This plan was frequently adopted to elude pursuit. Seven went to Macao, and from thence took their passage by the usual passenger steamer to Hong-Kong. The poor little urchin whom they had spared, but whose father had been drowned, was allotted to one of these seven.

Before the steamer reached her destination, the Captain noticed the boy, who appeared to be in much distress, and being a kind-hearted man (peace to his ashes!) asked what ailed him. On hearing the story I have just related, instead of running the steamer alongside the jetty at Hong-Kong, as was usual, he anchored in mid-stream, hailed the police-boat to come alongside, drew up the hundred odd Chinese passengers, and with the boy's assistance picked the seven men from amongst them. They were taken possession of by the police and locked up.

The previous evening, one of the eighty-two unfortunates who had been flung overboard arrived at Hong-Kong, and gave the same account as the boy did. This man's fate was evidently not drowning. It appeared when he found himself in the water, and going quickly to the bottom, he managed with a desperate effort to free his hands by slipping them through the lashing, and then bringing himself to the surface he soon got his feet free. Chinamen as a rule swim like fish, and fortunately for this one, he was no exception. He reached the nearest island safely, and from thence to Hong-Kong in a fishing-boat must have been a pleasant journey after the short but peculiar one he had just gone through. His account had been received previous to the boy's; both agreed, and in consequence I was sent out to examine, and, if possible, capture some of the other pirates. Of course it was useless; no trace whatever could be obtained.

The seven men were tried and condemned at Hong-Kong, and one morning I had the satisfaction of seeing them all hanged. I think a more cold-blooded affair could hardly be imagined than the above wholesale drowning of eighty-two fellow-countrymen.

I was cruising up the coast one day, merely on the look-out, having no definite information to go on, when, on passing a small island, two fishermen paddled off in a sanpan.

"Have got pilong," one immediately said.

"Where?" I asked.

"Can makee see," he replied, and on looking in the direction he pointed, I saw two small junks making the best of their way to sea. There was no wind, so I steamed quietly on, knowing they could not escape. About a dozen other smaller junks now put off, and opened fire at the two larger ones. Guns, jingalls, and other explosive instruments were discharged indiscriminately. As I ran alongside the nearest of the two junks, this fusilade ceased, and I soon had both junks secured. The crews I took on board the gun-boat, and steamed in and anchored off the town. The Mandarin, the governor of the place, at once came off, when the following conversation took place between us. First thanking me for my opportune appearance and capture of the two pirate junks, with their crews intact, numbering, all told, to twenty-one, he said—

"These two junks have given me a great deal of trouble for four days; they have blockaded the place; neither a fishing or trading junk has been able to get out."

"Do you mean to say," I answered, "that these two miserable junks, with twenty-one men between them, and mounting one two-pounder gun, have actually shut your port up for that time?"

"Yes," he said. "We are, my people are, very frightened of pilongs."

"Have you no troops?" I remarked; "your personal staff seems to consist of at least fifty."

"Oh yes," he replied; "I have 800 soldiers on shore!"

There were something like a hundred junks of all sizes, some large enough to have run over the pirates without feeling the shock.

"Why did you not put some of your brave men in the fishing-junks and capture these pirates?"

"Ah, you English are very brave," he replied; "my men are very easily frightened."

Well, I thought to myself, that seems pretty certain.

"How many inhabitants are there in the town?" I asked.

"More than 4000," was the answer.

"I think," I said, "if I were a Chinaman, I would turn pirate at once. They must lead very jolly independent lives."

"Yes, they do," answered this blue-buttoned warrior; " the only things they fear are English gunboats."

A score or so of fishing junks had assembled round. The crews, consisting of quite as many women as men, were making a fearful clamour, talking over the last four days, and their sleepless nights; and now their relief had come, and their dreaded enemies were captured.

"Give us the pirates," they cried; the women particularly bawled for their possession.

I had been a couple of days cruising along the eastern coast, anchoring at night, and examining during the day-time the numerous creeks, bays, and hiding-places, but without success of any kind. Towards evening of the second day I reached a favourite creek, which, bending back from the head of a deep bay, twenty miles from the open sea, expanded into an inland basin, with innumerable smaller creeks and passages, twisting and turning about amongst the hills in all directions. It was a grand place for pirates. By having men stationed on the peaks of the hills, signals were easily passed along very quickly to their junks inside, which warning generally was in time to allow them to escape by some of the interminable creeks.

Soon after anchoring I went on shore to see the missionary priest, a Roman Catholic and a Jesuit. I never met or heard of a Protestant missionary taking up his quarters in such situations as I am now speaking of, viz., amongst the poorer villagers far away from the open or treaty ports, where half the people live by piracy and robbery, in petty ways as well as in a more wholesale manner. A few words about this little man. He was an Italian of very good family, and had received an excellent education. Chinese he spoke like a native, besides six other languages as perfectly. He was a botanist, and full of intelligence on most subjects. Although he resided at this particular spot, his district was extensive, running inland about fifty miles, and to a greater distance along the coast. He had built a small chapel and school; how he managed this out of a monthly pittance of eight dollars was always a mystery to me. I believe, however, he made pilgrimages to Hong-Kong, and there, by his energy and charm of manner, managed to raise occasional help by subscriptions. Fifteen native children he entirely supported. He was the doctor, the friend, the counsellor of the village, and on more occasions than one had he, by his influence and the respect in which he was held in the surrounding district, not only kept the peace, but made villagers who had turned out against each other on some petty quarrel return home in friendship. His influence for good was very great; considering the people he was amongst, it was marvellous. His small, thin, delicate figure looked as if his life hung on a very slender thread.

"I suppose you are looking after pirates?" he remarked, as we walked up from the beach to his house. "A few days ago I had to cross the bay, and I feel sure there was a large piratical craft at anchor under one of the rocky points; they are a bad lot about here, I fear; but you won't, I know, ask me anything I do not voluntarily tell you about these things. Poor people, they have hard times of it."

"Why do you call them poor?" I asked.

"Because those who do not live by piracy are squeezed by those who do, and squeezed into the bargain by the Mandarins."

"No wonder they don't become rich," I said; "but I must tell you about a neighbour of yours, who now is rather a friend of mine, although he is an arrant rogue, and the head of a pirate gang. I find him, however, very useful sometimes; but I will tell you how I made his acquaintance. A fishing vessel belonging to Hong-Kong was attacked by a couple of pirate craft, and of course taken. I suppose they thought no ransom would be forthcoming for such poor people."

"Yes, I fear that is the way they work their mischief," answered my companion.

"The pirates quietly sailed away with his junk and all his property, having first landed the owner and his family. The fisherman reached Hong-Kong, gave information, and I, as usual, was sent out to recover, if possible, the junk, etc. Step by step I traced the pirates until I ran them to earth at Kato; here a good deal of the stolen property was found stowed away in the house belonging to the headman of the village, and it required a deal of perseverance before he would part with it; but after sending a twenty-four pound shot through the roof of his house, he thought better of his sins."

"It was time he did," laughingly rejoined Voluntari.

"He keeps fifteen junks employed robbing his own countrymen chiefly, but foreigners as well when a good opportunity to do so occurs. Since my first little episode with this worthy I have frequently called on him, and although, of course, I gain no news about his own craft, he has no objection to give information relating to the movements of his neighbours, or rather one of his neighbours, who happens to be a fellow-piratical chief. It was only about three weeks ago I took two large junks which I should never have found except through this unneighbourly rascal."

"I have heard of him," answered the priest, "and I fear he is a great rogue. The most wealthy men in many of these out-of-the-way villages live chiefly by piracy and plunder."

I decided to remain about the locality for a day or two longer, and early next morning got the gun-boat into a small bay, so narrow, and so perfectly hidden, that she had only just room to swing round her anchor, and until you came over the low hills which surrounded the spot, nothing of the little craft could be seen.

About three miles off I knew pheasants and partridges were to be found, and crossing the piece of water which intervened, I beat all the likely cover along the edges of the millet and maize fields. Toward midday I had bagged a few brace of each, some quail, and half-a-dozen snipe, and the sun being by this time warm enough to make a drink refreshing, I made for the village at the foot of the highest range in the neighbourhood, hoping to get some good water, or perhaps tea. As I reached the place, to my surprise it appeared deserted; not a human being, neither pig nor yelping cur, being visible. But as soon as I got amongst the houses, a face, then a head appeared, at an open casement; then another, until any number of heads popped out.

"Lofu! lofu!" (tiger! tiger!) they cried.

"Where?" I said, thinking of the No. 6 shot with which my gun was loaded.

"He come down just now, and walk through the village; he very hungry."

"I daresay he is," I answered, "but I don't see him; where did he go?" That, however, no one knew; probably picking up a pig, he had returned to the thick impenetrable cover, or the mountain-side.

Quietly walking down to the nearest village during the day-time certainly appeared a very cool proceeding, but I was assured this was by no means an unusual incident, and that generally a pig or calf disappeared. The inhabitants themselves, when it so happened, drove their animals into their houses, shut themselves in, and remained perfectly quiet until the tiger thought proper to walk away. Sometimes they send to Canton for professional huntsmen, who generally manage to bag one or two of these troublesome beasts in a year. Either finding the remains of the animal that has been carried off, or, if that cannot be done, setting a bait, they then fix a cross-bow some yards from the trail by which the tiger will probably come, a string being led from the trigger of the cross-bow across his path, and pressing against this string as he quietly passes along, he lets loose his own death-warrant, in the shape of a poisoned arrow, discharged with all the force that a bamboo bow twenty feet long is capable of giving. I have seen some very beautiful and fine skins taken from these tigers in the south.

Returning to the gun-boat, soon after leaving the village with its inhabitants in a happier state of mind that when I entered it, I found a couple of Chinamen on board, who had brought word that some large pirate junks were at anchor a few miles away, in quite a different creek, and entirely hidden and separated from where the gun-boat then was by a mass of mountains.

We were under weigh in ten minutes, steaming for the spot indicated. The course, however, led past my pirate friend's residence, and as we reached the village, a sanpan pulled vigorously off with a couple of men in her. On seeing them approach I stowed the first informers away, to ascertain, without their seeing each other, the news that these men evidently wished to give. They, too, had information in substance much the same as the first gentlemen.

I did not quite like this eagerness to show me where the said pirates were, but of course without disclosing my doubts, and keeping the informers out of sight of each other, on we went. The creek was reached; it was about half a mile wide, and very shallow at the extreme end,—the gunboat, in fact, could not get within a mile of the bottom of it,—so I anchored, and started with my two boats, taking about twenty men with me. As we pulled along the south side, within fifty yards of the shore, I noticed several men running along amongst the trees, which here grew thickly up the hill-side, and as they were all making for the head of the creek, as we were, I conjectured that those I saw thus hurrying on were bent on picking up odds and ends of spoil from the junks, which I now felt sure we should very soon find. My boat had got a couple of hundred yards ahead of the other, fortunately, and had just opened out the mastheads of a fine large junk hidden behind a low point covered with thick bushes and trees. "I have you, my friend," I inwardly said. At that moment, a flash, a report, and a shower of grape passed over our heads, ploughing up the water like hail on the other side of the boat. It passed through my mind instantly that I had been caught napping in a cleverly devised trap. Pulling short round, three strokes landed the boat in front of the battery, not five yards from their guns; another discharge, which certainly ought to have sent us all into the middle of next week, and the next moment we were amongst the pirates. Every bush and tree appeared to have a rascal behind it blazing away with a jingall; one fellow's eye I caught sight of along his barrel, and feeling at the moment rather vicious, pulled the trigger of my short rifle at him, but a wretched snap was the only result. However, he missed his object as well. The scuffle was soon over, the pirates being driven from their battery and junk into the thick surrounding woods and cover, where I did not care to follow them. The battery and junk now took my attention. The former was armed with 18-pounder carronades, one of which had evidently been loaded to the muzzle, the discharge having capsized it backwards. By allowing us to approach so near before opening fire they had missed their mark; if we had only been a hundred yards instead of fifty, I don't think many would have escaped. As it was, our luck had been extraordinary: not a man was touched either by jingall or gun.

On one occasion a fine clipper tea-ship, when on her way down the China Sea, got becalmed near the southeast part of Hainan. In a very short time fifteen junks appeared on the scene, and with the assistance of large sculls were soon within range, and opened fire. Fortunately for the vessel a light breeze sprang up, and with her lofty spars and quantity of light canvas she soon drew ahead out of range, and escaped closer quarters.

On the information reaching Hong-Kong I was ordered out to see if anything could be done towards capturing some of these junks. It was a lovely evening when we left, moonless but starlit, and as we steamed quietly through the shipping, and reached the open water to the west of the island, one could not help feeling how peaceful and quiet everything was. Keeping on during the night, we passed through the labyrinth of islands that extends nearly thirty miles to the south-west, and at daylight had reached the first of those that stud the south coast, directly west of the Canton river. A single junk was in sight, well inshore, and some miles ahead; but as it was quite calm the course I was steering would bring me within half a mile of her. Her great batwing-like sails flapped as the long swell lifted and rolled her from side to side, and on looking through the telescope I saw several neat round holes through her mat sails. I thought it strange, moreover, for an honest junk to be alone in that locality, knowing well that they usually went in small fleets for self-protection.

Deciding to have a better look at her, I altered course; but before the little gun-boat's head was round, a boat from the junk had been launched, a dozen men had jumped into her, and were pulling for the shore as hard as possible.

I first caught the sanpan, and then towing the junk to a favourite anchorage, burnt her; we then proceeded down the coast with the twenty-four pirates on board, whom I handed over to the Governor of the nearest province. Three exceptions I made—one because the rogue had once actually belonged to the *Opossum*, the gun-boat I commanded; another, because he was quite a youth, and had been to England; and the third because he was only fourteen years old, and I thought at that age he might learn a new trade, although he had been seven years with the pirates. To shorten a long story, this junk had, about three months before, been taken by pirates, when in company with a small fleet of Hong-Kong trading junks. After killing the crew, the pirates had kept her. They had then been so fortunate in their depredations that their own companions had attacked them; but, being a good sailer, the junk outstripped her envious friends, and when we hove in sight was all but at her journey's end, Macao, where her crew would have divided 20,000 dollars, and dispersed.

As we steamed up to her I observed the rascals flinging things overboard, but little dreamed they were bags of dollars, which were thus reduced to something less than half the number mentioned when I got on board.

The prisoners were forwarded to Canton. Six or seven, however, managed to escape on the way. The remainder were tried, condemned, and executed. On their trial they swore that those who escaped bribed the Mandarin to allow them to do so; and that had they themselves only possessed, or been able to raise money, as their more fortunate companions had done, they also would have been allowed to take to their heels. The authorities, at any rate, believed these wretched men, and the Mandarin, a first-class, red-buttoned individual, was recalled from his station, degraded, and sent into retirement. Altogether it was a queer piece of justice. In time I managed to get the unfortunate man reinstated, so far as his rank went, but he was never again given the governorship of the province.

On leaving Quanghai I kept on to the west, intending to reach Tienpak, where I thought I might hear some news regarding the Hainan pirates.

Tienpak was a queer place to get to, situated five miles up a narrow creek, scarcely fifty yards wide, which at low water led through flat sands, but at high tide the whole immense extent of sand was covered with three or four feet of water. After the military Mandarin had been on board I returned his visit on shore, and found him comfortably settled in a temporary residence on the outskirts of the town. He had collected all the prettiest girls of the place to wait and attend upon him during his short stay at this rough village. None of these people had ever seen a European before, and their curiosity in consequence was greatly excited by my arrival.

One girl, as she handed me a cup of tea, begged to be allowed to touch my whiskers,—such articles being scarce, if not wholly wanting, amongst her own countrymen.

I jokingly asked them, "Who would like to live on board the gun-boat?" and next morning, rather to my consternation, half-a-dozen of these fair ones came off, got up in all their best robes and cosmetics. The rough but honest old Mandarin accompanied his harem. It was amusing to see these girls, who, I fear, really thought half of them might be chosen to remain on board, trying to make themselves useful at once, by dusting and arranging the different articles in my cabin.

But adieu we bade them, and started for Hainan,—Mandarin, two war-junks, and gun-boat.

A hundred miles west of Tienpak, I found a narrow entrance leading through some low sandhills into a spacious basin, which, on steaming across it, proved to be ten miles in width. No signs of junks were to be seen; but finding the mouth of a large river emptying itself into the north-west corner of the basin, I followed its course seven or eight miles up, passing several earth-batteries on either bank in that distance. Here we came across a large junk loading with oil, and from the crew ascertained that a couple of days before a fleet of pirates had been in the bay. This was bad luck, but there was nothing for it except the chance of finding them about Nowchow, an island just to the north of Hainan. Thither therefore we went, but the birds had flown from here also, probably for the southern parts of Hainan. It was rather more than provoking, considering that ten to one these were some of the very fellows who had attacked the clipper ship. However, better luck next time, I thought, as I turned the gunboat's head towards Hong-Kong. Our coal was getting very short, and we had only enough, and barely that, to take us back. We anchored for a couple of days *en route*, at a favourite snug bay, and landing early the following morning with my gun and setter, I soon picked up some snipe, a few teal, and several quail. In crossing a soft muddy patch in the marsh I came upon the print of a tiger's track, perfectly fresh. Probably the beast, after hunting about the skirts of the villages in the valley, had crossed the swamp on his way to the mountains. The four toes measured exactly seven inches across. Partridges, as the day advanced, began to utter their curious wild note, as they answered one another from almost every hillock along the lower ranges. Turning homewards, I soon added a brace or two to my bag, and felt well satisfied with my forenoon's sport and walk as I reached the beach. Almost as I stepped on the clear sand, a bullet whizzed past my head, and went with a thud into the bank a few feet off. The report had hardly done reverberating amongst the hills, before my telescope picked out the enemy, some 300 yards off on a grassy mound, and not a little to my astonishment, the enemy was one of my own marines. It appeared that during my absence a small pirate craft had turned up amongst the bushes which line the creek, and that I was taken for one of the crew by those who were hunting them up. During the night the quartermaster on watch believed he heard the tiger. I slept, however, too soundly after my week's work to be easily disturbed, and I don't know whether the man was dreaming or not. I have no doubt, if I had time, I might have got him, by watching at night with a calf or pig for a bait; as it was, I returned next day to Hong-Kong to find another piratical report waiting for me.

Cruising for Pirates and What We Caught

JOHN S. SEWALL

The following September, the *Saratoga* was again dispatched on a mission of vengeance. A Boston merchantman, the *Celestial*, while peaceably wending her way to Hong Kong, had run the gauntlet of a whole fleet of Chinese freebooters but had managed to elude them and escape. We were sent out to catch the miscreants, or any other red-rovers we might find practicing their art, and teach them the error of their ways.

Our orders were to cruise for a month down the coast as far as the Gulf of Tonquin—the first week off the Ladrones, the remaining three off the Taya Islands and Hainan. It was ugly weather, squally and threatening when we got up anchor and disappeared from Hong Kong. But it took us out clear of the islands in dashing style, and three or four hours brought us to our cruising ground. There under easy sail we stood off all day and night to the southward and westward, sharply scanning every sort of craft we met and looking into the harbors for any bandits that might be lurking there. The next forenoon we wore round and made a long stretch back toward the Ladrones. We gave chase to a sinister-looking scow that proved to be an innocent trader bound to Macao, whither he had fled, badly frightened as soon as we let him off. One evening we met a fleet of eight junks coming in, and we promptly put about and overhauled them. They were as panic-stricken as the other. The sudden apparition of a big man-of-war pouncing upon them like a hawk upon a brood of chickens sent them scampering off to all points of the compass, burning joss paper and wildly beating their gongs for help from the Chinese pantheon.

At last the week off the Ladrones was duly completed. The helm was put up and round we went, bound for "fresh fields and pastures new." A fair breeze was sweeping us smoothly down the seas when suddenly our foreyard determined otherwise. To the best of our knowledge and belief it had always been robust and healthy, a well-behaved stick of sound and positive convictions. But all at once it was discovered that an internal disorder was preying on its vitals; whereupon the carpenter bluntly reported to the officer of the deck, and the officer of the deck to the first lieutenant, and the first lieutenant to the captain, that the foreyard was rotten in the slings. No sailor need be reminded what that would mean in a gale of wind. Round the ship spun again on her heel and bracing sharp up began to beat back for the nearest known port; which haven of refuge proved to be a cove in an island variously called Sancian, Sanchuen, and St. John's. Occupied by fishermen, it was a quiet place some seventy-five miles to the southwest of Macao. High bluffs, projecting ledges, with patches of sandy beach below and between, and the whole plentifully bestrewn with boulders, which were the relics of some far away glacial period—that was the type of scenery.

At the head of a bay some three or four miles off, we could see a fishing hamlet and a fleet of small craft at anchor before it or slipping in and out with the tide. Close by us, a few rocky farms, out of which the tenants managed to scratch a living by coaxing out of the gravel small crops of bananas, oranges, pineapples, sweet potatoes, and beans, wherever the jealous boulders would permit.

This was the place where the Portuguese were first permitted to trade in 1517, before the founding of Macao. For a few years they had here a bustling colony. But a neighbor island, Lampacao, proved more attractive and gradually drew away from Sancian both the trade and the traders. Macao in turn did the same for Lampacao, and the site was so entirely abandoned that now the very location of the ancient city is quite unknown.

The dim memory of Lampacao and all her vanished commerce was as nothing, however, beside our interest in one man, who finished a great life and breathed his last on the shores of this obscure islet. It was in 1552 that St. Francis Xavier died on Sancian. It was in 1852, just three centuries after, that a party of us stood reverently on the strand from which the body of the heroic missionary had been borne away to be entombed in a distant church in Goa. From that day to this, though of different faith, I have felt a sense of possession in the memory and deeds of the famous East Indian apostle, simply from having walked the beach he trod and looked on the rugged scenery that was the last vision to his closing eyes.

The delinquent spar was speedily down on deck, stripped of its harness, laid on its back, and made ready for surgery. A bad case of appendicitis, or internal cancer, or worse. The carpenter and his crew went at it *con amore*, dug out the cankerous sludge, filled in with sound timber, and fished the whole with extra spars laid on and heavily clamped along the middle of the yard. A reasonably fair job, and as strong as tools and wood could make it, but awkward and bungling; the carpenter himself declared that he would not trust it in a gale of wind. If we had had that stick aloft in the typhoon we encountered a fortnight later, very likely we should have lost our masts and gone to the bottom; in which case any possible readers who may be sauntering with me through these devious pages would have been spared the labor. But the carpenter's verdict and an official survey of the bandaged spar changed all that. The captain decided to put back to Macao and get a new foreyard.

I need not hint to you how incensed the commodore was that we should dare to leave our cruising ground, nor how he set all the carpenters to work from all three ships to make the new spar out of our spare main topmast and the *Susquehanna's* spare jib-boom, and when done, hustled us out of port in short order to finish our cruise. At any rate, we got out of that neighborhood as fast as canvas and breeze could take us and went to look for the other pirates. Outside, a fair wind swept us down off the Taya Islands. There we tried a ruse; ran the guns in, closed the ports, concealed our multitudinous crew, and did our best to look like an innocent merchantman, hoping to decoy some red-rover, or perhaps a whole fleet of them, to an attack. No result; pious fraud does not seem to work with pirates. So we kept on down the coast, passed the false Tinhosa, and ran in for Tinhosa the real, which proved to be a steep, rocky, mountainous island nearly halfway down the eastern shore of Hainan. Another long stretch, and the delusive current swept us far to the southward and westward of Gaalong Bay, and doubtless chuckled all over its foamy surface to see us laboriously beating back in the teeth of an increasing gale. If you have ever gone fishing for pirates in these outlandish parts, these unfamiliar names may assist the geographical side of your memory. We meant to run to Gaalong Bay for shelter, but in the rising storm we could not fetch in, and so ran for the open main in order to get plenty of sea room in which to meet whatever was coming.

And it was coming, sure. This "Thing" of the sea had been getting itself together and lying in wait for us; a demoniac octopus of the air whose tentacles were already spitefully snatching at us from afar. Let us get a look at the monster before it actually arrives, as we did not at the Madjicosima storm a few pages back.

Our unlucky cruise was just about timed with the autumnal change of monsoon. In the China seas the regular semi-annual shift of atmospheric currents occurs in September and October; when, the sun having returned into the southern hemisphere, the southwest monsoon gradually retreats from its invasion of northern zones and the northeast trades chase it back to its home. It is not a sudden change. There is a kind of tricky recess, a belt of calms and erratic weather. This is the happy hunting ground of the typhoon. As M. Reclus explains in his entertaining book, *The Ocean*, "It is at this epoch of the change of the seasons that the powerful aerial masses, charged with electricity, engage in strife for the supremacy, and by their encounter produce those great eddies which are developed in spirals across the seas and the continents." The statement which he draws from another meteorologist that of 365 West Indian hurricanes recorded between 1493 and 1855, more than two-thirds came in October, when "the strongly heated coasts of South America begin to attract toward themselves the colder and denser air of the northern continent," might stand as a fair account of the situation in the East Indies also. The furnace heat of the tropics, the enormous expansion and elevation of the lower atmospheric levels, the velocity of the other masses rushing in, their collision with island peaks and mountain ranges, their sharp concussion with each other and the attendant electric explosions—these are the fierce dynamics of the air out of which are gendered those revolving storms that descend to the earth and go spinning their dance of death over a much enduring surface.

In point of size, they vary from the tornado, which mows its narrow swath through the woods, to the full-grown cyclone whose circle sweeps half an ocean. The hurricane of 1839 was about three hundred miles in diameter at the Antilles, five hundred when it reached the Bermudas, and nearly eighteen hundred when it crashed upon Ireland. A furious cyclone encountered between Japan and Formosa in July 1853 by the *Saratoga* and three other vessels of the Japan expedition, which was afterwards described and mapped by Mr. Redfield, was at least a thousand miles in diameter. Still larger was the storm that overtook our flagship the *Mississippi*, not far from the same region in October of the following year. It was from fifteen hundred to two thousand miles across, and traveled for six days at a rate of from twelve to forty miles an hour. By contrast, the tornado that crossed the state of Indiana in April 1852, leaving a track littered with wreckage of forests and cattle and towns, was only a mile wide. The destructive cyclone in Iowa in 1882 averaged half a mile. One which obliterated a village near Springfield, Missouri, in April 1880, sweeping its very site so bare that scarcely the splinters could be found, cut a path nowhere broader than 150 rods. And, finally, the tornado that tore its way through Tuscumbia, Alabama, on a quiet Sabbath evening in the autumn of 1874, bursting the stoutest buildings into fragments and killing a number of the inhabitants, measured in diameter less than four hundred feet.

The height of the column is as variable as its diameter. Two miles is an unusual elevation; and the other extreme might be not more than a hundred yards. A lofty mountain range is a wall against which it beats in vain. It cannot climb. It can only pass by doubling the huge buttresses and promontories. Sometimes it is flattened down to a shallow disk on the surface of the sea, spinning like a horizontal flywheel, dark, angry, furious, deadly, while the sea birds congregate out of harm's way in the calm regions a few hundred feet above, and the sun looks serenely down on the black delirium beneath.

This was the case with the typhoon just referred to as having caught in its toils so many of the ships of our squadron on their way back from Japan. Some of the officers noticed that "even when the wind was piping loudest, when the water was whirled violently by in perfect sheets, the scud moved overhead at a remarkably slow rate, and the upper layer of clouds seemed scarcely to be stirred at all." On one of those grim nights, while our rolling ship was lying to off the chain of islands that stretches from Japan to Lew Chew, not daring to run through in such a tempest and on such imperfect charts, I remember how the moon struggled almost through the weltering haze and what a ghastly glare she cast on the boiling sea. Strange that a few hundred feet of altitude should make all the difference between a calm and a hurricane—between paradise and hell.

The prognostics of these storms are well fitted to inspire alarm. Nature is not uniform. A western tornado will sometimes burst upon its victims with little or no warning. But those that come in the daytime can frequently be seen at a distance making their lurid preparations. A writer in the signal service describes it thus—it is likely that he has seen one coming: "The first sign of a tornado is generally a tumultuous, strange appearance in the southwest; and then the whirling funnel comes in sight writhing and swinging from side to side, now rising and again seeming to plunge down to the ground; its winds tear limbs from trees and roofs from houses, and suck them upwards with clouds of dust and debris. As it sweeps over a village, the houses on its path are not blown over, but exploded, and their walls fall outward on all sides. Heavy wagons, beams, and chains are all picked up and transported through the air. Lighter objects, such as boards, shingles, clothing, and papers, are often carried miles away before they fall."

Another observer gives a still more circumstantial account: "Innumerable descriptions show that the cloud in the northwest is heavy, black, and comparatively slow in its movement, until struck by a light, rather smoky, and more rapidly moving cloud from the southwest. Then the clouds rush to a common center, and there is a violent conflict of currents, driving clouds in every direction, up and down, round and round. Clouds like great sheets of white smoke dash about in a frightful manner, with such unnatural velocity that the observer is often panic-stricken and flees to the nearest cellar for safety. Finally a black, threatening mass descends slowly toward the earth, whirling violently, but still manifesting confusion in form. This soon gives place to the peculiar funnel-like shape, with definite outline so well-known. It appears intensely black, like coal smoke issuing from a locomotive, and its trunk-like form sometimes has a wrenching spiral motion, like a snake hung up by the head and writhing in agony. As white clouds approach and are drawn into the vortex, the funnel-shaped trunk sways like an elastic column. It sometimes rises, falls, and careens from side to side like a balloon. Branches and trunks of trees, rails, treetops, pieces of houses, straw, furniture, stoves, roofs, iron-work, lumber, and other debris are seen flying about in the central part of the cloud, but are gradually drawn upward and thrown out near the top, usually not until the storm has progressed a mile or two farther on from a given point. Dark masses of cloud are seen to shoot downward on either side of the funnel, to enter it just above the ground, and to apparently rush upward through the center and out at the top in a terrific manner. Sometimes the funnel pauses and whirls with apparently increased velocity, reducing everything to splinters, and leaving scarcely a vestige of a house or clump of trees, all being ground comparatively fine and carried away as chaff. The people at Westwood describe the roar of the tornado as having a peculiar hollow, humming sound. It somewhat resembles the rumbling of cars, or the booming of the sea. The sound is indescribable and unlike any other in nature. It is so loud that the falling of heavy trees against the side of a house and the crash of falling buildings are lost in the general roar."

The more formidable cyclones that ravage the deep usually send their dread heralds in advance. M. Reclus in describing their approach indulges in some vivid rhetoric. "Some days before the terrible hurricane is unchained, nature, already gloomy, and as if veiled, seems to anticipate a disaster. The little white clouds which float in the heights of air with the counter trade winds are hidden under a yellowish or dirty white vapor; the heavenly bodies are surrounded by vaguely iridescent halos and heavy layers of clouds, which in the evening present the most magnificent shadows of purple and of gold stretching far over the horizon, and the air is as stifling as if it came from the mouth of some great furnace. The cyclone, which already whirls in the upper regions, gradually approaches the surface of the ground or water. Torn fragments of reddish or black clouds are carried furiously along by the storm, which plunges and hurries through space; the column of mercury is wildly agitated in the barometer and sinks rapidly; the birds assemble as if to take counsel, then fly swiftly away so as to escape the tempest that pursues them. Soon a dark mass shows itself in the threatening part of the sky; this mass increases and spreads itself out, gradually covering the azure with a veil of a terrible darkness or a blood-colored hue. This is the cyclone, which fills and takes possession of its empire, twisting its immense spirals around the horizon. The roaring of the seas and skies succeeds to this awful silence."

These hurricanes have a will of their own, and revolve in opposite directions on opposite sides of the equator. In the southern hemisphere they wheel from left to right, like the hands of a watch; in the northern, from right to left. This is not their only motion. Occasionally one will spin on the same spot, like a top; but most of them, like the planets, not only revolve on their axis but at the same time travel in an orbit, sometimes with great velocity. The rate attained by the entire body of the storm varies from one mile per hour to forty, fifty, and even sixty. The distances traversed vary still more. A few hundred rods may exhaust the tornado. A few hundred miles would make a fair average for the cyclone.

Probably the most extensive track that has ever been traced and mapped was that of the great storm of 1885, which circumnavigated more than half the globe. It was generated near the southern coast of China in the latter part of September, "passed over Japan and the Aleutian archipelago, and entered the United States on 10 October. Crossing the Rocky Mountain range it proceeded through the northern states and Canada to Labrador and Davis Strait. In the Atlantic it was joined on the eighteenth by another disturbance which had come up from the Atlantic tropics, the junction of the two being followed by a cessation of progressive movement from the nineteenth to the twenty-fifth. During this period a severe gale that passed along the southern counties of England on the morning of the twenty-fourth—a storm the forecasting of which was shown to be impossible—was formed. Following in the wake of this storm, the parent cyclone reached the French coast on the twenty-seventh, its advent being marked by violent gales and extensive floods over the whole of western and central Europe and Algeria. Passing through France and the Netherlands, the disturbance showed signs of exhaustion, and on 1 November, in the Baltic, it quietly dispersed, after accomplishing a journey of more than sixteen thousand miles in thirty-six days."

The speed with which these portents travel along the surface is slow compared with their frightful gyrations on their own axis; a velocity which hurls weighty masses out of their path with the force of dynamite. In the hurricane of August 1837, at St. Thomas, an eyewitness writes, "The fort at the entrance of the harbor is leveled with the foundation and the twenty-four pounders thrown down; it looks as if it had been battered to pieces by cannon shot. ... One fine American ship, five hundred tons, was driven on shore near the citadel, and in an hour nothing could be seen of her but a few timbers." In the Iowa cyclone of 1882, trees, cattle, human beings, even houses, were sucked up into the enormous spirals, whisked through the air, and then dashed to atoms. This was the storm that was so fatal to the institution at Grinnell. Usually colleges investigate phenomena; this phenomenon investigated the college, and it did it with a scientific thoroughness that left nothing more to be further analyzed.

I have spoken of an "axis." An axis of course there is; but around it lies a central space of calms, which may be rods or even miles in diameter. The typhoon center is greatly dreaded by the navigator. A ship caught within the deadly enclosure wallows unmanageably in a tumbling sea and inside a cylinder of wind whose walls are whirling with a frightful speed. Violent squalls and waterspouts are sent tearing off from the revolving walls, and go thundering to and fro within the cylinder like a bedlam of demons.

In one of our many visits to Hong Kong, an English man-of-war came into port which had undergone a novel experience. In crossing the Indian Ocean she found a typhoon was making the same trip just north of her and about parallel with her own course. Her plucky commander was of an inquiring turn of mind and thought his ugly neighbor would bear investigation. He accordingly battened down his hatches and sailed in and out of the storm three times for the purpose of determining its size and course and verifying the direction and force of the wind. Then he hove to and waited, and when at a safe distance sailed across its wake. There he found a big ship over which the center had passed, waterlogged, dismasted, and terribly mangled in the mighty struggle. He had the happiness of picking off her crew before she went down.

Of all the apparatus of havoc that belongs to the hurricane, there is one more to be noted which is peculiarly fatal. It is the storm wave. The hurricane not only draws into its vortex the winds and lightnings and clouds; it sucks in the sea also and lifts a disk of water above the general level of the ocean almost as broad as its own diameter. This enormous tidal wave does not revolve with the wind at all, but is drawn forward and keeps pace with it. Like a murderous slave it does the bidding of the typhoon, and is ready to engulf fleets, submerge islands, demolish towns, desolate anything that may lie in its track. Read the list of hurricanes that have ravaged the West Indies and our own southern coast, from the first one noted by Columbus down to this present year of grace. In many cases the storm has carried with it appalling inundations that have buried villages and strewn the wrecks of vessels far inland.

In October 1864, this tempest-wave raised the Hoogly twenty-two feet for many miles above Calcutta, sweeping banks and islands with a fatal flood. A cyclone that struck the southern coast of India in 1789 led in its train three storm-waves that buried a city of thirty thousand inhabitants and lifted a whole fleet of vessels far up on the shore. In a similar catastrophe in 1876, which broke without warning in the night, three large islands and many smaller ones off the mouth of the Ganges were buried by a wave twenty feet deep, and more than two hundred fifty thousand hapless beings were swept into the sea. During a typhoon that passed over Kobe, Japan, in July 1871, scores of ships and junks were carried into the fields and forests far beyond the reach of the highest tides. In one of the violent hurricanes of the West Indies, the waves broke on the northern shores of the Barbados seventy-two feet above the mean level.

The memorable storm of October 1780 has been known as the most terrible cyclone of modern times. The ravages of its tidal wave were almost as destructive as those of the tempest itself. This frightful convulsion hurled its weight upon the hapless islands and fleets in its way more like an avalanche of the ocean than a mere tempest. It spared nothing. Squadrons were crushed like eggshells and sent to the bottom with all on board. An English fleet at anchor off St. Lucia went down on the spot. A French convoy with five thousand troops on board, several men-of-war on their way home, and a large number of merchantmen trading among the islands, were overtaken and sunk with their crews. Cities and plantations were ravaged as terribly as the deep. On the various islands nearly twenty thousand people were crushed under the wreck of their homes, or mangled by the countless missiles flying through the air, or swept off by the tidal wave.

A less extensive hurricane, but almost equally destructive, fell upon the southern coast of China in the autumn of 1874. Hong Kong was almost torn to pieces. Every vessel in the harbor or on the coast was crippled or sunk, and some eight thousand lives were lost. An officer of the Pacific mail steamer *Alaska* saw a fleet of more than one hundred Chinese junks founder all at once. The *Alaska* herself was driven on shore. Macao, seventy miles west, fared still worse. The storm obliterated whole streets and piled them with blocking ruins. To add to its horrors a band of pirates fired the city for purposes of plunder and seven hundred houses were consumed. Every vessel, foreign or native, was destroyed. Ten thousand lives were lost; and long before the dead could be disentangled for burial, the air became loaded with pestilence, and a wholesale cremation was ordered. The destruction of property reached a total of millions.

I trust the reader is in a forgiving mood, and our long delay in reaching this particular typhoon will be condoned. There is I believe a melancholy fascination about these grim tragedies of the sea; and I have gathered a few of the sad facts that demonstrate the power and the ferocity of this "sleeping giant" when it wakes in his wrath, creating havoc.

The ninth of October was creeping on. For some days the weather had been ugly and threatening. Somewhere a storm was mustering for the fray, and "Brooding its dreamy thunders far aloof."

The barometer fluttered for a day or two and then began to sink. The sky looked wicked. The wind was blowing hard and increasing. Sail had been gradually reduced. The waves had worked themselves into a most uncomfortable ferment. "Rocked in the cradle of the deep" is very romantic when you sing it, but not so nice when the cradle breaks your head and threatens to pitch you out. The timbers moaned and creaked, and the spars aloft groaned with the extra pressure when some deeper lurch swept them roaring back against the blast. I do not know a sound more dismal or ominous than the sepulchral tones wrung from the very fiber of the ship as she staggers reluctantly onward to meet the coming storm, perhaps to meet her doom. She seems to be groaning her own requiem beforehand.

When a tempest is on hand, sailors like to make all snug alow and aloft. Seamanship requires it. So does safety. The sailor is not the reckless being you think him when you see him at work astride a yardarm, or standing on a rope reefing topsails seventy-five feet in the air. He is a prehensile animal, and has methods of clinging that are not recognized in common philosophy. By noon we were in a state of uncomfortable preparation; royal and topgallant yards and masts sent down and stowed on deck; spare spars and boats made fast with extra lanyards; guns secured with double lashings; hatches battened down, and life-lines stretched along the decks.

A man-of-war is built for offensive warfare; but in an encounter with a tempest she is wholly on the defensive. She cannot attack the storm, it is the storm that attacks her. She cannot even strike back. There is no brilliant maneuver with which she can flank her omnipresent antagonist. Her petty array of battery, pikes, carbines, and cutlasses, with which she plays battle with other toy ships like herself, are worse than useless in the presence of a foe that scours around the horizon, skirmishes at her from invisible distances, blinds her with Egyptian darkness, crazes her with a savage drunken sea, and gathering its forces into successive paroxysms of wrath swoops down upon her with the weight and plunge of half the heavens falling. Then her battery is her deadliest burden, and her sharpest weapons make her only a more bristling target for the lightnings. She cannot screen herself. She cannot ward off the pitiless blows. She can only lie there on the devilish sea and take unresisting all the fury and ferocity with which her grim adversary can belabor her. The "Thing" that was coming was evidently a cyclone or, in the vernacular of the East, a typhoon. Either term is sufficiently hideous to anyone whose judgment of the sign is at all guided by his experience of the thing signified.

With the data at hand it would not be easy to determine where this particular hurricane originated, or in the throes of what atmospheric convulsion it may have been brought to the agony of birth. There was a villainous gale the same day at Madras, with a fearful score of wrecks and lives; but that was two thousand miles to the west of us, and our assailant came from the area of southeast. The October mail steamer was badly damaged by a typhoon a few days before us in nearly the same spot, but that storm had vanished; thus ours could not have been its residuum.

The *Sobrao*, a Portuguese ship, was caught in a typhoon off the Bashees which lasted ten days, and finally, mangled, dismasted, and utterly exhausted, she held together long enough for an American barque to pick off her crew, then sullenly gave up the fight and went down. This was two days before our hurricane and seven hundred or eight hundred miles to the east. It is possible that the vortex in which we were entrapped may have been an eddy sent tearing off from this larger sphere. If so, its path must have been a curve cutting diagonally across Luzon or down its western shores before it struck off over the seas in quest of other prey. The weather record of Manila for the autumn of 1852, if our Filipino friends kept such records then, would easily determine.

We never knew what other havoc it may have inflicted, with the single exception of one comrade in distress, an English ship that started for California and had the ill luck to be beset by three cyclones in succession. The last of the three was ours, and it well nigh finished her. It was "too much typhoon," as our Celestial friends admitted; and in process of time she came limping back into Hong Kong, halt, crippled, masts gone, bulwarks and everything else swept clean with the deck from forecastle to cabin. Logically she ought to have gone to the bottom; but her three tormentors were considerate enough not to come all at once. It was an unusually bad season. Many were the giant storms that stalked over the waves and many the craft that attempted to run the gauntlet. Some succeeded and escaped into more amiable seas; some were baffled and put back for help; and some left their mangled ribs to garnish the reefs, or vanished in the still depths where the storms send their victims and plunder but can never go themselves.

We had been all day standing out to the northward and eastward on the port tack, with the wind from the northward and westward. The farther we got, the more violent was the gale and the heavier the sea. No wonder, for we were plunging straight into the storm. The path of the cyclone was just to the north of us. It was crossing the China Sea on a west-nor'west course. We entered its southwest quarter, and were therefore heading straight for its center nearly all the afternoon. Any East Indian navigator who may chance to read this account would say that we were on the wrong tack. Yes, we were; but to a ship on a lee shore, Hobson's choice may be the only one open. Our position at noon that day was latitude 17° 41', longitude 110° 34', southeast of Gaalong Bay. It had been the captain's intention to run in, but the wind was contrary, in every sense of the term, and the coveted shelter of Gaalong was impossible. Our special danger was from the Paracels—an immense tract of reefs and shoals something like a hundred square miles, without an island or rock above the level of the sea on which a poor waif might find refuge in case he outlived the boiling surge and the tearing coral. We were just to windward of this sunken trap.

With the Paracels on one side and a typhoon on the other, it was worse than being caught "between the devil and the deep sea." It was not inspiring to reflect that if we did not founder before reaching it we might go smashing upon it at any moment. In the desperate effort to claw off, the ship was staggering under a press of canvas which otherwise she would not have dared to carry. The farther out we got, the more furious and brutal the sea. A stunning blow from the crest of a wave dashed in upon the starboard head, the decks had long been flooded. At every lurch, mountains of brine tumbled on board. Sail had been gradually reduced to foresail and main topsail, both close-reefed, with main trysail and fore storm-staysail. But the violence of the wind, instead of driving her forward, pressed her over almost on her beam ends, and she was drifting bodily to leeward. But that way lay the Paracels. That would not do. The canvas must come off.

Meanwhile all hands on deck; all the officers were summoned to the cabin. The first lieutenant had taken the deck. His stentorian voice could roar like a bull of Bashan; but in the fury of the storm even his voice could not be heard six inches from his lips. The orders were given in the cabin and were carried forward among the men by the other officers who picked their way desperately along the life lines. It is a serious job to shorten sail in a hurricane; commonly the hurricane does not wait for you but does it itself. The first rope started might take the masts out of her. But there was no alternative. And after a hard fight of two hours with the whole crew at the ropes, the poor *Saratoga* was lying under bare poles, wallowing, pitching, rolling, plunging, almost sinking in the pitiless sea; the foresail clewed up and stowed after a fashion, the storm-staysail blown out of the bolt-ropes, the trysail ripped into shreds and wound in all impossible ways about the main shrouds and running rigging. The main topsail gave the poor fellows the toughest work and the greatest danger. By superhuman effort it was clewed up, and the boatswain, a powerfully muscular man, led the crew of maintopmen up to furl it. He managed to crawl into the slings of the yard, but not a man would follow him. Brave as they were, the scene was enough to defy human power. The yard, though of course down on the cap, was still seventy-five feet and more from the deck. The great sail was flapping and writhing and tugging like a Titan, and threatened to rip yard and all into the sea. The mast whirled in giddy circles, sometimes dipping the yard-arms in the foam; and with such sudden and furious jerks that it required all one's strength to hold on and keep from being flung overboard. The air was full of driving scud and black as pitch. The wind scooped off the tops of the waves and sent them hissing through the rigging with the force of a chain shot. And the ghastly phosphorescence of the sea as it boiled around the ship and through the broken ports and then over hammock nettings cast a deathly glare over the scene that served to make the darkness visible. The men crept down and abandoned the sail to its fate.

It had four reefs in it, and these held; but all below them was stripped into ragged ribbons. Next morning the poor topsail, which was nearly new, was a curiosity fit for a museum.

All this time we were heading to the northward and eastward on the port tack. It was certain that the Paracels were right under our lee; how near, we could only conjecture. And though we were forging slowly ahead, yet we were drifting very much faster toward those fatal rocks. It was decided to get the ship about if possible, set some patch of canvas that might perhaps hold, and run her out into wider sea room. Then we could resume that port tack whenever the shift of wind should indicate that the storm had traveled far enough to bring us out of its southwestern quarter into the southeastern. Any shipmaster will understand how a vessel caught in a typhoon to windward of the Paracels and entering it from the south would find the port tack the wrong one to get into the storm and the right one to get out of it.

With infinite difficulty and risk, the ship was got round on the starboard tack and headed about southwest. She met her new course with a frightful lurch and then a bound and plunge as if determined to do her best. But it was asking too much. She made no headway, and those dread rocks, like a magnet, were dragging her to leeward as fast as before. Three or four hours must settle our fate. We watched the barometer. Will it never stop falling? Does it mean that we are nearing the center? Shall we go down in that horrible vortex? Or will the storm keep us up until it can dash us on those ghastly reefs? If the cyclone is of great diameter, or is passing slowly, the wind must hold from the same quarter for a long time and there will be no escaping the shoals. Better be on the port tack. That might give us a ghost of a chance. Preparations were made accordingly for wearing ship. But by this time she had become quite unmanageable. In that weltering mob of a sea, with enormous pyramids of black water rushing at her from all directions at once, half submerging her and then in the next breath pitching her out on the tip of a roaring billow, she would not mind her helm, nor pay the least attention to any of the more common arts of seamanship.

As a last resort a desperate experiment was tried, which I had read of but had never expected to witness. The ship was under bare poles and not a rag of canvas could live on her for a moment. With an immense deal of persuasion, some of it more force than suasion, a hundred or more of the men were driven into the weather fore rigging from twenty to fifty feet above deck, where they formed a dense mass against which the hurricane drove with tremendous pressure. This was attempted by a man-of-war caught in the disastrous hurricane at Samoa in 1889; in this case the men being massed in the mizzen shrouds instead of the fore.

I have often thought of those men thus hung in mid air, and congratulated myself that it was not one of the duties of a captain's clerk to be among them. Drenched with the salt spray, benumbed, yet clinging like death to the slippery shrouds, whirled and jerked through the air by the writhing ship beneath, swept over the boiling caldron of waters now on the one side and the next instant on the other, it was a miracle that they were not every man of them snapped off and shot headlong into the sea; and all the while the black night made lurid and infernal by the phosphorescent foam, and the elements roaring together with a din more deafening and horrible than 40 million parks of artillery and as many more locomotives, all thundering, howling, booming, and screeching at once. While these poor fellows were hanging on for dear life in the fore shrouds, other men were stationed with axes to cut away the mizzenmast. The helm was put hard up. But the poor ship, lacerated and exhausted, seemed unable to make any further effort and lay helplessly wallowing and tumbling like a log. A desperate half-hour had passed since the men crept into the rigging. It seemed a week. The order was on the lips of the first lieutenant to cut away, when at last as if awaking to the situation and rousing from some dreadful swoon, she showed signs of returning life. She began to feel her helm and the terrific pressure of the wind on that black swarm in the fore rigging, and slowly and painfully began to pay off. It was a perilous moment as she swung round into the trough of the sea. Will she live through it? More likely she will roll herself under and go down. We braced ourselves and held our breath. Then both batteries went under, as indeed they had been doing all the evening. But there was good stuff in her yet.

As she came to her course, with a few tremendous lurches she shook herself clear of the mountains of water on her decks and rose heavily and wearily on the next wave. Once fairly round on the port tack it was found that the change had come that the far-seeing barometer had already predicted. The wind was hauling to the westward. This meant that the center of the storm was directly north of us and was rapidly passing. It meant also that we were not to leave our bones on the Paracels. As it proved, the evolution had been performed under the fiercest blast we had that night. It was nine o'clock when we wore ship. The storm continued to rage with fury, but the squalls came less frequently and were less spiteful. By midnight it had so far spent itself that it was safe to begin to make sail. With the close-reefed foresail on her again she was steadier, and, crippled as she was, did her best to crawl out of the dread neighborhood in which she had so nearly met her doom. What that doom would have been you can imagine from the memory of scores of proud ships that have sailed out on the mysterious sea, from which no tidings have ever come back to the wives and mothers who watched and wept and prayed. Or if the grim Paracels had been our sepulchre, death would have been still more tragic. There are no islands in that submerged continent of graves; no friendly strand on which a drowning waif might possibly be cast; nothing but murderous ledges and wild tearing coral reefs. Had the *Saratoga* struck there, five minutes would have sufficed to rend ship and crew into shreds and scatter them throughout miles of quite angry surf.

The next morning was a peaceful Sabbath. When I went on deck at six bells, the sun was shining. The sea had quieted down, and a languid breeze was wafting us gently along; sky and ocean demurely innocent—apparently no recollection of the wild orgies of the night before. The morning watch was sending down the fragments of split sails and bending others in their stead. The decks were still lumbered with debris and everything drenched and soaked. You may remember how Bessus, the poltroon in one of Beaumont and Fletcher's plays, described his memorable drubbing: "I think I have been cudgelled by all nations, and almost all religions." If our poor old belabored craft could have put herself into rhetoric, that is doubtless the way in which she would have expressed her feelings. Three boats were missing, torn away davits and all. Spare spars in the main chains were gone, ports smashed in, and loads of the smaller deck furniture, battle-axes, cutlasses, handspikes, life buoys, halyard racks, and the like, washed overboard. During the night the spanker boom had got adrift and taken command of the poop, sweeping it clean of everything; and cutting up the heavy iron rail on both sides had twirled it into the mizzen rigging like so much wire.

There was no loss of life. Many of the crew were half drowned in the scuppers, or cut and bruised as they were swept to and fro across the decks in avalanches of waves, ropes, spars, men, and everything movable in a jumble together. But the "Thing" was passed, and we had come out alive. It was an immense satisfaction to find that we were still on top of the ocean instead of the ocean on top of us. A week sufficed to repair damages and make things shipshape. And we started up the seas again to renew our quest of pirates and glory.

Neither glory nor pirates were to be had for the asking. But we had the luck to encounter one episode that is pleasant to remember. One forenoon, a fortnight after our mauling by the tempest, the lookout at the masthead sung out, "Sail ho!" It was but a speck on the distant waves, perhaps a derelict, or a tangle of jetsam from some foundering bark. But as we approached we could see something moving on board. It proved to be a Chinese fishing boat, dismasted in a typhoon three days after ours. The wretched survivors were waving frantic signals of distress. We sent a boat and took them off. For nearly a fortnight they had been drifting about on the waves, provisions gone, and nothing left but to surrender to starvation or the merciless sea. They were helped on board, six gaunt skeletons; and the first thing they did was to drop on their knees and knock their foreheads on the deck, worshiping officers and crew alike for rescuing them from death. I never saw a more pathetic sight. The next thing was to turn them over to the medical department for such mild nutrition as would save them from starving. Then we went to quarters, cast loose the guns, and began blazing away at the dismasted junk in order to sink her out of the way of passing ships. But somehow the balls were contrary; the sea was rough, and she got only four shots out of a whole broadside. As she did not seem disposed to be good and go to the bottom, another boat was sent to set her on fire. We filled away and left her blazing astern.

Another week and our time was up. We plodded our way back to the old berth, and without pirates, without glory, but with a lot of experience, we came to anchor as usual in Macao roads.

An Indictment for Piracy, 1812

At the Circuit Court of the United States, for the First Circuit, holden at Boston, within and for the District of Massachusetts, on the twentieth day of October, A. D. 1812, before

Hon. JOSEPH STORY, *Presiding Judge*,
Hon. JOHN DAVIS, *District Judge*.

The Grand Jurors returned *three Bills of Indictment* against SAMUEL TULLEY and JOHN DALTON, of Philadelphia, in the State of Pennsylvania, mariners. One for PIRACY, on the Statute of the U. S. passed 30th April, 1790—for piratically and feloniously running away with the schooner *George Washington*, from the care, custody, and possession of Uriah Phillips Levy, her master. Another for the MURDER of George Cummings, on the high seas, on the 20th day of January last. Another for *feloniously scuttling* and *casting away said vessel* on the high seas, on the 21st day of January last, against the provisions of a law of Congress in such case made and provided. Copies of these several Indictments, and a list of thirty-six Jurors to be called at the trial, were given to the prisoners, and in pursuance of a statute provision for the assignment of causes, JAMES T.

Austin and Peter O. Thacher Esquires, were assigned them by the court to assist them in their defence. On Tuesday, 28th October, the prisoners were brought into court, and arraigned on the first Indictment.

The Indictment was then read in the following words:

United States of America, $\Big\}$
Massachusetts District, s. s.

At a Circuit Court of the United States for the First Circuit, began and held at Boston, within and for the District of Massachusetts, on the twentieth day of October, in the year of our Lord eighteen hundred and twelve.

The Jurors for the United States, within and for the District and Circuit aforesaid, upon their oath, present that Samuel Tulley, late of the city of Philadelphia, in the District of Pennsylvania, mariner, and John Dalton, late also of the same city of Philadelphia, mariner, on the tenth day of January now last past, with force and arms upon the high seas, near a place called the Isle of May, one of the Cape Verd Islands, and out of the jurisdiction of any particular state, they, the said Samuel Tulley and John Dalton, being then and there mariners of a certain vessel of the United States, being a schooner, called the George Washington, then and there belonging, and appertaining to a certain citizen or citizens of the United States, to the Jurors aforesaid as yet unknown; of which said vessel, one Uriah Phillips Levy, a citizen of the said United States, was then and there master and commander, piratically and feloniously did then and there run away with the aforesaid vessel called the George Washington, and with certain goods and merchandize, that is to say, fourteen quarter casks of Teneriffe wine, and two thousand Spanish milled dollars, being altogether of the value of five thousand dollars, which were then and there on board of the vessel aforesaid; they, the said Samuel Tulley and John Dalton, during all the time aforesaid, being then and there mariners of the said vessel, and in and on board of the same on the high seas as aforesaid, against the peace and dignity of the United States, and the force of the statute in such case made and provided.

And the Jurors aforesaid, upon their oath aforesaid, do further present, that the said Samuel Tulley and John Dalton, on the said tenth day of January now last past, then being mariners of, in and on board the said schooner or vessel called the George Washington, belonging and appertaining to certain citizens of the United States, (to the Jurors aforesaid as yet unknown,) with force and arms upon the high seas aforesaid, and out of the jurisdiction of any particular state, near a place called the Isle of May, one of the Cape Verd Islands, in and on board the said schooner or vessel called the George Washington, whereof the said Uriah Phillips Levy, a citizen of the said United States, then and there was master as aforesaid; the same schooner or vessel, and the tackle and apparel thereof, of the value of five thousand dollars of lawful money of the United States, and certain goods and merchandize, to wit, fourteen quarter casks of Teneriffe wine, of the value of one thousand dollars of like lawful money, and two thousand Spanish milled dollars, of the value of two thousand dollars of like lawful money, of the goods and chattels of certain citizens of the said United States, (to the Jurors aforesaid as yet unknown,) then and there being in the said schooner or vessel, under the care and custody, and in the possession of the said Uriah Phillips Levy as master of the said schooner or vessel, then and there upon the high seas aforesaid, near the said Isle of May, and out of the jurisdiction of any particular state, with force and arms as aforesaid, from the care, custody, and possession of the said Uriah Phillips Levy, piratically and feloniously did steal, take and run away with. They, (the said Samuel Tulley and John Dalton,) then and there being mariners of the said vessel, and in and board the said vessel, upon the high seas as aforesaid—against the peace and dignity of the said United States, and the force of the Statute in such case made and provided.

And the Jurors aforesaid, upon their oath aforesaid, do further present, that after the commission of the said offences, to wit, on the fifteenth of July now last past, the said Samuel and John, the offenders aforesaid, were first brought into the said Massachusetts District, and that the said Massachusetts District, is the District into which the said offenders were as aforesaid first brought.

A true Bill,

HUMPHREY DEVEREUX, *Foreman*

GEORGE BLAKE, { *U. S. Attorney, for Massachusetts District.*

Whereupon the Clerk of the court asked them, if they were guilty or not guilty? to which they severally answered, not guilty; and it was then demanded of them, how they would be tried? to which they said, by God and their country; and the Clerk rejoined, God send you a good deliverance. The prisoners being ready for trial, a Jury was empannelled, and after several challenges by the prisoners, the following gentlemen were sworn to pass between them and the United States.

WILLIAM STEARNS, of *Salem*, Foreman;
SAMUEL HARRINGTON, of *Worcester*;
JOHN CLARK, of *Cambridge*;
JOTHAM LINCOLN, of *Hingham*;
ABRAHAM TUCKERMAN, of *Boston*;
HAWKES FEARING, Jun. of *Hingham*;
SAMUEL GATES, of *Worcester*;
SOLOMON RICHARDS, of *Roxbury*;
BENJAMIN SEAVER, *Do.*
JOSIAH SEAVERNS, *Do.*
JAMES LEWIS, of *Dorchester*;
ISAAC N. FIELD, *Do.*

The case was then opened by George Blake, Esq. *Attorney for the United States.* He said it was his painful, but necessary duty, to lay before the Court and Jury, the law on which the Indictment was founded, and the evidence which would support the charge against the prisoners at the bar; and in order to enable them more fully to understand the story which the witnesses would substantiate, he should present them with a general outline of what he expected the government would be able to offer in evidence. The Attorney then read the law as follows:

"If any person or persons shall commit upon the high seas, or in any river, haven, bason or bay out of the jurisdiction of any particular state, murder or robbery, or any other offence, which, if committed within the body of a county, would be punishable with death; or if any captain or mariner of any ship or other vessel, shall piratically and feloniously run away with such ship or vessel, or any goods or merchandize to the value of fifty dollars, or yield up such ship or vessel voluntarily to any pirate, or if any seaman shall lay violent hands upon his commander, thereby to hinder and prevent his fighting in defence of his ship or goods committed to his trust, or shall make a revolt in the ship, every such offender shall be deemed, taken, and adjudged to be a pirate and felon, and being thereof convicted, shall suffer death. And the trial of crimes committed on the high seas, or in any place out of the jurisdiction of any particular state, shall be in the district where the offender is apprehended, or where he may first be brought."

The Attorney then gave a summary and candid statement of the expected evidence, and proceeded to call the witnesses.

JAMES HOLMES called and sworn.

He said he brought the prisoners at the bar, together with John Owen, a black man, from the Island of St. Lucie to the United States; that they were delivered to him as prisoners by the authority of the Island, to be brought to the United States; that the first port lie made was Martha's Vineyard; that the three men were delivered to the civil authority, and committed to prison in New-Bedford, and afterwards brought to Boston.

URIAH PHILLIPS LEVY called and sworn.

He said he was the master of the schooner George Washington, and a part-owner jointly with two other American citizens; that she was a new vessel, American registered; was built in the state of Delaware, and had not been to sea till the voyage in question. On the 17th October, 1811, he sailed from the Delaware, on a voyage to Teneriffe and elsewhere. His crew consisted of Samuel Tulley his mate, John Dalton a foremost hand—the prisoners; a sailor called Neal, Daniel Hopkins, George Cummings, and John Owen, cook. On the 13th day of December the schooner arrived at Teneriffe, landed the cargo and took on board 14 quarter casks of wine, and $2500 in specie. On 23d December sailed from Teneriffe to the Isle of May, one of the Cape de Verd Islands, where they arrived on the fourth of January. That a proper and convenient place for anchorage was pointed out to him by an American captain who lay there, and the schooner was moored in about ten fathoms of water, by two cables, one 9½ the other 8½ inch, 75 and 60 fathoms. On the ninth of January, at 3 o'clock P. M. went on shore and left all hands on board, directing the mate to send the boat on board the brig Lambert, capt. Levi Joy, then lying there, at sun down. Joseph Neal and Daniel Hopkins came with the boat at that time, and he ordered them to return and come again for him in an hour or two. At eight o'clock Joseph and Daniel came again; they stated to him a conversation between themselves and the mate on board the schooner, which the witness was not permitted to repeat. That he immediately looked out for his vessel, but saw she had gone from the place she was moored in, and he never has seen her from that time to the present. That the next day he caused the search to be made for the anchors, which he found and weighed. The cables were fastened to them, but both cables had been cut with some sharp instrument, and from an examination of the length, he had not the least doubt they had been cut at the windlass.

On cross-examination he said, the anchorage in the Isle of May was in an open road; that there is a strong current, which is felt immediately on leaving the bay; that the schooner was a good sailer, required some pumping, and on her outward passage with a cargo of corn, they used to pump every half hour; that the last time he saw the vessel, they had been swaying up the foresail; the topsail was in the cabin; the foreyards, gib-boom and foresail were on deck; the fore-rigging had been set up and rattled down; that the vessel might have been got ready for sea in five minutes; that at the time there was only a moderate breeze, and all sail could have been set; that when he first knew the schooner had gone, it was rather dark, yet light enough to have discovered her if she had been in the bay; that no vessel was there capable of pursuing with any hope of overtaking her; that there was generally a heavy sea and swell running into the bay, and that the windlass had been whelped with four pieces of board over each end. He often left the schooner in the care of the mate before this time. Dalton complained of being sick on the voyage, but always did his duty. Joseph and Daniel left the Isle of May with his consent, in a vessel bound to the United States; he has made very careful inquiry for them, but has not been able to gain any intelligence of them, nor can he say where they are. He sent circular letters respecting his loss into every part of the United States and the West Indies, but has never obtained any information respecting his schooner. The American consul gave him such intelligence respecting men detained at St. Lucie as induced him to go there, where he received from the commanding officer 1350 dollars and his clothes, the balance being detained for expenses. The prisoners had left the Island before his arrival.

JOHN OWEN called and sworn.

He said that he lately belonged to the American schooner George Washington, commanded by captain Levy, and a few months since, sailed from Philadelphia in the said vessel to the Island of Teneriffe, and from thence to the Isle of May. Whilst lying at the Isle of May, one day after dinner, the Captain went aboard an American vessel likewise lying there, and desired the mate to send the boat for him at sunset, which was done accordingly; but the Captain did not return, and desired the boat again to be sent for him, at eight o'clock. The witness, being cook of the vessel, prepared supper at about eight o'clock in the evening, of which the mate, Samuel Tulley, partook; but the George overboard; the Mate saying, "overboard he shall go at the risque of my life;" and George was in this manner by them thrown overboard, and left in the sea.

The next day after George had been thus thrown overboard, land was seen from the vessel; it was time of evening and the Mate made the vessel lie too till morning. The Mate then caused the long boat to be hoisted out; put into it the Captain's large chest and several other things according to his wish, together with the trunks of Jack and this witness. Then made this witness get into the boat, fastened it to a line, and let the line run out (he, Owen, remaining in the boat) to a great length, then the line being made fast the boat was towed by the vessel; afterwards the boat was hauled up along side the vessel and the Mate and Jack came into it; and he knows, by what was said by the Mate and Jack, afterwards, whilst in the boat, that during the time he was towed in the boat, those two men bored holes in the bottom of the vessel in order to occasion her to sink; but so long as she remained in sight from the boat, the vessel did not sink.

When the boat had thus quitted the vessel, the Mate distributed to Jack and this witness money, consisting of dollars, which he knew to have belonged to the Captain; the Mate saying they must all keep secret every thing that had happened, and keep the money for themselves. The same evening, the boat came near to land, but being afraid of the reefs, it was made to stand out to sea again; and the next day again approached, and coming ashore, they found the land which he did not know before, to be the Island of St. Lucie in the West Indies. After they got on shore, they went to the first house on the Island, which was inhabited by persons who spoke only French, and they could not make themselves understood. The Mate and Dalton repeatedly enjoined upon the witness not to tell what had happened, but to keep it secret and to say they had run foul of a wreck and were cast away, and that the Captain had taken one boat and they another. The Mate went to town. Witness and Dalton staid till he returned, which he did after a short time, in company with the harbour master, who took them all in a boat and rowed round to the town. Dalton then went to one place to live, and the witness and the Mate lived together at another. He continued to repeat the story in which he had been instructed. He however grew uneasy in mind at being obliged to tell a lie to every body who questioned him, and resolved to disclose the whole affair; for which purpose he went one evening to captain Taylor's, an American captain, and told the truth as he has now related it. Thereupon they were all arrested, and after sometime being confined were brought here as prisoners.

On his cross-examination he said that when the vessel was said to be adrift, it was candle light, but that he could see the land from the deck. That Dalton assisted in lowering down the boat but cannot say whether he asked for leave to go ashore or not; the night was dark, cannot tell what course they steered; they set the mainsail, foresail and gib. During most of the night the Mate kept the helm; when he left it, Dalton stood at helm. He does not know if any attempts were made to put back, but the next morning there was no land in sight. From the remains of the cables, he knows both must have been cut with an axe or knife. George, the deceased, was a foreigner; the morning before he died he gave the witness his earrings and breastpin and said he should not live to see land. When the witness came upon deck and saw George struggling, he had in one hand a knife and in the other a hammer; the Mate was wounded badly in the cheek and back of his ear with the knife, and on the back of his head with the hammer; he also received a wound across his hand, which has left a scar. To a question of one of the Jurors, witness said he never heard either the Mate or Dalton express any regret for the loss of the man or seem to lay it to heart. The money which he received of the Mate, the witness said he never expended, nor did he go into any company or place of amusement in St. Lucie; and when he was arrested there, the money was taken by the officers of government.

The Attorney for the United States rested the case on this testimony.

The Counsel for the prisoners then called CAPT. BENJAMIN HARRIS, *who was accordingly sworn.* He stated that he was an experienced seaman, having been for many years conversant with the sea; that he had been at the Isle of May and the other Cape de Verd Islands. That there is a pretty regular trade wind prevailing there, which blows off the coast; that sometimes there are what is called heavy rollers, which he explained, by saying they were great billows or waves, driven in by the force of the winds or other causes, and that these were frequent in the hurricane months, but not usual in the month of January. That the anchorage at the Isle of May is very bad, by means of many anchors being lost there, which are apt to cut off the cables of vessels riding there. Vessels are apt to part their cables and drift out. His own vessel was driven out in that manner at Bona Vesta. That when a vessel was found to be adrift, an experienced seaman would in the first place make sail and endeavour to beat to windward. That in moderate weather, although there is a strong current off the Isle of May, he should not think it difficult to get back or to make the Isle of Jago, where vessels usually touch.

CAPT. MICHAEL HOPKINS called and sworn.

He corroborated the testimony of Captain Harris. He said that the anchorage ground was bad, that there were many foul anchors in the bay, vessels frequently part their cables and drift out; that in the months of August, September and November it is very rough with heavy swells and rollers; that it is not incredible that a vessel, situated as the George Washington was and short manned, might be driven off and find it very difficult to return; though he should think there would be no great difficulty, in moderate weather, in returning. That when the vessel was found to have parted her cables, it was judicious and seamanlike to make sail.

At this stage of the cause, the Court adjourned for one hour. The Jury were directed to continue together and not to converse on the case before them, but to keep their minds perfectly unbiassed until the whole cause was finished, and with the consent of the prisoners, they were permitted to take moderate refreshment.

AFTERNOON.

Court opened.—Present as before.

J. T. Austin and Peter O. Thacher Esquires, severally addressed the Jury at great length, on behalf of the prisoners; and the Reporter regrets, that he has not been permitted to make an extract from their briefs. Three points, however, were relied upon in the defence.

1st. That the whole evidence, if the witnesses for the government were credited, was not inconsistent with the accidental departure of the schooner, or at least without any criminal agency on the part of the Mate or Dalton; and that whatever events might have occurred at sea, rendering a concealment necessary when they arrived at St. Lucie, that the fact of feloniously and piratically *running away* was not made out in evidence.

2dly. That the principal witness in the case, and the witness from whom alone the facts came, by which the defendants could be charged, was John Owen, the cook, who was a single witness, suspicious in his character, and from his own testimony, although he does not *confess* himself guilty, must be deemed to be an accomplice in whatever crimes were committed. The Jury, therefore, were not only warranted in laying his evidence out of the case, but it would be their duty so to do. That to convict one man of a capital offence, on the credibility of a single witness, even of honest character, was risking too much, and incurring a greater responsibility and hazard than a Jury were warranted in assuming; but to condemn two men on the testimony of a single witness of very suspicious character, a perfect stranger, of a class of society not usually well instructed in moral principles and the obligation of an oath, swearing for his own liberty and deeply interested in the event of the prosecution, was an event which no Jury would venture to produce; and that although it might by possibility be true, that this dark coloured accomplice had told a correct story, yet that on evidence so suspicious and so liable to mistake, it was the safest and most rational judgment to pronounce, not indeed that the defendants were innocent men, but that they were not proved, by satisfactory and unimpeachable evidence, to be guilty.

3dly. That the facts, if credited, do not amount to the crime of PIRACY. The defendants, it was said, were indicted on the statute for *piratically*, as well as feloniously, running away with the schooner George Washington, from the care, custody and possession of Uriah P. Levy, the master. The word feloniously referred to the disposition and temper of mind, what in law is called *animus furandi;* and the word *piratically*, to the manner in which this disposition was exercised; and that nothing could amount to the crime of *piratically* running away with the vessel, but a larceny of the property, TOGETHER WITH such personal violence or putting in fear, as would change the crime of larceny into the more aggravated crime of robbery, if it had been committed on shore. The distinction was illustrated by the following case. If a gentleman left his horse in the care of his servant while he alighted, and the servant went off with the horse and sold him, or converted him to his own use in any other way, it would be larceny in the servant, but not robbery; but if the servant or any other person, while the master was riding his horse, had with force and violence, or by threats compelled the master to dismount, and the servant had then rode off with the horse, this would be robbery. This addition of force changes the nature of the crime and increases the punishment—and by the laws of the U. S. the robber is punished with death, while the thief is subjected to a limited imprisonment. The Counsel contended, that the same distinction existed between the crimes of larceny and piracy; and they quoted from a variety of law writers, and from analogous reasoning to prove their position, and finally said, that if the mate or seamen, who were the servants of capt. Levy, had exercised any personal violence upon him and threatened him, and then run away with the schooner, it would be *piratical;* but if they had watched an opportunity in the absense of the captain, when they could get possession without such force or threats, and had run away with her, it was not piracy, but larceny; and the prisoners, although amenable to justice on another Indictment, for an offence less heinous and not capital, could not be found guilty of the crime charged upon them in this Indictment.

A distinction was also attempted to be made in the operation of the evidence on the defendants separately, with a view to shew that in whatever light the conduct of Tulley might be viewed, Dalton was not a principal, but only accessary.

In concluding his remarks, Mr. Austin, of Counsel for the prisoners, addressed the Jury in words of the following import, as nearly as we can repeat them from our minutes.

The defendants, gentlemen, are in your hands. If there exists a reasonable doubt as to the law or the evidence, that doubt will save them. Fortunately for our country, a scene like the present rarely presents itself in our Courts of Justice. I persuade myself, the times in which we live have not destroyed the sensibility which such a scene should excite. We hear, indeed, almost on every gale, the dreadful deeds of war and battle, and grow more and more familiar with death. Among the many who are falling around us, two lives like those of the unhappy men at the bar, may not be thought much addition to the melancholy catalogue. Yet, gentlemen, when the law, which is made for the protection of human life, deems it necessary to put that life in jeopardy, not for any injury to the lives of other members of the community, but for a mere injury to personal property; there is much, very much for a Jury to consider.

If by your verdict, the defendants should be called to pass through the dark valley of the shadow of death, they will at least have the consolation of knowing, that their fate has been sealed by an impartial and honourable Jury. But if the reverse of this should be the case; if your verdict opens their prison doors, and restores them to a new existence, chastened by the dangers they have incurred, and bound to honesty by the perils they have passed, the reflection of having returned to them their lives, which the law this day puts into your hands, will be to you a source of the sweetest consolation, at that awful hour when your lives shall be required by the great Judge of Nature. Gentlemen, the defendants are in your power: I can only repeat for them the humane wish of the law—"GOD send them a good deliverance."

After the defence had been concluded by the Counsel for the prisoners, GEORGE BLAKE, Esq. addressed the Jury on the part of the prosecution, and applied the evidence to the several points on which it was necessary for the Jury to be satisfied. He contended that it was utterly impossible, under the circumstances which had been stated, that the schooner could have drifted by accident from her moorings, and equally so, that any other persons than the prisoners could have been instrumental in the perpetration of the crime. He enforced to the Jury the strong and violent presumptions of guilt, which the testimony of capt. Levy alone furnished against the prisoners. From his testimony it was beyond contradiction, that the vessel had been at the Isle of May, and that suddenly she departed, and had never since been heard of; that the Mate and Dalton were on board, and the Mate having her in charge. That the Captain's chest of clothes, and some of his money had been carried by the prisoners to St. Lucie, where they were found by capt. Levy, who received them from the hands of the legal authority. That the vessel was feloniously taken, is also apparent from his testimony, because the fact to which he swears positively, that on examination the cables were found to have been cut, is irreconcilable with any other supposition. The testimony of Owen, the cook, is therefore not *necessary*, although in a case of this kind it is satisfactory to obtain all the information which the nature of the case admits. His statement is in affirmance of capt. Levy's, and is corroborated by it so far as both witnesses were capable of knowing the same facts. It is only an enlarged and more circumstantial story to which he testifies. The Captain had given the outlines of the horrible picture, Owen had filled up the dark particulars of the scene. In law, even an accomplice was admissable as a witness, and by every principle of common sense, his evidence would be credited if it was probable, consistent, and corroborated by facts independent of it, and known to exist. His statement of the departure from the Isle of May and arrival at St. Lucie, are not only probably, but certainly true; his story is consistent, clear, and uncontradicted in any of its parts; after an able and most ingenious cross-examination, nothing appears to make his statement in the least degree ambiguous or uncertain. He tells a plain, unvarnished tale of his whole course of life. The great advantage of a trial by Jury is, that Jurors have an opportunity of seeing the witnesses, and judging of the credit due them by the manner in which they testify. In this instance he left it to the Jury to determine whether they ever saw a more unembarrassed, and intelligent, and cautious witness; and whether he was an accomplice or not, it was impossible to resist the force of his testimony.

But was he an accomplice? His own statement, and the circumstances he has related, shew that he was not. He had, probably, no will of his own. In the most menial capacity, a mere drudge, necessary to the new masters of the vessel, but too insignificant to be for a moment consulted, he had no choice but to obey their commands. He was a man more sinned against, than sinning; and as soon as he had an opportunity, evinced his regard for the laws of God and man, which he had seen so flagrantly violated, by voluntarily giving evidence to the first American captain whom he was able to meet, by means of which, the defendants were arrested and brought to the bar of their country.

The Attorney considered at large, and replied to the various arguments which had been urged by the Counsel for the prisoners, and contended that every felonious running away with a vessel on the high seas, was a piratical act within the statute; and if the Jury believed the testimony which had been adduced, the crime contemplated by law and charged in the Indictment had been perpetrated, and the Jury would not hesitate in a verdict of Guilty.

After the arguments had closed, the learned Judges severally addressed the Jury. Each of them recapitulated the testimony, and stated in a very fair, perspicuous, and impartial manner, the operation and effect of it, as well in favour as against the prisoners at the bar. On the question of law, which they said had been very properly raised by the Counsel for the defendants, they had bestowed as much attention as was possible during the course of the trial; and both their Honours stated explicitly their opinion, that a felonious running away with the vessel, was a piratical act within the meaning of the act of Congress, and subjected the perpetrators to capital punishment. The prisoners had had a fair and patient hearing; the Jury had paid close attention to the evidence, and the arguments which had been addressed to them. It was a question of evidence, and they were the sole and exclusive arbitrators. It was also a question to be settled by the judgment, and not by the feelings. The powerful appeal, that had been made to their sensibility, might cause them to regret the obligations imposed upon them; but as Jurors, the oath of God was upon them. They had a duty to do, which it would be criminal in them to omit. They were bound as well by their allegiance to their country, as by their tenderness for the prisoners. This duty might be painful, but it was, nevertheless, imperious. If in their consciences they believed the defendants were guilty, they were bound to say so, and leave the consequences to Providence. Theirs was a duty prescribed by justice; the more delightful attribute of mercy, was, by the law, placed in other hands; in hands which never failed to exercise it, where the circumstances of the case warranted the interposition of executive favour. A reasonable doubt would operate in favour of life; but the doubt must be reasonable; not the mere suggestions of fancy, and the airy creations of mere possibility, but a reasonable and conscientious doubt. To such, a Juror was bound to listen; with such a doubt he never ought to condemn. If such a doubt remained, the prisoners were entitled to an acquital.

The trial commenced at ten o'clock in the morning, and it was eleven at night when the case was given in charge to the Jury. Officers were sworn to keep them in some convenient place until they had agreed upon a verdict, and not to suffer any person to speak to them unless by order of Court, and the Court adjourned until the next day, (Wednesday,) at nine o'clock, A.M.

Wednesday. The Court opened. Present Judges Story and Davis. The prisoners were brought into Courtand the Jury came in; being called, they severally answered to their names. It was then asked of them whether they had agreed on a verdict, to which the foreman answered they had NOT. The Court thereupon inquired if any further explanation of the law was necessary, to which the foreman replied that the Jury could not agree, that the facts in the case amounted to *Piracy*. The Court then repeated the substance of their former charge on this point, and ordered the Jury to withdraw for further consideration. The Jury accordingly retired. In about three hours they came again into Court. The prisoners were also brought in, and answered to their names.

Clerk. Gentlemen of the Jury, have you agreed upon a verdict?

Jury. Yes.

Clerk. Who shall speak for you?

Jury. The Foreman.

Clerk. Mr. Foreman, rise and look upon the prisoners. Prisoners, look upon the Foreman. Mr. Foreman, what say you? Is Samuel Tulley, *one of the prisoners at the Bar,* Guilty *or not* Guilty?

Foreman. GUILTY!

Clerk. Mr. Foreman, what say you? Is John Dalton, *one of the prisoners at the Bar,* Guilty, *or not* Guilty?

Foreman. GUILTY!

The next day the following motion was filed by the Prisoner's counsel.

United States of America,
District of Massachusetts. }

Circuit Court of U. S. October Term, 1812.

The United States by Indictment *vs.*

SAMUEL TULLY AND JOHN DALTON.

And now after verdict and before judgment the said Samuel and John, by their counsel assigned them by the Court, now move the Court here for a new trial of the issue joined on the said indictment for the following causes, viz.

1. Because the honorable Court in committing the cause to the jury who tried the same misdirected them in a material point of law; in this, that they directed the jury if they believed from the evidence in the case that the defendants feloniously run away with the vessel and merchandize mentioned in the indictment, it constituted the crime of piracy within the meaning of the statue on which the indictment is founded.

2. Because the verdict of the jury was rendered against the weight of evidence, they having found the defendants guilty of *piratically* and feloniously running away with the vessel and merchandize mentioned in the indictment from the care, custody and possession of Uriah Phillips Levy, the master thereof, although no evidence was offered them to show that any force or violence were exercised on the said Levy, or that he or any other person were thereby put in fear, but the evidence on the part of the government proved the contrary.

PETER O. THACHER.
JAMES T. AUSTIN.

J. T. AUSTIN addressed the Court. He said that having had a very fair and full opportunity of addressing the Court through the Jury at the trial on the subject matter of the present motion, the Counsel for the prisoners did not propose to occupy the further time of their Honors with a recapitulation of former arguments. In justice, however, to the defence which the Court had entrusted to their care, they deemed it proper to present these objections in the present shape, that they might command the deliberate reflection and judgment, which their immense importance to the prisoners entitled them to receive. They were the only planks in the shipwreck of their hopes, on which they had any prospect of floating to a shore of safety. It would be for their Honors to decide, whether this too should fail them.

On the subject of a new trial, he would merely remark, that, although in capital cases it had not been very usual, yet the case of United States *vs.* Fries, in the Circuit Court of the United States, for the District of Pennsylvania, and the case of Commonwealth *vs.* Hardy, in the Supreme Judicial Court of this State, in both of which cases, after verdict of Guilty, new trials had been awarded, were, in point to shew the power and practice of the Court, where circumstances authorised the interference of their discretion.

The motion was received by the Court and held under consideration until Monday, 9th November. The prisoners were then again brought into Court and opinion of their Honors were severally delivered.

His Honor Judge Davis. A pirate is one, says Hawkins, who, to enrich himself, either by surprise or force, sets upon merchants or other traders by sea to spoil them of their goods; this description, as is observed by a respectable writer of our own country, is applicable merely to piracy by the law of nations. Piracy by the common law consists in committing those acts of robbery and depredation upon the high seas, which if committed on shore would amount to felony there.

The description of the offence in the first part of the 8th Section of our statutes is analogous to the common law description, but the statute proceeds in correspondence with the statute of 11 and 12 of William 3, to make certain other acts piracy, which would not be so at common law, and among the rest an atrocious breach of trust, by any Captain or mariner of any ship or vessel, in running away with such ship or vessel, or any goods or merchandize, to the value of fifty dollars. To constitute this offence, the act must be done as the statute expresses it, piratically and feloniously. Unlawful depredation, says a respectable writer of the civil law, is of the essence of piracy, and this, I apprehend is true relative to the piracy thus created by statute as to piracies by common law. The *animus depredandi*, as it is expressed by Molloy, is to be determined by the Jury, from facts and circumstances given in evidence, and is comprehended in the term *feloniously*, which refers to the mind, will or intention. If the Jury find the act of running away with the ship or vessel and goods, to be done feloniously, they find it to be done without any justification or excuse; they find it to be done wilfully and fraudulently, animo furandi, lucricausa; and having been committed with the other qualities and accidents mentioned in the statutes, i. e. at sea, by persons bearing the relation to the ship, of Captain or mariners, and the property plundered, amounting to fifty dollars—such felonious act is in contemplation of the Statute piratical.

Thus the Jury were instructed, and aker the serious deliberation which the nature and magnitude of the case necessarily impose, I do not think the direction erroneous.

In regard to the second objection, if force were necessary to be proved in order to constitute piracy, there was sufficient evidence in the case of a forcible taking of the property in question; nor can it be contended, I think, from the evidence, that no person was put in fear. But it is said that no evidence was offered to shew, that any force or violence were exercised on Levy, the master, in whose care, custody, and possession, the vessel and goods were alleged to be; or that he was put in fear. This objection is grounded on an analogy to robbery on land; an analogy too strictly pursued in the argument on this head. Even at common law, piracy might be committed without the characteristics, which this objection considers as essential. If a ship shall ride at anchor, says Molloy, and the mariners shall be part in their ship's boat, and the rest on shore, and none shall be in the ship, yet if a pirate shall attack and rob her, the same is piracy. And on this Statute there can be no question, as appears to me, that actual force on the master or other person in possession, is not necessary to constitute the offence. The Statute had in view the prevention of atrocious violation of trust by persons standing in particular relations to the ship. Officers and mariners may combine feloniously to run away with the ship and cargo, without any person being put in fear in the sense considered in the objection, and yet it would be clearly a piratical act with in the true intent and meaning of the Statute.

It is not necessary now to consider whether a new trial could properly be directed by the Court, if the objections, or either of them were well founded. Being persuaded that the Jury were not misdirected in matter of law, and that the Indictment is legally maintainable without proof of actual force or violence on the master or others, or that they were put in fear, I am of opinion that the motion be over-ruled.

The honourable JUDGE STORY stated at full length his reasons on this point, which concurring with those of Hon. Judge Davis, it is not necessary to recapitulate. The motion was accordingly over-ruled.

GEORGE BLAKE, ESQ. then rose and addressed the Court in a solemn and impressive speech, in which he recapitulated the proceedings on the indictment, the verdict of the Jury, and the law which denounced capital punishment on such conviction; and concluded, by stating it to be his duty to move, and he accordingly did now move the Court to proceed to pronounce the sentence of the law.

HIS HONOR JUDGE STORY then addressed the prisoners as follows:

SAMUEL TULLEY—JOHN DALTON,

You have been charged by the Grand Inquest of the United States, for the District of Massachusetts, with the crime of piratically and feloniously running away with the schooner George Washington, commanded by Uriah Phillips Levy, against the Statute of the United States in such cases made and provided. You have been duly furnished with copies of the Indictment, and also with lists of the Jury, who, upon your trial, were to pass between you and the United States. You have had counsel assigned you by the Court, according to the benign provision of the law in capital cases. You have been arraigned on the Indictment, and have severally pleaded not guilty. You have been tried by an impartial Jury of your country, and at the trial had assistance and arguments of able, and learned, and eloquent counsel in your defence. You have been severally found guilty by the verdict of your peers. You have excepted to the opinions of the Court in matters of law at your trial. These exceptions have been fully considered by the Court, and upon mature deliberation have been over-ruled. You have now been brought into Court to receive the judgment of the law, and the District Attorney has now, in your presence, moved the Court to proceed to judgment.

What reasons have you now to shew to the Court, why they should not pronounce sentence against you?

No reasons being shewn, the learned Judge proceeded as follows:

Before I proceed to the painful duty imposed upon me by the law, a cup of bitterness which I would most willingly put aside, I shall make a few remarks, which I hope will impress your minds with the most solemn conviction of the turpitude of your offence, and with the mercy of God, incline your hearts to contrition and repentance.

The crime of which you have been convicted is of a most odious nature; it is wilful, malicious, deliberate piracy. Among all civilized nations it is esteemed as an offence, which places you in enmity with the whole world, which banishes you from the hospitality and the protection of society, and consigns you to an ignominious death. In the present case, it has been attended with still more aggravated circumstances than usually attend the depredations of unauthorized plunderers of the property of their fellow-men. You were a part of a crew of a vessel navigated under the flag of the United States, entrusted by the owners, with their confidence and property, and urged by every honorable motive to an honest discharge of your respective duties.

The security of the commerce of the country, the maintenance of the good order of society, and the lives of thousand of your fellow-citizens are intimately connected with the good faith and honesty of seamen. How have you repaid the confidence reposed in you by the esteem of your commander? You have been treacherous and deceitful. You have had no adequate temptations, and no apology for your deliberate violations of the law.

You sought the darkness of night to cover deeds which would not bear the light. You had time to consider and reflect. The midnight stars shone with disastrous light on your wickedness; the deep silence of the hour, when nature pauses as upon the brink of dissolution, gravely warned you of your fate. The morning rose in its splendour to call you back to repentance; yet you returned not; yet you sought not the forgiveness of the world, by returning to the bosom of society, and repenting of your sin. Shall I stop or shall I proceed? One crime leads on the way to another, and every step in guilt is but a new incitement to urge another. One of your companions bowed down in spirit, overwhelmed with self-humiliation, approached you in the fulness of his sorrow, and repented and implored your mercy. Did your bowels yearn with mercy towards him?

Did you endeavour to soften his woe or to seek with him the path of future peace by a return to virtue? I dread even to remember the hateful tale! His tears and entreaties were of no effect.

I would not willingly accuse, much less would I unheard condemn you. The hour of his fate drew nigh; in the deep gloom of the night there was a most foul and unnatural murder. You heard his dying groans; you saw his last struggle; you took his lifeless corpse and plunged it amid the sullen waves. The ocean received him to its bosom, and returned back its short, but awful murmurs. Were you guilty of this atrocious crime? I will not say; let your own hearts and consciences declare. The morrow saw no tears and no contrition. The deeds of night were but the precursors of a new destruction. The vessel was herself the next object of ruin; and she was wantonly scuttled and left to sink to the bottom of the sea. Foul and deliberate falsehoods closed the horrible history of your crime.

Yet though these transactions were veiled from human eyes, think not that they escaped the all-seeing eyes of that being who createth and governeth the universe. At the solemn hour when deep sleep falls upon the sons of men, his ever-watchful mind is awake. When darkness surrounds the plunder of the public pirate, he is ever present and marks the wanderings of wickedness. When MURDER riots in supposed security, he hears the voice of dying innocence, and HIS OWN RIGHT ARM SHALL AVENGE THE DEEP DAMNATION OF THE DEED.

I would not willingly afflict you in your fallen condition, but I must awaken your consciences to an awful sense of your impending fate. You are now soon to be cut off from life, and these cheering beams which now surround you will soon be shut forever from your sight. The grave will become your cold and and solitary residence, and the places that now know you shall know you no more. You are in the bloom and vigour of your days, yet society has found it necessary to arrest them, and to send you, *with all your imperfections on your heads*, to another world. Think, oh think, after what has happened how you can appear before that dread tribunal, and that OMNIPOTENT JUDGE who searcheth the hearts and trieth the reins of all men. From his sentence there is no appeal, and before him you must soon appear to render an account of all the deeds done in the body. There can be no concealment or shelter there; the accusing spirit of conscience will rise in judgment against you, and the voice of your poor unfortunate brother will be heard from the very depths of the ocean.

Let me entreat you, tenderly and earnestly entreat you, as dying sinners, to turn from your wicked thoughts; to ponder on the errors of your ways, and with penitence and humiliation to seek the altars of our holy religion. Let me entreat you to pray for mercy and forgiveness from that righteous God, whom you have so justly offended. The time, perhaps, may not be too late.

The glory of CHRISTIANITY may yet brighten your declining days, and THE SPIRIT OF REDEEM-ING GRACE may drop a tear on your sins and blot them out forever.

I now proceed to pronounce the awful sentence of the law upon your crime:

WHEREUPON all and singular the premises being seen, and by the said Judges of the said Court here fully understood—it is considered by the Court here, that the said Samuel Tulley and John Dalton be, and they hereby are severally deemed, taken, and adjudged to be pirates and fel-ons;—and that they, the said Samuel Tulley and John Dalton, and each of them, be hanged by the neck until they, and each of them, be dead. And it is further ordered and considered by the Court here, that the Marshal of this District do, on peril of what may fall thereon, cause execution to be done in the premises aforesaid, upon them, the said Samuel Tulley and John Dalton, on the tenth day of December next ensuing, between the hours of ten o'clock in the forenoon, and three in the afternoon of the same day; and that they, the said Samuel Tulley and John Dalton, be now taken from hence to the gaol in Boston, in the District of Massachusetts, from whence they came, there, or in some other safe and convenient prison within the District aforesaid, to be closely kept until the day of execution, and from thence, on the day appointed for execution as aforesaid, to be taken to the place of execution in Boston aforesaid, there to be hanged as aforesaid.

I recommend you to the mercy of ALMIGHTY GOD, before whom we shall all one day appear; and I pray that he may succour and support you in the hour of trial, and I now bid you AN ETER-NAL FAREWELL.

The Last of the Sea Rovers: The Riff Coast Pirates

W. B. LORD

O nay, O nay, then said our King,
   O nay, this must not be,
To yield to such a rover
   Myself will not agree;
He hath deceived the Frenchman,
   Likewise the King of Spain,
And how can he be true to me,
   That hath been false to twain?

OLD SEA SONG OF THE YEAR 1620.

Probably by this time the greater part of the piratical craft along the Riff coast has been destroyed, and the long-promised Moorish gunboat stationed there to protect foreign shipping. These steps have doubtless been hastened by the fact that the pirates, unfortunately for themselves, attacked a vessel some little time ago belonging to the Sultan of Morocco. For years past the Governments of several European Powers have sought to put friendly pressure upon the Sultan of Morocco to effectually stop the depredations of the Riffian coast pirates. No strong measures, however, were really taken until the above episode occurred. It is said that in early days the Moors were some time in accustoming themselves to the perils of the deep. At first they marvelled greatly at "those that go down to the sea in ships, and have their business in great waters," but they did not hasten to follow their example. One eminent ruler of ancient times, in that region, when asked what the sea was like, replied, "The sea is a huge beast which silly folk ride like worms on logs." But it afterwards became clear that the Moors had a strong fancy for the "worms" and "logs" too. They gave up marvelling at those who went to sea, and went on it themselves in search of plunder. The risk, the uncertainty, the danger, the sense of superior skill and ingenuity, that attract the adventurous spirit, and the passion for sport, are stated by some writers to have brought such a state of things into existence. One fact seems to be pretty certain, that when these depredations were first made, they took the form of reprisals upon the Spaniards. No sooner was Granada fallen, than thousands of desperate Moors left the land, disdaining to live under a Spanish yoke. Settling along a portion of the northern coast of Africa, they immediately proceeded to first attack all Spanish vessels that could be found. Their quickness and knowledge of the coasts gave them the opportunity of reprisals for which they longed. Probably this got monotonous in course of time, for in their wild sea courses they took to harrying the vessels belonging to other nations, and so laid the foundation for a race of pirates, which has continued down to quite recently. As nowadays, the Moors cruised in boats from the commencement of their marauding expeditions. Each man pulled an oar, and knew how to fight as well as row. Drawing little water, a small squadron of these craft could be pushed up almost any creek, or lie hidden behind a rock, till the enemy came in sight. Then oars out, and a quick stroke for a few minutes. Next they were alongside their unsuspecting prey, and pouring in a first volley. Ultimately the prize was usually taken, the crew put in irons, and the pirates returned home with their capture, no doubt being received with acclamation upon their arrival.

As far back as the sixteenth century the Spanish forts at Alhucemas—not to mention other places—were established for the purpose of repressing piracy in its vicinity. Considerable interest is attached to several of the piracies committed during the past few years, as they culminated in strong representations being made to the Sultan of Morocco by the various Governments under whose flag the respective vessels sailed. Some of them went so far as to send warships to cruise along the Riffian coast. This step apparently had some moral effect upon the pirates, for from that time onwards attacks upon foreign vessels practically ceased. Something more than this, however, was needed, for no one could say how soon the marauding expeditions might be renewed upon a larger scale than ever, so as to make up for lost opportunities. On August 14, 1897, the Italian three-masted schooner *Fiducia* was off the coast of Morocco, in the Mediterranean, homeward bound from Pensacola to Marseilles. Here she got becalmed, and while in that condition two boats approached her from the shore. At first the crew of the *Fiducia* thought they were native fishing boats. When, however, the latter got within a hundred yards or so of the helpless vessel, the suspicions of the crew were aroused. The captain warned the Moors not to approach any nearer; a volley of bullets was returned by way of reply, followed by a regular fusillade as the boats advanced. There were only three revolvers on board the schooner, and with these the crew prepared to defend themselves. Soon, however, their supply of ammunition became exhausted, and the pirates boarded the schooner without further opposition. The vessel was at once ransacked, even the clothes of the crew being taken. The ship's own boat was lowered, and into this the marauders put their booty, and took it ashore, also carrying the captain and one of the crew with them. About an hour later another boat, containing about twenty pirates, came off and fired on the ship. The crew, seeing that they could offer no effective resistance, hid themselves away in the hold. The other pirates had left very little for the new arrivals to take, and this seemed to annoy them so much that they gave vent to their ill-feelings in several ways, not the least wanton being the pollution of the ship's fresh water. They also smashed the vessel's compass, and tore up the charts. For the next two days the crew existed on a few biscuits, which the pirates had left behind. The following day the British steamship *Oanfa*, of London, hove in sight. The crew of the schooner hoisted a shirt as a signal, which was fortunately seen, and a boat sent off in response thereto. Assistance was promptly rendered, and the *Fiducia* put in a position to resume her voyage. This was done until spoken by the Italian cruiser *Ercole*, which assisted the schooner to her destination.

In October, 1896, the French barque *Prosper Corue* was lying becalmed off Alhucemas, a place fortified by the Spaniards to keep the pirates in check, when several boats full of armed Moors seized the vessel and made the crew prisoners. They then completely pillaged the ship, removing almost everything of any use or value. While the miscreants were thus busily engaged a Spanish merchant steamship, named the *Sevilla*, happened to come along, and was in time to capture one boat and rescue several of the prisoners. The *Sevilla* then made towards the barque, but the pirates opened fire on the steamer, killing and wounding some of the crew. The Spaniard was compelled to retire, leaving the captain of the barque in the hands of the Moors. Subsequently the barque was picked up in an abandoned condition by the British steamship *Oswin*, and towed into Almeria. An arrangement was afterwards made with the pirates to release the captains of the *Fiducia* and the Portuguese barque *Rosita Faro*—a much earlier capture—and some members of both crews, in exchange for the Riffians captured by the Spanish steamer *Sevilla* and a ransom of 3,000 dollars. It was only after prolonged negotiations and a large sum of money that a French warship succeeded in obtaining the freedom of the captain of the *Prosper Corue* and a few other Frenchmen. For some reason or other, the pirates seemed very much disinclined to part with these prisoners. Only a short time before the attack on the French barque took place, a notice was issued by the British Board of Trade, in which the attention of ship-owners and masters of vessels was called to the dangers attending navigation off the coast of Morocco. The document then proceeded to detail the case of the British schooner *Mayer*, of Gibraltar, which was boarded about 10 miles from the Riff coast by twenty Moors armed with rifles and daggers. As usual, the pirates ransacked the vessel, destroyed the ensign and ship's papers, brutally assaulted the men on board, and then made off in their boat. Scarcely had the foregoing notice been generally circulated than another case of a similar character happened in connection with the Italian schooner *Scatuola*. Again, there is the Spanish cutter *Jacob*. She was running along the Moorish coast one fine summer's evening a few years since, when a boat full of pirates suddenly came alongside, and speedily upset the quietness which had previously reigned on board the *Jacob*. Five of the crew managed to escape in the cutter's boat and were picked up some days later by a passing vessel. Those who remained on board the cutter fared very badly. After the vessel had been pillaged, the rigging and sails destroyed, the men were all securely bound and left to their fate. Fortunately the weather continued fine, and the *Jacob* drifted towards the Spanish coast, where she was seen and assistance promptly rendered.

The captain of another Spanish vessel had quite a "thrilling" adventure among these pirates in May, 1892. He left Gibraltar in command of the barque *San Antonio* for Alhucemas, and when about six miles from Peñon de la Gomera a boat manned by thirteen Moors was observed to be approaching the vessel. When near enough they opened fire, and ordered the captain to lower his sails, which was done, as the Spaniards were, practically speaking, without arms. The Moors then boarded the *San Antonio* and took her in tow. When close to the land the captain was rowed ashore, and the pirates spent part of the night in unloading the cargo. Next morning the *San Antonio* was seen drifting out to sea, and the captain, who was afraid of being put to death, suggested that he should go on board and bring her back to the anchorage. Probably thinking that some of their comrades were on the barque, but unable to set the necessary canvas to return, only two Moors were sent off with the captain, and these remained in the boat when the vessel was reached. Upon gaining the deck of the barque the captain was surprised to find himself alone. Without hesitating for a moment he released the crew, who were confined below, hoisted sail and stood out to sea. The Moors who had been left in the boat were speedily cut adrift, much to their amazement, for it so happened that none of the pirates had stayed on board. No doubt they were eager to find a safe hiding-place for their plunder, and, thinking the barque quite secure till morning, took no further heed of the matter. A few days later the *San Antonio* arrived at Gibraltar, where full particulars of the outrage were furnished to the authorities. Space will not admit of details being given of the attacks on the Spanish barque *Goleta,* the Portuguese barque *Rosita Faro,* the British felucca *Joven Enrique,* and other vessels. It should be mentioned, however, that several famous British and foreign sailing yachts upon various occasions have had remarkably narrow escapes from being captured by these sea ruffians.

It is sincerely to be hoped that the Sultan of Morocco is carrying out his task in such a manner as will induce the inhabitants of the Riff coast to follow some occupation in future which is more likely to be appreciated by those who have to navigate vessels in the Mediterranean. Previous to stern measures being taken by the Sultan, it was not at all uncommon for his envoys to the native tribes—for the purpose of obtaining the release of captives—to be received with derision. Often, too, they were maltreated to such an extent that they were glad to escape with their lives. Some of the neighboring tribes continually endeavored to purchase captives for the pleasure of killing them, but it is satisfactory to learn that no sales are recorded, as the anticipated ransom was always largely in excess of the sums offered by the bloodthirsty natives.

Pirates and Coast-Guards

HENRI DE MONFREID AND IDA TREAT

From Khor Ali we made directly for Djibouti. I thought it wise to spend the day in town, ostensibly purchasing supplies, while my men spread discreetly through the native quarter news of my successful trip to the Arab coast. Late in the afternoon we hoisted sail, presumably for Mascali. I counted on reaching Sowaba Island, where we had buried the arms, under cover of the night.

During the day I was disquieted by the news Abdi picked up along the docks that the sea turtle season had opened. A boutre had arrived in Djibouti the day before with the first catch of the year. Catching sea turtles (which furnish the tortoise shell of commerce) was almost exclusively the work of Arabs who trapped the creatures on moonlit nights when the females left the water to lay their eggs. According to Abdi, the little Archipelago of Sowaba furnished a high percentage of all tortoise shell in the Djibouti market.

This unforeseen complication disturbed me considerably. It did not seem improbable that an Arab crew, spending the day in idleness on the islands, might have discovered traces of our excavations. Even if the secret of the buried arms was still safe, I had no intention of digging them up again under the eyes of spectators.

We left Djibouti that same afternoon at four, a land breeze carrying us briskly across the gulf. By eleven we had weathered the Ras Bir, and towards two in the morning we sighted the peaked silhouette of the largest of the islands. As we approached, a spark glowed in the shadow of the base. Someone had landed on Sowaba. Steering straight for the island, I kept my night binoculars fixed on the point of light. Suddenly it disappeared—a bad sign—for it looked as if our sail, visible in the moonlight, had disturbed the campers on the beach.

When we were half a mile from shore, the black triangle of a sail detached itself from the dark mass of the island, gliding west towards the open sea. My gloomiest forebodings seemed justified. Under normal circumstances, no native boutre hoists sail at three in the morning. I was convinced that our cache had been discovered and looted. Abdi, wiser than I in the customs of the coast, shared the conviction.

Veering away from Sowaba, I headed straight for the boutre, a *zaroug*, carrying more canvas than the *Sahala*. In the open sea, we could not hope to overtake it. But I calculated that to avoid the reef, the *zaroug* would be obliged to haul close to the wind—a manœuvre which would give me a chance to cover part of the distance that lay between us.

Casting about for an effective means of overhauling the fugitive, I remembered a length of fine steel chain fastened about a sea chest belonging to one of my men. I had on board a 12-calibre shotgun. With a knife I ripped the charge of shot from two cartridges which I then placed in the chambers. In each of the gun barrels I inserted a segment of the chain, about twenty-four inches long. With that charge, I counted on tearing the sail of the *zaroug*, provided I could get near enough to fire.

As foreseen, the *zaroug* was forced to tack about to avoid the reef. The breeze freshened— the eastern monsoon was rising as dawn approached. The *Sahala* gained rapidly, for we could sail large while the *zaroug* hugged the wind. Its crew was invisible; evidently they feared I might fire—and had no weapons. As the distance shrunk between us, I heard the sound of muffled blows in the hold of the *zaroug*, a sound which removed my last floating doubt as to the theft of the buried arms.

The Arabs were trying to open the rifle cases. If they succeeded, we were assured of a reception! I comforted myself with the thought that native boats carry no tools of any sort; and

I remembered the solid planks of the rifle-cases, reinforced by iron bands. All the same, I had my men build a barricade of rice and durra sacks around the helm.

When still a cable's length away, hammer-blows in the *zaroug* growing more vigorous, I ordered my Somalis to open fire with the Gras rifles, aiming at the water line to demoralise the amateur carpenters in the hold. The blows ceased instantly. But like ourselves, the *zaroug* was sailing large. Had it passed the end of the reef? To my despair, I saw the stretch of water widen between us. We were still too far behind to risk sending the shot of steel chain through their mainsail. That trick could not be counted on to succeed at more than 150 yards.

Suddenly I saw the *zaroug* veer to the wind again; the helmsman must have sighted the reef. In his haste, he brought to; the sail slapped emptily in the wind. Fear of our gun shots made the *zaroug* crew work sail with prudence; so prudently indeed, that we gained half a cable length before the Arab boat got under way again. We pushed even closer; but just as I prepared to try out my double charge of chain, the *zaroug* veered large—it had made the end of the reef.

At that, I emptied the two barrels of the shot gun—our last hope. A miracle kept the arm from bursting (the charge weighed fully three times as much as the shot I had removed). One barrel twisted slightly, but that was all.

At the same instant, the *zaroug's* taut sail split as if by magic through its entire length. A minute later, the wind had torn the light canvas to ribbons. The crew hastened to lower the sail-yard; too late—the wind had pushed the *zaroug* on the reef. It struck while we were still a few yards away. To avoid a like fate, we accosted them on the side towards the open sea. Only then the *nakhoda* of the *zaroug* seemed to find his voice.

"What do you want with us?" he shouted angrily. I looked him square in the eyes.

"Give back the arms you stole on Sowaba—or I will shoot every man of you." His crew did not wait for the command. With a chorus of terrified yells, "Yahallah! O Yahallah!" they emptied the hold: four cases of rifles and five of cartridges. They had not uncovered all our trenches.

"We did not know they were yours," the *nakhoda* muttered by way of excuse when the last case had been carried aboard the *Sahala*; "Awad Omar is no thief."

"You thought the turtles had laid them?" Abdi inquired jocularly.

Meantime, the deck of the *zaroug* was awash and it was rapidly settling on the reef. To avoid the rock ourselves—for with the morning wind the sea had grown rougher—I ordered the Arabs on board the *Sahala*, and took the *zaroug* in tow (it still floated though full of water; it had run afoul of the very point), and made for the open sea.

Afraid lest I hand them over to the authorities in Djibouti, the *nakhoda* begged me to let him and his crew return to their boat.

"Do you want to drown?" I inquired. "You have a hole in the boutre as big as my two fists." The *nakhoda* shook his head.

"*Mafish ghof!* (No fear!) Give me rice."

From Awad Omar, pirate, arms-smuggler, and in his leisure moments fisher of sea turtles, I learned a trick for stopping leaks, which stood me in good stead less than twenty-four hours later. He took about six pounds of rice, rolling it in a piece of sailcloth like a sausage. This he introduced in the hole the reef had dug in the port side of the *zaroug*. In a few minutes the rice swelled, blocking the aperture completely. In fair weather, according to the Arab, you could count on the patch resisting safely for forty-eight hours. As soon as the leak was stopped, the crew of the *zaroug* started baling. Half an hour later I set them adrift, and hoisting a jib they made off in the direction of the Arab coast. I kept as hostage the *nakhoda's* son, a fifteen-year-old boy of great beauty, to assure the discretion of his father and his father's sailors. When my cargo had been safely delivered, they could talk as they pleased—but for another twenty-four hours I did not care to have our adventure noised abroad. In three days, I told the *nakhoda*, he could send for the young Ibrahim Awad at Djibouti.

The *nakhoda* did not protest. Arabs are good losers; the fortunes of war they accept as a matter of course—as a rule they bear no grudge against the victor. Drive a shrewd bargain with an Arab, he will respect you and become your friend; but let him get the better of you through incapacity, weakness, or even amiability—he will never forgive you. "*Ghashim!*" (Imbecile) he dubs you disdainfully, as one who cannot see beyond his own nose!

Awad Omar and his crew, I observed, found something mysterious and inexplicable in our arrival at Sowaba while they were still loading the *zaroug* with the stolen arms. What had been mere coincidence they preferred to interpret as second sight on my part. Nor had they been able, to explain—except as evidence of divine intervention—the "miraculous" destruction of their sail. Even had I taken no hostage, chances were that not one of them would have risked mentioning our encounter, for fear of occult and supernatural reprisals.

After this episode, we returned to the island without further incident. I did not like to lie at anchor there in broad daylight, but for me it was a point of honour to arrive on time at Khor Ali that evening. We loaded the remaining cases as rapidly as possible, and at noon, when all were safely on board, I headed the *Sahala* south-west towards the entrance of the gulf.

As we neared the Dankali coast, I saw on the horizon sails leaving Tajura for Djibouti. To escape recognition I ran as close to land as I dared and anchored there, lowering the sail. I kept my glasses fixed on the heights above Khor Ali, but seeing no smoke signal anywhere, I concluded the coast was clear.

Though it was not yet dark, I decided to enter and wait there for the signal, for I thought I ran a greater risk of being seen out in the gulf. Besides, I wanted to be sure of landing my cargo before the tide ran out. We had barely dropped anchor when a Dankali swam out to us from shore.

"Abd el Hai," he called guardedly from the water. "A message from Sheik Mâki. There was no time to bring the camels here. Go first to Ambabo."

Ambabo, a little beach with an oasis of date palms, lies ten miles west of Tajura. We reached it at nightfall. Sighting what I took to be a fire signal, I replied with a flare. We dropped anchor 500 yards from the coast, and as nothing stirred along the beach, I swam ashore to find out if arrangements had been made for unloading the arms. I found Bourham Bey, alone on the edge of the oasis. Rapidly he explained.

I was to land half my cargo at Ambabo and deliver the rest twenty-four hours later to Dîni, my second customer, at Khor Ali. A storm on the Mabla had held up the camels. Bourham Bey's own caravan would not reach the coast for another hour or two. In my impatience at the delay, I volunteered to bring the arms to shore myself. The transport proved even more difficult than at Sowaba Island; we carried the heavy cases through 500 yards of shallow water and surf and across a beach strewn with sharp stones. I worked with my Somalis until the last case had been brought to land. On the final trip to the beach, I split the sole of my left foot on a shell, and smashed a great toe as we lowered the last box of rifles to the sand. But these were the only accidents, and long before the moon rose, we were already under sail for Mascali, for I preferred a flying visit to the island to a day tacking in the gulf under the torrid sun, or risking anchorage in full view of the coast.

Morning had not yet come when the island showed dark ahead—a welcome sight, for all of us showed signs of fatigue. The tide was not yet full; skirting the southern end of Mascali I found barely enough water to carry us over the reef. I hastened ashore, for my feet pained badly. I had had nothing on board to bandage them with and had washed my wounds with sea water and let it go at that.

As we approached the camp, I hailed Ahmed Baket, a Soudanese whom I had left in charge.

"Ahmed—O," I called cheerily, "wake up and make us coffee." To my surprise, I received no answer, but in the dark I collided smartly with the Soudanese, who at the call had rushed out to meet me.

"*Yallah roh! Fissa fissa* (leave at once)!" he chattered in great excitement. "The Government *doueri* is moored on the other side of the island!"

I waited for no explanations; wheeling in my tracks, I limped in all haste back to the beach. There was nothing to do but leave by the route over which we had come. I adjusted the antiquated out-motor purchased second-hand at Djibouti some weeks before and for once the unruly machine, on a rare streak of good behaviour, propelled us soberly along the reef. Black water was in sight, when I felt a slight shock. A point of rock had torn the rudder from its sockets; a moment later the *Sahala* grounded. At the jolt the entire crew dived overboard. I succeeded, presently, in fishing up the rudder intact, which was luck, but the boutre, caught midkeel, turned like a top on its axis, and refused to budge. In the east, the horizon paled; I had visions of our being caught like flies in glue. As we tugged and hauled, the breeze freshened, blocking the channel; not even the out-motor, I feared, would push against it, and the motor, besides, seemed to have gone dead.

I ordered my men to hoist the mainsail. As the yard climbed the mast, the *Sahala* leaned far to starboard. The keel cleared the rock. Throwing all my weight against the bar, I headed her straight south-west, across the reef, trusting to luck alone that the rocks would spare us. Three times we hit a block of coral—the shock checked us, but each time, after an endless second, the boutre lunged forward. In five minutes we reached deep water and I drew a deep long breath. We had sprung a leak—not a bad one—the *Sahala* was a solid boat. Like nearly all the boutres of the coast, it was built of Indian teak. The men worked at the pumps, emptying water from the hold as fast as it came in. There was no time to examine our damage; the sun had reached the horizon. We must be out of sight at once.

To my annoyance, looking back towards Mascali—flat as a table, like all the islands of the region—I saw across the island a white triangle of canvas moving slowly towards the west. The *doueri* was passing through the channel that separated Mascali from Moucha. Our route to the open sea was cut off. No choice was ours but to continue south-west into the Gulf of Tajura.

In half an hour, the *doueri* rounded the western point of Mascali, and veering south-west, headed straight towards us. At the distance, it would have been impossible to identify the *Sahala* with any certainty. If the *doueri* gave chase, it was probably only because of our proximity to Mascali at that early hour.

We continued south-west into the gulf, skirting the Issa coast—a desolate wall of black rock overgrown with a burnt vegetation of thorns. Two hours and the Government boat had gained three miles of the nine that lay between us. If the wind held, it was bound to overtake us. In which case, what was there to do but throw overboard the remaining cases of arms. Which still left us to account for our presence in the gulf, and headlong flight from Mascali with a leaky boat? The idea of failure on that first arms venture of mine was intolerable. Rather stake all on a last card, however improbable success.

A mile ahead, Ras Debeleba stretched its long black cape into the gulf. I resolved, past the cape, to sink, not the cases of arms, but the *Sahala* itself in the Marsa Debeleba; and let the *doueri* continue its phantom pursuit to the end of the gulf. A mad scheme, but at the time nothing looked too desperate.

We rounded the cape and I prepared to put the plan into execution. But a surprise awaited us:—close to the beach, a boutre lay at anchor and half a dozen Arabs were busy loading it with faggots. My heart sank. Adieu my self-imposed shipwreck! ... no longer feasible with six curious Arabs as spectators ... and eventual informers. The game was up. And yet, as often in our life, when reason has demonstrated that defeat is inevitable and imminent, something stirs. An inner voice cries: "You cannot fail, *you cannot*. All this is mere appearance. Carry on!"

There, in the anchorage of Marsa Debeleba, after an instant of dejection, I had a sudden inspiration. Arabs who gathered firewood on the Issa coast had first to obtain permission at Djibouti, which entailed the payment of a fee. Most likely that boutre behind Debeleba was there illegally. Heading towards shore I hailed the *nakhoda*.

"The *doueri* is behind the point. *Yallah roh!*" The words produced a magic effect. Hurling the faggots aboard pell-mell, the Arabs scrambled into their craft, and hoisting sail, made all speed out of the bay. On the *Sahala*, too, things moved quickly. Everything water could spoil was tossed into the dugout. Everything that could float went overboard for the waves to carry ashore, even the mast and yard. With a gimlet, I drilled two rows of holes through her side, and with a mallet struck out the plank between the rows. The water rushed in; in less than a quarter of an hour the *Sahala* filled and sank. Only the bowsprit and the stern rail showed at the surface. So slightly as to be invisible a few hundred yards away. Freed of its ballast—all but the cases of cartridges which I had left intentionally in the hold—the boutre did not go to the bottom, but floated "between waters," as the French say, kept from drifting by the two anchors.

Leaving the crew to keep watch, Abdi and I climbed to the top of the cape to follow through binoculars the progress of the *doueri*. To my astonishment, I saw that it had altered its course; it was hot on the trail of the Arab boutre, apparently mistaken for mine! What remorse I might have felt for a sorry trick on a humble smuggler of firewood was forgotten. The Arabs relying on the speed of their craft had obliqued towards the Dankali coast and the entrance to the gulf. While Abdi watched the chase, I hurried back to salvage the *Sahala*, sunk to no purpose.

The rice trick learned from Awad Omar came in handy. We stopped the leak with a poultice of rice (as an additional precaution we covered the holes on the outside with squares of tin *tanika* nailed fast), my men pumped and baled. In a couple of hours the boutre was above water again, none the worse for its bath, though it still leaked from its morning blow on the reef. The cases of arms, being waterproof, suffered not at all.

When all was ready again, the whole crew except the boy Moussa, and Abdi still at his post of observation, went ashore—stretched in the shade of the bushes to sleep. Towards nightfall, Abdi woke me with the news that the *doueri* had given up the chase, and headed off towards Djibouti. Cheered, I roused the Somalis, and we hoisted sail for Khor Ali, where four hours later I deposited my contraband in the hands of Dini, the Dankali, who was waiting there with the Bedouins and camels.

What had provoked the visit of the Government boat to Mascali—and the ensuing chase in the waters of Tajura—I could only guess. But I thought it wise to run the *Sahala*, its wounds still plastered with rice, over to Djibouti the next day for repairs. While I worked with Arab carpenters on the beach, my men spread through the port a story of how we had run aground while fishing and had been obliged to take shelter on the Issa coast—a good enough alibi in view of the obvious damage to the *Sahala's* hull to explain our absence from Mascali Island.

PART II

The Captains

Captain Singleton

DANIEL DEFOE

As it is usual for great Persons whose Lives have been remarkable, and whose Actions deserve Recording to Posterity, to insist much upon their Originals, give full Accounts of their Families, and the Histories of their Ancestors: So, that I may be methodical, I shall do the same, tho' I can look but a very little Way into my Pedigree as you will see presently.

If I may believe the Woman, whom I was taught to call Mother, I was a little Boy, of about two Years old, very well dress'd, had a Nursery Maid to tend me, who took me out on a fine Summer's Evening into the Fields towards *Islington*, as she pretended, to give the Child some Air, a little Girl being with her of Twelve or Fourteen Years old, that lived in the Neighbourhood. The Maid, whether by Appointment or otherwise, meets with a Fellow, her Sweet-heart, as I suppose; he carries her into a Publick-House, to give her a Pot and a Cake; and while they were toying in the House, the Girl plays about with me in her Hand in the Garden, and at the Door, sometimes in Sight, sometimes out of Sight, thinking no Harm.

At this Juncture comes by one of those Sort of People, who, it seems, made it their Business to Spirit away little Children. This was a Hellish Trade in those Days, and chiefly practised where they found little Children very well drest, or for bigger Children, to sell them to the Plantations.

The Woman pretending to take me up in her Arms and kiss me, and play with me, draws the Girl a good Way from the House, till at last she makes a fine Story to the Girl, and bids her go back to the Maid, and tell her where she was with the Child; that a Gentlewoman had taken a Fancy to the Child, and was kissing of it, but she should not be frighted, or to that Purpose; for they were but just there; and so while the Girl went, she carries me quite away.

From this time it seems I was disposed of to a Beggar-Woman that wanted a pretty little Child to set out her Case, and after that to a Gypsey, under whose Government I continued till I was about Six Years old; and this Woman, tho' I was continually dragged about with her, from one Part of the Country to another, yet never let me want for any thing, and I called her Mother; tho' she told me at last, she was not my Mother, but that she bought me for Twelve Shillings of another Woman, who told her how she came by me, and told her that my Name was *Bob Single-ton*, not *Robert*, but plain *Bob*; for it seems they never knew by what Name I was Christen'd.

It is in vain to reflect here, what a terrible Fright the careless Hussy was in, that lost me; what Treatment she received from my justly enraged Father and Mother, and the Horror these must be in at the Thoughts of their Child being thus carry'd away; for as I never knew any thing of the Matter, but just what I have related, nor who my Father and Mother were, so it would make but a needless Digression to talk of it here.

My good *Gypsey Mother*, for some of her worthy Actions *no doubt*, happened in Process of Time to be hang'd; and as this fell out something too soon for me to be perfected in the Strolling Trade, the Parish where I was left, which for my Life I can't remember, took some Care of me to be sure; for the first thing I can remember of my self afterwards, was, that I went to a Parish-School, and the Minister of the Parish used to talk to me to be a good Boy; and that tho' I was but a poor Boy, if I minded my Book, and served God, I might make a good Man.

I believe I was frequently removed from one Town to another, perhaps as the Parishes disputed my supposed Mother's last Settlement. Whether I was so shifted by Passes! or otherwise, I know not; but the Town where I last was kept, whatever its Name was, must be not far off from the Sea Side; for a Master of a Ship who took a Fancy to me, was the first that brought me to a Place not far from *Southampton*, which I afterwards knew to be

Busselton, and there I tended the Carpenters, and such People as were employ'd in Building a Ship for him; and when it was done, tho' I was not above Twelve Years old, he carried me to Sea with him, on a Voyage to *Newfoundland*.

I lived well enough, and pleased my Master so well, that he called me his own Boy; and I would have called him Father, but he would not allow it, for he had Children of his own. I went three or four Voyages with him, and grew a great sturdy Boy, when coming Home again from the Banks of *Newfoundland*, we were taken by an *Algerine* Rover, or Man of War; which, if my Account stands right, was about the Year 1695, for you may be sure I kept no Journal.

I was not much concerned at the Disaster, tho' I saw my Master, after having been wounded by a Splinter in the Head during the Engagement, very barbarously used by the *Turks; I say*, I was not much concerned, till upon some unlucky thing I said, which, as I remember, was about abusing my Master, they took me and beat me most unmercifully with a flat Stick on the Soles of my Feet, so that I could neither go or stand for several Days together.

But my good Fortune was my Friend upon this Occasion; for as they were sailing away with our Ship in Tow as a Prize, steering for the Streights, and in Sight of the Bay of *Cadiz*, the *Turkish* Rover was attack'd by two great *Portuguese* Men of War, and taken and carried into *Lisbon*.

As I was not much concerned at my Captivity, not indeed understanding the Consequences of it, if it had continued; so I was not suitably sensible of my Deliverance: Nor indeed was it so much a Deliverance to me, as it would otherwise ha' been; for my Master, who was the only Friend I had in the World, died at *Lisbon* of his Wounds; and I being then almost reduced to my primitive State, *viz.* of Starving, had this Addition to it, that it was in a foreign Country too, where I knew no body, and could not speak a Word of their Language. However, I fared better here than I had Reason to expect; for when all the rest of our Men had their Liberty to go where they would, I that knew not whither to go, staid in the Ship for several Days, till at length one of the Lieutenants seeing me, enquired what that young *English* Dog did there, and why they did not turn him on Shore?

I heard him, and partly understood what he meant, tho' not what he said, and began then to be in a terrible Fright; for I knew not where to get a Bit of Bread; when the Pilot of the Ship, an old Seaman, seeing me look very dull, came to me, and speaking broken *English* to me, told me, I must be gone. Whither must I go (said I?) Where you will, (said he), Home to your own Country, if you will. How must I go thither (said I?) Why have you no Friend (said he?) No, (said I) not in the World, but that Dog, pointing to the Ship's Dog, (who having stole a Piece of Meat just before, had brought it close by me, and I had taken it from him, and eat it) for he has been a good Friend, and brought me my Dinner.

Well, well, says he, *you must have your Dinner*; *Will you go with me? Yes*, says I, *with all my Heart*. In short, the old Pilot took me Home with him, and used me tolerably well, tho' I fared hard enough, and I lived with him about two Years, during which time he was solliciting his Business, and at length got to be Master or Pilot under *Don Garcia de Pimentesia de Carravallas*, Captain of a *Portuguese* Gallion, or Carrack, which was bound to *Goa* in the *East-Indies*; and immediately having gotten his Commission, put me on Board to look after his Cabbin, in which he had stored himself with Abundance of Liquors, Succades, Sugar, Spices, and other things for his Accommodation in the Voyage, and laid in afterwards a considerable Quantity of *European* Goods, fine Lace, and Linnen; and also Bays, Woollen, Cloath, Stuffs, *&c.* under the Pretence of his Clothes.

I was too young in the Trade to keep any Journal of this Voyage, tho' my Master, who was for a *Portuguese* a pretty good Artist, prompted me to it: But my not understanding the Language, was one Hindrance; at least, it served me for an Excuse. However, after some time I began to look into his Charts and Books; and as I could write a tolerable Hand, understood some *Latin*, and began to have a Smattering of the *Portuguese* Tongue; so I began to get a little superficial Knowledge of Navigation, but not such as was likely to be sufficient to carry me thro' a Life of Adventure, as mine was to be. *In short*, I learnt several material Things in this Voyage among the *Portuguese:* I learnt particularly to be an errant Thief and a bad Sailor; and I think I may say they are the best Masters for Teaching both these, of any Nation in the World.

We made our Way for the *East-Indies*, by the Coast of *Brasil;* not that it is in the Course of Sailing the Way thither; but our Captain, either on his own Account, or by the Direction of the Merchants, went thither first, where at *All Saints Bay*, or as they call it in *Portugal*, the *Rio de Todos los Santos*, we delivered near an Hundred Ton of Goods, and took in a considerable Quantity of Gold, with some Chests of Sugar, and Seventy or Eighty great Rolls of Tobacco, every Roll weighing at least 100 Weight.

Here being lodged on Shore by my Master's Order, I had the Charge of the Captain's Business, he having seen me very diligent for my own Master; and in Requital for his mistaken Confidence, I found Means to secure, that is to say, to steal about twenty Moydores out of the Gold that was Shipt on Board by the Merchants, and this was my first Adventure.

We had a tolerable Voyage from hence to the Cape *de bona Speranza;* and I was reputed as a mighty diligent Servant to my Master, and very faithful (I was diligent indeed, but I was very far from honest; however, they thought me honest, which by the Way, was their very great Mistake) upon this very Mistake, the Captain took a particular Liking to me, and employ'd me frequently on his own Occasions; and on the other Hand, in Recompence for my Officious Diligence,

I received several particular Favours from him; particularly, I was by the Captain's Command, made a kind of a Steward under the Ship's Steward, for such Provisions as the Captain demanded for his own Table. He had another Steward for his private Stores besides, but my Office concerned only what the Captain called for of the Ship's Stores, for his private Use.

However, by this Means I had Opportunity particularly to take Care of my Master's Man, and to furnish my self with sufficient Provisions to make me live much better than the other People in the Ship; for the Captain seldom ordered any thing out of the Ship's Stores, as above, but I snipt some of it for my own Share. We arrived at *Goa* in the *East-Indies*, in about seven Months, from *Lisbon*, and remained there eight more; during which Time I had indeed nothing to do, my Master being generally on Shore, but to learn every thing that is wicked among the *Portuguese*, a Nation the most perfidious and the most debauch'd, the most insolent and cruel, of any that pretend to call themselves Christians, in the World.

Thieving, Lying, Swearing, Forswearing, joined to the most abominable Lewdness, was the stated Practice of the Ship's Crew; *adding to it*, that with the most unsufferable Boasts of their new Courage, they were generally speaking the most compleat Cowards that I ever met with; and the Consequence of their Cowardice was evident upon many Occasions. However, there was here and there one among them that was not so bad as the rest; and as my Lot fell among them, it made me have the most contemptible Thoughts of the rest, as indeed they deserved.

I was exactly fitted for their Society indeed; for I had no Sense of Virtue or Religion upon me. I had never heard much of either, except what a good old Parson had said to me when I was a Child of about Eight or Nine Years old; nay, I was preparing, and growing up apace, to be as wicked as any Body could be, or perhaps ever was. Fate certainly thus directed my Beginning, knowing that I had Work which I had to do in the World, which nothing but one hardened against all Sense of Honesty or Religion, could go thro'; and yet even in this State of Original Wickedness, I entertained such a settled Abhorrence of the abandon'd Vileness of the *Portuguese*, that I could not but hate them most heartily from the Beginning, and all my Life afterwards. They were so brutishly wicked, so base and perfidious, not only to Strangers, but to one another; so meanly submissive when subjected; so insolent, or barbarous and tyrannical when superior, that I thought there was something in them that shock'd my very Nature. Add to this, that 'tis natural to an *Englishman* to hate a Coward, it all joined together to make the Devil and a *Portuguese* equally my Aversion.

However, according to the *English* Proverb, *He that is Shipp'd with the Devil must sail with the Devil;* I was among them, and I manag'd my self as well as I could. My Master had consented that I should assist the Captain in the Office as above; but as I understood afterwards, that the

Captain allowed my Master Half a Moydore a Month for my Service, and that he had my Name upon the Ship's Books also, I expected that when the Ship came to be paid four Months Wages at the *Indies*, as they it seems always do, my Master would let me have something for my self.

But I was wrong in my Man, for he was none of that Kind: He had taken me up as in Distress, and his Business was to keep me so, and make his Market of me as well as he could; which I began to think of after a different Manner than I did at first; for at first I thought he had entertained me in meer Charity, upon seeing my distrest Circumstances, but did not doubt, but when he put me on Board the Ship, I should have some Wages for my Service.

But he thought, it seems, quite otherwise; and when I procured one to speak to him about it when the Ship was paid at *Goa*, he flew into the greatest Rage imaginable, and called me *English Dog*, young *Heretick*, and threaten'd to put me into Inquisition. Indeed of all the Names the Four and Twenty Letters could make up, he should not have called me *Heretick*; for as I knew nothing about Religion, neither *Protestant* from *Papist*, or either of them from a *Mahometan*, I could never be a Heretick. However, it pass'd but a little, but as young as I was, I had been carried into the Inquisition; and there, if they had ask'd me, if I was a *Protestant* or a *Catholick*, I should have said Yes to that which came first. If it had been the *Protestant* they had ask'd first, it had certainly made a Martyr of me for I did not know what.

But the very Priest they carried with them, or Chaplain of the Ship, as we call him, saved me; for seeing me a Boy entirely ignorant of Religion, and ready to do or say any thing they bid me, he ask'd me some Questions about it, which he found I answered so very simply, that he took it upon him to tell them, he would answer for my being a good Catholick; and he hoped he should be the Means of saving my Soul; and he pleased himself, that it was to be a Work of Merit to him; so he made me as good a *Papist* as any of them in about a Week's Time.

I then told him my Case about my Master how, it is true, he had taken me up in a miserable Case, on Board a Man of War at *Lisbon*; and I was indebted to him for bringing me on Board this Ship; that if I had been left at *Lisbon*, I might have starv'd, and the like: And therefore I was willing to serve him; but that I hop'd he would give me some little Consideration for my Service, or let me know how long he expected I should serve him for nothing.

It was all one; neither the Priest or any one else could prevail with him, but that I was not his Servant but his Slave; that he took me in the *Algerine*; and that I was a *Turk*, only pretended to be an *English* Boy, to get my Liberty, and he would carry me to the Inquisition as a *Turk*.

This frighted me out of my Wits; for I had no body to vouch for me what I was, or from whence I came; but the good *Padre Antonio*, for that was his Name, cleared me of that Part by a Way I did not understand: For he came to me one Morning with two Sailors, and told me they must search me, to bear Witness that I was not a *Turk*. I was amazed at them, and frighted; and did not understand them; nor could I imagine what they intended to do to me. However, stripping me, they were soon satisfy'd; and Father *Anthony* bad me be easy, for they could all Witness that I was no *Turk*. So I escaped that Part of my Master's Cruelty.

And now I resolved from that time to run away from him if I could; but there was no doing of it there; for there were not Ships of any Nation in the World in that Port, except two or three *Persian* Vessels from *Ormus*; so that if I had offer'd to go away from him, he would have had me seized on Shore, and brought on Board by Force. So that I had no Remedy but Patience, and this he brought to an End too as soon as he could; for after this he began to use me ill, and not only to straiten my Provisions, but to beat and torture me in a barbarous Manner for every Trifle; so that in a Word my Life began to be very miserable.

The Violence of this Usage of me, and the Impossibility of my Escape from his Hands, set my Head a-working upon all Sorts of Mischief; and in particular, I resolved, after studying all other Ways to deliver my self, and finding all ineffectual; I say, I resolved to murther him. With this Hellish Resolution in my Head, I spent whole Nights and Days contriving how to put it in Execution, the Devil prompting me very warmly to the Fact. I was indeed entirely at a Loss for the Means; for I had neither Gun or Sword, nor any Weapon to assault him with. Poison I had my Thoughts much upon, but knew not where to get any; or if I might have got it, I did not know the Country Word for it, or by what Name to ask for it.

In this Manner I quitted the Fact intentionally a Hundred and a Hundred Times; but Providence, either for his sake, or for mine, always frustrated my Designs, and I could never bring it to pass; so I was obliged to continue in his Chains till the Ship, having taken in her Loading, set Sail for *Portugal*.

I can say nothing here to the Manner of our Voyage; for as I said, I kept no Journal; but this I can give an Account of, that having been once as high as the *Cape of Good Hope*, as we call it; or *Cabo de bona Speranza*, as they call it, we were driven back again by a violent Storm from the W. S. W. which held us six Days and Nights, a great Way to the Eastward; and after that standing afore the Wind for several Days more, we at last came to an Anchor on the Coast of *Madagascar*.

The Storm had been so violent, that the Ship had received a great deal of Damage, and it required some time to repair her; so standing in nearer the Shore, the Pilot, *My Master*, brought the Ship into a very good Harbour, where we rid in Twenty six Fathom Water, about Half a Mile from the Shore.

While the Ship rode here, there happen'd a most desperate Mutiny among the Men, upon Account of some Deficiency in their Allowance, which came to that Height, that they threaten'd the Captain to set him on Shore, and go back with the Ship to *Goa*. I wish'd they would, with all my Heart, for I was full of Mischief in my Head, and ready enough to do any. So, tho' I was but a Boy, as they called me, yet I prompted the Mischief all I could, and embarked in it so openly, that I escap'd very little being hang'd in the first and most early Part of my Life; for the Captain had some Notice, that there was a Design laid by some of the Company to murther him; and having partly by Money and Promises, and partly by Threatning and Torture, brought two Fellows to confess the Particulars, and the Names of the Persons concerned, they were presently apprehended, till one accusing another, no less than sixteen Men were seized, and put into Irons, whereof I was one.

The Captain, who was made desperate by his Danger, resolving to clear the Ship of his Enemies, try'd us all, and we were all condemned to die. The Manner of his Process I was too young to take Notice of; but the Purser and one of the Gunners were hang'd immediately, and I expected it with the rest. I do not remember any great Concern I was under about it, only that I cry'd very much; for I knew little then of this World, and nothing at all of the next.

However, the Captain contented himself with executing these two; and some of the rest, upon their humble Submission, and Promise of future good Behaviour, were pardoned; but five were ordered to be set on Shore on the Island, and left there, of which I was one. My Master used all his Interest with the Captain to have me excused, but could not obtain it; for somebody having told him that I was one of them, who was singled out to have killed him, when my Master desired I might not be set on Shore, the Captain told him, I should stay on Board if he desired it, but then I should be hang'd; so he might chuse for me which he thought best: The Captain, it seems, was particularly provok'd at my being concerned in the Treachery, because of his having been so kind to me, and of his having singled me out to serve him, as I have said above; and this perhaps obliged him to give my Master such a rough Choice, either to set me on Shore, or to have me hang'd on Board: And had my Master indeed known what good Will I had for him, he would not ha' been long in chusing for me; for I had certainly determined to do him a Mischief the first Opportunity I had had for it. This was therefore a good Providence for me, to keep me from dipping my Hands in Blood, and it made me more tender afterwards in Matters of Blood, than I believe I should otherwise have been. But as to my being one of them that was to kill the Captain, that I was wrong'd in, for I was not the Person; but it was really one of them that were pardoned, he having the good Luck not to have that Part discovered.

I was now to enter upon a Part of independent Life, a thing I was indeed very ill prepared to manage; for I was perfectly loose and dissolute in my Behaviour, bold and wicked while I was under Government, and now perfectly unfit to be trusted with Liberty; for I was as ripe for any

Villainy, as a young Fellow that had no solid Thought ever placed in his Mind could be supposed to be. Education, as you have heard, I had none; and all the little Scenes of Life I had pass'd thro', had been full of Dangers and desperate Circumstances; but I was either so young, or so stupid, that I escaped the Grief and Anxiety of them, for want of having a Sense of their Tendency and Consequences.

This thoughtless, unconcern'd Temper had one Felicity indeed in it; that it made me daring and ready for doing any Mischief, and kept off the Sorrow which otherwise ought to have attended me when I fell into any Mischief; that this Stupidity was instead of a Happiness to me, for it left my Thoughts free to act upon Means of Escape and Deliverance in my Distress, however great it might be; whereas my Companions in the Misery, were so sunk by their Fear and Grief, that they abandoned themselves to the Misery of their Condition, and gave over all Thought but of their perishing and starving, being devoured by wild Beasts, murthered, and perhaps eaten by *Cannibals, and the like.*

I was but a young Fellow about 17 or 18; but hearing what was to be my Fate, I received it with no Appearance of Discouragement; but I asked what my Master said to it, and being told that he had used his utmost Interest to save me, but the Captain had answered I should either go on Shore or be hanged on Board, which he pleased; I then gave over all Hope of being received again: I was not very thankful in my Thoughts to my Master for his solliciting the Captain for me, because I knew that what he did was not in Kindness to me, so much as in Kindness to himself; I mean to preserve the Wages which he got for me, which amounted to above six Dollars a Month, including what the Captain allowed him for my particular Service to him.

When I understood that my Master was so apparently kind, I asked if I might not be admitted to speak with him, and they told me I might, if my Master would come down to me, but I could not be allowed to come up to him; so then I desired my Master might be spoke to to come to me, and he accordingly came to me; I fell on my Knees to him, and begg'd he would forgive me what I had done to displease him; and indeed the Resolution I had taken to murther him, lay with some Horrour upon my Mind just at that Time, so that I was once just a-going to confess it, and beg him to forgive me, but I kept it in: He told me he had done all he could to obtain my Pardon of the Captain, but could not; and he knew no Way for me but to have Patience, and submit to my Fate; and if they came to speak with any Ship of their Nation at the Cape, he would endeavour to have them stand in, and fetch us off again if we might be found.

Then I begg'd I might have my Clothes on Shore with me. He told me he was afraid I should have little Need of Clothes, for he did not see how we could long subsist on the Island, and that he had been told that the Inhabitants were *Cannibals* or *Men-eaters* (tho' he had no

Reason for that Suggestion) and we should not be able to live among them. I told him I was not so afraid of that, as I was of starving for want of Victuals; and as for the Inhabitants being *Cannibals*, I believed we should be more likely to eat them, than they us, if we could but get at them: But I was mightily concerned, I said, we should have no Weapons with us to defend our selves, and I begg'd nothing now, but that he would give me a Gun and a Sword, with a little Powder and Shot.

He smiled and said, they would signify nothing to us, for it was impossible for us to pretend to preserve our Lives among such a populous and desperate Nation as the People of the Island were. I told him, that however it would do us this Good, for we should not be devoured or destroy'd immediately; so I begged hard for the Gun. At last he told me, he did not know whether the Captain would give him Leave to give me a Gun, and if not, he durst not do it; but he promised to use his Interest to obtain it for me, which he did, and the next Day he sent me a Gun, with some Ammunition, but told me, the Captain would not suffer the Ammunition to be given us, till we were set all on Shore, and till he was just going to set Sail. He also sent me the few Clothes I had in the Ship, which indeed were not many.

Two days after this we were all carried on Shore together; the rest of my Fellow-Criminals hearing I had a Gun, and some Powder and Shot, sollicited for Liberty to carry the like with them, which was also granted them; and thus we were set on Shore to shift for our selves.

At our first coming into the Island, we were terrified exceedingly with the Sight of the barbarous People; whose Figure was made more terrible to us than really it was, by the Report we had of them from the Seamen; but when we came to converse with them a while, we found they were not *Cannibals*, as was reported, or such as would fall immediately upon us and eat us up; but they came and sat down by us, and wondered much at our Clothes and Arms, and made Signs to give us some Victuals, such as they had, which was only Roots and Plants dug out of the Ground, for the present, but they brought us Fowls and Flesh afterwards in good Plenty.

This encouraged the other four Men that were with me very much, for they were quite dejected before; but now they began to be very familiar with them, and made Signs, that if they would use us kindly, we would stay and live with them; which they seemed glad of, tho' they knew little of the Necessity we were under to do so, or how much we were afraid of them.

However, upon other Thoughts, we resolved that we would only stay in that Part so long as the Ship rid in the Bay, and then making them believe we were gone with the Ship, we would go and place our selves, if possible, where there were no Inhabitants to be seen, and so live as we could, or perhaps watch for a Ship that might be driven upon the Coast, as we were.

The Ship continued a Fortnight in the Road repairing some Damage which had been done her in the late Storm, and taking in Wood and Water; and during this time the Boat coming often on Shore, the Men brought us several Refreshments, and the Natives believing we only belong'd to the Ship, were civil enough. We lived in a kind of a Tent on the Shore, or rather a Hut, which we made with the Boughs of Trees, and sometimes in the Night retired to a Wood a little out of their Way, to let them think we were gone on board the Ship. However, we found them barbarous, treacherous and villainous enough in their Nature, only civil for Fear, and therefore concluded we should soon fall into their Hands when the Ship was gone.

The Sense of this wrought upon my Fellow-Sufferers even to Distraction; and one of them, being a Carpenter, in his mad Fit, swam off to the Ship in the Night, tho' she lay then a League to Sea, and made such pitiful Moan to be taken in, that the Captain was prevailed with at last to take him in, tho' they let him lye swimming three Hours in the Water before he consented to it.

Upon this, and his humble Submission, the Captain received him, and, in a word, the Importunity of this Man (who for some time petition'd to be taken in, tho' they hanged him as soon as they had him) was such as could not be resisted; for, after he had swam so long about the Ship, he was not able to have reached the Shore again; and the Captain saw evidently that the Man must be taken on Board, or suffered to drown, and the whole Ship's Company offering to be bound for him for his good Behaviour, the Captain at last yielded, and he was taken up, but almost dead with his being so long in the Water.

When this Man was got in, he never left Importuning the Captain and all the rest of the Officers in Behalf of us that were behind, but to the very last Day the Captain was inexorable; when, at the time their Preparations were making to sail, and Orders given to hoist the Boats into the Ship, all the Seamen in a Body came up to the Rail of the Quarter-Deck, where the Captain was walking with some of his Officers, and appointing the Boatswain to speak for them, he went up, and falling on his Knees to the Captain, begged of him in the humblest manner, possible, to receive the four Men on Board again, offering to answer for their Fidelity, or to have them kept in Chains till they came to *Lisbon*, and there to be delivered up to Justice, rather than, as they said, to have them left to be murthered by Savages, or devoured by wild Beasts. It was a great while e'er the Captain took any Notice of them, but when he did he ordered the Boatswain to be seized, and threatned to bring him to the Capstern for speaking for them.

Upon this Severity, one of the Seamen, bolder than the rest, but still with all possible Respect to the Captain, besought his Honour, as he called him, that he would give Leave to some more of them to go on Shore, and die with their Companions, or, if possible, to assist them to resist the Barbarians. The Captain, rather provoked than cowd with this, came to the Barricado of the Quarter-Deck, and speaking very prudently to the Men, (for, had he spoken roughly, two Thirds of them would have left the Ship, if not all of them) he told them, it was for their Safety as well as his own, that he had been obliged to that Severity; that Mutiny on board a Ship was the same thing as Treason in the King's Palace, and he could not answer it to his Owners and Employers to trust the Ship and Goods Committed to his Charge, with Men who had entertained Thoughts of the worst and blackest Nature; that he wished heartily that it had been any where else that they had been set on Shore, where they might have been in less Hazard from the Savages; that if he had designed they should be destroyed, he could as well have executed them on board as the other two; that he wished it had been in some other Part of the World, where he might have delivered them up to the Civil Justice, or might have left them among Christians; but that it was better their Lives were put in Hazard, than his Life, and the Safety of the Ship; and that tho' he did not know that he had deserved so ill of any of them, as that they should leave the Ship, rather than do their Duty; yet if any of them were resolved to do so unless he would consent to take a Gang of Traytors on board, who, as he had proved before them all, had conspired to murther him, he would not hinder them, nor, for the present, would he resent their Importunity; but if there was no body left in the Ship but himself, he would never consent to take them on board.

This Discourse was delivered so well, was in it self so reasonable, was managed with so much Temper, yet so boldly concluded with a Negative, that the greatest Part of the Men were satisfied for the present: However, as it put the Men into Juncto's and Cabals, and they were not composed for some Hours; the Wind also slackening towards Night, the Captain ordered not to weigh till next Morning.

The same Night 23 of the Men, among whom was the Gunner's Mate, the Surgeon's Assistant, and two Carpenters, applying to the Chief Mate, told him, that as the Captain had given them Leave to go on Shore to their Comerades, they begged, that he would speak to the Captain not to take it ill that they were desirous to go and die with their Companions; and that they thought they could do no less in such an Extremity, than go to them; because if there was any way to save their Lives, it was by adding to their Numbers, and making them strong enough to assist one another in defending themselves against the Savages, till perhaps they might one time or other find Means to make their Escape, and get to their own Country again.

The Mate told them in so many Words, that he durst not speak to the Captain upon any such Design, and was very sorry they had no more respect for him, than to desire him to go of such an Errand; but if they were resolved upon such an Enterprize, he would advise them to take the Long-Boat in the Morning betimes, and go off, seeing the Captain had given them Leave, and leave a civil Letter behind them to the Captain, and to desire him to send his Men on Shore for the Boat, which should be delivered very honestly, and he promised to keep their Counsel so long.

Accordingly an Hour before Day, those 23 Men, with every Man a Fire-lock and Cutlass, with some Pistols, three Halbards or Half-Pikes, and good Store of Powder and Ball, without any Provision but about Half an Hundred of Bread, but with all their Chests and Clothes, Tools, Instruments, Books, &c. embarked themselves so silently, that the Captain got no Notice of it till they were gotten half the Way on Shore.

As soon as the Captain heard of it, he called for the Gunner's Mate, *the Chief Gunner being at that time sick in his Cabbin*, and ordered to fire at them; but, to his great Mortification, the Gunner's Mate was one of the Number, and was gone with them; and indeed it was by his Means they got so many Arms, and so much Ammunition. When the Captain found how it was, and that there was no Help for it, he began to be a little appeased, made light of it, and called up the Men, spoke kindly to them, and told them he was very well satisfied in the Fidelity and Ability of those that were now left; and that he would give to them, for their Encouragement, to be divided among them, the Wages which was due to the Men that were gone; and that it was a great Satisfaction to him that the Ship was freed from such a mutinous Rabble, who had not the least Reason for their Discontent.

The Men seemed very well satisfied, and particularly the Promise of the Wages of those that were gone, went a great way with them. After this the Letter which was left by the Men was given to the Captain, by his Boy, with whom, it seems, the Men had left it. The Letter was much to the same Purpose of what they had said to the Mate, and which he declined to say for them; only that at the End of their Letter they told the Captain, that as they had no dishonest Design, so they had taken nothing away with them which was not their own, except some Arms and Ammunition, such as were absolutely necessary to them, as well for their Defence against the Savages, as to kill Fowls or Beasts for their Food, that they might not perish; and as there were considerable Sums due to them for Wages, they hoped he would allow the Arms and Ammunition upon their Accounts. They told him, that as to the Ship's Long-Boat which they had taken to bring them on Shore, they knew it was necessary to him, and they were very willing to restore it to him; and if he pleased to send for it, it should be very honestly delivered to his Men, and not the least Injury offered to any of those who came for it, nor the least Perswasion or Invitation made use of to any of them to stay with them; and at the Bottom of the Letter they very humbly besought him, that for their Defence, and for the Safety of their Lives he would be pleased to send them a Barrel of Powder, and some Ammunition, and give them Leave to keep the Mast and Sail of the Boat, that if it was possible for them to make themselves a Boat of any kind, they might shift off to Sea to save themselves in such Part of the World as their Fate should direct them to.

Upon this the Captain, who had won much upon the rest of his Men by what he had said to them, and was very easy as to the General Peace; (for it was very true, that the most mutinous of the Men were gone) came out to the Quarter-Deck, and calling the Men together, let them know the Substance of the Letter; and told the Men, that however they had not deserved such Civility from him, yet he was not willing to expose them more than they were willing to expose themselves, he was inclined to send them some Ammunition; and as they had desired but one Barrel of Powder, he would send them two Barrels, and Shot, or Lead, and Moulds to make Shot in proportion: and, to let them see that he was civiller to them than they deserved, he ordered a Cask of Arrack, and a great Bag of Bread to be sent them for Subsistence, till they should be able to furnish themselves.

The rest of the Men applauded the Captain's Generosity, and every one of them sent us some thing or other; and about three in the Afternoon the Pinnace came on Shore, and brought us all these things, which we were very glad of, and returned the Long-Boat accordingly; and as to the Men that came with the Pinnace, as the Captain had singled out such Men as he knew would not come over to us, so they had positive Orders not to bring any one of us on board again, upon Pain of Death; and indeed both were so true to our Points, that we neither asked them to stay, nor they us to go.

We were now a good Troop, being in all 27 Men, very well armed and provided with every thing but Victuals; we had two Carpenters among us, a Gunner, and, which was worth all the rest, a Surgeon or Doctor, that is to say, he was an Assistant to a Surgeon at *Goa*, and was entertained as Supernumerary with us: The Carpenters had brought all their Tools, the Doctor all his Instruments and Medicines, and indeed we had a great deal of Baggage, that is to say, in the whole, for some of us had little more than the Clothes on our Backs, of whom I was one; but I had one thing which none of them had *viz.* I had the 22 Moydores of Gold, which I stole at the *Brasils*, and two Pieces of Eight. The two Peices of Eight I shewed, and one Moydore, but no more; and none of them ever suspected that I had any more Money in the World, having been known to be only a poor Boy taken up in Charity, as you have heard, and used like a Slave, and in the worst Manner of a Slave, by my cruel Master the Pilot.

It will be easy to imagine we four, that were left at first, were joyful, nay, even surprized with Joy, at the coming of the rest, tho' at first we were frighted, and thought they came to fetch us back to hang us; but they took ways quickly to satisfy us that they were in the same Condition with us, only with this additional Circumstance, that theirs was voluntarily, and ours by Force.

The first Piece of News they told us after the short History of their coming away, was, that our Companion was on board, but how he got thither we could not imagine; for he had given us the Slip, and we never imagined he could swim so well as to venture off to the Ship, which lay at so great a Distance; nay, we did not so much as know that he could swim at all, and not thinking any thing of what really happen'd, we thought that he must have wandered into the Woods, and was devoured, or was fallen into the Hands of the Natives and was murthered; and these Thoughts filled us with Fears enough, and of several kinds, about its being some time or other our Lot to fall into their Hands also.

But hearing how he had with much Difficulty been received on board the Ship again, and pardon'd, we were much better satisfied than before.

Being now, as I have said, a considerable Number of us, and in Condition to defend our selves, the first thing we did was to give every one his Hand, that we would not separate from one another upon any Occasion whatsoever, but that we would live and die together; that we would kill no Food, but that we would distribute it in publick; and that we would be in all things guided by the Majority, and not insist upon our own Resolutions in any thing, if the Majority were against it; that we would appoint a Captain among us to be out Governour or Leader during Pleasure; that while he was in Office, we would obey him without Reserve, on Pain of Death; and that every one should take Turn, but the Captain was not to act in any particular thing without Advice of the rest, and by the Majority.

Having established these Rules, we resolved to enter into some Measures for our Food, and for conversing with the Inhabitants or Natives of the Island, for our Supply; as for Food, they were at first very useful to us, but we soon grew weary of them, being an ignorant, ravenous, brutish sort of People, even worse than the Natives of any other Country that we had seen; and we soon found that the principal Part of our Subsistance was to be had by our Guns, shooting of Deer and other Creatures, and Fowls of all other Sorts, of which there is Abundance.

We found the Natives did not disturb or concern themselves much about us; nor did they enquire, or perhaps know whether we stay'd among them or not, much less that our Ship was gone quite away, and had cast us off, as was our Case; for the next Morning after we had sent back the Long-Boat, the Ship stood away to the South-East, and in four Hours time was out of our Sight.

The next Day two of us went out into the Country one Way, and two another, to see what kind of a Land we were in; and we soon found the Country was very pleasant and fruitful, and a convenient Place enough to live in; but as before, inhabited by a Parcel of Creatures scarce human, or capable of being made sociable on any Account whatsoever.

We found the Place full of Cattle and Provisions; but whether we might venture to take them where we could find them, or not, we did not know; and tho' we were under a Necessity to get Provisions, yet we were loath to bring down a whole Nation of Devils upon us at once, and therefore some of our Company agreed to try to speak with some of the Country, if we could, that we might see what Course was to be taken with them. Eleven of our Men went of this Errand, well armed, and furnished for Defence. They brought Word, that they had seen some of the Natives, who appeared very civil to them, but very shy and afraid, seeing their Guns; for it was easy to perceive, that the Natives knew what their Guns were, and what Use they were of.

They made Signs to the Natives for some Food, and they went and fetched several Herbs and Roots, and some Milk; but it was evident they did not design to give it away, but to sell, making Signs to know what our Men would give them.

Our Men were perplexed at this, for they had nothing to Barter; however, one of the Men pulled out a Knife and shewed them, and they were so fond of it, that they were ready to go together by the Ears for the Knife: The Seaman seeing that, was willing to make a good Market for his Knife, and keeping them chaffering about it a good while, some offered him Roots, and others Milk; at last one offered him a Goat for it, which he took. Then another of our Men shewed them another Knife, but they had nothing good enough for that; whereupon one of them made Signs that he would go and fetch something; so our Men stay'd three Hours for their Return, when they came back and brought him a small sized, thick, short Cow, very fat, and good Meat, and gave him for his Knife.

This was a good Market, but our Misfortune was we had no Merchandize; for our Knives were as needful to us as to them, and but that we were in Distress for Food, and must of Necessity have some, these Men would not have parted with their Knives.

However, in a little time more we found that the Woods were full of living Creatures which we might kill for our Food, and that without giving Offence to them; so that our Men went daily out a Hunting, and never failed to kill something or other; for as to the Natives, we had no Goods to Barter; and for Money, all the Stock among us would not have subsisted us long; however, we called a general Council to see what Money we had, and to bring it all together, that it might go as far as possible; and when it came to my Turn, I pulled out a Moydore and the two Dollars I spoke of before.

This Moydore I ventured to shew, that they might not despise me too much for adding too little to the Store, and that they might not pretend to search me; and they were very civil to me upon the Presumption that I had been so faithful to them as not to conceal any thing from them.

But our Money did us little Service, for the People neither knew the Value of the Use of it, nor could they justly rate the Gold in Proportion with the Silver; so that all our Money, which was not much when it was all put together, would go but a little way with us, that is to say, to buy us Provisions.

Our next Consideration was to get away from this cursed Place, and whether to go; when my Opinion came to be asked, I told them I would leave that all to them, and I told them I had rather they would let me go into the Woods to get them some Provisions, than consult with me, for I would agree to whatever they did; but they would not agree to that, for they would not consent that any of us should go into the Woods alone; for tho' we had yet seen no Lions or Tygers in the Woods, we were assured there were many in the Island, besides other Creatures as dangerous, and, perhaps worse, as we afterwards found by our own Experience.

We had many Adventures in the Woods for our Provisions, and often met with wild and terrible Beasts, which we could not call by their Names, but as they were like us seeking their Prey, but were themselves good for nothing, so we disturbed them as little as possible.

Our Consultations concerning our Escape from this Place, which as I have said, we were now upon, ended in this only, that as we had two Carpenters among us, and that they had Tools almost of all Sorts with them, we should try to build us a Boat to go off to Sea with, and that then perhaps we might, find our way back to *Goa*, or land on some more proper Place to make our Escape. The Counsels of this Assembly were not of great Moment, yet as they seem to be introductory of many more remarkable Adventures which happened under my Conduct hereabouts many Years after, I think this Miniature of my future Enterprizes may not be unpleasant to relate.

To the Building of a Boat I made no Objection, and away they went to work immediately; but as they went on, great Difficulties occurred, such as want of Saws to cut out Plank; Nails, Bolts, and Spikes, to fasten the Timbers, Hemp, Pitch and Tar, to Caulk and Pay her Seams, *and the like:* At length one of the Company proposed, that instead of building a Bark or Sloop, or Shalloup, or whatever they would call it, which they found was so difficult, they should rather make a large *Periagua*, or Canoe, which might be done with great Ease.

It was presently objected, that we could never make a Canoe large enough to pass the great Ocean, which we were to go over, to get to the Coast of *Malabar,* that it not only would not bear the Sea, but it would never bear the Burthen; for we were not only Twenty seven Men of us, but had a great deal of Luggage with us, and must, for our Provision, take in a great deal more.

I never proposed to speak in their General Consultations before; but finding they were at some Loss about what kind of Vessel they should make, and how to make it; and what would be fit for our Use, and what not; I told them I found they were at a full Stop in their Counsels of every kind; that it was true we could never pretend to go over to *Goa*, or the Coast of *Malabar* in a Canoe, which tho' we could all get into it, and that it would bear the Sea well enough, yet would not hold our Provisions, and especially we could not put fresh Water enough into it for the Voyage; and to make such an Adventure would be nothing but meer running into certain Destruction, and yet that nevertheless I was for making a Canoe.

They answered, that they understood all I had said before well enough, but what I meant by telling them first how dangerous and impossible it was to make our Escape in a Canoe, and yet then to advise making a Canoe, that they could not understand.

To this I answer'd, that I conceiv'd our Business was not to attempt our Escape in a Canoe, but that as there were other Vessels at Sea besides our Ship, and that there were few Nations that lived on the Sea-Shore that were so barbarous, but that they went to Sea in some Boats or other, our Business was to cruise along the Coast of the Island, which was very long, and to seize upon the first we could get that was better than our own, and so from that to another, till perhaps we might at last get a good Ship to carry us whither ever we pleased to go.

Excellent Advice, says one of them, admirable Advice, says another. Yes, yes, says the third, which was the Gunner, the *English* Dog has given excellent Advice; but it is just the way to bring us all to the Gallows; the Rogue has given Devilish Advice, indeed, to go a Thieving, till from a little Vessel we come to a great Ship, and so we shall turn downright Pyrates, the End of which is to be hanged.

You may call us Pyrates, says another, if you will, and if we fall into bad Hands, we may be used like Pyrates; but I care not for that, I'll be a Pyrate, or any thing, nay, I'll be hang'd for a Pyrate, rather than starve here; and therefore I think the Advice is very good; and so they cry'd all, Let us have a Canoe. The Gunner over-ruled by the rest; submitted; but as we broke up the Council, he came to me, takes me by the Hand, and looking into the Palm of my Hand, and into my Face too, very gravely, My Lad, *says he*, thou art born to do a World of Mischief; thou hast commenced Pyrate very young, but have a Care of the Gallows, young Man; have a Care, I say, for thou wilt be an eminent Thief.

I laugh'd at him, and told him, I did not know what I might come to hereafter; but as our Case was now, I should make no Scruple to take the first Ship I came at, to get our Liberty: I only wish'd we could see one, and come at her. Just while we were talking, one of our Men that was at the Door of our Hutt, told us, that the Carpenter, who, it seems, was upon a Hill at a Distance, cried out, *a Sail, a Sail.*

We all turn'd out immediately; but tho' it was very clear Weather, we could see nothing; but the Carpenter continuing to holloo to us, *a Sail, a Sail,* away we run up the Hill, and there we saw a Ship plainly; but it was at a very great Distance, too far for us to make any Signal to her.

However, we made a Fire upon the Hill, with all the Wood we could get together, and made as much Smoke as possible. The Wind was down, and it was almost calm; but as we thought by a Perspective Glass which the Gunner had in his Pocket, her Sails were full, and she stood away large with the Wind at E. N. E. taking no Notice of our Signal, but making for the Cape *de bona Speranza*; so we had no Comfort from her.

We went therefore immediately to Work about our intended Canoe, and having singled out a very large Tree to our Mind, we fell to Work with her; and having three good Axes among us, we got it down, but it was four Days time first, tho' we worked very hard too. I do not remember what Wood it was, or exactly what Dimensions; but I remember that it was a large one, and we were as much encouraged when we launched it, and found it swam upright and steady, as we would have been at another time, if we had a good Man of War at our Command.

She was so very large, that she carried us all very easily, and would have carried two or three Ton of Baggage with us; so that we began to consult about going to Sea directly to *Goa*; but many other Considerations check'd that Thought, especially when we came to look nearer into it; such as Want of Provisions, and no Casks for fresh Water; no Compass to steer by; no Shelter from the Breach of the high Sea, which would certainly founder us; no Defence from the Heat of the Weather, and the like; so that they all came readily into my Project, to cruise about where we were, and see what might offer.

Accordingly, to gratify our Fancy, we went one Day all out to Sea in her together, and we were in a very fair Way to have had enough of it; for when she had us all on Board, and that we were gotten about Half a League to Sea, there happening to be a pretty high Swell of the Sea, tho' little or no Wind, yet she wallow'd so in the Sea, that we all of us thought she would at last wallow her self Bottom up; so we set all to Work to get her in nearer the Shore, and giving her fresh Way in the Sea, she swam more steady, and with some hard Work we got her under the Land again.

We were now at a great Loss; the Natives were civil enough to us, and came often to discourse with us; one time they brought one whom they shew'd Respect to as a King, with them, and they set up a long Pole between them and us, with a great Tossel of Hair hanging, not on the Top, but something above the Middle of it, adorn'd with little Chains, Shells, Bits of Brass, and the like; and this we understood afterwards was a Token of Amity and Friendship, and they brought down to us Victuals in Abundance, Cattel, Fowls, Herbs, Roots, but we were in the utmost Confusion on our Side; for we had nothing to buy with, or exchange for; and as to giving us things for nothing, they had no Notion of that again. As to our Money, it was meer Trash to them, they had no Value for it; so that we were in a fair Way to be starved. Had we had but some Toys and Trinckets, Brass Chains, Baubles, Glass Beads, or in a Word, the veriest Trifles that a Ship Loading would not have been worth the Freight, we might have bought Cattel and Provisions enough for an Army, or to Victual a Fleet of Men of War, but for Gold or Silver we could get nothing.

Upon this we were in a strange Consternation. I was but a young Fellow, but I was for falling upon them with our Fire Arms; and taking all the Cattel from them, and send them to the Devil to stop their Hunger, rather than be starved our selves; but I did not consider that this might have brought Ten Thousand of them down upon us the next Day; and tho' we might have killed a vast Number of them, and perhaps have frighted the rest, yet their own Desperation, and our small Number, would have animated them so, that one time or other they would have destroy'd us all.

In the Middle of our Consultation, one of our Men who had been a kind of a Cutler, or Worker in Iron, started up, and ask'd the Carpenter, if among all his Tools he could not help him to a File. Yes, says the Carpenter, I can, but it is a small one. The smaller the better, says the other. Upon this he goes to Work, and first by heating a Piece of an old broken Chissel in the Fire, and then with the Help of his File, he made himself several Kinds of Tools for his Work; and then he takes three or four Pieces of Eight, and beats them out with a Hammer upon a Stone, till they were very broad and thin, then he cut them out into the Shape of Birds and Beasts: he made little Chains of them for Bracelets and Necklaces, and turn'd them into so many Devices, of his own Head, that it is hardly to be exprest.

When he had for about a Fortnight exercised his Head and Hands at this Work, we try'd the Effect of his Ingenuity; and having another Meeting with the Natives, were surprized to see the Folly of the poor People. For a little Bit of Silver cut out in the Shape of a Bird, we had two Cows; and, which was our Loss, if it had been in Brass, it had been still of more Value. For one of the Bracelets made of Chain-work, we had as much Provision of several Sorts, as would fairly have been worth in *England*, Fifteen or Sixteen Pounds; and so of all the rest. Thus, that which when it was in Coin was not worth Six-pence to us, when thus converted into Toys and Trifles, was worth an Hundred Times its real Value, and purchased for us any thing we had Occasion for.

In this Condition, we lived upwards of a Year, but all of us began to be very much tir'd of it, and whatever came of it, resolv'd to attempt to Escape. We had furnished our selves with no less than three very good Canoes; and as the *Monsoones*, or Trade-Winds, generally affect that Country, blowing in most Parts of this Island one six Months of a Year one Way, and the other six Months another Way, we concluded we might be able to bear the Sea well enough. But always when we came to look nearer into it, the Want of fresh Water was the thing that puts us off from such an Adventure, for it is a prodigious Length, and what no Man on Earth could be able to perform without Water to drink.

Being thus prevailed upon by our own Reason to set the Thoughts of that Voyage aside, we had then but two things before us; one was, to put to Sea the other Way, *viz.* West, and go away for the *Cape of Good Hope*, where first or last we should meet with some of our own Country Ships, or else to put for the main Land of *Africa*, and either travel by Land, or sail along the Coast towards the Red Sea, where we should first or last find a Ship of some Nation or other, that would take us up, or perhaps we might take them up; which, by the bye, was the thing that always run in my Head.

It was our ingenious Cutler, whom ever after we called *Silver-Smith*, that proposed this; but the Gunner told him, that he had been in the Red Sea, in a *Malabar* Sloop, and he knew this, that if we went into the Red Sea, we should either be killed by the wild *Arabs*, or taken and made Slaves of by the *Turks*; and therefore he was not for going that Way.

Upon this I took Occasion to put in my Vote again. *Why*, said I, *do we talk of being killed by the* Arabs, *or made Slaves of by the* Turks? *Are we not able to board almost any Vessel we shall meet with in those Seas; and instead of their taking us, we to take them?* Well done, *Pyrate*, said the Gunner, he that had look'd in my Hand, and told me I should come to the Gallows; *I'll say that for him*, says he, *he always looks the same Way. But I think o' my Conscience, 'tis our only Way now.* Don't tell me, *says I*, of being a Pyrate, *we must be Pyrates, or any thing, to get fairly out of this cursed Place.*

In a Word, they concluded all by my Advice, that our Business was to cruize for any thing we could see. Why then, *said I* to them, our first Business is to see, if the People upon this Island have no Navigation, and what Boats they use; and if they have any better or bigger than ours, let us take one of them. First indeed all our Aim was to get, if possible, a Boat with a Deck and a Sail; for then we might have saved our Provisions, which otherwise we could not.

We had, to our great good Fortune, one Sailor among us, who had been Assistant to the Cook, he told us, that he would find a Way how to preserve our Beef, without Cask or Pickle; and this he did effectually by curing it in the Sun, with the Help of Salt-Petre, of which there was great Plenty in the Island; so that before we found any Method for our Escape, we had dry'd the Flesh of six or seven Cows and Bullocks, and ten or twelve Goats, and it relished so well, that we never gave our selves the Trouble to boil it when we eat it, but either broiled it, or eat it dry: But our main Difficulty about fresh Water still remained; for we had no Vessel to put any into, much less to keep any for our going to Sea.

But our first Voyage being only to coast the Island, we resolved to venture, whatever the Hazard or Consequence of it might be; and in order to preserve as much fresh Water as we could, our Carpenter made a Well thwart the Middle of one of our Canoes, which he separated from the other Parts of the Canoe, so as to make it tight to hold the Water, and cover'd so as we might step upon it; and this was so large, that it held near a Hogshead of Water very well. I cannot better describe this Well, than by the same kind which the small Fisher-Boats in *England* have to preserve their Fish alive in; only, that this, instead of having Holes to let the Salt Water in, was made sound every Way to keep it out; and it was the first Invention, I believe, of its Kind, for such an Use: But Necessity is a Spur to Ingenuity, and the Mother of Invention.

It wanted but a little Consultation to resolve now upon our Voyage. The first Design was only to coast it round the Island, as well to see if we could seize upon any Vessel fit to embark our selves in, as also to take hold of any Opportunity which might present for our passing over to the Main; and therefore our Resolution was to go on the Inside, or West Shore of the Island, where at least at one Point, the Land stretching a great Way to the North-West, the Distance is not extraordinary great from the Island to the Coast of *Africk*.

Such a Voyage, and with such a desperate Crew, I believe was never made; for it is certain we took the worst Side of the Island to look for any Shipping, especially for Shipping of other Nations, this being quite out of the Way: However, we put to Sea, after taking all our Provisions and Ammunition, Bag and Baggage on Board; we had made both Mast and Sail for our two large Periagua's, and the other we paddl'd along as well as we could; but when a Gale sprung up, we took her in Tow.

We sail'd merrily forward for several Days, meeting with nothing to interrupt us. We saw several of the Natives in small Canoes, catching Fish, and sometimes we endeavoured to come near enough to speak with them, but they were always shye, and afraid of us, making in for the Shore, as soon as we attempted it; till one of our Company remember'd the Signal of Friendship which the Natives made us from the South Part of the Island, *viz.* of setting up a long Pole and put us in Mind, that perhaps it was the same thing to them as a Flag of Truce was to us: So we resolved to try it and accordingly the next time we saw any of their Fishing Boats at Sea, we put up a Pole in our Canoe that had no Sail, and rowed towards them. As soon as they saw the Pole, they staid for us, and as we came nearer, paddl'd towards us When they came to us, they shewed themselves very much pleased, and gave us some large Fish, of which we did not know the Names, but they were very good. It was our Misfortune still, that we had nothing to give them in Return; but our Artist, of whom I spoke before, gave them two little thin Plates of Silver, beaten, as I said before, out of a Piece of Eight; they were cut in a Diamond Square, longer one way than t'other, and a Hole punch'd at one of the longest Corners. This they were so fond of, that they made us stay till they had cast their Lines and Nets again, and gave us as many Fish as we cared to have.

All this while we had our Eyes upon their Boats, view'd them very narrowly, and examined whether any of them were fit for our Turn; but they were poor sorry things; their Sail was made of a large Matt, only one that was of a Piece of Cotton Stuff, fit for little, and their Ropes were twisted Flags, of no Strength; so we concluded we were better as we were, and let them alone. We went forward to the North, keeping the Coast close on Board for twelve Days together; and having the Wind at East, and E. S. E. we made very fresh Way. We saw no Towns on the Shore, but often saw some Hutts by the Water Side, upon the Rocks, and always Abundance of People about them, who we could perceive run together to stare at us.

It was as odd a Voyage as ever Men went: We were a little Fleet of three Ships, and an Army of between Twenty and Thirty as dangerous Fellows as ever they had among them; and had they known what we were they would have compounded to give us every thing we desired, to be rid of us.

On the other Hand, we were as miserable as Nature could well make us to be; for we were upon *a* Voyage and *no* Voyage, we were bound *some* where and *no* where; for tho' we knew what we intended to do, we did really not know what we were doing: We went forward and forward by a Northerly Course; and as we advanced, the Heat increased, which began to be intolerable to us who were upon the Water, without any Covering from Heat or Wet; besides we were now in the Month of *October*, or thereabouts, in a Southern Latitude, and as we went every Day nearer the Sun, the Sun came also every Day nearer to us, till at last we found our selves in the Latitude of 20 Degrees, and having past the Tropick about five or six Days before that, in a few Days more the Sun would be in the Zenith, just over our Heads.

Upon these Considerations we resolved to seek for a good Place to go on Shore again, and pitch our Tents till the Heat of the Weather abated. We had by this time measured Half the Length of the Island, and were come to that Part where the Shore tending away to the North-West, promised fair to make our Passage over to the main Land of *Africk*, much shorter than we expected. But notwithstanding that, we had good Reason to believe it was about 120 Leagues.

So, the Heats consider'd, we resolved to take Harbour; besides, our Provisions were exhausted, and we had not many Days Store left. Accordingly, putting in for the Shore early in the Morning, as we usually did once in three or four Days, for fresh Water, we sat down and considered, whether we should go on, or take up our Standing there; but upon several Considerations too long to repeat here, we did not like the Place, so we resolved to go on for a few Days longer.

After Sailing on N. W. by N. with a fresh Gale at S. E. about six Days, we found at a great Distance, a large Promontory, or Cape of Land, pushing out a long Way into the Sea; and as we were exceeding fond of seeing what was beyond the Cape, we resolved to double it before we took into Harbour; so we kept on our Way, the Gale continuing, and yet it was four Days more before we reach'd the Cape. But it is not possible to express the Discouragement and Melancholy that seized us all when we came thither; for when we made the Head Land of the Cape, we were surprized to see the Shore fall away on, the other Side, as much as it had advanced on this Side, and a great deal more; and that, in short, if we would adventure over to the Shore of *Africk*, it must be from hence; for that if we went further, the Breadth of the Sea still increased, and to what Breadth it might increase, we knew not.

While we mused upon this Discovery, we were surprized with very bad Weather, and especially violent Rains, with Thunder and Lightning most unusually terrible to us. In this Pickle we run for the Shore, and getting under the Lee of the Cape, run our Frigates into a little Creek, where we saw the Land overgrown with Trees, and made all the Haste possible to get on Shore, being exceeding wet, and fatigued with the Heat, the Thunder, Lightning and Rain.

Here we thought our Case was very deplorable indeed, and therefore our Artist, of whom I have spoken so often, set up a great Cross of Wood on the Hill, which was within a Mile of the Head Land, with these Words, but in the *Portuguese* Language,

Point Desperation. Jesus have Mercy!

We set to work immediately to build us some Hutts, and to get our Clothes dry'd, and tho' I was young, and had no Skill in such Things, yet I shall never forget the little City we built, for it was no less; and we fortify'd it accordingly; and the Idea is so fresh in my Thought, that I cannot but give a short Description of it.

Our Camp was on the South Side of a little Creek on the Sea, and under the Shelter of a steep Hill, which lay, tho' on the other Side of the Creek, yet within a Quarter of a Mile of us N. W. by N. and very happily intercepted the Heat of the Sun all the after Part of the Day. The Spot we pitched on had a little fresh Water, Brook, or a Stream running into the Creek by us, and we saw Cattle feeding in the Plains and low Ground, East and to the South of us a great Way.

Here we set up twelve little Hutts, like Soldiers Tents, but made of the Boughs of Trees stuck into the Ground, and bound together on the Top with Withes, and such other things as we could get; the Creek was our Defence on the North, a little Brook on the West, and the South and East Sides we fortify'd with a Bank, which entirely covered our Hutts; and being drawn oblique from the North West to the South East, made our City a Triangle. Behind the Bank, or Line, our Hutts stood, having three other Hutts behind them at a good Distance. In one of these, which was a little one, and stood further off, we put our Gun-powder, and nothing else, for fear of Danger; in the other, which was bigger, we drest our Victuals, and put all our Necessaries; and in the third, which was biggest of all, we eat our Dinners, called our Councils, and sat and diverted our selves with such Conversation as we had one with another, which was but indifferent truly at that time.

Our Correspondence with the Natives was absolutely necessary, and our Artist, the Cutler, having made Abundance of those little Diamond cut Squares of Silver, with these we made Shift to Traffick with the black People for what we wanted; for indeed they were pleased wonderfully with them: And thus we got Plenty of Provisions. At first, and in particular, we got about fifty Head of Black Cattel and Goats, and our Cook's Mate took care to cure them, and dry them, salt and preserve them for our grand Supply; nor was this hard to do, the Salt and Salt-Petre being very good, and the Sun excessively hot; and here we lived about four Months.

The Southern Solstice was over, and the Sun gone back towards the *Equinoctial*, when we considered of our next Adventure, which was to go over the Sea of *Zanquebar*, as the *Portuguese* call it, and to land, if possible, upon the Continent of *Africa*.

We talked with many of the Natives about it, such as we could make our selves intelligible to; but all that we could learn from them was, that there was a great Land of Lions beyond the Sea, but that it was a great Way off; we knew as well as they that it was a long Way, but our People differed mightily about it: Some said it was 150 Leagues, others not above 100. One of our Men that had a Map of the World shewed us by his Scale, that it was not above 80 Leagues. Some said there were Islands all the Way to touch at; some that there were no Islands at all: For my Part, I knew nothing of this Matter one way or another, but heard it all without Concern, whether it was near or far off; however, this we learned from an Old Man who was blind, and led about by a Boy, that if we stay'd till the End of *August,* we should be sure of the Wind to be fair, and the Sea smooth all the Voyage.

This was some Encouragement, but staying again was very unwelcome News to us, because that then the Sun would be returning again to the South, which was what our Men were very unwilling to. At last we called a Council of our whole Body; their Debates were too tedious to take Notice of, only to note, that when it came to *Captain Bob,* (for so they called me ever since I had taken State upon me before one of their great Princes) truly I was on no Side, it was not one Farthing Matter to me, I told them, whether we went or stayed, I had no home, and all the World was alike to me; so I left it entirely to them to determine.

In a Word, they saw plainly there was nothing to be done where we were, without Shipping; that if our Business indeed was only to eat and drink, we could not find a better Place in the

World; but if our Business was to get away, and get home into our own Country, we could not find a Worse.

I confess, I liked the Country wonderfully, and even then had strange Notions of coming again to live there; and I used to say to them very often, that if I had but a Ship of 20 Guns, and a Sloop, and both well Manned, I would not desire a better Place in the World to make my self as rich as a King.

But to return to the Consultations they were in about going: Upon the whole, it was resolved to venture over for the Main; and venture we did, madly enough, indeed; for it was the wrong time of the Year to undertake such a Voyage in that Country; for, as the Winds hang Easterly all the Months from *September* to *March,* so they generally hang Westerly all the rest of the Year, and blew right in our Teeth, so that as soon as we had, with a kind of a Land Breeze, stretched over about 15 or 20 Leagues, and, as I may say, just enough to lose our selves, we found the Wind set in a steady fresh Gale or Breeze from the Sea, at West W. S. W. or S. W. by W. and never further from the West; so that, in a Word we could make nothing of it.

On the other Hand, the Vessel, such as we had would not lye close upon a Wind; if so, we might have stretched away N. N. W. and have met with a great many Islands in our Way, as we found afterwards; but we could make nothing of it, tho' we tried, and by the trying had almost undone us all; for, stretching away to the North, as near the Wind as we could, we had forgotten the Shape and Position of the Island of *Madagascar* it self; how that we came off at the Head of a Promontory or Point of Land that lies about the Middle of the Island, and that stretches out West a great way into the Sea; and that now being run a Matter of 40 Leagues to the North, the Shore of the Island fell off again above 200 Miles to the East, so that we were by this Time in the wide Ocean, between the Island and the Main, and almost 100 Leagues from both.

Indeed as the Winds blew fresh at West, as before, we had a smooth Sea, and we found it pretty good going before it, and so taking our smallest Canoe in Tow, we stood in for the Shore with all the Sail we could make. This was a terrible Adventure; for if the least Gust of Wind had come, we had been all lost, our Canoes being deep, and in no Condition to make Way in a high Sea.

This Voyage, however, held us eleven Days in all, and at length having spent most of our Provisions, and every Drop of Water we had, we spied Land, to our great Joy, tho' at the Distance of ten or eleven Leagues, and as under the Land, the Wind came off like a Land Breeze, and blew hard against us, we were two Days more before we reached the Shore, having all that while excessive hot Weather, and not a Drop of Water, or any other Liquor, except some Cordial Waters, which one of our Company had a little of left in a Case of Bottles.

This gave us a Taste of what we should have done, if we had ventured forward with a scant Wind and uncertain Weather, and gave us a Surfeit of our Design for the Main, at least 'till we might have some better Vessels under us; so we went on Shore again, and pitched our Camp, as before; in as convenient Manner as we could, fortifying our selves against any Surprize; but the Natives here were exceeding courteous, and much civiller than on the South Part of the Island; and tho' we could not understand what they said, or they us, yet we found Means to make them understand that we were Sea-faring Men, and Strangers; and that we were in Distress for want of Provisions.

The first Proof we had of their Kindness was, that, as soon as they saw us come on Shore, and begin to make our Habitation, one of their Captains or Kings, for we knew not what to call them, came down with five or six Men and some Women, and brought us five Goats and two young fat Steers, and gave them to us for nothing; and when we went to offer them any thing, the Captain, or the King, would not let any of them touch it, or take any thing of us. About two Hours after came another King or Captain, with forty or fifty Men after him; we began to be afraid of him, and laid Hands upon our Weapons; but he perceiving it, caused two Men to go before him carrying two long Poles in their Hands, which they held upright, as high as they could, which we presently perceiv'd was a Signal of Peace, and these two Poles they set up afterwards sticking them up in the Ground; and when the King and his Men came to these two Poles, they stuck all their Lances up in the Ground, and came on unarmed, leaving their Lances, as also their Bows and Arrows behind them.

This was to satisfy us, that they were come as Friends, and we were very glad to see it; for we had no Mind to quarrel with them, if we could help it. The Captain of this Gang seeing some of our Men making up their Hutts, and that they did it but bunglingly, he becken'd to some of his Men to go and help us. Immediately 15 or 16 of them came and mingled among us, and went to Work for us; and, indeed, they were better Workmen than we were, for they run up three or four Hutts for us in a Moment, and much handsomer done than ours.

After this they sent us Milk, Plantanes, Pumpkins, and Abundance of Roots and Greens that were very good, and then took their Leave, and would not take any thing from us that we had. One of our Men offer'd the King or Captain of these Men a Dram, which he drank, and was mightily pleased with it, and held out his Hand for another, which we gave him; and, in a Word, after this, he hardly failed coming to us two or three times a Week, always bringing us something or other, and one time sent us seven Head of Black Cattle, some of which we cured and dried as before.

And here I cannot but remember one thing, which afterwards stood us in great stead, *viz.* that the Flesh of their Goats and their Beef also, but especially the former, when we had dried and cured it, looked red, and eat hard and firm, as dry'd Beef in *Holland*; they were so pleased with it, and it was such a Dainty to them, that at any time after they would Trade with us for it, not knowing, or so much as imagining, what it was; so that for Ten or Twelve Pound Weight of smoked dry'd Beef, they would give us a whole Bullock, or Cow, or any thing else we could desire.

Here we observed two Things that were very material to us, even essentially so; first, we found they had a great deal of Earthen-Ware here, which they make use of many ways, as we did: Particularly they had long deep Earthen Pots, which they used to sink into the Ground to keep the Water which they drank cool and pleasant; and the other was, that they had larger Canoes than their Neighbours had.

By this we were prompted to enquire if they had no larger Vessels than those we saw there; or if any other of the Inhabitants had not such. They signified presently, that they had no larger Boats than that they shewed us; but that on the other Side of the Island they had larger Boats, and that with Decks upon them, and large Sails; and this made us resolve to Coast round the whole Island to see them; so we prepared and victualled our Canoe for the Voyage, and, in a Word, went to Sea for the third time.

It cost us a Month or six Weeks time to perform this Voyage, in which time we went on Shore several times for Water and Provisions, and found the Natives always very free and courteous; but we were surprized one Morning early; being at the Extremity of the Northermost Part of the Island, when one of our Men cried out *a Sail, a Sail*: We presently saw a Vessel a great Way out at Sea; but after we had looked at it with our Perspective Glasses, and endeavoured all we could to make out what it was, we could not tell what to think of it; for it was neither Ship, Ketch, Gaily, Galliot, or like any thing that we had ever seen before: All that we could make of it was, that it went from us standing out to Sea. In a Word, we soon lost Sight of it, for we were in no Condition to chase any thing, and we never saw it again, but by all we could perceive of it, from what we saw of such things afterwards, it was some *Arabian* Vessel which had been trading to the Coast of *Mosambique*, or *Zanguebar*, the same Place where we afterwards went, as you shall hear.

I kept no Journal of this Voyage, nor indeed did I all this while understand any thing of Navigation, more than the common Business of a Fore-mast Man; so I can say nothing to the Latitudes or Distances of any Places we were at, how long we were going, or how far we sailed in a Day; but this I remember, that being now come round the Island, we sailed up the Eastern Shore due South, as we had done down the Western Shore due North before.

Nor do I remember that the Natives differed much from one another, either in Stature or Complexion, or in their Manners, their Habits their Weapons, or indeed in any thing; and yet we could not perceive that they had any Intelligence one with another; but they were extremely kind and civil to us on this Side, as well as on the other.

We continued our Voyage South for many Weeks, tho' with several Intervals of going on Shore to get Provisions and Water. At length, coming round at Point of Land which lay about a League farther than ordinary into the Sea, we were agreeably surprized with a Sight, which, no doubt, had been as disagreeable to those concern'd, as it was pleasant to us. This was the Wreck of an *European* Ship, which had been cast away upon the Rocks, which in that Place run a great Way into the Sea.

We could see plainly at Low Water, a great deal of the Ship lay dry; even at High Water, she was not entirely covered; and that at most she did not lye above a League from the Shore. It will easily be believ'd, that our Curiosity led us, the Wind and Weather also permitting, to go directly to her, which we did without any Difficulty, and presently found that it was a *Dutch*-built Ship, and that she could not have been very long in that Condition, a great deal of the upper Work of her Stern remaining firm, with the Mizen Mast standing. Her Stern seem'd to be jaum'd in between two Ridges of the Rock, and so remained fast, all the Fore-part of the Ship having been beaten to Pieces.

We could see nothing to be gotten out of the Wreck that was worth our while; but we resolv'd to go on Shore, and stay sometime thereabouts, to see if perhaps we might get any Light into the Story of her, and we were not without Hopes that we might hear something more particular about her Men, and perhaps find some of them on Shore there, in the same Condition that we were in, and so might encrease our Company.

It was a very pleasant Sight to us, when coming on Shore, we saw all the Marks and Tokens of a Ship-Carpenter's Yard; as a Launch Block and Craddles, Scaffolds and Planks, and Pieces of Planks, the Remains of the Building a Ship or Vessel; and, in a Word, a great many things that fairly invited us to go about the same Work, and we soon came to understand, that the Men belonging to the Ship that was lost, had saved themselves on Shore, perhaps in their Boat, and had built themselves a Bark or Sloop, and so were gone to Sea again; and enquiring of the Natives which Way they went, they pointed to the South and South-West, by which we could easily understand that they were gone away to the *Cape of Good Hope.*

No body will imagine we could be so dull as not to gather from hence, that we might take the same Method for our Escapes; so we resolved first in general, that we would try, if possible, to build us a Boat of one Kind or other, and go to Sea as our Fate should direct.

In order to this, our first Work was to have the two Carpenters search about to see what Materials the *Dutchmen* had left behind them that might be of Use; and in particular, they found one that was very useful, and which I was much employ'd about, and that was a Pitch-Kettle,[1] and a little Pitch in it.

When we came to set close to this Work, we found it very laborious and difficult, having but few Tools, no Iron Work, no Cordage, no Sails; so that, in short, whatever we built, we were oblig'd to be our own Smiths, Rope-Makers, Sail-Makers, and indeed to practice twenty Trades that we knew little or nothing of: However, Necessity was the Spur to Invention, and we did many things which before we thought impracticable, that is to say, in our Circumstances.

After our two Carpenters had resolved upon the Dimensions of what they would build, they set us all to Work, to go off in our Boats, and split up the Wreck of the old Ship, and to bring away every thing we could; and particularly, that, if possible, we should bring away the Mizen Mast, which was left standing, which with much Difficulty we effected, after above twenty Days Labour of fourteen of our Men.

At the same time we got out a great deal of Iron-Work; as Bolts, Spikes, Nails, &c. all which our Artist, of whom I have spoken already, who was now grown a very dexterous Smith, made us Nails and Hinges for our Rudder, and Spikes such as we wanted.

But we wanted an Anchor, and if we had had an Anchor, we could not have made a Cable; so we contented our selves with making some Ropes with the Help of the Natives, of such Stuff as they made their Matts of, and with these we made such a kind of cable or *Tow Line*, as was sufficient to fasten our Vessel to the Shore, which we contented our selves with for that time.

To be short, we spent four Months here, and work'd very hard too; at the End of which time we launch'd our Frigate, which, in a few Words, had many Defects, but yet, all things considered, it was as well as we could expect it to be.

In short, it was a kind of a Sloop, of the Burthen of near 18 or 20 Ton, and had we had Masts and Sails; standing, and running Rigging, as is usual in such Cases, and other Conveniences, the Vessel might have carry'd us wherever we could have had a Mind to go; but of all the Materials we wanted, this was the worst, *viz.* that we had no Tar or Pitch to pay the Seams, and secure the Bottom; and tho' we did what we could with Tallow and Oil, to make a Mixture to supply that Part, yet we could not bring it to answer our End fully; and when we launch'd her into the Water, she was so leaky, and took in the Water so fast, that we thought all our Labour had been lost, for we had much ado to make her swim; and as for Pumps, we had none, nor had we any Means to make one.

But at length one of the Natives, a black *Negro-man*, shewed us a Tree, the Wood of which being put into the Fire, sends forth a Liquid that is as glutinous, and almost as strong as Tar, and of which, by boiling, we made a Sort of Stuff which serv'd us for Pitch, and this answered our End effectually; for we perfectly made our Vessel sound and tight, so that we wanted no Pitch or Tar at all. This Secret has stood me in stead upon many Occasions since that time, in the same Place.

Our Vessel being thus finished, out of the Mizen Mast of the Ship, we made a very good Mast to her, and fitted our Sails to it as well as we could; then we made a Rudder and Tiller; and, in a Word, every thing that our present Necessity called upon us for; and having victualled her, and put as much fresh Water on Board as we thought we wanted, or as we knew how to stow (for we were yet without Casks) we put to Sea with a fair Wind.

We had spent near another Year in these Rambles, and in this Piece of Work; for it was now, as our Men said, about the Beginning of our *February*, and the Sun went from us apace, which was much to our Satisfaction, for the Heats were exceeding violent. The Wind, as I said, was fair, for as I have since learnt, the Winds generally spring up to the Eastward, as the Sun goes from them to the North.

Our Debate now was, which Way we should go, and never were Men so irresolute; some were for going to the East, and stretching away directly for the Coast of *Malabar*; but others who considered more seriously the Length of that Voyage, shook their Heads at the Proposal, knowing very well, that neither our Provisions, especially of Water; or our Vessel, were equal to such a Run as that is, of near 2000 Miles, without any Land to touch at in the Way.

These Men too had all along had a great Mind to a Voyage for the main Land of *Africk*, where they said we should have a fair Cast for our Lives, and might be sure to make our selves rich which Way soever we went, if we were but able to make our Way through, whether by Sea or by Land.

Besides, as the Case stood with us, we had not much Choice for our Way; for if we had resolv'd for the East, we were at the wrong Season of the Year, and must have staid till *April* or *May* before we had gone to Sea. At length, as we had the Wind at S. E. and E. S. E. and fine promising Weather, we came all into the first Proposal, and resolved for the Coast of *Africa*; nor were we long in disputing as to our Coasting the Island, which we were upon; for we were now on the wrong Side of the Island for the Voyage we intended; So we stood away to the North, and having rounded the Cape, we hall'd away Southward under the Lee of the Island, thinking to reach the West Point of Land, which, as I Observed before, runs out so far towards the Coast of *Africa*, as would have shorten'd our Run almost 100 Leagues. But when we had sailed about thirty Leagues, we found the Winds variable under the Shore, and right against us; so we concluded to stand over directly, for then we had the Wind fair, and our Vessel was but very ill fitted to lye near the Wind, or any Way indeed but just afore it.

Having resolv'd upon it therefore, we put in to the Shore, to furnish our selves again with fresh Water and other Provisions, and about the latter End of *March*, with more Courage than Discretion, more Resolution than Judgment, we launch'd for the main Coast of *Africa*.

As for me, I had no Anxieties about it; so that we had but a View of reaching some Land or other, I cared not what or where it was to be, having at this time no Views of what was before me, nor much Thought of what might, or might not befal me; but with as little Consideration as any one can be supposed to have at my Age, I consented to every thing that was proposed, however hazardous the thing it self, however improbable the Success.

Captain Hook

J. M. BARRIE

The Pirate Ship

One green light squinting over Kidd's Creek, which is near the mouth of the pirate river, marked where the brig, the *Jolly Roger*, lay, low in the water; a rakish-looking craft foul to the hull, every beam in her detestable like ground strewn with mangled feathers. She was the cannibal of the seas, and scarce needed that watchful eye, for she floated immune in the horror of her name.

She was wrapped in the blanket of night, through which no sound from her could have reached the shore. There was little sound, and none agreeable save the whir of the ship's sewing machine at which Smee sat, ever industrious and obliging, the essence of the commonplace, pathetic Smee. I know not why he was so infinitely pathetic, unless it were because he was so pathetically unaware of it; but even strong men had to turn hastily from looking at him, and more than once on summer evenings he had touched the fount of Hook's tears and made it flow. Of this, as of almost everything else, Smee was quite unconscious.

A few of the pirates leant over the bulwarks drinking in the miasma of the night; others sprawled by barrels over games of dice and cards; and the exhausted four who had carried the little house lay prone on the deck, where even in their sleep they rolled skilfully to this side or that out of Hook's reach, lest he should claw them mechanically in passing.

Hook trod the deck in thought. O man unfathomable. It was his hour of triumph. Peter had been removed for ever from his path, and all the other boys were on the brig, about to walk the plank. It was his grimmest deed since the days when he had brought Barbecue to heel; and knowing as we do how vain a tabernacle is man, could we be surprised had he now paced the deck unsteadily, bellied out by the winds of his success?

But there was no elation in his gait, which kept pace with the action of his sombre mind. Hook was profoundly dejected.

He was often thus when communing with himself on board ship in the quietude of the night. It was because he was so terribly alone. This inscrutable man never felt more alone than when surrounded by his dogs. They were socially so inferior to him.

Hook was not his true name. To reveal who he really was would even at this date set the country in a blaze; but as those who read between the lines must already have guessed, he had been at a famous public school; and its traditions still clung to him like garments, with which indeed they are largely concerned. Thus it was offensive to him even now to board a ship in the same dress in which he grappled her; and he still adhered in his walk to the school's distinguished slouch. But above all he retained the passion for good form.

Good form! However much he may have degenerated, he still knew that this is all that really matters.

From far within him he heard a creaking as of rusty portals, and through them came a stern tap-tap-tap, like hammering in the night when one cannot sleep. 'Have you been good form today?' was their eternal question.

'Fame, fame, that glittering bauble, it is mine,' he cried.

'Is it quite good form to be distinguished at anything?' the tap-tap from his school replied.

'I am the only man whom Barbecue feared,' he urged; 'and Flint himself feared Barbecue.'

'Barbecue, Flint – what house?' came the cutting retort.

Most disquieting reflection of all, was it not bad form to think about good form?

His vitals were tortured by this problem. It was a claw within him sharper than the iron one; and as it tore him, the perspiration dripped down his sallow countenance and streaked his doublet. Ofttimes he drew his sleeve across his face, but there was no damming that trickle.

Ah, envy not Hook.

There came to him a presentiment of his early dissolution. It was as if Peter's terrible oath had boarded the ship. Hook felt a gloomy desire to make his dying speech, lest presently there should be no time for it.

'Better for Hook,' he cried, 'if he had had less ambition.' It was in his darkest hours only that he referred to himself in the third person.

'No little children love me.'

Strange that he should think of this, which had never troubled him before; perhaps the sewing machine brought it to his mind. For long he muttered to himself, staring at Smee, who was hemming placidly, under the conviction that all children feared him.

Feared him! Feared Smee! There was not a child on board the brig that night who did not already love him. He had said horrid things to them and hit them with the palm of his hand, because he could not hit with his fist; but they had only clung to him the more. Michael had tried on his spectacles.

To tell poor Smee that they thought him lovable! Hook itched to do it, but it seemed too brutal. Instead, he revolved this mystery in his mind: why do they find Smee lovable? He pursued the problem like the sleuth hound that he was. If Smee was lovable, what was it that made him so? A terrible answer suddenly presented itself: 'Good form?'

Had the bo'sun good form without knowing it, which is the best form of all?

He remembered that you have to prove you don't know you have it before you are eligible for Pop.

With a cry of rage he raised his iron hand over Smee's head; but he did not tear. What arrested him was this reflection:

'To claw a man because he is good form, what would that be?'

'Bad form!'

The unhappy Hook was as impotent as he was damp, and he fell forward like a cut flower.

His dogs thinking him out of the way for a time, discipline instantly relaxed; and they broke into a bacchanalian dance, which brought him to his feet at once; all traces of human weakness gone, as if a bucket of water had passed over him.

'Quiet, you scugs,' he cried, 'or I'll cast anchor in you': and at once the din was hushed. 'Are all the children chained, so they cannot fly away?'

'Ay, ay.'

'Then hoist them up.'

The wretched prisoners were dragged from the hold, all except Wendy, and ranged in line in front of him. For a time he seemed unconscious of their presence. He lolled at his ease, humming, not unmelodiously, snatches of a rude song, and fingering a pack of cards. Ever and anon the light from his cigar gave a touch of colour to his face.

'Now then, bullies,' he said briskly, 'six of you walk the plank to-night, but I have room for two cabin boys. Which of you is it to be?'

'Don't irritate him unnecessarily,' had been Wendy's instructions in the hold; so Tootles stepped forward politely. Tootles hated the idea of signing under such a man, but an instinct told him that it would be prudent to lay the responsibility on an absent person; and though a some-what silly boy, he knew that mothers alone are always willing to be the buffer. All children know this about mothers, and despise them for it, but make constant use of it.

So Tootles explained prudently, 'You see, sir, I don't think my mother would like me to be a pirate. Would your mother like you to be a pirate, Slightly?'

He winked at Slightly, who said mournfully, 'I don't think so,' as if he wished things had been otherwise. 'Would your mother like you to be a pirate, Twin?'

'I don't think so,' said the first twin, as clever as the others. 'Nibs, would—'

'Stow this gab,' roared Hook, and the spokesmen were dragged back. 'You, boy,' he said, addressing John, 'you look as if you had a little pluck in you. Didst never want to be a pirate, my hearty?'

Now John had sometimes experienced this hankering at maths prep., and he was struck by Hook's picking him out.

'I once thought of calling myself Red-handed Jack,' he said diffidently.

'And a good name too. We'll call you that here, bully, if you join.'

'What do you think, Michael?' asked John.

'What would you call me if I join?' Michael demanded.

'Blackbeard Joe.'

Michael was naturally impressed. 'What do you think, John?' He wanted John to decide, and John wanted him to decide.

'Shall we still be respectful subjects of the King?' John inquired.

Through Hook's teeth came the answer: 'You would have to swear, "Down with the King."'

Perhaps John had not behaved very well so far, but he shone out now.

'Then I refuse,' he cried, banging the barrel in front of Hook.

'And I refuse,' cried Michael.

'Rule Britannia!' squeaked Curly.

The infuriated pirates buffeted them in the mouth; and Hook roared out, 'That seals your doom. Bring up their mother. Get the plank ready.'

They were only boys, and they went white as they saw Jukes and Cecco preparing the fatal plank. But they tried to look brave when Wendy was brought up.

No words of mine can tell you how Wendy despised those pirates. To the boys there was at least some glamour in the pirate calling, but all that she saw was that the ship had not been scrubbed for years. There was not a port-hole, on the grimy glass of which you might not have written with your finger 'Dirty pig'; and she had already written it on several. But as the boys gathered round her she had no thought, of course, save for them.

'So, my beauty,' said Hook, as if he spoke in syrup, 'you are to see your children walk the plank.'

Fine gentleman though he was, the intensity of his communings had soiled his ruff, and suddenly he knew that she was gazing at it. With a hasty gesture he tried to hide it, but he was too late.

'Are they to die?' asked Wendy, with a look of such frightful contempt that he nearly fainted.

'They are,' he snarled. 'Silence all,' he called gloatingly, 'for a mother's last words to her children.'

At this moment Wendy was grand. 'These are my last words, dear boys,' she said firmly. 'I feel that I have a message to you from your real mothers, and it is this: "We hope our sons will die like English gentlemen."'

Even the pirates were awed; and Tootles cried out hysterically, 'I am going to do what my mother hopes. What are you to do, Nibs?'

'What my mother hopes. What are you to do, Twin?'

'What my mother hopes. John, what are—'

But Hook had found his voice again.

'Tie her up,' he shouted.

It was Smee who tied her to the mast. 'See here, honey,' he whispered, 'I'll save you if you promise to be my mother.'

But not even for Smee would she make such a promise. 'I would almost rather have no children at all,' she said disdainfully.

It is sad to know that not a boy was looking at her as Smee tied her to the mast; the eyes of all were on the plank: that last little walk they were about to take. They were no longer able to hope that they would walk it manfully, for the capacity to think had gone from them; they could stare and shiver only.

Hook smiled on them with his teeth closed, and took a step toward Wendy. His intention was to turn her face so that she should see the boys walking the plank one by one. But he never reached her, he never heard the cry of anguish he hoped to wring from her. He heard something else instead.

It was the terrible tick-tick of the crocodile.

They all heard it – pirates, boys, Wendy; and immediately every head was blown in one direction; not to the water whence the sound proceeded, but toward Hook. All knew that what was about to happen concerned him alone, and that from being actors they were suddenly become spectators.

Very frightful was it to see the change that came over him. It was as if he had been clipped at every joint. He fell in a little heap.

The sound came steadily nearer; and in advance of it came this ghastly thought, 'The crocodile is about to board the ship.'

Even the iron claw hung inactive; as if knowing that it was no intrinsic part of what the attacking force wanted. Left so fearfully alone, any other man would have lain with his eyes shut where he fell: but the gigantic brain of Hook was still working, and under its guidance he crawled on his knees along the deck as far from the sound as he could go. The pirates respectfully cleared a passage for him, and it was only when he brought up against the bulwarks that he spoke.

'Hide me,' he cried hoarsely.

They gathered round him; all eyes averted from the thing that was coming aboard. They had no thought of fighting it. It was Fate.

Only when Hook was hidden from them did curiosity loosen the limbs of the boys so that they could rush to the ship's side to see the crocodile climbing it. Then they got the strangest surprise of this Night of Nights; for it was no crocodile that was coming to their aid. It was Peter

He signed to them not to give vent to any cry of admiration that might rouse suspicion. Then he went on ticking.

'Hook or Me This Time'

Odd things happen to all of us on our way through life without our noticing for a time that they have happened. Thus, to take an instance, we suddenly discover that we have been deaf in one ear for we don't know how long, but, say, half an hour. Now such an experience had come that night to Peter. When last we saw him he was stealing across the island with one finger to his lips and his dagger at the ready. He had seen the crocodile pass by without noticing anything peculiar about it, but by and by he remembered that it had not been ticking. At first he thought this eerie, but soon he concluded rightly that the clock had run down.

Without giving a thought to what might be the feelings of a fellow-creature thus abruptly deprived of its closest companion, Peter at once considered how he could turn the catastrophe to his own use; and he decided to tick, so that wild beasts should believe he was the crocodile and let him pass unmolested. He ticked superbly, but with one unforeseen result. The crocodile was among those who heard the sound, and it followed him, though whether with the purpose of regaining what it had lost, or merely as a friend under the belief that it was again ticking itself, will never be certainly known, for, like all slaves to a fixed idea, it was a stupid beast.

Peter reached the shore without mishap, and went straight on; his legs encountering the water as if quite unaware that they had entered a new element. Thus many animals pass from land to water, but no other human of whom I know. As he swam he had but one thought: 'Hook or me this time.' He had ticked so long that he now went on ticking without knowing that he was doing it. Had he known he would have stopped, for to board the brig by the help of the tick, though an ingenious idea, had not occurred to him.

On the contrary, he thought he had scaled her side as noiseless as a mouse; and he was amazed to see the pirates cowering from him, with Hook in their midst as abject as if he had heard the crocodile.

The crocodile! No sooner did Peter remember it than he heard the ticking. At first he thought the sound did come from the crocodile, and he looked behind him swiftly. Then he realised that he was doing it himself, and in a flash he understood the situation. 'How clever of me,' he thought at once, and signed to the boys not to burst into applause.

It was at this moment that Ed Teynte the quartermaster emerged from the forecastle and came along the deck. Now, reader, time what happened by your watch. Peter struck true and deep. John clapped his hands on the ill-fated pirate's mouth to stifle the dying groan. He fell forward. Four boys caught him to prevent the thud. Peter gave the signal, and the carrion was cast overboard. There was a splash, and then silence. How long has it taken?

'One!' (Slightly had begun to count.)

None too soon, Peter, every inch of him on tiptoe, vanished into the cabin; for more than one pirate was screwing up his courage to look round. They could hear each other's distressed breathing now, which showed them that the more terrible sound had passed.

'It's gone, captain,' Smee said, wiping his spectacles. 'All's still again.'

Slowly Hook let his head emerge from his ruff, and listened so intently that he could have caught the echo of the tick. There was not a sound, and he drew himself up firmly to his full height.

'Then here's to Johnny Plank,' he cried brazenly, hating the boys more than ever because they had seen him unbend. He broke into the villainous ditty:

> 'Yo ho, yo ho, the frisky plank,
> You walks along it so,
> Till it goes down and you goes down
> To Davy Jones below!'

To terrorise the prisoners the more, though with a certain loss of dignity, he danced along an imaginary plank, grimacing at them as he sang; and when he finished he cried, 'Do you want a touch of the cat before you walk the plank?'

At that they fell on their knees. 'No, no,' they cried so piteously that every pirate smiled.

'Fetch the cat, Jukes,' said Hook; 'it's in the cabin.'

The cabin! Peter was in the cabin! The children gazed at each other.

'Ay, ay,' said Jukes blithely, and he strode into the cabin. They followed him with their eyes; they scarce knew that Hook had resumed his song, his dogs joining in with him:

> 'Yo ho, yo ho, the scratching cat,
> Its tails are nine, you know,
> And when they're writ upon your back—'

What was the last line will never be known, for of a sudden the song was stayed by a dreadful screech from the cabin. It wailed through the ship, and died away. Then was heard a crowing sound which was well understood by the boys, but to the pirates was almost more eerie than the screech.

'What was that?' cried Hook.

'Two,' said Slightly solemnly.

The Italian Cecco hesitated for a moment and then swung into the cabin. He tottered out, haggard.

'What's the matter with Bill Jukes, you dog?' hissed Hook, towering over him.

'The matter wi' him is he's dead, stabbed,' replied Cecco in a hollow voice.

'Bill Jukes dead!' cried the startled pirates.

'The cabin's as black as a pit,' Cecco said, almost gibbering, 'but there is something terrible in there: the thing you heard crowing.'

The exultation of the boys, the lowering looks of the pirates, both were seen by Hook.

'Cecco,' he said in his most steely voice, 'go back and fetch me out that doodle-doo.'

Cecco, bravest of the brave, cowered before his captain, crying 'No, no': but Hook was purring to his claw.

'Did you say you would go, Cecco?' he said musingly.

Cecco went, first flinging up his arms despairingly. There was no more singing, all listened now; and again came a death-screech and again a crow.

No one spoke except Slightly. 'Three,' he said.

Hook rallied his dogs with a gesture. ' 'Sdeath and odds fish,' he thundered, 'who is to bring me that doodle-doo?'

'Wait till Cecco comes out,' growled Starkey, and the others took up the cry.

'I think I heard you volunteer, Starkey,' said Hook, purring again.

'No, by thunder!' Starkey cried.

'My hook thinks you did,' said Hook, crossing to him. 'I wonder if it would not be advisable, Starkey, to humour the hook?'

'I'll swing before I go in there,' replied Starkey doggedly, and again he had the support of the crew.

'Is it mutiny?' asked Hook more pleasantly than ever. 'Starkey's ringleader.'

'Captain, mercy,' Starkey whimpered, all of a tremble now.

'Shake hands, Starkey,' said Hook, proffering his claw.

Starkey looked round for help, but all deserted him. As he backed Hook advanced, and now the red spark was in his eye. With a despairing scream the pirate leapt upon Long Tom and precipitated himself into the sea.

'Four,' said Slightly.

'And now,' Hook asked courteously, 'did any other gentleman say mutiny?' Seizing a lantern and raising his claw with a menacing gesture, 'I'll bring out that doodledoo myself,' he said, and sped into the cabin.

'Five.' How Slightly longed to say it. He wetted his lips to be ready, but Hook came staggering out, without his lantern.

'Something blew out the light,' he said a little unsteadily.

'Something!' echoed Mullins.

'What of Cecco?' demanded Noodler.

'He's as dead as Jukes,' said Hook shortly.

His reluctance to return to the cabin impressed them all unfavourably, and the mutinous sounds again broke forth. All pirates are superstitious; and Cookson cried, 'They do say the surest sign a ship's accurst is when there's one on board more than can be accounted for.'

'I've heard,' muttered Mullins, 'he always boards the pirate craft at last. Had he a tail, captain?'

'They say,' said another, looking viciously at Hook, 'that when he comes it's in the likeness of the wickedest man aboard.'

'Had he a hook, captain?' asked Cookson insolently; and one after another took up the cry. 'The ship's doomed.' At this the children could not resist raising a cheer. Hook had wellnigh forgotten his prisoners, but as he swung round on them now his face lit up again.

'Lads,' he cried to his crew, 'here's a notion. Open the cabin door and drive them in. Let them fight the doodledoo for their lives. If they kill him, we're so much the better; if he kills them, we're none the worse.'

For the last time his dogs admired Hook, and devotedly they did his bidding. The boys, pretending to struggle, were pushed into the cabin and the door was closed on them.

'Now, listen,' cried Hook, and all listened. But not one dared to face the door. Yes, one, Wendy, who all this time had been bound to the mast. It was for neither a scream nor a crow that she was watching; it was for the reappearance of Peter.

She had not long to wait. In the cabin he had found the thing for which he had gone in search: the key that would free the children of their manacles; and now they all stole forth, armed with such weapons as they could find. First signing to them to hide, Peter cut Wendy's bonds, and then nothing could have been easier than for them all to fly off together; but one thing barred the way, an oath, 'Hook or me this time.' So when he had freed Wendy, he whispered to her to conceal herself with the others, and himself took her place by the mast, her cloak around him so that he should pass for her. Then he took a great breath and crowed.

To the pirates it was a voice crying that all the boys lay slain in the cabin; and they were panic-stricken. Hook tried to hearten them; but like the dogs he had made them they showed him their fangs, and he knew that if he took his eyes off them now they would leap at him.

'Lads,' he said, ready to cajole or strike as need be, but never quailing for an instant, 'I've thought it out. There's a Jonah aboard.'

'Ay,' they snarled, 'a man wi' a hook.'

'No, lads, no, it's the girl. Never was luck on a pirate ship wi' a woman on board. We'll right the ship when she's gone.'

Some of them remembered that this had been a saying of Flint's. 'It's worth trying,' they said doubtfully.

'Fling the girl overboard,' cried Hook; and they made a rush at the figure in the cloak.

'There's none can save you now, missy,' Mullins hissed jeeringly.

'There's one,' replied the figure.

'Who's that?'

'Peter Pan the avenger!' came the terrible answer; and as he spoke Peter flung off his cloak. Then they all knew who 'twas that had been undoing them in the cabin, and twice Hook essayed to speak and twice he failed. In that frightful moment I think his fierce heart broke.

At last he cried, 'Cleave him to the brisket,' but without conviction.

'Down, boys, and at them,' Peter's voice rang out; and in another moment the clash of arms was resounding through the ship. Had the pirates kept together it is certain that they would have won; but the onset came when they were all unstrung, and they ran hither and thither, striking wildly, each thinking himself the last survivor of the crew. Man to man they were the stronger; but they fought on the defensive only, which enabled the boys to hunt in pairs and choose their quarry. Some of the miscreants leapt into the sea; others hid in dark recesses, where they were found by Slightly, who did not fight, but ran about with a lantern which he flashed in their faces, so that they were half blinded and fell an easy prey to the reeking swords of the other boys. There was little sound to be heard but the clang of weapons, an occasional screech or splash, and Slightly monotonously counting – five – six – seven – eight – nine – ten – eleven.

I think all were gone when a group of savage boys surrounded Hook, who seemed to have a charmed life, as he kept them at bay in that circle of fire. They had done for his dogs, but this man alone seemed to be a match for them all. Again and again they closed upon him, and again and again he hewed a clear space. He had lifted up one boy with his hook, and was using him as a buckler, when another, who had just passed his sword through Mullins, sprang into the fray.

'Put up your swords, boys,' cried the newcomer, 'this man is mine.'

Thus suddenly Hook found himself face to face with Peter. The others drew back and formed a ring round them.

For long the two enemies looked at one another; Hook shuddering slightly, and Peter with the strange smile upon his face.

'So, Pan,' said Hook at last, 'this is all your doing.'

'Ay, James Hook,' came the stern answer, 'it is all my doing.'

'Proud and insolent youth,' said Hook, 'prepare to meet thy doom.'

'Dark and sinister man,' Peter answered, 'have at thee.'

Without more words they fell to, and for a space there was no advantage to either blade. Peter was a superb swordsman, and parried with dazzling rapidity; ever and anon he followed up a feint with a lunge that got past his foe's defence, but his shorter reach stood him in ill stead, and he could not drive the steel home. Hook, scarcely his inferior in brilliancy, but not quite so nimble in wrist play, forced him back by the weight of his onset, hoping suddenly to end all with a favourite thrust, taught him long ago by Barbecue at Rio; but to his astonishment he found this thrust turned aside again and again. Then he sought to close and give the quietus with his iron hook, which all this time had been pawing the air; but Peter doubled under it and, lunging fiercely, pierced him in the ribs. At sight of his own blood, whose peculiar colour, you remember, was offensive to him, the sword fell from Hook's hand, and he was at Peter's mercy.

'Now!' cried all the boys; but with a magnificent gesture Peter invited his opponent to pick up his sword. Hook did so instantly, but with a tragic feeling that Peter was showing good form.

Hitherto he had thought it was some fiend fighting him, but darker suspicions assailed him now.

'Pan, who and what art thou?' he cried huskily.

'I'm youth, I'm joy,' Peter answered at a venture, 'I'm a little bird that has broken out of the egg.'

This, of course, was nonsense; but it was proof to the unhappy Hook that Peter did not know in the least who or what he was, which is the very pinnacle of good form.

'To't again,' he cried despairingly.

He fought now like a human flail, and every sweep of that terrible sword would have severed in twain any man or boy who obstructed it; but Peter fluttered round him as if the very wind it made blew him out of the danger zone. And again and again he darted in and pricked.

Hook was fighting now without hope. That passionate breast no longer asked for life; but for one boon it craved: to see Peter bad form before it was cold for ever.

Abandoning the fight he rushed into the powder magazine and fired it.

'In two minutes,' he cried, 'the ship will be blown to pieces.'

Now, now, he thought, true form will show.

But Peter issued from the powder magazine with the shell in his hands, and calmly flung it overboard.

What sort of form was Hook himself showing? Misguided man though he was, we may be glad, without sympathising with him, that in the end he was true to the traditions of his race. The other boys were flying around him now, flouting, scornful; and as he staggered about the deck striking up at them impotently, his mind was no longer with them; it was slouching in the playing fields of long ago, or being sent up for good, or watching the wall-game from a famous wall. And his shoes were right, and his waistcoat was right, and his tie was right, and his socks were right.

James Hook, thou not wholly unheroic figure, farewell.

For we have come to his last moment.

Seeing Peter slowly advancing upon him through the air with dagger poised, he sprang upon the bulwarks to cast himself into the sea. He did not know that the crocodile was waiting for him; for we purposely stopped the clock that this knowledge might be spared him: a little mark of respect from us at the end.

He had one last triumph, which I think we need not grudge him. As he stood on the bulwark looking over his shoulder at Peter gliding through the air, he invited him with a gesture to use his foot. It made Peter kick instead of stab.

At last Hook had got the boon for which he craved.

'Bad form,' he cried jeeringly, and went content to the crocodile.

Thus perished James Hook.

'Seventeen,' Slightly sang out; but he was not quite correct in his figures. Fifteen paid the penalty for their crimes that night; but two reached the shore: Starkey to be captured by the redskins, who made him nurse for all their papooses, a melancholy come-down for a pirate; and Smee, who henceforth wandered about the world in his spectacles, making a precarious living by saying he was the only man that James Hook had feared.

Wendy, of course, had stood by taking no part in the fight, though watching Peter with glistening eyes; but now that all was over she became prominent again. She praised them equally, and shuddered delightfully when Michael showed her the place where he had killed one; and then she took them into Hook's cabin and pointed to his watch which was hanging on a nail. It said 'half-past-one'!

The lateness of the hour was almost the biggest thing of all. She got them to bed in the pirates' bunks pretty quickly, you may be sure; all but Peter, who strutted up and down the deck, until at last he fell asleep by the side of Long Tom. He had one of his dreams that night, and cried in his sleep for a long time, and Wendy held him tight.

The Adventures and Execution of Captain John Rackam

CHARLES ELLMS

This John Rackam was quarter-master to Vane's company, till the crew were divided, and Vane turned out of it for refusing to board a French man-of-war, Rackam being voted captain of the division that remained in the brigantine. The 24th of November 1718, was the first day of his command; his first cruise was among the Carribbee Islands, where he took and plundered several vessels.

We have already taken notice, that when Captain Woods Rogers went to the island of Providence with the king's pardon to such of the pirates as should surrender, this brigantine, which Rackam commanded, made its escape through another passage, bidding defiance to the mercy that was offered.

To the windward of Jamaica, a Madeira-man fell into the pirate's way, which they detained two or three days, till they had their market out of her, and then they gave her back to the master, and permitted one Hosea Tidsel, a tavern keeper at Jamaica, who had been picked up in one of their prizes, to depart in her, she being bound for that island.

After this cruise they went into a small island, and cleaned, and spent their Christmas ashore, drinking and carousing as long as they had any liquor left, and then went to sea again for more.

They succeeded but too well, though they took no extraordinary prize for above two months, except a ship laden with convicts from Newgate, bound for the plantations, which in a few days was retaken, with all her cargo, by an English man-of-war that was stationed in those seas.

Rackam stood towards the island of Bermuda, and took a ship bound to England from Carolina, and a small pink from New England, both of which he brought to the Bahama Islands, where, with the pitch, tar and stores they cleaned again, and refitted their own vessel; but staying too long in that neighborhood, Captain Rodgers, who was Governor of Providence, hearing of these ships being taken, sent out a sloop well manned and armed, which retook both the prizes, though in the mean while the pirate had the good fortune to escape.

From hence they sailed to the back of Cuba, where Rackam kept a little kind of a family, at which place they stayed a considerable time, living ashore with their Delilahs, till their money and provisions were expended, and they concluded it time to look out for more. They repaired their vessel, and were making ready to put to sea, when a guarda de costa came in with a small English sloop, which she had taken as an interloper on the coast. The Spanish guard-ship attacked the pirate, but Rackam being close in behind a little island, she could do but little execution where she lay; the Dons therefore warped into the channel that evening, in order to make sure of her the next morning. Rackam finding his case desperate, and that there was hardly any possibility of escaping, resolved to attempt the following enterprize. The Spanish prize lying for better security close into the land, between the little island and the Main, our desperado took his crew into the boat with their cutlasses, rounded the little island, and fell aboard their prize silently in the dead of the night without being discovered, telling the Spaniards that were aboard her, that if they spoke a word, or made the least noise, they were all dead men; and so they became masters of her. When this was done he slipped her cable, and drove out to sea. The Spanish man-of-war was so intent upon their expected prize, that they minded nothing else, and as soon as day broke, they made a furious fire upon the empty sloop; but it was not long before they were rightly apprised of the matter, when they cursed themselves sufficiently for a company of fools, to be bit out of a good rich prize, as she proved to be, and to have nothing but an old crazy hull in the room of her.

Rackam and his crew had no occasion to be displeased at the exchange, as it enabled them to continue some time longer in a way of life that suited their depraved minds. In August 1720, we find him at sea again, scouring the harbours and inlets of the north and west parts of Jamaica, where he took several small crafts, which proved no great booty to the rovers; but they had but few men, and therefore were obliged to run at low game till they could increase their company and their strength.

In the beginning of September, they took seven or eight fishing boats in Harbour Island, stole their nets and other tackle, and then went off to the French part of Hispaniola, where they landed, and took the cattle away, with two or three Frenchmen whom they found near the water-side, hunting wild hogs in the evening. The Frenchmen came on board, whether by consent or compulsion is not certainly known. They afterwards plundered two sloops, and returned to Jamaica, on the north coast of which island, near Porto Maria Bay, they took a schooner, Thomas Spenlow, master, it being then the 19th of October, The next day Rackam seeing a sloop in Dry Harbour Bay, stood in and fired a gun; the men all ran ashore, and he took the sloop and lading; but when those ashore found that they were pirates, they hailed the sloop, and let them know they were all willing to come on board of them.

Rackam's coasting the island in this manner proved fatal to him; for intelligence of his expedition came to the governor by a canoe which he had surprised ashore in Ocho Bay: upon this a sloop was immediately fitted out, and sent round the island in quest of him, commanded by Captain Barnet, and manned with a good number of hands. Rackam, rounding the island, and drawing round the western point, called Point Negril, saw a small pettiaga, which, at the sight of the sloop, ran ashore and landed her men, when one of them hailed her. Answer was made that they were Englishmen, and begged the pettiaga's men to come on board and drink a bowl of punch, which they prevailed upon them to do. Accordingly, the company, in an evil hour, came all aboard of the pirate, consisting of nine persons; they were armed with muskets and cutlasses, but what was their real design in so doing we will not pretend to say. They had no sooner laid down their arms and taken up their pipes, than Barnet's sloop, which was in pursuit of Rackam's, came in sight.

The pirates, finding she stood directly towards them, feared the event, and weighed their anchor, which they had but lately let go, and stood off. Captain Barnet gave them chase, and, having advantage of little breezes of wind which blew off the land, came up with her, and brought her into Port Royal, in Jamaica.

About a fortnight after the prisoners were brought ashore, viz. November 16, 1720, Captain Rackam and eight of his men were condemned and executed. Captain Rackam and two others were hung in chains.

But what was very surprising, was the conviction of the nine men that came aboard the sloop on the same day she was taken. They were tried at an adjournment of the court on the 24th of January, the magistracy waiting all that time, it is supposed, for evidence to prove the piratical intention of going aboard the said sloop; for it seems there was no act or piracy committed by them, as appeared by the witnesses against them, two Frenchmen, taken by Rackam off the island of Hispaniola, who merely deposed that the prisoners came on board without any compulsion.

The court considered the prisoners' cases, and the majority of the commissioners being of opinion that they were all guilty of the piracy and felony they were charged with, viz. the going over with a piratical intent to John Rackam, &c. then notorious pirates, and by them known to be so, they all received sentence of death, and were executed on the 17th of February at Gallows Point at Port Royal.

Nor holy bell, nor pastoral bleat,
In former days within the vale,
Flapped in the bay the pirate's sheet,
Curses were on the gale;
Rich goods lay on the sand, and murdered men,
Pirate and wreckers kept their revels there.

THE BUCCANEER.

Mutiny!—Captain Howel Davis and His Crew

CAPTAIN CHARLES JOHNSON

Captain Howel Davis was born at Milford, in Monmouthshire, and was, from a boy, brought up to sea. The last voyage he made from England was in the *Cadogan* snow, of Bristol, Captain Skinner commander, bound for the coast of Guinea, of which snow Davis was chief mate. They were no sooner arrived at Sierra Leone on the aforesaid coast, but they were taken by the Pirate England, who plundered them; and Skinner was barbarously murdered.

After the death of Captain Skinner, Davis pretended that he was mightily solicited by England to engage with him, but that he resolutely answered he would sooner be shot to death than sign the Pirates' articles. Upon which England, pleased with his bravery, sent him and the rest of the men again on board the snow, appointing him captain of her in the room of Skinner, commanding him to pursue his voyage. He also gave him a written paper sealed up, with orders to open it when he should come into a certain latitude, and at the peril of his life follow the orders therein set down. This was an act of grandeur like what princes practice to their admirals and generals. It was punctually complied with by Davis who read it to the ship's company. It contained no less than a generous deed of gift of the ship and cargo to Davis and the crew, ordering him to go to Brazil and dispose of the lading to the best advantage, and to make a fair and equal dividend with the rest.

Davis proposed to the crew whether they were willing to follow their directions, but to his great surprise found the majority of them altogether averse to it; wherefore, in a rage, he bade them be damned, and go where they would. They knew that part of the cargo was consigned to certain merchants at Barbados, wherefore they steered for that island. When they arrived they related to these merchants the unfortunate death of Skinner, and the proposal which had been made to them by Davis. Upon which Davis was seized and committed to prison, where he was kept three months. However, as he had been in no act of piracy, he was discharged without being brought to any trial; yet he could not expect any employment there. Wherefore, knowing that the Island of Providence was a kind of rendezvous of Pirates, he was resolved to make one amongst them, if possible, and to that purpose found means of shipping himself for that island. But he was again disappointed, for when he arrived there, the Pirates had newly surrendered to Captain Woodes Rogers and accepted of the Act of Grace which he had just brought from England.

However, Davis was not long out of business, for Captain Rogers having fitted out two sloops for trade, one called the *Buck*, the other the *Mumvil Trader*, Davis found an employment on board one of them. The lading of these sloops was of considerable value, consisting of European goods, in order to be exchanged with the French and Spaniards; and many of the hands on board of them were the Pirates lately come in upon the late Act of Grace. The first place they touched at was the Island of Martinique, belonging to the French; where Davis, having conspired with some others, rose in the night, secured the master and seized the sloop. As soon as this was done they called to the other sloop, which lay a little way from them, among whom they knew there were a great many hands ripe for rebellion, and ordered them to come on board of them. They did so, and the greatest part of them agreed to join with Davis. Those who were otherwise inclined were sent back on board the *Mumvil* sloop to go where they pleased, Davis having first taken out of her everything which he thought might be of use.

After this, a council of war was called over a large bowl of punch, at which it was proposed to choose a commander. The election was soon over, for it fell upon Davis by a great majority of legal pollers; there was no scrutiny demanded, for all acquiesced in the choice. As soon as he was possessed of his command he drew up articles which were signed and sworn to by himself and the rest, then he made a short speech, the sum of which was a declaration of war against the whole world.

After this, they consulted about a proper place where they might clean their sloop, a light pair of heels being of great use either to take or escape being taken. For this purpose they made choice of Coxon's Hole, at the east end of the Island of Cuba, a place where they might secure themselves from surprise, the entrance being so narrow that one ship might keep out a hundred.

Here they cleaned with much difficulty, for they had no carpenter in their company, a person of great use upon such exigencies. From hence they put to sea, making to the north side of the island of Hispaniola. The first sail which fell in their way was a French ship of twelve guns. It must be observed that Davis had but thirty-five hands, yet provisions began to grow short with him; wherefore he attacked this ship. She soon struck and he sent twelve of his hands on board of her in order to plunder. This was no sooner done but a sail was spied, a great way to windward of them. They inquired of the Frenchman what she might be; he answered that he had spoke with a ship the day before, of 24 guns and 60 men, and he took this to be the same.

Davis then proposed to his men to attack her, telling them she would be a rare ship for their use; but they looked upon it to be an extravagant attempt, and discovered no fondness for it. But he assured them he had a stratagem in his head would make all safe; wherefore he gave chase, and ordered his prize to do the same. The prize being a slow sailer, Davis first came up with the enemy, and standing alongside of them, showed his piratical colors. They, much surprised, called to Davis telling him they wondered at his impudence in venturing to come so near them, and ordered him to strike. But he answered, that he intended to keep them in play till his consort came up, who was able to deal with them, and that if they did not strike to him they should have but bad quarter. Whereupon he gave them a broadside, which they returned.

In the meantime the prize drew near, who obliged all the prisoners to come upon deck in white shirts, to make a show of force, as they had been directed by Davis. They also hoisted a dirty tarpaulin, by way of black flag, they having no other, and fired a gun. The Frenchmen were so intimidated by this appearance of force that they struck. Davis called out to the captain to come on board of him with twenty of his hands. He did so, and they were all, for the greater security, clapped into irons, the captain excepted. Then he sent four of his own men on board the first prize, and in order still to carry on the cheat spoke aloud that they should give his service to the captain and desire him to send some hands on board the prize, to see what they had got; but at the same time gave them a written paper with instructions what to do. Here he ordered them to nail up the guns in the little prize, to take out all the small arms and powder, and to go, every man of them, on board the second prize. When this was done, he ordered that more of the prisoners should be removed out of the great prize into the little one, by which he secured himself from any attempt which might be feared from their numbers; for those on board of him were fast in irons, and those in the little prize had neither arms nor ammunition.

Thus the three ships kept company for 2 days, when, finding the great prize to be a very dull sailer, he thought she would not be fit for his purpose; wherefore he resolved to restore her to the captain, with all his hands. But first, he took care to take out all her ammunition, and everything else which he might possibly want. The French captain was in such a rage at being so outwitted that when he got on board his own ship he was going to throw himself overboard, but was prevented by his men.

Having let go both his prizes, he steered northward, in which course he took a small Spanish sloop; after this, he made towards the Western Islands [Azores] but met with no booty thereabouts. Then he steered for the Cape Verde Islands. They cast anchor at St. Nicholas, hoisting English colors; the Portuguese inhabiting there took him for an English privateer, and Davis going ashore, they both treated him very civilly and also traded with him. Here he remained five weeks, in which time he and half his crew, for their pleasure, took a journey to the chief town of the island, which was 19 miles up the country. Davis making a good appearance was caressed by the Governor and the inhabitants, and no diversion was wanting which the Portuguese could show or money could purchase. After about a week's stay he came back to the ship, and the rest of the crew went to take their pleasure up to the town in their turn.

At their return they cleaned their ship and put to sea, but not with their whole company, for five of them, like Hannibal's men, were so charmed with the luxuries of the place and the free conversation of some women, that they stayed behind; and one of them, whose name was Charles Franklin, a Monmouthshire man, married and settled himself, and lives there to this day.

From hence they sailed to Bonavista, and looked into that harbor, but finding nothing, they steered for the Isle of Mayo. When they arrived here, they met with a great many ships and vessels in the road, all of which they plundered, taking out of them whatever they wanted; and also strengthening themselves with a great many fresh hands, who most of them entered voluntarily. One of the ships they took to their own use, mounted her with twenty-six guns and called her the *King James*. There being no fresh water hereabouts, they made towards St. Jago, belonging to the Portuguese, in order to lay in a store. Davis, with a few hands, going ashore to find the most commodious place to water at, the Governor with some attendants came himself and examined who they were and whence they came. And not liking Davis's account of himself, the Governor was so plain to tell them he suspected them to be Pirates. Davis seemed mightily affronted, standing much upon his honor, replying to the Governor he scorned his words. However, as soon as his back was turned, for fear of accidents he got on board again as fast as he could. Davis related what had happened, and his men seemed to resent the affront which had been offered him. Davis, upon this, told them he was confident he could surprise the fort in the night; they agreed with him to attempt it, and accordingly, when it grew late, they went ashore well armed, and the guard which was kept, was so negligent that they got within the fort before any alarm was given. When it was too late there was some little resistance made, and three men killed on Davis's side. Those in the fort, in their hurry ran into the Governor's house to save themselves, which they barricaded so strongly that Davis's party could not enter it. However they threw in grenado shells, which not only ruined all the furniture but killed several men within.

When it was day the whole country was alarmed and came to attack the Pirates; wherefore, it not being their business to stand a siege, they made the best of their way on board their ship again, after having dismounted the guns of the fort. By this enterprise they did a great deal of mischief to the Portuguese, and but very little good to themselves.

Having put to sea they mustered their hands, and found themselves near seventy strong. Then it was proposed what course they should steer, and differing in their opinions, they divided, and by a majority it was carried for Gambia, in the coast of Guinea. Of this opinion was Davis; he having been employed in that trade and was acquainted with the coast. He told them that there was a great deal of money always kept in Gambia Castle, and that it would be worth their while to make an attempt upon it. They asked him how it was possible, since it was garrisoned? He desired they would leave the management of it to him, and he would undertake to make them masters of it. They began now to conceive so high an opinion of his conduct, as well as courage, that they thought nothing impossible to him, therefore they agreed to obey him without inquiring further into his design.

Having come within sight of the place, he ordered all his men under deck, except as many as were absolutely necessary for working the ship, that those from the forts, seeing a ship with so few hands, might have no suspicion of her being any other than a trading vessel. Then he ran close under the fort and there cast anchor; and having ordered out the boat, he commanded six men in her, in old ordinary jackets, while he himself with the master and the doctor, dressed themselves like gentlemen; his design being that the men should look like common sailors, and they like merchants. In rowing ashore he gave his men instructions what to say in case any questions should be asked them.

Being come to the landing place, he was received by a file of musketeers, and conducted into the fort, where the Governor accosting them civilly, asked them who they were and whence they came? They answered they were of Liverpool, bound for the river of Senegal, to trade for gum and elephants' teeth, but that they were chased on that coast by two French men-of-war, and narrowly escaped being taken, having a little the heel of them; but now they were resolved to make the best of a bad market and would trade here for slaves. Then the Governor asked them what was the chief of their cargo? They answered, iron and plate, which were good things there. The Governor told them he would slave them to the full value of their cargo, and asked them if they had any European liquor on board. They answered, a little for their own use; however, a hamper should be at his service. The Governor then very civilly invited them all to stay and dine with him. Davis told him that being commander of the ship, he must go on board to see her well moored and give some other orders, but those two gentlemen might stay, and that he himself would also return before dinner, and bring the hamper of liquor with him.

While he was in the fort, his eyes were very busy in observing how things lay. He took notice there was a sentry at the entrance, and a guardhouse just by it, where the soldiers upon duty commonly waited, their arms standing in a corner in a heap; he saw, also, a great many small arms in the Governor's hall. Now when he came on board he assured his men of success, desiring them not to get drunk, and that as soon as they saw the flag upon the Castle struck, they might conclude he was master, and send twenty hands immediately ashore. In the meantime, there being a sloop at anchor near them, he sent some hands in a boat to secure the master and all the men, and bring them on board of him, lest they, observing any bustle or arming in his ship, might send ashore and give intelligence.

These precautions being taken, he ordered his men who were to go in the boat with him, to put two pair of pistols each under their clothes, he doing the like himself, and gave them directions to go into the guard-room, and to enter into conversation with the soldiers and observe, when he should fire a pistol through the Governor's window, to start up at once and secure the arms in the guard-room.

When Davis arrived, dinner not being ready, the Governor proposed that they should pass their time in making a bowl of punch till dinnertime. It must be observed that Davis's coxswain waited upon them, who had an opportunity of going about all parts of the house, to see what strength they had. He whispered to Davis, there being no person in the room, but he (Davis), the master, the doctor, the coxswain and the Governor. Davis on a sudden drew out a pistol, clapped it to the Governor's breast, telling him he must surrender the fort and all the riches in it, or he was a dead man. The Governor being no ways prepared for such an attack, promised to be very passive and do all they desired, therefore they shut the door, took down all the arms that hung in the hall, and loaded them. Davis fired his pistol through the window, upon which his men without, executed their part of the scheme like heroes in an instant; getting betwixt the soldiers and their arms, all with their pistols cocked in their hands, while one of them carried the arms out. When this was done they locked the soldiers into the guard-room, and kept guard without.

In the meantime one of them struck the Union flag on the top of the Castle, at which signal those on board sent on shore a reinforcement of hands, and they got possession of the fort without the least hurry or confusion, or so much as a man lost on either side.

Davis harangued the soldiers, upon which a great many of them took on with him, those who refused he sent on board the little sloop; and because he would not be at the trouble of a guard for them, he ordered all the sails and cables out of her, which might hinder them from attempting to get away.

This day was spent in a kind of rejoicing, the Castle firing her guns to salute the ship and the ship the Castle. But the next day they minded their business, that is, they fell to plundering. But they found things fall vastly short of their expectation; for they discovered that a great deal of money had been lately sent away. However, they met with the value of about £2,000 sterling in bar-gold, and a great many other rich effects. Everything they liked, which was portable, they brought aboard their ship; some things which they had no use for they were so generous as to make a present of to the master and crew of the little sloop, to whom they also returned his vessel again; and then they fell to work in dismounting the guns and demolishing the fortifications.

After they had done as much mischief as they could, and were weighing anchor to be gone, they spied a ship bearing down upon them in full sail. They soon got their anchors up, and were in a readiness to receive her. This ship proved to be a French Pirate of fourteen guns and sixty-four hands, half French, half negroes. The captain's name was La Bouse. He expected no less than a rich prize, which made him so eager in the chase; but when he came near enough to see their guns and the number of their hands upon deck, he began to think he should catch a Tartar, and supposed her to be a small English man-of-war. However, since there was no escaping, he resolved to do a bold and desperate action, which was to board Davis. As he was making towards her for this purpose, he fired a gun and hoisted his black colors. Davis returned the salute and hoisted his black colors also. The Frenchman was not a little pleased at this happy escape; they both hoisted out their boats, and the captains went to meet and congratulate one another with a flag of truce in their sterns. A great many civilities passed between them, and La Bouse desired Davis that they might sail down the coast together, that he (La Bouse) might get a better ship. Davis agreed to it, and very courteously promised him that the first ship he took fit for his use he would give him, as being willing to encourage a willing brother.

The first place they touched at was Sierra Leone where at first going in, they spied a tall ship at anchor. Davis being the best sailer first came up with her, and wondering that she did not try to make off, suspected her to be a ship of force. As soon as he came alongside of her, she brought a spring upon her cable and fired a whole broadside upon Davis, at the same time hoisting a black flag. Davis hoisted his black flag in like manner and fired one gun to leeward.

In fine, she proved to be a Pirate ship of twenty-four guns, commanded by one Cocklyn, who expecting these two would prove prizes, let them come in lest his getting under sail might frighten them away.

The satisfaction was great on all sides at this junction of confederates and brethren in iniquity. Two days they spent in improving their acquaintance and friendship, the third day Davis and Cocklyn agreed to go in La Bouse's brigantine and attack the fort. They contrived it so as to get up thither by high water. Those in the fort suspected them to be what they really were, and therefore stood upon their defense; when the brigantine came within musket shot, the fort fired all their guns upon her, the brigantine did the like upon the fort, and so held each other in play for several hours, when the two confederate ships were come up to the assistance of the brigantine. Those who defended the fort, seeing such a number of hands on board these ships, had not the courage to stand it any longer, but abandoning the fort, left it to the mercy of the Pirates.

They took possession of it, and continued there near seven weeks, in which time they all cleaned their ships. We should have observed that a galley came in to the road while they were there, which Davis insisted should be yielded to La Bouse, according to his word of honor before given. Cocklyn did not oppose it, so La Bouse went into her with his crew, and cutting away her half deck, mounted her with twenty-four guns.

Having called a council of war they agreed to sail down the coast together, and for the greater grandeur, appointed a commodore, which was Davis. But they had not kept company long when, drinking together on board of Davis, they had like to have fallen together by the ears, the strong liquor stirring up a spirit of discord among them, and they quarreled; but Davis put an end to it by this short speech:—*Harke ye, you Cocklyn and La Bouse, I find by strengthening you I have put a rod into your hands to whip myself, but I am still able to deal with you both. But since we met in love, let us part in love, for I find that three of a trade can never agree.* Upon which the other two went on board their respective ships and immediately parted, each steering a different course.

Davis held on his way down the coast, and making Cape Appollonia he met with two Scotch and one English vessel, which he plundered and then let go. About five days after he fell in with a Dutch interloper, of thirty guns and ninety men (half being English) off Cape Three Points Bay.

Davis coming up alongside of her, the Dutchman gave the first fire, and pouring in a broadside upon Davis, killed nine of his men. Davis returned it and a very hot engagement followed, which lasted from one o'clock at noon till nine next morning, when the Dutchman struck and yielded herself their prize.

Davis fitted up the Dutch ship for his own use and called her the *Rover*, aboard of which he mounted thirty-two guns and twenty-seven swivels, and proceeded with her and the *King James* to Anamabo. He entered the bay betwixt the hours of twelve and one at noon, and found there three ships lying at anchor, who were trading for negroes, gold, and teeth [ivory]. The names of these ships were the *Hink* pink, Captain Hall commander; the *Princess*, Captain Plumb, of which Roberts, who will make a considerable figure in the sequel of this history, was second mate; and the *Morrice* sloop, Captain Fin. He takes these ships without any resistance, and having plundered them, he makes a present of one of them, *viz.*, the *Morrice* sloop, to the Dutchmen, on board of which alone were found a hundred and forty negroes, besides dry goods, and a considerable quantity of gold-dust.

It happened there were several canoes alongside of this last when Davis came in, who saved themselves and got ashore. These gave notice at the fort that these ships were Pirates, upon which the fort fired upon them, but without any execution, for their metal was not of weight enough to reach them. Davis, therefore, by way of defiance, hoisted his Black Flag and returned their compliment.

The same day he sailed with his three ships, making his way down the coast towards Prince's, a Portuguese colony. The next day, after he left Anamabo, early in the morning the man at the masthead espied a sail. It must be observed they kept a good look-out; for, according to their articles, he who first espies a sail, if she proves a prize, is entitled to the best pair of pistols on board over and above his dividend, in which they take a singular pride; and a pair of pistols has sometimes been sold for £30, from one to another.

Immediately they gave chase and soon came up with her. The ship proved to be a Hollander, and being betwixt Davis and the shore, she made all the sail she could, intending to run aground. Davis guessed her design, and putting out all his small sails, came up with her before she could effect it, and fired a broadside, upon which she immediately struck and called for quarter. It was granted, for according to Davis's articles, it was agreed that quarter should be given whenever it was called for, upon pain of death.

This ship proved a very rich prize, having the Governor of Accra on board, with all his effects, going to Holland. There was, in money, to the value of £15,000 sterling, besides other valuable merchandise, all of which they brought on board of themselves.

Upon this new success they restored Captain Hall and Captain Plumb, before-mentioned, to their ships again, but strengthened their [own] company with thirty-five hands, all white men, taken out of these two and the *Morrice* sloop. They also restored the Dutch their ship, after having plundered her as is mentioned.

Before they got to the Island of Prince's, one of their ships *viz.*, that called the *King James*, sprang a leak. Davis ordered all hands out of her on board his own ship, with everything else of use, and left her at an anchor at High Cameroon. As soon as he came in sight of the island he hoisted English colors; the Portuguese observing a large ship sailing towards them, sent out a little sloop to examine what she might be. This sloop hailing of Davis, he told them he was an English man-of-war in quest of Pirates, and that he had received intelligence there were some upon that coast. Upon this they received him as a welcome guest and piloted him into the harbor. He saluted the fort, which they answered, and he came to an anchor just under their guns, and hoisted out the pinnace, man-of-war fashion, ordering nine hands and a coxen in it to row him ashore.

The Portuguese, to do him the greater honor, sent down a file of musketeers to receive him and conduct him to the Governor. The Governor, not in the least suspecting what he was, received him very civilly, promising to supply him with whatever the island afforded. Davis thanked him, telling him the King of England would pay for whatever he should take; so after several civilities passed between him and the Governor, he returned again on board.

It happened a French ship came in there to supply itself with some necessaries, which Davis took into his head to plunder. But to give the thing a color of right, he persuaded the Portuguese that she had been trading with the Pirates, and that he found several Pirates' goods on board which he seized for the King's use. This story passed so well upon the Governor that he commended Davis's diligence.

A few days after, Davis, with about fourteen more, went privately ashore, and walked up the country towards a village where the Governor and the other chief men of the island kept their wives, intending as we may suppose, to supply their husbands' places with them. But being discovered, the women fled to a neighboring wood, and Davis and the rest retreated to their ship without effecting their design. The thing made some noise, but as nobody knew them, it passed over.

Having cleaned his ship and put all things in order, his thoughts now were turned upon the main business, *viz.*, the plunder of the island; and not knowing where the treasure lay, a stratagem came into his head to get it (as he thought) with little trouble. He consulted his men upon it and they liked the design. His scheme was to make a present to the Governor of a dozen negroes, by way of return for the civilities received from him, and afterwards to invite him with the chief men and some of the friars on board his ship, to an entertainment. The minute they came on board they were to be secured in irons and there kept till they should pay a ransom of £40,000 sterling.

But this stratagem proved fatal to him, for a Portuguese negro swam ashore in the night, and discovered the whole plot to the Governor, and also let him know that it was Davis who had made the attempt upon their wives. However, the Governor dissembled, received the Pirates' invitation civilly and promised that he and the rest would go.

The next day Davis went on shore himself, as if it were out of greater respect, to bring the Governor on board. He was received with the usual civility, and he and other principal Pirates who, by the way, had assumed the title of lords (and as such took upon them to advise or council their captain upon any important occasion, and likewise held certain privileges which the common Pirates were debarred from, as walking the quarterdeck, using the great cabin, going ashore at pleasure, and treating with foreign powers, that is, with the captains of ships they made prize of), I say, Davis and some of the lords were desired to walk up to the Governor's house, to take some refreshment before they went on board. They accepted it without the least suspicion, but never returned again, for an ambuscade was laid. A signal being given, a whole volley was fired upon them; they every man dropped except one, this one fled back and escaped into the boat and got on board the ship. Davis was shot through the bowels, yet he rose again, and made a weak effort to get away, but his strength soon forsook him and he dropped down dead. Just as he fell he perceived he was followed and drawing out his pistols, fired them at his pursuers. Thus, like a game cock, giving a dying blow that he might not fall unrevenged.

Captain Charles Vane

ARCHIBALD HURD

It will be remembered that one of the chief steps taken by the English government to suppress the West Atlantic piracy of the early eighteenth century was the occupation of the island of New Providence in the Bahamas, the chief pirate rendezvous in those waters. For that purpose, as we have seen, Captain Woodes Rogers with a couple of men-of-war was dispatched to the island in the year 1718, armed in the first place with the King's pardon for all who would take the oath of loyalty and undertake to reform their ways, and in the second with authority to suppress sea-robbery to the full extent of his powers. We have also seen that most of the pirates—at any rate in the formal sense—took advantage of the offered amnesty, and that these included such characters as Teach or Blackbeard, Major Stede Bonnet and many another hardly less famous. The majority of these probably took the oath of allegiance with their tongues in their cheeks, and a considerable number were soon at their old trade again. But there was one experienced practitioner who entirely declined to accept the pardon except upon his own terms, and this exception was that same Charles Vane to whom we have already had occasion to refer. It was he, as we have noted, under whom John Rackam, the companion of Anne Bonny and Mary Read, gained some of his earlier experiences; and it was he whom the gallant Colonel Rhett of South Carolina turned aside to chase—as it proved in vain—on his way to capture Stede Bonnet. In fact, in his own beat, as it were, the coast-line of the North American colonies, Jamaica, and the Bay of Honduras, Charles Vane was as familiar and feared a character as any of his more widely-known contemporaries.

Nor was he disposed to follow the herd in their surrender to Captain Woodes Rogers, and finding himself in the harbour of New Providence with an appreciable amount of recently acquired treasure, he decided to open negotiations on his own account with this quite unnecessary and unwelcome newcomer. He therefore sent him a letter stating that he would only consent to surrender if he could dispose of his spoil in any way he liked, and as he received no reply to this, he decided to bid Rogers defiance and make for the open sea unencumbered with a pardon. For this purpose he took a sloop belonging to one of his men named Yeates, and with a crew of ninety men made a dash for it, helped, as it happened, by the geography of the harbour. For the entrance to this was divided by a small island into two definite channels, one of which remained commanded by Captain Woodes Rogers' men-of-war. Having first fired his prizes, therefore, Yeates headed for the free channel, discharged a parting volley at the surprised men-of-war, and successfully got to sea, leaving his more amenable or subtler fellows to make their terms with the government's representative. A couple of days later he secured himself a consort in the shape of a captured Barbados sloop, and in this he placed Yeates with twenty-five hands, taking another merchantman two days afterwards. It had been a propitious start for his next campaign. He had satisfied his pride and outwitted Rogers. And he accordingly repaired to an out-of-the-way island to divide his new plunder and celebrate the event in customary fashion.

That was in the summer of 1718, and having rested and refreshed his men, Vane next beat his way south and south-east along the coast of the island of Hispaniola. Here or hereabouts he secured his next victim, a Spanish vessel on passage to Havana in Cuba, plundering her and setting her on fire, and casting her crew adrift in one of their own boats. His chief needs at the moment, however, were provisions and a reinforcement of necessary marine stores, and these he presently obtained from a captured brigantine in the neighbourhood of the island of St. Christopher. He then turned north towards the North American colonies, and in August was operating off the coast of South Carolina, taking his toll of that hard-pressed little community but a few weeks after Blackbeard and Bonnet had held up the citizens of Charlestown. He seized several English vessels in the North American colonial trade, as well as a ship hailing from Barbados under the command of Captain Dill, another from Antigua under the command of Captain Cook, a vessel from the Dutch island of Curaçao under the command of Captain Richards, and a brigantine from the Gulf of Guinea in West Africa with a cargo of ninety negro slaves, under the command of Captain Thompson. None of these vessels was kept by him and the negroes were transferred to the sloop of which his subordinate Yeates was in charge.

As so frequently happened, however, in these pirate fraternities, there had been for some time a growing ill-feeling between Yeates and his commander, as well as between the crews of the two vessels. Little incidents, in which there had been a difference of opinion, had become magnified, and Yeates had already made up his mind to part company with Vane on the first convenient opportunity. With Captain Thompson's negroes on board, and being in the vicinity of a civilized community, as well as upon a coast with many natural advantages, Yeates decided that his moment had come, and accordingly began to manœuvre for departure. The two pirate vessels were now some thirty miles south of Charlestown, and in the neighbourhood of the North Edisto River, and it was up this river, guarded as it was by a bar, that Yeates decided to take his vessel. But Vane, already probably somewhat suspicious as to his chief officer's intentions, quickly divined what was in Yeates' mind, and furiously angry at once set sail in chase of his vanishing colleague. He quickly gained on him, but Yeates' start proved just sufficient to carry him into safety, and he successfully crossed the bar before Vane could overhaul him, and fired a parting broadside at his late chief. Having made his way up the river, he then sent messengers to Governor Johnson of Charlestown, offering to surrender with all his hands and his valuable contingent of negroes on condition that the Governor would allow him to take advantage of the King's pardon. To this Johnson agreed, and a few days later the pirates entered the town, Captain Thompson, to his great satisfaction, receiving his lost negroes back again.

Meanwhile, Vane had been wrathfully cruising outside the bar of the North Edisto River waiting for Yeates to reappear, and had taken, during his vigil, two more vessels homeward bound to England from Charlestown. News of Vane had also, during this time, been brought into the little capital of South Carolina by the various captains whose ships he had plundered, and Colonel Rhett, whom, as we have already seen, was fitting out the two vessels with which he afterwards captured Stede Bonnet in the Cape Fear River, decided to put out in chase of him. Vane was too old a bird, however, not to have realized that some measures of retaliation would probably be taken against him, and had allowed tidings to escape to the effect that he was proposing to cruise southward. Sailing on September 15th, Rhett therefore missed him, as we have already recorded, Vane having made his way north towards the New England colonies, where he next meant to operate.

While Rhett had thus given him up and was following in his wake on the resumed task of hunting down and destroying Bonnet, Vane was well on his way towards the scene of his next recorded capture. But in the interval there occurred a picturesque incident which is perhaps worth recording, for as he approached Ocracoke Inlet, some little distance south of Cape Hatteras, he fell in with his even more notorious fellow-pirate, Captain Teach or Blackbeard, and the two saluted each other with formal salvoes of guns, afterwards engaging in mutual courtesies, not to say orgies, for several days. Vane then pushed farther north, and on October 23rd, captured a small brigantine, bound from Jamaica to the port of Salem on the Delaware River. This he plundered and let go, and for some further weeks met with no other success, his next encounter being with the French man-of war, to which we have already referred in the story of the two women pirates. For it was as a result of this encounter that John Rackam, Anne Bonny's future lover, succeeded in obtaining command of Vane's vessel after having deposed his chief, although in all the circumstances, Vane's disputed conduct on this occasion was probably dictated by the sounder judgment. Indeed the incident might have had a disastrous issue for all the pirates concerned, for after confidently approaching the Frenchman in the belief that she was a harmless merchantman, they suddenly found themselves in the presence of a very powerfully armed man-of-war, who promptly received them with a broadside. Vane at once went about, whereupon the Frenchman gave chase, and it was then that Rackam, who was apparently Yeates' successor, led the section of the crew that wished to come and engage the pursuer. For though it was true, as Rackam admitted, that "she had more Guns and a greater weight of Mettal," yet he was all for making alongside and endeavouring to board her when, as he said, "the best Boys would carry the day."

Hardened old pirate as he was, however, Vane refused to be over-persuaded, pointing out, we are told, "that it was too rash and desperate an Enterprise, the Man of War appearing to be twice their Force; and that their Brigantine might be sunk by her before they could reach on board." For the, moment, too, he carried his point, the Frenchman being safely eluded. But after a council of war the next day he was formally found guilty of cowardice and set adrift in a small boat with the fifteen members of the crew who had taken his part, including one Robert Deal, one of his chief officers. In view of his past exploits, however, and no doubt of a certain lingering affection for their old leader, Vane was given an ample supply of provisions together with some ammunition, so that, if he cared, he could make a fresh start elsewhere. This he resolved to do, and accordingly made his way south again towards the Bay of Honduras, eventually taking three small ships off the northwest coast of Jamaica, one of which he kept for a consort, while from all of them he recruited likely hands for his service.

The end of the year was now approaching, and on the 15th December, Vane with his augmented company fell in with an armed vessel, the *Pearl*, of Jamaica, under Captain Rowling. As the approaching pirate vessel showed no colours, Rowling opened fire upon them.

But when Vane at once responded, at the same time breaking the Black Flag from his mast, Rowling surrendered, and his vessel was carried off to a small island safely out of reach of possible investigators. On the way to this island Vane captured yet another vessel, which he also took with him, the spoils being divided, according to his usual procedure when his destination was reached. Here he remained lurking in safe obscurity till February of the following year, probably in entire ignorance of the fate that had meanwhile overtaken Blackbeard, with whom he had so lately been exchanging courtesies. In February, however, he decided to take the high seas again, and with one of his prizes as consort, set out upon the voyage that Fate had determined was to prove his last.

For hardly had he put to sea when he ran into one of the cyclones that occasionally devastate these West Indian islands, and was soon separated from his consort and driving helplessly before the wind. Finally he was driven upon a small uninhabited island, where his little ship was broken to pieces upon the shore, most of the men being drowned and Vane himself barely escaping with his life. But he had already escaped from too many tight corners not to make the most of every reprieve, and for some weeks he succeeded in keeping himself alive, thanks to the convenient visit to the island of a handful of poor fishermen in search of turtles. Moreover, by another chance that seemed at first equally fortunate, a Jamaica trader put into the island for water, and proved to belong to an old acquaintance of his, a sturdy buccaneer named Captain Holford.

But between the buccaneer and the pirate such as Vane there was a distinct if somewhat narrow gulf, and Holford, knowing his man, proved less amenable than Vane had hoped. "Charles," he seems to have said frankly, "I shan't have you aboard my ship unless I carry you a Prisoner; for I shall have you caballing with my Men, knock me on the Head, and run away with my Ship a pyrating"—a surmise that seems, on the face of it, not to have been improbable, although Vane strenuously denied it. But Holford was not to be shaken and pointed out to Vane that "He might easily find a Way to get off, if he had a Mind to it," adding, "I am now going down the Bay and shall return hither in about a Month; and if I find you upon the island when I come back, I'll carry you to Jamaica and hang you."

"But how can I get away?" replied Vane.

"Are there no Fishermen's Dories," said Holford, "upon the Beach? Can't you take one of them?"

"What," said Vane properly shocked, "would you have me steal a Dory then?"

But as regards Holford, at any rate, Vane had come to the end of his tether.

"Do you make it a matter of Conscience," he said, "to steal a Dory, when you have been a common Robber and Pyrate, stealing Ships and Cargoes, and plundering all Mankind that fell in your Way? Stay there and be d—d, if you are so squeamish," whereupon the ex-buccaneer, we are told, sailed away.

Even then, however, Vane might have succeeded in escaping, for a few days later a second vessel put into the island, homeward bound for Jamaica. The captain of this had never met Vane, who now represented himself under another name as a poor ship-wrecked sailor only too anxious to prove his honest worth in return for a passage. The captain agreed to take him; Vane went aboard, and the vessel continued upon its way, when by the most ironical chance of all, the captain met an old friend, also homeward bound. This was none other than Holford, who was invited on board to dinner, and who chanced, as he went by, to glance down into the hold, where he caught sight of Charles Vane virtuously at work. Calling his host, he pointed him out, giving a brief summary of Vane's immediate past. It was ultimately arranged that Holford should take him over and carry him as a prisoner to Jamaica. Holford accordingly sent his mate, suitably armed, and a stout boat's crew to fetch the unfortunate pirate, who was then placed in irons on board Holford's vessel and safely lodged in prison at Port Royal. Here, not long before, Vane's principal subordinate, Robert Deal, had been caught and hanged, and in due course, Charles Vane, after being tried and found guilty, paid his long overdue penalty.

The Life of Captain Lewis

CHARLES ELLMS

Captain Lewis was at an early age associated with pirates. We first find him a boy in company with the pirate Banister, who was hanged at the yard arm of a man-of-war, in sight of Port Royal, Jamaica. This Lewis and another boy were taken with him, and brought into the island hanging by the middle at the mizen peak. He had a great aptitude for languages, and spoke perfectly well that of the Mosquil Indians, French, Spanish, and English. I mention our own, because it is doubted whether he was French or English, for we cannot trace him back to his origin. He sailed out of Jamaica till he was a lusty lad, and was then taken by the Spaniards at the Havana, where he tarried some time; but at length he and six more ran away with a small canoe, and surprised a Spanish periagua, out of which two men joined them, so that they were now nine in company. With this periagua they surprised a turtling sloop, and forced some of the hands to take on with them; the others they sent away in the periagua.

He played at this small game, surprising and taking coasters and turtlers, till with forced men and volunteers he made up a company of 40 men. With these he took a large pink built ship, bound from Jamaica to the bay of Campeachy, and after her, several others bound to the same place; and having intelligence that there lay in the bay a fine Bermuda built brigantine of 10 guns, commanded by Captain Tucker, he sent the captain of the pink to him with a letter, the purport of which was, that he wanted such a brigantine, and if he would part with her, he would pay him 10,000 pieces of eight; if he refused this, he would take care to lie in his way, for he was resolved, either by fair or foul means to have the vessel. Captain Tucker, having read the letter, sent for the masters of vessels then lying in the bay, and told them, after he had shown the letter, that if they would make him up 54 men, (for there were about ten Bermuda sloops,) he would go out and fight the pirates. They said no, they would not hazard their men, they depended on their sailing, and every one must take care of himself as well as he could.

However, they all put to sea together, and spied a sail under the land, which had a breeze while they lay becalmed. Some said he was a turtler; others, the pirate, and so it proved; for it was honest Captain Lewis, who putting out his oars, got in among them. Some of the sloops had four guns, some two, some none. Joseph Dill had two, which he brought on one side, and fired smartly at the pirate, but unfortunately one of them split, and killed three men. Tucker called to all the sloops to send him men, and he would fight Lewis, but to no purpose; nobody came on board him. In the mean while a breeze sprung up, and Tucker, trimming his sails, left them, who all fell a prey to the pirate; into whom, however, he fired a broadside at going off. One sloop, whose master I will not name, was a very good sailer, and was going off; but Lewis firing a shot, brought her to, and he lay by till all the sloops were visited and secured. Then Lewis sent on board him, and ordered the master into his sloop. As soon as he was on board, he asked the reason of his lying by, and betraying the trust his owners had reposed in him, which was doing like a knave and coward, and he would punish him accordingly; for, said he, *you might have got off, being so much a better sailer than my vessel.* After this speech, he fell upon him with a rope's end, and then snatching up his cane, drove him about the decks without mercy. The master, thinking to pacify him, told him he had been out trading in that sloop several months, and had on board a good quantity of money, which was hid, and which, if he would send on board a black belonging to the owners, he would discover to him. This had not the desired effect, but one quite contrary; for Lewis told him he was a rascal and villain for this discovery, and he would pay him for betraying his owners, and redoubled his strokes. However, he sent and took the money and negro, who was an able sailor. He took out of his prizes what he had occasion for, forty able negro sailors, and a white carpenter. The largest sloop, which was about ninety tons, he took for his own use, and mounted her with 12 guns. His crew was now about eighty men, whites and blacks.

After these captures, he cruised in the Gulf of Florida, laying in wait for the West India homeward bound ships that took the leeward passage, several of which, falling into his hands, were plundered by him, and released. From hence he went to the coast of Carolina, where he cleaned his sloop, and a great many men whom he had forced, ran away from him. However, the natives traded with him for rum and sugar, and brought him all he wanted, without the government's having any knowledge of him, for he had got into a very private creek; though he was very much on his guard, that he might not be surprised from the shore.

From Carolina he cruised on the coast of Virginia, where he took and plundered several merchantmen, and forced several men, and then returned to the coast of Carolina, where he did abundance of mischief. As he had now an abundance of French on board, who had entered with him, and Lewis, hearing the English had a design to maroon them, he secured the men he suspected, and put them in a boat, with all the other English, ten leagues from shore, with only ten pieces of beef, and sent them away, keeping none but French and negroes. These men, it is supposed, all perished in the sea.

From the coast of Carolina he shaped his course for the banks of Newfoundland, where he overhauled several fishing vessels, and then went into Trinity Harbor in Conception Bay, where there lay several merchantmen, and seized a 24 gun galley, called the Herman. The commander, Captain Beal, told Lewis, if he would send his quarter master ashore he would furnish him with necessaries. He being sent ashore, a council was held among the masters, the consequence of which was, the seizing the quarter master, whom they carried to Captain Woodes Rogers. He chained him to a sheet anchor which was ashore, and planted guns at the point, to prevent the pirate getting out, but to little purpose; for the people at one of these points firing too soon, Lewis quitted the ship, and, by the help of oars and the favor of the night, got out in his sloop, though she received many shot in her hull. The last shot that was fired at the pirate did him considerable damage.

He lay off and on the harbor, swearing he would have his quarter master, and intercepted two fishing shallops, on board of one of which was the captain of the galley's brother. He detained them, and sent word, if his quarter master did not immediately come off, he would put all his prisoners to death. He was sent on board without hesitation. Lewis and the crew inquired how he had been used, and he answered, very civilly. "It's well," said the pirate, "for had you been ill treated, I would have put all these rascals to the sword." They were dismissed, and the captain's brother going over the side, the quarter master stopped him, saying, he must drink the gentlemen's health ashore, particularly Captain Rogers' and, whispering him in the ear, told him, if they had known of his being chained all night, he would have been cut in pieces, with all his men. After this poor man and his shallop's company were gone, the quarter master told the usage he had met with, which enraged Lewis, and made him reproach his quarter master, whose answer was, that he did not think it just the innocent should suffer for the guilty.

The masters of the merchantmen sent to Capt. Tudor Trevor, who lay at St. John's in the Sheerness man-of-war. He immediately got under sail, and missed the pirate but four hours. She kept along the coast and made several prizes, French and English, and put into a harbor where a French ship lay making fish. She was built at the latter end of the war, for a privateer, was an excellent sailer, and mounted 24 guns. The commander hailed him: the pirate answered, *from Jamaica with rum and sugar.* The Frenchman bid him go about his business; that a pirate sloop was on the coast, and he might be the rogue; if he did not immediately sheer off, he would fire a broadside into him. He went off and lay a fortnight out at sea, so far as not to be descried from shore, with resolution to have the ship. The Frenchman being on his guard, in the meanwhile raised a battery on the shore, which commanded the harbor. After a fortnight, when he was thought to be gone off, he returned, and took two of the fishing shallops belonging to the Frenchman, and manning them with pirates, they went in. One shallop attacked the battery; the other surprised, boarded and carried the ship, just as the morning star appeared, for which reason he gave her that name. In the engagement the owner's son was killed, who made the voyage out of curiosity only. The ship being taken, seven guns were fired, which was the signal, and the sloop came down and lay alongside the ship. The captain told him he supposed he only wanted his liquor; but Lewis made answer he wanted his ship, and accordingly hoisted all his ammunition and provision into her. When the Frenchman saw they would have his ship, he told her trim, and Lewis gave him the sloop; and excepting what he took for provision, all the fish he had made. Several of the French took on with him, who, with others, English and French, had by force or voluntarily, made him up 200 men.

From Newfoundland he steered for the coast of Guinea, where he took a great many ships, English, Dutch and Portuguese. Among these ships was one belonging to Carolina, commanded by Capt. Smith. While he was in chase of this vessel a circumstance occurred, which made his men believe he dealt with the devil; his fore and main top-mast being carried away, he, Lewis, running up the shrouds to the main-top, tore off a handful of hair, and throwing it into the air used this expression, *good devil, take this till I come.* And it was observed, that he came afterwards faster up with the chase than before the loss of his top-masts.

Smith being taken, Lewis used him very civilly, and gave him as much or more in value than he took from him, and let him go, saying, he would come to Carolina when he had made money on the coast, and would rely on his friendship.

They kept some time on the coast, when they quarrelled among themselves, the French and English, of which the former were more numerous, and they resolved to part. The French therefore chose a large sloop newly taken, thinking the ship's bottom, which was not sheathed, damaged by the worms. According to this agreement they took on board what ammunition and provision they thought fit out of the ship, and put off, choosing one Le Barre captain. As it blew hard, and the decks were encumbered, they came to an anchor under the coast, to stow away their ammunition, goods, &c. Lewis told his men they were a parcel of rogues, and he would make them refund; accordingly he run alongside, his guns being all loaded and new primed, and ordered him to cut away his mast or he would sink him. Le Barre was obliged to obey. Then he ordered them all ashore. They begged the liberty of carrying their arms, goods, &c. with them, but he allowed them only their small arms and cartridge boxes. Then he brought the sloop alongside, put every thing on board the ship, and sunk the sloop.

Le Barre and the rest begged to be taken on board. However, though he denied them, he suffered Le Barre and some few to come, with whom he and his men drank plentifully. The negroes on board Lewis told him the French had a plot against him. He answered, he could not withstand his destiny; for the devil told him in the great cabin he should be murdered that night.

In the dead of the night, the rest of the French came on board in canoes, got into the cabin and killed Lewis. They fell on the crew; but, after an hour and a half's dispute, the French were beaten off, and the quarter master, John Cornelius, an Irishman, succeeded Lewis.

—"He was the mildest manner'd man,
That ever scuttled ship or cut a throat;
With such true breeding of a gentleman,
You never could discern his real thought.
Pity he loved an adventurous life's variety,
He was so great a loss to good society."

Tom Sawyer, Pirate King

MARK TWAIN

Tom's mind was made up now. He was gloomy and desperate. He was a forsaken, friendless boy, he said; nobody loved him; when they found out what they had driven him to, perhaps they would be sorry; he had tried to do right and get along, but they would not let him; since nothing would do them but to be rid of him, let it be so; and let them blame *him* for the consequences—why shouldn't they? What right had the friendless to complain? Yes, they had forced him to it at last: he would lead a life of crime. There was no choice.

By this time he was far down Meadow Lane, and the bell for school to "take up" tinkled faintly upon his ear. He sobbed, now, to think he should never, never hear that old familiar sound any more—it was very hard, but it was forced on him; since he was driven out into the cold world, he must submit—but he forgave them. Then the sobs came thick and fast.

Just at this point he met his soul's sworn comrade, Joe Harper—hard-eyed, and with evidently a great and dismal purpose in his heart. Plainly here were "two souls with but a single thought." Tom, wiping his eyes with his sleeve, began to blubber out something about a resolution to escape from hard usage and lack of sympathy at home by roaming abroad into the great world never to return; and ended by hoping that Joe would not forget him.

But it transpired that this was a request which Joe had just been going to make of Tom, and had come to hunt him up for that purpose. His mother had whipped him for drinking some cream which he had never tasted and knew nothing about; it was plain that she was tired of him and wished him to go; if she felt that way, there was nothing for him to do but succumb; he hoped she would be happy, and never regret having driven her poor boy out into the unfeeling world to suffer and die.

As the two boys walked sorrowing along, they made a new compact to stand by each other and be brothers and never separate till death relieved them of their troubles. Then they began to lay their plans. Joe was for being a hermit, and living on crusts in a remote cave, and dying, some time, of cold, and want, and grief; but after listening to Tom, he conceded that there were some conspicuous advantages about a life of crime, and so he consented to be a pirate.

Three miles below St. Petersburg, at a point where the Mississippi River was a trifle over a mile wide, there was a long, narrow, wooded island, with a shallow bar at the head of it, and this offered well as a rendezvous. It was not inhabited; it lay far over toward the further shore, abreast a dense and almost wholly unpeopled forest. So Jackson's Island was chosen. Who were to be the subjects of their piracies, was a matter that did not occur to them. Then they hunted up Huckleberry Finn, and he joined them promptly, for all careers were one to him; he was indifferent. They presently separated to meet at a lonely spot on the river bank two miles above the village at the favorite hour—which was midnight. There was a small log raft there which they meant to capture. Each would bring hooks and lines, and such provision as he could steal in the most dark and mysterious way—as became outlaws. And before the afternoon was done, they had all managed to enjoy the sweet glory of spreading the fact that pretty soon the town would "hear something." All who got this vague hint were cautioned to "be mum and wait."

About midnight Tom arrived with a boiled ham and a few trifles, and stopped in a dense undergrowth on a small bluff overlooking the meeting-place. It was starlight, and very still. The mighty river lay like an ocean at rest. Tom listened a moment, but no sound disturbed the quiet. Then he gave a low, distinct whistle. It was answered from under the bluff. Tom whistled twice more; these signals were answered in the same way. Then a guarded voice said:

"Who goes there?"

"Tom Sawyer, the Black Avenger of the Spanish Main. Name your names."

"Huck Finn the Red-Handed, and Joe Harper the Terror of the Seas." Tom had furnished these titles, from his favorite literature.

" 'Tis well. Give the countersign."

Two hoarse whispers delivered the same awful word simultaneously to the brooding night:

"BLOOD!"

Then Tom tumbled his ham over the bluff and let himself down after it, tearing both skin and clothes to some extent in the effort. There was an easy, comfortable path along the shore under the bluff, but it lacked the advantages of difficulty and danger so valued by a pirate.

The Terror of the Seas had brought a side of bacon, and had about worn himself out with getting it there. Finn the Red-Handed had stolen a skillet and a quantity of half-cured leaf tobacco, and had also brought a few corn-cobs to make pipes with. But none of the pirates smoked or "chewed" but himself. The Black Avenger of the Spanish Main said it would never do to start without some fire. That was a wise thought; matches were hardly known there in that day. They saw a fire smoldering upon a great raft a hundred yards above, and they went stealthily thither and helped themselves to a chunk. They made an imposing adventure of it, saying, "Hist!" every now and then, and suddenly halting with finger on lip; moving with hands on imaginary dagger-hilts; and giving orders in dismal whispers that if "the foe" stirred, to "let him have it to the hilt," because "dead men tell no tales." They knew well enough that the raftsmen were all down at the village laying in stores or having a spree, but still that was no excuse for their conducting this thing in an unpiratical way.

They shoved off, presently, Tom in command, Huck at the after oar and Joe at the forward. Tom stood amidships, gloomy-browed, and with folded arms, and gave his orders in a low, stern whisper:

"Luff, and bring her to the wind!"

"Aye-aye, sir!"

"Steady, steady-y-y-y!"

"Steady it is, sir!"

"Let her go off a point!"

"Point it is, sir!"

As the boys steadily and monotonously drove the raft toward midstream it was no doubt understood that these orders were given only for "style," and were not intended to mean anything in particular.

"What sail's she carrying?"

"Courses, tops'ls, and flying-jib, sir."

"Send the r'yals up! Lay out aloft, there, half a dozen of ye—foretopmaststuns'l! Lively, now!"

"Aye-aye, sir!"

"Shake out that maintogalans'l! Sheets and braces! *Now*, my hearties!"

"Aye-aye, sir!"

"Hellum-a-lee—hard a port! Stand by to meet her when she comes! Port, port! *Now*, men! With a will! stead-y-y-y!"

"Steady it is, sir!"

The raft drew beyond the middle of the river; the boys pointed her head right, and then lay on their oars. The river was not high, so there was not more than a two- or three-mile current. Hardly a word was said during the next three-quarters of an hour. Now the raft was passing before the distant town. Two or three glimmering lights showed where it lay, peacefully sleeping, beyond the vague vast sweep of star-gemmed water, unconscious of the tremendous event that, was happening. The Black Avenger stood still with folded arms, "looking his last" upon the scene of his former joys and his later sufferings, and wishing "she" could see him now, abroad on the wild sea, facing peril and death with dauntless heart, going to his doom with a grim smile on his lips. It was but a small strain on his imagination to remove Jackson's Island beyond eyeshot of the village, and so he "looked his last" with a broken and satisfied heart. The other pirates were looking their last, too; and they all looked so long that they came near letting the current drift them out of the range of the island. But they discovered the danger in time, and made shift to avert it. About two o'clock in the morning the raft grounded on the bar two hundred yards above the head of the island, and they waded back and forth until they had landed their freight. Part of the little raft's belongings consisted of an old sail, and this they spread over a nook in the bushes for a tent to shelter their provisions; but they themselves would sleep in the open air in good weather, as became outlaws.

They built a fire against the side of a great log twenty or thirty steps within the somber depths of the forest, and then cooked some bacon in the frying-pan for supper, and used up half of the corn "pone" stock they had brought. It seemed glorious sport to be feasting in that wild free way in the virgin forest of an unexplored and uninhabited island, far from the haunts of men, and they said they never would return to civilization. The climbing fire lit up their faces and threw its ruddy glare upon the pillared tree-trunks of their forest temple, and upon the varnished foliage and festooning vines.

When the last crisp slice of bacon was gone, and the last allowance of corn pone devoured, the boys stretched themselves out on the grass, filled with contentment. They could have found a cooler place, but they would not deny themselves such a romantic feature as the roasting campfire.

"*Ain't* it gay?" said Joe.

"It's *nuts!*" said Tom. "What would the boys say if they could see us?"

"Say? Well, they'd just die to be here—hey, Hucky?"

"I reckon so," said Huckleberry; "anyways, *I*'m suited. I don't want nothing better'n this. I don't ever get enough to eat, gen'ally—and here they can't come and pick at a feller and bullyrag him so."

"It's just the life for me," said Tom. "You don't have to get up, mornings, and you don't have to go to school, and wash, and all that blame foolishness. You see a pirate don't have to do *anything*, Joe, when he's ashore, but a hermit *he* has to be praying considerable, and then he don't have any fun, anyway, all by himself, that way."

"Oh, yes, that's so," said Joe, "but I hadn't thought much about it, you know. I'd a good deal rather be a pirate, now that I've tried it."

"You see," said Tom, "people don't go much on hermits, nowadays, like they used to in old times, but a pirate's always respected. And a hermit's got to sleep on the hardest place he can find, and put sackcloth and ashes on his head, and stand out in the rain, and—"

"What does he put sackcloth and ashes on his head for?" inquired Huck.

"*I* dono. But they've *got* to do it. Hermits always do. You'd have to do that if you was a hermit."

"Dern'd if I would," said Huck.

"Well, what would you do?"

"I dunno. But I wouldn't do that."

"Why, Huck, you'd *have* to. How'd you get around it?"

"Why, I just wouldn't stand it. I'd run away."

"Run away! Well, you *would* be a nice old slouch of a hermit. You'd be a disgrace."

The Red-Handed made no response, being better employed. He had finished gouging out a cob, and now he fitted a weed stem to it, loaded it with tobacco, and was pressing a coal to the charge and blowing a cloud of fragrant smoke—he was in the full bloom of luxurious contentment. The other pirates envied him this majestic vice, and secretly resolved to acquire it shortly. Presently Huck said:

"What does pirates have to do?"

Tom said:

"Oh, they have just a bully time—take ships and burn them, and get the money and bury it in awful places in their island where there's ghosts and things to watch it, and kill everybody in the ships—make 'em walk a plank."

"And they carry the women to the island," said Joe; "they don't kill the women."

"No," assented Tom, "they don't kill the women—they're too noble. And the women's always beautiful, too."

"And don't they wear the bulliest clothes! Oh, no! All gold and silver and di'monds," said Joe, with enthusiasm.

"Who?" said Huck.

"Why, the pirates."

Huck scanned his own clothing forlornly.

"I reckon I ain't dressed fitten for a pirate," said he, with a regretful pathos in his voice; "but I ain't got none but these."

But the other boys told him the fine clothes would come fast enough, after they should have begun their adventures. They made him understand that his poor rags would do to begin with, though it was customary for wealthy pirates to start with a proper wardrobe.

Gradually their talk died out and drowsiness began to steal upon the eyelids of the little waifs. The pipe dropped from the fingers of the Red-Handed, and he slept the sleep of the conscience-free and the weary. The Terror of the Seas and the Black Avenger of the Spanish Main had more difficulty in getting to sleep. They said their prayers inwardly, and lying down, since there was nobody there with authority to make them kneel and recite aloud; in truth, they had a mind not to say them at all, but they were afraid to proceed to such lengths as that, lest they might call down a sudden and special thunderbolt from Heaven. Then at once they reached and hovered upon the imminent verge of sleep—but an intruder came, now, that would not "down." It was conscience. They began to feel a vague fear that they had been doing wrong to run away; and next they thought of the stolen meat, and then the real torture came. They tried to argue it away by reminding conscience that they had purloined sweetmeats and apples scores of times; but conscience was not to be appeased by such thin plausibilities; it seemed to them, in the end, that there was no getting around the stubborn fact that taking sweetmeats was only "hooking," while taking bacon and hams and such valuables was plain simple *stealing*—and there was a command against that in the Bible. So they inwardly resolved that so long as they remained in the business, their piracies should not again be sullied with the crime of stealing. Then conscience granted a truce, and these curiously inconsistent pirates fell peacefully to sleep.

Ann Bonny *and* Mary Read *convicted of Piracy Nov.ʳ 28ᵗʰ 1720 at a Court of Vice Admiralty held at* S.ᵗ Jago de la Vega *in ỹ Island of Jamaica.*

Anne Bonney and Mary Read

CHARLES ELLMS

Anne Bonney

This female pirate was a native of Cork. Her father was an attorney, and, by his activity in business, rose to considerable respectability in that place. Anne was the fruit of an unlawful connexion with his own servant maid, with whom he afterwards eloped to America, leaving his own affectionate and lawful wife. He settled at Carolina, and for some time followed his own profession; but soon commenced merchant, and was so successful as to purchase a considerable plantation. There he lived with his servant in the character of his wife; but she dying, his daughter Anne superintended the domestic affairs of her father.

During her residence with her parent she was supposed to have a considerable fortune, and was accordingly addressed by young men of respectable situations in life. It happened with

Anne, however, as with many others of her youth and sex, that her feelings, and not her interest, determined her choice of a husband. She married a young sailor without a shilling. The avaricious father was so enraged, that, deaf to the feelings of a parent, he turned his own child out of doors. Upon this cruel usage, and the disappointment of her fortune, Anne and her husband sailed for the island of Providence, in the hope of gaining employment.

Acting a part very different from that of Mary Read, Anne's affections were soon estranged from her husband by Captain Rackam; and eloping with him, she went to sea in men's clothes. Proving with child, the captain put her on shore, and entrusted her to the care of some friends until her recovery, when she again accompanied him in his expeditions.

Upon the king's proclamation offering a pardon to all pirates, he surrendered, and went into the privateering business, as we have related before: he, however, soon embraced an opportunity to return to his favorite employment. In all his piratical exploits Anne accompanied him; and, as we have already recorded, displayed such courage and intrepidity, that she, along with Mary Read and a seaman, were the last three who remained on board when the vessel was taken.

Anne was known to many of the planters in Jamaica, who remembered to have seen her in her father's house, and they were disposed to intercede in her behalf. Her unprincipled conduct, in leaving her own husband and forming an illicit connexion with Rackam, tended, however, to render her friends less active. By a special favor, Rackam was permitted to visit her the day before he was executed; but, instead of condoling with him on account of his sad fate, she only observed, that she was sorry to see him there, but if he had fought like a man he needed not have been hanged like a dog. Being with child, she remained in prison until her recovery, was reprieved from time to time, and though we cannot communicate to our readers any particulars of her future life, or the manner of her death, yet it is certain that she was not executed.

Mary Read

The attention of our readers is now to be directed to the history of two female pirates,—a history which is chiefly remarkable from the extraordinary circumstance of the softer sex assuming a character peculiarly distinguished for every vice that can disgrace humanity, and at the same time for the exertion of the most daring, though brutal, courage.

Mary Read was a native of England, but at what place she was born is not recorded. Her mother married a sailor when she was very young, who, soon after their marriage, went to sea, and never returned. The fruit of that marriage was a sprightly boy. The husband not returning, she again found herself with child, and to cover her shame, took leave of her husband's relations, and went to live in the country, taking her boy along with her. Her son in a short time died, and she was relieved from the burden of his maintenance and education. The mother had not resided long in the country before Mary Read, the subject of the present narrative, was born.

After the birth of Mary, her mother resided in the country for three or four years, until her money was all spent, and her ingenuity was set at work to contrive how to obtain a supply. She knew that her husband's mother was in good circumstances, and could easily support her child, provided she could make her pass for a boy, and her son's child. But it seemed impossible to impose upon an old experienced mother. She, however, presented Mary in the character of her grandson. The old woman proposed to take the boy to live with her, but the mother would not on any account part with her boy; the grandmother, therefore, allowed a crown per week for his support.

The ingenuity of the mother being successful, she reared the daughter as a boy. But as she grew up, she informed her of the secret of her birth, in order that she might conceal her sex. The grandmother, however, dying, the support from that quarter failed, and she was obliged to hire her out as a footboy to a French lady. The strength and manly disposition of this supposed boy increased with her years, and leaving that servile employment, she engaged on board a man-of-war.

The volatile disposition of the youth did not permit her to remain long in this station, and she next went into Flanders, and joined a regiment of foot as a cadet. Though in every action she conducted herself with the greatest bravery, yet she could not obtain a commission, as they were in general bought and sold. She accordingly quitted that service, and enlisted into a regiment of horse; there she behaved herself so valiantly, that she gained the esteem of all her officers. It, however, happened, that her comrade was a handsome young Fleming, and she fell passionately in love with him. The violence of her feelings rendered her negligent of her duty, and effected such a change in her behaviour as attracted the attention of all. Both her comrade and the rest of the regiment deemed her mad. Love, however, is inventive, and as they slept in the same tent, she found means to discover her sex without any seeming design. He was both surprised and pleased, supposing that he would have a mistress to himself; but he was greatly mistaken, and he found that it was necessary to court her for his wife. A mutual attachment took place, and, as soon as convenient, women's clothes were provided for her, and they were publicly married.

The singularity of two troopers marrying caused a general conversation, and many of the officers honored the ceremony with their presence, and resolved to make presents to the bride, to provide her with necessaries. After marriage they were desirous to quit the service, and their discharge being easily obtained, they set up an ordinary under the sign of the "Three Shoes," and soon acquired a considerable run of business.

But Mary Read's felicity was of short duration; the husband died, and peace being concluded, her business diminished. Under these circumstances she again resumed her man's dress, and going into Holland, enlisted into a regiment of foot quartered in one of the frontier towns. But there being no prospect of preferment in time of peace, she went on board a vessel bound for the West Indies.

During the voyage, the vessel was captured by English pirates, and as Mary was the only English person on board, they detained her, and having plundered the vessel of what they chose, allowed it to depart. Mary continued in that unlawful commerce for some time, but the royal pardon being tendered to all those in the West Indies, who should, before a specified day, surrender, the crew to which she was attached, availed themselves of this, and lived quietly on shore with the fruits of their adventures. But from the want of their usual supplies, their money became exhausted; and being informed that Captain Rodgers, in the island of Providence, was fitting out some vessels for privateering, Mary, with some others, repaired to that island to serve on board his privateers. We have already heard, that scarcely had the ships sailed, when some of their crews mutinied, and ran off with the ships, to pursue their former mode of life. Among these was Mary Read. She indeed, frequently declared, that the life of a pirate was what she detested, and that she was constrained to it both on the former and present occasion. It was, however, sufficiently ascertained, that both Mary Read and Anne Bonney were among the bravest and most resolute fighters of the whole crew; that when the vessel was taken, these two heroines, along with another of the pirates, were the last three upon deck; and that Mary, having in vain endeavored to rouse the courage of the crew, who had fled below, discharged a pistol amongst them, killing one and wounding another.

Nor was Mary less modest than brave; for though she had remained many years in the character of a sailor, yet no one had discovered her sex, until she was under the necessity of doing so to Anne Bonney. The reason of this was, that Anne, supposing her to be a handsome fellow, became greatly enamored of her, and discovered her sex and wishes to Mary, who was thus constrained to reveal her secret to Anne. Rackam being the paramour of Bonney, and observing her partiality towards Mary, threatened to shoot her lover; so that to prevent any mischief, Anne also informed the captain of the sex of her companion.

Rackam was enjoined to secrecy, and here he behaved honorably; but love again assailed the conquered Mary. It was usual with the pirates to retain all the artists who were captured in the trading-vessels; among these was a very handsome young man, of engaging manners, who vanquished the heart of Mary. In a short time her love became so violent, that she took every opportunity of enjoying his company and conversation; and, after she had gained his friendship, discovered her sex. Esteem and friendship were speedily converted into the most ardent affection, and a mutual flame burned in the hearts of these two lovers. An occurrence soon happened that put the attachment of Mary to a severe trial. Her lover having quarrelled with one of the crew, they agreed to fight a duel on shore. Mary was all anxiety for the fate of her lover, and she manifested a greater concern for the preservation of his life than that of her own; but she could not entertain the idea that he could refuse to fight, and so be esteemed a coward. Accordingly she quarrelled with the man who challenged her lover, and called him to the field two hours before his appointment with her lover, engaged him with sword and pistol, and laid him dead at her feet.

Though no esteem or love had formerly existed, this action was sufficient to have kindled the most violent flame. But this was not necessary, for the lover's attachment was equal, if not stronger than her own; they pledged their faith, which was esteemed as binding as if the ceremony had been performed by a clergyman.

Captain Rackam one day, before he knew that she was a woman, asked her why she followed a line of life that exposed her to so much danger, and at last to the certainty of being hanged. She replied, that, "As to hanging, she thought it no great hardship, for were it not for that, every cowardly fellow would turn pirate, and so infest the seas; and men of courage would starve. That if it was put to her choice, she would not have the punishment less than death, the fear of which kept some dastardly rogues honest; that many of those who are now cheating the widows and orphans, and oppressing their poor neighbors who have no money to obtain justice, would then rob at sea, and the ocean would be as crowded with rogues as the land: so that no merchants would venture out, and the trade in a little time would not be worth following."

Being with child at the time of her trial, her execution was delayed; and it is probable that she would have found favor, but in the mean time she fell sick and died.

Mary Read was of a strong and robust constitution, capable of enduring much exertion and fatigue. She was vain and bold in her disposition, but susceptible of the tenderest emotions, and of the most melting affections. Her conduct was generally directed by virtuous principles, while at the same time, she was violent in her attachments. Though she was inadvertently drawn into that dishonorable mode of life which has stained her character, and given her a place among the criminals noticed in this work, yet she possessed a rectitude of principle and of conduct, far superior to many who have not been exposed to such temptations to swerve from the path of female virtue and honor.

Jaddi, the Malay Pirate

THE INDIAN ANTIQUARY

Long before that action with the English man-of-war which drove me to Singapore, I sailed in a fine fleet of prahus belonging to the Rajah of Johore [Sultân Mahmâd Shâh]. We were all then very rich—ah! such numbers of beautiful wives and such feasting!—but, above all, we had a great many most holy men in our force! When the proper monsoon came, we proceeded to sea to fight the Bugismen [of Celebes] and Chinamen bound from Borneo and the Celebes to Java; for you must remember our Rajah was at war with them. (Jadee always maintained that the proceedings in which he had been engaged partook of a purely warlike, and not of a piratical character.)

Our thirteen prahus had all been fitted out in and about Singapore. I wish you could have seen them, Touhan [*Tüan*, Sir]. These prahus we see here are nothing to them, such brass guns, such long pendants, such creeses [Malay *kris,* dagger]! Allah-il-Allah! Our Datoos [*datuk,* a chief] were indeed great men!

Sailing along the coast as high as Patani, we then crossed over to Borneo, two Illanoon prahus acting as pilots, and reached a place called Sambas [West-Borneo]: there we fought the Chinese and Dutchmen, who ill-treat our countrymen, and are trying to drive the Malays out of that country. Gold-dust and slaves in large quantities were here taken, most of the latter being our countrymen of Sumatra and Java, who are captured and sold to the planters and miners of the Dutch settlements.

"Do you mean to say," I asked, "that the Dutch countenance such traffic?"

"The Hollanders," replied Jadee, "have been the bane of the Malay race; no one knows the amount of villainy, the bloody cruelty of their system towards us. They drive us into our prahus to escape their taxes and laws, and then declare us pirates and put us to death. There are natives in our crew, Touhan, of Sumatra and Java, of Bianca [Banka] and Borneo; ask them why they hate the Dutchmen; why they would kill a Dutchman. It is because the Dutchman is a false man, not like the white man [English]. The Hollander stabs in the dark; he is a liar!"

However, from Borneo we sailed to Biliton [island between Banka and Borneo] and Bianca, and there waited for some large junks that were expected. Our cruise had been so far successful, and we feasted away—fighting cocks, smoking opium and eating white rice. At last our scouts told us that a junk was in sight. She came, a lofty-sided one of Fokien [Fuhkien]. We knew these Amoy men would fight like tiger-cats for their sugar and silks; and as the breeze was fresh, we only kept her in sight by keeping close inshore and following her. Not to frighten the China-men, we did not hoist sail but made our slaves pull. "Oh!" said Jadee, warming up with the recollection of the event—"oh! it was fine to feel what brave fellows we then were!"

Towards night we made sail and closed upon the junk, and at daylight it fell a stark calm, and we went at our prize like sharks. All our fighting men put on their war-dresses; the Illanoons danced their war-dance, and all our gongs sounded as we opened out to attack her on different sides.

But those Amoy men are pigs! They burnt joss-paper; sounded their gongs, and received us with such showers of stones, hot-water, long pikes, and one or two well-directed shots that we hauled off to try the effect of our guns, sorry though we were to do it, for it was sure to bring the Dutchmen upon us. Bang! bang! we fired at them, and they at us; three hours did we persevere, and whenever we tried to board, the Chinese beat us back every time, for her side was as smooth and as high as a wall, with galleries overhanging.

We had several men killed and hurt; a council was called; a certain charm was performed by one of our holy men, a famous chief, and twenty of our best men devoted themselves to effecting a landing on the junk's deck, when our look-out prahus made the signal that the Dutchmen were coming; and sure enough some Dutch gun-boats came sweeping round a headland. In a moment we were round and pulling like demons for the shores of Biliton, the gun-boats in chase of us, and the Chinese howling with delight. The sea-breeze freshened and brought up a schooner-rigged boat very fast. We had been at work twenty-four hours and were heartily tired; our slaves could work no longer, so we prepared for the Hollanders; they were afraid to close upon us and commenced firing at a distance. This was just what we wanted; we had guns as well as they, and by keeping up the fight until dark, we felt sure of escape. The Dutchmen, however, knew this too, and kept closing gradually upon us; and when they saw our prahus bailing out water and blood, they knew we were suffering and cheered like devils. We were desperate; surrender to Dutchmen we never would; we closed together for mutual support, and determined at last, if all hope of escape ceased, to run our prahus ashore, burn them, and lie hid in the jungle until a future day. But a brave Datoo with his shattered prahus saved us; he proposed to let the Dutchmen board her, creese [stab with a *kris*] all that did so, and then trust to Allah for his escape.

It was done immediately; we all pulled a short distance away and left the brave Datoo's prahu like a wreck abandoned. How the Dutchmen yelled and fired into her! The slaves and cowards jumped out of the prahu, but our braves kept quiet; at last, as we expected, one gun-boat dashed alongside of their prize and boarded her in a crowd. Then was the time to see how the Malay man could fight; the creese was worth twenty swords, and the Dutchmen went down like sheep. We fired to cover our countrymen, who, as soon as their work was done, jumped overboard and swam to us; but the brave Datoo, with many more died as brave Malays should do, running a-muck against a host of enemies.

The gun-boats were quite scared by this punishment, and we lost no time in getting away as rapidly as possible; but the accursed schooner, by keeping more in the offing, held the wind and preserved her position, signaling all the while for the gun-boats to follow her. We did not want to fight any more; it was evidently an unlucky day. On the opposite side of the channel to that we were on, the coral reefs and shoals would prevent the Hollanders following us: it was determined at all risks to get there in spite of the schooner. With the first of the land-wind in the evening we set sail before it and steered across for Bianca. The schooner placed herself in our way like a clever sailor, so as to turn us back; but we were determined to push on, take her fire, and run all risks.

It was a sight to see us meeting one another; but we were desperate: we had killed plenty of Dutchmen; it was their turn now. I was in the second prahu, and well it was so, for when the headmost one got close to the schooner, the Dutchman fired all his guns into her, and knocked her at once into a wrecked condition. We gave one cheer, fired our guns and then pushed on for our lives. "Ah! sir, it was a dark night indeed for us. Three prahus in all were sunk and the whole force dispersed."

To add to our misfortunes a strong gale sprang up. We were obliged to carry canvas; our prahu leaked from shot-holes; the sea continually broke into her; we dared not run into the coral reefs on such a night, and bore up for the Straits of Malacca. The wounded writhed and shrieked in their agony, and we had to pump, we fighting men, and bale like *black fellows* [Caffre or negro slaves]! By two in the morning we were all worn out. I felt indifferent whether I was drowned or not, and many threw down their buckets and sat down to die. The wind increased and, at last, as if to put us out of our misery, just such a squall as this came down upon us. I saw it was folly contending against our fate, and followed the general example. "God is great!" we exclaimed, but the Rajah of Johore came and reproved us. "Work until daylight," he said, "and I will ensure your safety." We pointed at the black storm which was approaching. "Is that what you fear?" he replied, and going below he produced just such a wooden spoon and did what you have seen me do, and I tell you, my captain, as I would if the "Company Sahib" stood before me, that the storm was nothing, and that we had a dead calm one hour afterwards and were saved. God is great and Mahomet is his prophet!—but there is no charm like the Johore one for killing the wind!

A True Account of Three Notorious Pirates

HOWARD PYLE

Captain Teach *alias* Black-beard

Edward Teach was a Bristol man born, but had sailed some time out of Jamaica, in privateers, in the late French war; yet though he had often distinguished himself for his uncommon boldness and personal courage, he was never raised to any command, till he went a-pirating, which, I think, was at the latter end of the year 1716, when Captain Benjamin Hornygold put him into a sloop that he had made prize of, and with whom he continued in consortship till a little while before Hornygold surrendered.

In the spring of the year 1717 Teach and Hornygold sailed from Providence, for the main of America, and took in their way a billop from the Havana, with 120 barrels of flour, as also a sloop from Bermuda, Thurbar master, from whom they took only some gallons of wine, and then let him go; and a ship from Madeira to South Carolina, out of which they got plunder to a considerable value.

After cleaning on the coast of Virginia, they returned to the West Indies, and in the latitude of 24, made prize of a large French Guineaman, bound to Martinico, which, by Hornygold's consent, Teach went aboard of as captain, and took a cruise in her. Hornygold returned with his sloop to Providence, where, at the arrival of Captain Rogers, the governor, he surrendered to mercy, pursuant to the king's proclamation.

Aboard of this Guineaman Teach mounted forty guns, and named her the *Queen Ann's Revenge;* and cruising near the island of St. Vincent, took a large ship, called the *Great Allen,* Christopher Taylor, commander; the pirates plundered her of what they thought fit, put all the men ashore upon the island above mentioned, and set fire to the ship.

A few days after Teach fell in with the *Scarborough,* man-of-war, of thirty guns, who engaged him for some hours; but she, finding the pirate well-manned, and having tried her strength, gave over the engagement and returned to Barbadoes, the place of her station, and Teach sailed towards the Spanish America.

In this way he met with a pirate sloop of ten guns, commanded by one Major Bonnet, lately a gentleman of good reputation and estate in the island of Barbadoes, whom he joined; but in a few days after, Teach, finding that Bonnet knew nothing of a maritime life, with the consent of his own men, put in another captain, one Richards, to command Bonnet's sloop, and took the Major on board his own ship, telling him, that as he had not been used to the fatigues and care of such a post, it would be better for him to decline it and live easy, at his pleasure, in such a ship as his, where he would not be obliged to perform the necessary duties of a sea-voyage.

At Turniff, ten leagues short of the Bay of Honduras, the pirates took in fresh water, and while they were at anchor there, they saw a sloop coming in, whereupon Richards, in the sloop called the *Revenge,* slipped his cable and run out to meet her; who, upon seeing the black flag hoisted, struck his sail and came to under the stern of Teach, the commodore. She was called the *Adventure,* from Jamaica, David Harriot, master. They took him and his men aboard the great ship, and sent a number of other hands with Israel Hands, master of Teach's ship, to man the sloop for the piratical account.

The 9th of April they weighed from Turniff, having lain there about a week, and sailed to the bay, where they found a ship and four sloops; three of the latter belonged to Jonathan Bernard, of Jamaica, and the other to Captain James. The ship was of Boston, called the *Protestant Cæsar,* Captain Wyar, commander. Teach hoisted his black colors and fired a gun, upon which Captain Wyar and all his men left their ship and got ashore in their boat. Teach's quartermaster and eight of his crew took possession of Wyar's ship, and Richards secured all the sloops, one of which they burnt out of spite to the owner. The *Protestant Cæsar* they also burnt, after they had plundered her, because she belonged to Boston, where some men had been hanged for piracy, and the three sloops belonging to Bernard they let go.

From hence the rovers sailed to Turkill, and then to the Grand Caimanes, a small island about thirty leagues to the westward of Jamaica, where they took a small turtler, and so to the Havana, and from thence to the Bahama Wrecks; and from the Bahama Wrecks they sailed to Carolina, taking a brigantine and two sloops in their way, where they lay off the bar of Charles Town for five or six days. They took here a ship as she was coming out, bound for London, commanded by Robert Clark, with some passengers on board for England. The next day they took another vessel coming out of Charles Town, and also two pinks coming into Charles Town; likewise a brigantine with fourteen negroes aboard; all of which, being done in the face of the town, struck so great a terror to the whole province of Carolina, having just before been visited by Vane, another notorious pirate, that they abandoned themselves to despair, being in no condition to resist their force. There were eight sail in the harbor, ready for the sea, but none dared to venture out, it being almost impossible to escape their hands. The inward bound vessels were under the same unhappy dilemma, so that the trade of this place was totally interrupted. What made these misfortunes heavier to them was a long, expensive war the colony had had with the natives, which was but just ended when these robbers infested them.

Teach detained all the ships and prisoners, and, being in want of medicines, resolved to demand a chest from the government of the province. Accordingly, Richards, the captain of the *Revenge* sloop, with two or three more pirates, were sent up along with Mr. Marks, one of the prisoners whom they had taken in Clark's ship, and very insolently made their demands, threatening that if they did not send immediately the chest of medicines and let the pirate ambassadors return, without offering any violence to their persons, they would murder all their prisoners, send up their heads to the governor, and set the ships they had taken on fire.

Whilst Mr. Marks was making application to the council, Richards and the rest of the pirates walked the streets publicly in the sight of all people, who were fired with the utmost indignation, looking upon them as robbers and murderers, and particularly the authors of their wrongs and oppressions, but durst not so much as think of executing their revenge for fear of bringing more calamities upon themselves, and so they were forced to let the villains pass with impunity. The government was not long in deliberating upon the message, though it was the greatest affront that could have been put upon them, yet, for the saving so many men's lives (among them Mr. Samuel Wragg, one of the council), they complied with the necessity and sent aboard a chest, valued at between three and four hundred pounds, and the pirates went back safe to their ships.

Black-beard (for so Teach was generally called, as we shall hereafter show), as soon as he had received the medicines and his brother rogues, let go the ships and the prisoners, having first taken out of them in gold and silver about £1,500 sterling, besides provisions and other matters.

From the bar of Charles Town they sailed to North Carolina, Captain Teach in the ship, which they called the man-of-war, Captain Richards and Captain Hands in the sloops, which they termed privateers, and another sloop serving them as a tender. Teach began now to think of breaking up the company and securing the money and the best of the effects for himself and some others of his companions he had most friendship for, and to cheat the rest. Accordingly, on pretense of running into Topsail inlet to clean, he grounded his ship, and then, as if it had been done undesignedly and by accident, he orders Hands' sloop to come to his assistance and get him off again, which he, endeavoring to do, ran the sloop on shore near the other, and so were both lost. This done, Teach goes into the tender sloop, with forty hands, and leaves the *Revenge* there, then takes seventeen others and maroons them upon a small sandy island, about a league from the main, where there was neither bird, beast, or herb for their subsistence, and where they must have perished if Major Bonnet had not, two days after, taken them off.

Teach goes up to the governor of North Carolina, with about twenty of his men, and they surrender to his Majesty's proclamation, and receive certificates thereof from his Excellency; but it did not appear that their submitting to this pardon was from any reformation of manners, but only to await a more favorable opportunity to play the same game over again; which he soon after effected, with greater security to himself, and with much better prospect of success, having in this time cultivated a very good understanding with Charles Eden, Esq., the governor above mentioned.

The first piece of service this kind governor did to Black-beard was to give him a right to the vessel which he had taken when he was a-pirating in the great ship called the *Queen Ann's Revenge,* for which purpose a court of vice-admiralty was held at Bath Town, and, though Teach had never any commission in his life, and the sloop belonging to the English merchants, and taken in time of peace, yet was she condemned as a prize taken from the Spaniards by the said Teach. These proceedings show that governors are but men.

Before he sailed upon his adventures, he married a young creature of about sixteen years of age, the governor performing the ceremony. As it is a custom to marry here by a priest, so it is there by a magistrate; and this, I have been informed, made Teach's fourteenth wife whereof about a dozen might be still living.

In June, 1718, he went to sea upon another expedition, and steered his course towards Bermudas. He met with two or three English vessels in his way, but robbed them only of provisions, stores, and other necessaries, for his present expense; but near the island before mentioned, he fell in with two French ships, one of them was laden with sugar and cocoa, and the other light, both bound to Martinico. The ship that had no lading he let go, and putting all the men of the loaded ship aboard her, he brought home the other with her cargo to North Carolina, where the governor and the pirates shared the plunder.

When Teach and his prize arrived he and four of his crew went to his Excellency and made affidavit that they found the French ship at sea without a soul on board her; and then a court was called, and the ship condemned. The governor had sixty hogsheads of sugar for his dividend, and one Mr. Knight, who was his secretary and collector for the province, twenty, and the rest was shared among the other pirates.

The business was not yet done; the ship remained, and it was possible one or other might come into the river that might be acquainted with her, and so discover the roguery. But Teach thought of a contrivance to prevent this, for, upon a pretence that she was leaky, and that she might sink, and so stop up the mouth of the inlet or cove where she lay, he obtained an order from the governor to bring her out into the river and set her on fire, which was accordingly executed, and she was burnt down to the water's edge, her bottom sunk, and with it their fears of her ever rising in judgment against them.

Captain Teach, alias Black-beard, passed three or four months in the river, sometimes lying at anchor in the coves, at other times sailing from one inlet to another, trading with such sloops as he met for the plunder he had taken, and would often give them presents for stores and provisions he took from them; that is, when he happened to be in a giving humor; at other times he made bold with them, and took what he liked, without saying "By your leave," knowing well they dared not send him a bill for the payment. He often diverted himself with going ashore among the planters, where he revelled night and day. By these he was well received, but whether out of love or fear I cannot say. Sometimes he used them courteously enough, and made them presents of rum and sugar in recompense of what he took from them; but, as for liberties, which it is said he and his companions often took with the wives and daughters of the planters, I cannot take upon me to say whether he paid them *ad valorem* or no. At other times he carried it in a lordly manner towards them, and would lay some of them under contribution; nay, he often proceeded to bully the governor, not that I can discover the least cause of quarrel between them, but it seemed only to be done to show he dared do it.

The sloops trading up and down this river being so frequently pillaged by Black-beard, consulted with the traders and some of the best planters what course to take. They saw plainly it would be in vain to make an application to the governor of North Carolina, to whom it properly belonged to find some redress; so that if they could not be relieved from some other quarter, Black-beard would be like to reign with impunity; therefore, with as much secrecy as possible, they sent a deputation to Virginia, to lay the affair before the governor of that colony, and to solicit an armed force from the men-of-war lying there to take or destroy this pirate.

This governor consulted with the captains of the two men-of-war, viz., the *Pearl* and *Lime,* who had lain in St. James's river about ten months. It was agreed that the governor should hire a couple of small sloops, and the men-of-war should man them. This was accordingly done, and the command of them given to Mr. Robert Maynard, first lieutenant of the *Pearl,* an experienced officer, and a gentleman of great bravery and resolution, as will appear by his gallant behavior in this expedition. The sloops were well manned, and furnished with ammuition and small arms, but had no guns mounted.

About the time of their going out the governor called an assembly, in which it was resolved to publish a proclamation, offering certain rewards to any person or persons who, within a year after that time, should take or destroy any pirate. The original proclamation, being in our hands, is as follows:—

By his Majesty's Lieutenant-Governor and Commander-in-Chief of the Colony and Dominion of Virginia.

A PROCLAMATION,

Publishing the Rewards given for apprehending or killing Pirates.

Whereas, by an Act of Assembly, made at a Session of Assembly, begun at the capital in Williamsburg, the eleventh day of November, in the fifth year of his Majesty's reign, entitled, An Act to Encourage the Apprehending and Destroying of Pirates: It is, amongst other things, enacted, that all and every person, or persons, who, from and after the fourteenth day of November, in the Year of our Lord one thousand seven hundred and eighteen, and before the fourteenth day of November, which shall be in the Year of our Lord one thousand seven hundred and nineteen, shall take any pirate, or pirates, on the sea or land, or, in case of resistance, shall kill any such pirate, or pirates, between the degrees of thirty-four and thirty-nine of northern latitude, and within one hundred leagues of the continent of Virginia, or within the provinces of Virginia, or North Carolina, upon the conviction, or making due proof of the killing of all and every such pirate, and pirates, before the Governor and Council, shall be entitled to have, and receive out of the public money, in the hands of the Treasurer of this Colony, the several rewards following: that is to say, for Edward Teach, commonly called Captain Teach, or Black-beard, one hundred pounds; for every other commander of a pirate ship, sloop, or vessel, forty pounds; for every lieutenant, master, or quartermaster, boatswain, or carpenter, twenty pounds; for every other inferior officer, fifteen pounds; and for every private man taken on board such ship, sloop, or vessel, ten pounds; and that for every pirate which shall be taken by any ship, sloop, or vessel, belonging to this colony, or North Carolina, within the time aforesaid, in any place whatsoever, the like rewards shall be paid according to the quality and condition of such pirates. Wherefore, for the encouragement of all such persons as shall be willing to serve his Majesty, and their country, in so just and honourable an undertaking as the suppressing a sort of people who may be truly called enemies to mankind: I have thought fit, with the advice and consent of his Majesty's Council, to issue this Proclamation, hereby declaring the said rewards shall be punctually and justly paid, in current money of Virginia, according to the directions of the said Act. And I do order and appoint this proclamation to be published by the sheriffs at their respective country houses, and by all ministers and readers in the several churches and chapels throughout this colony.

Given at our Council-Chamber at Williamsburgh, this 24th day of November, 1718, in the fifth year of his Majesty's reign.

GOD SAVE THE KING.

A. Spotswood.

The 17th of November, 1718, the lieutenant sailed from Kicquetan, in James river in Virginia, and the 31st, in the evening, came to the mouth of Okerecock inlet, where he got sight of the pirate. This expedition was made with all imaginable secrecy, and the officer managed with all the prudence that was necessary, stopping all boats and vessels he met with in the river from going up, and thereby preventing any intelligence from reaching Black-beard, and receiving at the same time an account from them all of the place where the pirate was lurking. But notwithstanding this caution, Black-beard had information of the design from his Excellency of the province; and his secretary, Mr. Knight, wrote him a letter particularly concerning it, intimating "that he had sent him four of his men, which were all he could meet with in or about town, and so bid him be upon his guard." These men belonged to Black-beard, and were sent from Bath Town to Okerecock inlet, where the sloop lay, which is about twenty leagues.

Black-beard had heard several reports, which happened not to be true, and so gave the less credit to this advice; nor was he convinced till he saw the sloops. Then it was time to put his vessel in a posture of defense. He had no more than twenty-five men on board, though he gave out to all the vessels he spoke with that he had forty. When he had prepared for battle he sat down and spent the night in drinking with the master of a trading sloop, who, it was thought, had more business with Teach than he should have had.

Lieutenant Maynard came to an anchor, for the place being shoal, and the channel intricate, there was no getting in where Teach lay that night; but in the morning he weighed, and sent his boat ahead of the sloops to sound, and coming within gun-shot of the pirate, received his fire; whereupon Maynard hoisted the king's colors, and stood directly towards him with the best way that his sails and oars could make. Black-beard cut his cable, and endeavored to make a running fight, keeping a continual fire at his enemies with his guns. Mr. Maynard, not having any, kept a constant fire with small arms, while some of his men labored at their oars. In a little time Teach's sloop ran aground, and Mr. Maynard's, drawing more water than that of the pirate, he could not come near him; so he anchored within half gun-shot of the enemy, and, in order to lighten his vessel, that he might run him aboard, the lieutenant ordered all his ballast to be thrown overboard, and all the water to be staved, and then weighed and stood for him; upon which Black-beard hailed him in this rude maner: "Damn you for villains, who are you; and from whence came you?" The lieutenant made him answer, "You may see by our colors we are no pirates." Black-beard bid him send his boat on board that he might see who he was; but Mr. Maynard replied thus: "I cannot spare my boat, but I will come aboard of you as soon as I can with my sloop." Upon this Black-beard took a glass of liquor, and drank to him with these words: "Damnation seize my soul if I give you quarter, or take any from you." In answer to which Mr. Maynard told him "that he expected no quarter from him, nor should he give him any."

By this time Black-beard's sloop fleeted as Mr. Maynard's sloops were rowing towards him, which being not above a foot high in the waist, and consequently the men all exposed, as they came near together (there being hitherto little or no execution done on either side), the pirate fired a broadside charged with all manner of small shot. A fatal stroke to them!—the sloop the lieutenant was in having twenty men killed and wounded, and the other sloop nine. This could not be helped, for there being no wind, they were obliged to keep to their oars, otherwise the pirate would have got away from him, which it seems, the lieutenant was resolute to prevent.

After this unlucky blow Black-beard's sloop fell broadside to the shore; Mr. Maynard's other sloop, which was called the *Ranger*, fell astern, being for the present disabled. So the lieutenant, finding his own sloop had way and would soon be on board of Teach, he ordered all his men down, for fear of another broadside, which must have been their destruction and the loss of their expedition. Mr. Maynard was the only person that kept the deck, except the man at the helm, whom he directed to lie down snug, and the men in the hold were ordered to get their pistols and their swords ready for close fighting, and to come up at his command; in order to which two ladders were placed in the hatchway for the more expedition. When the lieutenant's sloop boarded the other Captain Teach's men threw in several new-fashioned sort of grenades, viz., case-bottles filled with powder and small shot, slugs, and pieces of lead or iron, with a quick-match in the mouth of it, which, being lighted without side, presently runs into the bottle to the powder, and, as it is instantly thrown on board, generally does great execution besides putting all the crew into a confusion. But, by good Providence, they had not that effect here, the men being in the hold. Black-beard, seeing few or no hands aboard, told his men "that they were all knocked to head, except three or four; and therefore," says he, "let's jump on board and cut them to pieces."

Whereupon, under the smoke of one of the bottles just mentioned, Black-beard enters with fourteen men over the bows of Maynard's sloop, and were not seen by him until the air cleared. However, he just then gave a signal to his men, who all rose in an instant, and attacked the pirates with as much bravery as ever was done upon such an occasion. Black-beard and the lieutenant fired the first shots at each other, by which the pirate received a wound, and then engaged with swords, till the lieutenant's unluckily broke, and stepping back to cock a pistol, Black-beard, with his cutlass, was striking at that instant that one of Maynard's men gave him a terrible wound in the neck and throat, by which the lieutenant came off with only a small cut over his fingers.

They were now closely and warmly engaged, the lieutenant and twelve men against Black-beard and fourteen, till the sea was tinctured with blood round the vessel. Black-beard received a shot into his body from the pistol that Lieutenant Maynard discharged, yet he stood his ground, and fought with great fury till he received five-and-twenty wounds, and five of them by shot. At length, as he was cocking another pistol, having fired several before, he fell down dead; by which time eight more out of the fourteen dropped, and all the rest, much wounded, jumped overboard and called out for quarter, which was granted, though it was only prolonging their lives a few days. The sloop *Ranger* came up and attacked the men that remained in Black-beard's sloop with equal bravery, till they likewise cried for quarter.

Here was an end of that courageous brute, who might have passed in the world for a hero had he been employed in a good cause.

The lieutenant caused Black-beard's head to be severed from his body, and hung up at the boltsprit end; then he sailed to Bath Town, to get relief for his wounded men.

In rummaging the pirate's sloop, they found several letters and written papers, which discovered the correspondence between Governor Eden, the secretary and collector, and also some traders at New York, and Black-beard. It is likely he had regard enough for his friends to have destroyed these papers before action, in order to hinder them from falling into such hands, where the discovery would be of no use either to the interest or reputation of these fine gentlemen, if it had not been his fixed resolution to have blown up together, when he found no possibility of escaping.

When the lieutenant came to Bath Town, he made bold to seize from the governor's storehouse the sixty hogsheads of sugar, and from honest Mr. Knight, twenty; which it seems was their dividend of the plunder taken in the French ship. The latter did not survive this shameful discovery, for, being apprehensive that he might be called to an account for these trifles, fell sick, it is thought, with the fright, and died in a few days.

After the wounded men were pretty well recovered, the lieutenant sailed back to the men-of-war in James River, in Virginia, with Black-beard's head still hanging at the boltsprit end, and fifteen prisoners, thirteen of whom were hanged, it appearing, upon trial, that one of them, viz., Samuel Odell, was taken out of the trading sloop but the night before the engagement. This poor fellow was a little unlucky at his first entering upon his new trade, there appearing no less than seventy wounds upon him after the action; notwithstanding which he lived and was cured of them all. The other person that escaped the gallows was one Israel Hands, the master of Blackbeard's sloop, and formerly captain of the same, before the *Queen Ann's Revenge* was lost in Topsail inlet.

The aforesaid Hands happened not to be in the fight, but was taken afterwards ashore at Bath Town, having been sometime before disabled by Black-beard, in one of his savage humors, after the following manner: One night, drinking in his cabin with Hands, the pilot, and another man, Black-beard, without any provocation, privately draws out a small pair of pistols, and cocks them under the table, which being perceived by the man, he withdrew and went upon deck, leaving Hands, the pilot, and the captain together. When the pistols were ready he blew out the candle, and, crossing his hands, discharged them at his company; Hands, the master, was shot throgh the knee and lamed for life, the other pistol did no execution. Being asked the meaning of this, he only answered by damning them, that "if he did not now and then kill one of them, they would forget who he was."

Hands being taken, was tried and condemned, but just as he was about to be executed a ship arrived at Virginia with a proclamation for prolonging the time of his Majesty's pardon to such of the pirates as should surrender by a limited time therein expressed. Notwithstanding the sentence, Hands pleaded the pardon, and was allowed the benefit of it, and was alive some time ago in London, begging his bread.

Now that we have given some account of Teach's life and actions, it will not be amiss that we speak of his beard, since it did not a little contribute towards making his name so terrible in those parts.

Plutarch and other grave historians have taken notice that several great men amongst the Romans took their surnames from certain odd marks in their countenances—as Cicero, from a mark, or vetch, on his nose—so our hero, Captain Teach, assumed the cognomen of Blackbeard, from that large quantity of hair which, like a frightful meteor, covered his whole face, and frightened America more than any comet that has appeared there a long time.

This beard was black, which he suffered to grow of an extravagant length; as to breadth, it came up to his eyes. He was accustomed to twist it with ribbons, in small tails, after the manner of our Ramilie wigs, and turn them about his ears. In time of action he wore a sling over his shoulders, with three brace of pistols hanging in holsters like bandaliers, and stuck lighted matches under his hat, which, appearing on each side of his face, his eyes naturally looking fierce and wild, made him altogether such a figure that imagination cannot form an idea of a fury from hell to look more frightful.

If he had the look of a fury, his humors and passions were suitable to it.

In the commonwealth of pirates, he who goes the greatest length of wickedness is looked upon with a kind of envy amongst them as a person of a more extraordinary gallantry, and is thereby entitled to be distinguished by some post, and if such a one has but courage, he must certainly be a great man. The hero of whom we are writing was thoroughly accomplished this way, and some of his frolics of wickedness were so extravagant, as if he aimed at making his men believe he was a devil incarnate; for being one day at sea, and a little flushed with drink, "Come," says he, "let us make a hell of our own, and try how long we can bear it." Accordingly he, with two or three others, went down into the hold, and closing up all the hatches, filled several pots full of brimstone and other combustible matter, and set it on fire, and so continued till they were almost suffocated, when some of the men cried out for air. At length he opened the hatches, not a little pleased that he held out the longest.

The night before he was killed he sat up and drank till the morning with some of his own men and the master of a merchantman; and having had intelligence of the two sloops coming to attack him, as has been before observed, one of his men asked him, in case anything should happen to him in the engagement with the sloops, whether his wife knew where he had buried his money? He answered, "That nobody but himself and the devil knew where it was, and the longest liver should take all.

Those of his crew who were taken alive told a story which may appear a little incredible; however, we think it will not be fair to omit it since we had it from their own mouths. That once upon a cruise they found out that they had a man on board more than their crew; such a one was seen several days amongst them, sometimes below and sometimes upon deck, yet no man in the ship could give an account who he was, or from whence he came, but that he disappeared a little before they were cast away in their great ship; but it seems they verily believed it was the devil.

One would think these things should induce them to reform their lives, but so many reprobates together, encouraged and spirited one another up in their wickedness, to which a continual course of drinking did not a little contribute, for in Black-beard's journal, which was taken, there were several memorandums of the following nature found writ with his own hand: Such a day rum all out; our company somewhat sober; a damned confusion amongst us; rouges a-plotting; great talk of separation; so I looked sharp for a prize; such a day took one with a great deal of liquor on board, so kept the company hot, damned hot, then all things went well again.

Thus it was these wretches passed their lives, with very little pleasure or satisfaction in the possession of what they violently take away from others, and sure to pay for it at last by an ignominious death.

The names of the pirates killed in the engagement, are as follows:—

Edward Teach, commander; Philip Morton, gunner; Garret Gibbens, boatswain; Owen Roberts, carpenter; Thomas Miller, quartermaster; John Husk, Joseph Curtice, Joseph Brooks (1), Nath. Jackson. All the rest, except the two last, were wounded, and afterwards hanged in Virginia:—John Carnes, Joseph Brooks (2), James Blake, John Gills, Thomas Gates, James White, Richard Stiles, Cæsar, Joseph Philips, James Robbins, John Martin, Edward Salter, Stephen Daniel, Richard Greensail, Israel Hands, pardoned, Samuel Odel, acquitted.

There were in the pirate sloops, and ashore in a tent near where the sloops lay, twenty-five hogsheads of sugar, eleven teirces, and one hundred and forty-five bags of cocoa, a barrel of indigo, and a bale of cotton; which, with what was taken from the governor and secretary, and the sale of the sloop, came to £2,500, besides the rewards paid by the governor of Virginia, pursuant to his proclamation; all which was divided among the companies of the two ships, *Lime* and *Pearl,* that lay in James River; the brave fellows that took them coming in for no more than their dividend amongst the rest, and were paid it not till four years afterwards.

Captain William Kid

We are now going to give an account of one whose name is better known in England than most of those whose histories we have already related; the person we mean is Captain Kid, whose public trial and execution here rendered him the subject of all conversation, so that his actions have been chanted about in ballads; however, it is now a considerable time since these things passed, and though the people knew in general that Captain Kid was hanged, and that his crime was piracy, yet there were scarce any, even at that time, who were acquainted with his life or actions, or could account for his turning pirate.

In the beginning of King William's war, Captain Kid commanded a privateer in the West Indies, and by several adventurous actions acquired the reputation of a brave man, as well as an experienced seaman. About this time the pirates were very troublesome in those parts, wherefore Captain Kid was recommended by the Lord Bellamont, then governor of Barbadoes, as well as by several other persons, to the Government here, as a person very fit to be entrusted with the command of a Government ship, and to be employed in cruising upon the pirates, as knowing those seas perfectly well, and being acquainted with all their lurking places; but what reasons governed the politics of those times I cannot tell, but this proposal met with no encouragement here, though it is certain it would have been of great consequence to the subject, our merchants suffering incredible damages by those robbers.

Upon this neglect the Lord Bellamont and some others, who knew what great captures had been made by the pirates, and what a prodigious wealth must be in their possession, were tempted to fit out a ship at their own private charge, and to give the command of it to Captain Kid; and to give the thing a great reputation, as well as to keep their seamen under the better command, they procured the King's Commission for the said Captain Kid, of which the following is an exact copy:—

"William Rex,—William the Third, by the grace of God, King of England, Scotland, France, and Ireland, Defender of the Faith, &c. To our trusty and well-beloved Captain William Kid, Commander of the ship the *Adventure* galley, or to any other the commander of the same for the time being, greeting; Whereas we are informed, that Captain Thomas Too, John Ireland, Captain Thomas Wake, and Captain William Maze, or Mace, and other subjects, natives or inhabitants of New York, and elsewhere, in our plantations in America, have associated themselves, with divers others, wicked and ill-disposed persons, and do, against the law of nations, commit many and great piracies, robberies, and depredations on the seas upon the parts of America, and in other parts, to the great hindrance and discouragement of trade and navigation, and to the great danger and hurt of our loving subjects, our allies, and all others, navigating the seas upon their lawful occasions. Now know ye, that we being desirous to prevent the aforesaid mischiefs, and, as much as in us lies, to bring the said pirates, freebooters and sea-rovers to justice, have thought fit, and do hereby give and grant to the said William Kid (to whom our Commissioners for exercising the office of Lord High

Admiral of England, have granted a commission as a private man-of-war, bearing date December 11, 1695), and unto the commander of the said ship for the time being, and unto the officers, mariners, and others, which shall be under your command, full power and authority to apprehend, seize, and take into your custody as well the said Captain Thomas Too, John Ireland, Captain Thomas Wake, and Captain William Maze, or Mace, as all such pirates, freebooters and sea-rovers, being either our subjects, or of other nations associated with them, which you shall meet with upon the seas or coasts of America, or upon any other seas or coasts, with all their ships and vessels; and all such merchandises, money, goods, and wares as shall be found on board, or with them, in case they shall willingly yield themselves; but if they will not yield without fighting, then you are by force to compel them to yield. And we do also require you to bring, or cause to be brought, such pirates, freebooters, or sea-rovers, as you shall seize, to a legal trial, to the end they may be proceeded against according to the law in such cases. And we do hereby command all our officers, ministers, and other our loving subjects whatsoever, to be aiding and assisting to you in the premisses. And we do hereby enjoin you to keep an exact journal of your proceedings in the execution of the premisses, and set down the names of such pirates, and of their officers and company, and the names of such ships and vessels as you shall by virtue of these presents take and seize, and the quantities of arms, ammunition, provision, and lading of such ships, and the true value of the same, as near as you judge. And we do hereby strictly charge and command you as you will answer the contrary at your peril, that you do not, in any manner, offend or molest our friends or allies, their ships, or subjects, by colour or pretence of these presents, or the authority thereby granted. In witness whereof we have caused our Great Seal of England to be affixed to these presents. Given at our Court of Kensington, the 26th day of January, 1695, in the seventh year of our reign."

Captain Kid had also another commission, which was called a Commission of Reprisals; for it being then war time, this commission was to justify him in the taking of French merchant ships, in case he should meet with any.

With these two commissions he sailed out of Plymouth in May, 1696, in the *Adventure* galley of thirty guns and eighty men. The place he first designed for was New York; in his voyage thither he took a French banker, but this was no act of piracy, he having a commission for that purpose, as we have just observed.

When he arrived at New York he put up articles for engaging more hands, it being necessary to his ship's crew, since he proposed to deal with a desperate enemy. The terms he offered were that every man should have a share of what was taken, reserving for himself and owners forty shares. Upon which encouragement he soon increased his company to a hundred and fifty-five men.

With this company he sailed first for Madeira where he took in wine and some other necessaries; from thence he proceeded to Bonavist, one of the Cape de Verde islands, to furnish the ship with salt, and from thence went immediately to St. Jago, another of the Cape de Verde islands, in order to stock himself with provisions. When all this was done he bent his course to Madagascar, the known rendezvous of pirates. In his way he fell in with Captain Warren, commodore of three men-of-war; he acquainted them with his design, kept them company two or three days, and then leaving them made the best way for Madagascar, where he arrived in February, 1696, just nine months from his departure from Plymouth.

It happened that at this time the pirate ships were most of them out in search of prey, so that, according to the best intelligence Captain Kid could get, there was not one of them at this time about the island, wherefore, having spent some time in watering his ship and taking in more provisions, he thought of trying his fortune on the coast of Malabar, where he arrived in the month of June following, four months from his reaching Madagascar. Hereabouts he made an unsuccessful cruise, touching sometimes at the island of Mahala, sometimes at that of Joanna, between Malabar and Madagascar. His provisions were every day wasting, and his ship began to want repair; wherefore, when he was at Joanna, he found means of borrowing a sum of money from some Frenchmen who had lost their ship, but saved their effects, and with this he purchased materials for putting his ship in good repair.

It does not appear all this while that he had the least design of turning pirate, for near Mahala and Joanna both he met with several Indian ships richly laden, to which he did not offer the least violence, though he was strong enough to have done what he pleased with them; and the first outrage or depredation I find he committed upon mankind was after his repairing his ship and leaving Joanna. He touched at a place called Mabbee, upon the Red Sea, where he took some Guinea corn from the natives, by force.

After this he sailed to Bab's Key, a place upon a little island at the entrance of the Red Sea. Here it was that he first began to open himself to his ship's company, and let them understand that he intended to change his measures; for, happening to talk of the Moca fleet which was to sail that way, he said, "We have been unsuccessful hitherto; but courage, my boys, we'll make our fortunes out of this fleet." And finding that none of them appeared averse to it he ordered a boat out, well manned, to go upon the coast to make discoveries, commanding them to take a prisoner and bring to him, or get intelligence any way they could. The boat returned in a few days, bringing him word that they saw fourteen or fifteen ships ready to sail, some with English, some with Dutch, and some with Moorish colors.

We cannot account for this sudden change in his conduct, otherwise than by supposing that he first meant well, while he had hopes of making his fortune by taking of pirates; but now, weary of ill-success, and fearing lest his owners, out of humor at their great expenses, should dismiss him, and he should want employment, and be marked out for an unlucky man—rather, I say, than run the hazard of poverty, he resolved to do his business one way, since he could not do it another.

He therefore ordered a man continually to watch at the mast-head, lest this fleet should go by them; and about four days after, towards evening it appeared in sight, being convoyed by one English and one Dutch man-of-war. Kid soon fell in with them, and, getting into the midst of them, fired at a Moorish ship which was next him; but the men-of-war, taking the alarm, bore down upon Kid, and, firing upon him, obliged him to sheer off, he not being strong enough to contend with them. Now he had begun hostilities he resolved to go on, and therefore he went and cruised along the coast of Malabar. The first prize he met was a small vessel belonging to Aden; the vessel was Moorish, and the owners were Moorish merchants, but the master was an Englishman; his name was Parker. Kid forced him and a Portuguese that was called Don Antonio, which were all the Europeans on board, to take on with them; the first he designed as a pilot, and the last as an interpreter. He also used the men very cruelly, causing them to be hoisted up by the arms, and drubbed with a naked cutlass, to force them to discover whether they had money on board, and where it lay; but as they had neither gold nor silver on board he got nothing by his cruelty; however, he took from them a bale of pepper, and a bale of coffee, and so let them go.

A little time after he touched at Carawar, a place upon the same coast, where, before he arrived, the news of what he had done to the Moorish ship had reached them; for some of the English merchants there had received an account of it from the owners, who corresponded with them; wherefore, as soon as Kid came in, he was suspected to be the person who committed this piracy, and one Mr. Harvey and Mr. Mason, two of the English factory, came on board and asked for Parker and Antonio, the Portuguese, but Kid denied that he knew any such persons, having secured them both in a private place in the hold, where they were kept for seven or eight days, that is till Kid sailed from thence.

However, the coast was alarmed, and a Portuguese man-of-war was sent out to cruise. Kid met with her, and fought her about six hours, gallantly enough; but finding her too strong to be taken, he quitted her, for he was able to run away from her when he would. Then he went to a place called Porco, where he watered the ship, and bought a number of hogs of the natives to victual his company.

Soon after this he came up with a Moorish ship, the master whereof was a Dutchman, called Schipper Mitchel, and chased her under French colors, which, they observing, hoisted French colors too. When he came up with her he hailed her in French, and they, having a Frenchman on board, answered him in the same language; upon which he ordered them to send their boat on board. They were obliged to do so, and having examined who they were, and from whence they came, he asked the Frenchman, who was a passenger, if he had a French pass for himself? The Frenchman gave him to understand that he had. Then he told the Frenchman he must pass for captain, and "by G—d," says he, "you are the captain." The Frenchman durst not refuse doing as he would have him. The meaning of this was, that he would seize the ship as fair prize, and as if she had belonged to French subjects, according to a commission he had for that purpose; though, one would think, after what he had already done, that he need not have recourse to a quibble to give his actions a color.

In short, he took the cargo and sold it some time after; yet still he seemed to have some fears upon him lest these proceedings should have a bad end, for, coming up with a Dutch ship some time, when his men thought of nothing but attacking her, Kid opposed it; upon which a mutiny arose, and the majority being for taking the said ship, and arming themselves to man the boat to go and seize her, he told them, such as did, never should come on board him again, which put an end to the design, so that he kept company with the said ship some time, without offering her any violence. However, this dispute was the occasion of an accident, upon which an indictment was afterwards grounded against Kid; for Moor, the gunner, being one day upon deck, and talking with Kid about the said Dutch ship, some words arose between them, and Moor told Kid that he had ruined them all; upon which Kid, calling him dog, took up a bucket and struck him with it, which, breaking his skull, he died the next day.

But Kid's penitential fit did not last long, for, coasting along Malabar, he met with a great number of boats, all which he plundered. Upon the same coast he also lighted upon a Portuguese ship, which he kept possession of a week, and then, having taken out of her some chests of Indian goods, thirty jars of butter, with some wax, iron, and a hundred bags of rice, he let her go.

Much about the same time he went to one of the Malabar islands for wood and water, and his cooper, being ashore, was murdered by the natives; upon which Kid himself landed, and burnt and pillaged several of their houses, the people running away; but having taken one, he caused him to be tied to a tree, and commanded one of his men to shoot him; then putting to sea again he took the greatest prize which fell into his hands while he followed his trade. This was a Moorish ship of four hundred tons, richly laden, named the *Queda*, merchant, the master whereof was an Englishman—he was called Wright, for the Indians often make use of English or Dutch men to command their ships, their own mariners not being so good artists in navigation. Kid chased her under French colors, and, having come up with her, he ordered her to hoist out her boat and to send on board of him, which, being done, he told Wright he was his prisoner; and informing himself concerning the said ship, he understood there were no Europeans on board except two Dutch, and one Frenchman, all the rest being Indians or Armenians, and that the Armenians were part owners of the cargo. Kid gave the Armenians to understand that if they would offer anything that was worth his taking for their ransom, he would hearken to it; upon which they proposed to pay him twenty thousand rupees, not quite three thousand pounds sterling; but Kid judged this would be making a bad bargain, wherefore he rejected it, and setting the crew on shore at different places on the coast, he soon sold as much of the cargo as came to near ten thousand pounds. With part of it he also trafficked, receiving in exchange provisions or such other goods as he wanted. By degrees he disposed of the whole cargo, and when the division was made it came to about two hundred pounds a man, and, having reserved forty shares to himself, his dividend amounted to about eight thousand pounds sterling.

The Indians along the coast came on board and trafficked with all freedom, and he punctually performed his bargains, till about the time he was ready to sail; and then, thinking he should have no further occasion for them, he made no scruple of taking their goods and setting them on shore without any payment in money or goods, which they little expected; for as they had been used to deal with pirates, they always found them men of honor in the way of trade—a people, enemies to deceit, and that scorned to rob but in their own way.

Kid put some of his men on board the *Queda*, merchant, and with this ship and his own sailed for Madagascar. As soon as he was arrived and had cast anchor there came on board of him a canoe, in which were several Englishmen who had formerly been well acquainted with Kid. As soon as they saw him they saluted him and told him they were informed he was come to take them, and hang them, which would be a little unkind in such an old acquaintance. Kid soon dissipated their doubts by swearing he had no such design, and that he was now in every respect their brother, and just as bad as they, and, calling for a cup of bomboo, drank their captain's health.

These men belonged to a pirate ship, called the *Resolution*, formerly the *Mocco*, merchant, where of one Captain Culliford was commander, and which lay at an anchor not far from them. Kid went on board with them, promising them his friendship and assistance, and Culliford in his turn came on board of Kid; and Kid, to testify his sincerity in iniquity, finding Culliford in want of some necessaries, made him a present of an anchor and some guns, to fit him out for the sea again.

The *Adventure* galley was now so old and leaky that they were forced to keep two pumps continually going, wherefore Kid shifted all the guns and tackle out of her into the *Queda*, merchant, intending her for his man-of-war; and as he had divided the money before, he now made a division of the remainder of the cargo. Soon after which the greatest part of the company left him, some going on board Captain Culliford, and others absconding in the country, so that he had not above forty men left.

He put to sea and happened to touch at Amboyna, one of the Dutch spice islands, where he was told that the news of his actions had reached England, and that he was there declared a pirate.

The truth of it is, his piracies so alarmed our merchants that some motions were made in Parliament, to inquire into the commission that was given him, and the persons who fitted him out. These proceedings seemed to lean a little hard upon the Lord Bellamont, who thought himself so much touched thereby that he published a justification of himself in a pamphlet after Kid's execution. In the meantime it was thought advisable, in order to stop the course of these piracies, to publish a proclamation, offering the king's free pardon to all such pirates as should voluntarily surrender themselves, whatever piracies they had been guilty of at any time, before the last day of April, 1699. That is to say, for all piracies committed eastward of the Cape of Good Hope, to the longitude and meridian of Socatora and Cape Camorin. In which proclamation Avery and Kid were excepted by name.

When Kid left Amboyna he knew nothing of this proclamation, for certainly had he had notice of his being excepted in it he would not have been so infatuated to run himself into the very jaws of danger; but relying upon his interest with the Lord Bellamont, and fancying that a French pass or two he found on board some of the ships he took would serve to countenance the matter, and that part of the booty he got would gain him new friends—I say, all these things made him flatter himself that all would be hushed, and that justice would but wink at him. Wherefore he sailed directly for New York, where he was no sooner arrived but by the Lord Bellamont's orders he was secured with all his papers and effects. Many of his fellow-adventurers who had forsook him at Madagascar, came over from thence passengers, some to New England, and some to Jersey, where, hearing of the king's proclamation for pardoning of pirates, they surrendered themselves to the governor of those places. At first they were admitted to bail, but soon after were laid in strict confinement, where they were kept for some time, till an opportunity happened of sending them with their captain over to England to be tried.

Accordingly, a Sessions of Admiralty being held at the Old Bailey, in May, 1701, Captain Kid, Nicholas Churchill, James How, Robert Lumley, William Jenkins, Gabriel Loff, Hugh Parrot,

Richard Barlicorn, Abel Owens, and Darby Mullins, were arraigned for piracy and robbery on the high seas, and all found guilty except three: these were Robert Lumley, William Jenkins, and Richard Barlicorn, who, proving themselves to be apprentices to some of the officers of the ship, and producing their indentures in court, were acquitted.

The three above mentioned, though they were proved to be concerned in taking and sharing the ship and goods mentioned in the indictment, yet, as the gentlemen of the long robe rightly distinguished, there was a great difference between their circumstances and the rest; for there must go an intention of the mind and a freedom of the will to the committing an act of felony or piracy. A pirate is not to be understood to be under constraint, but a free agent; for, in this case, the bare act will not make a man guilty, unless the will make it so.

Kid was tried upon an indictment of murder also—viz., for killing Moor, the gunner—and found guilty of the same.

As to Captain Kid's defense, he insisted much upon his own innocence, and the villainy of his men. He said he went out in a laudable employment, and had no occasion, being then in good circumstances, to go a-pirating; that the men often mutinied against him, and did as they pleased; that he was threatened to be shot in his cabin, and that ninety-five left him at one time, and set fire to his boat, so that he was disabled from bringing his ship home, or the prizes he took, to have them regularly condemned, which he said were taken by virtue of a commission under the broad seal, they having French passes. The captain called one Colonel Hewson to his reputation, who gave him an extraordinary character, and declared to the court that he had served under his command, and been in two engagements with him against the French, in which he fought as well as any man he ever saw; that there were only Kid's ship and his own against Monsieur du Cass, who commanded a squadron of six sail, and they got the better of him. But this being several years before the facts mentioned in the indictment were committed, proved of no manner of service to the prisoner on his trial.

As to the friendship shown to Culliford, a notorious pirate, Kid denied, and said he intended to have taken him, but his men, being a parcel of rogues and villains, refused to stand by him, and several of them ran away from his ship to the said pirate. But the evidence being full and particular against him, he was found guilty as before mentioned.

When Kid was asked what he had to say why sentence should not pass against him, he answered that "he had nothing to say, but that he had been sworn against by perjured, wicked people." And when sentence was pronounced, he said, "My lord, it is a very hard sentence. For my part I am the innocentest person of them all, only I have been sworn against by perjured persons."

Wherefore, about a week after, Captain Kid, Nicholas Churchill, James How, Gabriel Loff, Hugh Parrot, Abel Owen, and Darby Mullins, were executed at Execution Dock, and afterwards hung up in chains, at some distance from each other down the river, where their bodies hung exposed for many years.

Captain Bartholomew Roberts and His Crew

Bartholomew Roberts sailed in an honest employ from London, aboard of the *Princess,* Captain Plumb, commander, of which ship he was second mate. He left England November, 1719, and arrived at Guinea about February following and being at Anamaboe, taking in slaves for the West Indies, was taken in the said ship by Captain Howel Davis. In the beginning he was very averse to this sort of life, and would certainly have escaped from them had a fair opportunity presented itself; yet afterwards he changed his principles, as many besides him have done upon another element, and perhaps for the same reason too, viz., preferment; and what he did not like as a private man he could reconcile to his conscience as a commander.

Davis having been killed in the Island of Princes whilst planning to capture it with all its inhabitants, the company found themselves under the necessity of filling up his post, for which there appeared two or three candidates among the select part of them that were distinguished by the title of Lords—such were Sympson, Ashplant, Anstis, &c.—and on canvassing this matter, how shattered and weak a condition their government must be without a head, since Davis had been removed in the manner before mentioned, my Lord Dennis proposed, it is said, over a bowl, to this purpose:

"That it was not of any great signification who was dignified with title, for really and in good truth all good governments had, like theirs, the supreme power lodged with the community, who might doubtless depute and revoke as suited interest or humor. We are the original of this claim," says he, "and should a captain be so saucy as to exceed prescription at any time, why, down with him! It will be a caution after he is dead to his successors of what fatal consequence any sort of assuming may be. However, it is my advice that while we are sober we pitch upon a man of courage and skilled in navigation, one who by his council and bravery seems best able to defend this commonwealth, and ward us from the dangers and tempests of an unstable element, and the fatal consequences of anarchy; and such a one I take Roberts to be—a fellow, I think, in all respects worthy your esteem and favor."

This speech was loudly applauded by all but Lord Sympson, who had secret expectations himself, but on this disappointment grew sullen and left them, swearing "he did not care who they chose captain so it was not a papist, for against them he had conceived an irreconcilable hatred, for that his father had been a sufferer in Monmouth's rebellion."

Roberts was accordingly elected, though he had not been above six weeks among them. The choice was confirmed both by the Lords and Commoners, and he accepted of the honor, saying that, since he had dipped his hands in muddy water and must be a pirate, it was better being a commander than a common man.

As soon as the government was settled, by promoting other officers in the room of those that were killed by the Portuguese, the company resolved to avenge Captain Davis's death, he being more than ordinarily respected by the crew for his affability and good nature, as well as his conduct and bravery upon all occasions; and, pursuant to this resolution, about thirty men were landed, in order to make an attack upon the fort, which must be ascended to by a steep hill against the mouth of the cannon. These men were headed by one Kennedy, a bold, daring fellow, but very wicked and profligate; they marched directly up under the fire of their ship guns, and as soon as they were discovered, the Portuguese quitted their post and fled to the town, and the pirates marched in without opposition, set fire to the fort, and threw all the guns off the hill into the sea, which after they had done they retreated quietly to their ship.

But this was not looked upon as a sufficient satisfaction for the injury they received, therefore most of the company were for burning the town, which Roberts said he would yield to if any means could be proposed of doing it without their own destruction, for the town had a securer situation than the fort, a thick wood coming almost close to it, affording cover to the defendants, who, under such an advantage, he told them, it was to be feared, would fire and stand better to their arms; beside, that bare houses would be but a slender reward for their trouble and loss. This prudent advice prevailed; however, they mounted the French ship they seized at this place with twelve guns, and lightened her, in order to come up to the town, the water being shoal, and battered down several houses; after which they all returned on board, gave back the French ship to those that had most right to her, and sailed out of the harbor by the light of two Portuguese ships, which they were pleased to set on fire there.

Roberts stood away to the southward, and met with a Dutch Guineaman, which he made prize of, but, after having plundered her, the skipper had his ship again. Two days after he took an English ship, called the *Experiment*, Captain Cornet, at Cape Lopez; the men went all into the pirate service, and having no occasion for the ship they burnt her and then steered for St. Thome, but meeting with nothing in their way, they sailed for Annabona, and there watered, took in provisions, and put it to a vote of the company whether their next voyage should be to the East Indies or to Brazil. The latter being resolved on, they sailed accordingly, and in twenty-eight days arrived at Ferdinando, an uninhabited island on that coast. Here they watered, boot-topped their ship, and made ready for the designed cruise.

Upon this coast our rovers cruised for about nine weeks, keeping generally out of sight of land, but without seeing a sail, which discouraged them so that they determined to leave the station and steer for the West Indies; and, in order thereto, stood in to make the land for the taking of their departure; and thereby they fell in unexpectedly with a fleet of forty-two sail of Portuguese ships off the bay of Los Todos Santos, with all their lading in, for Lisbon, several of them of good force, who lay-to waiting for two men-of-war of seventy guns each, their convoy. However, Roberts thought it should go hard with him, but he would make up his market among them, and thereupon mixed with the fleet, and kept his men hid till proper resolutions could be formed. That done, they came close up to one of the deepest, and ordered her to send the master on board quietly, threatening to give them no quarter if any resistance or signal of distress was made. The Portuguese, being surprised at these threats, and the sudden flourish of cutlasses from the pirates, submitted without a word, and the captain came on board. Roberts saluted him after a friendly manner telling him that they were gentlemen of fortune, but that their business with him was only to be informed which was the richest ship in that fleet; and if he directed them right he should be restored to his ship without molestation, otherwise he must expect immediate death.

Whereupon this Portuguese master pointed to one of forty guns and a hundred and fifty men, a ship of greater force than the *Rover;* but this no ways dismayed them; they were Portuguese, they said, and so immediately steered away for him. When they came within hail, the master whom they had prisoner was ordered to ask "how Seignior Captain did?" and to invite him on board, "for that he had a matter of consequence to impart to him;" which being done, he returned for answer that "he would wait upon him presently," but by the bustle that immediately followed, the pirates perceived that they were discovered, and that this was only a deceitful answer to gain time to put their ship in a posture of defense; so without further delay they poured in a broadside, boarded, and grappled her. The dispute was short and warm, wherein many of the Portuguese fell, and two only of the pirates. By this time the fleet was alarmed: signals of top-gallant sheets flying and guns fired to give notice to the men-of-war, who rid still at an anchor, and made but scurvy haste out to their assistance; and if what the pirates themselves related to be true, the commanders of those ships were blameable to the highest degree, and unworthy the title, or so much as the name, of men. For Roberts, finding the prize to sail heavy, and yet resolving not to lose her, lay by for the headmost of them, which much outsailed the other, and prepared for battle, which was ignominiously declined, though of such superior force;

for, not daring to venture on the pirate alone, he tarried so long for his consort as gave them both time leisurely to make off.

They found this ship exceedingly rich, being laden chiefly with sugar, skins, and tobacco, and in gold forty thousand moidores, besides chains and trinkets of considerable value; particularly a cross set with diamonds designed for the king of Portugal, which they afterwards presented to the governor of Caiana, by whom they were obliged.

Elated with this booty, they had nothing now to think of but some safe retreat where they might give themselves up to all the pleasures that luxury and wantonness could bestow; and for the present pitched upon a place called the Devil's Islands in the river of Surinam, on the coast of Caiana, where they arrived, and found the civilest reception imaginable, not only from the governor and factory, but their wives, who exchanged wares, and drove a considerable trade with them.

They seized in this river a sloop, and by her gained intelligence that a brigantine had also sailed in company with her from Rhode Island, laden with provisions for the coast—a welcome cargo! They growing short in the sea store, and, as Sancho says, "No adventures to be made without belly-timber." One evening, as they were rummaging their mine of treasure, the Portuguese prize, this expected vessel was descried at the masthead, and Roberts, imagining nobody could do the business so well as himself, takes forty men in the sloop, and goes in pursuit of her; but a fatal accident followed this rash, though inconsiderable adventure, for Roberts, thinking of nothing less than bringing in the brigantine that afternoon, never troubled his head about the sloop's provision, nor inquired what there was on board to subsist such a number of men; but out he sails after his expected prize, which he not only lost further sight of, but after eight days' contending with contrary winds and currents, found themselves thirty leagues to leeward. The current still opposing their endeavors, and perceiving no hopes of beating up to their ship, they came to an anchor, and inconsiderately sent away the boat to give the rest of the company notice of their condition, and to order the ship to them; but too soon—even the next day—their wants made them sensible of their infatuation, for their water was all expended, and they had taken no thought how they should be supplied till either the ship came or the boat returned, which was not likely to be under five or six days. Here, like Tantalus, they almost famished in sight of the fresh streams and lakes, being drove to such extremity at last that they were forced to tear up the floor of the cabin and patch up a sort of tub or tray with ropeyarns to paddle ashore and fetch off immediate supplies of water to preserve life.

After some days the long-wished-for boat came back, but with the most unwelcome news in the world; for Kennedy, who was lieutenant, and left, in absence of Roberts, to command the privateer and prize, was gone off with both. This was mortification with a vengeance, and you may imagine they did not depart without some hard speeches from those that were left and had suffered by their treachery. And that there need be no further mention of this Kennedy, I shall leave Captain Roberts to vent his wrath in a few oaths and execrations, and follow the other, whom we may reckon from that time as steering his course towards Execution Dock.

Kennedy was now chosen captain of the revolted crew, but could not bring his company to any determined resolution. Some of them were for pursuing the old game, but the greater part of them seemed to have inclinations to turn from those evil courses, and get home privately, for there was no act of pardon in force; therefore they agreed to break up, and every man to shift for himself, as he should see occasion. The first thing they did was to part with the great Portuguese prize, and having the master of the sloop (whose name, I think, was Cane) aboard, who, they said, was a very honest fellow—for he had humored them upon every occasion—told them of the brigantine that Roberts went after; and when the pirates first took him he complimented them at any odd rate, telling them they were welcome to his sloop and cargo, and wished that the vessel had been larger and the loading richer for their sakes. To this good-natured man they gave the Portuguese ship, which was then above half loaded, three or four negroes, and all his own men, who returned thanks to his kind benefactors, and departed.

Captain Kennedy, in the *Rover,* sailed to Barbadoes, near which island they took a very peaceable ship belonging to Virginia. The commander was a Quaker, whose name was Knot; he had neither pistol, sword, nor cutlass on board; and Mr. Knot appearing so very passive to all they said to him, some of them thought this a good opportunity to go off; and accordingly eight of the pirates went aboard, and he carried them safe to Virginia. They made the Quaker a present of ten chests of sugar, ten rolls of Brazil tobacco, thirty moidores, and some gold dust, in all to the value of about £250. They also made presents to the sailors, some more, some less, and lived a jovial life all the while they were upon their voyage, Captain Knot giving them their way; nor, indeed, could he help himself, unless he had taken an opportunity to surprise them when they were either drunk or asleep, for awake they wore arms aboard the ship and put him in a continual terror, it not being his principle (or the sect's) to fight, unless with art and collusion. He managed these weapons well till he arrived at the Capes; and afterwards four of the pirates went off in a boat, which they had taken with them for the more easily making their escapes, and made up the bay towards Maryland, but were forced back by a storm into an obscure place of the country, where, meeting with good entertainment among the planters, they continued several days without being discovered to be pirates. In the meantime Captain Knot, leaving four others on board his ship who intended to go to North Carolina, made what haste he could to discover to Mr. Spotswood, the governor, what sort of passengers he had been forced to bring with him, who, by good fortune, got them seized; and search being made after the others, who were revelling about the country, they were also taken, and all tried, convicted, and hanged; two Portuguese Jews, who were taken on the coast of Brazil and whom they brought with them to Virginia, being the principal evidences. The latter had found means to lodge part of their wealth with the planters, who never brought it to account. But Captain Knot surrendered up everything that belonged to them that were taken aboard, even what they presented to him, in lieu of such things as they had plundered him of in their passage, and obliged his men to do the like.

Some days after the taking of the Virginiaman last mentioned, in cruising in the latitude of Jamaica, Kennedy took a sloop bound thither from Boston, loaded with bread and flour; aboard of this sloop went all the hands who were for breaking the gang, and left those behind that had a mind to pursue further adventures. Among the former was Kennedy, their captain, of whose honor they had such a despicable notion that they were about to throw him overboard when they found him in the sloop, as fearing he might betray them all at their return to England; he having in his childhood been bred a pick-pocket, and before he became a pirate a house-breaker; both professions that these gentlemen have a very mean opinion of. However, Captain Kennedy, by taking solemn oaths of fidelity to his companions, was suffered to proceed with them.

In this company there was but one that pretended to any skill in navigation (for Kennedy could neither write nor read, he being preferred to the command merely for his courage, which indeed he had often signalized, particularly in taking the Portuguese ship), and he proved to be a pretender only; for, shaping their course to Ireland, where they agreed to land, they ran away to the north-west coast of Scotland, and there were tossed about by hard storms of wind for several days without knowing where they were, and in great danger of perishing. At length they pushed the vessel into a little creek and went all ashore, leaving the sloop at an anchor for the next comers.

The whole company refreshed themselves at a little village about five miles from the place where they left the sloop, and passed there for shipwrecked sailors, and no doubt might have travelled on without suspicion, but the mad and riotous manner of their living on the road occasioned their journey to be cut short, as we shall observe presently.

Kennedy and another left them here, and, travelling to one of the seaports, shipped themselves for Ireland, and arrived there in safety. Six or seven wisely withdrew from the rest, travelled at their leisure, and got to their much-desired port of London without being disturbed or suspected, but the main gang alarmed the country wherever they came, drinking and roaring at such a rate that the people shut themselves up in their houses, in some places not daring to venture out among so many mad fellows. In other villages they treated the whole town, squandering their money away as if, like æsop, they wanted to lighten their burthens. This expensive manner of living procured two of their drunken stragglers to be knocked on the head, they being found murdered in the road and their money taken from them. All the rest, to the number of seventeen, as they drew nigh to Edinburgh, were arrested and thrown into gaol upon suspicion of they knew not what; however, the magistrates were not long at a loss for proper accusations, for two of the gang offering themselves for evidences were accepted of, and the others were brought to a speedy trial, whereof nine were convicted and executed.

Kennedy having spent all his money, came over from Ireland and kept a public-house on Deptford Road, and now and then it was thought, made an excursion abroad in the way of his former profession, till one of his household gave information against him for a robbery, for which he was committed to Bridewell; but because she would not do the business by halves she found out a mate of a ship that Kennedy had committed piracy upon, as he foolishly confessed to her. This mate, whose name was Grant, paid Kennedy a visit in Bridewell, and knowing him to be the man, procured a warrant, and had him committed to the Marshalsea prison.

The game that Kennedy had now to play was to turn evidence himself; accordingly he gave a list of eight or ten of his comrades, but, not being acquainted with their habitations, one only was taken, who, though condemned, appeared to be a man of a fair character, was forced into their service, and took the first opportunity to get from them, and therefore received a pardon; but Walter Kennedy, being a notorious offender, was executed July 19, 1721, at Execution Dock.

The rest of the pirates who were left in the ship *Rover* stayed not long behind, for they went ashore to one of the West India islands. What became of them afterwards I cannot tell, but the ship was found at sea by a sloop belonging to *St. Christophers*, and carried into that island with only nine negroes aboard.

Thus we see what a disastrous fate ever attends the wicked, and how rarely they escape the punishment due to their crimes, who, abandoned to such a profligate life, rob, spoil, and prey upon mankind, contrary to the light and law of nature, as well as the law of God. It might have been hoped that the examples of these deaths would have been as marks to the remainder of this gang, how to shun the rocks their companions had split on; that they would have surrendered to mercy, or divided themselves for ever from such pursuits, as in the end they might be sure would subject them to the same law and punishment, which they must be conscious they now equally deserved; impending law, which never let them sleep well unless when drunk. But all the use that was made of it here, was to commend the justice of the court that condemned Kennedy, for he was a sad dog, they said, and deserved the fate he met with.

But to go back to Roberts, whom we left on the coast of Caiana, in a grievous passion at what Kennedy and the crew had done, and who was now projecting new adventures with his small company in the sloop; but finding hitherto they had been but as a rope of sand, they formed a set of articles to be signed and sworn to for the better conservation of their society, and doing justice to one another, excluding all Irishmen from the benefit of it, to whom they had an implacable aversion upon the account of Kennedy. How, indeed, Roberts could think that an oath would be obligatory where defiance had been given to the laws of God and man, I cannot tell, but he thought their greatest security lay in this—"that it was every one's interest to observe them, if they minded to keep up so abominable a combination."

The following is the substance of articles as taken from the pirates own informations:—

I

Every man has a vote in affairs of moment, has equal title to the fresh provisions or strong liquors at any time seized, and may use them at pleasure, unless a scarcity (no uncommon thing among them) make it necessary for the good of all to vote a retrenchment.

II

Every man to be called fairly in turn by list, on board of prizes, because, over and above their proper share, they were on these occasions allowed a shift of clothes. But if they defrauded the company to the value of a dollar, in plate, jewels, or money, marooning was their punishment. (This was a barbarous custom of putting the offender on shore, on some desolate or uninhabited cape or island, with a gun, a few shot, a bottle of water, a bottle of powder, to subsist with or starve.) If the robbery was only between one another, they contented themselves with slitting the ears and nose of him that was guilty, and set him on shore, not in an uninhabited place, but somewhere where he was sure to encounter hardships.

III

No person to game at cards or dice for money.

IV

The lights and candles to be put out at eight o'clock at night. If any of the crew after that hour still remained inclined for drinking, they were to do it on the open deck. (Which Roberts believed would give a check to their debauches, for he was a sober man himself, but found at length that all his endeavors to put an end to this debauch proved ineffectual.)

V

To keep their piece, pistols, and cutlass clean, and fit for service. (In this they were extravagantly nice, endeavoring to outdo one another in the beauty and richness of their arms, giving sometimes at an auction—at the mast—£30 or £40 a pair for pistols. These were slung in time of service, with different colored ribbons, over their shoulders, in a way peculiar to these fellows, in which they took great delight.)

VI

No boy or woman to be allowed amongst them. If any man were found seducing any of the latter sex, and carried her to sea disguised, he was to suffer death. (So that when any fell into their hands, as it chanced in the *Onslow*, they put a sentinel immediately over her to prevent ill consequences from so dangerous an instrument of division and quarrel; but then here lies the roguery—they contend who shall be sentinel, which happens generally to one of the greatest bullies.)

VII

To desert the ship or their quarters in battle, was punished with death or marooning.

VIII

No striking one another on board, but every man's quarrel to be ended on shore, at sword and pistol. Thus the quartermaster of the ship, when the parties will not come to any reconciliation, accompanies them on shore with what assistance he thinks proper, and turns the disputants back to back at so many paces distance. At the word of command they turn and fire immediately, or else the piece is knocked out of their hands. If both miss, they come to their cutlasses, and then he is declared victor who draws the first blood.

IX

No man to talk of breaking up their way of living till each had shared £1,000. If, in order to this, any man should lose a limb, or become a cripple in their service, he was to have 800 dollars out of the public stock, and for lesser hurts proportionably.

X

The captain and quartermaster to receive two shares of a prize; the master, boatswain, and gunner, one share and a half, the other officers one and a quarter.

XI

The musicians to have rest on the Sabbath-day, but the other six days and nights none without special favor.

These, we are assured, were some of Roberts's articles, but as they had taken care to throw overboard the original they had signed and sworn to, there is a great deal of room to suspect the remainder contained something too horrid to be disclosed to any, except such as were willing to be sharers in the iniquity of them. Let them be what they will, they were together the test of all newcomers, who were initiated by an oath taken on a Bible, reserved for that purpose only, and were subscribed to in presence of the worshipful Mr. Roberts. And in case any doubt should arise concerning the construction of these laws, and it should remain a dispute whether the party had infringed them or no, a jury was appointed to explain them, and bring in a verdict upon the case in doubt.

Since we are now speaking of the laws of this company, I shall go on, and, in as brief a manner as I can, relate the principal customs and government of this roguish commonwealth, which are pretty near the same with all pirates.

For the punishment of small offences which are not provided for by the articles, and which are not of consequence enough to be left to a jury, there is a principal officer among the pirates, called the quartermaster, of the men's own choosing, who claims all authority this way, excepting in time of battle. If they disobey his command, are quarrelsome and mutinous with one another, misuse prisoners, plunder beyond his order, and in particular, if they be negligent of their arms, which he musters at discretion, he punishes at his own arbitrament, with drubbing or whipping, which no one else dare do without incurring the lash from all the ship's company. In short, this officer is trustee for the whole, is the first on board any prize, separating for the company's use what he pleases, and returning what he thinks fit to the owners, exceping gold and silver, which they have voted not returnable.

After a description of the quartermaster and his duty, who acts as a sort of civil magistrate on board a pirate ship, I shall consider their military officer, the captain; what privileges he exerts in such anarchy and unruliness of the members. Why, truly very little—they only permit him to be captain, on condition that they may be captain over him; they separate to his use the great cabin, and sometimes vote him small parcels of plate and china (for it may be noted that Roberts drank his tea constantly), but then every man, as the humor takes him, will use the plate and china, intrude into his apartment, swear at him, seize a part of his victuals and drink, if they like it, without his offering to find fault or contest it. Yet Roberts, by a better management than usual, became the chief director in everything of moment; and it happened thus:—The rank of captain being obtained by the suffrage of the majority, it falls on one superior for knowledge and boldness—pistol proof, as they call it—who can make those fear who do not love him. Roberts is said to have exceeded his fellows in these respects, and when advanced, enlarged the respect that followed it by making a sort of privy council of half a dozen of the greatest bullies, such as were his competitors, and had interest enough to make his government easy; yet even those, in the latter part of his reign, he had run counter to in every project that opposed his own opinion; for which, and because he grew reserved and would not drink and roar at their rate, a cabal was formed to take away his captainship, which death did more effectually.

The captain's power is uncontrollable in chase or in battle, drubbing, cutting, or even shooting any one who dares deny his command. The same privilege he takes over prisoners, who receive good or ill usage mostly as he approves of their behavior, for though the meanest would take upon them to misuse a master of a ship, yet he would control herein when he sees it, and merrily over a bottle give his prisoners this double reason for it: first, that it preserved his precedence; and secondly, that it took the punishment out of the hands of a much more rash and mad set of fellows than himself. When he found that rigor was not expected from his people (for he often practiced it to appease them), then he would give strangers to understand that it was pure inclination that induced him to a good treatment of them, and not any love or partiality to their persons; for, says he, "there is none of you but will hang me, I know, whenever you can clinch me within your power."

And now, seeing the disadvantages they were under for pursuing their plans, viz., a small vessel ill repaired, and without provisions or stores, they resolved, one and all, with the little supplies they could get, to proceed for the West Indies, not doubting to find a remedy for all these evils and to retrieve their loss.

In the latitude of Deseada, one of the islands, they took two sloops, which supplied them with provisions and other necessaries, and a few days afterwards took a brigantine belonging to Rhode Island, and then proceeded to Barbadoes, off of which island they fell in with a Bristol ship of ten guns, in her voyage out, from whom they took abundance of clothes, some money, twenty-five bales of goods, five barrels of powder, a cable, hawser, ten casks of oatmeal, six casks of beef, and several other goods, besides five of their men; and after they had detained her three days let her go, who, being bound for the aforesaid island, she acquainted the governor with what had happened as soon as she arrived.

Whereupon a Bristol galley that lay in the harbor was ordered to be fitted out with all imaginable expedition, of 20 guns and 80 men, there being then no man-of-war upon that station, and also a sloop with 10 guns and 40 men. The galley was commanded by one Captain Rogers, of Bristol, and the sloop by Captain Graves, of that island, and Captain Rogers, by a commission from the governor, was appointed commodore.

The second day after Rogers sailed out of the harbor he was discovered by Roberts, who, knowing nothing of their design, gave them chase. The Barbadoes ships kept an easy sail till the pirates came up with them, and then Roberts gave them a gun, expecting they would have immediately struck to his piratical flag; but instead thereof, he was forced to receive the fire of a broadside, with three huzzas at the same time, so that an engagement ensued; but Roberts, being hardly put to it, was obliged to crowd all the sail the sloop would bear to get off. The galley, sailing pretty well, kept company for a long while, keeping a constant fire, which galled the pirate; however, at length, by throwing over their guns and other heavy goods, and thereby lightening the vessel, they, with much ado, got clear; but Roberts could never endure a Barbadoes man afterwards, and when any ships belonging to that island fell in his way, he was more particularly severe to them than others.

Captain Roberts sailed in the sloop to the island of Dominico, where he watered and got provisions of the inhabitants, to whom he gave goods in exchange. At this place he met with thirteen Englishmen, who had been set ashore by a French Guard de la Coste, belonging to Martinico, taken out of two New England ships that had been seized as prizes by the said French sloop. The men willingly entered with the pirates, and it proved a seasonable recruiting.

They stayed not long here, though they had immediate occasion for cleaning their sloop, but did not think this a proper place; and herein they judged right, for the touching at this island had like to have been their destruction, because they, having resolved to go away to the Granada Islands for the aforesaid purpose, by some accident it came to be known to the French colony, who, sending word to the governor of Martinico, he equipped and manned two sloops to go in quest of them. The pirates sailed directly for the Granadilloes, and hall'd into a lagoon at Corvocoo, where they cleaned with unusual dispatch, staying but a little above a week, by which expedition they missed of the Martinico sloops only a few hours, Roberts sailing overnight and the French arriving the next morning. This was a fortunate escape, especially considering that it was not from any fears of their being discovered that they made so much haste from the island, but, as they had the impudence themselves to own, for the want of wine and women.

Thus narrowly escaped, they sailed for Newfoundland, and arrived upon the banks the latter end of June, 1720. They entered the harbor of Trepassi with their black colors flying, drums beating, and trumpets sounding. There were two-and-twenty vessels in the harbor, which the men all quitted upon the sight of the pirate, and fled ashore. It is impossible particularly to recount the destruction and havoc they made here, burning and sinking all the shipping except a Bristol galley, and destroying the fisheries and stages of the poor planters without remorse or compunction; for nothing is so deplorable as power in mean and ignorant hands—it makes men wanton and giddy, unconcerned at the misfortunes they are imposing on their fellow-creatures, and keeps them smiling at the mischiefs that bring themselves no advantage. They are like madmen that cast fire-brands, arrows, and death, and say, Are not we in sport?

Captain Gow of the Orkneys

ARCHIBALD HURD

Hitherto in considering the reign of the eighteenth century pirates it is to the outer seas that their adventures have taken us. In the West Atlantic, with its half-settled tropical islands, with its long coast-line dotted with struggling settlements separated by huge areas of still untamed wilderness; along the west coast of Africa, with its tiny trading centres or "forts"; and in the Indian Ocean—these were the natural haunts of the privateers men thrown out of employment at the end of the long wars with France. Here were rich trading-vessels far from home and but scantily protected by naval power. Here were innumerable natural harbours remote from the interference of the law. And here also were isolated communities far from civilization, providing a ready and not too inquisitive market for cheaply acquired goods. In the last of our characters, however, John Gow, we come upon a pirate in home waters, and a crew of boys, for most of them were but little more than this, who made the Channel, the Mediterranean, and the coast of Scotland the scene of their exploits. Indeed, their story is rather that of a single raid than a definite pirate career, but Gow is an interesting figure in that he was probably the original of Sir Walter Scott's "Pirate," as well, possibly, as of Defoe's "Captain Singleton."

Born at Wick in Caithness somewhere about 1697, he was the son of a respectable Scottish merchant and his wife, and his early life seems to have been spent chiefly in the Orkney Islands. Very little is known of this, however, and it is at the age of twenty-seven as bo'sun of an English vessel homeward bound from Lisbon that he first figured as the ringleader in an unsuccessful plot to capture the ship upon which he was employed. By this time, of course, and even in the more distant seas where effective policing was infinitely harder, most of the more famous pirates had already run their course and come to their appointed ends. In Ocracoke inlet on the Virginian coast the black-visaged Teach had died fighting. The tarred corpses of Bartholomew Roberts' companions were still probably swinging in chains at Cape Coast Castle. England was begging for food, if he had not already died, upon the shores of Madagascar. Bonnet and Rackam, Vane and Davis, and a dozen others had met their fate, and to all intents and purposes the reign of the pirates was already becoming a thing of the past. The enterprise of Gow must therefore either have argued a complete ignorance of the real factors of the situation, a totally unbalanced judgment, or a passion for wild and unlawful adventure that shouldered all other considerations aside.

As we have said, however, his first effort was a failure, but by the time the details of his plot had become known, Gow himself was out of the country on his way to Holland. Here in August, 1724, he signed on as an ordinary seaman in a Guernsey vessel lying in the river Texel, which was bound for Santa Cruz to take a cargo of leather, cloth, and beeswax to Genoa in Italy. Her captain was of French extraction, one Captain Oliver Ferneau, and owing to the fact that Holland and Turkey were then at war, it was found convenient by the Amsterdam shippers to employ a foreign crew. Of the twenty-three hands, therefore, the majority were British, and during the voyage to Santa Cruz, Gow so pleased Ferneau that the latter made him his second mate, an office he combined with that of gunner. Eventually to be known as the *George Galley*, it seems probable, though not certain, that when she left Amsterdam this 200-ton Guernsey-man was sailing under the name of the *Caroline*, and after an uneventful voyage she arrived safely at her first port of destination. She remained there for two months, taking in her cargo, and it was during this time that Gow laid his plans to make himself her master. In this his chief confederates were two fellow Scotsmen, William Melvin and Dan Macaulay, aged respectively seventeen and twenty, an Irish boy of sixteen named Michael Moore, a Welshman, John Williams, a young

Dane, John Peterson, and a couple of Swedes, John Winter and Peter Rollson; and just as the vessel sailed, Gow succeeded in manufacturing a plausible grievance as the first step of his active campaign. Ferneau was annoyed, but behaved with considerable discretion, so that the vessel put to sea with an ostensibly contented crew, but with signs of impending trouble, which he observed and which he confided to his first mate.

After discussing the matter they decided it would be well to have their firearms handy, but unfortunately for them their conversation was overheard by one of the conspirators, while by the irony of fate it was Gow, the unsuspected plotter in the background, to whom as chief gunner the captain's orders would have come. Hurriedly, in view of this, the conspirators consulted, and since by the next morning the captain's party would be well armed, it was decided that it was a case of now or never, and they resolved to make their attack that night. All was apparently peaceful, however, when at eight o'clock the crew, according to custom, marshalled for prayers in the chief cabin, and a couple of hours later, in the November darkness, the captain was alone on the quarter-deck. Down below, the first mate, the surgeon, and the supercargo were all asleep in their hammocks, as were those members of the crew who were not on duty or had not been informed of what was on foot. For Gow's purposes it was the ideal moment. A solitary binnacle light glimmered on the deck. And when, at a given signal, the murdering began, Captain Ferneau was quickly overpowered. Wheeling round at the muffled sound of a shot, he was seized and pinioned by Winter, Melvin and Rollston, and after a fierce struggle, in which he was stabbed and finally twice shot by Gow, he was thrown overboard.

Meanwhile, down below, the mate, surgeon, and supercargo had all been similarly put to death, the mate being shot by the boy Michael Moore under the orders of Williams, who was destined to be Gow's chief officer. With the exception of one Belbin, who readily joined them, the rest of the crew were imprisoned for the night in the great cabin, and the next morning were told that if they accepted the new régime and did their duty willingly no harm would befall them. The ship was then christened the *Revenge*, and in addition to the twelve guns which she already mounted, six more were brought up from the hold, giving her an effective armament of eighteen guns. Her course was set for the coast of Spain, and her career as a pirate had begun.

Her first prize was an English vessel, the *Delight* of Poole, on her way to Cadiz from Newfoundland with a cargo of fish; and this ship was eventually sunk, her captain, Thomas Wise, and crew of five being put in chains on board the *Revenge*. She was not much of a capture, nor was her successor, a Scottish vessel, the *Sarah*, under the command of Captain Somerville, bound for Genoa, and also disappointingly laden with fish, the chief desire of the pirates being for a fresh supply of wine and liquor. After being plundered she too was despatched to the bottom, a couple of her men agreeing to sail under Gow; one of them was the carpenter, John Menzies, and the other an apprentice of eighteen, Alexander Robb—the latter being placed in charge of his late skipper and fellow crew, who were imprisoned in the *Revenge's* powder room.

So far Gow's venture had not been particularly successful, and soon afterwards a French vessel eluded him, evidently being suspicious of the *Revenge's* appearance and giving her a fruitless three days' chase. Moreover, his water supply was now beginning to run low, and Gow therefore decided to make for Madeira, the nearest land to him, where he sent an armed boat's crew into the harbour, giving them discretion to obtain what they could in any way that seemed most promising. Once again, however, the *Revenge* and her representatives failed to convince her observers, and Gow was obliged to leave the island as poor as he came, heading next for the little island of Porto Santo, where he hoisted the British colours and sent his respects and a present to the governor. The latter was highly gratified, at once giving him the desired permission to purchase supplies and take in water, and even paid a personal visit to the *Revenge*, where Gow received him with equal courtesy. But there was some delay in respect of the arrival of provisions, and Gow decided to make use of the governor's presence, informing him that he must remain a prisoner until the *Revenge's* requirements had been fully satisfied. This was satisfactorily accomplished upon the following morning, when the governor was given a further present, and departed ashore amid mutual protestations of respect and with a formal salute of guns.

Fully equipped with arms and ammunition, and reasonably well supplied with victuals, Gow now headed his ship towards Cape St. Vincent and next took an American merchantman bound for Lisbon. Like her predecessors, however, she proved a poor bargain, the bulk of her cargo being timber, and all that the pirates secured from her was some bread and some barrels of beef and pork. This was on December 18th, and Gow took the opportunity of unloading into her Captain Wise and her crew with the exception of a little cabin boy whom he retained. The American skipper, Captain Cross, he kept aboard the *Revenge*, forcibly recruiting some of his hands. Then, nine days later, he made a capture of rather more value in the shape of a French vessel, the *Lewis Joseph*, with a cargo of wine, fruit and oil, to say nothing of several guns and a good supply of fire-arms and ammunition. Her master and crew of eleven were taken on board the *Revenge*, while the two imprisoned skippers, Cross and Somerville, together with such of their men as had not been forced to join the pirates, were placed—each with a small present!—upon the *Lewis Joseph* and sent on their way.

Gow had now taken four vessels, and his next encounter was with a large Frenchman in the neighbourhood of Cape Finisterre, and this led to a contretemps with his chief officer Williams that very nearly had a fatal issue. For Williams had already cleared the *Revenge* for action when, on drawing nearer to the Frenchman, it was discovered that she was a vessel of thirty-two guns with a crew of at least a hundred. Gow at once pointed out that it would be folly to attack her, whereupon Williams accused him of cowardice, and finally, after a heated controversy in which Gow kept full control of himself, Williams drew his pistol and fired at his captain point blank. The pistol did not however go off, and at the same moment Winter and Peterson both fired at Williams, wounding him in the arm and stomach, while others of the crew at once seized him. In spite of his wounds, however, he broke free from them, and running towards the powder room threatened to blow up the ship, being again seized and disarmed just in time. Gow had now every excuse to make short shrift of his lieutenant, and most of the crew were anxious to throw him overboard—a fate that he himself had several times repeatedly urged as the proper portion for the other prisoners. But Gow decided instead to keep him in irons and hand him over to the next vessel that they captured, with orders that he was then to be delivered as a pirate to the first man-of-war encountered. Williams had not long to wait, for on January 6th Gow took a Bristol vessel, the *Triumvirate*, which was destined to be the last of his prizes as a pirate on the high seas. Nor was she much more to boast of than the others had been, and all that she yielded to Gow was a boat and some tackle, some rum and brandy, a watch, a few spoons, and a silver cup. But she was a convenient receptacle for all his remaining prisoners, including the wounded mate, and these were afterwards handed over by the captain of the *Triumvirate* to H.M.S. *Argyle*, whom he met at Lisbon.

But it was now clear, at any rate to Gow himself, that news of his proceedings would soon be public property, and that if he did not very speedily seek another theatre of operation, he would be having a man-of-war upon his own heels. He therefore called his crew together and put the position before them, discussing the various alternatives with which they were faced. The traditional pirate grounds of the Gulf of Guinea, the West Indies, and the coast of North America, were all canvassed, but it was decided that the *Revenge* was not sufficiently equipped for a long-distance voyage with possible hard fighting. But Gow had already formed a plan, which he put before his men, for making his way to the Orkney Islands, where, as he shrewdly said, they would hardly be searched for, and where he knew various houses near the coast that might easily be plundered. The majority of his men agreed, and having altered the vessel's name to the *George Galley*, Gow arrived off Stromness harbour in the middle of January, 1725.

Here the pirates had agreed to represent themselves to the inhabitants of the little town as bound from Cadiz to Stockholm, but prevented by adverse weather from passing the Sound, and as having decided therefore to put into Stromness to refit and take in water and provisions. Two or three other vessels were also in the harbour, and with these Gow, under the name of Smith, began to do a strictly legitimate trade, his crew being bound under penalty of death to maintain the story that had been agreed upon. He also liberally entertained, and was entertained by, the leading men of the town, and there is even a legend that he won the affections of the daughter of one of the most prominent of these.

But Fate was now beginning to close upon him, and upon the shrewd mind of these northern observers it began to dawn that there was something a little strange about this dashing young captain and his prosperous and undisciplined crew. By an extraordinary chance, too, there happened to be lying in this remote harbour a vessel called the *Margaret*, whose skipper, Captain Andrew Watt, had known the *Caroline* at Amsterdam, a ship indeed to which two of his own apprentices had deserted. The *George Galley* had therefore seemed familiar to him, but had not particularly aroused his suspicions until he heard one day that his erstwhile apprentices, Macaulay and Jamieson, had been seen ashore. That decided Captain Watt to put aboard her, where he had an interview with Gow, who refused to part with the boys, but was unable to prevent Captain Watt from making a very careful scrutiny of his surroundings. This more than confirmed him in his belief that all had not gone well with the former *Caroline*, and that the *George Galley* was something very different from the peaceful merchantman that she professed to be. But a few days later he had definite evidence from the boy Jamieson, who came to him while ashore and made a full confession of all that had happened since the vessel left Santa Cruz. Watt then tried to persuade Jamieson to desert at once, but the lad was afraid that, if he did so, his fellow pirates would destroy the *Margaret*, and he also had hopes of a general break-away on the part of a majority of the crew who were discontented, he said, and were hoping to get command of the vessel. This they did not succeed in doing, although about a dozen were of them made their escape in the ship's long-boat and succeeded in reaching the mainland of Scotland near Duncansby Head.

Meanwhile, about the same time, another of the crew, Robert Read, finding himself ashore, decided to bolt for it and made for the hills. Here he took refuge in an outlying farm, and borrowing a horse from the farmer, made his way to Kirkwall, where he gave full details to the authorities. Captain Watt also, who had just sailed in the *Margaret*, had laid information before leaving, while certain minor robberies and the mysterious disappearance of one or two likely local lads had now thoroughly alarmed the neighbourhood and especially the local lairds who had been Gow's objective. Moreover, by yet another unhappy chance for Gow, there had just arrived at Stranraer the French vessel in which he had placed the two plundered captains, Cross and Somerville. Of this Gow was ignorant, but it was sufficiently clear to him that the vanished members of his crew would not be long in getting him into trouble, and having cajoled or pressed into his service an adequate number of substitutes he resolved to leave Stromness at once.

This was on the 10th of February when his refitting was only half accomplished, and it is pleasant to record that just before he sailed, young Jamieson succeeded in escaping, disguised in women's clothes, together with the little cabin boy who had been forcibly retained after the capture of the *Delight* of Poole. On the same night, before he finally put to sea, Gow sent an armed force to attack the house of one of the local gentry, a Mr. Honeyman, who lived on the eastern coast of the Bay some two miles distant. This gentleman was High Sheriff of Orkney and was away from home, probably in connection with the affairs of Gow himself; and Mrs. Honeyman and her daughter together with the servants, were left to deal with the attack.

With great presence of mind Mrs. Honeyman, at the first alarm, succeeded in emptying her husband's money-chest of most of its treasure, and bluffed her way past the sentinel with the bags of gold concealed about her person. Meanwhile, the daughter, as quick-witted as her mother, had bolted upstairs and secured the most important of her father's documents, tying them up in a cloth and throwing them out of the window—afterwards escaping herself by the same route. All that Gow seems to have obtained, therefore, was a few spoons and about seven pounds in gold, although tradition asserts that the pirates returned to their boats to the triumphant accompaniment of bagpipes and with three abducted servant maids.

Such was the end of his Stromness visit, and sailing at once on the return of the raiding party, he arrived three days later off the little island of Eday, having taken in water and landed his female captives at another small island en route. But Eday, as it turned out, was to be the scene of his doom, for in spite of having entrusted himself to a local pilot, the *George Galley* ran ashore, and but for her anchors, would quickly have been broken up. Even as it was, she was in a dangerous plight, since the stolen long-boat was not available for towing purposes, while the inhabitants of the island, of whom the chief proprietor was James Fea, had already received warning of what they might expect. Moreover, James Fea was a man of great subtlety and resource, and as soon as it became clear from observation, as well as from messengers despatched by Gow in his little remaining yawl, that the *George Galley* was in trouble, he had his own big boat dismounted, and the oars of all the smaller ones hidden away.

Meanwhile he sent a tactful letter back to Gow by the hands of one Laing, a relative of his and a local merchant, who returned from the pirate bearing the offer of a substantial reward in return for Fea's assistance in floating his vessel. To this Fea made no definite reply, but placed six men—all that the little island could muster—at various points of observation. Later in the evening, the yawl again put ashore from the *George Galley*, under the command of Belbin, William's successor, and with her crew of five men armed to the teeth. Fea, who was himself unarmed, then took one or two of his men with him to meet them, and with the rest of his force concealed in the neighbourhood, warmly protested against the evidence of hostility with which Belbin and his fellows had landed. To this they replied that they meant to have a boat, if not by fair means then by foul. But in the matter of diplomacy they had found in Fea one who was much more than their master.

Pointing out to them how awkwardly he was placed, with all the other Orkney gentry in arms against Gow, he suggested a conference in a neighbouring inn as to the best method of procedure. Belbin agreed to this, and with his followers accompanied Fea to the house in question, Fea having taken the opportunity of ordering one of his men to summon him, in about a quarter of an hour's time, to the side of his wife, who was at that time ill. The call duly came, and excusing himself, Fea rapidly completed his plans. It was now dark, and arranging an ambush about half-way between his house and the inn, he presently returned and invited Belbin to accept his hospitality while he was making what arrangements he could to meet Gow's demand. Again Belbin agreed, probably the more inclined thereto by the liquor with which he and his comrades had been plied, though he took the precaution of first attending to the loading of his pistols. A few minutes later, however, he was promptly and effectively overpowered, his four companions being similarly rushed as they sat drinking in the inn.

The *George Galley* was now boatless. Express messengers had been sent by Fea to Kirkwall for reinforcements, and beacons of alarm had been lit on the island hill-tops. Moreover, a strong wind was blowing, the seas were running high, and Gow must have realized that he was now in an extremely tight corner. Towards evening, however, on the next day, Sunday, the wind shifted, giving the *George Galley* a chance had her anchor-cable been cut at the right moment. But unfortunately for Gow, it was severed just as the *George's* bow was swinging towards the shore, and in a couple of minutes she was faster than ever upon the small island, known as the Calf of Eday, about three-quarters of a mile from the main island. Then at last Gow saw that his case was hopeless and hoisted a white flag, whereupon Fea came down to the shore and opened negotiations through a speaking trumpet. As a result of these, Gow agreed to an interview, and Fea accordingly sent a cousin of his, accompanied by five armed men, across the channel to the opposite island. Before doing so, however, he took the precaution of placing observers on the roof of his house who were to signal to the landing party if any armed men left the stranded vessel.

It was a wise precaution, for just as Gow's proxy—he had decided at the last minute not to come himself—approached Fea's cousin and his men, the observers on Eday saw a body of armed pirates rapidly hurrying to the scene of conference. They at once signalled, whereupon the islanders retreated to their boat, the proxy afterwards denying that he had had any knowledge of the treachery that had thus been foiled. The pirates being recalled, Fea's cousin then agreed to send a hostage on board the *George* in return for the presence of Gow himself. Gow therefore came in person, but Fea, who had been watching events from the opposite shore, and who had not authorized the delivery of a hostage, at once put across with some of the recruits that had now reached him, and succeeded in obtaining the return of the hostage. He then arrested Gow—an act for which he was subsequently criticized—and further succeeded in persuading Gow to send for some of his men, whom he also made prisoners. He took them all back with him to Eday, where he placed them under a strong guard, and soon afterwards, realizing that their sorry game was up, the remainder of the *George's* crew surrendered.

Later they were transported to London for trial, where they found Williams awaiting them, and in the following June, Gow himself, together with Macaulay, Melvin, Peterson, Rollson, Winter, Robb, Belbin and Williams paid the due penalty at Wapping. The story of their adventures and trial had created enormous public interest, and the gallows, which had been erected at the low watermark, according to custom, was surrounded by a huge crowd, the ships in the river being similarly thronged with eager spectators. Indeed, so great was the anxiety to see the last of the pirates that several lives, we are told, were lost both in the water and on shore—a sordid enough ending to one of the most pitiful and least romantic of pirate enterprises.

A Crew of the "Bloody Forties"

CAPTAIN SAMUEL SAMUELS

It fell to my lot to ship a full crew of these pirates, as there happened to be just thirty of them in Liverpool at the same time. No remonstrance from my friends could induce me to change my mind.

Justice Mansfield used to send me many boys in whom he thought there were some good traits. Instead of sending them to jail, he would turn them over to me to make sailors of, and bring out their better nature. Some, I am happy to say, grew up to be excelllent officers. The justice manifested much interest when he heard that thirty of the "Bloodies" were going with me. It was an open secret that I was to be dealt with after a fashion of their own. The magistrate informed me through his detectives of a plot that had been agreed upon in Mrs. Riley's den which meant trouble for me. Some of the fellows were a part of the crew on board the *Columbia* when Captain Bryer was murdered on the voyage homeward the winter previous. We were anchored in the river ready for sea, waiting for the emigrant officers to clear the ship, when Captain Shomburg, who came on board to give me my clearance, remarked,

"I never saw such a set of pirates in my life, and advise you not to take them."

"Never fear; I will draw their teeth," said I. Then, addressing the crew,

"Men, you know the rules of the ship. Pass by the carpenter shop and have the ends of your knives broken."

"What for?" they asked.

"You heard the order. Obey it."

It was done, but not with very good grace, as the grumblings around the shop indicated. The grumblings drew my attention, so I ordered,

"Lay aft here, all hands."

They came in a sort of dogged, insolent manner.

"Men," I said, "you have a right to growl, but let it be in the forecastle, not in the hearing of myself or officers. Obey orders promptly. Don't shamble your feet as you walk, but raise them and move quickly. When you are spoken to, answer so as to be heard."

"Ay, ay, sir."

"I noticed you coming aft just now. The saucy manner you assumed is insulting, and some of you know it. Finnigan, you and Casey have sailed with me before, and therefore know me. I know you to be the ringleaders of the Bloody Forties, thirty of whom I see before me now. I know that you have banded yourselves together, and that you took an oath in Mrs. Riley's den to clip the wings of the bloody old *Dreadnought*, and give the skipper a swim. You think that the lid of Davy Jones's locker has been open long enough for me. You intend to do as you please, and have your own way on the ship. Now you see that I know, and do not fear you, but am glad to have such men, as I think I can teach you a lesson that will last you through life. Sweeney, you and I were together in the Mobile jail. What was in me there as a boy is now fully developed in me as a man, but divested of the villainous associations. Now, men, stand where you are while the officers search you for hidden weapons."

Afterwards the officers searched the forecastle.

"According to your behavior," I concluded, "you shall have watch and watch, and an occasional glass of grog. As I see some of you shivering for the want of it, you shall have one now."

After they had finished it they manned the windlass and hove up the anchor. The tug took us as far as Point Lynas. There was a moderate breeze from the south-west, and we stood across the Channel to the Irish shore, then tacked again, and worked down the Channel with a steady royal breeze from the westward. The weather was clear.

The next morning, the 12th of July, 1859, at 4 A.M., we tacked ship to the northward. We were then close to St. David's Head, and I gave the order to put the helm down, which the man at the wheel did without repeating the order. The next order was "hard a-lee," at which time the head sheets should be let go. As this was not done promptly, it nearly caused the ship to mis-stay. The next order, as she slowly came to, was, "Raise tacks and sheets." As she was head to the wind, swinging around, the next order was, "Maintop-sail haul." Then, "Let go and haul." Then, "Haul taut the weather main-brace."

I then called all hands aft, and the men who were slow in letting go the sheets were sharply reprimanded, and the man at the wheel who failed to answer when spoken to was told that the next time he neglected this rule of the ship he would be punished.

The movements of the men plainly showed that there was trouble brewing, and I cautioned the officers to be very prudent in the management of the crew.

The wind backed to the southward, so that the ship luffed up to her course down the Channel. At noon, off Queenstown, while the crew were at dinner, I was walking the quarter-deck watching the course, and noticing that the man at the wheel was not steering steadily, I said.

"Steer steady!"

He made no reply.

"Did you hear me speak to you, sir?"

"I am steering steady," he answered, in a sullen manner.

The impertinent tone of his voice caused me to jump towards him. He attempted to draw his sheath-knife. Seeing my danger, I struck the man, knocking him senseless leeward of the wheel. Wallace, my dog, then took charge of him, and kept his fore paws on his chest. I took the knife from him, and called the officers to handcuff him. He was then put in the after-house, and locked up.

This scene was enacted so quickly that the crew knew nothing of it, except what they heard from the passengers immediately after.

The second mate took the wheel until two bells, or one o'clock. Orders were given to "Turn to, and haul taut the weather main-brace." The crew came aft to the quarter-deck without any attempt to obey the order, which was repeated.

"Why don't you obey the order?" I asked.

"We want Mike let out of irons," was their reply.

"From this time, men, you shall see who is master. You have acted so insolently that I see no kind treatment on my part will deter you from carrying out the compact made with your pals in Liverpool. For the remainder of the voyage I shall stop your watch and watch, and treat you as you deserve. Again I repeat, Haul taut the weather main-brace. The refusal to obey an order given places you in mutiny."

Not a man moved. It was a very exciting time. The emigrants had all huddled aft as far as the main-mast—they were not allowed on the quarter-deck—to witness what would happen. I felt as if blood would be shed. With right on my side and might on theirs the contest would appear unequal.

I turned to go into the cabin to arm myself when the crew ran forward. The knife which had been taken away from the man at the wheel had been repointed, which led me to believe that the knives of the rest of the crew had been treated in the same manner, and that mischief was intended.

When I came out of the cabin I had on a raglan, to conceal my weapons. I ordered the emigrants to go below. I went forward, followed by my faithful dog, but unaccompanied by the officers. They were of no possible use except one. The first officer was an old man, the second a coward, the third, Mr. Whitehorn, who had been with me for many years, and was as brave as a lion though small in stature, had taken the wheel, as the man had deserted it to join his shipmates.

I reached the galley door, which was about six feet from the forward end of the house. The passage which I had traversed between the water-cask and the rail was less than five feet wide. I still advanced to the end of the house, when, with a yell like that of demons let loose, the crew rushed at me with their knives.

The time had come for me to prove to these men that moral courage was superior to brute force. With a pistol in each hand, pointed at the heads of those nearest to me, and a cutlass at my side, I stood immovable. The screaming of the women and children below, blended with the noise on deck, beggars all description. Not a man dared to come nearer than about twelve feet from me, knowing that another step forward would seal his doom. My pistol practice had been heard of, and it was well known that with either hand I was a dead shot. The pistols had hair-triggers, and carried each an ounce minie-ball. During a momentary lull, when I could be heard, I said,

"Men, you have found your master."

Finding that they would not listen to what I had to say I retreated. With a yell they attempted to rush upon me as I was about to turn.

Suddenly wheeling again, and pointing my pistols at them, and with a voice that could be heard above the din, I said,

"The first man that advances another step dies."

Then backing through the passage-way as far as the main-hatch, I turned and walked aft.

During the afternoon the passengers came to me and requested me to go into Queenstown, which was bearing north about eight miles. I replied that the ship was bound to New York, not Queenstown, and that they need have no fear of their lives.

At 6 P.M. I went forward to reason with the men, but it was of no use. The yells and the language they used were the worst I have ever heard. Finnigan bared his breast and dared me to shoot, calling me an outrageous name. For a moment they thought Finnigan would be a dead man when I raised my pistol at him point-blank, with hammer uplifted. Finnigan receded a step or two, and a deadly silence prevailed.

"You cowardly dog, you shall bite the dust for this," I said.

At the same time, taking advantage of the momentary stillness, I called upon the crew to return to their duty. This they refused to do unless I gave them watch and watch.

"I am here to command," I replied, "and you to obey my orders. You shall neither eat nor drink until you return to duty."

This was met with yells and jeers. "Let's kill the old devil now," they cried.

"Stand back, you cowardly villains," I said.

"Shoot! shoot! shoot!" they yelled.

"I would if I feared you. The law gives me the right, but I prefer to teach you a lesson. Perhaps you will come to your senses when you are hungry."

"Oh! we will help ourselves when we d—n please."

"I am responsible for the ship and all on board. Any one who attempts either to injure or rob I will look upon as a pirate and treat him as such. If one of you attempts to come abaft the main-mast I will blow your brains out."

This was met with a brandishing of knives and a volley of oaths. Seeing that no impression could be made upon them, I walked aft.

That night the men, fearing that the forecastle would be battened down upon them, set a watch of four, while the others turned in. At midnight we passed Cape Clear, with a six-knot breeze. During the night I walked the deck. The officers relieved one another at the wheel every two hours. There was no sleep for us aft that night.

At seven bells the following morning I went forward again to reason with the crew, but the same scene was enacted as on the day before. At noon the breeze freshened, and I ordered, in a voice which could be heard fore and aft,

"Take in the royals."

The order was met with, "Go to h—!" from forward.

The sails were furled, however, by the officers and boys. The wind still freshened, and we headed the ship off to north-north-west. By midnight the ship was tearing through the water at the rate of twelve knots, and seeing a heavy squall coming down upon us, we lowered the top-gallant sails to the caps. The sea was making rapidly, and the ship was pitching and burying her forecastle, filling the lee gangway. The spray from the weather bow made a clear breach over us. I never carried sails so hard in my life. I had to keep the top-sails set, for had I lowered them the after-guard would have been too light to hoist them again.

At 4 A.M. the wind moderated, and at 8 A.M it was nearly calm. We then set the top-gallant sails again. Afterwards I went forward to see what could be done with the men; but the result was the same as before, except that they said if they got their breakfast they would turn to.

"You shall work before you eat," I answered.

"D—n you! then we will help ourselves to the best grub in the ship."

At 11 A.M. we exchanged signals with one of the Inman steamers, bound east. At noon we tacked ship to the south-west, and I went forward with the third officer to work tacks and sheets, as the men had threatened to throw any one overboard that came forward on the forecastle.

During the day several of the passengers came aft to ask me to give the men something to eat. One or two of the roughest went so far as to say that if the request was not complied with they would supply them themselves.

"I am sorry to see that you sympathize with the mutineers," I said. "If they conquer me they will scuttle the ship, after having committed the greatest outrages on those whom you hold most dear; and at night, while you are asleep, the hatches will be battened down and the ship sunk, while they will take to the boats, expecting to be picked up by a passing ship, and making up such stories as have frequently been told—that the ship had sprung a leak and sunk, leaving them the only survivors. These men know now that according to marine laws they have subjected themselves to five years in State-prison, and a fine of five thousand dollars. This virtually means imprisonment for life. You see, therefore, that these men intend to take my life and to escape in the boats rather than subject themselves to such penalty. I mean to bring them to subjection through hunger, and I forbid you to give them food or aid them in any way in their mutinous conduct. If you disobey, you are subject to the same penalty to which they are liable. The sympathy you have already shown them has protracted this difficulty; let me see no more of it. I have now warned you."

Except upon two or three, my remarks made a very favorable impression. To these I said,

"Understand me. I have the same authority over you that I have over my crew, and if I see a possibility of your joining them I will put you in irons."

One of them defied me to do so, and after a short tussle Mr. Whitehorn and I succeeded in putting the irons on him, without any interference from the rest of the passengers, who were ordered to leave the decks and go below.

As the sunset was clear, with a nice breeze from the north-west, the sea smooth, and the ship running eight knots on a wind, I went forward again to talk to the men. The result was as before. They demanded watch and watch, and I refused it. However, they appeared in a better frame of mind.

"Now, men, hear what I have to say. To all those who will throw their knives overboard and go to work I will forgive this mutinous conduct, except Finnigan, Casey, and Sweeney."

The offer was received with yells and howls. I then went aft, and the crew set their watch as before.

Fifty-six hours had passed without sleep aft or food forward. This state of things would have to have an ending very soon, and there was not the slightest doubt in my mind that some one would be killed.

At 8 P.M. I ordered Mr. Whitehorn to take charge of the deck, and shoot the first man that came abaft the main-mast.

I went into the cabin, and passed into the after-steerage, where the Germans were partitioned off from the other passengers. I addressed them in their own language. My remarks were the same as those addressed to the other passengers. I pointed out their danger should I be killed.

"Germans," I said, "most of you have served in the army, and have the reputation of being brave men. I therefore call upon you to defend your wives and little ones, and join me in quelling this mutiny."

With a shout they said, "Order us, captain, and we will obey."

I was reinforced by seventeen brave fellows. I armed them with iron bars taken from the cargo, and cut in handy lengths. The night was dark, and the time near midnight. All the passengers were below. A deathlike stillness prevailed, when suddenly a low growl from Wallace drew our attention to the gangway forward, between the houses and rail, where two men were discovered crawling aft, close under the rails. I fancied that I saw their knives in their hands. I was standing at the break of the quarter-deck, Mr. Whitehorn was near by.

"Shall I shoot?" he asked.

"No, there are only two."

"Shall I go down into the cabin and call up the Germans?"

"No, not now."

I waited till the men got aft as far as the capstan, which was about twenty feet from where I stood, when I said,

"Move no farther. Stand and throw up your arms, or I will put a bullet through you."

The order was obeyed instantly.

"Now walk aft and let me see who you are. What do you want?"

"Captain, you said you would forgive any one who joined you. We are married men, and ask your forgiveness."

"All right," I answered. "Throw your knives overboard. Now, one of you take the wheel, but mark me, if I find any treachery you will be the first ones to fall."

They were then searched for concealed weapons, but none were found.

"Men, what were your motives for joining me?"

"We all took an oath to stand by one another and kill you if you came forward of the house to-night; and if you did not come forward we were to burst in the galley at eight bells and help ourselves. When Dutch Bill said, 'Boys, we had better go to work,' he was struck on the head with a serving-mallet by Sweeney, and knocked senseless. He was lying in that condition when we left him to take our watch on deck. Joe and Tom, who are now on deck, are willing to come aft and join you when we call them. If you will trust us four with arms, we will help you to bring the rest to terms."

One of these men was sent forward to tell the others to take no notice of what was being done, and not to join us just yet, but go below as usual, and if asked what had become of the other two men in their watch, to say that they had deserted to join the captain. And at the same time they were told that when I came forward in the morning to ask the men to go to work, at the proper moment, when they could be well heard, they were to say, "Well, boys, here goes my knife," and with that to throw their knives overboard.

"I will attend to the rest," I said.

At five bells the Germans were brought out of the cabin. The pig-pen was placed across the port side as a barricade, and four men were put behind it. The rest were so distributed on the top of the house and elsewhere as to prevent the crew from surrounding me.

The ladders leading down the steerage were hauled up, and the hatches fastened down, to guard against the steerage passengers joining the crew.

At daybreak (seven bells) the two sailors who had the watch forward were to be relieved by four others. Among them were Casey and Sweeney. I had learned from the two men who had joined us aft that the attack was to be made on the galley and store-room, in which many of the provisions were kept.

At 3.45 A.M. Mr. Whitehorn and I, with Wallace in advance, walked forward on the starboard side, prepared for the encounter. When abreast of the galley, not seeing any of the men, I said,

"Go ahead, Wallace."

When the dog reached the corner of the house a deep growl indicated that some one was hidden forward of it. Having learned that Casey and Sweeney were the ones to make the attack, I proceeded cautiously, with pistol in hand, to the edge of the house, when they both jumped from behind it towards me, with arms uplifted and knives in hand, ready to strike.

In an instant I leveled my pistol at Casey, while the dog jumped at Sweeney's throat. Casey, seeing his danger, backed to the forecastle scuttle, while the other two men yelled down the forecastle.

"Jump up, boys! We've got him! Let's murder him now!"

With shouts and oaths they rushed on deck, determined to finish their work. They had planned during the night that some were to go around, while others were to clamber over the house and make an attack on flank and rear. In this movement they were checked, however, by the Germans, who arose from behind their barricade and felled the ringleaders with their iron bars. Seeing themselves defeated and me reinforced, they retreated to the starboard side forward, where I held them at bay, with pistol levelled and hammer raised.

"Death to the first man who dares advance! I will give you one moment to throw your knives overboard."

Finnigan now spoke up.

"You shall be the first to go, you d—d psalm-singing——!"

"Throw your knives overboard and go to work."

"What guarantee shall we have, captain, if we throw our knives overboard, that you will not shoot us?" asked one of the men.

"If I do not fear you armed with knives, I certainly will not unarmed, and to show how little I fear you, I will give my pistols into the custody of any passenger you name as soon as I see your knives thrown overboard."

"Will you give us watch and watch again, and promise not to prosecute us when we get ashore?"

"I will make no bargain with you. Throw your knives overboard and go to work."

"Well, boys, it's no use," said one of the men. "He is too much for us. Here goes mine."

With that one knife after the other went spinning overboard to leeward just as the sun was rising. A more gratifying sight I never saw than those gleaming blades dropping into the ocean. After this I discharged my pistols.

"Now, men, to let you see that I keep faith with you, name the man who is to take charge of these pistols. Finnigan, you insulted me just now, calling me a coward and other vile names. You are the leader of this gang and the bully of the forecastle. Now ask my pardon at once. I never take an insult from any one without resenting it, and certainly not from a brute like you."

"And I never have and never will ask pardon of any man," he answered.

The spirit of the muscular Christian seized me for the time, and the blow I dealt him sent him headlong down the forecastle, in front of which he had been standing.

"Stand back, men," I said. "Whitehorn, go bring that fellow up."

He found him lying at the foot of the ladder, unconscious. A rope was tied around him, and he was hauled on deck and placed in charge of the doctor. While Whitehorn was putting the rope around him, he found a knife concealed under his shirt. Upon this I drew my cutlass, and pointing it at Casey and Sweeney, ordered them to throw up their arms, which they did instantly, asking if I meant to kill them now.

Mr. Whitehorn searched them at my request, and found, as in Finnigan's case, a bowie-knife on each: one had it under his jumper, and the other had it in his boot. The rest were searched, but nothing was found upon them.

"Now, men, let it be understood. You are to jump when you are spoken to, and instead of walking you are to run to obey the orders given. I will treat you as you deserve. The last order I gave you, and which you disobeyed, was, 'Haul taut the weather main-brace.' I now repeat it, 'Haul taut the weather main-brace!'"

With one voice they called, "Ay, ay, sir!" and ran to obey. From the way they hauled on that brace, I feared they would spring the yard.

"Belay there, men!" I sang out; and then, "Boy, tell the cook to get the men's coffee ready. Whitehorn, turn the men to holy-stoning decks."

By this time Finnigan, under the doctor's care, had recovered from the effects of the rough handling, and was sitting aft near the break of the poop-deck, where he had been ordered to remain until I came aft. When again asked if he would apologize, he made no reply. I ordered him bucked, and put into the sweat-box. In less than half an hour he cried out for mercy, and was ready to say or do anything to be let out of irons. A few minutes afterwards he was brought unshackled to the quarter-deck, where all hands were holy-stoning.

"Men, listen to what your recent leader and bully has to say. He would have led you to murder and to the gallows."

"Captain," he said, "I have had enough. To say this does not make a coward of a man when he has found his master."

"This won't do. You must take back your insulting language," I replied.

"Well, then, captain, whoever calls you a coward is a d—d liar."

"Leave out the 'd—d.' You know that swearing is prohibited, and if there is to be any I claim the first privilege. Now down on your knees and holy-stone."

"Ay, ay, sir."

At seven bells all hands were ordered to breakfast. At eight bells they turned to again. The order was scarcely given when the men were on deck, scrubbing, stoning, and polishing brasswork with such a will that one would think that when they got through they were to have forty-eight hours' leave of absence on shore and a month's pay, after a year's cruise.

The day was lovely. All the emigrants were ordered on deck, and the 'tween-decks thoroughly cleaned and fumigated. At noon the wind backed to the south-west. We tacked ship to the northward, and the way they made the yards fly around was only equalled in the race we had with the clipper-ship *Lightning* the winter previous in the Channel. The men were put through a day's work that would make up for lost time. One could hardly realize that a few hours before there had been such a serious time on board. I insisted that the officers should treat the men as though nothing had happened. At seven o'clock (six bells) the men were called aft.

"Men," I said, "I think we understand each other."

"Please, captain, make the punishment as light as possible," they replied.

The ordinary ship's work was carried on for the rest of the voyage without any watch below, and a smarter set of men I never had. My heart was very much softened when several of the crew attended divine worship on Sunday, and they were all allowed a glass of grog before dinner. On a beautiful August morning the Highland lights hove in sight right ahead at four bells, and at the same time we took a pilot on board. At daylight all hands were turned to after they had had their coffee, which was always served out at this time in the morning. The order was given to reeve the signal halyards fore and aft, which was instantly obeyed, although the men might expect that the signals were to be set for assistance. I had told them at the height of the mutiny that they could not hope to escape punishment, as I would run up the signals for the *Harriet Lane* Revenue cutter. Signals were run up, but not such ones as the men had expected. All hands were ordered into the forecastle, where I joined them with the ship's articles. I told them that I had come to say a few words to them. I then reviewed a part of my forecastle life. I told them how I had been as they were, a prey to the sharks ashore—how I had been drugged, bought, sold, and robbed. I begged them to break the chains that bound them to the depraved life they were leading, and assert the manhood God had given them for a better purpose than to be the slaves of boardinghouse keepers and crimps. I told them there was no reason why they should not become officers, captains, or merchants, and drew a picture of a home life with wives and children which I set in contrast with another dark picture showing the end that would overtake them if they gave way to their unbridled passions. "And now," I said, "I forgive you as freely for what has passed as I hope to be forgiven in the world to come. I beg you to repent your past sins, and pray to God to give you a new life." I ended with a prayer which brought tears to the eyes of most of these hardened men.

"I leave with you," said I, "the ship's articles which you have signed, or had signed for you. On the back of these are the marine laws, wherein you will see the penalty you have subjected yourselves to. I have one request to make, which is that you will not leave the ship until she is moored to the dock with rigging stopped up, and you have received from me yourselves what little pay there is due you. I want you to do this instead of deserting the ship in the usual fashion, and allowing the landlords or the sailor lawyers to collect your money. They generally cheat you out of most of it. I know you will do this, to show me that you mean to lead better lives, and by so doing you will convince me that my forbearance has taught you a lesson of repentance. If what has happened has been the means of converting all or any of you, I shall feel that this has been the most fortunate voyage of my life." I then went aft.

A short time afterwards Finnigan, who had been the ringleader, brought the articles to me, saying that he had come to return them and, in behalf of the crew, to thank me for my forbearance. He had the most to be thankful for, he said. He declared that they would do all I asked them, and would try to be better men.

Abreast of the light-ship we were taken in tow by the tug. We furled the sails, and squared everything man-of-war fashion. At ten o'clock we arrived at quarantine, and were passed by the doctor. We discharged our passengers in barges, to be taken to Castle Garden. During the short time the ship was detained at quarantine the news of the mutiny had spread all over the city like wildfire, and by the time we were moored at the dock we were besieged by all the runners and sailor thieves in New York, expecting to see a row, in which they were quite ready to take a hand. These villains had no love for me, whom they considered their natural enemy, standing between them and their prey. Much to their astonishment, the men, instead of deserting in the usual way by jumping to the wharf or overboard, prevented the runners from coming on board. It would be impossible to describe the taunts and jeers of these rascals at what they called the cowardice of the crew in not daring to come ashore without liberty. They suggested among other things that I must have licked the whole lot of them. No attention was paid to these jeers by the crew, who were stowing away hawsers, sweeping decks, and giving the brasswork an extra polish. I paid the men off in the cabin. When about half were paid, the *Kangaroo*, of the Inman line, left the dock above us for Liverpool. Our men on deck called to those in the cabin to come up and give her three cheers. This was done with a will, and her crew with equal heartiness returned three cheers for the "bully *Dreadnought*," whereupon our men gave three cheers for me.

I finished paying off the crew. When everything was ship-shape alow and aloft the men took their seats on the spars, evidently waiting for something. This being reported to me, I went on deck and walked to the capstan, where the men surrounded me, with their hats in their hands, each urging the other to speak. Understanding that they wanted to make a speech, I said, "I think I know what you wish to say. Your actions speak plainer than words. Let me say that I would trust any of you hereafter with my life. I never had or expect to have a better set of sailors with me. The moral lesson which God has given me the privilege to teach you I know will make you better men. When I am ready to go to sea again, if any of you want to ship I shall be glad to take you." This was met with three rousing cheers for "the wild boat of the Atlantic." They expressed their willingness to sail to the ends of the world, or to h—l, with me. I wished them good-by, and expressed the hope that they would find their wives, children, and friends as well as they could wish them to be. With a "God bless you, captain," they left the ship.

Superintendent Kennedy with a posse of police arrived on the scene just in time to clear the docks and ask what was the matter. Mr. Ogden, the ship's agent, had sent him word that the crew, aided by the runners, had attacked the officers and myself.

"There has been a mistake, Kennedy," I said. "As you see, the crew are going ashore very peaceably."

"What about the mutiny? Shall I arrest the men?"

"No. I would ship them to-morrow, if I wanted a crew."

Poor Jack has a hard enough time at the best of it. He is a prey to plunderers ashore, and the sport and plaything of the wild elements of the deep, and he is at the mercy of officers who are too often ready to exert to a tyrannous extent the authority they possess. It is little wonder that his heart should be warped at times until it seemed to be almost dead in his bosom. But let us remember that a little kindness and consideration, joined with firm justice on the part of his superiors, will often melt that obdurate nature, and make that heart full and warm again.

King's Evidence Against a Pirate

FROM STATE TRIALS, 1812

[*Edinburgh, 27th March*, 1705.] In the presence of Mr. James Graham, Judge of the High Court of Admiralty, George Haines, one of the crew of the *Worcester*, being desirous to make a confession of what he knew in relation to the crimes for which he and the rest of the crew are pursued, declared, that when the ship the *Worcester* was in the Downs, the declarant received a letter from a friend in London, telling him that it was surmised in London, that their ship was going out upon some ill design; and that he had likeways another letter from his father to the same effect, and heard the gunner, James Simpson, say, he had also another of the same nature. The declarant declares that thereafter he used all his endeavours to go ashore, and accordingly he having got leave to see some friends aboard the Fleet frigate that was then riding in the Downs, he got into her long boat that was then going ashore, but some of the frigate's crew having received notice where the declarant was, after he went ashore, they came to him, and having drunk with him to some pitch, persuaded him to go aboard his own ship again; and the declarant was accordingly carried aboard, in one of the boats belonging to the town of Deal. And some time thereafter the declarant designed likewise to have got into a man-of-war, riding hard by their ship; but Mr. Callant, the supercargo, came after him and brought him back: and the declarant believes the name of the man-of-war was the *Salisbury*. That the ship *Worcester* sailed from Downs the 8th of March, 1702, in the morning. That in the month of June or July thereafter, the ship arrived at Delagoa, where their sloop was built of timber, and other materials which they had brought from England aboard the ship. That having sailed from Delagoa, some few days before they came upon the coast of Malabar, he heard some of the crew, and particularly John Bruckley, the cooper, talk of turning pirates, and persuading others of the crew to go in with them. That when they came upon the coast of Malabar, and had been there about a month, they endeavoured to take a large country boat; and for that end the sloop endeavoured to pass between the said boat and the shore, that so the ship might come up with the said boat; but there being several hands aboard, and the boat having fifty oars, outsailed both ship and sloop and got off; declares, that Coge Commodo was aboard the ship the time of the aforesaid chase, and that he drew his sabre and encouraged the crew of the *Worcester*; declares, that hereafter the ship and sloop sailed for Cochin, with a design to have cleaned both at that place (the sloop being much spoiled with worms); but the governor would not allow them to be cleaned there; and therefore they went up to Callecut, where the sloop was cleaned and refitted, and manned with about eight men and two guns, two patteraroes, and other small arms and ammunition put aboard; and then the sloop alone sailed up towards Tillicherry, and stayed away from the ship about eight days; declares, that the sloop took no goods with her when she went out; but when she returned she had aboard eight hogsheads of rack, and knows not how she came by them. But John Roberts, one of the crew who had been with the sloop at that time, was very melancholy after his return; and the declarant having a coconut full of rack in his hand, desired Roberts to take a part; but he would not, and went down to his hammock mightily concerned; and afterwards told the declarant, that the reason of his concern and melancholy was that he was accessory to the cutting off of some men's heads at Sacrifice Rock, betwixt Tillicherry and Callecut; declares that the sloop did sail by herself from Callecut thereafter, and the ship followed down to Callicoiloan, and did there meet with the sloop; and having discovered a ship coming as from the southward, the sloop was put under sail, and made to pass in betwixt the said ship and the offing, that so she might not get to sea: and the ship coming nearer to the *Worcester*, in which the declarant was at the time, the *Worcester* slipped her anchors and made towards the aforesaid ship, and at length came up with her, and fired a sharp shot to cause her to come to, which she did accordingly, by breaking her head sails back to her masts; and that thereafter she was boarded; declares, that the ship was about seventy tons burden, and square-sterned, and painted in the quarters with red and yellow; and that she had a main deck and quarter deck, and a little forecastle, and was of the Indian build; and that there were in the ship, when boarded, about twelve or fourteen men, all white and sickly, as the declarant clearly perceived before the ship was boarded. But when the declarant was endeavouring to know of what country the men were, Edward Carry, one of the *Worcester's* crew, knocked him down with a hand-spike into the midship hatch; but he afterwards heard amongst the crew that the men of the taken ship were Britons; declares, that he knew not what became of the men who were aboard of the taken ship, not having been able to come above deck, with the stroke which he received from Edward Carry, and whereof he yet bears the mark; but declares that the sloop went off before he came above deck and stayed away for three or four days, and that the declarant thereafter heard that the men were put into the sloop. And what was done with the said men of the taken ship he cannot tell, but doubts not they were murdered and made away, because they could not be put ashore at any place at hand on that coast; there being English and Dutch factories all along the coast, very near each other; declares, that those of the crew who went with the sloop from the ship at that time were Mr. Loveday, Thomas Calcate, Andrew Robertson, gunner of the sloop, John Roberts, Edward Carry, Duncan Mackay, Alexander Taylor, and Antonio Ferdinando, the black; but cannot be positive who besides there were; declares, that the next evening after the action, the ship which was taken the day before was carried in by some of the crew to Callicoiloan and sold to Coge Commodo for 1,500 rupees, and that the goods of the said taken ship were some bails and mats of China roots and four chests of copper, which chests were afterwards sold at Bengal to a Bannion merchant named Tagodas; declares, that some days after the action the declarant was sent ashore with a letter to the supercargo, and that he then heard that Coge Commodo, to whom the ship was sold, was a great assister of all pirates, and was very serviceable to Kidd and Avery when upon that coast, and bought off their goods, as the declarant was credibly informed by the people on that coast. And declares, that the time the declarant was on shore, the supercargo, Mr. Linsteed, Reynolds, Hammond, and the doctor were ashore. And the declarant did likewise see Antonio Ferdinando, the black, at the Ibeck of Callicoiloan, who complained of a wound in his arm; declares, that after the action, and before the declarant went ashore, the doctor, Charles May, came aboard from the Ibeck of Callicoiloan; and seeing the chests, which had come out of the taken ship up on the deck, he asked Captain Madder, What did all that lumber upon the deck? And that Madder answered him with a curse, and told him to mind his plaster-box and ask no questions; declares, that while the ship was upon the coast of Malabar she sprang a leak in the strake next the keel, which made the crew to pump constantly; however, they went not into any place upon the coast of Malabar to refit her, but sailed to Bengal, which was about five weeks' sailing; and there the ship was refitted, not only of the leak, but of a hurt which the ship got in the action, in the plank betwixt the midship's crupper and the chestree, and a new plank put in, in the larboard side, where the hurt was; declares, that the declarant did keep a note, by way of journal, during the voyage, which contained the substance of what he now declares in relation to the above particulars; and that when the ship was seized in the road of Leith, he heaved the same over board, lest it should have fallen in the seizer's hands; declares, that he would have emitted this declaration and confession sooner, but that he was always made believe by Captain Green's agents that the defences made for the crew would certainly bring them off; and if they did all agree in one mind, and keep close mouths, there would be no fear; for nothing could be other-ways proven that could do them harm. And declares, that Wilcocks, the chirurgeon's mate, told the declarant, that he saw a letter from the owners of the *Worcester*, in London, to Captain Green, which bore, that although the crew were condemned in Scotland, they had pardons ready to send down to them. And this the declarant was likeways informed of, by the carpenter's wife.

Ja. Graham.   George Haines.

[*Edinburgh, March* 28, 1705.] In presence of Sir Robert Forbes, Judge of the High Court of Admiralty, compeared George Haines, one of the crew of the ship the *Worcester*, and declared that he now adds to his former declaration: that after the ship therein mentioned was seized he saw the men who were therein killed and murdered with pole-axes and cutlasses, and saw their dead bodies put into the sloop and thereafter thrown overboard; and to the best of the declarant's knowledge the said men so killed were Scotsmen, the declarant having heard them speak the Scots language. And further declares, that the said ship then seized was understood by the crew of the *Worcester* to have been Captain Drummond his ship; and particularly, he heard Captain Madder, John Bruckley, and the deceased Edward Carry say so. And further adds that he would have emitted what is above before this time but was afraid lest his mentioning the ship so seized to belong to Captain Drummond, and the men aboard the same to have been murdered, might have rendered the government offended and obliged them to deal hardly with the declarant. And this he declares to be the truth, as he shall answer to God.

Robr. Forbes.   George Haines.

From the "Trial of Captain Green and his Crew, for Piracy, A.D. 1705," in *State Trials*, Vol. XIV, 1812.

The Life of Lafitte

CHARLES ELLMS

The Famous Pirate of the Gulf of Mexico

Jean Lafitte, was born at St. Maloes in France, in 1781, and went to sea at the age of thirteen; after several voyages in Europe, and to the coast of Africa, he was appointed mate of a French East Indiaman, bound to Madras. On the outward passage they encountered a heavy gale off the Cape of Good Hope, which sprung the main-mast and otherwise injured the ship, which determined the captain to bear up for the Mauritius, where he arrived in safety; a quarrel having taken place on the passage out between Lafitte and the captain, he abandoned the ship and refused to continue the voyage. Several privateers were at this time fitting out at this island, and Lafitte was appointed captain of one of these vessels; after a cruise during which he robbed the vessels of other nations, besides those of England, and thus committing piracy, he stopped at the Seychelles, and took in a load of slaves for the Mauritius; but being chased by an English frigate as far north as the equator, he found himself in a very awkward condition; not having provisions enough on board his ship to carry him back to the French Colony. He therefore conceived the bold project of proceeding to the Bay of Bengal, in order to get provisions from on board some English ships. In his ship of two hundred tons, with only two guns and twenty-six men, he attacked and took an English armed schooner with a numerous crew. After putting nineteen of his own crew on board the schooner, he took the command of her and proceeded to cruise upon the coast of Bengal. He there fell in with the Pagoda, a vessel belonging to the English East India Company, armed with twenty-six twelve pounders and manned with one hundred and fifty men. Expecting that the enemy would take him for a pilot of the Ganges, he manœuvred accordingly. The Pagoda manifested no suspicions, whereupon he suddenly darted with his brave followers upon her decks, overturned all who opposed them, and speedily took the ship. After a very successful cruise he arrived safe at the Mauritius, and took the command of La Confiance of twenty-six guns and two hundred and fifty men, and sailed for the coast of British India. Off the Sand Heads in October, 1807, Lafitte fell in with the Queen East Indiaman, with a crew of near four hundred men, and carrying forty guns; he conceived the bold project of getting possession of her. Never was there beheld a more unequal conflict; even the height of the vessel compared to the feeble privateer augmented the chances against Lafitte; but the difficulty and danger far from discouraging this intrepid sailor, acted as an additional spur to his brilliant valor. After electrifying his crew with a few words of hope and ardor, he manœuvred and ran on board of the enemy. In this position he received a broadside when close too; but he expected this, and made his men lay flat upon the deck. After the first fire they all rose, and from the yards and tops, threw bombs and grenades into the forecastle of the Indiaman. This sudden and unforeseen attack caused a great havoc. In an instant, death and terror made them abandon a part of the vessel near the mizen-mast. Lafitte, who observed every thing, seized the decisive moment, beat to arms, and forty of his crew prepared to board, with pistols in their hands and daggers held between their teeth. As soon as they got on deck, they rushed upon the affrighted crowd, who retreated to the steerage, and endeavored to defend themselves there. Lafitte thereupon ordered a second division to board, which he headed himself; the captain of the Indiaman was killed, and all were swept away in a moment. Lafitte caused a gun to be loaded with grape, which he pointed towards the place where the crowd was assembled, threatening to exterminate them. The English deeming resistance fruitless, surrendered, and Lafitte hastened to put a stop to the slaughter. This exploit, hitherto unparalleled, resounded through India, and the name of Lafitte became the terror of English commerce in these latitudes.

As British vessels now traversed the Indian Ocean under strong convoys, game became scarce, and Lafitte determined to visit France; and after doubling the Cape of Good Hope, he coasted up to the Gulf of Guinea, and in the Bight of Benin, took two valuable prizes loaded with gold dust, ivory, and Palm Oil; with this booty he reached St. Maloes in safety. After a short stay at his native place he fitted out a brigantine, mounting twenty guns and one hundred and fifty men, and sailed for Gaudaloupe; amongst the West India Islands, he made several valuable prizes; but during his absence on a cruise the island having been taken by the British, he proceeded to Carthagena, and from thence to Barrataria. After this period, the conduct of Lafitte at Barrataria does not appear to be characterized by the audacity and boldness, of his former career; but he had amassed immense sums of booty, and as he was obliged to have dealings with the merchants of the United States, and the West Indies, who frequently owed him large sums, and the cautious dealings necessary to found and conduct a colony of Pirates and Smugglers in the very teeth of a civilized nation, obliged Lafitte to cloak as much as possible his real character.

As we have said before, at the period of the taking of Gaudaloupe by the British, most of the privateers commissioned by the government of that island, and which were then on a cruise, not being able to return to any of the West India Islands, made for Barrataria, there to take in a supply of water and provisions, recruit the health of their crews, and dispose of their prizes, which could not be admitted into any of the ports of the United States, we being at that time in peace with Great Britain. Most of the commissions granted to privateers by the French government at Gaudaloupe, having expired sometime after the declaration of the independence of Carthagena, many of the privateers repaired to that port, for the purpose of obtaining from the new government commissions for cruising against Spanish vessels. Having duly obtained their commissions, they in a manner blockaded for a long time all the ports belonging to the royalists, and made numerous captives, which they carried into Barrataria. Under this denomination is comprised part of the coast of Louisiana to the west of the mouths of the Mississippi, comprehended between Bastien bay on the east, and the mouths of the river or bayou la Fourche on the west. Not far from the sea are lakes called the great and little lakes of Barrataria, communicating with one another by several large bayous with a great number of branches. There is also the island of Barrataria, at the extremity of which is a place called the Temple, which denomination it owes to several mounds of shells thrown up there by the Indians. The name of Barrataria is also given to a large basin which extends the whole length of the cypress swamps, from the Gulf of Mexico to three miles above New Orleans. These waters disembogue into the gulf by two entrances of the bayou Barrataria, between which lies an island called Grand Terre, six miles in length, and from two to three miles in breadth, running parallel with the coast. In the western entrance is the great pass of Barrataria, which has from nine to ten feet of water. Within this pass about two leagues from the open sea, lies the only secure harbor on the coast, and accordingly this was the harbor frequented by the *Pirates*, so well known by the name of Barratarians.

At Grand Jerre, the privateers publicly made sale by auction, of the cargoes of their prizes. From all parts of Lower Louisiana, people resorted to Barrataria, without being at all solicitous to conceal the object of their journey. The most respectable inhabitants of the state, especially those living in the country, were in the habit of purchasing smuggled goods coming from Barrataria.

The government of the United States sent an expedition under Commodore Patterson, to disperse the settlement of marauders at Barrataria; the following is an extract of his letter to the secretary of war.

Sir—I have the honor to inform you that I departed from this city on the 11th June, accompanied by Col. Ross, with a detachment of seventy of the 44th regiment of infantry. On the 12th, reached the schooner Carolina, of Plaquemine, and formed a junction with the gun vessels at the Balize on the 13th, sailed from the southwest pass on the evening of the 15th, and at half past 8 o'clock, A. M. on the 16th, made the Island of Barrataria, and discovered a number of vessels in the harbor, some of which shewed Carthagenian colors. At 2 o'clock, perceived the pirates forming their vessels, ten in number, including prizes, into a line of battle near the entrance of the harbor, and making every preparation to offer me battle. At 10 o'clock, wind light and variable, formed the order of battle with six gun boats and the Sea Horse tender, mounting one six pounder and fifteen men, and a launch mounting one twelve pound carronade; the schooner Carolina, drawing too much water to cross the bar. At half past 10 o'clock, perceived several smokes along the coasts as signals, and at the same time a white flag hoisted on board a schooner at the fort, an American flag at the mainmast head and a Carthagenian flag (under which the pirates cruise) at her topping lift; replied with a white flag at my main; at 11 o'clock, discovered that the pirates had fired two of their best schooners; hauled down my white flag and made the *signal for battle*; hoisting with a large white flag bearing the words "Pardon for Deserters"; having heard there was a number on shore from the army and navy. At a quarter past 11 o'clock, two gun boats grounded and were passed agreeably to my previous orders, by the other four which entered the harbor, manned by my barge and the boats belonging to the grounded vessels, and proceeded in to my great disappointment. I perceived that the pirates abandoned their vessels, and were flying in all directions. I immediately sent the launch and two barges with small boats in pursuit of them. At meridian, took possession of all their vessels in the harbor consisting of six schooners and one felucca, cruisers, and prizes of the pirates, one brig, a prize, and two armed schooners under the Carthagenian flag, both in the line of battle, with the armed vessels of the pirates, and apparently with an intention to aid them in any resistance they might make against me, as their crews were at quarters, tompions out of their guns, and matches lighted. Col. Ross at the same time landed, and with his command took possession of their establishment on shore, consisting of about forty houses of different sizes, badly constructed, and thatched with palmetto leaves.

When I perceived the enemy forming their vessels into a line of battle I felt confident from their number and very advantageous position, and their number of men, that they would have fought me; their not doing so I regret; for had they, I should have been enabled more effectually to destroy or make prioners of them and their leaders; but it is a subject of great satisfaction to me, to have effected the object of my enterprise, without the loss of a man.

The enemy had mounted on their vessels twenty pieces of cannon of different calibre; and as I have since learnt, from eight hundred, to one thousand men of all nations and colors.

Early in the morning of the 20th, the Carolina at anchor, about five miles distant, made the signal of a "strange sail in sight to eastward"; immediately after she weighed anchor, and gave chase the strange sail, standing for Grand Terre, with all sail; at half past 8 o'clock, the chase hauled her wind off shore to escape; sent acting Lieut. Spedding with four boats manned and armed to prevent her passing the harbor; at 9 o'clock, A. M., the chase fired upon the Carolina, which was returned; each vessel continued firing during the chase, when their long guns could reach. At 10 o'clock, the chase grounded outside of the bar, at which time the Carolina was from the shoalness of the water obliged to haul her wind off shore and give up the chase; opened a fire upon the chase across the island from the gun vessels. At half past 10 o'clock, she hauled down her colors and was taken possession of. She proved to be the armed schooner Gen. Boliver; by grounding she broke both her rudder pintles and made water; took from her her armament, consisting of one long brass eighteen pounder, one long brass six pounder, two twelve pounders, small arms, &c., and twenty-one packages of dry goods. On the afternoon of the 23d, got underway with the whole squadron, in all seventeen vessels, but during the night one escaped, and the next day arrived at New Orleans with my whole squadron.

At different times the English had sought to attack the pirates at Barrataria, in hopes of taking their prizes, and even their armed vessels. Of these attempts of the British, suffice it to instance that of June 23d, 1813, when two privateers being at anchor off Cat Island, a British sloop of war anchored at the entrance of the pass, and sent her boats to endeavor to take the privateers; but they were repulsed with considerable loss.

Such was the state of affairs, when on the 2d Sept., 1814, there appeared an armed brig on the coast opposite the pass. She fired a gun at a vessel about to enter, and forced her to run aground; she then tacked and shortly after came to an anchor at the entrance of the pass. It was not easy to understand the intentions of this vessel, who, having commenced with hostilities on her first appearance now seemed to announce an amicable disposition. Mr. Lafitte then went off in a boat to examine her, venturing so far that he could not escape from the pinnace sent from the brig, and making towards the shore, bearing British colors and a flag of truce. In this pinnace were two naval officers. One was Capt. Lockyer, commander of the brig. The first question they asked was, where was Mr. Lafitte? he not choosing to make himself known to them, replied that the person they inquired for was on shore. They then delivered to him a packet directed to Mr. Lafitte, Barrataria, requesting him to take particular care of it, and to deliver it into Mr. Lafitte's hands. He prevailed on them to make for the shore, and as soon as they got near enough to be in his power, he made himself known, recommending to them at the same time to conceal the business on which they had come. Upwards of two hundred persons lined the shore, and it was a general cry amongst the crews of the privateers at Grand Terre, that those British officers should be made prisoners and sent to New Orleans as spies. It was with much difficulty that Lafitte dissuaded the multitude from this intent, and led the officers in safety to his dwelling. He thought very prudently that the papers contained in the packet might be of importance towards the safety of the country and that the officers if well watched could obtain no intelligence that might turn to the detriment of Louisiana. He now examined the contents of the packet, in which he found a proclamation addressed by Col. Edward Nichalls, in the service of his Brittanic Majesty, and commander of the land forces on the coast of Florida, to the inhabitants of Louisiana. A letter from the same to Mr. Lafitte, the commander of Barrataria; an official letter from the honorable W. H. Percy, captain of the sloop of war Hermes, directed to Lafitte. When he had perused these letters, Capt. Lockyer enlarged on the subject of them and proposed to him to enter into the service of his Britannic Majesty with the rank of post captain and to receive the command of a 44 gun frigate. Also all those under his command, or over whom he had sufficient influence. He was also offered thirty thousand dollars, payable at Pensacola, and urged him not to let slip this opportunity of acquiring fortune and consideration. On Lafitte's requiring a few days to reflect upon these proposals, Capt. Lockyer observed to him that no reflection could be necessary, respecting proposals that obviously precluded hesitation, as he was a Frenchman and proscribed by the American government. But to all his splendid promises and daring insinuations, Lafitte replied that in a few days he would give a final answer; his object in this procrastination being to gain time to inform the officers of the state government of this nefarious project. Having occasion to go to some distance for a short time, the persons who had proposed to send the British officers prisoners to New Orleans, went and seized them in his absence, and confined both them and the crew of the pinnace, in a secure place, leaving a guard at the door. The British officers sent for Lafitte; but he, fearing an insurrection of the crews of the privateers, thought it advisable not to see them until he had first persuaded their captains and officers to desist from the measures on which they seemed bent. With this view he represented to the latter that, besides the infamy that would attach to them if they treated as prisoners people who had come with a flag of truce, they would lose the opportunity of discovering the projects of the British against Louisiana.

Early the next morning Lafitte caused them to be released from their confinement and saw them safe on board their pinnace, apologizing the detention. He now wrote to Capt. Lockyer the following letter.

To Captain Lockyer.

Barrataria, 4th Sept. 1814.

Sir—The confusion which prevailed in our camp yesterday and this morning, and of which you have a complete knowledge, has prevented me from answering in a precise manner to the object of your mission; nor even at this moment can I give you all the satisfaction that you desire; however, if you could grant me a fortnight, I would be entirely at your disposal at the end of that time. This delay is indispensable to enable me to put my affairs in order. You may communicate with me by sending a boat to the eastern point of the pass, where I will be found. You have inspired me with more confidence than the admiral, your superior officer, could have done himself; with you alone, I wish to deal, and from you also I will claim, in due time the reward of the services, which I may render to you.

Yours, &c.

J. LAFITTE.

His object in writing that letter was, by appearing disposed to accede to their proposals, to give time to communicate the affair to the officers of the state government, and to receive from them instructions how to act, under circumstances so critical and important to the country. He accordingly wrote on the 4th September to Mr. Blanque, one of the representatives of the state, sending him all the papers delivered to him by the British officers with a letter addressed to his excellency, Gov. Claiborne of the state of Louisiana.

To Gov. CLAIBORNE.

Barrataria, Sept. 4th, 1814.

Sir—In the firm persuasion that the choice made of you to fill the office of first magistrate of this state, was dictated by the esteem of your fellow citizens, and was conferred on merit, I confidently address you on an affair on which may depend the safety of this country. I offer to you to restore to this state several citizens, who perhaps in your eyes have lost that sacred title. I offer you them, however, such as you could wish to find them, ready to exert their utmost efforts in defence of the country. This point of Louisiana, which I occupy, is of great importance in the present crisis. I tender my services to defend it; and the only reward I ask is that a stop be put to the proscription against me and my adherents, by an act of oblivion, for all that has been done hitherto. I am the stray sheep wishing to return to the fold. If you are thoroughly acquainted with the nature of my offences, I should appear to you much less guilty, and still worthy to discharge the duties of a good citizen. I have never sailed under any flag but that of the republic of Carthagena, and my vessels are perfectly regular in that respect. If I could have brought my lawful prizes into the ports of this state; I should not have employed the illicit means that have caused me to be proscribed. I decline saying more on the subject, until I have the honor of your excellency's answer, which I am persuaded can be dictated only by wisdom. Should your answer not be favorable to my ardent desires, I declare to you that I will instantly leave the country, to avoid the imputation of having cooperated towards an invasion on this point, which cannot fail to take place, and to rest secure in the acquitttal of my conscience.

I have the honor to be your excellency's, &c.

J. LAFITTE.

The contents of these letters do honor to Lafitte's judgment, and evince his sincere attachment to the American cause. On the receipt of this packet from Lafitte, Mr. Blanque immediately laid its contents before the governor, who convened the committee of defence lately formed of which he was president; and Mr. Rancher the bearer of Lafitte's packet, was sent back with a verbal answer to desire Lafitte to take no steps until it should be determined what was expedient to be done;

the message also contained an assurance that, in the meantime no steps should be taken against him for his past offences against the laws of the United States.

At the expiration of the time agreed on with Captain Lockyer, his ship appeared again on the coast with two others, and continued standing off and on before the pass for several days. But he pretended not to perceive the return of the sloop of war, who tired of waiting to no purpose put out to sea and disappeared.

Lafitte having received a guarantee from General Jackson for his safe passage from Barrataria to New Orleans and back, he proceeded forthwith to the city where he had an interview with Gov. Claiborne and the General. After the usual formalities and courtesies had taken place between these gentlemen, Lafitte addressed the Governor of Louisiana nearly as follows. I have offered to defend for you that part of Louisianna I now hold. But not as an outlaw, would I be its defender. In that confidence, with which you have inspired me, I offer to restore to the state many citizens, now under my command. As I have remarked before, the point I occupy is of great importance in the present crisis. I tender not only my own services to defend it, but those of all I command; and the only reward I ask is, that a stop be put to the proscription against me and my adherents, by an act of oblivion for all that has been done hitherto.

"My dear sir," said the Governor, who together with General Jackson, was impressed with admiration of his sentiments, "your praiseworthy wishes shall be laid before the council of the state, and I will confer with my august friend here present, upon this important affair, and send you an answer to-morrow." At Lafitte withdrew, the General said farewell; when we meet again, I trust it will be in the ranks of the American army. The result of the conference was the issuing the following order.

The Governor of Louisiana, informed that many individuals implicated in the offences heretofore committed against the United States at Barrataria, express a willingness at the present crisis to enroll themselves and march against the enemy.

He does hereby invite them to join the standard of the United States and is authorised to say, should their conduct in the field meet the approbation of the Major General, that that officer will unite with the governor in a request to the president of the United States, to extend to each and every individual, so marching and acting, a free and full pardon. These general orders were placed in the hands of Lafitte, who circulated them among his dispersed followers, most of whom readily embraced the conditions of pardon they held out. In a few days many brave men and skillful artillerists, whose services contributed greatly to the safety of the invaded state, flocked to the standard of the United States, and by their conduct, received the highest approbation of General Jackson.

BY THE PRESIDENT OF THE UNITED STATES OF AMERICA.

A Proclamation

"Among the many evils produced by the wars, which, with little intermission, have afflicted Europe, and extended their ravages into other quarters of the globe, for a period exceeding twenty years, the dispersion of a considerable portion of the inhabitants of different countries, in sorrow and in want, has not been the least injurious to human happiness, nor the least severe in the trial of human virtue.

"It had been long ascertained that many foreigners, flying from the dangers of their own home, and that some citizens, forgetful of their duty, had co-operated in forming an establishment on the island of Barrataria, near the mouth of the river Mississippi, for the purpose of a clandestine and lawless trade. The government of the United States caused the establishment to be broken up and destroyed; and, having obtained the means of designating the offenders of every description, it only remained to answer the demands of justice by inflicting an exemplary punishment.

"But it has since been represented that the offenders have manifested a sincere penitence; that they have abandoned the prosecution of the worst cause for the support of the best, and, particularly, that they have exhibited, in the defence of New Orleans, unequivocal traits of courage and fidelity. Offenders, who have refused to become the associates of the enemy in the war, upon the most seducing terms of invitation; and who have aided to repel his hostile invasion of the territory of the United States, can no longer be considered as objects of punishment, but as objects of a generous forgiveness.

"It has therefore been seen, with great satisfaction, that the General Assembly of the State of Louisiana earnestly recommend those offenders to the benefit of a full pardon; And in compliance with that recommendation, as well as in consideration of all the other extraordinary circumstances in the case, I, *James Madison*, President of the United States of America, do issue this proclamation, hereby granting, publishing and declaring, a free and full pardon of all offences committed in violation of any act or acts of the Congress of the said United States, touching the revenue, trade and navigation thereof, or touching the intercourse and commerce of the United States with foreign nations, at any time before the eighth day of January, in the present year one thousand eight hundred and fifteen, by any person or persons whatsoever, being inhabitants of New Orleans and the adjacent country, or being inhabitants of the said island of Barrataria, and the places adjacent; *Provided*, that every person, claiming the benefit of this full pardon, in order to entitle himself thereto, shall produce a certificate in writing from the governor of the State of Louisiana, stating that such person has aided in the defence of New Orleans and the adjacent country, during the invasion thereof as aforesaid.

"And I do hereby further authorize and direct all suits, indictments, and prosecutions, for fines, penalties, and forfeitures, against any person or persons, who shall be entitled to the benefit of this full pardon, forthwith to be stayed, discontinued and released: All civil officers are hereby required, according to the duties of their respective stations, to carry this proclamation into immediate and faithful execution.

"Done at the City of Washington, the sixth day of February, in the year one thousand eight hundred and fifteen, and of the independence of the United States the thirty-ninth.

"By the President,
"JAMES MADISON

"JAMES MONROE,
Acting Secretary of State."

The morning of the eighth of January, was ushered in with the discharge of rockets, the sound of cannon, and the cheers of the British soldiers advancing to the attack. The Americans, behind the breastwork, awaited in calm intrepidity their approach. The enemy advanced in close column of sixty men in front, shouldering their muskets and carrying fascines and ladders. A storm of rockets preceded them, and an incessant fire opened from the battery, which commanded the advanced column. The musketry and rifles from the Kentuckians and Tennesseeans, joined the fire of the artillery, and in a few moments was heard along the line a ceaseless, rolling fire, whose tremendous noise resembled the continued reverberation of thunder. One of these guns, a twenty-four pounder, placed upon the breastwork in the third embrasure from the river, drew, from the fatal skill and activity with which it was managed, even in the heat of battle, the admiration of both Americans and British; and became one of the points most dreaded by the advancing foe.

Here was stationed Lafitte and his lieutenant Dominique and a large band of his men, who during the continuance of the battle, fought with unparalleled bravery. The British already had been twice driven back in the utmost confusion, with the loss of their Commander-in-chief, and two general officers.

Two other batteries were manned by the Barratarians, who served their pieces with the steadiness and precision of veteran gunners. In the first attack of the enemy, a column pushed forward between the levee and river; and so precipitate was their charge that the outposts were forced to retire, closely pressed by the enemy. Before the batteries could meet the charge, clearing the ditch, they gained the redoubt through the embrasures, leaping over the parapet, and overhelming by their superior force the small party stationed there.

Lafitte, who was commanding in conjunction with his officers, at one of the guns, no sooner saw the bold movement of the enemy, than calling a few of his best men by his side, he sprung forward to the point of danger, and clearing the breastwork of the entrenchments, leaped, cutlass in hand, into the midst of the enemy, followed by a score of his men, who in many a hard fought battle upon his own deck, had been well tried.

Astonished at the intrepidity which could lead men to leave their entrenchments and meet them hand to hand, and pressed by the suddenness of the charge, which was made with the recklessness, skill and rapidity of practised boarders bounding upon the deck of an enemy's vessel, they began to give way, while one after another, two British officers fell before the cutlass of the pirate, as they were bravely encouraging their men. All the energies of the British were now concentrated to scale the breastwork, which one daring officer had already mounted. While Lafitte and his followers, seconding a gallant band of volunteer riflemen, formed a phalanx which they in vain assayed to penetrate.

The British finding it impossible to take the city and the havock in their ranks being dreadful, made a precipitate retreat, leaving the field covered with their dead and wounded.

General Jackson, in his correspondence with the secretary of war did not fail to notice the conduct of the "Corsairs of Barrataria," who were, as we have already seen, employed in the artillery service. In the course of the campaign they proved, in an unequivocal manner, that they had been misjudged by the enemy, who a short time previous to the invasion of Louisiana, had hoped to enlist them in his cause. Many of them were killed or wounded in the defence of the country. Their zeal, their courage, and their skill, were remarked by the whole army, who could no longer consider such brave men as criminals. In a few days peace was declared between Great Britian and the United States.

The piratical establishment of Barrataria having been broken up and Lafitte not being content with leading an honest, peaceful life, procured some fast sailing vessels, and with a great number of his followers, proceeded to Galvezton Bay, in Texas, during the year 1819; where he received a commission from General Long; and had five vessels generally cruising and about 300 men. Two open boats bearing commissions from General Humbert, of Galvezton, having robbed a plantation on the Marmento river, of negroes, money, &c., were captured in the Sabine river, by the boats of the United States schooner Lynx. One of the men was hung by Lafitte, who dreaded the vengeance of the American government. The Lynx also captured one of his schooners, and her prize that had been for a length of time smuggling in the Carmento. One of his cruisers, named the Jupiter, returned safe to Galvezton after a short cruise with a valuable cargo, principally specie; she was the first vessel that sailed under the authority of Texas. The American government well knowing that where Lafitte was, piracy and smuggling would be the order of the day, sent a vessel of war to cruise in the Gulf of Mexico, and scour the coasts of Texas. Lafitte having been appointed governor of Galvezton and one of the cruisers being stationed off the port to watch his motions, it so annoyed him that he wrote the following letter to her commander, Lieutenant Madison.

To the commandant of the American cruiser, off the port of Galvezton.

Sir—I am convinced that you are a cruiser of the navy, ordered by your government. I have therefore deemed it proper to inquire into the cause of your living before this port without communicating your intention. I shall by this message inform you, that the port of Galvezton belongs to and is in the possession of the republic of Texas, and was made a port of entry the 9th October last. And whereas the supreme congress of said republic have thought proper to appoint me as governor of this place, in consequence of which, if you have any demands on said government, or persons belonging to or residing in the same, you will please to send an officer with such demands, whom you may be assured will be treated with the greatest politeness, and receive every satisfaction required. But if you are ordered, or should attempt to enter this port in a hostile manner, my oath and duty to the government compels me to rebut your intentions at the expense of my life.

To prove to you my intentions towards the welfare and harmony of your government I send enclosed the declaration of several prisoners, who were taken in custody yesterday, and by a court of inquiry appointed for that purpose, were found guilty of robbing the inhabitants of the United States of a number of slaves and specie. The gentlemen bearing this message will give you any reasonable information relating to this place, that may be required.

Yours, &c.
J. LAFITTE.

About this time one Mitchell, who had formerly belonged to Lafitte's gang, collected upwards of one hundred and fifty desperadoes and fortified himself on an island near Barrataria, with several pieces of cannon; and swore that he and all his comrades would perish within their trenches before they would surrender to any man. Four of this gang having gone to New Orleans on a frolic, information was given to the city watch, and the house surrounded, when the whole four with cocked pistols in both hands sallied out and marched through the crowd which made way for them and no person dared to make an attempt to arrest them.

The United States cutter, Alabama, on her way to the station off the mouth of the Mississippi, captured a piratical schooner belonging to Lafitte; she carried two guns and twenty-five men, and was fitted out at New Orleans, and commanded by one of Lafitte's lieutenants, named Le Fage; the schooner had a prize in company and being hailed by the cutter, poured into her a volley of musketry; the cutter then opened upon the privateer and a smart action ensued which terminated in favor of the cutter, which had four men wounded and two of them dangerously; but the pirate had six men killed; both vessels were captured and brought into the Bayou St. John. An expedition was now sent to dislodge Mitchell and his comrades from the island he had taken possession of; after coming to anchor, a summons was sent for him to surrender, which was answered by a brisk cannonade from his breastwork. The vessels were warped close in shore; and the boats manned and sent on shore whilst the vessels opened upon the pirates; the boat's crews landed under a galling fire of grape shot and formed in the most undaunted manner; and although a severe loss was sustained they entered the breastwork at the point of the bayonet; after a desperate fight the pirates gave way, many were taken prisoners but Mitchell and the greatest part escaped to the cypress swamps where it was impossible to arrest them.

A large quantity of dry goods and specie together with other booty was taken. Twenty of the pirates were taken and brought to New Orleans, and tried before Judge Hall, of the Circuit Court of the United States, sixteen were brought in guilty; and after the Judge had finished pronouncing sentence of death upon the hardened wretches, several of them cried out in open court, *Murder—by God.*

Accounts of these transactions having reached Lafitte, he plainly perceived there was a determination to sweep all his cruisers from the sea; and a war of extermination appeared to be waged against him.

In a fit of desperation he procured a large and fast sailing brigantine mounting sixteen guns and having selected a crew of one hundred and sixty men he started without any commission as a regular pirate determined to rob all nations and neither to give or receive quarter. A British sloop of war which was cruising in the Gulf of Mexico, having heard that Lafitte himself was at sea, kept a sharp look out from the mast head; when one morning as an officer was sweeping the horizon with his glass he discovered a long dark looking vessel, low in the water, but having very tall masts, with sails white as the driven snow. As the sloop of war had the weather gage of the pirate and could outsail her before the wind, she set her studding sails and crowded every inch of canvass in chase; as soon as Lafitte ascertained the character of his opponent, he ordered the awnings to be furled and set his big square-sail and shot rapidly through the water; but as the breeze freshened the sloop of war came up rapidly with the pirate, who, finding no chance of escaping, determined to sell his life as dearly as possible; the guns were cast loose and the shot handed up; and a fire opened upon the ship which killed a number of men and carried away her fore-topmast, but she reserved her fire until within cable's distance of the pirate; when she fired a general discharge from her broadside, and a volley of small arms; the broadside was too much elevated to hit the low hull of the brigantine, but was not without effect; the foretopmast fell, the jaws of the main gaff were severed and a large proportion of the rigging came rattling down on deck; ten of the pirates were killed, but Lafitte remained unhurt. The sloop of war entered her men over the starboard bow and a terriffic contest with pistols and cutlasses ensued; Lafitte received two wounds at this time which disabled him, a grape shot broke the bone of his right leg and he received a cut in the abdomen, but his crew fought like tigers and the deck was ankle deep with blood and gore; the captain of the boarders received such a tremendous blow on the head from the butt end of a musket, as stretched him senseless on the deck near Lafitte, who raised his dagger to stab him to the heart. But the tide of his existence was ebbing like a torrent, his brain was giddy, his aim faltered and the point descended in the Captain's right thigh; dragging away the blade with the last convulsive energy of a death struggle, he lacerated the wound. Again the reeking steel was upheld, and Lafitte placed his left hand near the Captain's heart, to make his aim more sure; again the dizziness of dissolution spread over his sight, down came the dagger into the captain's left thigh and Lafitte was a corpse.

The upper deck was cleared, and the boarders rushed below on the main deck to complete their conquest. Here the slaughter was dreadful, till the pirates called out for quarter, and the carnage ceased; all the pirates that surrendered were taken to Jamaica and tried before the Admiralty court where sixteen were condemned to die, six were subsequently pardoned and ten executed.

Thus perished Lafitte, a man superior in talent, in knowledge of his profession, in courage, and moreover in physical strength; but unfortunately his reckless career was marked with crimes of the darkest dye.

Barbarossa—King of the Corsairs

E. HAMILTON CURREY, RN

At the coming of spring Barbarossa was at sea again with thirty-two ships ready for any eventuality, his crews aflame with ardor for revenge against those by whom they had been so roughly handled. He chose for the scene of operations a place on the coast of Majorca some fifteen miles from Palma; from here he commanded the route of the Spaniards from their country to the African coast, and it was against this nation that he felt a great bitterness owing to recent events. Eagerly did the corsair and his men watch for the Spanish ships, the heavier vessels lying at anchor, but the light, swift galleys ranging and questing afar so that none might be missed. Very soon the vigilance of the Moslems was rewarded by the capture of a number of vessels, sent by Bernard de Mendoza laden with Turkish and Moorish slaves, destined to be utilized as rowers in the Spanish galleys. These men were hailed as a welcome reinforcement, and joyfully joined the forces of Kheyr-ed-Din when he moved on Minorca, captured the castle by a surprise assault, raided the surrounding country, and captured five thousand seven hundred Christians, amongst whom were eight hundred men who had been wounded in the attack on Tunis—all these unfortunates were sent to refill the bagnio of Algiers.

This private war of revenge was, however, destined soon to come to an end, as Soliman the Magnificent in this year became involved in disputes with the Venetian Republic, and recalled "that veritable man of the sea," as Barbarossa had been described by Ibrahim, to Constantinople.

In this city by the sea there had taken place a tragedy which, although it only involved the death of a single man, was nevertheless far-reaching in its consequences; for the man was none other than that great statesman Ibrahim, Grand Vizier, and the only trusted counsellor of the Padishah. He who had been originally a slave had risen step by step in the favor of his master until he arrived at the-giddy eminence which he occupied at the time of his death. It is a somewhat curious commentary on the essentially democratic status of an autocracy that a man could thus rise to a position second only to that of the autocrat himself; and, in all probability, wielding quite as much power.

Ibrahim had for years been treated by Soliman more as a brother than as a dependent, which, in spite of his Grand Viziership, he was in fact. They lived in the very closest communion, taking their meals together, and even sleeping in the same room, Soliman, a man of high intelligence himself, and a ruler who kept in touch with all the happenings which arose in his immense dominions, desiring always to have at hand the man whom he loved; from whom, with his amazing grip of political problems and endless fertility of resource, he was certain of sympathy and sound advice. But in an oriental despotism there are other forces at work besides those of *la haute politique*, and Ibrahim had one deadly enemy who was sworn to compass his destruction. The Sultana Roxalana was the light of the harem of the Grand Turk. This supremely beautiful woman, originally a Russian slave, was the object of the most passionate devotion on the part of Soliman; but she was as ambitious as she was lovely, and brooked no rival in the affections of Soliman, be that person man, woman, or child. In her hands the master of millions, the despot whose nod was death, became a submissive slave; the undisciplined passions of this headstrong woman swept aside from her path all those whom she suspected of sharing her influence, in no matter how remote a fashion. At her dictation had Soliman caused to be murdered his son Mustafa, a youth of the brightest promise, because, in his intelligence and his winning ways he threatened to eclipse Selim, the son of Roxalana herself.

This woman possessed a strong natural intelligence, albeit she was totally uneducated; she saw and knew that Ibrahim was all-powerful with her lover, and this roused her jealousy to fever-heat. She was not possessed of a cool judgment, which would have told her that Ibrahim was a statesman dealing with the external affairs of the Sublime Porte, and that with her and with her affairs he neither desired, nor had he the power, to interfere. What, however, the Sultana did know was that in these same affairs of State her opinion was dust in the balance when weighed against that of the Grand Vizier.

Soliman had that true attribute of supreme greatness, the unerring aptitude for the choice of the right man. He had picked out Ibrahim from among his immense entourage, and never once had he regretted his choice. As time went on and the intellect and power of the man became more and more revealed to his master, that sovereign left in his hands even such matters as despots are apt to guard most jealously. We have seen how, in spite of the murmurings of the whole of his capital, and the almost insubordinate attitude of his navy, he had persevered in the appointment of Kheyr-ed-Din Barbarossa, because the judgment of Ibrahim was in favor of its being carried out. This, to Roxalana, was gall and wormwood; well she knew that, as long as the Grand Vizier lived, her sovereignty was at best but a divided one. There was a point at which her blandishments stopped short; this was when she found that her opinion did not coincide with that of the minister. She was, as we have seen in the instance of her son, not a woman to stick at trifles, and she decided that Ibrahim must die.

There could be no hole-and-corner business about this; he must die, and when his murder had been accomplished she would boldly avow to her lover what she had done and take the consequences, believing in her power over him to come scatheless out of the adventure. In those days, when human life was so cheap, she might have asked for the death of almost any one, and her whim would have been gratified by a lover who had not hesitated to put to death his own son at her dictation. But with Ibrahim it was another matter; he was the familiar of the Sultan, his *alter ego* in fact. It says much for the nerve of the Sultana that she dared so greatly on this memorable and lamentable occasion.

On March 5th, 1536, Ibrahim went to the royal seraglio, and, following his ancient custom, was admitted to the table of his master, sleeping after the meal at his side. At least so it was supposed, but none knew save those engaged in the murder what passed on that fatal night; the next day his dead body lay in the house of the Sultan.

Across the floor of jasper, in that palace which was a fitting residence for one rightly known as "The Magnificent," the blood of Ibrahim flowed to the feet of Roxalana. The disordered clothing, the terrible expression of the face of the dead man, the gaping wounds which he had received, bore witness that there had taken place a grim struggle before that iron frame and splendid intellect had been leveled with the dust. This much leaked out afterwards, as such things will leak out, and then the Sultana took Soliman into her chamber and gazed up into his eyes. The man was stunned by the immensity of the calamity which had befallen him and his kingdom, but his manhood availed him not against the wiles of this Circe. Ibrahim had been foully done to death in his own palace, and this woman clinging so lovingly round his neck now was the murderess. The heart's blood of his best friend was coagulating on the threshold of his own apartment when he forgave her by whom his murder had been accomplished. This was the vengeance of Roxalana, and who shall say that it was not complete?

The Ottoman Empire was the poorer by the loss of its greatest man, the jealousy of the Sultana was assuaged, the despot who had permitted this un-avenged murder was still on the throne, thrall to the woman who had first murdered his son and then his friend and minister. But the deed carried with it the evil consequences which were only too likely to occur when so capable a head of the State was removed at so critical a time. Renewed strife was in the air, and endless squabbles between Venice and the Porte were taking place. With these we have no concern, but, in addition to other complaints, there were loud and continuous ones concerning the corsairs. Venice, "The Bride of the Sea," had neither rest nor peace; the pirates swarmed in Corfu, in Zante, in Candia, in Cephalonia, and the plunder and murder of the subjects of the Republic was the theme of the perpetual representations to the Sultan. The balance of advantage in this guerilla warfare was with the corsairs until Girolame Canale, a Venetian captain, seized one of the Moslem leaders known as "The Young Moor of Alexandria." The victory of Canale was somewhat an important one as he captured the galley of "The Young Moor" and four others; two more were sunk, and three hundred Janissaries and one thousand slaves fell into the hands of the Venetian commander. There being an absence of nice feeling on the part of the Venetians, the Janissaries were at once beheaded to a man.

The whole story is an illustration of the extraordinary relations existing among the Mediterranean States at this time. Soliman the Magnificent, Sultan of Turkey, had lent three hundred of his Janissaries, his own picked troops, to assist the corsairs in their depredations on Venetian commerce. Having done this, and the Janissaries having been caught and summarily and rightly put to death as pirates, the Sultan, as soon as he heard of what had occurred, sent an ambassador, one Yonis Bey, to Venice to demand satisfaction for the insult passed upon him by the beheading of his own soldiers turned pirates. The conclusion of the affair was that the Venetians released "The Young Moor of Alexandria" as soon as he was cured of the eight wounds which he had received in the conflict, and sent him back to Africa with such of his galleys as were left. There was one rather comical incident in connection with this affair, which was that when Yonis Bey was on his way from Constantinople to Venice he was chased by a Venetian fleet, under the command of the Count Grandenico, and driven ashore. The Count was profuse in his apologies when he discovered that he had been chasing a live ambassador; but the occurrence so exasperated Soliman that he increased his demands in consequence.

Barbarossa, who had spent his time harrying the Spaniards at sea ever since the fall of Tunis, was shortly to appear on the scene again. He received orders from the Sultan, and came as fast as a favoring wind would bring him. Kheyr-ed-Din had been doing well in the matter of slaves and plunder, but he knew that, with the backing of the Grand Turk, he would once again be in command of a fleet in which he might repeat his triumph of past years, and prove himself once more the indispensable "man of the sea."

Soon after his arrival his ambitions were gratified, and he found himself with a fleet of one hundred ships. Since the death of Ibrahim, and the incident which terminated with the dispatch of Yonis Bey to Venice, the relations between the Grand Turk and the Venetian Republic had become steadily worse, and at last the Sultan declared war. On May 17th, 1537, Soliman, accompanied by his two sons, Selim and Mohammed, left Constantinople. With the campaign conducted by the Sultan we are not concerned here; it was directed against the Ionian Islands, which had been in the possession of Venice since 1401. On August 18th Soliman laid siege to Corfu, and was disastrously beaten, re-embarking his men on September 7th, after losing thousands in a fruitless attack on the fortress. He returned to Constantinople utterly discomfited. It was the seventh campaign which the Sultan had conducted in person, but the first in which the ever-faithful Ibrahim had not been by his side.

This defeat at the hands of the Venetians was not, however, the only humiliation which he was destined to experience in this disastrous year; for once again Doria, that scourge of the Moslem, was loose upon the seas, and was making his presence felt in the immediate neighborhood of Corfu, where the Turks had been defeated. On July 17th Andrea had left the port of Messina with twenty-five galleys, had captured ten richly laden Turkish ships, gutted and burned them. Kheyr-ed-Din was at sea at the time, but the great rivals were not destined to meet on this occasion. Instead of Barbarossa, Andrea fell in with Ali-Chabelli, the lieutenant of Sandjak Bey of Gallipoli.

On July 22nd the Genoese admiral and the Turkish commander from the Dardanelles met to the southward of Corfu, off the small island of Paxo, and a smart action ensued. It ended in the defeat of Ali-Chabelli, whose galleys were captured and towed by Doria into Paxo. That veteran fighter was himself in the thickest of the fray, and, conspicuous in his crimson doublet, had been an object of attention to the marksmen of Chabelli during the entire action. In spite of the receipt of a severe wound in the knee, the admiral refused to go below until victory was assured. He was surrounded at this time by a devoted band of nobles sworn to defend the person of their admiral or to die in his defense. His portrait has been sketched for us at this time by the Dominican Friar, Padre Alberto Guglielmotto, author of "La guerra dei Pirati e la marina Pontifica dal 1500 al 1560." The description runs thus: "Andrea Doria was of lofty stature, his face oval in shape, forehead broad and commanding, his neck was powerful, his hair short, his beard long and fan-shaped, his lips were thin, his eyes bright and piercing."

Once again had he defeated an officer of the Grand Turk; and it may be remarked that Ibrahim was probably quite right in the estimation, or rather in the lack of estimation, in which he held the sea-officers of his master, as they seem to have been deficient in every quality save that of personal valor, and in their encounters with Doria and the knights were almost invariably worsted. For the sake of Islam, for the prestige of the Moslem arms at sea, it was time that Barbarossa should take matters in hand once more.

The autumn of this year 1537 proved that the old Sea-wolf had lost none of his cunning, that his followers were as terrible as ever. What did it seem to matter that Venetian and Catalan, Genoese and Frenchman, Andalusian and the dwellers in the Archipelago, were all banded together in league against this common foe? Did not the redoubtable Andrea range the seas in vain, and were not all the efforts of the Knights of Saint John futile, when the son of the renegado from Mitylene and his Christian wife put forth from the Golden Horn? What was the magic of this man, it was asked despairingly, that none seemed able to prevail against him? Had it not been currently reported that Carlos Quinto, the great Emperor, had driven him forth from Tunis a hunted fugitive, broken and penniless, with never a galley left, without one ducat in his pocket? Was he so different, then, from all the rest of mankind that his followers would stick to him in evil report as well as in the height of his prosperity? Men swore and women crossed themselves at the mention of his name.

"Terrible as an army with banners," indeed, was Kheyr-ed-Din in this eventful summer: things had gone badly with the crescent flag, the Padishah was unapproachable in his palace, brooding perchance on that "might have been" had he not sold his honor and the life of his only friend to gratify the malice of a she-devil; those in attendance on the Sultan trembled, for the humor of the despot was black indeed.

But "the veritable man of the sea" was in some sort to console him for that which he had lost; as never in his own history—and there was none else with which it could be compared—had the Corsair King made so fruitful a raid. He ravaged the coasts of the Adriatic and the islands of the Archipelago, sweeping in slaves by the thousand, and by the end of the year he had collected eighteen thousand in the arsenal at Stamboul. Great was the jubilation in Constantinople when the Admiralissimo himself returned from his last expedition against the infidel; stilled were the voices which hinted disaffection—who among them all could bring back four hundred thousand pieces of gold? What mariner could offer to the Grand Turk such varied and magnificent presents?

Upon his arrival Barbarossa asked permission to kiss the threshold of the palace of the Sultan, which boon being graciously accorded to him, he made his triumphal entry. Two hundred captives clad in scarlet robes carried cups of gold and flasks of silver; behind them came thirty others, each staggering under an enormous purse of sequins; yet another two hundred brought collars of precious stones or bales of the choicest goods; and a further two hundred were laden with sacks of small coin. Certainly if Soliman the Magnificent had lost a Grand Vizier he had succeeded in finding an admiral!

All through the earlier months of 1538 the dockyards of Constantinople hummed with a furious activity, for Soliman had decreed that the maritime campaign of this year was to begin with no less than one hundred and fifty ships. His admiral, however, did not agree with this decision; to the Viziers he raged and stormed. "Listen," he said, "O men of the land who understand naught of the happenings of the sea. By this time Saleh-Reis must have quitted Alexandria convoying to the Bosphorus twenty sail filled with the richest merchandise; should he fall in with the accursed Genoese, Doria, where then will be Saleh-Reis and his galleys and his convoy? I will tell you: the ships in Genoa, the galleys burned, Saleh-Reis and all his mariners chained to the rowers' bench."

The Viziers trembled as men did when Barbarossa stormed and turned upon them those terrible eyes which knew neither fear not pity. "We be but men," they answered, "and our lord the Sultan has so ordained it."

"I have forty galleys," replied the corsair; "you have forty more. With these I will take the sea; but, mark you," he continued, softening somewhat, "you do right to fear the displeasure of the Sultan, and I also have no wish to encounter it; but vessels raised and equipped in a hurry will be of small use to me. In the name of Allah the compassionate and his holy Prophet give me my eighty galleys and let me go."

In Kheyr-ed-Din Barbarossa sound strategical instinct went hand in hand with the desperate valor of the corsair. To dally in the Golden Horn while so rich a prey was at sea to be picked up by his Christian foes was altogether opposed to his instincts: never to throw away a chance in the game of life had ever been his guiding principle.

Soliman, great man as he undoubtedly was, had not the adamantine hardness of character which enabled his admiral to risk all on the hazards of the moment; or possibly the Grand Turk was deficient in that clearness of strategical instinct which never in any circumstances foregoes a present advantage for something which may turn out well in a problematical future. Soliman, sore, sullen, and unapproachable, dwelt in his palace brooding over the misfortunes which had been his lot since the death of Ibrahim. Barbarossa, who so recently had lost practically all that he possessed, and who had reached an age at which most men have no hopes for the future, was as clear in intellect, as undaunted in spirit, as if he had been half a century younger: to be even once more with those by whom he had been defeated and dispossessed was the only thing now in his mind. The capture of Saleh-Reis and his convoy would be a triumph of which he could not bear to think. Further, it would add to the demoralization of the sea forces of the Sultan, which were sadly in need of some striking success after the defeats which had so recently been their portion. The Sultan had decided that one hundred and fifty ships were necessary; his admiral thought otherwise. There was too much at stake for him to dally at Constantinople; his fiery energy swept all before it, and in the end he had his way. On June 7th, 1538, he finally triumphed over the hesitations of the Viziers and put to sea with eighty sail.

The Sultan, from his kiosk, the windows of which opened on the Bosphorus, counted the ships.

"Only eighty sail; is that all?" he asked.

The trembling Viziers prostrated themselves before him.

"O our Lord, the Padishah," they cried, "Saleh-Reis comes from Alexandria with a rich convoy; somewhere lurking is Andrea Doria, the accursed; it was necessary, O Magnificent, to send succor."

There was a pause, in which the hearts of men beat as do those who know not but that the next moment may be their last on earth.

The Sultan stared from his window at the retreating ships in a silence like the silence of the grave. At last he turned:

"So be it," he answered briefly; "but see to it that reinforcements do not lag upon the road."

If there had been activity in the dockyards before it was as nothing to the strenuous work that was to be done henceforward.

Before starting on this expedition Kheyr-ed-Din had made an innovation in the manning of some of the most powerful of his galleys, which was of the utmost importance, and which was to add enormously to the success of his future maritime enterprises. The custom had always been that the Ottoman galleys had been rowed by Christians, captured and enslaved; of course the converse was true in the galleys of their foes. There were, for the size of the vessels, an enormous number of men carried in the galleys of the sixteenth century, and an average craft of this description would have on board some four hundred men; of these, however, the proportion would be two hundred and fifty slaves to one hundred and fifty fighting men. That which Kheyr-ed-Din now insisted upon was that a certain proportion of his most powerful units should be rowed by Moslem fighting men, so that on the day of battle the oarsmen could join in the fray instead of remaining chained to their benches, as was the custom with the slaves. It is, however, an extraordinary testimony to the influnece which the corsair had attained in Constantinople that he had been able to effect this change in the composition of some of his crews; it must have been done with the active coöperation of the Sultan, as no authority less potent than that of the sovereign himself could have induced free men to undertake the terrible toil of rower in a galley. This was reserved for the unfortunate slave on either side owing to the intolerable hardship of the life, and results, in the pace at which a galley proceeded through the water, were usually obtained by an unsparing use of the lash on the naked bodies of the rowers.

This human material was used up in the most prodigal manner possible, as those in command had not the inducement of treating the rowers well, from that economic standpoint which causes a man to so use his beast of burden as to get the best work from him. In the galley, when a slave would row no more he was flung overboard and another was put in his place.

The admiral, however, even when backed by the Padishah, could not man a large fleet of galleys with Moslem rowers, and, as there was a shortage in the matter of propelling power, his first business was to collect slaves, and for this purpose he visited the islands of the Archipelago. The lot of the unhappy inhabitants of these was indeed a hard one. They were nearer to the seat of the Moslem power than any other Christians; they were in those days totally unable to resist an attack in force, and in consequence were swept off in their thousands.

Seven islands cover the entrance to the Gulf of Volo. The nearest to the coast is Skiathos, which is also the most important; it was defended by a castle built upon a rock. This castle was attacked by Barbarossa, who bombarded it for six days, carried it by assault, and massacred the garrison. He spared the lives of the inhabitants of the island, and by this means secured three thousand four hundred rowers for his galleys. He had to provide motor-power for the reinforcements which he expected. In July he was reinforced from Constantinople by ninety galleys, while from Egypt came Saleh-Reis, who had succeeded in avoiding the terrible Doria, with twenty more; the fleet was thus complete.

PART III

Pirate Song and Verse

The Corsair

LORD BYRON

The First Canto

"————nessun maggior dolore,
Che ricordarsi del tempo felice
Nelle miseria,"

DANTE

I

"O'er the glad waters of the dark blue sea,
Our thoughts as boundless, and our souls as free
Far as the breeze can bear, the billows foam,
Survey our empire, and behold our home!
These are our realms, no limits to their sway –
Our flag the sceptre all who meet obey.
Ours the wild life in tumult still to range
From toil to rest, and joy in every change.
Oh, who can tell? not thou, luxurious slave!
Whose soul would sicken o'er the heaving wave;
Not thou, vain lord of wantonness and ease!
Whom slumber soothes not – pleasure cannot please –
Oh, who can tell, save he whose heart hath tried,
And danced in triumph o'er the waters wide,
The exulting sense – the pulse's maddening play,
That thrills the wanderer of that trackless way?
That for itself can woo the approaching fight,
And turn what some deem danger to delight;
That seeks what cravens shun with more than zeal,
And where the feebler faint can only feel –
Feel – to the rising bosom's inmost core,
Its hope awaken and its spirit soar?
No dread of death if with us die our foes –
Save that it seems even duller than repose:
Come when it will – we snatch the life of life –
When lost – what recks it but disease or strife?
Let him who crawls enamour'd of decay,
Cling to his couch, and sicken years away:
Heave his thick breath, and shake his palsied head;
Ours – the fresh turf; and not the feverish bed.
While gasp by gasp he falters forth his soul,
Ours with one pang – one bound – escapes control.
His corse may boast its urn and narrow cave,

And they who loath'd his life may gild his grave:
Ours are the tears, though few, sincerely shed,
When Ocean shrouds and sepulchres our dead.
For us, even banquets fond regret supply
In the red cup that crowns our memory;
And the brief epitaph in danger's day,
When those who win at length divide the prey,
And cry, Remembrance saddening o'er each brow,
How had the brave who fell exulted now!"

II

Such were the notes that from the Pirate's isle
Around the kindling watch-fire rang the while:
Such were the sounds that thrill'd the rocks along,
And unto ears as rugged seem'd a song!
In scatter'd groups upon the golden sand,
They game – carouse – converse – or whet the brand:
Select the arms – to each his blade assign,
And careless eye the blood that dims its shine.
Repair the boat, replace the helm or oar,
While others straggling muse along the shore:
For the wild bird the busy springes set,
Or spread beneath the sun the dripping net:
Gaze where some distant sail a speck supplies
With all the thirsting eve of Enterprise:
Tell o'er the tales of many a night of toil,
And marvel where they next shall seize a spoil:
No matter where – their chief's allotment this;
Theirs, to believe no prey nor plan amiss.
But who that CHIEF? his name on every shore
Is famed and fear'd – they ask and know no more.
With these he mingles not but to command;
Few are his words, but keen his eye and hand.
Ne'er seasons he with mirth their jovial mess

But they forgive his silence for success.
Ne'er for his lip the purpling cup they fill,
That goblet passes him untasted still –
And for his fare – the rudest of his crew
Would that, in turn, have pass'd untasted too;
Earth's coarsest bread, the garden's homeliest roots,
And scarce the summer luxury of fruits,
His short repast in humbleness supply
With all a hermit's board would scarce deny.
But while he shuns the grosser joys of sense,
His mind seems nourish'd by that abstinence.
"Steer to that shore!" – they sail. "Do this!" – 'tis done:
"Now form and follow me!" – the spoil is won.
Thus prompt his accents and his actions still,
And all obey and few inquire his will;
So to such, brief answer and contemptuous eye
Convey reproof, nor further deign reply.

III

"A sail! – sail!" – a promised prize to Hope!
Her nation – flag – how speaks the telescope?
No prize, alas! but yet a welcome sail:
The blood-red signal glitters in the gale.
Yes – she is ours – a home-returning bark –
Blow fair thou breeze! – she anchors ere the dark.
Already doubled is the cape – our bay
Receives that prow which proudly spurns the spray.
How gloriously her gallant course she goes!
Her white wings flying – never from her foes –
She walks the waters like a thing of life,
And seems to dare the elements to strife.
Who would not brave the battle-fire, the wreck,
To move the monarch of her peopled deck?

IV

Hoarse o'er her side the rustling cable rings;
The sails are furl'd; and anchoring round she swings;
And gathering loiterers on the land discern
Her boat descending from the latticed stem.
'Tis mann'd – the oars keep concert to the strand,
Till grates her keel upon the shallow sand.
Hail to the welcome shout! – the friendly speech!
When hand grasps hand uniting on the beach;
The smile, the question, and the quick reply,
And the heart's promise of festivity!

V

The tidings spread, and gathering grows the crowd;
The hum of voices, and the laughter loud,
And woman's gentler anxious tone is heard –
Friends', husbands', lovers' names in each dear word:
"Oh! are they safe? we ask not of success –
But shall we see them? Will their accents bless?
From where the battle roars, the billows chafe
They doubtless boldly did – but who are safe?
Here let them haste to gladden and surprise,
And kiss the doubt from these delighted eyes!"

VI

"Where is our chief? for him we bear report –
And doubt that joy – which hails our coming short;
Yet thus sincere, 'tis cheering, though so brief;
But, Juan! instant guide us to our chief:
Our greeting paid, we'll feast on our return,
And all shall hear what each may wish to learn."
Ascending slowly by the rock-hewn way,
To where his watch-tower beetles o'er the bay,

By bushy brake, and wild flowers blossoming,
And freshness breathing from each silver spring,
Whose scatter'd streams from granite basins burst,
Leap into life, and sparkling woo your thirst;
From crag to cliff they mount – near yonder cave,
What lonely straggler looks along the wave?
In pensive posture leaning on the brand,
Not oft a resting-staff to that red hand?
" 'Tis he 'tis Conrad – here, as wont, alone;
On – Juan! – on – and make our purpose known.
The bark he views – and tell him we would greet
His ear with tidings he must quickly meet:
We dare not yet approach – thou know'st his mood
When strange or uninvited steps intrude."

VII

Him Juan sought, and told of their intent; –
He spake not, but a sign express'd assent.
These Juan calls – they come – to their salute
He bends him slightly, but his lips are mute.
"These letters, Chief, are from the Greek – the spy,
Who still proclaims our spoil or peril nigh:
Whate'er his tidings, we can well report,
Much that" – "Peace, peace!" – he cuts their prating short.
Wondering they turn, abash'd, while each to each
Conjecture whispers in his muttering speech:
They watch his glance with many a stealing look
To gather how that eye the tidings took;
But, this as if he guess'd, with head aside,
Perchance from some emotion, doubt, or pride,
He read the scroll – "My tablets, Juan, hark –
Where is Gonsalvo?"
"In the anchor'd bark"
"There let him stay – to him this order bear –

Back to your duty – for my course prepare:
Myself this enterprise to-night will share."
"To-night, Lord Conrad!"
"Ay! at set of sun:
The breeze will freshen when the day is done.
My corslet, cloak – one hour and we are gone.
Sling on thy bugle – see that free from rust
My carbine-lock springs worthy of my trust.
Be the edge sharpen'd of my boarding-brand,
And give its guard more room to fit my hand.
This let the armourer with speed dispose
Last time, it more fatigued my arm than foes:
Mark that the signal-gun be duly fired,
To tell us when the hour of stay's expired."

VIII

They make obeisance, and retire in haste,
Too soon to seek again the watery waste:
Yet they repine not – so that Conrad guides;
And who dare question aught that he decides?
That man of loneliness and mystery
Scarce seen to smile, and seldom heard to sigh;
Whose name appals the fiercest of his crew,
And tints each swarthy cheek with sallower hue;
Still sways their souls with that commanding art
That dazzles, leads, yet chills the vulgar heart.
What is that spell, that thus his lawless train
Confess and envy, yet oppose in vain?
What should it be, that thus their faith can bind?
The power of Thought – the magic of the Mind!
Link'd with success, assumed and kept with skill,
That moulds another's weakness to its will;
Wields with their hands, but, still to these unknown,
Makes even their mightiest deeds appear his own

Such hath it been shall be – beneath the sun
The many still must labour for the one!
'Tis Nature's doom – but let the wretch who toils
Accuse not, hate not him who wears the spoils.
Oh! if he knew the weight of splendid chains,
How light the balance of his humbler pains!

IX

Unlike the heroes of each ancient race,
Demons in act, but Gods at least in face,
In Conrad's form seems little to admire,
Though his dark eyebrow shades a glance of fire:
Robust but not Herculean – to the sight
No giant frame sets forth his common height;
Yet, in the whole, who paused to look again,
Saw more than marks the crowd of vulgar men;
They gaze and marvel how – and still confess
That thus it is, but why they cannot guess.
Sun-burnt his cheek, his forehead high and pale
The sable curls in wild profusion veil;
And oft perforce his rising lip reveals
The haughtier thought it curbs, but scarce conceals
Though smooth his voice, and calm his general mien
Still seems there something he would not have seen
His features' deepening lines and varying hue
At times attracted, yet perplex'd the view,
As if within that murkiness of mind
Work'd feelings fearful, and yet undefined
Such might it be – that none could truly tell –
Too close inquiry his stern glance would quell.
There breathe but few whose aspect might defy
The full encounter of his searching eye;
He had the skill, when Cunning's gaze would seek

To probe his heart and watch his changing cheek
At once the observer's purpose to espy,
And on himself roll back his scrutiny,
Lest he to Conrad rather should betray
Some secret thought, than drag that chief's to day.
There was a laughing Devil in his sneer,
That raised emotions both of rage and fear;
And where his frown of hatred darkly fell,
Hope withering fled, and Mercy sigh'd farewell!

X

Slight are the outward signs of evil thought,
Within – within – 'twas there the spirit wrought!
Love shows all changes – Hate, Ambition, Guile,
Betray no further than the bitter smile;
The lip's least curl, the lightest paleness thrown
Along the govern'd aspect, speak alone
Of deeper passions; and to judge their mien,
He, who would see, must be himself unseen.
Then – with the hurried tread, the upward eye,
The clenched hand, the pause of agony,
That listens, starting, lest the step too near
Approach intrusive on that mood of fear;
Then – with each feature working from the heart,
With feelings, loosed to strengthen – not depart,
That rise, convulse, contend – that freeze, or glow
Flush in the cheek, or damp upon the brow;
Then, Stranger! if thou canst, and tremblest not
Behold his soul – the rest that soothes his lot!
Mark how that lone and blighted bosom sears
The scathing thought of execrated years!
Behold – but who hath seen, or e'er shall see,
Man as himself – the secret spirit free?

XI

Yet was not Conrad thus by Nature sent
To lead the guilty – guilt's worse instrument –
His soul was changed, before his deeds had driven
Him forth to war with man and forfeit heaven
Warp'd by the world in Disappointment's school,
In words too wise, in conduct there a fool;
Too firm to yield, and far too proud to stoop,
Doom'd by his very virtues for a dupe,
He cursed those virtues as the cause of ill,
And not the traitors who betray'd him still;
Nor deem'd that gifts bestow'd on better men
Had left him joy, and means to give again
Fear'd, shunn'd, belied, ere youth had lost her force,
He hated man too much to feel remorse,
And thought the voice of wrath a sacred call,
To pay the injuries of some on all.
He knew himself a villain – but he deem'd
The rest no better than the thing he seem'd
And scorn'd the best as hypocrites who hid
Those deeds the bolder spirit plainly did.
He knew himself detested, but he knew
The hearts that loath'd him, crouch'd and dreaded too.
Lone, wild, and strange, he stood alike exempt
From all affection and from all contempt;
His name could sadden, and his acts surprise;
But they that fear'd him dared not to despise;
Man spurns the worm, but pauses ere he wake
The slumbering venom of the folded snake:
The first may turn, but not avenge the blow;
The last expires, but leaves no living foe;
Fast to the doom'd offender's form it clings,
And he may crush – not conquer – still it stings!

XII

None are all evil – quickening round his heart
One softer feeling would not yet depart
Oft could he sneer at others as beguiled
By passions worthy of a fool or child;
Yet 'gainst that passion vainly still he strove,
And even in him it asks the name of Love!
Yes, it was love – unchangeable – unchanged,
Felt but for one from whom he never ranged;
Though fairest captives daily met his eye,
He shunn'd, nor sought, but coldly pass'd them by;
Though many a beauty droop'd in prison'd bower,
None ever sooth'd his most unguarded hour.
Yes – it was Love – if thoughts of tenderness
Tried in temptation, strengthen'd by distress
Unmoved by absence, firm in every clime,
And yet – oh more than all! untired by time;
Which nor defeated hope, nor baffled wile,
Could render sullen were she near to smile,
Nor rage could fire, nor sickness fret to vent
On her one murmur of his discontent;
Which still would meet with joy, with calmness part,
Lest that his look of grief should reach her heart;
Which nought removed, nor menaced to remove –
If there be love in mortals – this was love!
He was a villain – ay, reproaches shower
On him – but not the passion, nor its power,
Which only proved, all other virtues gone,
Not guilt itself could quench this loveliest one!

XIII

He paused a moment – till his hastening men
Pass'd the first winding downward to the glen.

"Strange tidings! – many a peril have I pass'd
Nor know I why this next appears the last!
Yet so my heart forebodes, but must not fear
Nor shall my followers find me falter here.
'Tis rash to meet, but surer death to wait
Till here they hunt us to undoubted fate;
And, if my plan but hold, and Fortune smile,
We'll furnish mourners for our funeral pile.
Ay, let them slumber – peaceful be their dreams!
Morn ne'er awoke them with such brilliant beams
As kindle high to – flight (but blow, thou breeze!)
To warm these slow avengers of the sea
Now to Medora – oh! my sinking heart,
Long may her own be lighter than thou art!
Yet was I brave – mean boast where all are brave!
Ev'n insects sting for aught they seek to save.
This common courage which with brutes we share
That owes its deadliest efforts to despair,
Small merit claims – but 'twas my nobler hope
To teach my few with numbers still to cope;
Long have I led them – not to vainly bleed:
No medium now – we perish or succeed;
So let it be – it irks not me to die;
But thus to urge them whence they cannot fly.
My lot hath long had little of my care,
But chafes my pride thus baffled in the snare:
Is this my skill? my craft? to set at last
Hope, power, and life upon a single cast?
Oh, Fate! – accuse thy folly, not thy fate!
She may redeem thee still, not yet too late."

XIV

Thus with himself communion held he, till
He reach'd the summit of his towercrown'd hill:

There at the portal paused – or wild and soft
He heard those accents never heard too oft
Through the high lattice far yet sweet they rung,
And these the notes his bird of beauty sung:

1

"Deep in my soul that tender secret dwells,
    Lonely and lost to light for evermore,
Save when to thine my heart responsive swells,
    Then trembles into silence as before.

2

"There, in its centre a sepulchral lamp
    Burns the slow flame, eternal, but unseen;
Which not the darkness of despair can damp,
    Though vain its ray as it had never been.

3

"Remember me – oh! pass not thou my grave
    Without one thought whose relics there recline
The only pang my bosom dare not brave
    Must be to find forgetfulness in thine.

4

"My fondest, faintest, latest accents hear–
    Grief for the dead not virtue can reprove;
Then give me all I ever ask'd – a tear,
    The first – last – sole reward of so much love! –
He pass'd the portal, cross'd the corridor,

And reach'd the chamber as the strain gave o'er:
"My own Medora! sure thy song is sad–"
"In Conrad's absence wouldst thou have it glad?
Without thine ear to listen to my lay,
Still must my song my thoughts, my soul betray:

Still must each action to my bosom suit,
My heart unhush'd, although my lips were mute!
Oh! many a night on this lone couch reclined,
My dreaming fear with storms hath wing'd the wind,
And deem'd the breath that faintly fann'd thy sail
The murmuring prelude of the ruder gale;
Though soft, it seem'd the low prophetic dirge,
That mourn'd thee floating on the savage surge;
Still would I rise to rouse the beacon fire,
Lest spies less true should let the blaze expire;
And many a restless hour outwatch'd each star,
And morning came – and still thou wert afar.
Oh! how the chill blast on my bosom blew,
And day broke dreary on my troubled view,
And still I gazed and gazed – and not a prow
Was granted to my tears, my truth, my vow!
At length 'twas noon – I hail'd and blest the mast
That met my sight – it near'd – Alas! it pass'd!
Another came – oh God! 'twas thine at last!
Would that those days were over! wilt thou ne'er,
My Conrad! learn the joys of peace to share?
Sure thou hast more than wealth, and many a home
As bright as this invites us not to roam:
Thou know'st it is not peril that I fear,
I only tremble when thou art not here;
Then not for mine, but that far dearer life,
Which flies from love and languishes for strife –
How strange that heart, to me so tender still,
Should war with nature and its better will!"
"Yea, strange indeed – that heart hath long been changed;
Worm-like 'twas trampled, adder-like avenged,
Without one hope on earth beyond thy love,
And scarce a glimpse of mercy from above.
Yet the same feeling which thou dost condemn,

My very love to thee is hate to them,
So closely mingling here, that disentwined,
I cease to love thee when I love mankind:
Yet dread not this – the proof of all the past
Assures the future that my love will last;
But – oh, Medora! nerve thy gentler heart;
This hour again – but not for long – we part."
"This hour we part – my heart foreboded this:
Thus ever fade my fairy dreams of bliss.
This hour – it cannot be – this hour away!
Yon bark hath hardly anchor'd in the bay:
Her consort still is absent, and her crew
Have need of rest before they toil anew:
My love! thou mock'st my weakness; and wouldst steel
My breast before the time when it must feel;
But trifle now no more with my distress,
Such mirth hath less of play than bitterness.
Be silent, Conrad! – dearest! come and share
The feast these hands delighted to prepare;
Light toil! to cull and dress thy frugal fare!
See, I have pluck'd the fruit that promised best,
And where not sure, perplex'd, but pleased, I guess'd
At such as seem'd the fairest; thrice the hill
My steps have wound to try the coolest rill;
Yes! thy sherbet tonight will sweetly flow,
See how it sparkles in its vase of snow!
The grapes' gay juice thy bosom never cheers;
Thou more than Moslem when the cup appears:
Think not I mean to chide – for I rejoice
What others deem a penance is thy choice.
But come, the board is spread; our silver lamp
Is trimm'd, and heeds not the sirocco's damp:
Then shall my handmaids while the time along,
And join with me the dance, or wake the song;

Or my guitar, which still thou lov'st to hear,
Shall soothe or lull – or, should it vex thine ear
We'll turn the tale by Ariosto told,
Of fair Olympia loved and left of old.
Why, thou wert worse than he who broke his vow
To that lost damsel, shouldst thou leave me now;
Or even that traitor chief – I've seen thee smile,
When the dear sky show'd Ariadne's Isle,
Which I have pointed from these cliffs the while:
And thus half sportive, half in fear, I said,
Lest time should rake that doubt to more than dread,
Thus Conrad, too, win quit me for the main;
And he deceived me – for he came again!"
"Again, again – and oft again – my love!
If there be life below, and hope above,
He will return – but now, the moments bring
The time of parting with redoubled wing:
The why, the where – what boots it now to tell?
Since all must end in that wild word – farewell!
Yet would I fain – did time allow disclose –
Fear not – these are no formidable foes
And here shall watch a more than wonted guard,
For sudden siege and long defence prepared:
Nor be thou lonely, though thy lord's away,
Our matrons and thy handmaids with thee stay;
And this thy comfort – that, when next we meet,
Security shall make repose more sweet.
List! – 'tis the bugle!" – Juan shrilly blew –
"One kiss – one more – another – oh! Adieu!"
She rose – she sprung – she clung to his embrace,
Till his heart heaved beneath her hidden face:
He dared not raise to his that deep-blue eye,
Which downcast droop'd in tearless agony.
Her long fair hair lay floating o'er his arms,

In all the wildness of dishevell'd charms;
Scarce beat that bosom where his image dwelt
So full – that feeling seem'd almost Unfelt!
Hark – peals the thunder of the signal-gun
It told 'twas sunset, and he cursed that sun.
Again – again – that form he madly press'd,
Which mutely clasp'd, imploringly caress'd!
And tottering to the couch his bride he bore,
One moment gazed, as if to gaze no more;
Felt that for him earth held but her alone,
Kiss'd her cold forehead – turn'd – is Conrad gone?

XV

"And is he gone?" on sudden solitude
How oft that fearful question will intrude
" 'Twas but an instant past, and here he stood!
And now" – without the portal's porch she rush'd,
And then at length her tears in freedom gush'd;
Big, bright, and fast, unknown to her they fell;
But still her lips refused to send – "Farewell!"
For in that word – that fatal word – how e'er
We promise, hope, believe, there breathes despair.
O'er every feature of that still, pale face,
Had sorrow fix'd what time can ne'er erase:
The tender blue of that large loving eye
Grew frozen with its gaze on vacancy,
Till – oh? how far! – it caught a glimpse of him,
And then it flow'd, and phrensied seem'd to swim
Through those long, dark, and glistening lashes dew'd
With drops of sadness oft to be renew'd.
"He's gone!" – against her heart that hand is driven,
Convulsed and quick – then gently raised to heaven:
She look'd and saw the heaving of the main;
The white sail set she dared not look again;

But turn'd with sickening soul within the gate
"It is no dream – and I am desolate!"

.

XVI

From crag to crag descending, swiftly sped
Stern Conrad down, nor once he turn'd his head;
But shrunk whene'er the windings of his way
Forced on his eye what he would not survey,
His lone but lovely dwelling on the steep,
That hail'd him first when homeward from the deep
And she – the dim and melancholy star,
Whose ray of beauty reach'd him from afar
On her he must not gaze, he must not think,
There he might rest – but on Destruction's brink:
Yet once almost he stopp'd, and nearly gave
His fate to chance, his projects to the wave:
But no – it must not be – a worthy chief
May melt, but not betray to woman's grief.
He sees his bark, he notes how fair the wind,
And sternly gathers all his might of mind:
Again he hurries on – and as he hears
The clang of tumult vibrate on his ears,
The busy sounds, the bustle of the shore,
The shout, the signal, and the dashing oar;
As marks his eye the seaboy on the mast,
The anchors rise, the sails unfurling fast,
The waving kerchiefs of the crowd that urge
That mute adieu to those who stem the surge;
And more than all, his blood-red flag aloft,
He marvell'd how his heart could seem so soft.
Fire in his glance, and wildness in his breast
He feels of all his former self possest;
He bounds – he flies – until his footsteps reach
The verge where ends the cliff, begins the beach,

There checks his speed; but pauses less to breathe
The breezy freshness of the deep beneath,
Than there his wonted statelier step renew;
Nor rush, disturb'd by haste, to vulgar view:
For well had Conrad learn'd to curb the crowd,
By arts that veil and oft preserve the proud;
His was the lofty port, the distant mien,
That seems to shun the sight – and awes if seen:
The solemn aspect, and the high-born eye,
That checks low mirth, but lacks not courtesy;
All these he wielded to command assent:
But where he wish'd to win, so well unbent
That kindness cancell'd fear in those who heard,
And others' gifts show'd mean beside his word,
When echo'd to the heart as from his own
His deep yet tender melody of tone:
But such was foreign to his wonted mood,
He cared not what he soften'd, but subdued:
The evil passions of his youth had made
Him value less who loved – than what obey'd.

XVII

Around him mustering ranged his ready guard,
Before him Juan stands – "Are all prepared?"
"They are – nay more – embark'd: the latest boat
Waits but my Chief –"
                          "My sword, and my capote."
Soon firmly girded on, and lightly slung,
His belt and cloak were o'er his shoulders flung:
"Call Pedro here!" He comes – and Conrad bends,
With all the courtesy he deign'd his friends;
"Receive these tablets, and peruse with care,
Words of high trust and truth are graven there;
Double the guard, and when Anselmo's bark

Arrives, let him alike these orders mark:
In three days (serve the breeze) the sun shall shine
On our return – till then all peace be thine!"
This said, his brother Pirate's hand he wrung,
Then to his boat with haughty gesture sprung.
Flash'd the dipt oars, and sparkling with the stroke,
Around the waves' phosphoric brightness broke;
They gain the vessel – on the deck he stands, –
Shrieks the shrill whistle, ply the busy hands –
He marks how well the ship her helm obeys,
How gallant all her crew, and deigns to praise.
His eyes of pride to young Gonsalvo turn –
Why doth he start, and inly seem to mourn?
Alas! those eyes beheld his rocky tower
And live a moment o'er the parting hour;
She – his Medora – did she mark the prow?
Ah! never loved he half so much as now!
But much must yet be done ere dawn of day –
Again he mans himself and turns away;
Down to the cabin with Gonsalvo bends,
And there unfolds his plan, his means, and ends;
Before them burns the lamp, and spreads the chart,
And all that speaks and aids the naval art;
They to the midnight watch protract debate;
To anxious eyes what hour is ever late?
Meantime, the steady breeze serenely blew,
And fast and falcon-like the vessel flew;
Pass'd the high headlands of each clustering isle,
To gain their port – long – long ere morning smile:
And soon the night-glass through the narrow bay
Discovers where the Pacha's galleys lay.
Count they each sail, and mark how there supine
The lights in vain o'er heedless Moslem shine.
Secure, unnoted, Conrad's prow pass'd by,

And anchor'd where his ambush meant to lie;
Screen'd from espial by the jutting cape,
That rears on high its rude fantastic shape.
Then rose his band to duty – not from sleep –
Equipp'd for deeds alike on land or deep;
While lean'd their leader o'er the fretting flood,
And calmly talk'd –and yet he talk'd of blood!

The Second Canto

"Conoscestci dubiosi desiri?" – Dante

I

In Coron's bay floats many a galley light,
Through Coron's lattices the lamps are bright
For Seyd, the Pacha, makes a feast to-night:
A feast for promised triumph yet to come,
When he shall drag the fetter'd Rovers home;
This hath he sworn by Allah and his sword,
And faithful to his firman and his word,
His summon'd prows collect along the coast,
And great the gathering crews, and loud the boast;
Already shared the captives and the prize,
Though far the distant foe they thus despise
'Tis but to sail – no doubt to-morrow's Sun
Will see the Pirates bound, their haven won!
Meantime the watch may slumber, if they will,
Nor only wake to war, but dreaming kill.
Though all, who can, disperse on shore and seek
To flesh their glowing valour on the Greek;
How well such deed becomes the turban'd brave –
To bare the sabre's edge before a slave!
Infest his dwelling – but forbear to slay,
Their arms are strong, yet merciful to-day,

And do not deign to smite because they may!
Unless some gay caprice suggests the blow,
To keep in practice for the coming foe.
Revel and rout the evening hours beguile,
And they who wish to wear a head must smile
For Moslem mouths produce their choicest cheer,
And hoard their curses, till the coast is clear.

II

High in his hall reclines the turban'd Seyd;
Around – the bearded chiefs he came to lead,
Removed the banquet, and the last pilaff –
Forbidden draughts, 'tis said, he dared to quaff,
Though to the rest the sober berry's juice
The slaves bear round for rigid Moslems' use;
The long chibouque's dissolving cloud supply,
While dance the Almas to wild minstrelsy.
The rising morn will view the chiefs embark;
But waves are somewhat treacherous in the dark:
And revellers may more securely sleep
On silken couch than o'er the rugged deep:
Feast there who can – nor combat till they must,
And less to conquest than to Korans trust:
And yet the numbers crowded in his host
Might warrant more than even the Pacha's boast.

III

With cautious reverence from the outer gate
Slow stalks the slave, whose office there to wait,
Bows his bent head, his hand salutes the floor,
Ere yet his tongue the trusted tidings bore:
"A captive Dervise, from the Pirate's nest
Escaped, is here – himself would tell the rest."
He took the sign from Seyd's assenting eye,

And led the holy man in silence nigh.
His arms were folded on his dark-green vest,
His step was feeble, and his look deprest;
Yet worn he seem'd of hardship more than years,
And pale his cheek with penance, not from fears.
Vow'd to his God – his sable locks he wore,
And these his lofty cap rose proudly o'er:
Around his form his loose long robe was thrown
And wrapt a breast bestow'd on heaven alone;
Submissive, yet with self-possession mann'd,
He calmly, met the curious eyes that scann'd;
And question of his coming fain would seek,
Before the Pacha's will allow'd to speak.

IV

"Whence com'st thou, Dervise?'
"From the outlaw's den,
A fugitive –"
"Thy capture where and when?"
"From Scalanova's port to Scio's isle,
The Saick was bound; but Allah did not smile
Upon our course – the Moslem merchant's gains
The Rovers won; our limbs have worn their chains.
I had no death to fear, nor wealth to boast
Beyond the wandering freedom which I lost;
At length a fisher's humble boat by night
Afforded hope, and offer'd chance of flight;
I seized the hour, and find my safety here –
With thee – most mighty Pacha! who can fear?"
"How speed the outlaws? stand they well prepared,
Their plunder'd wealth, and robber's rock, to guard?
Dream they of this our preparation, doom'd
To view with fire their scorpion nest consumed?"
"Pacha! the fetter'd captive's mourning eye,

That weeps for flight, but ill can play the spy;
I only heard the reckless waters roar
Those waves that would not bear me from the shore;
I only mark'd the glorious sun and sky,
Too bright, too blue, or my captivity;
And felt that all which Freedom's bosom cheers
Must break my chain before it dried my tears.
This may'st thou judge, at least, from my escape,
They little deem of aught in peril's shape;
Else vainly had I pray'd or sought the chance
That leads me here – if eyed with vigilance
The careless guard that did not see me fly
May watch as idly when thy power is nigh.
Pacha! my limbs are faint – and nature craves
Food for my hunger, rest from tossing waves:
Permit my absence – peace be with thee! Peace
With all around! – now grant repose – release."
"Stay, Dervise! I have more to question – stay,
I do command thee – sit – dost hear? – obey!
More I must ask, and food the slaves shall bring
Thou shalt not pine where all are banqueting:
The supper done – prepare thee to reply,
Clearly and full – I love not mystery."
'Twere vain to guess what shook the pious man,
Who look'd not lovingly on that Divan;
Nor show'd high relish for the banquet prest,
And less respect for every fellow guest.
'Twas but a moment's peevish hectic pass'd
Along his cheek, and tranquillised as fast:
He sate him down in silence, and his look
Resumed the calmness which before forsook:
This feast was usher'd in, but sumptuous fare
He shunn'd as if some poison mingled there.
For one so long condemn'd to toil and fast,

Methinks he strangely spares the rich re-past.
"What ails thee, Dervise? eat – dost thou suppose
This feast a Christian's? or my friends thy foes?
Why dost thou shun the salt? that sacred pledge,
Which once partaken, blunts the sabre's edge,
Makes ev'n contending tribes in peace unite,
And hated hosts seem brethren to the sight!"
"Salt seasons dainties – and my food is still
The humblest root, my drink the simplest rill;
And my stern vow and order's laws oppose
To break or mingle bread with friends or foes;
It may seem strange – if there be aught to dread,
That peril rests upon my single head;
But for thy sway – nay more – thy Sultan's throne,
I taste nor bread nor banquet – save alone;
Infringed our order's rule, the Prophet's rage
To Mecca's dome might bar my pilgrimage."
"Well – as thou wilt – ascetic as thou art –
One question answer; then in peace depart.
How many? – Ha! it cannot sure be day?
What star – what sun is bursting on the bay?
It shines a lake of fire! – away – away!
Ho! treachery! my guards! my scimitar!
The galleys feed the flames – and I afar!
Accursed Dervise! – these thy tidings – thou
Some villain spy – seize cleave him – slay him now!"
Up rose the Dervise with that burst of light,
Nor less his change of form appall'd the sight:
Up rose that Dervise – not in saintly garb,
But like a warrior bounding on his barb,
Dash'd his high cap, and tore his robe away –
Shone his mail'd breast, and flash'd his sabre's ray!
His close but glittering casque, and sable plume,
More glittering eye, and black brow's sabler gloom,

Glared on the Moslems' eyes some Afrit sprite,
Whose demon death-blow left no hope for fight.
The wild confusion, and the swarthy glow
Of flames on high, and torches from below;
The shriek of terror, and the mingling yell –
For swords began to dash and shouts to swell –
Flung o'er that spot of earth the air of hell!
Distracted, to and fro, the flying slaves
Behold but bloody shore and fiery waves;
Nought heeded they the Pacha's angry cry,
They seize that Dervise! – seize on Zatanai!
He saw their terror – check'd the first dispair
That urged him but to stand and perish there,
Since far too early and too well obey'd,
The flame was kindled ere the signal made;
He saw their terror – from his baldric drew
His bugle – brief the blast – but shrilly blew;
'Tis answered – "Well ye speed, my gallant crew!
Why did I doubt their quickness of career?
And deem design had left me single here?"
Sweeps his long arm – that sabre's whirling sway
Sheds fast atonement for its first delay;
Completes his fury what their fear begun,
And makes the many basely quail to one.
The cloven turbans o'er the chamber spread,
And scarce an arm dare rise to guard its head:
Even Seyd, convulsed, o'erwhelm'd, with rage surprise,
Retreats before him, though he still defies.
No craven he – and yet he dreads the blow,
So much Confusion magnifies his foe!
His blazing galleys still distract his sight,
He tore his beard, and foaming fled the fight;
For now the pirates pass'd the Haram gate,
And burst within – and it were death to wait

Where wild Amazement shrieking – kneeling throws
The sword aside – in vain the blood o'erflows!
The Corsairs pouring, haste to where within
Invited Conrad's bugle, and the din
Of groaning victims, and wild cries for life,
Proclaim'd how well he did the work of strife.
They shout to find him grim and lonely there,
A glutted tiger mangling in his lair!
But short their greeting, shorter his reply
" 'Tis well but Seyd escapes, and he must die –
Much hath been done, but more remains to do –
Their galleys blaze – why not their city too?"

V

Quick at the word they seized him each a torch
And fire the dome from minaret to porch.
A stern delight was fix'd in Conrad's eye,
But sudden sunk – for on his ear the cry
Of women struck, and like a deadly knell
Knock'd at that heart unmoved by battle's yell.
"Oh! burst the Haram – wrong not on your lives
One female form remember – we have wives.
On them such outrage Vengeance will repay;
Man is our foe, and such 'tis ours to slay:
But still we spared – must spare the weaker prey.
Oh! I forgot – but Heaven will not forgive
If at my word the helpless cease to live;
Follow who will – I go – we yet have time
Our souls to lighten of at least a crime."
He climbs the crackling stair, he bursts the door,
Nor feels his feet glow scorching with the floor;
His breath choked gasping with the volumed smoke,
But still from room to room his way he broke.
They search – they find – they save: with lusty arms

Each bears a prize of unregarded charms;
Calm their loud fears; sustain their sinking frames
With all the care defenceless beauty claims
So well could Conrad tame their fiercest mood,
And check the very hands with gore imbrued.
But who is she? whom Conrad's arms convey
From reeking pile and combat's wreck away –
Who but the love of him he dooms to bleed?
The Haram queen – but still the slave of Seyd!

VI

Brief time had Conrad now to greet Gulnare,
Few words to re-assure the trembling fair
For in that pause compassion snatch'd from war,
The foe before retiring, fast and far,
With wonder saw their footsteps unpursued,
First slowlier fled – then rallied – then withstood.
This Seyd perceives, then first perceives how few?
Compared with his, the Corsair's roving crew,
And blushes o'er his error, as he eyes
The ruin wrought by panic and surprise.
Alla il Alla! Vengeance swells the cry –
Shame mounts to rage that must atone or die!
And flame for flame and blood for blood must tell,
The tide of triumph ebbs that flow'd too well –
When wrath returns to renovated strife,
And those who fought for conquest strike for life
Conrad beheld the danger – he beheld
His followers faint by freshening foes repell'd:
"One effort – one – to break the circling host!"
They form – unite – charge – waver – all is lost!
Within a narrower ring compress'd, beset,
Hopeless, not heartless, strive and struggle yet –
Ah! now they fight in firmest file no more,
Hemm'd in, cut off, cleft down, and trampled o'er,

But each strikes singly, silently, and home,
And sinks outwearied rather than o'ercome,
His last faint quittance rendering with his breath,
Till the blade glimmers in the grasp of death!

VII

But first, ere came the rallying host to blows,
And rank to rank, and hand to hand oppose,
Gulnare and all her Haram handmaids freed,
Safe in the dome of one who held their creed,
By Conrad's mandate safely were bestow'd
And dried those tears for life and fame that flow'd:
And when that dark-eyed lady, young Gulnare
Recall'd those thoughts late wandering in despair
Much did she marvel o'er the courtesy
That smooth'd his accents, soften'd in his eye:
'Twas strange – that robber thus with gore bedew'd
Seem'd gentler then than Seyd in fondest mood.
The Pacha woo'd as if he deem'd the slave
Must seem delighted with the heart he gave
The Corsair vow'd protection, soothed affright
As if his homage were a woman's right.
"The wish is wrong – nay, worse for female – vain:
Yet much I long to view that chief again;
If but to thank for, what my fear forget,
The life my loving lord remember'd not!"

VIII

And him she saw, where thickest carnage spread,
But gather'd breathing from the happier dead;
Far from his band, and battling with a host
That deem right dearly won the field he lost,
Fell'd – bleeding – baffled of the death he sought,
And snatch'd to expiate all the ills he wrought;
Preserved to linger and to live in vain,

While Vengeance ponder'd o'er new plans of pain,
And stanch'd the blood she saves to shed again –
But drop for drop, for Seyd's unglutted eye
Would doom him ever dying – ne'er to die!
Can this be he? triumphant late she saw
When his red hand's wild gesture waved a law!
'Tis he indeed – disarm'd but undeprest,
His sole regret the life he still possest;
His wounds too slight, though taken with that will,
Which would have kiss'd the hand that then could kill.
Oh were there none, of all the many given,
To send his soul – he scarcely ask'd to heaven?
Must he alone of all retain his breath,
Who more than all had striven and struck for death?
He deeply felt – what mortal hearts must feel,
When thus reversed on faithless fortune's wheel,
For crimes committed, and the victor's threat
Of lingering tortures to repay the debt –
He deeply, darkly felt; but evil pride
That led to perpetrate, now serves to hide.
Still in his stern and self-collected mien
A conqueror's more than captive's air is seen
Though faint with wasting toil and stiffening wound,
But few that saw – so calmly gazed around:
Though the far shouting of the distant crowd,
Their tremors o'er, rose insolently loud,
The better warriors who beheld him near,
Insulted not the foe who taught them fear;
And the grim guards that to his durance led,
In silence eyed him with a secret dread.

IX

The Leech was sent – but not in mercy – there,
To note how much the life yet left could bear;

He found enough to load with heaviest chain,
And promise feeling for the wrench of pain;
To-morrow – yea – tomorrow's evening gun
Will sinking see impalement's pangs begun
And rising with the wonted blush of morn
Behold how well or ill those pangs are borne.
Of torments this the longest and the worst,
Which adds all other agony to thirst,
That day by day death still forbears to slake,
While famish'd vultures flit around the stake.
"Oh! Water – water!" smiling Hate denies
The victim's prayer, for if he drinks he dies.
This was his doom; – the Leech, the guard were gone,
And left proud Conrad fetter'd and alone.

X

'Twere vain to paint to what his feelings grew –
It even were doubtful if their victim knew.
There is a war, a chaos of the mind,
When all its elements convulsed, combined,
Lie dark and jarring with perturbed force,
And gnashing with impenitent Remorse –
That juggling fiend, who never spake before
But cries "I warn'd thee!" When the deed is o'er.
Vain voice! the spirit burning but unbent
May writhe, rebel – the weak alone repent!
Even in that lonely hour when most it feels,
And, to itself; all, all that self reveals, –
No single passion, and no ruling thought
That leaves the rest, as once, unseen, unsought,
But the wild prospect when the soul reviews,
All rushing through their thousand avenues –
Ambition's dreams expiring, love's regret,
Endanger'd glory, life itself beset:

The joy untasted, the contempt or hate
'Gainst those who fain would triumph in our fate
The hopeless past, the hasting future driven
Too quickly on to guess of hell or heaven;
Deeds, thoughts, and words, perhaps remember'd not
So keenly till that hour, but ne'er forgot;
Things light or lovely in their acted time,
But now to stern reflection each a crime;
The withering sense of evil unreveal'd,
Not cankering less because the more conceal'd –
All, in a word, from which all eyes must start,
That opening sepulchre – the naked heart
Bares with its buried woes, till Pride awake,
To snatch the mirror from the soul – and break
Ay, Pride can veil, and courage brave it all –
All – all – before – beyond – the deadliest fall.
Each hath some fear, and he who least betrays,
The only hypocrite deserving praise:
Not the loud recreant wretch who boasts and flies;
But he who looks on death – and silent dies.
So steel'd by pondering o'er his far career,
He half-way meets him should he menace near!

XI

In the high chamber of his highest tower
Sate Conrad, fetter'd in the Pacha's power.
His palace perish'd in the flame – this fort
Contain'd at once his captive and his court.
Not much could Conrad of his sentence blame,
His foe, if vanquish'd, had but shared the same: –
Alone he sate – in solitude had scann'd
His guilty bosom, but that breast he mann'd:
One thought alone he could not – dared not meet –
"Oh, how these tidings will Medora greet?"

Then – only then – his clanking hands he raised,
And strain'd with rage the chain on which he gazed
But soon he found, or feign'd, or dream'd relief,
And smiled in self-derision of his grief,
"And now come torture when it will – or may,
More need of rest to nerve me for the day!"
This said, with languor to his mat he crept,
And, whatsoe' er his visions, quickly slept
'Twas hardly midnight when that fray begun,
For Conrad's plans matured, at once were done:
And Havoc loathes so much the waste of time,
She scarce had left an uncommitted crime.
One hour beheld him since the tide he stemm'd –
Disguised, discover'd, conquering, ta'en, condemn'd –
A chief on land, an outlaw on the deep
Destroying, saving, prison'd, and asleep!

XII

He slept in calmest seeming, for his breath
Was hush'd so deep – Ah! happy if in death!
He slept – Who o'er his placid slumber bends?
His foes are gone, and here he hath no friends;
Is it some seraph sent to grant him grace?
No, 'tis an earthly form with heavenly face!
Its white arm raised a lamp – yet gently hid,
Lest the ray flash abruptly on the lid
Of that closed eye, which opens but to pain,
And once unclosed – but once may close again
That form, with eye so dark, and cheek so fair,
And auburn waves of gemm'd and braided hair;
With shape of fairy lightness – naked foot,
That shines like snow, and falls on earth as mute –
Through guards and dunnest night how came it there?
Ah! rather ask what will not woman dare?

Whom youth and pity lead like thee, Gulnare!
She could not sleep – and while the Pacha's rest
In muttering dreams yet saw his pirate-guest
She left his side – his signet-ring she bore
Which oft in sport adorn'd her hand before –
And with it, scarcely question'd, won her way
Through drowsy guards that must that sign obey.
Worn out with toil, and tired with changing blows
Their eyes had envied Conrad his repose;
And chill and nodding at the turret door,
They stretch their listeless limbs, and watch no more;
Just raised their heads to hail the signet-ring,
Nor ask or what or who the sign may bring.

XIII

She gazed in wonder, "Can he calmly sleep,
While other eyes his fall or ravage weep?
And mine in restlessness are wandering here –
What sudden spell hath made this man so dear?
True – 'tis to him my life, and more, I owe,
And me and mine he spared from worse than woe:
'Tis late to think – but soft, his slumber breaks –
How heavily he sighs! – he starts – awakes!"
He raised his head, and dazzled with the light,
His eye seem'd dubious if it saw aright:
He moved his hand – the grating of his chain
Too harshly told him that he lived again.
"What is that form? if not a shape of air,
Methinks, my jailor's face shows wondrous fair!"
"Pirate! thou know'st me not – but I am one,
Grateful for deeds thou hast too rarely done;
Look on me – and remember her, thy hand
Snatch'd from the flames, and thy more fearful band.
I come through darkness and I scarce know why –

Yet not to hurt – I would not see thee die."
"If so, kind lady! thine the only eye
That would not here in that gay hope delight:
Theirs is the chance – and let them use their right.
But still I thank their courtesy or thine,
That would confess me at so fair a shrine!"
Strange though it seem – yet with extremest grief
Is link'd a mirth – it doth not bring relief –
That playfulness of Sorrow ne'er beguiles,
And smiles in bitterness – but still it smiles;
And sometimes with the wisest and the best,
Till even the scaffold echoes with their jest!
Yet not the joy to which it seems akin –
It may deceive all hearts, save that within.
Whate'er it was that flash'd on Conrad, now
A laughing wildness half unbent his brow
And these his accents had a sound of mirth,
As if the last he could enjoy on earth;
Yet 'gainst his nature – for through that short life,
Few thoughts had he to spare from gloom and strife.

XIV

"Corsair! thy doom is named – but I have power
To soothe the Pacha in his weaker hour.
Thee would I spare – nay more – would save thee now,
But this – time – hope – nor even thy strength allow;
But all I can, I will: at least, delay
The sentence that remits thee scarce a day.
More now were ruin – even thyself were loth
The vain attempt should bring but doom to both."
"Yes! loth indeed: – my soul is nerved to all,
Or fall'n too low to fear a further fall:
Tempt not thyself with peril – me with hope
Of flight from foes with whom I could not cope:

Unfit to vanquish, shall I meanly fly,
The one of all my band that would not die?
Yet there is one to whom my memory clings,
Till to these eyes her own wild softness springs.
My sole resources in the path I trod
Were these – my bark, my sword, my love, my God!
The last I left in youth! – he leaves me now –
And Man but works his will to lay me low.
I have no thought to mock his throne with prayer
Wrung from the coward crouching of despair;
It is enough – I breathe, and I can bear.
My sword is shaken from the worthless hand
That might have better kept so true a brand;
My bark is sunk or captive – but my love –
For her in sooth my voice would mount above:
Oh! she is all that still to earth can bind –
And this will break a heart so more than kind,
And blight a form – till thine appear'd, Gulnare!
Mine eye ne'er ask'd if others were as fair."
"Thou lov'st another then? – but what to me
Is this – 'tis nothing – nothing e'er can be:
But yet – thou lov'st – and – oh! I envy those
Whose hearts on hearts as faithful can repose,
Who never feel the void – the wandering thought
That sighs o'er vision – such as mine hath wrought."
"Lady – methought thy love was his, for whom
This arm redeem'd thee from a fiery tomb."
"My love stern Seyd's! Oh – No – No – not my love –
Yet much this heart, that strives no more, once strove
To meet his passion but it would not be.
I felt – I feel – love dwells with – with the free.
I am a slave, a favour'd slave at best,
To share his splendour, and seem very blest!
Oft must my soul the question undergo,

Of – 'Dost thou love?' and burn to answer, 'No!'
Oh! hard it is that fondness to sustain,
And struggle not to feel averse in vain;
But harder still the heart's recoil to bear,
And hide from one – perhaps another there.
He takes the hand I give not, nor withhold –
Its pulse nor check'd, nor quicken'd – calmly cold:
And when resign'd, it drops a lifeless weight
From one I never loved enough to hate.
No warmth these lips return by his imprest,
And chill'd remembrance shudders o'er the rest.
Yes – had lever proved that passion's zeal,
The change to hatred were at least to feel:
But still he goes unmourn'd, returns unsought,
And oft when present – absent from my thought.
Or when reflection comes – and come it must –
I fear that henceforth 'twill but bring disgust;
I am his slave – but, in despite of pride,
'Twere worse than bondage to become his bride.
Oh! that this dotage of his breast would cease:
Or seek another and give mine release,
But yesterday – I could have said, to peace!
Yes, if unwonted fondness now I feign,
Remember captive! 'tis to break thy chain;
Repay the life that to thy hand I owe
To give thee back to all endear'd below,
Who share such love as I can never know.
Farewell, morn breaks, and I must now away:
'Twill cost me dear – but dread no death to-day!"

XV

She press'd his fetter'd fingers to her heart,
And bow'd her head, and turn'd her to depart,
And noiseless as a lovely dream is gone.

And was she here? and is he now alone?
What gem hath dropp'd and sparkles o'er his chain?
The tear most sacred, shed for others' pain,
That starts at once – bright – pure – from Pity's mine
Already polish'd by the hand divine!
Oh! too convincing – dangerously dear –
In woman's eye the unanswerable tear
That weapon of her weakness she can wield,
To save, subdue at once her spear and shield:
Avoid it – Virtue ebbs and Wisdom errs,
Too fondly gazing on that grief of hers!
What lost a world, and bade a hero fly?
The timid tear in Cleopatra's eye.
Yet be the soft triumvir's fault forgiven;
By this – how many lose not earth – but heaven!
Consign their souls to man's eternal foe,
And seal their own to spare some wanton's woe!

XVI

'Tis morn, and o'er his alter'd features play
The beams – without the hope of yester-day.
What shall he be ere night? perchance a thing
O'er which the raven flaps her funeral wing
By his closed eye unheeded and unfelt;
While sets that sun, and dews of evening melt,
Chin wet, and misty round each stiffen'd limb,
Refreshing earth – reviving all but him!

The Third Canto

"Come vedi – ancor non m'abbandona" – Dante

I

Slow sinks, more lovely ere his race be run,
Along Morea's hills the setting sun;
Not, as in Northern climes, obscurely bright,
But one unclouded blaze of living light!
O'er the hush'd deep the yellow beam he throws,
Gilds the green wave, that trembles as it glows.
On old Agina's rock and Idra's isle,
The god of gladness sheds his parting smile;
O'er his own regions lingering, loves to shine,
Though there his altars are no more divine.
Descending fast the mountain shadows kiss
Thy glorious gulf; unconquer'd Salamis!
Their azure arches through the long expanse
More deeply purpled meet his mellowing glance,
And tenderest tints, along their summits driven,
Mark his gay course, and own the hues of heaven;
Till, darkly shaded from the land and deep,
Behind his Delphian cliff he sinks to sleep.
On such an eve, his palest beam he cast,
When – Athens! here thy Wisest look'd his last.
How watch'd thy better sons his farewell ray,
That closed their murder'd sage's latest day!
Not yet – not yet – Sol pauses on the hill –
The precious hour of parting lingers still;
But sad his light to agonising eyes,
And dark the mountain's once delightful dyes:
Gloom o'er the lovely land he seem'd to pour,
The land, where Phoebus never frown'd before;
But ere he sank below Cithæron's head,

The cup of woe was quaff'd – the spirit fled
The soul of him who scorn'd to fear or fly –
Who lived and died, as none can live or die!
But lo! from high Hymettus to the plain,
The queen of night asserts her silent reign.
No murky vapour, herald of the storm,
Hides her fair face, nor girds her glowing form:
With cornice glimmering as the moon-beams play,
There the white column greets her grateful ray,
And, bright around with quivering beams beset,
Her emblem sparkles o'er the minaret:
The groves of olive scatter'd dark and wide
Where meek Cephisus pours his scanty tide,
The cypress saddening by the sacred mosque,
The gleaming turret of the gay kiosk,
And, dun and sombre 'mid the holy calm,
Near Theseus' fane yon solitary palm,
All tinged with varied hues arrest the eye –
And dull were his that pass'd them heedless by.
Again the Agean, heard no more afar,
Lulls his chafed breast from elemental war;
Again his waves in milder tints unfold
Their long array of sapphire and of gold,
Mix'd with the shades of many a distant isle,
That frown – where gentler ocean seems to smile.

II

Not now my theme – why turn my thoughts to thee?
Oh! who can look along thy native sea.
Nor dwell upon thy name, whate'er the tale
So much its magic must o'er all prevail?
Who that beheld that Sun upon thee set,
Fair Athens! could thine evening face for get?
Not he – whose heart nor time nor distance frees,
Spell-bound within the clustering Cyclades!

Nor seems this homage foreign to its strain,
His Corsair's isle was once thine own domain –
Would that with freedom it were thine again!

III

The Sun hath sunk – and, darker than the night,
Sinks with its beam upon the beacon height
Medora's heart – the third day's come and gone –
With it he comes not – sends not – faithless one!
The wind was fair though light; and storms were none.
Last eve Anselmo's bark return'd, and yet
His only tidings that they had not met!
Though wild, as now, far different were the tale
Had Conrad waited for that single sail.
The night-breeze freshens – she that day had pass'd
In watching all that Hope proclaim'd a mast;
Sadly she sate on high – Impatience bore
At last her footsteps to the midnight shore,
And there she wander'd, heedless of the spray
That dash'd her garments oft, and warn'd away:
She saw not, felt not this – nor dared depart,
Nor deem'd it cold – her chill was at her heart;
Till grew such certainty from that suspense
His very sight had shock'd from life or sense!
It came at last – a sad and shatter'd boat,
Whose inmates first beheld whom first they sought;
Some bleeding – all most wretched – these the few –
Scarce knew they how escaped – this all they knew.
In silence, darkling, each appear'd to wait
His fellow's mournful guess at Conrad's fate:
Something they would have said; but seem'd to fear
To trust their accents to Medora's ear.
She saw at once, yet sunk not – trembled not –
Beneath that grief, that loneliness of lot;
Within that meek fair form were feelings high,

That deem'd not, till they found, their energy
While yet was Hope they soften'd, flutter'd wept –
All lost – that softness died not – but it slept;
And o'er its slumber rose that Strength which said,
"With nothing left to love, there's nought to dread."
'Tis more than nature's; like the burning night
Delirium gathers from the fever's height.
"Silent you stand – nor would I hear you tell
What – speak not – breathe not – for I know it well –
Yet would I ask – almost my lip denies
The – quick your answer – tell me where he lies."
"Lady! we know not – scarce with life we fled
But here is one denies that he is dead:
He saw him bound: and bleeding – but alive."
She heard no further – 'twas in vain to strive –
So throbb'd each vein – each thought – till then withstood;
Her own dark soul – these words at once subdued:
She totters – falls – and senseless had the wave
Perchance but snatched her from another grave,
But that with hands though rude, yet weeping eyes,
They yield such aid as Pity's haste supplies:
Dash o'er her deathlike cheek the ocean dew,
Raise, fan, sustain – till life returns anew;
Awake her handmaids, with the matrons leave
That fainting form o'er which they gaze and grieve;
Then seek Anselmo's cavern, to report
The tale too tedious – when the triumph short.

IV

In that wild council words wax'd warm and strange
With thoughts of ransom, rescue, and revenge;
All, save repose or flight: still lingering there
Breathed Conrad's spirit; and forbade despair
Whate'er his fate – the breasts he form'd and led

Will save him living, or appease him dead
Woe to his foes! there yet survive a few
Whose deeds are daring, as their hearts are true.

V

Within the Haram's Secret chamber sate
Stern Seyd, still pondering o'er his Captive's fate;
His thoughts on love and hate alternate dwell,
Now with Gulnare, and now in Conrad's cell;
Here at his feet the lovely slave reclined
Surveys his brow – would soothe his gloom of mind;
While many an anxious glance her large dark eye
Sends in its idle search for sympathy,
His only bends in seeming o'er his beads,
But inly views his victim as he bleeds,
"Pacha! the day is time; and on the crest
Sits Triumph – Conrad taken – fall'n the rest!
His doom is fix'd – he dies; and well his fate
Was earn'd – yet much too worthless for thy hate:
Methinks, a short release, for ransom told
With all his treasure, not unwisely sold;
Report speaks largely of his pirate-hoard –
Would that of this my Pacha were the lord!
While baffled, weaken'd by this fatal fray –
Watch'd – follow'd – he were then an easier prey;
But once cut off – the remnant of his band
Embark their wealth, and seek a safer strand."
"Gulnare! – if for each drop of blood a gem
Were offer'd rich as Stamboul's diadem;
If for each hair of his a massy mine
Of virgin ore should supplicating shine;
If all our Arab tales divulge or dream
Of wealth were here – that gold should not redeem!
It had not now redeem'd a single hour,

But that I know him fetter'd, in my power;
And, thirsting for revenge, I ponder still
On pangs that longest rack, and latest kill."
"Nay, Seyd! I seek not to restrain thy rage,
Too justly moved for mercy to assuage;
My thoughts were only to secure for thee
His riches – thus released, he were not free:
Disabled, shorn of half his might and band,
His capture could but wait thy first command."
"His capture could! shall I then resign
One day to him – the wretch already mine?
Release my foe! – at whose remonstrance? – thine!
Fair suitor! – to thy virtuous gratitude,
That thus repays this Giaour's relenting mood,
Which thee and thine alone of all could spare,
No doubt – regardless if the prize were fair,
My thanks and praise alike are due – now hear!
I have a counsel for thy gentler ear:
I do mistrust thee, woman! and each word
Of thine stamps truth on all Suspicion heard.
Borne in his arms through fire from yon Serai –
Say, wert thou lingering there with him to fly?
Thou need'st not answer – thy confession speaks
Already reddening on thy guilty cheeks;
Then, lovely dame, bethink thee! and beware:
'Tis not his: life alone may claim such care!
Another word and – nay – I need no more.
Accursed was the moment when he bore
Thee from the flames, which better far – but no –
I then had mourn'd thee with a lover's woe –
Now 'tis thy lord that warns – deceitful thing!
Know'st thou that I can clip thy wanton wing?
In words alone I am not wont to chafe:
Look to thyself – nor deem thy falsehood safe!"

He rose – and slowly, sternly thence withdrew,
Rage in his eye and threats in his adieu:
Ah! little reck'd that chief of womanhood –
Which frowns ne'er quell'd, nor menaces subdued
And little deem'd he what thy heart, Gulnare!
When soft could feel, and when incensed could dare.
His doubts appear'd to wrong – nor yet she knew
How deep the root from whence compassion grew –
She was a slave – from such may captives claim
A fellow-feeling, differing but in name;
Still half unconscious – heedless of his wrath,
Again she ventured on the dangerous path,
Again his rage repell'd – until arose
That strife of thought, the source of woman's woes!

VI

Meanwhile, long, anxious, weary, still the same
Roll'd day and night: his soul could terror tame –
This fearful interval of doubt and dread,
When every hour might doom him worse than dead,
When every step that echo'd by the gate,
Might entering lead where axe and stake await;
When every voice that grated on his ear
Might be the last that he could ever hear;
Could terror tame – that spirit stern and high
Had proved unwilling as unfit to die;
'Twas worn – perhaps decay'd – yet silent bore
That conflict, deadlier far than all before:
The heat of fight, the hurry of the gale,
Leave scarce one thought inert enough to quail;
But bound and fix'd in fetter'd solitude,
To pine, the prey of every changing mood;
To gaze on thine own heart; and meditate
Irrevocable faults, and coming fate –

Too late the last to shun – the first to mend –
To count the hours that struggle to thine end,
With not a friend to animate, and tell
To other ears that death became thee well;
Around thee foes to forge the ready lie,
And blot life's latest scene with calumny;
Before thee tortures, which the soul can dare,
Yet doubts how well the shrinking flesh may bear
But deeply feels a single cry would shame –
To valour's praise thy last and dearest claim;
The life thou leav'st below, denied above
By kind monopolists of heavenly love;
And more than doubtful paradise – thy heaven
Of earthly hope – thy loved one from thee riven.
Such were the thoughts that outlaw must sustain,
And govern pangs surpassing mortal pain:
And those sustain'd he – boots it well or ill?
Since not to sink beneath, is something still!

VII

The first day pass'd – he saw not her – Gulnare –
The second, third – and still she came not there;
But what her words avouch'd, her charms had done,
Or else he had not seen another sun.
The fourth day roll'd along, and with the night
Came storm and darkness in their mingling might.
Oh! how he listen'd to the rushing deep,
That ne'er till now so broke upon his sleep;
And his wild spirit wilder wishes sent,
Roused by the roar of his own element!
Oft had he ridden on that winged wave,
And loved its roughness for the speed it gave;
And now its dashing echo'd on his ear,
Along known voice – alas! too vainly near!

Loud sung the wind above; and, doubly
Shook o'er his turret cell the thunder-cloud;
And flash'd the lightning by the latticed bar,
To him more genial than the midnight star:
Close to the glimmering grate he dragg'd his chain
And hoped that peril might not prove in vain.
He raised his iron hand to Heaven, and pray'd
One pitying flash to mar the form it made:
His steel and impious prayer attract alike –
The storm roll'd onward, and disdain'd to strike;
Its peal wax'd fainter – eased – he felt alone,
As if some faithless friend had spurn'd his groan!

VIII

The midnight pass'd, and to the massy door
A light step came – it paused – it moved once more;
Slow turns the grating bolt and sullen key:
'Tis as his heart foreboded – that fair she!
Whate'er her sins, to him a guardian saint,
And beauteous still as hermit's hope can paint;
Yet changed since last within that cell she came,
More pale her cheek, more tremulous her frame:
On him she cast her dark and hurried eye,
Which spoke before her accents – "Thou must die!
Yes, thou must die – there is but one resource
The last – the worst – if torture were not worse."
"Lady! I look to none; my lips proclaim
What last proclaim'd they – Conrad still the same:
Why shouldst thou seek an outlaw's life to spare,
And change the sentence I deserve to bear?
Well have I earn'd – nor here alone – the meed
Of Seyd's revenge, by many a lawless deed."
"Why should I seek? Because – Oh! didst thou not
Redeem my life from worse than slavery's lot?

Why should I seek? – hath misery made thee blind
To the fond workings of a woman's mind?
And must I say? – albeit my heart rebel
With all that woman feels, but should not tell –
Because, despite thy crimes, that heart is moved:
It fear'd thee, thank'd thee, pitied, madden'd, loved.
Reply not, tell not now thy tale again,
Thou lov'st another, and I love in vain:
Though fond as mine her bosom, form more fair,
I rush through peril which she would not dare.
If that thy heart to hers were truly dear,
Were I thine own thou wert not lonely here:
An outlaw's spouse and leave her lord to roam!
What hath such gentle dame to do with home?
But speak not now – o'er thine and o'er my head
Hangs the keen sabre by a single thread;
If thou hast courage still, and wouldst be free,
Receive this poniard – rise and follow me!"
"Ay – in my chains! my steps will gently tread,
With these adornments, o'er each slumbering head!
Thou hast forgot – is this a garb for flight?
Or is that instrument more fit for fight?"
"Misdoubting Corsair! I have gain'd the guard,
Ripe for revolt, and greedy for reward.
A single word of mine removes that chain:
Without some aid how here could I remain?
Well, since we met, hath sped my busy time,
If in aught evil, for thy sake the crime:
The crime – 'tis none to punish those of Seyd.
That hated tyrant, Conrad – he must bleed!
I see thee shudder, but my soul is changed –
Wrong'd, spurn'd, reviled, and it shall be avenged –
Accused of what till now my heart disdain'd –
Too faithful, though to bitter bondage chain'd.

Yes, smile! – but he had little cause to sneer,
I was not treacherous then, nor thou too dear:
But he has said it – and the jealous well –
Those tyrants, teasing, tempting to rebel –
Deserve the fate their fretting lips foretell
I never loved – he bought me – somewhat high –
Since with me came a heart he could not buy.
I was a slave unmurmuring; he hath said,
But for his rescue I with thee had fled.
'Twas false thou know'st – but let such augurs rue,
Their words are omens insult renders true.
Nor was thy respite granted to my prayer;
This fleeting grace was only to prepare
New torments for thy life, and my despair.
Mine too he threatens; but his dotage still
Would fain reserve me for his lordly will:
When wearier of these fleeting charms and me,
There yawns the sack, and yonder rolls the sea!
What, am I then a toy for dotard's play,
To wear but till the gilding frets away?
I saw thee – loved thee – owe thee all – would save,
If but to show how grateful is a slave.
But had he not thus menaced fame and life –
(And well he keeps his oaths pronounced in strife) –
I still had saved thee, but the Pacha spared.
Now I am all thine own, for all prepared:
Thou lov'st me not, nor know'st – or but the worst.
Alas! this love – that hatred – are the first –
Oh! couldst thou prove my truth, thou wouldst not start,
Nor fear the fire that lights an Eastern heart;
'Tis now the beacon of thy safety – now
It points within the port a Mainote prow:
But in one chamber, where our path must lead,
There sleeps – he must not wake – the oppressor Seyd!"

"Gulnar – Gulnare – I never felt till now
My abject fortune, wither'd fame so low:
Seyd is mine enemy; had swept my band
From earth with ruthless but with open hand,
And therefore came I, in my bark of war,
To smite the smiter with the scimitar;
Such is my weapon – not the secret knife;
Who spares a woman's seeks not slumber's life.
Thine saved I gladly, Lady – not for this;
Let me not deem that mercy shown amiss.
Now fare thee well – more peace be with thy breast!
Night wears apace, my last of earthly rest!"
"Rest! rest! by sunrise must thy sinews shake,
And thy limbs writhe around the ready stake.
I heard the order – saw – I will not see –
If thou wilt perish, I will fall with thee.
My life, my love, my hatred – all below
Are on this cast – Corsair! 'tis but a blow!
Without it flight were idle – how evade
His sure pursuit? – my wrongs too unrepaid,
My youth disgraced, the long, long wasted years,
One blow shall cancel with our future fears;
But since the dagger suits thee less than brand,
I'll try the firmness of a female hand.
The guards, are gain'd – one moment all were o'er –
Corsair! we meet in safety or no more;
If errs my feeble hand, the morning cloud
Will hover o'er thy scaffold, and my shroud."

IX

She turn'd, and vanish'd ere he could reply,
But his glance follow'd far with eager eye;
And gathering, as he could, the links that bound
His form, to curl their length, and curb their sound,

Since bar and bolt no more his steps preclude,
He, fast as fetter'd limbs allow, pursued.
'Twas dark and winding, and he knew not where
That passage led; nor lamp nor guard was there:
He sees a dusky glimmering – shall he seek
Or shun that ray so indistinct and weak?
Chance guides his steps – a freshness seems to bear
Full on his brow, as if from morning air;
He reach'd an open gallery – on his eye
Gleam'd the last star of night, the clearing sky:
Yet scarcely heeded these – another light
From a lone chamber struck upon his sight.
Towards it he moved; a scarcely closing door
Reveal'd the ray within, but nothing more.
With hasty step a figure outward pass'd,
Then paused, and turn'd – and paused – 'tis she at last!
No poniard in that hand, nor sign of ill –
"Thanks to that softening heart – she could not kill!"
Again he look'd, the wildness of her eye
Starts from the day abrupt and fearfully.
She stopp'd – threw back her dark far-floating hair,
That nearly veil'd her face and bosom fair,
As if she late had bent her leaning head
Above some object of her doubt or dread.
They meet – upon her brow – unknown, forgot –
Her hurrying hand had left – 'twas but a spot
Its hue was all he saw, and scarce withstood –
Oh! slight but certain pledge of crime – 'tis blood!

X

He had seen battle – he had brooded lone
O'er promised pangs to sentenced guilt foreshown;
He had been tempted, chasten'd, and the chain
Yet on his arms might ever there remain:

But ne'er from strife, captivity, remorse –
From all his feelings in their inmost force –
So thrill'd, so shudder'd every creeping vein
As now they froze before that purple stain.
That spot of blood, that light but guilty streak,
Had banish'd all the beauty from her cheek!
Blood he had view'd, could view unmoved – but then
It flow'd in combat, or was shed by men!

XI

" 'Tis done – he nearly waked – but it is done.
Corsair! he perish'd – thou art dearly won.
All words would now be vain – away – away!
Our bark is tossing – 'tis already day.
The few gain'd over, now are wholly mine
And these thy yet surviving band shall join:
Anon my voice shall vindicate my hand,
When once our sail forsakes this hated strand."

XII

She clapp'd her hands, and through the gallery pour,
Equipp'd for flight, her vassals – Greek and Moor;
Silent but quick they stoop, his chains unbind;
Once more his limbs are free as mountain wind!
But on his heavy heart such sadness sate,
As if they there transfer'd that iron weight.
No words are utter'd – at her sign, a door
Reveals the secret passage to the shore:
The city lies behind – they speed, they reach
The glad waves dancing on the yellow beach;
And Conrad following, at her beck, obey'd,
Nor cared he now if rescued or betray'd;
Resistance were as useless as if Seyd
Yet lived to view the doom his ire decreed.

XIII

Embark'd, the sail unfurl'd, the light breeze blew –
How much had Conrad's memory to re-view!
Sunk be in contemplation, till the cape
Where last he anchor'd rear'd its giant shape.
Ah! since that fatal night, though brief the time,
Had swept an age of terror, grief, and crime.
As its far shadow frown'd above the mast,
He veil'd his face, and sorrow'd as he pass'd;
He thought of all – Gonsalvo and his band,
His fleeting triumph and his failing hand;
He thought on her afar, his lonely bride:
He turn'd and saw – Gulnare, the homicide!

XIV

Sbe watch'd his features till she could not bear
Their freezing aspect and averted air;
And that strange fierceness, foreign to her eye,
Fell quench'd in tears, too late to shed or dry.
She knelt beside him and his hand she press'd,
"Thou may'st forgive, though Allah's self detest;
But for that deed of darkness what wert thou?
Reproach me – but not yet – Oh! spare me now!
I am not what I seem – this fearful night
My brain bewilder'd – do not madden quite
If I had never loved though less my guilt,
Thou hadst not lived to – hate me – if thou wilt."

XV

She wrongs his thoughts, they more himself upbraid
Than her, though undesign'd' the wretch be made;
But speechless all, deep, dark, and unexprest,
They bleed within that silent cell – his breast
Still onward, fair the breeze, nor rough the surge,

The blue waves sport around the stern they urge;
Far on the horizon's verge appears a speck
A spot – a mast – a sail – an armed deck!
Their little bark her men of watch descry,
And ampler canvas woos the wind from high;
She bears her down majestically near,
Speed on her prow, and terror in her tier;
A flash is seen – the ball beyond their bow
Booms harmless, hissing to the deep below.
Uprose keen Conrad from his silent trance,
A long, long absent gladness in his glance;
" 'Tis mine – my blood-red flag! Again – again –
I am not all deserted on the main!"
They own the signal, answer to the ball,
Hoist out the boat at once, and slacken sail.
" 'Tis Conrad! Conrad!" shouting from the deck,
Command nor duty could their transport check!
With light alacrity and gaze of pride,
They view him mount once more his vessel's side;
A smile relaxing in each rugged face,
Their arms can scarce forbear a rough embrace.
He, half forgetting danger and defeat,
Returns their greeting as a chief may greet,
Wrings with a cordial grasp Anselmo's hand,
And feels he yet can conquer and command!

XVI

These greetings o'er, the feelings that o'erflow,
Yet grieve to win him back without a blow;
They sail'd prepared for vengeance – had they known
A woman's hand secured that deed her own,
She were their queen – less scrupulous are they
Than haughty Conrad how they win their way.
With many an asking smile, and wondering stare,

They whisper round, and gaze upon Gulnare;
And her – at once above – beneath her sex
Whom blood appall'd not, their regards perplex.
To Conrad turns her faint imploring eye,
She drops her veil, and stands in silence by;
Her arms are meekly folded on that breast,
Which – Conrad safe – to fate resign'd the rest.
Though worse than frenzy could that bosom fill,
Extreme in love or hate, in good or ill,
The worst of crimes had left her woman still!

XVII

This Conrad mark'd, and felt – ah! could he less? –
Hate of that deed, but grief for her distress;
What she has done no tears can wash away,
And Heaven must punish on its angry day:
But – it was done: he knew, whate'er her guilt,
For him that poniard smote, that blood was spilt;
And he was free! and she for him had given
Her all on earth, and more than all in heaven!
And now he turn'd him to that dark-eyed slave
Whose brow was bow'd beneath the glance he gave,
Who now seem'd changed and humbled, faint and meek,
But varying oft the colour of her cheek
To deeper shades of paleness – all its red
That fearful spot which stain'd it from the dead!
He took that hand – it trembled – now too late –
So soft in love, so wildly nerved in hate;
He clasp'd that hand – it trembled – and his own
Had lost its firmness, and his voice its tone.
"Gulnare!" – but she replied not – "dear Gulnare!"
She raised her eye – her only answer there –
At once she sought and sunk in his embrace:
If he had driven her from that resting-place,

His had been more or less than mortal heart,
But – good or ill – it bade her not depart.
Perchance, but for the bodings of his breast,
His latest virtue then had join'd the rest.
Yet even Medora might forgive the kiss
That ask'd from form so fair no more than this,
The first, the last that Frailty stole from Faith –
To lips where Love had lavish'd all his breath
To lips – whose broken sighs such fragrance fling,
As he had fann'd them freshly with his wing!

XVIII

They gain by twilight's hour their lonely isle
To them the very rocks appear to smile;
The haven hums with many a cheering sound,
The beacons him their wonted stations round,
The boats are darting o'er the curly bay,
And sportive dolphins bend them through the spray;
Even the hoarse sea-bird's shrill, discordant shriek
Greets like the welcome of his tuneless beak!
Beneath each lamp that through its lattice gleams,
Their fancy paints the friends that trim the beams
Oh! what can sanctify the joys of home,
Like Hope's gay glance from Ocean's troubled foam?

XIX

The lights are high on beacon and from bower,
And 'midst them Conrad seeks Medora's tower:
He looks in vain – 'tis strange – and all remark,
Amid so many, hers alone is dark
'Tis strange of yore its welcome never fall'd,
Nor now, perchance, extinguish'd, only veil'd.
With the first boat descends he for the shore,
And looks impatient on the lingering oar.

Oh! for a wing beyond the falcon's flight,
To bear him like an arrow to that height!
With the first pause the resting rowers gave,
He waits not, looks not – leaps into the wave,
Strives through the surge, bestrides the beach, and high
Ascends the path familiar to his eye.
He reach'd his turret door – he paused – no sound
Broke from within; and all was night around
He knock'd, and loudly – footstep nor reply
Announced that any heard or deem'd him nigh;
He knock'd, but faintly – for his trembling hand
Refused to aid his heavy heart's demand.
The portal opens – 'tis a well-known face,
But not the form he panted to embrace.
Its lips are silent – twice his own essay'd,
And fail'd to frame the question they delay'd;
It quits his grasp expiring in the fall.
He would not wait for that reviving ray –
As soon could he have linger'd there for day;
But, glimmering through the dusky corridor,
Another chequers o'er the shadow'd floor.
His steps the chamber gain – his eyes behold
All that his heart believed not – yet fortold!

XX

He turn'd not – spoke not – sunk not – fix'd his look,
And set the anxious frame that lately shook:
He gazed – how long we gaze despite of pain,
And know, but dare not own, we gaze in vain!
In life itself she was so still and fair,
That death with gender aspect wither'd there;
And the cold flowers her colder hand contain'd,
In that last grasp as tenderly were strain'd
As if she scarcely felt, but feign'd asleep,

And made it almost mockery yet to weep:
The long dark lashes fringed her lids of snow
And veil'd – thought shrinks from all that lurk'd below –
Oh! o'er the eye Death most exerts his might,
And hurls the spirit from her throne of light;
Sinks those blue orbs in that long last eclipse,
But spares, as yet, the charm around her lips –
Yet, yet they seem as they forbore to smile,
And wish'd repose, – but only for awhile;
But the white shroud, and each extended tress?
Long, fair – but spread in utter lifelessness,
Which, late the sport of every summer wind,
Escaped the baffled wreath that strove to bind;
These – and the pale pure cheek, became the bier –
But she is nothing – wherefore is he here?

XXI

He ask'd no question – all were answer'd now
By the first glance on that still, marble brow.
It was enough – she died – what reck'd it how?
The love of youth, the hope of better years,
The source of softest wishes, tenderest fears,
The only living thing he could not hate,
Was reft at once – and he deserved his fate,
But did not feel it less, – the good explore,
For peace, those realms where guilt can never soar:
The proud, the wayward – who have fix'd below
Their joy, and find this earth enough for woe,
Lose in that one their all – perchance a mite –
But who in patience parts with all delight?
Full many a stoic eye and aspect stern
Mask hearts where grief hath little left to learn;
And many a withering thought lies hid, not lost
In smiles that least befit who wear them most.

XXII

By those, that deepest feel, is ill exprest
The indistinctness of the suffering breast;
Where thousand thoughts begin to end in one,
Which seeks from all the refuge found in none;
No words suffice the secret soul to show,
For Truth denies all eloquence to Woe.
On Conrad's stricken soul exhaustion prest,
And stupor almost lull'd it into rest;
So feeble now – his mother's softness crept
To those wild eyes, which like an infant's wept:
It was the very weakness of his brain,
Which thus confess'd without relieving pain.
None saw his trickling tears – perchance if seen,
That useless flood of grief had never been:
Nor long they flow'd – he dried them to
In helpless – hopeless – brokenness of heart:
The sun goes forth, but Conrad's day is dim;
And the night cometh – ne'er to pass from him.
There is no darkness like the cloud of mind,
On Grief's vain eye – the blindest of the blind!
Which may not – dare not see but turns aside
To blackest shade – nor will endure a guide!

XXIII

His heart was form'd for softness – warp'd to wrong;
Betray'd too early, and beguiled too long;
Each feeling pure – as falls the dropping dew
Within the grot – like that had harden'd too;
Less clear perchance, its earthly trials pass'd,
But sunk, and chill'd, and petrified at last.
Yet tempests wear, and lightning cleaves the rock;
If such his heart, so shatter'd it the shock.
There grew one flower beneath its rugged brow,

Though dark the shade – it shelter'd – saved till now.
The thunder came – that bolt hath blasted both,
The Granite's firmness, and the Lily's growth:
The gentle plant hath left no leaf to tell
Its tale, but shrunk and wither'd where it fell
And of its cold protector, blacken round
But shiver'd fragments on the barren ground!

XXIV

'Tis morn – to venture on his lonely hour
Few dare; though now Anselmo sought his tower.
He was not there, nor seen along the shore;
Ere night, alarm'd, their isle is traversed o'er:
Another morn – another bids them seek,
And shout his name till echo waxeth weak;
Mount: grotto, cavern, valley search'd in vain,
They find on shore a sea-boat's broken chain:
Their hope revives – they follow o'er the main.
'Tis idle all – moons roll on moons away,
And Conrad comes not, came not since that day:
Nor trace, nor tidings of his doom declare
Where lives his grief, or perish'd his despair!
Long mourn'd his band whom none could mourn beside;
And fair the monument they gave his bride:
For him they raise not the recording stone –
His death yet dubious, deeds too widely known;
He left a Corsair's name to other times,
Link'd with one virtue, and a thousand crimes.

Shakespeare on Pirates

Antony and Cleopatra, I, 4

Messenger.

> Cæsar, I bring thee word,
> Menecrates and Menas, famous pirates,

Make the sea serve them, which they ear and wound
With keels of every kind: many hot inroads
They make in Italy; the borders maritime
Lack blood to think on't, and flush youth revolt;
No vessel can peep forth, but 'tis as soon
Taken as seen.

Hamlet, IV, 6

(*Hamlet's Letter to Horatio.*)

Horatio, when thou shalt have overlooked this, give these fellows some means to the king: they have letters for him. 'Ere we were two days old at sea, a pirate of very war-like appointment gave us chase. Finding ourselves too slow of sail, we put on a compelled valour, in the grapple I boarded them: on the instant they got clear of our ship, so I alone became their prisoner. They have dealt with me like thieves of mercy, but they knew what they did; I am to do a good turn for them . . . Farewell. He that thou knowest thine, Hamlet.

Measure for Measure, I, 2

Second Gentleman.

Amen!

Lucio.

Thou concludest like the sanctimonious pirate, that went to sea with the Ten Commandments, but scraped one out of the table.

Second Gentleman.

"Thou shalt not steal"?

Lucio.

Ay, that he razed.

The Merchant of Venice, I, 3

Shylock.

Ships are but boards, sailors but men: there be land-rats and water-rats, land-thieves and water-thieves—I mean, pirates.

Second Part of King Henry VI, IV, 1

Suffolk.

Small things make base men proud: this villain here,
Being captain of a pinnace, threatens more
Than Bargulus, the strong Illyrian pirate.

Ibid., IV, 9

King Henry.

Thus stands my state, 'twixt Cade and York distress'd;
Like to a ship, that, having scap'd a tempest,
Is straightway calm'd, and boarded with a pirate.

The Pirate's Song

ANONYMOUS

To the mast nail our flag it is dark as the grave,
Or the death which it bears while it sweeps o'er the wave;
Let our deck clear for action, our guns be prepared;
Be the boarding-axe sharpened, the scimetar bared:
Set the canisters ready, and then bring to me,
For the last of my duties, the powder-room key.
It shall never be lowered, the black flag we bear;
If the sea be denied us, we sweep through the air.

Unshared have we left our last victory's prey;
It is mine to divide it, and yours to obey:
There are shawls that might suit a sultana's white neck,
And pearls that are fair as the arms they will deck;
There are flasks which, unseal them, the air will disclose
Diametta's fair summers, the home of the rose.
I claim not a portion: I ask but as mine –
'Tis to drink to our victory – one cup of red wine.
Some fight, 'tis for riches – some fight, 'tis for fame:
The first I despise, and the last is a name.
I fight, 'tis for vengeance! I love to see flow,
At the stroke of my sabre, the life of my foe.
I strike for the memory of long-vanished years;
I only shed blood where another shed tears.
I come, as the lightning comes red from above,
O'er the race that I loathe, to the battle I love.

The Buccaneer

JOHN MASEFIELD

I

We are far from sight of the harbour lights,
    Of the sea-ports whence we came,
But the old sea calls and the cold wind bites,
    And our hearts are turned to flame.

And merry and rich is the goodly gear
    We'll win upon the tossing sea,

A silken gown for my dainty dear,
  And a gold doubloon for me.

It's the old, old road and the old, old quest
  Of the cut-throat sons of Cain,
South by west and a quarter west,
  And hey for the Spanish main.

II

There's a sea-way somewhere where all day long
  Is the hushed susurrus of the sea,
The mewing of the skuas, and the sailor's song,
  And the wind's cry calling me.

There's a haven somewhere where the quiet of the bay
  Is troubled with the shifting tide,
Where the gulls are flying, crying in the bright white spray,
  And the tan-sailed schooners ride.

III

The toppling rollers at the harbour mouth
  Are spattering the bows with foam,
And the anchor's catted, and she's heading for the south
  With her topsails sheeted home.

And a merry measure is the dance she'll tread
  (To the clanking of the staysail's hanks)
When the guns are growling and the blood runs red,
  And the prisoners are walking the planks.

The Pirate Song

ANONYMOUS

I

The storm it howled with hideous swell,
And loud the plunging waters fell
   Down Fara's deep defiles;
And many a cloud that awed the sight
Was hovering on that fatal night
   Around those western isles.
The tide was up, the winds were high,
   The sea-bird wildly wisped the air,

And all the powers of sea and sky
   Mingled in dread confusion there!
The pirate horde
Awhile had sheath'd the murd'rous sword,
And fearless of the tempest's brawl
Were glutting o'er their carnival;
Their boats lay floating to the shore
And mocked the waves that washed them o'er.
And on an isolated rock
   That rose just where the land-mark turned,
Regardless of the ocean's shock
   A high and lonely beacon burned;
   And though by many oft discerned,
Yet 'mongst those many few could tell
   Why gleamed aloft that nightly glare:
But there were some who knew too well
   How came it and what meant it there:
'Twas but a light that seemed to save—
   A hapless guidance to the grave!

II

Where yon ridge looks o'er the wood,
There the pirate castle stood;
And though from mortal sight concealed
By rocks which form a potent shield,
Yet in its front the eye might scan
The strong, the well built barbican,
Which, founded on the varying brow,
Looks proudly o'er the waves below.

   There was one path to this ancient pile,
And it wound beneath a dark defile,
Yet such, that all who dared oppose
This way, were counted harmless foes;

For so did stone and weed molest,
That two could scarcely walk abreast.

 There was another, but no one knew
Save those who bore their burdens through
To whence it led; and none could guess
Why always near yon craggy place

 The pirate boat was homeward steered,
And having passed the rifted base
 Among the cliffs, so disappeared!

III

He rose; around his vaulted room
 Full many a corselet met the eye,
And many an ancient warrior's plume
 Hung lightly from the tapestry;
And here and there the morning sun
Gleamed softly down on sword and gun.
Firm and unmoved his great intent,
He chose the new accoutrement;
Upon his head was proudly set
The strong and ponderous burganet;
And lightly o'er his armour slung,
The bandolier all fitted hung;

And in his hand he carried loose
The bright and well-proved arquebuse.
His corselet too, which lancet dinge
And stains of once a redder tinge
Had sullied much, could well declare
(And 'twas a just memorial there)
How oft its strength from foeman's hand
Had saved some corsair from that band.

The Rivals

E. H. VISIAK

'E's dead an' gone, is Morgan:
    Sir 'Enry's sailed away.
There weren't none other like him—
    Unless 'twere Lollonais!

For sacking of a city,
    For burning 'em like hay,
None 'eld a matchlight to 'im—
    Unless 'twere Lollonais!

For bearding of a gov'nor,
    For turning of 'em gray,
'E was the One an' Only—
    Unless 'twere Lollonais!

For reformating papists,
    For making padres pray,
I back Sir 'Enry Morgan—
    Or Frenchy Lollonais!

For diddling of old shipmates,
    For cutting with the pay,
I'd like to see 'is equal—
    It were not Lollonais!

The Song of Captain Kidd

ANONYMOUS

Oh, my name was Robert Kidd, as I sail'd, as I sail'd;
Oh, my name was Robert Kidd, as I sail'd.
My sinful footsteps slid; God's laws they did forbid;
But still wickedly I did, as I sail'd.

I'd a Bible in my hand, when I sail'd, when I sail'd;
I'd a Bible in my hand, when I sail'd.
I'd a Bible in my hand, by my father's great command,
And I sank it in the sand, when I sail'd.

I spied three ships of France, as I sail'd, as I sail'd;
I spied three ships of France, as I sail'd.
I spied three ships of France; to them I did advance,
And took them all by chance, as I sail'd.

I spied three ships of Spain, as I sail'd, as I sail'd;
I spied three ships of Spain, as I sail'd.
I spied three ships of Spain; I fired on them amain,
Till most of them were slain, as I sail'd.

I murdered William Moore, as I sail'd, as I sail'd;
I murdered William Moore, as I sail'd.
I murdered William Moore; and I left him in his grave,
Not many leagues from shore, as I sail'd.

I'd ninety bars of gold, as I sail'd, as I sail'd;
I'd ninety bars of gold, as I sail'd.
I'd dollars manifold, and riches uncontrolled,
And by these I lost my soul, as I sail'd.

The Tarry Buccaneer

JOHN MASEFIELD

I'm going to be a pirate with a bright brass pivot-gun,
And an island in the Spanish Main beyond the setting sun,
And a silver flagon full of red wine to drink when work is done,
Like a fine old salt-sea scavenger, like a tarry Buccaneer.

With a sandy creek to careen in, and a pig-tailed Spanish mate,
And under my main-hatches a sparkling merry freight
Of doubloons and double moidores and pieces of eight,
Like a fine old salt-sea scavenger, like a tarry Buccaneer.

With a taste for Spanish wine-shops and for spending my doubloons,
And a crew of swart mulattoes and black-eyed octaroons,
And a thoughtful way with mutineers of making them maroons,
Like a fine old salt-sea scavenger, like a tarry Buccaneer.

With a sash of crimson velvet and a diamond-hilted sword,
And a silver whistle about my neck secured to a golden cord,
And a habit of taking captives and walking them along a board,
Like a fine old salt-sea scavenger, like a tarry Buccaneer.

With a spy-glass tucked beneath my arm and a cocked hat cocked askew.
And a long low rakish schooner a-cutting of the waves in two,
And a flag of skull and cross-bones, the wickedest that ever flew,
Like a fine old salt-sea scavenger, like a tarry Buccaneer.

The Articles of Pirate Law

—From the Life of Captain Phillips

The first thing they had now to do, was to choose officers, draw up articles, and settle their little commonwealth, to prevent disputes and ranglings afterwards; so John Phillips was made captain, John Nutt, master, (or navigator) of the vessel; James Sparks, gunner; Thomas Fern, carpenter; and William White was the only private man in the whole crew: When this was done, one of them writ out the following articles (which we have taken verbatim) and all swore to 'em upon a hatchet for want of a bible.

The Articles on Board the Revenge.

1. Every Man shall obey civil Command; the Captain shall have one full Share and a half in all Prizes; the Master, Carpenter, Boatswain, & Gunner shall have one Share and quarter.
2. If any Man shall offer to run away, or keep any Secret from the Company, he shall be marrooned, with one Bottle of Powder, and Bottle of Water, one small Arm, and Shot.
3. If any Man shall steal any Thing in the Company, or Game, to the value of a Piece of Eight, he shall be marroon'd or shot.
4. If at any time we should meet another Marrooner [that is Pyrate,] that Man that shall sign his Articles without the Consent of our Company, shall suffer such Punishment as the Captain and Company shall think fit.
5. That Man that shall strike another whilst these Articles are in force, shall receive Moses's Law (that is, 40 Stripes lacking one) on the bare Back.
6. That Man that shall snap his Arms, or smoak Tobacco in the Hold, without a Cap to his Pipe, or carry a Candle lighted without a Lanthorn, shall suffer the same punishment as in the former Article.
7. That Man that shall not keep his Arms clean, fit for an Engagement, or neglect his Business, shall be cut off from his Share, & suffer such other punishment as the Captain & Company shall think fit.
8. If any Man shall lose a Joint in time of an Engagement, shall have 400 Pieces of Eight; if a Limb, 800.
9. If at any time you meet with a prudent Woman, that Man that offers to meddle with her, without her Consent, shall suffer present Death.

The Articles of Captain George Lowther, & his Company.

1. The Captain is to have two full Shares; the Master is to have one Share and a half; The Doctor, Mate, Gunner & Boatswain, one Share and a quarter.
2. He that shall be found Guilty of taking up any unlawful Weapon on Board the Privateer, or any Prize, by us taken, so as to strike or abuse one another, in any regard, shall suffer what Punishment the Captain and Majority of the Company shall think fit.
3. He that shall be found Guilty of Cowardize, in the Time of Engagement, shall suffer what Punishment the Captain and Majority shall think fit.
4. If any Gold, Jewels, Silver, &c. be found on Board of any Prize or Prizes, to the value of a Piece of Eight; & the Finder do not deliver it to the Quarter-Master, in the Space of 24 Hours, shall suffer what Punishment the Captain and Majority shall think fit.

5. He that is found Guilty of Gaming, or Defrauding another to the Value of a Shilling, shall suffer what Punishment the Captain and Majority of the Company shall think fit.
6. He that shall have the Misfortune to lose a Limb, in time of Engagement, shall have the sum of one hundred and fifty Pounds Sterling, and remain with the Company as long as he shall think fit.
7. Good Quarters be given when called for.
8. He that sees a Sail first, shall have the best Pistol, or Small-Arm, on Board her.

The Articles of Black Bart

    I. Every man has a vote in affairs of moment; has equal title to fresh provisions, or strong liquors, at any time seized, and may us them at his pleasure, unless a scarcity makes necessary for the good of all, to vote a retrenchment.
   II. If any man defrauds the company to the value of a pound in plate, jewels, or money, marooning is their punishment. If the robbery is betwixt one another, we content themselves with slitting the ears and nose of him that is guilty, and set him on shore, not in an inhabited place, but somewhere he is sure to encounter hardships.
  III. No person to game at dice for money.
  IV. The lights and candles to be put out at 8 o'clock at night; if any of the crew, after that hour still remained inclined for drinking, they are to do it on open deck.
   V. To keep their piece, pistols, and cutlass clean and fit for service.
  VI. If any man is found seducing any of the female sex, and carrying her to sea disguised, he is to suffer death.
 VII. To desert the ship, or quarters in battle, is punished with death or marooning.
VIII. No striking one another on board, but every man's quarrels to be ended on shore, at sword and pistol.
  IX. No man is to talk of breaking up their way of living, till each has shared 1000 pounds. If in order to do this, any man should lose a limb, or become a cripple in this service, he is to have 800 pounds out of the public stocks, and for lesser hurts, proportionately.
   X. The captain and quartermaster to receive two shares of prize; the master boatswain and gunner, one share and a half; and other officers, one and a quarter.
  XI. The musicians to have rest on the Sabbath day, only by night.

The Pirate's Parody

CAPTAIN CHARLES JOHNSON

They passed their time here in dancing, and other diversions agreeable to these sort of folks; and among the rest they appointed a mock court of judicature to try one another for piracy, and he that was a criminal one day was made judge another. I had an account given me of one of these merry trials, and as it appeared diverting, I shall give the readers a short acount of it.

The court and criminals being both appointed, as also council to plead, the judge got up in a tree, and had a dirty tarpaulin hung over his shoulders; this was done by way of robe, with a thrum cap on his head, and a large pair of spectacles upon his nose. Thus equipped, he settled himself in his place, and abundance of officers attending him below, with crows, handspikes, etc instead of wands, tipstaves, and such like. The criminals were brought out, making a thousand sour faces; and one who acted as attorney general opened the charge against them; their speeches were very laconic, and their whole proceedings concise. We shall give it by way of dialogue.

Attorn. Gen: An't please your Lordship, and you Gentlemen of the Jury, here is a Fellow before you that is a sad Dog, a sad sad Dog; & I humbly hope your Lordship will order him to be hanged out of the Way immediately. He has committed Pyracy upon the High Seas, and we shall prove, an't please your Lordship, that this Fellow, this sad Dog before you, has escaped a thousand Storms, nay, has got safe ashore when the Ship has been cast away, which was a certain Sign he was not born to be drown'd; yet not having the Fear of hanging before his Eyes, he went on robbing & ravishing, Man, Woman and Child, plundering Ships Cargoes fore & aft, burning & sinking Ship, Bark and Boat, as if the Devil had been in him. But this is not all, my Lord, he bas committed worse Villanies than all these, for we shall prove, that he has been guilty of drinking Small-Beer; and your Lordship knows, there never was a sober Fellow but what was a Rogue. My Lord, I should have spoke much finer than I do now, but that, as your Lordship knows our Rum is all out, and how should a Man speak good Law that has not drank a Dram. However, I hope, your Lordship will order the Fellow to be hang'd.

Judge: Heark'ee me, sirrah, you lousy, pittiful, ill-look'd Dog; what have you to say why you should not be tuck'd up immediately, & set a Sundrying like a Scare-crow? Are you guilty, or not guilty?

Pris: Not guilty, an't please your Worship.

Judge: Not guilty! say so again, sirrah, and I'll have you hang'd without any Tryal.

Pris: An't please your Worship's Honour, my Lord, I am as honest a poor Fellow as ever went between Stem and Stern of a Ship, and can hand, reef, steer, and clap two Ends of a Rope together, as well as e'er a He that ever cross'd salt Water; but I was taken by one George Bradley [the name of him that sat as judge], a notorious Pyrate, a sad Rogue as ever was unhang'd, and he forc'd me, an't please your Honour.

Judge: Answer me, Sirrah, how will you be try'd?

Pris: By G— and my Country.

Judge: The Devil you will. Why then, Gentlemen of the Jury, I think we have nothing to do but to proceed to Judgment.

Attor. Gen: Right, my Lord; for if the Fellow should be suffer'd to speak, he may clear himself, and that's an Affront to the Court.

Pris: Pray, my Lord, I hope your Lordship will consider–

Judge. Consider! How dare you talk of considering? Sirrah, Sirrah, I never consider'd in all my Life. I'll make it Treason to consider.

Pris: But, I hope, your Lordship will hear some Reason.

Judge: D'y hear how the Scoundrel prates? What have we to do with Reason? I'd have you to know, Raskal, we don't sit here to hear Reason; we go according to Law. Is our Dinner ready?

Attor. Gen: Yes, my Lord.

Judge: Then, heark'ee, you Raskal at the Bar; hear me, Sirrah, hear me. You must suffer, for three Reasons; first, because it is not fit I should sit here as Judge, and no Body be hang'd; secondly, you must be hang'd, because you have a damn'd hanging Look: And thirdly, you must be hang'd because I am hungry; for know, Sirrah, that 'tis a Custom, that whenever the Judge's Dinner is ready before the Tryal is over, the Prisoner is to be hang'd of Course.

There's Law for you, ye Dog. So take him away Gaoler.

This is the trial just as it was related to me; the design of my setting it down, is only to show how these fellows can jest upon things, the fear and dread of which, should make them tremble.

Last Words and Other Pirate Quotations

"Adios todos!"

—Last words of the pirate Benito de Soto
just before the gallows trap sprung

"Tip me the black spot."

—R. L. Stevenson
Treasure Island

"My Lord, it is a very hard sentence. For my part, I am the most innocent person of them all, only I have been sworn against by perjured persons."

—Captain Kidd, to the court, upon being sentenced to death for piracy

"That you shall go from hence to the place from whence you came, and from thence to the place of execution, where you shall be hang'd by the neck untill you are dead. And may the God of infinite Mercy be merciful to your Soul."

—Sentenced to death for piracy

"I am now going down the bay, and shall return hither in about a month; and if I find you upon the island when I come back, I'll carry you to Jamaica and hang you."

—A warning to the Pirate Charles Vane

Go tell your King, he is King of the Land;
But I am the King of the Sea!

—Barbarossa to Charles V

"Are you merchants destined to any port, or are you merely adventurers and pirates, who roam the seas without any place of destination, and live by rapine and ruin?"

—Old King Nestor to Telemachus
Homer's *Odyssey*

"Don't be in a fright, but put on your clothes, and I'll let you into a secret. You must know that I am Captain now. I am bound to Madagascar, with the design of making my own fortune, and that of all these brave fellows joined with me. If you have a mind to make one of us, we will receive you. And if you turn sober, and attend to business, perhaps in time I make make you one of my lieutenants. If not, here's a boat, and you shall be set on shore."

—The Pirate Avery to the Captain of a captured ship

"The next day I was told that they had determined to take the brig and money, and that they were the strongest party, and would murder the officers, and that he that informed would suffer with them. There was no arms on board; the conspiracy was known to the whole company, and had I informed, my life would have been taken, and though I knew that if I was found out, my life would be taken by law, which is the same thing, so I did not inform. I have committed murder and I know I must die for it."
The Court: "If you wish to add anything further you will still be heard."
The Accused Pirate Wansley: "No sir, I believe I have said enough."

— Thomas J. Wansley
In court, shortly before his execution

I THINK it very absurd and misplaced to call Raleigh and Drake, and others of our naval heroes of Elizabeth's age, pirates. No man is a *pirate*, unless his contemporaries agree to call him so. Drake said,—"The subjects of the king of Spain have done their best to ruin my country: *ergo*, I will try to ruin the king of Spain's country." Would it not be silly to call the Argonauts pirates in our sense of the word?

—COLERIDGE on Pirates
Table-Talk, Mar. 17th, 1832.

"There's nothing I can do. I cannot withstand my destiny. The devil told me last night in the great cabin that I shall be murdered."

—The Pirate Lewis on the night of his death

"Fear not the sea, for those born to be hanged will never drown."

—Old proverb

"It is, it is a glorious thing
To be a Pirate King"

—W. S. Gilbert
The Pirates of Penzance

"He was the mildest manner'd man,
That ever scuttled ship or cut a throat;
With such true breeding of a gentleman,
You never could discern his real thought.
Pity he loved an adventurous life's variety,
He was so great a loss to good society."

—Charles Ellms on Captain Lewis

HERE lies Buccaneer Bill,
Who drank his last, and drank his fill:
The King's men met Bill off Peru,
Saluted Bill with cannon-brew;
They brought Bill home to London Town,
They hoisted Bill high o'er clod and clown.
The King gave Bill an iron chain,
For deeds of daring on the main,
And granted Bill to hang in state,
Over against the city gate.
Sing all who read this pretty thing,
God save our sovereign lord the King.

—EPITAPH for a Pirate

The dying Declarations of John Rose Archer and William White, on the Day of their Execution at Boston, June 2, 1724, for the Crimes of Pyracy.

First, separately, of Archer.

I greatly bewail by Profanations of the Lord's Day, and my Disobedience to my Parents. And my Cursing & Swearing, and my blaspheming the Name of the glorious God.

Unto which I have added, the Sins of Unchastity. And I have provoked the Holy One, at length, to leave me unto the Crimes of Pyracy and Robbery; wherein, at last, I have brought my self under the Guilt of Murder also.

But one Wickedness that had led me as much as any, to all the rest, has been my brutish Drunkenness. By strong Drink I have been heated & hardened into the Crimes that are now more bitter than Death unto me.

I could wish that Masters of Vessels would not use their Men with so much Severity, so many of them do, which exposes to great Temptations.

And then of White.

I am now, with Sorrow, reaping the Fruits of my Disobedience to my Parents, who used their Endeavours to have me instructed in my Bible, & my Catechism.

And the Fruits of my neglecting the publick Worship of God, and prophaning the holy Sabbath.

And my blaspheming the Name of God, my Maker.

But my Drunkenness has had a great Hand in bringing my Ruin upon me. I was drunk when I was enticed aboard the Pirate.

And now, for all the vile Things I did aboard, I own the Justice of God and Man, in what is done unto me.

Of both together.

We hope, we truly hate the Sins, whereof we have the Burthen lying so heavy upon our Consciences.

We warn all People, and particularly young People against such Sins as these. We wish, all may take Warning by us.

We beg for Pardon, for the sake of Christ, our Saviour; and our Hope is in him alone. Oh! that in this Blood our Scarlet and Crimson Guilt may be all washed away!

We are sensible of an hard Heart in us, full of Wickedness. And we look upon God for his renewing Grace upon us.

We bless God for the Space of Repentance which he had given us; and that he has not cut us off in the Midst and Heighth of our Wickedness.

We are not without Hope, that God has been savingly at work upon our Souls.

We are made sensible of our absolute Need of the Righteousness of Christ; that we may stand justified before God in that. We renounce all Dependance on our own.

We are humbly thankful to the Ministers of Christ, for the great Pains they have taken for our Good. The Lord reward their Kindness.

We don't Despair of Mercy; but hope, through Christ, that when we dye, we shall find Mercy with God, and be received into his Kingdom.

We wish others, and especially the Sea-faring, may get Good by what they see this Day befalling of us.

"Fifteen Men on a dead man's chest!
Yo-ho-ho, and a bottle of rum!
Drink and the devil had done for the rest—
Yo-ho-ho, and a bottle of rum!"

—R. L. Stevenson
Treasure Island

"Avast belay, yo ho, heave to,
   A-pirating we go,
And if we're parted by a shot
   We're sure to meet below!
Yo ho, yo ho, the pirate life,
   The flag o' skull and bones,
A merry hour, a hempen rope,
   And hey for Davy Jones!
Avast belay, when I appear,
   By fear they're overtook;
Nought's left upon your bones when you
   Have shaken hands with Hook."

—The Pirate's song from *Peter Pan*

PART IV

The Tales

With the Buccaneers

HOWARD PYLE

Being an Account of Certain Adventures that Befell Henry Mostyn under Captain H. Morgan in the Year 1665–66.

I

Although this narration has more particularly to do with the taking of the Spanish Vice-Admiral in the harbor of Puerto Bello, and of the rescue therefrom of Le Sieur Simon, his wife and daughter (the adventure of which was successfully achieved by Captain Morgan, the famous buccaneer), we shall, nevertheless, premise something of the earlier history of Master Harry Mostyn, whom you may, if you please, consider as the hero of the several circumstances recounted in these pages.

In the year 1664 our hero's father embarked from Portsmouth, in England, for the Barbadoes, where he owned a considerable sugar plantation. Thither to those parts of America he transported with himself his whole family, of whom our Master Harry was the fifth of eight children—a great lusty fellow as little fitted for the Church (for which he was designed) as could be. At the time of this story, though not above sixteen years old, Master Harry Mostyn was as big and well-grown as many a man of twenty, and of such a reckless and dare-devil spirit that no adventure was too dangerous or too mischievous for him to embark upon.

At this time there was a deal of talk in those parts of the Americas concerning Captain Morgan, and the prodigious successes he was having pirating against the Spaniards.

This man had once been an indentured servant with Mr. Rolls, a sugar factor at the Barbadoes. Having served out his time, and being of lawless disposition, possessing also a prodigious appetite for adventure, he joined with others of his kidney, and, purchasing a caraval of three guns, embarked fairly upon that career of piracy the most successful that ever was heard of in the world.

Master Harry had known this man very well while he was still with Mr. Rolls, serving as a clerk at that gentleman's sugar wharf, a tall, broad-shouldered, strapping fellow, with red cheeks, and thick red lips, and rolling blue eyes, and hair as red as any chestnut. Many knew him for a bold, gruff-spoken man, but no one at that time suspected that he had it in him to become so famous and renowned as he afterwards grew to be.

The fame of his exploits had been the talk of those parts for above a twelvemonth, when, in the latter part of the year 1665, Captain Morgan, having made a very successful expedition against the Spaniards into the Gulf of Campeachy—where he took several important purchases from the plate fleet—came to the Barbadoes, there to fit out another such venture, and to enlist recruits.

He and certain other adventurers had purchased a vessel of some five hundred tons, which they proposed to convert into a pirate by cutting port-holes for cannon, and running three or four carronades across her main-deck. The name of this ship, be it mentioned, was the *Good Samaritan*, as ill-fitting a name as could be for such a craft, which, instead of being designed for the healing of wounds, was intended to inflict such devastation as those wicked men proposed.

Here was a piece of mischief exactly fitted to our hero's tastes; wherefore, having made up a bundle of clothes, and with not above a shilling in his pocket, he made an excursion into the town to seek for Captain Morgan. There he found the great pirate established at an ordinary, with a little court of ragamuffins and swashbucklers gathered about him, all talking very loud, and drinking healths in raw rum as though it were sugared water.

And what a fine figure our buccaneer had grown, to be sure! How different from the poor, humble clerk upon the sugarwharf! What a deal of gold braid! What a fine, silver-hilted Spanish sword! What a gay velvet sling, hung with three silver-mounted pistols! If Master Harry's mind had not been made up before, to be sure such a spectacle of glory would have determined it.

This figure of war our hero asked to step aside with him, and when they had come into a corner, proposed to the other what he intended, and that he had a mind to enlist as a gentleman adventurer upon this expedition. Upon this our rogue of a buccaneer Captain burst out a-laughing, and fetching Master Harry a great thump upon the back, swore roundly that he would make a man of him, and that it was a pity to make a parson out of so good a piece of stuff.

Nor was Captain Morgan less good than his word, for when the *Good Samaritan* set sail with a favoring wind for the island of Jamaica, Master Harry found himself established as one of the adventurers aboard.

II

Could you but have seen the town of Port Royal as it appeared in the year 1665 you would have beheld a sight very well worth while looking upon. There were no fine houses at that time, and no great counting-houses built of brick, such as you may find nowadays, but a crowd of board and wattled huts huddled along the streets, and all so gay with flags and bits of color that Vanity Fair itself could not have been gayer. To this place came all the pirates and buccaneers that infested those parts, and men shouted and swore and gambled, and poured out money like water, and then maybe wound up their merrymaking by dying of fever. For the sky in these torrid latitudes is all full of clouds overhead, and as hot as any blanket, and when the sun shone forth it streamed down upon the smoking sands so that the houses were ovens and the streets were furnaces; so it was little wonder that men died like rats in a hole. But little they appeared to care for that; so that everywhere you might behold a multitude of painted women and Jews and merchants and pirates, gaudy with red scarfs and gold braid and all sorts of odds and ends of foolish finery, all fighting and gambling and bartering for that ill-gotten treasure of the be-robbed Spaniard.

Here, arriving, Captain Morgan found a hearty welcome, and a message from the Governor awaiting him, the message bidding him attend his Excellency upon the earliest occasion that offered. Whereupon, taking our hero (of whom he had grown prodigiously fond) along with him, our pirate went, without any loss of time, to visit Sir Thomas Modiford, who was then the royal Governor of all this devil's brew of wickedness.

They found his Excellency seated in a great easy-chair, under the shadow of a slatted veranda, the floor whereof was paved with brick. He was clad, for the sake of coolness, only in his shirt, breeches, and stockings, and he wore slippers on his feet. He was smoking a great cigarro of tobacco, and a goblet of limejuice and water and rum stood at his elbow on a table. Here, out of the glare of the heat, it was all very cool and pleasant, with a sea-breeze blowing violently in through the slats, setting them a-rattling now and then, and stirring Sir Thomas's long hair, which he had pushed back for the sake of coolness.

The purport of this interview, I may tell you, concerned the rescue of one Le Sieur Simon, who, together with his wife and daughter, was held captive by the Spaniards.

This gentleman adventurer (Le Sieur Simon) had, a few years before, been set up by the buccaneers as Governor of the island of Santa Catherina. This place, though well fortified by the Spaniards, the buccaneers had seized upon, establishing themselves thereon, and so infesting the commerce of those seas that no Spanish fleet was safe from them. At last the Spaniards, no longer able to endure these assaults against their commerce, sent a great force against the free-booters to drive them out of their island stronghold. This they did, retaking Santa Catherina, together with its Governor, his wife, and daughter, as well as the whole garrison of buccaneers.

This garrison were sent by their conquerors, some to the galleys, some to the mines, some to no man knows where. The Governor himself—Le Sieur Simon—was to be sent to Spain, there to stand his trial for piracy.

The news of all this, I may tell you, had only just been received in Jamaica, having been brought thither by a Spanish captain, one Don Roderiguez Sylvia, who was, besides, the bearer of despatches to the Spanish authorities relating the whole affair.

Such, in fine, was the purport of this interview, and as our hero and his Captain walked back together from the Governor's house to the ordinary where they had taken up their inn, the buccaneer assured his companion that he purposed to obtain those despatches from the Spanish captain that very afternoon, even if he had to use force to seize them.

All this, you are to understand, was undertaken only because of the friendship that the Governor and Captain Morgan entertained for Le Sieur Simon. And, indeed, it was wonderful how honest and how faithful were these wicked men in their dealings with one another. For you must know that Governor Modiford and Le Sieur Simon and the buccaneers were all of one kidney— all taking a share in the piracies of those times, and all holding by one another as though they were the honestest men in the world. Hence it was they were all so determined to rescue Le Sieur Simon from the Spaniards.

III

Having reached his ordinary after his interview with the Governor, Captain Morgan found there a number of his companions, such as usually gathered at that place to be in attendance upon him—some, those belonging to the *Good Samaritan;* others, those who hoped to obtain benefits from him; others, those ragamuffins who gathered around him because he was famous, and because it pleased them to be of his court and to be called his followers. For nearly always your successful pirate had such a little court surrounding him.

Finding a dozen or more of these rascals gathered there, Captain Morgan informed them of his present purpose—that he was going to find the Spanish captain to demand his papers of him, and calling upon them to accompany him.

With this following at his heels, our buccaneer started off down the street, his lieutenant, a Cornishman named Bartholomew Davis, upon one hand and our hero upon the other. So they paraded the streets for the best part of an hour before they found the Spanish captain. For whether he had got wind that Captain Morgan was searching for him, or whether, finding himself in a place so full of his enemies, he had buried himself in some place of hiding, it is certain that the buccaneers had traversed pretty nearly the whole town before they discovered that he was lying at a certain auberge kept by a Portuguese Jew. Thither they went, and thither Captain Morgan entered with the utmost coolness and composure of demeanor, his followers crowding noisily in at his heels.

The space within was very dark, being lighted only by the doorway and by two large slatted windows or openings in the front.

In this dark, hot place—not over-roomy at the best—were gathered twelve or fifteen villanous-appearing men, sitting at tables and drinking together, waited upon by the Jew and his wife. Our hero had no trouble in discovering which of this lot of men was Captain Sylvia, for not only did Captain Morgan direct his glance full of war upon him, but the Spaniard was clad with more particularity and with more show of finery than any of the others who were there.

Him Captain Morgan approached and demanded his papers, whereunto the other replied with such a jabber of Spanish and English that no man could have understood what he said. To this Captain Morgan in turn replied that he must have those papers, no matter what it might cost him to obtain them, and thereupon drew a pistol from his sling and presented it at the other's head.

At this threatening action the innkeeper's wife fell a-screaming, and the Jew, as in a frenzy, besought them not to tear the house down about his ears.

Our hero could hardly tell what followed, only that all of a sudden there was a prodigious uproar of combat. Knives flashed everywhere, and then a pistol was fired so close to his head that he stood like one stunned, hearing some one crying out in a loud voice, but not knowing whether it was a friend or a foe who had been shot. Then another pistol-shot so deafened what was left of Master Harry's hearing that his ears rang for above an hour afterwards. By this time the whole place was full of gunpowder smoke, and there was the sound of blows and oaths and outcrying and the clashing of knives.

As Master Harry, who had no great stomach for such a combat, and no very particular interest in the quarrel, was making for the door, a little Portuguese, as withered and as nimble as an ape, came ducking under the table and plunged at his stomach with a great long knife, which, had it effected its object, would surely have ended his adventures then and there. Finding himself in such danger, Master Harry snatched up a heavy chair, and, flinging it at his enemy, who was preparing for another attack, he fairly ran for it out of the door, expecting every instant to feel the thrust of the blade betwixt his ribs.

A considerable crowd had gathered outside, and others, hearing the uproar, were coming running to join them. With these our hero stood, trembling like a leaf, and with cold chills running up and down his back like water at the narrow escape from the danger that had threatened him.

Nor shall you think him a coward, for you must remember he was hardly sixteen years old at the time, and that this was the first affair of the sort he had encountered. Afterwards, as you shall learn, he showed that he could exhibit courage enough at a pinch.

While he stood there endeavoring to recover his composure, the while the tumult continued within, suddenly two men came running almost together out of the door, a crowd of the combatants at their heels. The first of these men was Captain Sylvia; the other, who was pursuing him, was Captain Morgan.

As the crowd about the door parted before the sudden appearing of these, the Spanish captain, perceiving, as he supposed, a way of escape opened to him, darted across the street with incredible swiftness towards an alleyway upon the other side. Upon this, seeing his prey like to get away from him, Captain Morgan snatched a pistol out of his sling, and resting it for an instant across his arm, fired at the flying Spaniard, and that with so true an aim that, though the street was now full of people, the other went tumbling over and over all of a heap in the kennel, where he lay, after a twitch or two, as still as a log.

At the sound of the shot and the fall of the man the crowd scattered upon all sides, yelling and screaming, and the street being thus pretty clear, Captain Morgan ran across the way to where his victim lay, his smoking pistol still in his hand, and our hero following close at his heels.

Our poor Harry had never before beheld a man killed thus in an instant who a moment before had been so full of life and activity, for when Captain Morgan turned the body over upon its back he could perceive at a glance, little as he knew of such matters, that the man was stone dead. And, indeed, it was a dreadful sight for him who was hardly more than a child. He stood rooted for he knew not how long, staring down at the dead face with twitching fingers and shuddering limbs. Meantime a great crowd was gathering about them again.

As for Captain Morgan, he went about his work with the utmost coolness and deliberation imaginable, unbuttoning the waistcoat and the shirt of the man he had murdered with fingers that neither twitched nor shook. There were a gold cross and a bunch of silver medals hung by a whip-cord about the neck of the dead man. This Captain Morgan broke away with a snap, reaching the jingling baubles to Harry, who took them in his nerveless hand and fingers that he could hardly close upon what they held.

The papers Captain Morgan found in a wallet in an inner breast-pocket of the Spaniard's waistcoat. These he examined one by one, and finding them to his satisfaction, tied them up again, and slipped the wallet and its contents into his own pocket.

Then for the first time he appeared to observe Master Harry, who, indeed, must have been standing the perfect picture of horror and dismay. Whereupon, bursting out a-laughing, and slipping the pistol he had used back into its sling again, he fetched poor Harry a great slap upon the back, bidding him be a man, for that he would see many such sights as this.

But, indeed, it was no laughing matter for poor Master Harry, for it was many a day before his imagination could rid itself of the image of the dead Spaniard's face; and as he walked away down the street with his companions, leaving the crowd behind them, and the dead body where it lay for its friends to look after, his ears humming and ringing from the deafening noise of the pistol-shots fired in the close room, and the sweat trickling down his face in drops, he knew not whether all that had passed had been real, or whether it was a dream from which he might presently awaken.

IV

The papers Captain Morgan had thus seized upon as the fruit of the murder he had committed must have been as perfectly satisfactory to him as could be, for having paid a second visit that evening to Governor Modiford, the pirate lifted anchor the next morning and made sail towards the Gulf of Darien. There, after cruising about in those waters for about a fortnight without falling in with a vessel of any sort, at the end of that time they overhauled a caravel bound from Puerto Bello to Cartagena, which vessel they took, and finding her loaded with nothing better than raw hides, scuttled and sunk her, being then about twenty leagues from the main of Cartagena. From the captain of this vessel they learned that the plate fleet was then lying in the harbor of Puerto Bello, not yet having set sail thence, but waiting for the change of the winds before embarking for Spain. Besides this, which was a good deal more to their purpose, the Spaniards told the pirates that the Sieur Simon, his wife, and daughter were confined aboard the vice-admiral of that fleet, and that the name of the vice-admiral was the *Santa Maria y Valladolid.*

So soon as Captain Morgan had obtained the information he desired he directed his course straight for the Bay of Santo Blaso, where he might lie safely within the cape of that name without any danger of discovery (that part of the main-land being entirely uninhabited) and yet be within twenty or twenty-five leagues of Puerto Bello.

Having come safely to this anchorage, he at once declared his intentions to his companions, which were as follows:

That it was entirely impossible for them to hope to sail their vessel into the harbor of Puerto Bello, and to attack the Spanish vice-admiral where he lay in the midst of the armed flota; wherefore, if anything was to be accomplished, it must be undertaken by some subtle design rather than by open-handed boldness. Having so prefaced what he had to say, he now declared that it was his purpose to take one of the ship's boats and to go in that to Puerto Bello, trusting for some opportunity to occur to aid him either in the accomplishment of his aims or in the gaining of some further information. Having thus delivered himself, he invited any who dared to do so to volunteer for the expedition, telling them plainly that he would constrain no man to go against his will, for that at best it was a desperate enterprise, possessing only the recommendation that in its achievement the few who undertook it would gain great renown, and perhaps a very considerable booty.

And such was the incredible influence of this bold man over his companions, and such was their confidence in his skill and cunning, that not above a dozen of all those aboard hung back from the undertaking, but nearly every man desired to be taken.

Of these volunteers Captain Morgan chose twenty—among others our Master Harry—and having arranged with his lieutenant that if nothing was heard from the expedition at the end of three days he should sail for Jamaica to await news, he embarked upon that enterprise, which, though never heretofore published, was perhaps the boldest and the most desperate of all those that have since made his name so famous. For what could be a more unparalleled undertaking than for a little open boat, containing but twenty men, to enter the harbor of the third strongest fortress of the Spanish mainland with the intention of cutting out the Spanish vice-admiral from the midst of a whole fleet of powerfully armed vessels, and how many men in all the world do you suppose would venture such a thing?

But there is this to be said of that great buccaneer: that if he undertook enterprises so desperate as this, he yet laid his plans so well that they never went altogether amiss. Moreover, the very desperation of his successes was of such a nature that no man could suspect that he would dare to undertake such things, and accordingly his enemies were never prepared to guard against his attacks. Aye, had he but worn the King's colors and served under the rules of honest war, he might have become as great and as renowned as Admiral Blake himself!

But all that is neither here nor there; what I have to tell you now is that Captain Morgan in this open boat with his twenty mates reached the Cape of Salmedina towards the fall of day. Arriving within view of the harbor they discovered the plate fleet at anchor, with two men-of-war and an armed galley riding as a guard at the mouth of the harbor, scarce half a league distant from the other ships. Having spied the fleet in this posture, the pirates presently pulled down their sails and rowed along the coast, feigning to be a Spanish vessel from Nombre de Dios. So hugging the shore, they came boldly within the harbor, upon the opposite side of which you might see the fortress a considerable distance away.

Being now come so near to the consummation of their adventure, Captain Morgan required every man to make an oath to stand by him to the last, whereunto our hero swore as heartily as any man aboard, although his heart, I must needs confess, was beating at a great rate at the approach of what was to happen. Having thus received the oaths of all his followers, Captain Morgan commanded the surgeon of the expedition that, when the order was given, he, the medico, was to bore six holes in the boat, so that, it sinking under them, they might all be compelled to push forward, with no chance of retreat. And such was the ascendency of this man over his followers, and such was their awe of him, that not one of them uttered even so much as a murmur, though what he had commanded the surgeon to do pledged them either to victory or to death, with no chance to choose between. Nor did the surgeon question the orders he had received, much less did he dream of disobeying them.

By now it had fallen pretty dusk, whereupon, spying two fishermen in a canoe at a little distance, Captain Morgan demanded of them in Spanish which vessel of those at anchor in the harbor was the vice-admiral, for that he had despatches for the captain thereof. Whereupon the fishermen, suspecting nothing, pointed to them a galleon of great size riding at anchor not half a league distant.

Towards this vessel accordingly the pirates directed their course, and when they had come pretty nigh, Captain Morgan called upon the surgeon that now it was time for him to perform the duty that had been laid upon him. Where upon the other did as he was ordered, and that so thoroughly that the water presently came gushing into the boat in great streams, whereat all hands pulled for the galleon as though every next moment was to be their last.

And what do you suppose were our hero's emotions at this time? Like all in the boat, his awe of Captain Morgan was so great that I do believe he would rather have gone to the bottom than have questioned his command, even when it was to scuttle the boat. Nevertheless, when he felt the cold water gushing about his feet (for he had taken off his shoes and stockings) he became possessed with such a fear of being drowned that even the Spanish galleon had no terrors for him if he could only feel the solid planks thereof beneath his feet.

Indeed, all the crew appeared to be possessed of a like dismay, for they pulled at the oars with such an incredible force that they were under the quarter of the galleon before the boat was half filled with water.

Here, as they approached, it then being pretty dark and the moon not yet having risen, the watch upon the deck hailed them, whereupon Captain Morgan called out in Spanish that he was Captain Alvarez Mendazo, and that he brought despatches for the vice-admiral.

But at that moment, the boat being now so full of water as to be logged, it suddenly tilted upon one side as though to sink beneath them, whereupon all hands, without further orders, went scrambling up the side, as nimble as so many monkeys, each armed with a pistol in one hand and a cutlass in the other, and so were upon deck before the watch could collect his wits to utter any outcry or to give any other alarm than to cry out, "Jesu bless us! who are these?" at which words somebody knocked him down with the butt of a pistol, though who it was our hero could not tell in the darkness and the hurry.

Before any of those upon deck could recover from their alarm or those from below come up upon deck, a part of the pirates, under the carpenter and the surgeon, had run to the gunroom and had taken possession of the arms, while Captain Morgan, with Master Harry and a Portuguese called Murillo Braziliano, had flown with the speed of the wind into the great cabin.

Here they found the captain of the vice-admiral playing at cards with the Sieur Simon and a friend, Madam Simon and her daughter being present.

Captain Morgan instantly set his pistol at the breast of the Spanish captain, swearing with a most horrible fierce countenance that if he spake a word or made any outcry he was a dead man. As for our hero, having now got his hand into the game, he performed the same service for the Spaniard's friend, declaring he would shoot him dead if he opened his lips or lifted so much as a single finger.

All this while the ladies, not comprehending what had occurred, had sat as mute as stones; but now having so far recovered themselves as to find a voice, the younger of the two fell to screaming, at which the Sieur Simon called out to her to be still, for these were friends who had come to help them, and not enemies who had come to harm them.

All this, you are to understand, occupied only a little while, for in less than a minute three or four of the pirates had come into the cabin, who, together with the Portuguese, proceeded at once to bind the two Spaniards hand and foot, and to gag them. This being done to our buccaneer's satisfaction, and the Spanish captain being stretched out in the corner of the cabin, he instantly cleared his countenance of its terrors, and bursting forth into a great loud laugh, clapped his hand to the Sieur Simon's, which he wrung with the best will in the world. Having done this, and being in a fine humor after this his first success, he turned to the two ladies. "And this, ladies," said he, taking our hero by the hand and presenting him, "is a young gentleman who has embarked with me to learn the trade of piracy. I recommend him to your politeness."

Think what a confusion this threw our Master Harry into, to be sure, who at his best was never easy in the company of strange ladies! You may suppose what must have been his emotions to find himself thus introduced to the attention of Madam Simon and her daughter, being at the time in his bare feet, clad only in his shirt and breeches, and with no hat upon his head, a pistol in one hand and a cutlass in the other. However, he was not left for long to his embarrassments, for almost immediately after he had thus far relaxed, Captain Morgan fell of a sudden serious again, and bidding the Sieur Simon to get his ladies away into some place of safety, for the most hazardous part of this adventure was yet to occur, he quitted the cabin with Master Harry and the other pirates (for you may call him a pirate now) at his heels.

Having come upon deck, our hero beheld that a part of the Spanish crew were huddled forward in a flock like so many sheep (the others being crowded below with the hatches fastened upon them), and such was the terror of the pirates, and so dreadful the name of Henry Morgan, that not one of those poor wretches dared to lift up his voice to give any alarm, nor even to attempt an escape by jumping overboard.

At Captain Morgan's orders, these men, together with certain of his own company, ran nimbly aloft and began setting the sails, which, the night now having fallen pretty thick, was not for a good while observed by any of the vessels riding at anchor about them.

Indeed, the pirates might have made good their escape, with at most only a shot or two from the men-of-war, had it not then been about the full of the moon, which, having arisen, presently discovered to those of the fleet that lay closest about them what was being done aboard the vice-admiral.

At this one of the vessels hailed them, and then after a while, having no reply, hailed them again. Even then the Spaniards might not immediately have suspected anything was amiss but only that the vice-admiral for some reason best known to himself was shifting his anchorage, had not one of the Spaniards aloft—but who it was Captain Morgan was never able to discover—answered the hail by crying out that the vice-admiral had been seized by the pirates.

At this the alarm was instantly given and the mischief done, for presently there was a tremendous bustle through that part of the fleet lying nighest the vice-admiral—a deal of shouting of orders, a beating of drums, and the running hither and thither of the crews.

But by this time the sails of the vice-admiral had filled with a strong land breeze that was blowing up the harbor, whereupon the carpenter, at Captain Morgan's orders, having cut away both anchors, the galleon presently bore away up the harbor, gathering headway every moment with the wind nearly dead astern. The nearest vessel was the only one that for the moment was able to offer any hinderance. This ship, having by this time cleared away one of its guns, was able to fire a parting shot against the vice-admiral, striking her somewhere forward, as our hero could see by a great shower of splinters that flew up in the moonlight.

At the sound of the shot all the vessels of the flota not yet disturbed by the alarm were aroused at once, so that the pirates had the satisfaction of knowing that they would have to run the gantlet of all the ships between them and the open sea before they could reckon themselves escaped.

And, indeed, to our hero's mind it seemed that the battle which followed must have been the most terrific cannonade that was ever heard in the world. It was not so ill at first, for it was some while before the Spaniards could get their guns clear for action, they being not the least in the world prepared for such an occasion as this. But by-and-by first one and then another ship opened fire upon the galleon, until it seemed to our hero that all the thunders of heaven let loose upon them could not have created a more prodigious uproar, and that it was not possible that they could any of them escape destruction.

By now the moon had risen full and round, so that the clouds of smoke that rose in the air appeared as white as snow. The air seemed full of the hiss and screaming of shot, each one of which, when it struck the galleon, was magnified by our hero's imagination into ten times its magnitude from the crash which it delivered and from the cloud of splinters it would cast up into the moonlight. At last he suddenly beheld one poor man knocked sprawling across the deck, who, as he raised his arm from behind the mast, disclosed that the hand was gone from it, and that the shirt-sleeve was red with blood in the moonlight. At this sight all the strength fell away from poor Harry, and he felt sure that a like fate or even a worse must be in store for him.

But, after all, this was nothing to what it might have been in broad daylight, for what with the darkness of night, and the little preparation the Spaniards could make for such a business, and the extreme haste with which they discharged their guns (many not understanding what was the occasion of all this uproar), nearly all the shot flew so wide of the mark that not above one in twenty struck that at which it was aimed.

Meantime Captain Morgan, with the Sieur Simon, who had followed him upon deck, stood just above where our hero lay behind the shelter of the bulwark. The captain had lit a pipe of tobacco, and he stood now in the bright moonlight close to the rail, with his hands behind him, looking out ahead with the utmost coolness imaginable, and paying no more attention to the din of battle than though it were twenty leagues away. Now and then he would take his pipe from his lips to utter an order to the man at the wheel. Excepting this he stood there hardly moving at all, the wind blowing his long red hair over his shoulders.

Had it not been for the armed galley the pirates might have got the galleon away with no great harm done in spite of all this cannonading, for the man-of-war which rode at anchor nighest to them at the mouth of the harbor was still so far away that they might have passed it by hugging pretty close to the shore, and that without any great harm being done to them in the darkness. But just at this moment, when the open water lay in sight, came this galley pulling out from behind the point of the shore in such a manner as either to head our pirates off entirely or else to compel them to approach so near to the man-of-war that that latter vessel could bring its guns to bear with more effect.

This galley, I must tell you, was like others of its kind such as you may find in these waters, the hull being long and cut low to the water so as to allow the oars to dip freely. The bow was sharp and projected far out ahead, mounting a swivel upon it, while at the stern a number of galleries built one above another into a castle gave shelter to several companies of musketeers as well as the officers commanding them.

Our hero could behold the approach of this galley from above the starboard bulwarks, and it appeared to him impossible for them to hope to escape either it or the man-of-war. But still Captain Morgan maintained the same composure that he had exhibited all the while, only now and then delivering an order to the man at the wheel, who, putting the helm over, threw the bows of the galleon around more to the larboard, as though to escape the bow of the galley and get into the open water beyond. This course brought the pirates ever closer and closer to the man-of-war, which now began to add its thunder to the din of the battle, and with so much more effect that at every discharge you might hear the crashing and crackling of splintered wood, and now and then the outcry or groaning of some man who was hurt. Indeed, had it been daylight, they must at this juncture all have perished, though, as was said, what with the night and the confusion and the hurry, they escaped entire destruction, though more by a miracle than through any policy upon their own part.

Meantime the galley, steering as though to come aboard of them, had now come so near that it, too, presently began to open its musketry fire upon them, so that the humming and rattling of bullets were presently added to the din of cannonading.

In two minutes more it would have been aboard of them, when in a moment Captain Morgan roared out of a sudden to the man at the helm to put it hard a starboard. In response the man ran the wheel over with the utmost quickness, and the galleon, obeying her helm very readily, came around upon a course which, if continued, would certainly bring them into collision with their enemy.

It is possible at first the Spaniards imagined the pirates intended to escape past their stern, for they instantly began backing oars to keep them from getting past, so that the water was all of a foam about them; at the same time they did this they poured in such a fire of musketry that it was a miracle that no more execution was accomplished than happened.

As for our hero, methinks for the moment he forgot all about everything else than as to whether or no his captain's manœuvre would succeed, for in the very first moment he divined, as by some instinct, what Captain Morgan purposed doing.

At this moment, so particular in the execution of this nice design, a bullet suddenly struck down the man at the wheel. Hearing the sharp outcry, our Harry turned to see him fall forward, and then to his hands and knees upon the deck, the blood running in a black pool beneath him, while the wheel, escaping from his hands, spun over until the spokes were all of a mist.

In a moment the ship would have fallen off before the wind had not our hero, leaping to the wheel (even as Captain Morgan shouted an order for some one to do so), seized the flying spokes, whirling them back again, and so bringing the bow of the galleon up to its former course.

In the first moment of this effort he had reckoned of nothing but of carrying out his captain's designs. He neither thought of cannon-balls nor of bullets. But now that his task was accomplished, he came suddenly back to himself to find the galleries of the galleon aflame with musket-shots, and to become aware with a most horrible sinking of the spirits that all the shots therefrom were intended for him. He cast his eyes about him with despair, but no one came to ease him of his task, which, having undertaken, he had too much spirit to resign from carrying through to the end, though he was well aware that the very next instant might mean his sudden and violent death. His ears hummed and rang, and his brain swam as light as a feather. I know not whether he breathed, but he shut his eyes tight as though that might save him from the bullets that were raining about him.

At this moment the Spaniards must have discovered for the first time the pirates' design, for of a sudden they ceased firing, and began to shout out a multitude of orders, while the oars lashed the water all about with a foam. But it was too late then for them to escape, for within a couple of seconds the galleon struck her enemy a blow so violent upon the larboard quarter as nearly to hurl our Harry upon the deck, and then with a dreadful, horrible crackling of wood, commingled with a yelling of men's voices, the galley was swung around upon her side, and the galleon, sailing into the open sea, left nothing of her immediate enemy but a sinking wreck, and the water dotted all over with bobbing heads and waving hands in the moonlight.

And now, indeed, that all danger was past and gone, there were plenty to come running to help our hero at the wheel. As for Captain Morgan, having come down upon the main-deck, he fetches the young helmsman a clap upon the back. "Well, Master Harry," says he, "and did I not tell you I would make a man of you?" Whereat our poor Harry fell a-laughing, but with a sad catch in his voice, for his hands trembled as with an ague, and were as cold as ice. As for his emotions, God knows he was nearer crying than laughing, if Captain Morgan had but known it.

Nevertheless, though undertaken under the spur of the moment, I protest it was indeed a brave deed, and I cannot but wonder how many young gentlemen of sixteen there are to-day who, upon a like occasion, would act as well as our Harry.

The Daughter of the Great Mogul

DANIEL DEFOE

In this time I pursued my voyage, coasted the whole Malabar shore, and met with no purchase but a great Portugal East India ship, which I chased into Goa, where she got out of my reach. I took several small vessels and barks, but little of value in them, till I entered the great Bay of Bengal, when I began to look about me with more expectation of success, though without prospect of what happened.

I cruised here about two months, finding nothing worth while; so I stood away to a port on the north point of the isle of Sumatra, where I made no stay; for here I got news that two large ships belonging to the Great Mogul were expected to cross the bay from Hoogly, in the Ganges, to the country of the King of Pegu, being to carry the granddaughter of the Great Mogul to Pegu, who was to be married to the king of that country, with all her retinue, jewels, and wealth.

This was a booty worth watching for, though it had been some months longer; so I resolved that we would go and cruise off Point Negaris, on the east side of the bay, near Diamond Isle; and here we plied off and on for three weeks, and began to despair of success; but the knowledge of the booty we expected spurred us on, and we waited with great patience, for we knew the prize would be immensely rich.

At length we spied three ships coming right up to us with the wind. We could easily see they were not Europeans by their sails, and began to prepare ourselves for a prize, not for a fight; but were a little disappointed when we found the first ship full of guns and full of soldiers, and in condition, had she been managed by English sailors, to have fought two such ships as ours were. However, we resolved to attack her if she had been full of devils as she was full of men.

Accordingly, when we came near them, we fired a gun with shot as a challenge. They fired again immediately three or four guns, but fired them so confusedly that we could easily see they did not understand their business; when we considered how to lay them on board, and so to come thwart them, if we could; but falling, for want of wind, open to them, we gave them a fair broadside. We could easily see, by the confusion that was on board, that they were frightened out of their wits; they fired here a gun and there a gun, and some on that side that was from us, as well as those that were next to us. The next thing we did was to lay them on board, which we did presently, and then gave them a volley of our small shot, which, as they stood so thick, killed a great many of them, and made all the rest run down under their hatches, crying out like creatures bewitched. In a word, we presently took the ship, and having secured her men, we chased the other two. One was chiefly filled with women, and the other with lumber. Upon the whole, as the granddaughter of the Great Mogul was our prize in the first ship, so in the second was her women, or, in a word, her household, her eunuchs, all the necessaries of her wardrobe, of her stables, and of her kitchen; and in the last, great quantities of household stuff, and things less costly, though not less useful.

But the first was the main prize. When my men had entered and mastered the ship, one of our lieutenants called for me, and accordingly I jumped on board. He told me he thought nobody but I ought to go into the great cabin, or, at least, nobody should go there before me; for that the lady herself and all her attendance was there, and he feared the men were so heated they would murder them all, or do worse.

I immediately went to the great cabin door, taking the lieutenant that called me along with me, and caused the cabin door to be opened. But such a sight of glory and misery was never seen by buccaneer before. The queen (for such she was to have been) was all in gold and silver, but frightened and crying, and, at the sight of me, she appeared trembling, and just as if she was going to die. She sat on the side of a kind of a bed like a couch, with no canopy over it, or any covering; only made to lie down upon. She was, in a manner, covered with diamonds, and I, like a true pirate, soon let her see that I had more mind to the jewels than to the lady.

However, before I touched her, I ordered the lieutenant to place a guard at the cabin door, and fastening the door, shut us both in, which he did. The lady was young, and, I suppose, in their country esteem, very handsome, but she was not very much so in my thoughts. At first, her fright, and the danger she thought she was in of being killed, taught her to do everything that she thought might interpose between her and danger, and that was to take off her jewels as fast as she could, and give them to me; and I, without any great compliment, took them as fast as she gave them me, and put them into my pocket, taking no great notice of them or of her, which frighted her worse than all the rest, and she said something which I could not understand. However, two of the other ladies came, all crying, and kneeled down to me with their hands lifted up. What they meant, I knew not at first; but by their gestures and pointings I found at last it was to beg the young queen's life, and that I would not kill her.

When the three ladies kneeled down to me, and as soon as I understood what it was for, I let them know I would not hurt the queen, nor let any one else hurt her, but that she must give me all her jewels and money. Upon this they acquainted her that I would save her life; and no sooner had they assured her of that but she got up smiling, and went to a fine Indian cabinet, and opened a private drawer, from whence she took another little thing full of little square drawers and holes. This she brings to me in her hand, and offered to kneel down to give it me. This innocent usage began to rouse some good-nature in me (though I never had much), and I would not let her kneel; but sitting down myself on the side of her couch or bed, made a motion to her to sit down too. But here she was frightened again, it seems, at what I had no thought of. But as I did not offer anything of that kind, only made her sit down by me, they began all to be easier after some time, and she gave me the little box or casket, I know not what to call it, but it was full of invaluable jewels. I have them still in my keeping, and wish they were safe in England; for I doubt not but some of them are fit to be placed on the king's crown.

Being master of this treasure, I was very willing to be good-humored to the persons; so I went out of the cabin, and caused the women to be left alone, causing the guard to be kept still, that they might receive no more injury than I would do them myself.

After I had been out of the cabin some time, a slave of the women's came to me, and made sign to me that the queen would speak with me again. I made signs back that I would come and dine with her majesty; and accordingly I ordered that her servants should prepare her dinner, and carry it in, and then call me. They provided her repast after the usual manner, and when she saw it brought in she appeared pleased, and more when she saw me come in after it; for she was exceedingly pleased that I had caused a guard to keep the rest of my men from her; and she had, it seems, been told how rude they had been to some of the women that belonged to her.

When I came in, she rose up, and paid me such respect as I did not well know how to receive, and not in the least how to return. If she had understood English, I could have said plainly, and in good rough words, "Madam, be easy; we are rude, roughhewn fellows, but none of our men should hurt you, or touch you; I will be your guard and protection; we are for money indeed, and we shall take what you have, but we will do you no other harm." But as I could not talk thus to her, I scarce knew what to say; but I sat down, and made signs to have her sit down and eat, which she did, but with so much ceremony that I did not know well what to do with it.

After we had eaten, she rose up again, and drinking some water out of a china cup, sat her down on the side of the couch as before. When she saw I had done eating, she went then to another cabinet, and pulling out a drawer, she brought it to me; it was full of small pieces of gold coin of Pegu, about as big as an English half-guinea, and I think there were three thousand of them. She opened several other drawers, and showed me the wealth that was in them, and then gave me the key of the whole.

We had revelled thus all day, and part of the next day, in a bottomless sea of riches, when my lieutenant began to tell me, we must consider what to do with our prisoners and the ships, for that there was no subsisting in that manner. Upon this we called a short council, and concluded to carry the great ship away with us, but to put all the prisoners—queen, ladies, and all the rest—into the lesser vessels, and let them go; and so far was I from ravishing this lady, as I hear is reported of me, that though I might rifle her of everything else, yet, I assure you, I let her go untouched for me, or, as I am satisfied, for any one of my men; nay, when we dismissed them, we gave her leave to take a great many things of value with her, which she would have been plundered of if I had not been so careful of her.

We had now wealth enough not only to make us rich, but almost to have made a nation rich; and to tell you the truth, considering the costly things we took here, which we did not know the value of, and besides gold and silver and jewels,—I say, we never knew how rich we were; besides which we had a great quantity of bales of goods, as well calicoes as wrought silks, which, being for sale, were perhaps as a cargo of goods to answer the bills which might be drawn upon them for the account of the bride's portion; all which fell into our hands, with a great sum in silver coin, too big to talk of among Englishmen, especially while I am living, for reasons which I may give you hereafter.

Cleveland

SIR WALTER SCOTT

Hark to the insult loud, the bitter sneer,
The fierce threat answering to the brutal jeer;
Oaths fly like pistol-shots, and vengeful words
Clash with each other like conflicting swords—
The robber's quarrel by such sounds is shown,
And true men have some chance to gain their own.

Captivity, a Poem.

When Cleveland, borne off in triumph from his assailants in Kirkwall, found himself once more on board the pirate-vessel, his arrival was hailed with hearty cheers by a considerable part of the crew, who rushed to shake hands with him, and offer their congratulations on his return; for the situation of a Buccaneer Captain raised him very little above the level of the lowest of his crew, who, in all social intercourse, claimed the privilege of being his equal.

When his faction, for so these clamorous friends might be termed, had expressed their own greetings, they hurried Cleveland forward to the stern, where Goffe, their present commander, was seated on a gun, listening in a sullen and discontented mood to the shout which announced Cleveland's welcome. He was a man betwixt forty and fifty, rather under the middle size, but so very strongly made, that his crew used to compare him to a sixty-four cut down. Black-haired, bull-necked, and beetle-browed, his clumsy strength and ferocious countenance contrasted strongly with the manly figure and open countenance of Cleveland, in which even the practice of his atrocious profession had not been able to eradicate a natural grace of motion and generosity of expression. The two piratical Captains looked upon each other for some time in silence, while the partisans of each gathered around him. The elder part of the crew were the principal adherents of Goffe, while the young fellows, among whom Jack Bunce was a principal leader and agitator, were in general attached to Cleveland.

At length Goffe broke silence.—"You are welcome aboard, Captain Cleveland.—Smash my taffrail! I suppose you think yourself commodore yet! but that was over when you lost your ship, and be d—d!"

And here, once for all, we may take notice, that it was the gracious custom of this commander to mix his words and oaths in nearly equal proportions, which he was wont to call *shotting* his discourse. As we delight not, however, in the discharge of such artillery, we shall only indicate by a space like this—the places in which these expletives occurred; and thus, if the reader will pardon a very poor pun, we will reduce Captain Goffe's volley of sharp-shot into an explosion of blank cartridges. To his insinuations that he was come on board to assume the chief command, Cleveland replied, that he neither desired, nor would accept, any such promotion, but would only ask Captain Goffe for a cast of the boat, to put him ashore in one of the other islands, as he had no wish either to command Goffe, or to remain in a vessel under his orders.

"And why not under my orders, brother?" demanded Goffe, very austerely; "— — — are you too good a man, — — — with your cheese-toaster and your jib there, — — — to serve under my orders, and be d—d to you, where there are so many gentlemen that are elder and better seamen than yourself?"

"I wonder which of these capital seamen it was," said Cleveland coolly, "that laid the ship under the fire of yon six-gun battery, that could blow her out of the water, if they had a mind, before you could either cut or slip? Elder and better sailors than I may like to serve under such a lubber, but I beg to be excused for my own share, Captain—that's all I have got to tell you."

"I think you are both mad!" said Hawkins the boatswain—"a meeting with sword and pistol may be devilish good fun in its way, when no better is to be had; but who the devil that had common sense, amongst a set of gentlemen in our condition, would fall a-quarrelling with each other, to let these duck-winged, web-footed islanders have a chance of knocking us all upon the head?"

"Well said, old Hawkins!" observed Derrick the quartermaster, who was an officer of very considerable importance among these rovers; "I say, if the two captains won't agree to live together quietly, and club both heart and head to defend the vessel, why, d—n me, depose them both, say I, and choose another in their stead!"

"Meaning yourself, I suppose, Master Quarter-master!" said Jack Bunce; "but that cock won't fight. He that is to command gentlemen, should be a gentleman himself, I think; and I give my vote for Captain Cleveland, as spirited and as gentlemanlike a man as ever daffed the world aside, and bid it pass!"

"What! *you* call yourself a gentleman, I warrant!" retorted Derrick; "why, —— your eyes! a tailor would make a better out of the worst suit of rags in your strolling wardrobe!—It is a shame for men of spirit to have such a Jack-a-dandy scarecrow on board!"

Jack Bunce was so incensed at these base comparisons, that without more ado, he laid his hand on his sword. The carpenter, however, and boatswain, interfered, the former brandishing his broad axe, and swearing he would put the skull of the first who should strike a blow past clouting, and the latter reminding them, that, by their articles, all quarrelling, striking, or more especially fighting, on board, was strictly prohibited; and that, if any gentleman had a quarrel to settle, they were to go ashore, and decide it with cutlass and pistol in presence of two of their messmates.

"I have no quarrel with any one, — — —!" said Goffe sullenly; "Captain Cleveland has wandered about among the islands here, amusing himself,— — —! and we have wasted our time and property in waiting for him, when we might have been adding twenty or thirty thousand dollars to the stock-purse. However, if it pleases the rest of the gentlemen-adventurers, — — —! why, I shall not grumble about it."

"I propose," said the boatswain, "that there should be a general council called in the great cabin, according to our articles, that we may consider what course we are to hold in this matter."

A general assent followed the boatswain's proposal; for every one found his own account in these general councils, in which each of the rovers had a free vote. By far the greater part of the crew only valued this franchise, as it allowed them, upon such solemn occasions, an unlimited quantity of liquor—a right which they failed not to exercise to the uttermost, by way of aiding their deliberations. But a few amongst the adventurers, who united some degree of judgment with the daring and profligate character of their profession, were wont, at such periods, to limit themselves within the bounds of comparative sobriety, and by these, under the apparent form of a vote of the general council, all things of moment relating to the voyage and undertakings of the pirates were in fact determined. The rest of the crew, when they recovered from their intoxication, were easily persuaded that the resolution adopted had been the legitimate effort of the combined wisdom of the whole senate.

Upon the present occasion the debauch had proceeded until the greater part of the crew were, as usual, displaying inebriation in all its most brutal and disgraceful shapes—swearing empty and unmeaning oaths—venting the most horrid imprecations in the mere gaiety of their heart—singing songs; and, from the middle of this earthly hell, the two captains, together with one or two of their principal adherents, as also the carpenter and boatswain, who always took a lead on such occasions, had drawn together into a pandemonium, or privy council of their own, to consider what was to be done; for, as the boatswain metaphorically observed, they were in a narrow channel, and behoved to keep sounding the tide-way.

When they began their consultations, the friends of Goffe remarked, to their great displeasure, that he had not observed the wholesome rule to which we have just alluded; but that, in endeavouring to drown his mortification at the sudden appearance of Cleveland, and the reception he met with from the crew, the elder Captain had not been able to do so without overflowing his reason at the same time. His natural sullen taciturnity had prevented this from being observed until the council began its deliberations, when it proved impossible to hide it.

The first person who spoke was Cleveland, who said, that, so far from wishing the command of the vessel, he desired no favour at any one's hand, except to land him upon some island or holm at a distance from Kirkwall, and leave him to shift for himself.

The boatswain remonstrated strongly against this resolution. "The lads," he said, "all knew Cleveland, and could trust his seamanship, as well as his courage; besides, he never let the grog get quite uppermost, and was always in proper trim, either to sail the ship, or to fight the ship, whereby she was never without some one to keep her course when he was on board.—And as for the noble Captain Goffe," continued the mediator, "he is as stout a heart as ever broke biscuit, and that I will uphold him; but then, when he has his grog aboard—I speak to his face—he is so d—d funny with his cranks and his jests, that there is no living with him. You all remember how nigh he had run the ship on that cursed Horse of Copinsha, as they call it, just by way of frolic; and then you know how he fired off his pistol under the table, when we were at the great council, and shot Jack Jenkins in the knee, and cost the poor devil his leg, with his pleasantry."

"Jack Jenkins was not a chip the worse," said the carpenter; "I took the leg off with my saw as well as any loblolly boy in the land could have done—heated my broad axe, and seared the stump—ay by—! and made a jury-leg that he shambles about with as well as ever he did—for Jack could never cut a feather."

"You are a clever fellow, carpenter," replied the boatswain, "but I had rather you tried your saw and red-hot axe upon the ship's knee-timbers than on mine, sink me!—But that here is not the case—The question is, if we shall part with Captain Cleveland here, who is a man of thought and action, whereby it is my belief it would be heaving the pilot overboard when the gale is blowing on a lee-shore. And, I must say, it is not the part of a true heart to leave his mates, who have been here waiting for him till they have missed stays. Our water is well-nigh out, and we have junketed till provisions are low with us. We cannot sail without provisions—we cannot get provisions without the good-will of the Kirkwall folks. If we remain here longer, the *Halcyon* frigate will be down upon us—she was seen off Peterhead two days since,—and we shall hang up at the yard-arm to be sun-dried. Now, Captain Cleveland will get us out of the hobble, if any can. He can play the gentleman with these Kirkwall folks, and knows how to deal with them on fair terms, and foul, too, if there be occasion for it."

"And so you would turn honest Captain Goffe a-grazing, would ye?" said an old weather-beaten pirate, who had but one eye; "what though he has his humours, and made my eye dowse the glim in his fancies and frolics, he is as honest a man as ever walked a quarter-deck, for all that; and d—n me but I stand by him so long as t'other lantern is lit!"

"Why, you would not hear me out," said Hawkins; "a man might as well talk to so many negers!—I tell you, I propose that Cleveland shall only be Captain from one, *post meridiem*, to five *a.m.*, during which time Goffe is always drunk."

The Captain of whom he last spoke gave sufficient proof of the truth of his words, by uttering an inarticulate growl, and attempting to present a pistol at the mediator Hawkins.

"Why, look ye now!" said Derrick, "there is all the sense he has, to get drunk on council-day, like one of these poor silly fellows!"

"Ay," said Bunce, "drunk as Davy's sow, in the face of the field, the fray, and the senate!"

"But, nevertheless," continued Derrick, "it will never do to have two captains in the same day. I think week about might suit better—and let Cleveland take the first turn."

"There are as good here as any of them," said Hawkins; "howsomdever, I object nothing to Captain Cleveland, and I think he may help us into deep water as well as another."

"Ay," exclaimed Bunce, "and a better figure he will make at bringing these Kirkwallers to order than his sober predecessor!—So Captain Cleveland for ever!"

"Stop, gentlemen," said Cleveland, who had hither-to been silent; "I hope you will not choose me Captain without my own consent?"

"Ay, by the blue vault of heaven will we," said Bunce, "if it be *pro bono publico!*"

"But hear me, at least," said Cleveland—"I do consent to take command of the vessel, since you wish it, and because I see you will ill get out of the scrape without me."

"Why, then, I say, Cleveland for ever, again!" shouted Bunce.

"Be quiet, prithee, dear Bunce!—honest Altamont!" said Cleveland.—"I undertake the business on this condition; that, when I have got the ship cleared for her voyage, with provisions, and so forth, you will be content to restore Captain Goffe to the command, as I said before, and put me ashore somewhere, to shift for myself—You will then be sure it is impossible I can betray you, since I will remain with you to the last moment."

"Ay, and after the last moment, too, by the blue vault! or I mistake the matter," muttered Bunce to himself.

The matter was now put to the vote; and so confident were the crew in Cleveland's superior address and management, that the temporary deposition of Goffe found little resistance even among his own partisans, who reasonably enough observed, "He might at least have kept sober to look after his own business—E'en let him put it to rights again himself next morning, if he will."

But when the next morning came, the drunken part of the crew, being informed of the issue of the deliberations of the council, to which they were virtually held to have assented, showed such a superior sense of Cleveland's merits, that Goffe, sulky and malcontent as he was, judged it wisest for the present to suppress his feelings of resentment, until a safer opportunity for suffering them to explode, and to submit to the degradation which so frequently took place among a piratical crew.

Cleveland, on his part, resolved to take upon him, with spirit and without loss of time, the task of extricating his ship's company from their perilous situation. For this purpose, he ordered the boat, with the purpose of going ashore in person, carrying with him twelve of the stoutest and best men of the crew, all very handsomely appointed (for the success of their nefarious profession had enabled the pirates to assume nearly as gay dresses as their officers), and above all, each man being sufficiently armed with cutlass and pistols, and several having pole-axes and poniards.

Cleveland himself was gallantly attired in a blue coat, lined with crimson silk, and laced with gold very richly, crimson damask waistcoat and breeches, a velvet cap, richly embroidered, with a white feather, white silk stockings, and red-heeled shoes, which were the extremity of finery among the gallants of the day. He had a gold chain several times folded round his neck, which sustained a whistle of the same metal, the ensign of his authority. Above all, he wore a decoration peculiar to those daring depredators, who, besides one, or perhaps two brace of pistols at their belt, had usually two additional brace, of the finest mounting and workmanship, suspended over their shoulders in a sort of sling or scarf of crimson ribbon. The hilt and mounting of the Captain's sword corresponded in value to the rest of his appointments, and his natural good mien was so well adapted to the whole equipment, that, when he appeared on deck, he was received with a general shout by the crew, who, as in other popular societies, judged a great deal by the eye.

Cleveland took with him in the boat, amongst others, his predecessor in office, Goffe, who was also very richly dressed, but who, not having the advantage of such an exterior as Cleveland's, looked like a boorish clown in the dress of a courtier, or rather like a vulgar-faced footpad decked in the spoils of some one whom he has murdered, and whose claim to the property of his garments is rendered doubtful in the eyes of all who look upon him, by the mixture of awkwardness, remorse, cruelty, and insolence, which clouds his countenance. Cleveland probably chose to take Goffe ashore with him, to prevent his having any opportunity, during his absence, to debauch the crew from their allegiance. In this guise they left the ship, and, swinging to their oars, while the water foamed higher at the chorus, soon reached the quay of Kirk-wall.

The command of the vessel was in the meantime entrusted to Bunce, upon whose allegiance Cleveland knew that he might perfectly depend, and, in a private conversation with him of some length, he gave him directions how to act in such emergencies as might occur.

These arrangements being made, and Bunce having been repeatedly charged to stand upon his guard alike against the adherents of Goffe and any attempt from the shore, the boat put off. As she approached the harbour, Cleveland displayed a white flag, and could observe that their appearance seemed to occasion a good deal of bustle and alarm. People were seen running to and fro, and some of them appeared to be getting under arms. The battery was manned hastily, and the English colours displayed. These were alarming symptoms, the rather that Cleveland knew, that, though there were no artillerymen in Kirkwall, yet there were many sailors perfectly competent to the management of great guns, and willing enough to undertake such service in case of need.

Noting these hostile preparations with a heedful eye, but suffering nothing like doubt or anxiety to appear on his countenance, Cleveland ran the boat right for the quay, on which several people, armed with muskets, rifles, and fowling-pieces, and others with half-pikes and whaling-knives, were now assembled, as if to oppose his landing. Apparently, however, they had not positively determined what measures they were to pursue; for, when the boat reached the quay, those immediately opposite bore back, and suffered Cleveland and his party to leap ashore without hindrance. They immediately drew up on the quay, except two, who, as their Captain had commanded, remained in the boat, which they put off to a little distance; a manœuvre which, while it placed the boat (the only one belonging to the sloop) out of danger of being seized, indicated a sort of careless confidence in Cleveland and his party, which was calculated to intimidate their opponents.

The Kirkwallers, however, showed the old Northern blood, put a manly face upon the matter, and stood upon the quay, with their arms shouldered, directly opposite to the rovers, and blocking up against them the street which leads to the town.

Cleveland was the first who spoke, as the parties stood thus looking upon each other.—"How is this, gentlemen burghers?" he said; "are you Orkney folks turned Highlandmen, that you are all under arms so early this morning; or have you manned the quay to give me the honour of a salute, upon taking the command of my ship?"

The burghers looked on each other, and one of them replied to Cleveland—"We do not know who you are; it was that other man," pointing to Goffe, "who used to come ashore as captain."

"That other gentleman is my mate, and commands in my absence," said Cleveland;—"but what is that to the purpose? I wish to speak with your Lord Mayor, or whatever you call him."

"The Provost is sitting in council with the Magistrates," answered the spokesman.

"So much the better," replied Cleveland.—"Where do their Worships meet?"

"In the Council-house," answered the other.

"Then make way for us, gentlemen, if you please, for my people and I are going there."

There was a whisper among the townspeople; but several were unresolved upon engaging in a desperate, and perhaps an unnecessary conflict, with desperate men; and the more determined citizens formed the hasty reflection that the strangers might be more easily mastered in the house, or perhaps in the narrow streets which they had to traverse, than when they stood drawn up and prepared for battle upon the quay. They suffered them, therefore, to proceed unmolested; and Cleveland, moving very slowly, keeping his people close together, suffering no one to press upon the flanks of his little detachment, and making four men, who constituted his rear-guard, turn round and face to the rear from time to time, rendered it, by his caution, a very dangerous task to make any attempt upon them.

In this manner they ascended the narrow street, and reached the Council-house, where the Magistrates were actually sitting, as the citizen had informed Cleveland. Here the inhabitants began to press forward, with the purpose of mingling with the pirates, and availing themselves of the crowd in the narrow entrance, to secure as many as they could, without allowing them room for the free use of their weapons. But this also had Cleveland foreseen, and, ere entering the Council-room, he caused the entrance to be cleared and secured, commanding four of his men to face down the street, and as many to confront the crowd who were thrusting each other from above. The burghers recoiled back from the ferocious, swarthy, and sunburnt countenances, as well as the levelled arms of these desperadoes, and Cleveland, with the rest of his party, entered the Council-room, where the Magistrates were sitting in council, with very little attendance. These gentlemen were thus separated effectually from the citizens, who looked to them for orders, and were perhaps more completely at the mercy of Cleveland, than he, with his little handful of men, could be said to be at that of the multitude by whom they were surrounded.

The Magistrates seemed sensible of their danger; for they looked upon each other in some confusion, when Cleveland thus addressed them:—

"Good morrow, gentlemen,—I hope there is no unkindness betwixt us. I am come to talk with you about getting supplies for my ship yonder in the roadstead—we cannot sail without them."

"Your ship, sir?" said the Provost, who was a man of sense and spirit,—"how do we know that you are her Captain?"

"Look at me," said Cleveland, "and you will, I think, scarce ask the question again."

The Magistrate looked at him, and accordingly did not think proper to pursue that part of the inquiry, but proceeded to say—"And if you are her Captain, whence comes she, and where is she bound for? You look too much like a man-of-war's man to be master of a trader, and we know that you do not belong to the British navy."

"There are more men-of-war on the sea than sail under the British flag," replied Cleveland; "but say that I were commander of a free-trader here, willing to exchange tobacco, brandy, gin, and such like, for cured fish and hides, why, I do not think I deserve so very bad usage from the merchants of Kirkwall as to deny me provisions for my money?"

"Look you, Captain," said the Town-clerk, "it is not that we are so very strait-laced neither—for, when gentlemen of your cloth come this way, it is as weel, as I tauld the Provost, just to do as the collier did when he met the devil,—and that is, to have naething to say to them, if they have naething to say to us;—and there is the gentleman," pointing to Goffe, "that was Captain before you, and may be Captain after you"—("The rascal speaks truth in that," muttered Goffe),—"he knows well how handsomely we entertained him, till he and his men took upon them to run through the town like hellicat devils.—I see one of them there!—that was the very fellow that stopped my servant-wench on the street, as she carried the lantern home before me, and insulted her before my face!"

"If it please your noble Mayorship's honour and glory," said Derrick, the fellow at whom the Town-clerk pointed, "it was not I that brought-to the bit of a tender that carried the lantern in the poop—it was quite a different sort of a person."

"Who was it, then, sir?" said the Provost.

"Why, please your majesty's worship," said Derrick, making several sea bows, and describing as nearly as he could, the exterior of the worthy Magistrate himself, "he was an elderly gentleman,—Dutch-built, round in the stern, with a white wig and a red nose—very like your majesty, I think;" then, turning to a comrade, he added, "Jack, don't you think the fellow that wanted to kiss the pretty girl with the lantern t'other night, was very like his worship?"

"Tom Derrick," answered the party appealed to, "I believe it is the very man!"

"This is insolence which we can make you repent of, gentlemen!" said the Magistrate, justly irritated at their effrontery; "you have behaved in this town, as if you were in an Indian village at Madagascar. You yourself, Captain, if captain you be, were at the head of another riot, no longer since than yesterday. We will give you no provisions till we know better whom we are supplying. And do not think to bully us; when I shake this handkerchief out at the window, which is at my elbow, your ship goes to the bottom. Remember she lies under the guns of our battery."

"And how many of these guns are honeycombed, Mr. Mayor?" said Cleveland. He put the question by chance; but instantly perceived, from a sort of confusion which the Provost in vain endeavoured to hide, that the artillery of Kirkwall was not in the best order. "Come, come, Mr. Mayor," he said, "bullying will go down with us as little as with you. Your guns yonder will do more harm to the poor old sailors who are to work them than to our sloop; and if we bring a broadside to bear on the town, why, your wives' crockery will be in some danger. And then to talk to us of seamen being a little frolicsome ashore, why, when are they otherwise? You have the Greenland whalers playing the devil among you every now and then; and the very Dutchmen cut capers in the streets of Kirkwall, like porpoises before a gale of wind. I am told you are a man of sense, and I am sure you and I could settle this matter in the course of a five-minutes' palaver."

"Well, sir," said the Provost, "I will hear what you have to say, if you will walk this way."

Cleveland accordingly followed him into a small interior apartment, and, when there, addressed the Provost thus: "I will lay aside my pistols, sir, if you are afraid of them."

"D—n your pistols!" answered the Provost, "I have served the King, and fear the smell of powder as little as you do!"

"So much the better," said Cleveland, "for you will hear me the more coolly.—Now, sir, let us be what perhaps you suspect us, or let us be anything else, what, in the name of Heaven, can you get by keeping us here, but blows and bloodshed? For which, believe me, we are much better provided than you can pretend to be. The point is a plain one—you are desirous to be rid of us—we are desirous to be gone. Let us have the means of departure, and we leave you instantly."

"Look ye, Captain," said the Provost, "I thirst for no man's blood. You are a pretty fellow, as there were many among the buccaneers in my time—but there is no harm in wishing you a better trade. You should have the stores and welcome for your money, so you would make these seas clear of you. But then, here lies the rub. The *Halcyon* frigate is expected here in these parts immediately; when she hears of you she will be at you; for there is nothing the white lapelle loves better than a rover—you are seldom without a cargo of dollars. Well, he comes down, gets you under his stern——"

"Blows us into the air, if you please," said Cleveland.

"Nay, that must be as *you* please, Captain," said the Provost; "but then what is to come of the good town of Kirkwall, that has been packing and peeling with the King's enemies? The burgh will be laid under a round fine, and it may be that the Provost may not come off so easily."

"Well then," said Cleveland, "I see where your pinch lies. Now, suppose that I run round this island of yours, and get into the roadstead at Stromness? We could get what we want put on board there, without Kirkwall or the Provost seeming to have any hand in it; or, if it should be ever questioned, your want of force, and our superior strength, will make a sufficient apology."

"That may be," said the Provost; "but if I suffer you to leave your present station, and go elsewhere, I must have some security that you will not do harm to the country."

"And we," said Cleveland, "must have some security on our side, that you will not detain us, by dribbling out our time till the *Halcyon* is on the coast. Now, I am myself perfectly willing to continue on shore as a hostage, on the one side, provided you will give me your word not to betray me, and send some magistrate, or person of consequence, aboard the sloop, where his safety will be a guarantee for mine."

The Provost shook his head, and intimated it would be difficult to find a person willing to place himself as hostage in such a perilous condition; but said he would propose the arrangement to such of the council as were fit to be trusted with a matter of such weight.

Captain Scarfield

HOWARD PYLE

The author of this narrative cannot recall that, in any history of the famous pirates, he has ever read a detailed and sufficient account of the life and death of Capt. John Scarfield. Doubtless some data concerning his death and the destruction of his schooner might be gathered from the report of Lieutenant

Mainwaring, now filed in the archives of the Navy Department, but beyond such bald and bloodless narrative the author knows of nothing, unless it be the little chap-book history published by Isaiah Thomas in Newburyport about the year 1821–22, entitled, "A True History of the Life and Death of Captain Jack Scarfield." This lack of particularity in the history of one so notable in his profession it is the design of the present narrative in a measure to supply, and, if the author has seen fit to cast it in the form of a fictional story, it is only that it may make more easy reading for those who see fit to follow the tale from this to its conclusion.

Captain Scarfield

I

Eleazer cooper, or Captain Cooper, as was his better-known title in Philadelphia, was a prominent member of the Society of Friends. He was an overseer of the meeting and an occasional speaker upon particular occasions. When at home from one of his many voyages he never failed to occupy his seat in the meeting both on First Day and Fifth Day, and he was regarded by his fellow townsmen as a model of business integrity and of domestic responsibility.

More incidental to this history, however, it is to be narrated that Captain Cooper was one of those trading skippers who carried their own merchandise in their own vessels which they sailed themselves, and on whose decks they did their own bartering. His vessel was a swift, large schooner, the *Eliza Cooper, of Philadelphia*, named for his wife. His cruising grounds were the West India Islands, and his merchandise was flour and corn meal ground at the Brandywine Mills at Wilmington, Delaware.

During the War of 1812 he had earned, as was very well known, an extraordinary fortune in this trading; for flour and corn meal sold at fabulous prices in the French, Spanish, Dutch, and Danish islands, cut off, as they were, from the rest of the world by the British blockade.

The running of this blockade was one of the most hazardous maritime ventures possible, but Captain Cooper had met with such unvaried success, and had sold his merchandise at such incredible profit that, at the end of the war, he found himself to have become one of the wealthiest merchants of his native city.

It was known at one time that his balance in the Mechanics' Bank was greater than that of any other individual depositor upon the books, and it was told of him that he had once deposited in the bank a chest of foreign silver coin, the exchanged value of which, when translated into American currency, was upward of forty-two thousand dollars—a prodigious sum of money in those days.

In person, Captain Cooper was tall and angular of frame. His face was thin and severe, wearing continually an unsmiling, mask-like expression of continent and unruffled sobriety. His manner was dry and taciturn, and his conduct and life were measured to the most absolute accord with the teachings of his religious belief.

He lived in an old-fashioned house on Front Street below Spruce—as pleasant, cheerful a house as ever a trading captain could return to. At the back of the house a lawn sloped steeply down toward the river. To the south stood the wharf and storehouses; to the north an orchard and kitchen garden bloomed with abundant verdure. Two large chestnut trees sheltered the porch and the little space of lawn, and when you sat under them in the shade you looked down the slope between two rows of box bushes directly across the shining river to the Jersey shore.

At the time of our story—that is, about the year 1820—this property had increased very greatly in value, but it was the old home of the Coopers, as Eleazer Cooper was entirely rich enough to indulge his fancy in such matters. Accordingly, as he chose to live in the same house where his father and his grandfather had dwelt before him, he peremptorily, if quietly, refused all offers looking toward the purchase of the lot of ground—though it was now worth five or six times its former value.

As was said, it was a cheerful, pleasant home, impressing you when you entered it with the feeling of spotless and all-pervading cleanliness—a cleanliness that greeted you in the shining brass doorknocker; that entertained you in the sitting room with its stiff, leather-covered furniture, the brass-headed tacks whereof sparkled like so many stars—a cleanliness that bade you farewell in the spotless stretch of sand-sprinkled hallway, the wooden floor of which was worn into knobs around the nail heads by the countless scourings and scrubbings to which it had been subjected and which left behind them an all-pervading faint, fragrant odor of soap and warm water.

Eleazer Cooper and his wife were childless, but one inmate made the great, silent, shady house bright with life. Lucinda Fairbanks, a niece of Captain Cooper's by his only sister, was a handsome, sprightly girl of eighteen or twenty, and a great favorite in the Quaker society of the city.

It remains only to introduce the final and, perhaps, the most important actor of the narrative—Lieut. James Mainwaring. During the past twelve months or so he had been a frequent visitor at the Cooper house. At this time he was a broad-shouldered, red-cheeked, stalwart fellow of twenty-six or twenty-eight. He was a great social favorite, and possessed the added romantic interest of having been aboard the *Constitution* when she fought the *Guerriere*, and of having, with his own hands, touched the match that fired the first gun of that great battle.

Mainwaring's mother and Eliza Cooper had always been intimate friends, and the coming and going of the young man during his leave of absence were looked upon in the house as quite a matter of course. Half a dozen times a week he would drop in to execute some little commission for the ladies, or, if Captain Cooper was at home, to smoke a pipe of tobacco with him, to sip a dram of his famous old Jamaica rum, or to play a rubber of checkers of an evening. It is not likely that either of the older people was the least aware of the real cause of his visits; still less did they suspect that any passages of sentiment had passed between the young people.

The truth was that Mainwaring and the young lady were very deeply in love. It was a love that they were obliged to keep a profound secret, for not only had Eleazer Cooper held the strictest sort of testimony against the late war—a testimony so rigorous as to render it altogether unlikely that one of so military a profession as Mainwaring practiced could hope for his consent to a suit for marriage, but Lucinda could not have married one not a member of the Society of Friends without losing her own birthright membership therein. She herself might not attach much weight to such a loss of membership in the Society, but her fear of, and her respect for, her uncle led her to walk very closely in her path of duty in this respect. Accordingly she and Mainwaring met as they could—clandestinely—and the stolen moments were very sweet. With equal secrecy Lucinda had, at the request of her lover, sat for a miniature portrait to Mrs. Gregory, which miniature, set in a gold medallion, Mainwaring, with a mild, sentimental pleasure, wore hung around his neck and beneath his shirt frill next his heart.

In the month of April of the year 1820 Mainwaring received orders to report at Washington. During the preceding autumn the West India pirates, and notably Capt. Jack Scarfield, had been more than usually active, and the loss of the packet *Marblehead* (which, sailing from Charleston, South Carolina, was never heard of more) was attributed to them. Two other coasting vessels off the coast of Georgia had been looted and burned by Scarfield, and the government had at last aroused itself to the necessity of active measures for repressing these pests of the West India waters.

Mainwaring received orders to take command of the *Yankee*, a swift, light-draught, heavily armed brig of war, and to cruise about the Bahama Islands and to capture and destroy all the pirates' vessels he could there discover.

On his way from Washington to New York, where the *Yankee* was then waiting orders, Mainwaring stopped in Philadelphia to bid good by to his many friends in that city. He called at the old Cooper house. It was on a Sunday afternoon. The spring was early and the weather extremely pleasant that day, being filled with a warmth almost as of summer. The apple trees were

Library Receipt
Onalaska - La Crosse County Library
Phone 781-9568
01/26/11 12:37PM
For TeleCirc call 789-7162
www.lacrossecountylibrary.org

Checkout Receipt

180540

The gigantic book of pirate stories /
33403004397763   Due: 02/16/11

TOTAL: 1

Thank you

already in full bloom and filled all the air with their fragrance. Everywhere there seemed to be the pervading hum of bees, and the drowsy, tepid sunshine was very delightful.

At that time Eleazer was just home from an unusually successful voyage to Antigua. Mainwaring found the family sitting under one of the still leafless chestnut trees, Captain Cooper smoking his long clay pipe and lazily perusing a copy of the *National Gazette*. Eleazer listened with a great deal of interest to what Mainwaring had to say of his proposed cruise. He himself knew a great deal about the pirates, and, singularly unbending from his normal, stiff taciturnity, he began telling of what he knew, particularly of Captain Scarfield—in whom he appeared to take an extraordinary interest.

Vastly to Mainwaring's surprise, the old Quaker assumed the position of a defendant of the pirates, protesting that the wickedness of the accused was enormously exaggerated. He declared that he knew some of the freebooters very well and that at the most they were poor, misdirected wretches who had, by easy gradation, slid into their present evil ways, from having been tempted by the government authorities to enter into privateering in the days of the late war. He conceded that Captain Scarfield had done many cruel and wicked deeds, but he averred that he had also performed many kind and benevolent actions. The world made no note of these latter, but took care only to condemn the evil that had been done. He acknowledged that it was true that the pirate had allowed his crew to cast lots for the wife and the daughter of the skipper of the *Northern Rose*, but there were none of his accusers who told how, at the risk of his own life and the lives of all his crew, he had given succor to the schooner *Halifax*, found adrift with all hands down with yellow fever. There was no defender of his actions to tell how he and his crew of pirates had sailed the pest-stricken vessel almost into the rescuing waters of Kingston harbor. Eleazer confessed that he could not deny that when Scarfield had tied the skipper of the *Baltimore Belle* naked to the foremast of his own brig he had permitted his crew of cutthroats (who were drunk at the time) to throw bottles at the helpless captive, who died that night of the wounds he had received. For this he was doubtless very justly condemned, but who was there to praise him when he had, at the risk of his life and in the face of the authorities, carried a cargo of provisions which he himself had purchased at Tampa Bay to the Island of Bella Vista after the great hurricane of 1818? In this notable adventure he had barely escaped, after a two days' chase, the British frigate *Ceres*, whose captain, had a capture been effected, would instantly have hung the unfortunate man to the yardarm in spite of the beneficent mission he was in the act of conducting.

In all this Eleazer had the air of conducting the case for the defendant. As he talked he became more and more animated and voluble. The light went out in his tobacco pipe, and a hectic spot appeared in either thin and sallow cheek. Mainwaring sat wondering to hear the severely peaceful Quaker preacher defending so notoriously bloody and cruel a cutthroat pirate as Capt. Jack Scarfield. The warm and innocent surroundings, the old brick house looking down upon them, the odor of apple blossoms and the hum of bees seemed to make it all the more incongruous. And still the elderly Quaker skipper talked on and on with hardly an interruption, till the warm sun slanted to the west and the day began to decline.

That evening Mainwaring stayed to tea and when he parted from Lucinda Fairbanks it was after nightfall, with a clear, round moon shining in the milky sky and a radiance pallid and unreal enveloping the old house, the blooming apple trees, the sloping lawn and the shining river beyond. He implored his sweetheart to let him tell her uncle and aunt of their acknowledged love and to ask the old man's consent to it, but she would not permit him to do so. They were so happy as they were. Who knew but what her uncle might forbid their fondness? Would he not wait a little longer? Maybe it would all come right after a while. She was so fond, so tender, so tearful at the nearness of their parting that he had not the heart to insist. At the same time it was with a feeling almost of despair that he realized that he must now be gone—maybe for the space of two years—without in all that time possessing the right to call her his before the world.

When he bade farewell to the older people it was with a choking feeling of bitter disappointment. He yet felt the pressure of her cheek against his shoulder, the touch of soft and velvet lips to his own. But what were such clandestine endearments compared to what might, perchance, be his—the right of calling her his own when he was far away and upon the distant sea? And, besides, he felt like a coward who had shirked his duty.

But he was very much in love. The next morning appeared in a drizzle of rain that followed the beautiful warmth of the day before. He had the coach all to himself, and in the damp and leathery solitude he drew out the little oval picture from beneath his shirt frill and looked long and fixedly with a fond and foolish joy at the innocent face, the blue eyes, the red, smiling lips depicted upon the satinlike, ivory surface.

II

For the better part of five months Mainwaring cruised about in the waters surrounding the Bahama Islands. In that time he ran to earth and dispersed a dozen nests of pirates. He destroyed no less than fifteen piratical crafts of all sizes, from a large half-decked whaleboat to a three-hundred-ton barkentine. The name of the *Yankee* became a terror to every sea wolf in the western tropics, and the waters of the Bahama Islands became swept almost clean of the bloody wretches who had so lately infested it.

But the one freebooter of all others whom he sought—Capt. Jack Scarfield—seemed to evade him like a shadow, to slip through his fingers like magic. Twice he came almost within touch of the famous marauder, both times in the ominous wrecks that the pirate captain had left behind him. The first of these was the waterlogged remains of a burned and still smoking wreck that he found adrift in the great Bahama channel. It was the *Water Witch*, *of Salem*, but he did not learn her tragic story until, two weeks later, he discovered a part of her crew at Port Maria, on the north coast of Jamaica. It was, indeed, a dreadful story to which he listened. The castaways said that they of all the vessel's crew had been spared so that they might tell the commander of the *Yankee*, should they meet him, that he might keep what he found, with Captain Scarfield's compliments, who served it up to him hot cooked.

Three weeks later he rescued what remained of the crew of the shattered, bloody hulk of the *Baltimore Belle*, eight of whose crew, headed by the captain, had been tied hand and foot and heaved overboard. Again, there was a message from Captain Scarfield to the commander of the *Yankee* that he might season what he found to suit his own taste.

Mainwaring was of a sanguine disposition, with fiery temper. He swore, with the utmost vehemence, that either he or John Scarfield would have to leave the earth.

He had little suspicion of how soon was to befall the ominous realization of his angry prophecy.

At that time one of the chief rendezvous of the pirates was the little island of San José, one of the southernmost of the Bahama group. Here, in the days before the coming of the *Yankee*, they were wont to put in to careen and clean their vessels and to take in a fresh supply of provisions, gunpowder, and rum, preparatory to renewing their attacks upon the peaceful commerce circulating up and down outside the islands, or through the wide stretches of the Bahama channel.

Mainwaring had made several descents upon this nest of freebooters. He had already made two notable captures, and it was here he hoped eventually to capture Captain Scarfield himself.

A brief description of this one-time notorious rendezvous of freebooters might not be out of place. It consisted of a little settlement of those wattled and mud-smeared houses such as you find through the West Indies. There were only three houses of a more pretentious sort, built of wood. One of these was a storehouse, another was a rum shop, and a third a house in which dwelt a mulatto woman, who was reputed to be a sort of left-handed wife of Captain Scarfield's. The population was almost entirely black and brown. One or two Jews and a half dozen Yankee traders, of hardly dubious honesty, comprised the entire white population. The rest consisted of a mongrel accumulation of negroes and mulattoes and half-caste Spaniards, and of a multitude of black or yellow women and children. The settlement stood in a bight of the beach forming a small harbor and affording a fair anchorage for small vessels, excepting it were against the beating of a southeasterly gale. The houses, or cabins, were surrounded by clusters of coco palms and growths of bananas, and a long curve of white beach, sheltered from the large Atlantic breakers that burst and exploded upon an outer bar, was drawn like a necklace around the semicircle of emerald-green water.

Such was the famous pirates' settlement of San José—a paradise of nature and a hell of human depravity and wickedness—and it was to this spot that Mainwaring paid another visit a few days after rescuing the crew of the *Baltimore Belle* from her shattered and sinking wreck.

As the little bay with its fringe of palms and its cluster of wattle huts opened up to view, Mainwaring discovered a vessel lying at anchor in the little harbor. It was a large and well-rigged schooner of two hundred and fifty or three hundred tons burden. As the *Yankee* rounded to under the stern of the stranger and dropped anchor in such a position as to bring her broadside battery to bear should the occasion require, Mainwaring set his glass to his eye to read the name he could distinguish beneath the overhang of her stern. It is impossible to describe his infinite surprise when, the white lettering starting out in the circle of the glass, he read, *The Eliza Cooper, of Philadelphia*.

He could not believe the evidence of his senses. Certainly this sink of iniquity was the last place in the world he would have expected to have fallen in with Eleazer Cooper.

He ordered out the gig and had himself immediately rowed over to the schooner. Whatever lingering doubts he might have entertained as to the identity of the vessel were quickly dispelled when he beheld Captain Cooper himself standing at the gangway to meet him. The impassive face of the friend showed neither surprise nor confusion at what must have been to him a most unexpected encounter.

But when he stepped upon the deck of the *Eliza Cooper* and looked about him, Mainwaring could hardly believe the evidence of his senses at the transformation that he beheld. Upon the main deck were eight twelve-pound carronade neatly covered with tarpaulin; in the bow a Long Tom, also snugly stowed away and covered, directed a veiled and muzzled snout out over the bowsprit.

It was entirely impossible for Mainwaring to conceal his astonishment at so unexpected a sight, and whether or not his own thoughts lent color to his imagination, it seemed to him that Eleazer Cooper concealed under the immobility of his countenance no small degree of confusion.

After Captain Cooper had led the way into the cabin and he and the younger man were seated over a pipe of tobacco and the invariable bottle of fine old Jamaica rum, Mainwaring made no attempt to refrain from questioning him as to the reason for this singular and ominous transformation.

"I am a man of peace, James Mainwaring," Eleazer replied, "but there are men of blood in these waters, and an appearance of great strength is of use to protect the innocent from the wicked. If I remained in appearance the peaceful trader I really am, how long does thee suppose I could remain unassailed in this place?"

It occurred to Mainwaring that the powerful armament he had beheld was rather extreme to be used merely as a preventive. He smoked for a while in silence and then he suddenly asked the other point-blank whether, if it came to blows with such a one as Captain Scarfield, would he make a fight of it?

The Quaker trading captain regarded him for a while in silence. His look, it seemed to Mainwaring, appeared to be dubitative as to how far he dared to be frank. "Friend James," he said at last, "I may as well acknowledge that my officers and crew are somewhat worldly. Of a truth they do not hold the same testimony as I. I am inclined to think that if it came to the point of a broil with those men of iniquity, my individual voice cast for peace would not be sufficient to keep my crew from meeting violence with violence. As for myself, thee knows who I am and what is my testimony in these matters."

Mainwaring made no comment as to the extremely questionable manner in which the Quaker proposed to beat the devil about the stump. Presently he asked his second question:

"And might I inquire," he said, "what you are doing here and why you find it necessary to come at all into such a wicked, dangerous place as this?"

"Indeed, I knew thee would ask that question of me," said the Friend, "and I will be entirely frank with thee. These men of blood are, after all, but human beings, and as human beings they need food. I have at present upon this vessel upward of two hundred and fifty barrels of flour which will bring a higher price here than anywhere else in the West Indies. To be entirely frank with thee, I will tell thee that I was engaged in making a bargain for the sale of the greater part of my merchandise when the news of thy approach drove away my best customer."

Mainwaring sat for a while in smoking silence. What the other had told him explained many things he had not before understood. It explained why Captain Cooper got almost as much for his flour and corn meal now that peace had been declared as he had obtained when the war and the blockade were in full swing. It explained why he had been so strong a defender of Captain Scarfield and the pirates that afternoon in the garden. Meantime, what was to be done? Eleazer confessed openly that he dealt with the pirates. What now was his—Mainwaring's—duty in the case? Was the cargo of the *Eliza Cooper* contraband and subject to confiscation? And then another question framed itself in his mind: Who was this customer whom his approach had driven away?

As though he had formulated the inquiry into speech the other began directly to speak of it. "I know," he said, "that in a moment thee will ask me who was this customer of whom I have just now spoken. I have no desire to conceal his name from thee. It was the man who is known as Captain Jack or Captain John Scarfield."

Mainwaring fairly started from his seat. "The devil you say!" he cried. "And how long has it been," he asked, "since he left you?"

The Quaker skipper carefully refilled his pipe, which he had by now smoked out. "I would judge," he said, "that it is a matter of four or five hours since news was brought overland by means of swift runners of thy approach. Immediately the man of wickedness disappeared." Here Eleazer set the bowl of his pipe to the candle flame and began puffing out voluminous clouds of smoke. "I would have thee understand, James Mainwaring," he resumed, "that I am no friend of this wicked and sinful man. His safety is nothing to me. It is only a question of buying upon his part and of selling upon mine. If it is any satisfaction to thee I will heartily promise to bring thee news if I hear anything of the man of Belial. I may furthermore say that I think it is likely thee will have news more or less directly of him within the space of a day. If this should happen, however, thee will have to do thy own fighting without help from me, for I am no man of combat nor of blood and will take no hand in it either way."

It struck Mainwaring that the words contained some meaning that did not appear upon the surface. This significance struck him as so ambiguous that when he went aboard the *Yankee* he confided as much of his suspicions as he saw fit to his second in command, Lieutenant Underwood. As night descended he had a double watch set and had everything prepared to repel any attack or surprise that might be attempted.

III

Nighttime in the tropics descends with a surprising rapidity. At one moment the earth is shining with the brightness of the twilight; the next, as it were, all things are suddenly swallowed into a gulf of darkness. The particular night of which this story treats was not entirely clear; the time of year was about the approach of the rainy season, and the tepid, tropical clouds added obscurity to the darkness of the sky, so that the night fell with even more startling quickness than usual. The blackness was very dense. Now and then a group of drifting stars swam out of a rift in the vapors, but the night was curiously silent and of a velvety darkness.

As the obscurity had deepened, Mainwaring had ordered lanthorns to be lighted and slung to the shrouds and to the stays, and the faint yellow of their illumination lighted the level white of the snug little war vessel, gleaming here and there in a starlike spark upon the brass trimmings and causing the rows of cannons to assume curiously gigantic proportions.

For some reason Mainwaring was possessed by a strange, uneasy feeling. He walked restlessly up and down the deck for a time, and then, still full of anxieties for he knew not what, went into his cabin to finish writing up his log for the day. He unstrapped his cutlass and laid it upon the table, lighted his pipe at the lanthorn and was about preparing to lay aside his coat when word was brought to him that the captain of the trading schooner was come alongside and had some private information to communicate to him.

Mainwaring surmised in an instant that the trader's visit related somehow to news of Captain Scarfield, and as immediately, in the relief of something positive to face, all of his feeling of restlessness vanished like a shadow of mist. He gave orders that Captain Cooper should be immediately shown into the cabin, and in a few moments the tall, angular form of the Quaker skipper appeared in the narrow, lanthorn-lighted space.

Mainwaring at once saw that his visitor was strangely agitated and disturbed. He had taken off his hat, and shining beads of perspiration had gathered and stood clustered upon his forehead. He did not reply to Mainwaring's greeting; he did not, indeed, seem to hear it; but he came directly forward to the table and stood leaning with one hand upon the open log book in which the lieutenant had just been writing. Mainwaring had reseated himself at the head of the table, and the tall figure of the skipper stood looking down at him as from a considerable height.

"James Mainwaring," he said, "I promised thee to report if I had news of the pirate. Is thee ready now to hear my news?"

There was something so strange in his agitation that it began to infect Mainwaring with a feeling somewhat akin to that which appeared to disturb his visitor. "I know not what you mean, sir!" he cried, "by asking if I care to hear your news. At this moment I would rather have news of that scoundrel than to have anything I know of in the world."

"Thou would? Thou would?" cried the other, with mounting agitation. "Is thee in such haste to meet him as all that? Very well; very well, then. Suppose I could bring thee face to face with him—what then? Hey? Hey? Face to face with him, James Mainwaring!"

The thought instantly flashed into Mainwaring's mind that the pirate had returned to the island; that perhaps at that moment he was somewhere near at hand.

"I do not understand you, sir," he cried. "Do you mean to tell me that you know where the villain is? If so, lose no time in informing me, for every instant of delay may mean his chance of again escaping."

"No danger of that!" the other declared, vehemently. "No danger of that! I'll tell thee where he is and I'll bring thee to him quick enough!" And as he spoke he thumped his fist against the open log book. In the vehemence of his growing excitement his eyes appeared to shine green in the lanthorn light, and the sweat that had stood in beads upon his forehead was now running in streams down his face. One drop hung like a jewel to the tip of his beaklike nose. He came a step nearer to Mainwaring and bent forward toward him, and there was something so strange and ominous in his bearing that the lieutenant instinctively drew back a little where he sat.

"Captain Scarfield sent something to you," said Eleazer, almost in a raucous voice, "something that you will be surprised to see." And the lapse in his speech from the Quaker "thee" to the plural "you" struck Mainwaring as singularly strange.

As he was speaking Eleazer was fumbling in a pocket of his long-tailed drab coat, and presently he brought something forth that gleamed in the lanthorn light.

The next moment Mainwaring saw leveled directly in his face the round and hollow nozzle of a pistol.

There was an instant of dead silence and then, "I am the man you seek!" said Eleazer Cooper, in a tense and breathless voice.

The whole thing had happened so instantaneously and unexpectedly that for the moment Mainwaring sat like one petrified. Had a thunderbolt fallen from the silent sky and burst at his feet he could not have been more stunned. He was like one held in the meshes of a horrid nightmare, and he gazed as through a mist of impossibility into the lineaments of the well-known, sober face now transformed as from within into the aspect of a devil. That face, now ashy white, was distorted into a diabolical grin. The teeth glistened in the lamplight. The brows, twisted into a tense and convulsed frown, were drawn down into black shadows, through which the eyes burned a baleful green like the eyes of a wild animal driven to bay. Again he spoke in the same breathless voice. "I am John Scarfield! Look at me, then, if you want to see a pirate!" Again there was a little time of silence, through which Mainwaring heard his watch ticking loudly from where it hung against the bulk-head. Then once more the other began speaking. "You would chase me out of the West Indies, would you? G—— you! What are you come to now? You are caught in your own trap, and you'll squeal loud enough before you get out of it. Speak a word or make a movement and I'll blow your brains out against the partition behind you! Listen to what I say or you are a dead man. Sing out an order instantly for my mate and my bos'n to come here to the cabin, and be quick about it, for my finger's on the trigger, and it's only a pull to shut your mouth forever."

It was astonishing to Mainwaring, in afterward thinking about it all, how quickly his mind began to recover its steadiness after that first astonishing shock. Even as the other was speaking he discovered that his brain was becoming clarified to a wonderful lucidity; his thoughts were becoming rearranged, and with a marvelous activity and an alertness he had never before experienced. He knew that if he moved to escape or uttered any outcry he would be instantly a dead man, for the circle of the pistol barrel was directed full against his forehead and with the steadiness of a rock. If he could but for an instant divert that fixed and deadly attention he might still have a chance for life. With the thought an inspiration burst into his mind and he instantly put it into execution; thought, inspiration, and action, as in a flash, were one. He must make the other turn aside his deadly gaze, and instantly he roared out in a voice that stunned his own ears: "Strike, bos'n! Strike, quick!"

Taken by surprise, and thinking, doubtless, that another enemy stood behind him, the pirate swung around like a flash with his pistol leveled against the blank boarding. Equally upon the instant he saw the trick that had been played upon him and in a second flash had turned again. The turn and return had occupied but a moment of time, but that moment, thanks to the readiness of his own invention, had undoubtedly saved Mainwaring's life. As the other turned away his gaze for that brief instant Mainwaring leaped forward and upon him. There was a flashing flame of fire as the pistol was discharged and a deafening detonation that seemed to split his brain. For a moment, with reeling senses, he supposed himself to have been shot, the next he knew he had escaped. With the energy of despair he swung his enemy around and drove him with prodigious violence against the corner of the table. The pirate emitted a grunting cry and then they fell together, Mainwaring upon the top, and the pistol clattered with them to the floor in their fall. Even as he fell, Mainwaring roared in a voice of thunder, "All hands repel boarders!" And then again, "All hands repel boarders!"

Whether hurt by the table edge or not, the fallen pirate struggled as though possessed of forty devils, and in a moment or two Mainwaring saw the shine of a long, keen knife that he had drawn from somewhere about his person. The lieutenant caught him by the wrist, but the other's muscles were as though made of steel. They both fought in despairing silence, the one to carry out his frustrated purposes to kill, the other to save his life. Again and again Mainwaring felt that the knife had been thrust against him, piercing once his arm, once his shoulder, and again his neck. He felt the warm blood streaming down his arm and body and looked about him in despair. The pistol lay near upon the deck of the cabin. Still holding the other by the wrist as he could, Mainwaring snatched up the empty weapon and struck once and again at the bald, narrow forehead beneath him. A third blow he delivered with all the force he could command, and then with a violent and convulsive throe the straining muscles beneath him relaxed and grew limp and the fight was won.

Through all the struggle he had been aware of the shouts of voices, of trampling of feet and discharge of firearms, and the thought came to him, even through his own danger, that the *Yankee* was being assaulted by the pirates. As he felt the struggling form beneath him loosen and dissolve into quietude, he leaped up, and snatching his cutlass, which still lay upon the table, rushed out upon the deck, leaving the stricken form lying twitching upon the floor behind him.

It was a fortunate thing that he had set double watches and prepared himself for some attack from the pirates, otherwise the *Yankee* would certainly have been lost. As it was, the surprise was so overwhelming that the pirates, who had been concealed in the large whaleboat that had come alongside, were not only able to gain a foothold upon the deck, but for a time it seemed as though they would drive the crew of the brig below the hatches.

But as Mainwaring, streaming with blood, rushed out upon the deck, the pirates became immediately aware that their own captain must have been overpowered, and in an instant their desperate energy began to evaporate. One or two jumped over board; one, who seemed to be the mate, fell dead from a pistol shot, and then, in the turn of a hand, there was a rush of a retreat and a vision of leaping forms in the dusky light of the lanthorns and a sound of splashing in the water below.

The crew of the *Yankee* continued firing at the phosphorescent wakes of the swimming bodies, but whether with effect it was impossible at the time to tell.

IV

The pirate captain did not die immediately. He lingered for three or four days, now and then unconscious, now and then semiconscious, but always deliriously wandering. All the while he thus lay dying, the mulatto woman, with whom he lived in this part of his extraordinary dual existence, nursed and cared for him with such rude attentions as the surroundings afforded. In the wanderings of his mind the same duality of life followed him. Now and then he would appear the calm, sober, self-contained, well-ordered member of a peaceful society that his friends in his far-away home knew him to be; at other times the nether part of his nature would leap up into life like a wild beast, furious and gnashing. At the one time he talked evenly and clearly of peaceful things; at the other time he blasphemed and hooted with fury.

Several times Mainwaring, though racked by his own wounds, sat beside the dying man through the silent watches of the tropical nights. Oftentimes upon these occasions as he looked at the thin, lean face babbling and talking so aimlessly, he wondered what it all meant. Could it have been madness—madness in which the separate entities of good and bad each had, in its turn, a perfect and distinct existence? He chose to think that this was the case. Who, within his inner consciousness, does not feel that same ferine, savage man struggling against the stern, adamantine bonds of morality and decorum? Were those bonds burst asunder, as it was with this man, might not the wild beast rush forth, as it had rushed forth in him, to rend and to tear? Such were the questions that Mainwaring asked himself. And how had it all come about? By what easy gradations had the respectable Quaker skipper descended from the decorum of his home life, step by step, into such a gulf of iniquity? Many such thoughts passed through Mainwaring's mind, and he pondered them through the still reaches of the tropical nights while he sat watching the pirate captain struggle out of the world he had so long burdened. At last the poor wretch died, and the earth was well quit of one of its torments.

A systematic search was made through the island for the scattered crew, but none was captured. Either there were some secret hiding places upon the island (which was not very likely) or else they had escaped in boats hidden somewhere among the tropical foliage. At any rate they were gone.

Nor, search as he would, could Mainwaring find a trace of any of the pirate treasure. After the pirate's death and under close questioning, the weeping mulatto woman so far broke down as to confess in broken English that Captain Scarfield had taken a quantity of silver money aboard his vessel, but either she was mistaken or else the pirates had taken it thence again and had hidden it somewhere else.

Nor would the treasure ever have been found but for a most fortuitous accident.

Mainwaring had given orders that the *Eliza Cooper* was to be burned, and a party was detailed to carry the order into execution. At this the cook of the *Yankee* came petitioning for some of the Wilmington and Brandywine flour to make some plum duff upon the morrow, and Mainwaring granted his request in so far that he ordered one of the men to knock open one of the barrels of flour and to supply the cook's demands.

The crew detailed to execute this modest order in connection with the destruction of the pirate vessel had not been gone a quarter of an hour when word came back that the hidden treasure had been found.

Mainwaring hurried aboard the *Eliza Cooper*, and there in the midst of the open flour barrel he beheld a great quantity of silver coin buried in and partly covered by the white meal.

A systematic search was now made. One by one the flour barrels were heaved up from below and burst open on the deck and their contents searched, and if nothing but the meal was found it was swept overboard. The breeze was whitened with clouds of flour, and the white meal covered the surface of the ocean for yards around.

In all, upward of one hundred and fifty thousand dollars was found concealed beneath the innocent flour and meal. It was no wonder the pirate captain was so successful, when he could upon an instant's notice transform himself from a wolf of the ocean to a peaceful Quaker trader selling flour to the hungry towns and settlements among the scattered islands of the West Indies, and so carrying his bloody treasure safely into his quiet Northern home.

In concluding this part of the narrative it may be added that a wide strip of canvas painted black was discovered in the hold of the *Eliza Cooper*. Upon it, in great white letters, was painted the name, "The Bloodhound." Undoubtedly this was used upon occasions to cover the real and peaceful title of the trading schooner, just as its captain had, in reverse, covered his sanguine and cruel life by a thin sheet of morality and respectability.

This is the true story of the death of Capt. Jack Scarfield.

The Newburyport chap-book, of which I have already spoken, speaks only of how the pirate disguised himself upon the ocean as a Quaker trader.

Nor is it likely that anyone ever identified Eleazer Cooper with the pirate, for only Mainwaring of all the crew of the *Yankee* was exactly aware of the true identity of Captain Scarfield. All that was ever known to the world was that Eleazer Cooper had been killed in a fight with the pirates.

In a little less than a year Mainwaring was married to Lucinda Fairbanks. As to Eleazer Cooper's fortune, which eventually came into the possession of Mainwaring through his wife, it was many times a subject of speculation to the lieutenant how it had been earned. There were times when he felt well assured that a part of it at least was the fruit of piracy, but it was entirely impossible to guess how much more was the result of legitimate trading.

For a little time it seemed to Mainwaring that he should give it all up, but this was at once so impracticable and so quixotic that he presently abandoned it, and in time his qualms and misdoubts faded away and he settled himself down to enjoy that which had come to him through his marriage.

In time the Mainwarings removed to New York, and ultimately the fortune that the pirate Scarfield had left behind him was used in part to found the great shipping house of Mainwaring & Bigot, whose famous transatlantic packet ships were in their time the admiration of the whole world.

The Attack

CAPTAIN MARRYAT

In the meantime, the sea-breeze had risen in the offing, and was sweeping along the surface to where the schooner was at anchor. The captain ordered a man to the cross-trees, directing him to keep a good lookout, while he walked the deck in company with his first mate.

"She may not have sailed until a day or two later," said the captain, continuing the conversation; "I have made allowance for that, and depend upon it, as she makes the eastern passage, we must soon fall in with her; if she does not heave in sight this evening by daylight, I shall stretch out in the offing; I know the Portuguese well. The sea-breeze has caught our craft; let them run up the inner jib, and see that she does not foul her anchor."

It was now late in the afternoon, and dinner had been sent into the cabin; the captain descended, and took his seat at the table with Francisco, who ate in silence. Once or twice the captain, whose wrath had subsided, and whose kindly feelings towards Francisco, checked for a time, had returned with greater force, tried, but in vain, to rally him into conversation, when "*Sail ho!*" was shouted from the mast-head.

"There she is," cried the captain, jumping from, and then, as if checking himself, immediately resuming, his seat.

Francisco put his hand to his forehead, covering his eyes as his elbow leant upon the table.

"A large ship, sir; we can see down to the second reef of her topsails," said Hawkhurst, looking down the skylight.

The captain hastily swallowed some wine from a flagon, cast a look of scorn and anger upon Francisco, and rushed on deck.

"Be smart, lads!" cried the captain, after a few seconds' survey of the vessel through his glass; "that's her: furl the awnings, and run the anchor up to the bows: there's more silver in that vessel, my lads, than your chests will hold; and the good saints of the churches at Goa will have to wait a little longer for their gold candlesticks."

The crew were immediately on the alert; the awnings were furled, and all the men, stretching aft the spring cable, walked the anchor up to the bows. In two minutes more the *Avenger* was standing out on the starboard tack, shaping her course so as to cut off the ill-fated vessel. The breeze freshened, and the schooner darted through the smooth water with the impetuosity of a dolphin after its prey. In an hour the hull of the ship was plainly to be distinguished; but the sun was near to the horizon, and before they could ascertain what their force might be, daylight had disappeared. Whether the schooner had been perceived or not, it was impossible to say; at all events, the course of the ship had not been altered, and if she had seen the schooner, she evidently treated her with contempt. On board the *Avenger*, they were not idle; the long gun in the centre had been cleared from the incumbrances which surrounded it, the other guns had been cast loose, shot handed up, and everything prepared for action, with all the energy and discipline of a man-of-war. The chase had not been lost sight of, and the eyes of the pirate captain were fixed upon her through a night-glass. In about an hour more the schooner was within a mile of the ship, and now altered her course so as to range up within a cable's length of her to leeward. Cain stood upon the gunwhale and hailed. The answer was in Portuguese.

"Heave to, or I'll sink you!" replied he in the same language.

carronades, and a heavy volley of muskets from the Portuguese, was the decided answer. The broadside, too much elevated to hit the low hull of the schooner, was not without effect—the foretopmast fell, the jaws of the main-gaff were severed, and a large proportion of the standing as well as the running rigging came rattling down on her decks. The volley of musketry was more fatal: thirteen of the pirates were wounded, some of them severely.

"Well done, John Portuguese!" cried Hawkhurst; "by the holy poker! I never gave you credit for so much pluck."

"Which they shall pay dearly for," was the cool reply of Cain, as he still remained in his exposed situation.

"Blood for blood! if I drink it," observed the second mate, as he looked at the crimson rivulet trickling down the fingers of his left hand from a wound in his arm—"just tie my handkerchief round this, Bill."

In the interim, Cain had desired his crew to elevate their guns, and the broadside was returned.

"That will do, my lads: starboard; ease off the boomsheet; let her go right round, Hawkhurst— we cannot afford to lose our men."

The schooner wore round, and ran astern of her opponent.

The Portuguese on board the ship, imagining that the schooner, finding she had met with unexpected resistance, had sheered off, gave a loud cheer.

"The last you will ever give, my fine fellows!" observed Cain, with a sneer.

In a few moments the schooner had run a mile astern of the ship.

"Now then, Hawkhurst, let her come to and about; man the long gun, and see that every shot is pitched into her, while the rest of them get up a new foretopmast, and knot and splice the rigging."

The schooner's head was again turned towards the ship; her position was right astern, about a mile distant or rather more; the long 32-pounder gun amidships was now regularly served, every shot passing through the cabin windows, or some other part of the ship's stern, raking her fore and aft. In vain did the ship alter her course, and present her broadside to the schooner; the latter was immediately checked in her speed, so as to keep the prescribed distance at which the carronades of the ship were useless, and the execution from the long gun decisive. The ship was at the mercy of the pirate; and as may be expected, no mercy was shown. For three hours did this murderous attack continue, when the gun, which, as before observed, was of brass, became so heated that the pirate captain desired his men to discontinue. Whether the ship had surrendered or not it was impossible to say, as it was too dark to distinguish: while the long gun was served, the foretopmast and main-gaff had been shifted, and all the standing and running rigging made good; the schooner keeping her distance, and following in the wake of the ship until daylight.

We must now repair on board of the ship: she was an Indiaman; one of the very few that occasionally are sent out by the Portuguese government to a country which once owned their undivided sway, but in which, at present, they hold but a few miles of territory. She was bound to

Goa, and had on board a small detachment of troops, a new governor and his two sons, a bishop and his niece, with her attendant. The sailing of a vessel with such a freight was a circumstance of rare occurrence, and was, of course, generally bruited about long before her departure. Cain had, for some months, received all the necessary intelligence relative to her cargo and destination; but, as usual with the Portuguese of the present day, delay upon delay had followed, and it was not until about three weeks previous that he had been assured of her immediate departure. He then ran down the coast to the bay we have mentioned that he might intercept her; and, as the event had proved, showed his usual judgment and decision. The fire of the schooner had been most destructive; many of the Indiaman's crew, as well as of the troops, had been mowed down one after another; until at last, finding that all their efforts to defend themselves were useless, most of those who were still unhurt had consulted their safety, and hastened down to the lowest recesses of the hold to avoid the raking and destructive shot. At the time that the schooner had discontinued her fire to allow the gun to cool, there was no one on deck but the Portuguese captain and one old weather-beaten seaman who stood at the helm. Below in the orlop-deck the remainder of the crew and the passengers were huddled together in a small space: some were attending to the wounded, who were numerous; others were invoking the saints to their assistance; the bishop, a tall, dignified person, apparently nearly sixty years of age, was kneeling in the centre of the group, which was dimly lighted by two or three lanterns, at one time in fervent prayer, at another, interrupted, that he might give absolution to those wounded men whose spirits were departing, and who were brought down and laid before him by their comrades. On one side of him knelt his orphan niece, a young girl of about seventeen years of age, watching his countenance as he prayed, or bending down with a look of pity and tearful eyes on her expiring countrymen, whose last moments were gladdened by his holy offices. On the other side of the bishop stood the governor, Don Philip de Ribiera, and his two sons, youths in their prime, and holding commissions in the king's service. There was melancholy on the brow of Don Ribiera; he was prepared for, and he anticipated, the worst. The eldest son had his eyes fixed upon the sweet countenance of Teresa de Silva—that very evening, as they walked together on the deck, had they exchanged their vows—that very evening they had luxuriated in the present, and had dwelt with delightful anticipation on the future. But we must leave them and return on deck.

The captain of the Portuguese ship had walked aft, and now went up to Antonio, the old seaman, who was standing at the wheel.

"I still see her with the glass, Antonio, and yet she has not fired for nearly two hours; do you think any accident has happened to her long gun? if so, we may have some chance."

Antonio shook his head. "We have but little chance, I am afraid, my captain; I knew by the ring of the gun, when she fired it, that it was brass; indeed, no schooner could carry a long iron gun of that calibre. Depend upon it, she only waits for the metal to cool and daylight to return: a long gun or two might have saved us; but now, as she has the advantage of us in heels, we are at her mercy."

"What can she be—a French privateer?"

"I trust it may be so; and I have promised a silver candlestick to St. Antonio that it may prove no worse: we then may have some chance of seeing our homes again; but I fear not."

"What, then, do you imagine her to be, Antonio?"

"The pirate which we have heard so much of."

"Jesu protect us! we must then sell our lives as dearly as we can."

"So I intend to do, my captain," replied Antonio, shifting the helm a spoke.

The day broke, and showed the schooner continuing her pursuit at the same distance astern, without any apparent movement on board. It was not until the sun was some degrees above the horizon that the smoke was again seen to envelop her bows, and the shot crashed through the timbers of the Portuguese ship. The reason for this delay was, that the pirate waited till the sun was up to ascertain if there were any other vessels to be seen, previous to his pouncing on his quarry. The Portuguese captain went aft and hoisted his ensign, but no flag was shown by the schooner. Again whistled the ball, and again did it tear up the decks of the unfortunate ship: many of those who had re-ascended to ascertain what was going on, now hastily sought their former retreat.

"Mind the helm, Antonio," said the Portuguese captain; "I must go down and consult with the governor."

"Never fear, my captain; as long as these limbs hold together, I will do my duty," replied the old man, exhausted as he was by long watching and fatigue.

The captain descended to the orlop-deck, where he found the major part of the crew and passengers assembled.

"My lords," said he, addressing the governor and bishop, "the schooner has not shown any colours, although our own are hoisted. I am come down to know your pleasure. Defence we can make none; and I fear that we are at the mercy of a pirate."

"A pirate!" ejaculated several, beating their breasts, and calling upon their saints.

"Silence, my good people, silence," quietly observed the bishop; "as to what it may be best to do," continued he, turning to the captain, "I cannot advise; I am a man of peace, and unfit to hold a place in a council of war. Don Ribiera, I must refer the point to you and your sons. Tremble not, my dear Teresa; are we not under the protection of the Almighty."

"Holy Virgin, pity us!" exclaimed Teresa.

"Come, my sons," said Don Ribiera, "we will go on deck and consult: let not any of the men follow us; it is useless risking lives which may yet be valuable."

Don Ribiera and his sons followed the captain to the quarter-deck, and with him and Antonio they held a consultation.

"We have but one chance," observed the old man, after a time; "let us haul down our colours as if in submission; they will then range up alongside, and either board us from the schooner, or from their boats; at all events, we shall find out what she is, and, if a pirate, we must sell our lives as dearly as we can. If, when we haul down the colours, she ranges up alongside, as I expect she will, let all the men be prepared for a desperate struggle."

"You are right, Antonio," replied the governor; "go aft, captain, and haul down the colours!—let us see what she does now. Down, my boys! and prepare the men to do their duty."

As Antonio had predicted, so soon as the colours were hauled down, the schooner ceased firing and made sail. She ranged up on the quarter of the ship, and up to her main peak soared the terrific black flag; her broadside was poured into the Indiaman, and before the smoke had cleared away there was a concussion from the meeting sides, and the bearded pirates poured upon her decks.

The crew of the Portuguese, with the detachment of troops, still formed a considerable body of men. The sight of the black flag had struck ice into every heart, but the feeling was resolved into one of desperation.

"Knives, men, knives!" roared Antonio, rushing on to the attack, followed by the most brave.

"Blood for blood!" cried the second mate, aiming a blow at the old man.

"You have it," replied Antonio, as his knife entered the pirate's heart, while, at the same moment, he fell and was himself a corpse.

The struggle was deadly, but the numbers and ferocity of the pirates prevailed. Cain rushed forward followed by Hawkhurst, bearing down all who opposed them. With one blow from the pirate-captain, the head of Don Ribiera was severed to the shoulder; a second struck down the eldest son, while the sword of Hawkhurst passed through the body of the other. The Portuguese captain had already fallen, and the men no longer stood their ground. A general massacre ensued, and the bodies were thrown overboard as fast as the men were slaughtered. In less than five minutes there was not a living Portuguese on the bloody decks of the ill-fated ship.

The Malay Proas

JAMES FENIMORE COOPER

We had cleared the Straits of Sunda early in the morning, and had made a pretty fair run in the course of the day, though most of the time in thick weather. Just as the sun set, however, the horizon became clear, and we got a sight of two small sail, seemingly heading in toward the coast of Sumatra, proas by their rig and dimensions. They were so distant, and were so evidently steering for the land, that no one gave them much thought, or bestowed on them any particular attention. Proas in that quarter were usually distrusted by ships, it is true; but the sea is full of them, and far more are innocent than are guilty of any acts of violence. Then it became dark soon after these craft were seen, and night shut them in. An hour after the sun had set, the wind fell to a light air, that just kept steerage-way on the ship. Fortunately, the *John* was not only fast, but she minded her helm, as a light-footed girl turns in a lively dance. I never was in a better-steering ship, most especially in moderate weather.

Mr. Marble had the middle watch that night, and, of course, I was on deck from midnight until four in the morning. It proved misty most of the watch, and for quite an hour we had a light drizzling rain. The ship the whole time was close-hauled, carrying royals. As everybody seemed to have made up his mind to a quiet night, one without any reefing or furling, most of the watch were sleeping about the decks, or wherever they could get good quarters, and be least in the way. I do not know what kept me awake, for lads of my age are apt to get all the sleep they can; but I believe I was thinking of Clawbonny, and Grace, and Lucy; for the latter, excellent girl as she was, often crossed my mind in those days of youth and comparative innocence. Awake I was, and walking in the weather-gangway, in a sailor's trot. Mr. Marble, he I do believe was fairly snoozing on the hen-coops, being, like the sails, as one might say, barely "asleep." At that moment I heard a noise, one familiar to seamen; that of an oar falling in a boat. So completely was my mind bent on other and distant scenes, that at first I felt no surprise, as if we were in a harbor surrounded by craft of various sizes, coming and going at all hours. But a second thought destroyed this illusion, and I looked eagerly about me. Directly on our weather-bow, distant, perhaps, a cable's length, I saw a small sail, and I could distinguish it sufficiently well to perceive it was a proa. I sang out "Sail ho! and close aboard!"

Mr. Marble was on his feet in an instant. He afterward told me that when he opened his eyes, for he admitted this much to me in confidence, they fell directly on the stranger. He was too much of a seaman to require a second look in order to ascertain what was to be done. "Keep the ship away—keep her broad off!" he called out to the man at the wheel. "Lay the yards square—call all hands, one of you. Captain Robbins, Mr. Kite, bear a hand up; the bloody proas are aboard us!" The last part of this call was uttered in a loud voice, with the speaker's head down the companion-way. It was heard plainly enough below, but scarcely at all on deck.

In the meantime everybody was in motion. It is amazing how soon sailors are wide awake when there is really anything to do! It appeared to me that all our people mustered on deck in less than a minute, most of them with nothing on but their shirts and trousers. The ship was nearly before the wind by the time I heard the captain's voice; and then Mr. Kite came bustling in among us forward, ordering most of the men to lay aft to the braces, remaining himself on the forecastle, and keeping me with him to let go the sheets. On the forecastle, the strange sail was no longer visible, being now abaft the beam; but I could hear Mr. Marble swearing there were two of them, and that they must be the very chaps we had seen to leeward, and standing in for the land at sunset. I also heard the captain calling out to the steward to bring him a powder-horn. Immediately after, orders were given to let fly all our sheets forward, and then I perceived that they were wearing ship. Nothing saved us but the prompt order of Mr. Marble to keep the ship away, by which means, instead of moving toward the proas, we instantly began to move from them. Although they went three feet to our two, this gave us a moment of breathing time.

As our sheets were all flying forward, and remained so for a few minutes, it gave me leisure to look about. I soon saw both proas, and glad enough was I to perceive that they had not approached materially nearer. Mr. Kite observed this also, and remarked that our movements had been so prompt as to "take the rascals aback." He meant they did not exactly know what we were at, and had not kept away with us.

At this instant, the captain and five or six of the oldest seamen began to cast loose all our starboard, or weather guns, four in all, and sixes. We had loaded these guns in the Straits of Banca, with grape and canister, in readiness for just such pirates as were now coming down upon us; and nothing was wanting but the priming and a hot loggerhead. It seems two of the last had been ordered in the fire, when we saw the proas at sunset; and they were now in excellent condition for service, live coals being kept around them all night by command. I saw a cluster of men busy with the second gun from forward, and could distinguish the captain pointing to it.

"There cannot well be any mistake, Mr. Marble?" the captain observed, hesitating whether to fire or not.

"Mistake, sir? Lord, Captain Robbins, you might cannonade any of the islands astern for a week, and never hurt an honest man. Let 'em have it, sir; I'll answer for it, you do good."

This settled the matter. The loggerhead was applied, and one of our sixes spoke out in a smart report. A breathless stillness succeeded. The proas did not alter their course, but neared us fast. The captain levelled his night-glass, and I heard him tell Kite, in a low voice, that they were full of men. The word was now passed to clear away all the guns, and to open the arm-chest, to come at the muskets and pistols. I heard the rattling of the boarding-pikes, too, as they were cut adrift from the spanker-boom, and fell upon the decks. All this sounded very ominous, and I began to think we should have a desperate engagement first, and then have all our throats cut afterward.

I expected now to hear the guns discharged in quick succession, but they were got ready only, not fired. Kite went aft, and returned with three or four muskets, and as many pikes. He gave the latter to those of the people who had nothing to do with the guns. By this time the ship was on a wind, steering a good full, while the two proas were just abeam, and closing fast. The stillness that reigned on both sides was like that of death. The proas, however, fell a little more astern; the result of their own manœuvering, out of all doubt, as they moved through the water much faster than the ship, seeming desirous of dropping into our wake, with a design of closing under our stern, and avoiding our broadside. As this would never do, and the wind freshened so as to give us four or five knot way, a most fortunate circumstance for us, the captain determined to tack while he had room. The *John* behaved beautifully, and came round like a top. The proas saw there was no time to lose, and attempted to close before we could fill again; and this they would have done with ninety-nine ships in a hundred. The captain knew his vessel, however, and did not let her lose her way, making everything draw again as it might be by instinct. The proas tacked, too, and, laying up much nearer to the wind than we did, appeared as if about to close on our lee-bow. The question was, now, whether we could pass them or not before they got near enough to grapple. If the pirates got on board us, we were hopelessly gone; and everything depended on coolness and judgment. The captain behaved perfectly well in this critical instant, commanding a dead silence, and the closest attention to his orders.

I was too much interested at this moment to feel the concern that I might otherwise have experienced. On the forecastle, it appeared to us all that we should be boarded in a minute, for one of the proas was actually within a hundred feet, though losing her advantage a little by getting under the lee of our sails. Kite had ordered us to muster forward of the rigging, to meet the expected leap with a discharge of muskets, and then to present our pikes, when I felt an arm thrown around my body, and was turned inboard, while another person assumed my place. This was Neb, who had thus coolly thrust himself before me, in order to meet the danger first. I felt vexed, even while touched with the fellow's attachment and self-devotion, but had no time to betray either feeling before the crews of the proas gave a yell, and discharged some fifty or sixty matchlocks at us. The air was full of bullets, but they all went over our heads. Not a soul on board the *John* was hurt. On our side, we gave the gentlemen the four sixes, two at the nearest and two at the stern-most proa, which was still near a cable's length distant. As often happens, the one seemingly farthest from danger, fared the worst. Our grape and canister had room to scatter, and I can at this distant day still hear the shrieks that arose from that craft! They were like the yells of fiends in anguish. The effect on that proa was instantaneous; instead of keeping on after her consort, she wore short round on her heel, and stood away in our wake, on the other tack, apparently to get out of the range of our fire.

I doubt if we touched a man in the nearest proa. At any rate, no noise proceeded from her, and she came up under our bows fast. As every gun was discharged, and there was not time to load them, all now depended on repelling the boarders. Part of our people mustered in the waist, where it was expected the proa would fall alongside, and part on the forecastle. Just as this distribution was made, the pirates cast their grapnel. It was admirably thrown, but caught only by a ratlin. I saw this, and was about to jump into the rigging to try what I could do to clear it, when Neb again went ahead of me, and cut the ratlin with his knife. This was just as the pirates had abandoned sails and oars, and had risen to haul up alongside. So sudden was the release, that twenty of them fell over by their own efforts. In this state the ship passed ahead, all her canvas being full, leaving the proa motionless in her wake. In passing, however, the two vessels were so near, that those aft in the *John* distinctly saw the swarthy faces of their enemies.

We were no sooner clear of the proas than the order was given, "Ready about!" The helm was put down, and the ship came into the wind in a minute. As we came square with the two proas, all our larboard guns were given to them, and this ended the affair. I think the nearest of the rascals got it this time, for away she went, after her consort, both running off toward the islands. We made a little show of chasing, but it was only a feint; for we were too glad to get away from them, to be in earnest. In ten minutes after we tacked the last time, we ceased firing, having thrown some eight or ten round-shot after the proas, and were close-hauled again, heading to the southwest.

Blueskin, the Pirate

HOWARD PYLE

I

Cape May and Cape Henlopen form, as it were, the upper and lower jaws of a gigantic mouth, which disgorges from its monstrous gullet the cloudy waters of the Delaware Bay into the heaving, sparkling blue-green of the Atlantic Ocean. From Cape Henlopen as the lower jaw there juts out a long, curving fang of high, smooth-rolling sand dunes, cutting sharp and clean against the still, blue sky above—silent, naked, utterly deserted, excepting for the squat, white-walled lighthouse standing upon the crest of the highest hill. Within this curving, sheltering hook of sand hills lie the smooth waters of Lewes Harbor, and, set a little back from the shore, the quaint old town, with its dingy wooden houses of clapboard and shingle, looks sleepily out through the masts of the shipping lying at anchor in the harbor, to the purple, clean-cut, level thread of the ocean horizon beyond.

Lewes is a queer, odd, old-fashioned little town, smelling fragrant of salt marsh and sea breeze. It is rarely visited by strangers. The people who live there are the progeny of people who have lived there for many generations, and it is the very place to nurse, and preserve, and care for old legends and traditions of bygone times, until they grow from bits of gossip and news into local history of considerable size. As in the busier world men talk of last year's elections, here these old bits, and scraps, and odds and ends of history are retailed to the listener who cares to listen—traditions of the War of 1812, when Beresford's fleet lay off the harbor threatening to bombard the town; tales of the Revolution and of Earl Howe's warships, tarrying for a while in the quiet harbor before they sailed up the river to shake old Philadelphia town with the thunders of their guns at Red Bank and Fort Mifflin.

With these substantial and sober threads of real history, other and more lurid colors are interwoven into the web of local lore—legends of the dark doings of famous pirates, of their mysterious, sinister comings and goings, of treasures buried in the sand dunes and pine barrens back of the cape and along the Atlantic beach to the southward.

Of such is the story of Blueskin, the pirate.

II

It was in the fall and the early winter of the year 1750, and again in the summer of the year following, that the famous pirate, Blueskin, became especially identified with Lewes as a part of its traditional history.

For some time—for three or four years—rumors and reports of Blueskin's doings in the West Indies and off the Carolinas had been brought in now and then by sea captains. There was no more cruel, bloody, desperate, devilish pirate than he in all those pirate-infested waters. All kinds of wild and bloody stories were current concerning him, but it never occurred to the good folk of Lewes that such stories were some time to be a part of their own history.

But one day a schooner came drifting into Lewes harbor—shattered, wounded, her fore-castle splintered, her foremast shot half away, and three great tattered holes in her mainsail. The mate with one of the crew came ashore in the boat for help and a doctor. He reported that the captain and the cook were dead and there were three wounded men aboard. The story he told to the gathering crowd brought a very peculiar thrill to those who heard it. They had fallen in with Blueskin, he said, off Fenwick's Island (some twenty or thirty miles below the capes), and the pirates had come aboard of them; but, finding that the cargo of the schooner consisted only of cypress shingles and lumber, had soon quitted their prize. Perhaps Blueskin was disappointed at not finding a more valuable capture; perhaps the spirit of deviltry was hotter in him that morning than usual; anyhow, as the pirate craft bore away she fired three broadsides at short range into the helpless coaster. The captain had been killed at the first fire, the cook had died on the way up, three of the crew were wounded, and the vessel was leaking fast, betwixt wind and water.

Such was the mate's story. It spread like wildfire, and in half an hour all the town was in a ferment. Fenwick's Island was very near home; Blueskin might come sailing into the harbor at any minute and then—! In an hour Sheriff Jones had called together most of the able-bodied men of the town, muskets and rifles were taken down from the chimney places, and every preparation was made to defend the place against the pirates, should they come into the harbor and attempt to land.

But Blueskin did not come that day, nor did he come the next or the next. But on the afternoon of the third the news went suddenly flying over the town that the pirates were inside the capes. As the report spread the people came running—men, women, and children—to the green before the tavern, where a little knot of old seamen were gathered together, looking fixedly out toward the offing, talking in low voices. Two vessels, one bark-rigged, the other and smaller a sloop, were slowly creeping up the bay, a couple of miles or so away and just inside the cape. There appeared nothing remarkable about the two crafts, but the little crowd that continued gathering upon the green stood looking out across the bay at them none the less anxiously for that. They were sailing close-hauled to the wind, the sloop following in the wake of her consort as the pilot fish follows in the wake of the shark.

But the course they held did not lie toward the harbor, but rather bore away toward the Jersey shore, and by and by it began to be apparent that Blueskin did not intend visiting the town. Nevertheless, those who stood looking did not draw a free breath until, after watching the two pirates for more than an hour and a half, they saw them—then about six miles away—suddenly put about and sail with a free wind out to sea again.

"The bloody villains have gone!" said old Captain Wolfe, shutting his telescope with a click.

But Lewes was not yet quit of Blueskin. Two days later a half-breed from Indian River bay came up, bringing the news that the pirates had sailed into the inlet—some fifteen miles below Lewes—and had careened the bark to clean her.

Perhaps Blueskin did not care to stir up the country people against him, for the half-breed reported that the pirates were doing no harm, and that what they took from the farmers of Indian River and Rehoboth they paid for with good hard money.

It was while the excitement over the pirates was at its highest fever heat that Levi West came home again.

III

Even in the middle of the last century the grist mill, a couple of miles from Lewes, although it was at most but fifty or sixty years old, had all a look of weather-beaten age, for the cypress shingles, of which it was built, ripen in a few years of wind and weather to a silvery, hoary gray, and the white powdering of flour lent it a look as though the dust of ages had settled upon it, making the shadows within dim, soft, mysterious. A dozen willow trees shaded with dappling, shivering ripples of shadow the road before the mill door, and the mill itself, and the long, narrow, shingle-built, one-storied, hip-roofed dwelling house. At the time of the story the mill had descended in a direct line of succession to Hiram White, the grandson of old Ephraim White, who had built it, it was said, in 1701.

Hiram White was only twenty-seven years old, but he was already in local repute as a "character." As a boy he was thought to be half-witted or "natural," and, as is the case with such unfortunates in small country towns where everybody knows everybody, he was made a common sport and jest for the keener, crueler wits of the neighborhood. Now that he was grown to the ripeness of manhood he was still looked upon as being—to use a quaint expression—"slack," or "not jest right." He was heavy, awkward, ungainly and loose-jointed, and enormously, prodigiously strong. He had a lumpish, thick-featured face, with lips heavy and loosely hanging, that gave him an air of stupidity, half droll, half pathetic. His little eyes were set far apart and flat with his face, his eyebrows were nearly white and his hair was of a sandy, colorless kind. He was singularly taciturn, lisping thickly when he did talk, and stuttering and hesitating in his speech, as though his words moved faster than his mind could follow. It was the custom for local wags to urge, or badger, or tempt him to talk, for the saké of the ready laugh that always followed the few thick, stammering words and the stupid drooping of the jaw at the end of each short speech. Perhaps Squire Hall was the only one in Lewes Hundred who misdoubted that Hiram was half-witted. He had had dealings with him and was wont to say that whoever bought Hiram White for a fool made a fool's bargain. Certainly, whether he had common wits or no, Hiram had managed his mill to pretty good purpose and was fairly well off in the world as prosperity went in southern Delaware and in those days. No doubt, had it come to the pinch, he might have bought some of his tormentors out three times over.

Hiram White had suffered quite a financial loss some six months before, through that very Blueskin who was now lurking in Indian River inlet. He had entered into a "venture" with Josiah Shippin, a Philadelphia merchant, to the tune of seven hundred pounds sterling. The money had been invested in a cargo of flour and corn meal which had been shipped to Jamaica by the bark *Nancy Lee*. The *Nancy Lee* had been captured by the pirates off Currituck Sound, the crew set adrift in the longboat, and the bark herself and all her cargo burned to the water's edge.

Five hundred of the seven hundred pounds invested in the unfortunate "venture" was money bequeathed by Hiram's father, seven years before, to Levi West.

Eleazer White had been twice married, the second time to the widow West. She had brought with her to her new home a good-looking, long-legged, black-eyed, black-haired ne'er-do-well of a son, a year or so younger than Hiram. He was a shrewd, quick-witted lad, idle, shiftless, willful, ill-trained perhaps, but as bright and keen as a pin. He was the very opposite to poor, dull Hiram. Eleazer White had never loved his son; he was ashamed of the poor, slack-witted oaf. Upon the other hand, he was very fond of Levi West, whom he always called "our Levi," and whom he treated in every way as though he were his own son. He tried to train the lad to work in the mill, and was patient beyond what the patience of most fathers would have been with his stepson's idleness and shiftlessness. "Never mind," he was used to say. "Levi'll come all right. Levi's as bright as a button."

It was one of the greatest blows of the old miller's life when Levi ran away to sea. In his last sickness the old man's mind constantly turned to his lost stepson. "Mebby he'll come back again," said he, "and if he does I want you to be good to him, Hiram. I've done my duty by you and have left you the house and mill, but I want you to promise that if Levi comes back again you'll give him a home and a shelter under this roof if he wants one." And Hiram had promised to do as his father asked.

After Eleazer died it was found that he had bequeathed five hundred pounds to his "beloved stepson, Levi West," and had left Squire Hall as trustee.

Levi West had been gone nearly nine years and not a word had been heard from him; there could be little or no doubt that he was dead.

One day Hiram came into Squire Hall's office with a letter in his hand. It was the time of the old French war, and flour and corn meal were fetching fabulous prices in the British West Indies. The letter Hiram brought with him was from a Philadelphia merchant, Josiah Shippin, with whom he had had some dealings. Mr. Shippin proposed that Hiram should join him in sending a "venture" of flour and corn meal to Kingston, Jamaica. Hiram had slept upon the letter overnight and now he brought it to the old Squire. Squire Hall read the letter, shaking his head the while. "Too much risk, Hiram!" said he. "Mr Shippin wouldn't have asked you to go into this venture if he could have got anybody else to do so. My advice is that you let it alone. I reckon you've come to me for advice?" Hiram shook his head. "Ye haven't? What have ye come for, then?"

"Seven hundred pounds," said Hiram.

"Seven hundred pounds!" said Squire Hall. "I haven't got seven hundred pounds to lend you, Hiram."

"Five hundred been left to Levi—I got hundred—raise hundred more on mortgage," said Hiram.

"Tut, tut, Hiram," said Squire Hall, "that'll never do in the world. Suppose Levi West should come back again, what then? I'm responsible for that money. If you wanted to borrow it now for any reasonable venture, you should have it and welcome, but for such a wildcat scheme—"

"Levi never come back," said Hiram—"nine years gone—Levi's dead."

"Mebby he is," said Squire Hall, "but we don't know that."

"I'll give bond for security," said Hiram.

Squire Hall thought for a while in silence. "Very well, Hiram," said he by and by, "if you'll do that. Your father left the money, and I don't see that it's right for me to stay his son from using it. But if it is lost, Hiram, and if Levi should come back, it will go well to ruin ye."

So Hiram White invested seven hundred pounds in the Jamaica venture and every farthing of it was burned by Blueskin, off Currituck Sound.

IV

Sally Martin was said to be the prettiest girl in Lewes Hundred, and when the rumor began to leak out that Hiram White was courting her the whole community took it as a monstrous joke. It was the common thing to greet Hiram himself with, "Hey, Hiram; how's Sally?" Hiram never made answer to such salutation, but went his way as heavily, as impassively, as dully as ever.

The joke was true. Twice a week, rain or shine, Hiram White never failed to scrape his feet upon Billy Martin's doorstep. Twice a week, on Sundays and Thursdays, he never failed to take his customary seat by the kitchen fire. He rarely said anything by way of talk; he nodded to the farmer, to his wife, to Sally and, when he chanced to be at home, to her brother, but he ventured nothing further. There he would sit from half past seven until nine o'clock, stolid, heavy, impassive, his dull eyes following now one of the family and now another, but always coming back again to Sally. It sometimes happened that she had other company—some of the young men of the neighborhood. The presence of such seemed to make no difference to Hiram; he bore whatever broad jokes might be cracked upon him, whatever grins, whatever giggling might follow those jokes, with the same patient impassiveness. There he would sit, silent, unresponsive; then, at the first stroke of nine o'clock, he would rise, shoulder his ungainly person into his overcoat, twist his head into his three-cornered hat, and with a "Good night, Sally, I be going now," would take his departure, shutting the door carefully to behind him.

Never, perhaps, was there a girl in the world had such a lover and such a courtship as Sally Martin.

V

It was one Thursday evening in the latter part of November, about a week after Blueskin's appearance off the capes, and while the one subject of talk was of the pirates being in Indian River inlet. The air was still and wintry; a sudden cold snap had set in and skims of ice had formed over puddles in the road; the smoke from the chimneys rose straight in the quiet air and voices sounded loud, as they do in frosty weather.

Hiram White sat by the dim light of a tallow dip, poring laboriously over some account books. It was not quite seven o'clock, and he never started for Billy Martin's before that hour. As he ran his finger slowly and hesitatingly down the column of figures, he heard the kitchen door beyond open and shut, the noise of footsteps crossing the floor and the scraping of a chair dragged forward to the hearth. Then came the sound of a basket of corncobs being emptied on the smoldering blaze and then the snapping and crackling of the reanimated fire. Hiram thought nothing of all this, excepting, in a dim sort of way, that it was Bob, the negro mill hand, or old black Dinah, the housekeeper, and so went on with his calculations.

At last he closed the books with a snap and, smoothing down his hair, arose, took up the candle, and passed out of the room into the kitchen beyond.

A man was sitting in front of the corncob fire that flamed and blazed in the great, gaping, sooty fireplace. A rough overcoat was flung over the chair behind him and his hands were spread out to the roaring warmth. At the sound of the lifted latch and of Hiram's entrance he turned his head, and when Hiram saw his face he stood suddenly still as though turned to stone. The face, marvelously altered and changed as it was, was the face of his stepbrother, Levi West. He was not dead; he had come home again. For a time not a sound broke the dead, unbroken silence excepting the crackling of the blaze in the fireplace and the sharp ticking of the tall clock in the corner. The one face, dull and stolid, with the light of the candle shining upward over its lumpy features, looked fixedly, immovably, stonily at the other, sharp, shrewd, cunning—the red wavering light of the blaze shining upon the high cheek bones, cutting sharp on the nose and twinkling in the glassy turn of the black, ratlike eyes. Then suddenly that face cracked, broadened, spread to a grin. "I have come back again, Hi," said Levi, and at the sound of the words the speechless spell was broken.

Hiram answered never a word, but he walked to the fireplace, set the candle down upon the dusty mantelshelf among the boxes and bottles, and, drawing forward a chair upon the other side of the hearth, sat down.

His dull little eyes never moved from his stepbrother's face. There was no curiosity in his expression, no surprise, no wonder. The heavy under lip dropped a little farther open and there was more than usual of dull, expressionless stupidity upon the lumpish face; but that was all.

As was said, the face upon which he looked was strangely, marvelously changed from what it had been when he had last seen it nine years before, and, though it was still the face of Levi West, it was a very different Levi West than the shiftless ne'er-do-well who had run away to sea in the Brazilian brig that long time ago. That Levi West had been a rough, careless, happy-go-lucky fellow; thoughtless and selfish, but with nothing essentially evil or sinister in his nature. The Levi West that now sat in a rush-bottom chair at the other side of the fireplace had that stamped upon his front that might be both evil and sinister. His swart complexion was tanned to an Indian copper. On one side of his face was a curious discoloration in the skin and a long, crooked, cruel scar that ran diagonally across forehead and temple and cheek in a white, jagged seam. This discoloration was of a livid blue, about the tint of a tattoo mark. It made a patch the size of a man's hand, lying across the cheek and the side of the neck. Hiram could not keep his eyes from this mark and the white scar cutting across it.

There was an odd sort of incongruity in Levi's dress; a pair of heavy gold earrings and a dirty red handkerchief knotted loosely around his neck, beneath an open collar, displaying to its full length the lean, sinewy throat with its bony "Adam's apple," gave to his costume somewhat the smack of a sailor. He wore a coat that had once been of fine plum color—now stained and faded—too small for his lean length, and furbished with tarnished lace. Dirty cambric cuffs hung at his wrists and on his fingers were half a dozen and more rings, set with stones that shone, and glistened, and twinkled in the light of the fire. The hair at either temple was twisted into a Spanish curl, plastered flat to the cheek, and a plaited oueue hung halfway down his back.

Hiram, speaking never a word, sat motionless, his dull little eyes traveling slowly up and down and around and around his stepbrother's person.

Levi did not seem to notice his scrutiny, leaning forward, now with his palms spread out to the grateful warmth, now rubbing them slowly together. But at last he suddenly whirled his chair around, rasping on the floor, and faced his stepbrother. He thrust his hand into his capacious coat pocket and brought out a pipe which he proceeded to fill from a skin of tobacco. "Well, Hi," said he, "d'ye see I've come back home again?"

"Thought you was dead," said Hiram, dully.

Levi laughed, then he drew a red-hot coal out of the fire, put it upon the bowl of the pipe and began puffing out clouds of pungent smoke. "Nay, nay," said he; "not dead—not dead by odds. But [puff] by the Eternal Holy, Hi, I played many a close game [puff] with old Davy Jones, for all that."

Hiram's look turned inquiringly toward the jagged scar and Levi caught the slow glance. "You're lookin' at this," said he, running his finger down the crooked seam. "That looks bad, but it wasn't so close as this"—laying his hand for a moment upon the livid stain. "A cooly devil off Singapore gave me that cut when we fell foul of an opium junk in the China Sea four years ago last September. This," touching the disfiguring blue patch again, "was a closer miss, Hi. A Spanish captain fired a pistol at me down off Santa Catharina. He was so nigh that the powder went under the skin and it'll never come out again. —— his eyes—he had better have fired the pistol into his own head that morning. But never mind that. I reckon I'm changed, ain't I, Hi?"

He took his pipe out of his mouth and looked inquiringly at Hiram, who nodded.

Levi laughed. "Devil doubt it," said he, "but whether I'm changed or no, I'll take my affidavy that you are the same old half-witted Hi that you used to be. I remember dad used to say that you hadn't no more than enough wits to keep you out of the rain. And, talking of dad, Hi, I hearn tell he's been dead now these nine years gone. D'ye know what I've come home for?"

Hiram shook his head.

"I've come for that five hundred pounds that dad left me when he died, for I hearn tell of that, too."

Hiram sat quite still for a second or two and then he said, "I put that money out to venture and lost it all."

Levi's face fell and he took his pipe out of his mouth, regarding Hiram sharply and keenly. "What d'ye mean?" said he presently.

"I thought you was dead—and I put—seven hundred pounds—into *Nancy Lee*—and Blueskin burned her—off Currituck."

"Burned her off Currituck!" repeated Levi. Then suddenly a light seemed to break upon his comprehension. "Burned by Blueskin!" he repeated, and thereupon flung himself back in his chair and burst into a short, boisterous fit of laughter. "Well, by the Holy Eternal, Hi, if that isn't a piece of your tarnal luck. Burned by Blueskin, was it?" He paused for a moment, as though turning it over in his mind. Then he laughed again. "All the same," said he presently, "d'ye see, I can't suffer for Blueskin's doings. The money was willed to me, fair and true, and you have got to pay it, Hiram White, burn or sink, Blueskin or no Blueskin." Again he puffed for a moment or two in reflective silence. "All the same, Hi," said he, once more resuming the thread of talk, "I don't reckon to be too hard on you. You be only half-witted, anyway, and I sha'n't be too hard on you. I give you a month to raise that money, and while you're doing it I'll jest hang around here. I've been in trouble, Hi, d'ye see. I'm under a cloud and so I want to keep here, as quiet as may be. I'll tell ye how it came about: I had a set-to with a land pirate in Philadelphia, and somebody got hurt. That's the reason I'm here now, and don't you say anything about it. Do you understand?"

Hiram opened his lips as though it was his intent to answer, then seemed to think better of it and contented himself by nodding his head.

That Thursday night was the first for a six-month that Hiram White did not scrape his feet clean at Billy Martin's doorstep.

VI

Within a week Levi West had pretty well established himself among his old friends and acquaintances, though upon a different footing from that of nine years before, for this was a very different Levi from that other. Nevertheless, he was none the less popular in the barroom of the tavern and at the country store, where he was always the center of a group of loungers. His nine years seemed to have been crowded full of the wildest of wild adventures and, happenings, as well by land as by sea, and, given an appreciative audience, he would reel off his yarns by the hour, in a reckless, devil-may-care fashion that set agape even old sea dogs who had sailed the western ocean since boyhood. Then he seemed always to have plenty of money, and he loved to spend it at the tavern taproom, with a lavishness that was at once the wonder and admiration of gossips.

At that time, as was said, Blueskin was the one engrossing topic of talk, and it added not a little to Levi's prestige when it was found that he had actually often seen that bloody, devilish pirate with his own eyes. A great, heavy, burly fellow, Levi said he was, with a beard as black as a hat—a devil with his sword and pistol afloat, but not so black as he was painted when ashore. He told of many adventures in which Blueskin figured and was then always listened to with more than usual gaping interest.

As for Blueskin, the quiet way in which the pirates conducted themselves at Indian River almost made the Lewes folk forget what he could do when the occasion called. They almost ceased to remember that poor shattered schooner that had crawled with its ghastly dead and groaning wounded into the harbor a couple of weeks since. But if for a while they forgot who or what Blueskin was, it was not for long.

One day a bark from Bristol, bound for Cuba and laden with a valuable cargo of cloth stuffs and silks, put into Lewes harbor to take in water. The captain himself came ashore and was at the tavern for two or three hours. It happened that Levi was there and that the talk was of Blueskin. The English captain, a grizzled old sea dog, listened to Levi's yarns with not a little contempt. He had, he said, sailed in the China Sea and the Indian Ocean too long to be afraid of any hog-eating Yankee pirate such as this Blueskin. A junk full of coolies armed with stink-pots was something to speak of, but who ever heard of the likes of Blueskin falling afoul of anything more than a Spanish canoe or a Yankee coaster?

Levi grinned. "All the same, my hearty," said he, "if I was you I'd give Blueskin a wide berth. I hear that he's cleaned the vessel that was careened awhile ago, and mebby he'll give you a little trouble if you come too nigh him."

To this the Englishman only answered that Blueskin might be—, and that the next afternoon, wind and weather permitting, he intended to heave anchor and run out to sea.

Levi laughed again. "I wish I might be here to see what'll happen," said he, "but I'm going up the river to-night to see a gal and mebby won't be back again for three or four days."

The next afternoon the English bark set sail as the captain promised, and that night Lewes town was awake until almost morning, gazing at a broad red glare that lighted up the sky away toward the southeast. Two days afterward a negro oysterman came up from Indian River with news that the pirates were lying off the inlet, bringing ashore bales of goods from their larger vessel and piling the same upon the beach under tarpaulins. He said that it was known down at Indian River that Blueskin had fallen afoul of an English bark, had burned her and had murdered the captain and all but three of the crew, who had joined with the pirates.

The excitement over this terrible happening had only begun to subside when another occurred to cap it. One afternoon a ship's boat, in which were five men and two women, came rowing into Lewes harbor. It was the longboat of the Charleston packet, bound for New York, and was commanded by the first mate. The packet had been attacked and captured by the pirates about ten leagues south by east of Cape Henlopen. The pirates had come aboard of them at night and no resistance had been offered. Perhaps it was that circumstance that saved the lives of all, for no murder or violence had been done. Nevertheless, officers, passengers and crew had been stripped of everything of value and set adrift in the boats and the ship herself had been burned. The longboat had become separated from the others during the night and had sighted Henlopen a little after sunrise.

It may be here said that Squire Hall made out a report of these two occurrences and sent it up to Philadelphia by the mate of the packet. But for some reason it was nearly four weeks before a sloop of war was sent around from New York. In the meanwhile, the pirates had disposed of the booty stored under the tarpaulins on the beach at Indian River inlet, shipping some of it away in two small sloops and sending the rest by wagons somewhere up the country.

VII

Levi had told the English captain that he was going upcountry to visit one of his lady friends. He was gone nearly two weeks. Then once more he appeared, as suddenly, as unexpectedly, as he had done when he first returned to Lewes. Hiram was sitting at supper when the door opened and Levi walked in, hanging up his hat behind the door as unconcernedly as though he had only been gone an hour. He was in an ugly, lowering humor and sat himself down at the table without uttering a word, resting his chin upon his clenched fist and glowering fixedly at the corn cake while Dinah fetched him a plate and knife and fork.

His coming seemed to have taken away all of Hiram's appetite. He pushed away his plate and sat staring at his stepbrother, who presently fell to at the bacon and eggs like a famished wolf. Not a word was said until Levi had ended his meal and filled his pipe. "Look'ee, Hiram," said he, as he stooped over the fire and raked out a hot coal. "Look'ee, Hiram! I've been to Philadelphia, d'ye see, a-settlin' up that trouble I told you about when I first come home. D'ye understand? D'ye remember? D'ye get it through your skull?" He looked around over his shoulder, waiting as though for an answer. But getting none, he continued: "I expect two gentlemen here from Philadelphia to-night. They're friends of mine and are coming to talk over the business and ye needn't stay at home, Hi. You can go out somewhere, d'ye understand?" And then he added with a grin, "Ye can go to see Sally."

Hiram pushed back his chair and arose. He leaned with his back against the side of the fireplace. "I'll stay at home," said he presently.

"But I don't want you to stay at home, Hi," said Levi. "We'll have to talk business and I want you to go!"

"I'll stay at home," said Hiram again.

Levi's brow grew as black as thunder. He ground his teeth together and for a moment or two it seemed as though an explosion was coming. But he swallowed his passion with a gulp. "You're a—— pig-headed, half-witted fool," said he. Hiram never so much as moved his eyes. "As for you," said Levi, whirling round upon Dinah, who was clearing the table, and glowering balefully upon the old negress, "you put them things down and git out of here. Don't you come nigh this kitchen again till I tell ye to. If I catch you pryin' around may I be ——, eyes and liver, if I don't cut your heart out."

In about half an hour Levi's friends came; the first a little, thin, wizened man with a very foreign look. He was dressed in a rusty black suit and wore gray yarn stockings and shoes with brass buckles. The other was also plainly a foreigner. He was dressed in sailor fashion, with petticoat breeches of duck, a heavy pea-jacket, and thick boots, reaching to the knees. He wore a red sash tied around his waist, and once, as he pushed back his coat, Hiram saw the glitter of a pistol butt. He was a powerful, thickset man, low-browed and bull-necked, his cheek, and chin, and throat closely covered with a stubble of blue-black beard. He wore a red kerchief tied around his head and over it a cocked hat, edged with tarnished gilt braid.

Levi himself opened the door to them. He exchanged a few words outside with his visitors, in a foreign language of which Hiram understood nothing. Neither of the two strangers spoke a word to Hiram: the little man shot him a sharp look out of the corners of his eyes and the burly ruffian scowled blackly at him, but beyond that neither vouchsafed him any regard.

Levi drew to the shutters, shot the bolt in the outer door, and tilted a chair against the latch of the one that led from the kitchen into the adjoining room. Then the three worthies seated themselves at the table which Dinah had half cleared of the supper china, and were presently deeply engrossed over a packet of papers which the big, burly man had brought with him in the pocket of his pea-jacket. The confabulation was conducted throughout in the same foreign language which Levi had used when first speaking to them—a language quite unintelligible to Hiram's ears. Now and then the murmur of talk would rise loud and harsh over some disputed point; now and then it would sink away to whispers.

Twice the tall clock in the corner whirred and sharply struck the hour, but throughout the whole long consultation Hiram stood silent, motionless as a stock, his eyes fixed almost unwinkingly upon the three heads grouped close together around the dim, flickering light of the candle and the papers scattered upon the table.

Suddenly the talk came to an end, the three heads separated and the three chairs were pushed back, grating harshly. Levi rose, went to the closet and brought thence a bottle of Hiram's apple brandy, as coolly as though it belonged to himself. He set three tumblers and a crock of water upon the table and each helped himself liberally.

As the two visitors departed down the road, Levi stood for a while at the open door, looking after the dusky figures until they were swallowed in the darkness. Then he turned, came in, shut the door, shuddered, took a final dose of the apple brandy and went to bed, without, since his first suppressed explosion, having said a single word to Hiram.

Hiram, left alone, stood for a while, silent, motionless as ever, then he looked slowly about him, gave a shake of the shoulders as though to arouse himself, and taking the candle, left the room, shutting the door noiselessly behind him.

VIII

This time of Levi West's unwelcome visitation was indeed a time of bitter trouble and tribulation to poor Hiram White. Money was of very different value in those days than it is now, and five hundred pounds was in its way a good round lump—in Sussex County it was almost a fortune. It was a desperate struggle for Hiram to raise the amount of his father's bequest to his stepbrother. Squire Hall, as may have been gathered, had a very warm and friendly feeling for Hiram, believing in him when all others disbelieved; nevertheless, in the matter of money the old man was as hard and as cold as adamant. He would, he said, do all he could to help Hiram, but that five hundred pounds must and should be raised—Hiram must release his security bond. He would loan him, he said, three hundred pounds, taking a mortgage upon the mill. He would have lent him four hundred but that there was already a first mortgage of one hundred pounds upon it, and he would not dare to put more than three hundred more atop of that.

Hiram had a considerable quantity of wheat which he had bought upon speculation and which was then lying idle in a Philadelphia storehouse. This he had sold at public sale and at a very great sacrifice; he realized barely one hundred pounds upon it. The financial horizon looked very black to him; nevertheless, Levi's five hundred pounds was raised, and paid into Squire Hall's hands, and Squire Hall released Hiram's bond.

The business was finally closed on one cold, gray afternoon in the early part of December. As Hiram tore his bond across and then tore it across again and again, Squire Hall pushed back the papers upon his desk and cocked his feet upon its slanting top. "Hiram," said he, abruptly, "Hiram, do you know that Levi West is forever hanging around Billy Martin's house, after that pretty daughter of his?"

So long a space of silence followed the speech that the Squire began to think that Hiram might not have heard him. But Hiram had heard. "No," said he, "I didn't know it."

"Well, he is," said Squire Hall. "It's the talk of the whole neighborhood. The talk's pretty bad, too. D'ye know that they say that she was away from home three days last week, nobody knew where? The fellow's turned her head with his sailor's yarns and his traveler's lies."

Hiram said not a word, but he sat looking at the other in stolid silence. "That stepbrother of yours," continued the old Squire presently, "is a rascal—he is a rascal, Hiram, and I misdoubt he's something worse. I hear he's been seen in some queer places and with queer company of late."

He stopped again, and still Hiram said nothing. "And look'ee, Hiram," the old man resumed, suddenly, "I do hear that you be courtin' the girl, too; is that so?"

"Yes," said Hiram, "I'm courtin' her, too."

"Tut! tut!" said the Squire, "that's a pity, Hiram. I'm afraid your cakes are dough."

After he had left the Squire's office, Hiram stood for a while in the street, bareheaded, his hat in his hand, staring unwinkingly down at the ground at his feet, with stupidly drooping lips and lackluster eyes. Presently he raised his hand and began slowly smoothing down the sandy shock of hair upon his forehead. At last he aroused himself with a shake, looked dully up and down the street, and then, putting on his hat, turned and walked slowly and heavily away.

The early dusk of the cloudy winter evening was settling fast, for the sky was leaden and threatening. At the outskirts of the town Hiram stopped again and again stood for a while in brooding thought. Then, finally, he turned slowly, not the way that led homeward, but taking the road that led between the bare and withered fields and crooked fences toward Billy Martin's.

It would be hard to say just what it was that led Hiram to seek Billy Martin's house at that time of day—whether it was fate or ill fortune. He could not have chosen a more opportune time to confirm his own undoing. What he saw was the very worst that his heart feared.

Along the road, at a little distance from the house, was a mock-orange hedge, now bare, naked, leafless. As Hiram drew near he heard footsteps approaching and low voices. He drew back into the fence corner and there stood, half sheltered by the stark network of twigs. Two figures passed slowly along the gray of the roadway in the gloaming. One was his stepbrother, the other was Sally Martin. Levi's arm was around her, he was whispering into her ear, and her head rested upon his shoulder.

Hiram stood as still, as breathless, as cold as ice. They stopped upon the side of the road just beyond where he stood. Hiram's eyes never left them. There for some time they talked together in low voices, their words now and then reaching the ears of that silent, breathless listener.

Suddenly there came the clattering of an opening door, and then Betty Martin's voice broke the silence, harshly, shrilly: "Sal!—Sal!—Sally Martin! You, Sally Martin! Come in yere. Where be ye?"

The girl flung her arms around Levi's neck and their lips met in one quick kiss. The next moment she was gone, flying swiftly, silently, down the road past where Hiram stood, stooping as she ran. Levi stood looking after her until she was gone; then he turned and walked away whistling.

His whistling died shrilly into silence in the wintry distance, and then at last Hiram came stumbling out from the hedge. His face had never looked before as it looked then.

IX

Hiram was standing in front of the fire with his hands clasped behind his back. He had not touched the supper on the table. Levi was eating with an appetite. Suddenly he looked over his plate at his stepbrother.

"How about that five hundred pounds, Hiram?" said he. "I gave ye a month to raise it and the month ain't quite up yet, but I'm goin' to leave this here place day after to-morrow—by next day at the furd'st—and I want the money that's mine."

"I paid it to Squire Hall to-day and he has it fer ye," said Hiram, dully.

Levi laid down his knife and fork with a, clatter. "Squire Hall!" said he, "what's Squire Hall got to do with it? Squire Hall didn't have the use of that money. It was you had it and you have got to pay it back to me, and if you don't do it, by G——, I'll have the law on you, sure as you're born."

"Squire Hall's trustee—I ain't your trustee," said Hiram, in the same dull voice.

"I don't know nothing about trustees," said Levi, "or anything about lawyer business, either. What I want to know is, are you going to pay me my money or no?"

"No," said Hiram, "I ain't—Squire Hall'll pay ye; you go to him."

Levi West's face grew purple red. He pushed back, his chair grating harshly. "You—bloody land pirate!" he said, grinding his teeth together. "I see through your tricks. You're up to cheating me out of my money. You know very well that Squire Hall is down on me, hard and bitter—writin' his —— reports to Philadelphia and doing all he can to stir up everybody agin me and to bring the bluejackets down on me. I see through your tricks as clear as glass, but ye sha'n't trick me. I'll have my money if there's law in the land ye bloody, unnatural thief ye, who'd go agin your dead father's will!"

Then—if the roof had fallen in upon him, Levi West could not have been more amazed— Hiram suddenly strode forward, and, leaning half across the table with his fists clenched, fairly glared into Levi's eyes. His face, dull, stupid, wooden, was now fairly convulsed with passion. The great veins stood out upon his temples like knotted whipcords, and when he spoke his voice was more a breathless snarl than the voice of a Christian man.

"Ye'll have the law, will ye?" said he. "Ye'll—have the law, will ye? You're afeared to go to law—Levi West—you try th' law—and see how ye like it. Who 're you to call me thief—ye bloody, murderin' villain ye! You're the thief—Levi West—you come here and stole my daddy from me—ye did. You make me ruin—myself to pay what oughter to been mine—then—ye—ye steal the gal I was courtin', to boot." He stopped and his lips writhed for words to say. "I know ye," said he, grinding his teeth. "I know ye! And only for what my daddy made me promise I'd a-had you up to the magistrate's before this."

Then, pointing with quivering finger: "There's the door—you see it! Go out that there door and don't never come into it again—if ye do—or if ye ever come where I can lay eyes on ye again—by th' Holy Holy I'll hale ye up to the Squire's office and tell all I know and all I've seen. Oh, I'll give ye your belly-fill of law if—ye want th' law! Git out of the house, I say!"

As Hiram spoke Levi seemed to shrink together. His face changed from its copper color to a dull, waxy yellow. When the other ended he answered never a word. But he pushed back his chair, rose, put on his hat and, with a furtive, sidelong look, left the house, without stopping to finish the supper which he had begun. He never entered Hiram White's door again.

X

Hiram had driven out the evil spirit from his home, but the mischief that it had brewed was done and could not be undone. The next day it was known that Sally Martin had run away from home, and that she had run away with Levi West. Old Billy Martin had been in town in the morning with his rifle, hunting for Levi and threatening if he caught him to have his life for leading his daughter astray.

And, as the evil spirit had left Hiram's house, so had another and a greater evil spirit quitted its harborage. It was heard from Indian River in a few days more that Blueskin had quitted the inlet and had sailed away to the southeast; and it was reported, by those who seemed to know, that he had finally quitted those parts.

It was well for himself that Blueskin left when he did, for not three days after he sailed away the *Scorpion* sloop-of-war dropped anchor in Lewes harbor. The New York agent of the unfortunate packet and a government commissioner had also come aboard the *Scorpion*.

Without loss of time, the officer in command instituted a keen and searching examination that brought to light some singularly curious facts. It was found that a very friendly understanding must have existed for some time between the pirates and the people of Indian River, for, in the houses throughout that section, many things—some of considerable value—that had been taken by the pirates from the packet, were discovered and seized by the commissioner. Valuables of a suspicious nature had found their way even into the houses of Lewes itself.

The whole neighborhood seemed to have become more or less tainted by the presence of the pirates.

Even poor Hiram White did not escape the suspicions of having had dealings with them. Of course the examiners were not slow in discovering that Levi West had been deeply concerned with Blueskin's doings.

Old Dinah and black Bob were examined, and not only did the story of Levi's two visitors come to light, but also the fact that Hiram was present and with them while they were in the house disposing of the captured goods to their agent.

Of all that he had endured, nothing seemed to cut poor Hiram so deeply and keenly as these unjust suspicions. They seemed to bring the last bitter pang, hardest of all to bear.

Levi had taken from him his father's love; he had driven him, if not to ruin, at least perilously close to it. He had run away with the girl he loved, and now, through him, even Hiram's good name was gone.

Neither did the suspicions against him remain passive; they became active.

Goldsmiths' bills, to the amount of several thousand pounds, had been taken in the packet and Hiram was examined with an almost inquisitorial closeness and strictness as to whether he had or had not knowledge of their whereabouts.

Under his accumulated misfortunes, he grew not only more dull, more taciturn, than ever, but gloomy, moody, brooding as well. For hours he would sit staring straight before him into the fire, without moving so much as a hair.

One night—it was a bitterly cold night in February, with three inches of dry and gritty snow upon the ground—while Hiram sat thus brooding, there came, of a sudden, a soft tap upon the door.

Low and hesitating as it was, Hiram started violently at the sound. He sat for a while, looking from right to left. Then suddenly pushing back his chair, he arose, strode to the door, and flung it wide open.

It was Sally Martin.

Hiram stood for a while staring blankly at her. It was she who first spoke. "Won't you let me come in, Hi?" said she. "I'm nigh starved with the cold and I'm fit to die, I'm so hungry. For God's sake, let me come in."

"Yes," said Hiram, "I'll let you come in, but why don't you go home?"

The poor girl was shivering and chattering with the cold; now she began crying, wiping her eyes with the corner of a blanket in which her head and shoulders were wrapped. "I have been home, Hiram," she said, "but dad, he shut the door in my face. He cursed me just awful, Hi—I wish I was dead!"

"You better come in," said Hiram. "It's no good standing out there in the cold." He stood aside and the girl entered, swiftly, gratefully.

At Hiram's bidding black Dinah presently set some food before Sally and she fell to eating ravenously, almost ferociously. Meantime, while she ate, Hiram stood with his back to the fire, looking at her face—that face once so round and rosy, now thin, pinched, haggard.

"Are you sick, Sally?" said he presently.

"No," said she, "but I've had pretty hard times since I left home, Hi." The tears sprang to her eyes at the recollection of her troubles, but she only wiped them hastily away with the back of her hand, without stopping in her eating.

A long pause of dead silence followed. Dinah sat crouched together on a cricket at the other side of the hearth, listening with interest. Hiram did not seem to see her. "Did you go off with Levi?" said he at last, speaking abruptly. The girl looked up furtively under her brows. "You needn't be afeared to tell," he added.

"Yes," said she at last, "I did go off with him, Hi."

"Where've you been?"

At the question, she suddenly laid down her knife and fork. "Don't you ask me that; Hi," said she, agitatedly, "I can't tell you that. You don't know Levi, Hiram; I darsn't tell you anything he don't want me to. If I told you where I been he'd hunt me out, no matter where I was, and kill me. If you only knew what I know about him, Hiram, you wouldn't ask anything about him."

Hiram stood looking broodingly at her for a long time; then at last he again spoke. "I thought a sight of you onc't, Sally," said he.

Sally did not answer immediately, but, after a while, she suddenly looked up. "Hiram," said she, "if I tell ye something will you promise on your oath not to breathe a word to any living soul?" Hiram nodded. "Then I'll tell you, but if Levi finds I've told he'll murder me as sure as you're standin' there. Come nigher—I've got to whisper it." He leaned forward close to her where she sat. She looked swiftly from right to left; then raising her lips she breathed into his ear: "I'm an honest woman, Hi. I was married to Levi West before I run away."

XI

The winter had passed, spring had passed, and summer had come. Whatever Hiram had felt, he had made no sign of suffering. Nevertheless, his lumpy face had begun to look flabby, his cheeks hollow, and his loose-jointed body shrunk more awkwardly together into its clothes. He was often awake at night, sometimes walking up and down his room until far into the small hours.

It was through such a wakeful spell as this that he entered into the greatest, the most terrible, happening of his life.

It was a sulphurously hot night in July. The air was like the breath of a furnace, and it was a hard matter to sleep with even the easiest mind and under the most favorable circumstances. The full moon shone in through the open window, laying a white square of light upon the floor, and Hiram, as he paced up and down, up and down, walked directly through it, his gaunt figure starting out at every turn into sudden brightness as he entered the straight line of misty light.

The clock in the kitchen whirred and rang out the hour of twelve, and Hiram stopped in his walk to count the strokes.

The last vibration died away into silence, and still he stood motionless, now listening with a new and sudden intentness, for, even as the clock rang the last stroke, he heard soft, heavy footsteps, moving slowly and cautiously along the pathway before the house and directly below the open window. A few seconds more and he heard the creaking of rusty hinges. The mysterious visitor had entered the mill. Hiram crept softly to the window and looked out. The moon shone full on the dusty, shingled face of the old mill, not thirty steps away, and he saw that the door was standing wide open. A second or two of stillness followed, and then, as he still stood looking intently, he saw the figure of a man suddenly appear, sharp and vivid, from the gaping blackness of the open doorway. Hiram could see his face as clear as day. It was Levi West, and he carried an empty meal bag over his arm.

Levi West stood looking from right to left for a second or two, and then he took off his hat and wiped his brow with the back of his hand. Then he softly closed the door behind him and left the mill as he had come, and with the same cautious step. Hiram looked down upon him as he passed close to the house and almost directly beneath. He could have touched him with his hand.

Fifty or sixty yards from the house Levi stopped and a second figure arose from the black shadow in the angle of the worm fence and joined him. They stood for a while talking together, Levi pointing now and then toward the mill. Then the two turned, and, climbing over the fence, cut across an open field and through the tall, shaggy grass toward the southeast.

Hiram straightened himself and drew a deep breath, and the moon, shining full upon his face, snowed it twisted, convulsed, as it had been when he had fronted his stepbrother seven months before in the kitchen. Great beads of sweat stood on his brow and he wiped them away with his sleeve. Then, coatless, hatless as he was, he swung himself out of the window, dropped upon the grass, and, without an instant of hesitation, strode off down the road in the direction that Levi West had taken.

As he climbed the fence where the two men had climbed it he could see them in the pallid light, far away across the level, scrubby meadow land, walking toward a narrow strip of pine woods.

A little later they entered the sharp-cut shadows beneath the trees and were swallowed in the darkness.

With fixed eyes and close-shut lips, as doggedly, as inexorably as though he were a Nemesis hunting his enemy down, Hiram followed their footsteps across the stretch of moonlit open. Then, by and by, he also was in the shadow of the pines. Here, not a sound broke the midnight hush. His feet made no noise upon the resinous softness of the ground below. In that dead, pulseless silence he could distinctly hear the distant voices of Levi and his companion, sounding loud and resonant in the hollow of the woods. Beyond the woods was a cornfield, and presently he heard the rattling of the harsh leaves as the two plunged into the tasseled jungle. Here, as in the woods, he followed them, step by step, guided by the noise of their progress through the canes.

Beyond the cornfield ran a road that, skirting to the south of Lewes, led across a wooden bridge to the wide salt marshes that stretched between the town and the distant sand hills. Coming out upon this road Hiram found that he had gained upon those he followed, and that they now were not fifty paces away, and he could see that Levi's companion carried over his shoulder what looked like a bundle of tools.

He waited for a little while to let them gain their distance and for the second time wiped his forehead with his shirt sleeve; then, without ever once letting his eyes leave them, he climbed the fence to the roadway.

For a couple of miles or more he followed the two along the white, level highway, past silent, sleeping houses, past barns, sheds, and haystacks, looming big in the moonlight, past fields, and woods, and clearings, past the dark and silent skirts of the town, and so, at last, out upon the wide, misty salt marshes, which seemed to stretch away interminably through the pallid light, yet were bounded in the far distance by the long, white line of sand hills.

Across the level salt marshes he followed them, through the rank sedge and past the glassy pools in which his own inverted image stalked beneath as he stalked above; on and on, until at last they had reached a belt of scrub pines, gnarled and gray, that fringed the foot of the white sand hills.

Here Hiram kept within the black network of shadow. The two whom he followed walked more in the open, with their shadows, as black as ink, walking along in the sand beside them, and now, in the dead, breathless stillness, might be heard, dull and heavy, the distant thumping, pounding roar of the Atlantic surf, beating on the beach at the other side of the sand hills, half a mile away.

At last the two rounded the southern end of the white bluff, and when Hiram, following, rounded it also, they were no longer to be seen.

Before him the sand hill rose, smooth and steep, cutting in a sharp ridge against the sky. Up this steep hill trailed the footsteps of those he followed, disappearing over the crest. Beyond the ridge lay a round, bowl-like hollow, perhaps fifty feet across and eighteen or twenty feet deep, scooped out by the eddying of the winds into an almost perfect circle. Hiram, slowly, cautiously, stealthily, following their trailing line of footmarks, mounted to the top of the hillock and peered down into the bowl beneath. The two men were sitting upon the sand, not far from the tall, skeleton-like shaft of a dead pine tree that rose, stark and gray, from the sand in which it may once have been buried, centuries ago.

XII

Levi had taken off his coat and waistcoat and was fanning himself with his hat. He was sitting upon the bag he had brought from the mill and which he had spread out upon the sand. His companion sat facing him. The moon shone full upon him and Hiram knew him instantly—he was the same burly, foreign-looking ruffian who had come with the little man to the mill that night to see Levi. He also had his hat off and was wiping his forehead and face with a red hand-kerchief. Beside him lay the bundle of tools he had brought—a couple of shovels, a piece of rope, and a long, sharp iron rod.

The two men were talking together, but Hiram could not understand what they said, for they spoke in the same foreign language that they had before used. But he could see his stepbrother point with his finger, now to the dead tree and now to the steep, white face of the opposite side of the bowl-like hollow.

At last, having apparently rested themselves, the conference, if conference it was, came to an end, and Levi led the way, the other following, to the dead pine tree. Here he stopped and began searching, as though for some mark; then, having found that which he looked for, he drew a tape-line and a large brass pocket compass from his pocket. He gave one end of the tape line to his companion, holding the other with his thumb pressed upon a particular part of the tree. Taking his bearings by the compass, he gave now and then some orders to the other, who moved a little to the left or the right as he bade. At last he gave a word of command, and, thereupon, his companion drew a wooden peg from his pocket and thrust it into the sand. From this peg as a base they again measured, taking bearings by the compass, and again drove a peg. For a third time they repeated their measurements and then, at last, seemed to have reached the point which they aimed for.

Here Levi marked a cross with his heel upon the sand.

His companion brought him the pointed iron rod which lay beside the shovels, and then stood watching as Levi thrust it deep into the sand, again and again, as though sounding for some object below. It was some while before he found that for which he was seeking, but at last the rod struck with a jar upon some hard object below. After making sure of success by one or two additional taps with the rod, Levi left it remaining where it stood, brushing the sand from his hands. "Now fetch the shovels, Pedro," said he, speaking for the first time in English.

The two men were busy for a long while, shoveling away the sand. The object for which they were seeking lay buried some six feet deep, and the work was heavy and laborious, the shifting sand sliding back, again and again, into the hole. But at last the blade of one of the shovels struck upon some hard substance and Levi stooped and brushed away the sand with the palm of his hand.

Levi's companion climbed out of the hole which they had dug and tossed the rope which he had brought with the shovels down to the other. Levi made it fast to some object below and then himself mounted to the level of the sand above. Pulling together, the two drew up from the hole a heavy iron-bound box, nearly three feet long and a foot wide and deep.

Levi's companion stooped and began untying the rope which had been lashed to a ring in the lid.

What next happened happened suddenly, swiftly, terribly. Levi drew back a single step, and shot one quick, keen look to right and to left. He passed his hand rapidly behind his back, and the next moment Hiram saw the moonlight gleam upon the long, sharp, keen blade of a knife. Levi raised his arm. Then, just as the other arose from bending over the chest, he struck, and struck again, two swift, powerful blows. Hiram saw the blade drive, lean and sharp, into the back, and heard the hilt strike with a dull thud against the ribs—once, twice. The burly, black-bearded wretch gave a shrill, terrible cry and fell staggering back. Then, in an instant, with another cry, he was up and clutched Levi with a clutch of despair by the throat and by the arm. Then followed a struggle, short, terrible, silent. Not a sound was heard but the deep, panting breath and the scuffling of feet in the sand, upon which there now poured and dabbled a dark-purple stream. But it was a one-sided struggle and lasted only for a second or two. Levi wrenched his arm loose from the wounded man's grasp, tearing his shirt sleeve from the wrist to the shoulder as he did so. Again and again the cruel knife was lifted, and again and again it fell, now no longer bright, but stained with red.

Then, suddenly, all was over. Levi's companion dropped to the sand without a sound, like a bundle of rags. For a moment he lay limp and inert; then one shuddering spasm passed over him and he lay silent and still, with his face half buried in the sand.

Levi, with the knife still gripped tight in his hand, stood leaning over his victim, looking down upon his body. His shirt and hand, and even his naked arm, were stained and blotched with blood. The moon lit up his face and it was the face of a devil from hell.

At last he gave himself a shake, stooped and wiped his knife and hand and arm upon the loose petticoat breeches of the dead man. He thrust his knife back into its sheath, drew a key from his pocket and unlocked the chest. In the moonlight Hiram could see that it was filled mostly with paper and leather bags, full, apparently of money.

All through this awful struggle and its awful ending Hiram lay, dumb and motionless, upon the crest of the sand hill, looking with a horrid fascination upon the death struggle in the pit below. Now Hiram arose. The sand slid whispering down from the crest as he did so, but Levi was too intent in turning over the contents of the chest to notice the slight sound.

Hiram's face was ghastly pale and drawn. For one moment he opened his lips as though to speak, but no word came. So, white, silent, he stood for a few seconds, rather like a statue than a living man, then, suddenly, his eyes fell upon the bag, which Levi had brought with him, no doubt, to carry back the treasure for which he and his companion were in search, and which still lay spread out on the sand where it had been flung. Then, as though a thought had suddenly flashed upon him, his whole expression changed, his lips closed tightly together as though fearing an involuntary sound might escape, and the haggard look dissolved from his face.

Cautiously, slowly, he stepped over the edge of the sand hill and down the slanting face. His coming was as silent as death, for his feet made no noise as he sank ankle-deep in the yielding surface. So, stealthily, step by step, he descended, reached the bag, lifted it silently. Levi, still bending over the chest and searching through the papers within, was not four feet away. Hiram raised the bag in his hands. He must have made some slight rustle as he did so, for suddenly Levi half turned his head. But he was one instant too late. In a flash the bag was over his head—shoulders—arms—body.

Then came another struggle, as fierce, as silent, as desperate as that other—and as short. Wiry, tough, and strong as he was, with a lean, sinewy, nervous vigor, fighting desperately for his life as he was, Levi had no chance against the ponderous strength of his stepbrother. In any case, the struggle could not have lasted long; as it was, Levi stumbled backward over the body of his dead mate and fell, with Hiram upon him. Maybe he was stunned by the fall; maybe he felt the hopelessness of resistance, for he lay quite still while Hiram, kneeling upon him, drew the rope from the ring of the chest and, without uttering a word, bound it tightly around both the bag and the captive within, knotting it again and again and drawing it tight. Only once was a word spoken. "If you'll lemme go," said a muffled voice from the bag, "I'll give you five thousand pounds—it's in that there box." Hiram answered never a word, but continued knotting the rope and drawing it tight.

XIII

The *Scorpion* sloop-of-war lay in Lewes harbor all that winter and spring, probably upon the slim chance of a return of the pirates. It was about eight o'clock in the morning and Lieutenant Maynard was sitting in Squire Hall's office, fanning himself with his hat and talking in a desultory fashion. Suddenly the dim and distant noise of a great crowd was heard from without, coming nearer and nearer. The Squire and his visitor hurried to the door. The crowd was coming down the street shouting, jostling, struggling, some on the footway, some in the roadway. Heads were at the doors and windows, looking down upon them. Nearer they came, and nearer; then at last they could see that the press surrounded and accompanied one man. It was Hiram White, hatless, coatless, the sweat running down his face in streams, but stolid and silent as ever. Over his shoulder he carried a bag, tied round and round with a rope. It was not until the crowd and the man it surrounded had come quite near that the Squire and the lieutenant saw that a pair of legs in gray-yarn stockings hung from the bag. It was a man he was carrying.

Hiram had lugged his burden five miles that morning without help and with scarcely a rest on the way.

He came directly toward the Squire's office and, still surrounded and hustled by the crowd, up the steep steps to the office within. He flung his burden heavily upon the floor without a word and wiped his streaming forehead.

The Squire stood with his knuckles on his desk, staring first at Hiram and then at the strange burden he had brought. A sudden hush fell upon all, though the voices of those without sounded as loud and turbulent as ever. "What is it, Hiram?" said Squire Hall at last.

Then for the first time Hiram spoke, panting thickly. "It's a bloody murderer," said he, pointing a quivering finger at the motionless figure.

"Here, some of you!" called out the Squire. "Come! Untie this man! Who is he?" A dozen willing fingers quickly unknotted the rope and the bag was slipped from the head and body.

Hair and face and eyebrows and clothes were powdered with meal, but, in spite of all and through all the innocent whiteness, dark spots and blotches and smears of blood showed upon head and arm and shirt. Levi raised himself upon his elbow and looked scowlingly around at the amazed, wonderstruck faces surrounding him.

"Why, it's Levi West!" croaked the Squire, at last finding his voice.

Then, suddenly, Lieutenant Maynard pushed forward, before the others crowded around the figure on the floor, and, clutching Levi by the hair, dragged his head backward so as to better see his face. "Levi West!" said he in a loud voice. "Is this the Levi West you've been telling me of? Look at that scar and the mark on his cheek! *This is Blueskin himself.*"

XIV

In the chest which Blueskin had dug up out of the sand were found not only the goldsmiths' bills taken from the packet, but also many other valuables belonging to the officers and the passengers of the unfortunate ship.

The New York agents offered Hiram a handsome reward for his efforts in recovering the lost bills, but Hiram declined it, positively and finally. "All I want," said he, in his usual dull, stolid fashion, "is to have folks know I'm honest." Nevertheless, though he did not accept what the agents of the packet offered, fate took the matter into its own hands and rewarded him not unsubstantially. Blueskin was taken to England in the *Scorpion*. But he never came to trial. While in Newgate he hanged himself to the cell window with his own stockings. The news of his end was brought to Lewes in the early autumn and Squire Hall took immediate measures to have the five hundred pounds of his father's legacy duly transferred to Hiram.

In November Hiram married the pirate's widow.

The Fleet of Captain Morgan

E. H. VISIAK

About midday the wind shifted into the north; and, continuing very high, it blew us from our course.

And, as we designed to touch at the Isle of Porto Rico, so we could not make it, but must go away under the great Island of Hispaniola. Hereupon the wind chopped back again, so that we sailed along the south side of the island. Soon after doubling the Cape of Lobos on the south western corner of Hispaniola, we descried at sea a fleet of full fifteen sail, that came towards us.

We misliked the appearance of them, yet held our course—albeit the Captain caused cutlashes and pistols to be served out, and had our ports opened and our guns run out. When we were come to about a quarter of a mile from those ships, the biggest of them fired a gun, and made a wiff to us to stand in the wind, or *lay to*, as mariners call it. This was very uneasy to my brother, and now he was sorry he had not borne up his helm and scampered away while there was yet time. Yea, it put him in so ill a temper, that I, who stood near him on the quarter-deck, was fain to remove to more peaceful ground. For, after he had ordered to obey the summons, he fell to pacing quickly up and down; and, as I stood a little in his path (or rather he pretended I did), he shoved me roughly to one side, as well as giving me a whirret on the ear for having, as he said, obstructed him.

The ships came a little nearer, and then brought to. Whereupon a dozen men put themselves into a big canoe, or periagua, which was towing astern of the Admiral, and pulled towards us. They came on but slowly, for the sea was heavy; but at length they laid aboard of us in the waist. They were all huge brawny seamen, sunburnt like red tiles, and very villainous.

When they had made fast their boat, the coxswain hallooed to my brother, and inquired of him whence we came. Being answered, "From England," he said he was come from Captain Morgan, who desired some provisions of bread, pork and cheese; in recompense whereof he had sent us some jars of excellent Peru wine.

Now, while the man spoke, I observed my brother gave a start and looked earnestly upon him; and, after he ceased, the Captain desired he would come aboard into the ship, but that the rest should stay in the boat. The rest, however, began to cry out against that.

"What! you won't treat us, Cap'n?" cries one, and "Let us see what liquor you brought from England," cries another, and "Why, you skinflint shark," quoth another, "if you drink not with us, we'll broach your fat hull!"

Hereupon these unruly rascals made to swarm the ship's side, and what the event of it had been I know not; but, on a sudden, a gun was shot off aboard the Admiral, which put a period to their brawling. They immediately fell quiet; and the coxswain said: "Cap'n Morgan's in haste, and I reckon we'd best be in haste also. Keep you still in the boat, while I go get the victuals. You'll not drink rumbo this bout!"

So he came up to us into the ship; and my brother took him into his cabin, shutting the door after, so that I know not what passed between them.

But when they came out, they talked very familiarly together; and, passing near me, I heard my brother say:

"Is Jolly Peter still with you?" whence I apprehended my brother had old acquaintance with these people. As to what they were, I doubted not, and now do know, they were nothing but a swarm of pirates. On board those fifteen vessels, indeed, was embarked the army of Captain Henry Morgan, a name soon to become so notorious and so dreadful. They were going to Maracaibo.

When such commodities as the pirates wanted had been laded into their boat (the jars of wine having been taken aboard the ship in the interim), that spokesman did very affectionately take leave of my brother, and returned into the boat. So they cast off and pulled away, singing a ribald song to keep the time.

After parting from the pirates, we hauled our wind and tacked in for the western shore of Hispaniola, to re-victual the ship and fill our water. Thereby, in the dusk of the evening, we hit a little bay, and came to an anchor within a mile from the shore, and lay there all night.

In the morning, so soon as it was light, I got up, and went on deck to view the landfall. Indeed, I was much inquisitive to behold this Island of Hispaniola; for a poor crooked mutilated man that lived in the village at home, had given me an account thereof, acquainting me with its varied fruitfulness and spacious and beautiful prospects, and with the curious customs of the hunters and planters there. He, when a boy, had been kidnapped, and transported into slavery on the plantations in the Isle of St. Christopher of the Caribbee Islands. There his master was one Bettesa, who did even excel in cruelty among a sort of people incredibly cruel to their slaves and servants, and used him with such barbarity as reduced his body to that miserable plight aforesaid. But at last, escaping from the clutches of this inhuman monster, he came to Hispaniola; where, after many days of hiding and wandering up and down the country, he fell in with a certain rich Spaniard, who proved his benefactor. For this generous-spirited man not only clothed and cared for that poor fugitive, but did also defray the charges of his passage to England on a ship that was departing thither; and, moreover, he gave him, in Spanish notes, a bounty sufficient to his support for the rest of his days.

Having mounted the poop, I looked very eagerly towards the land.

I beheld a low woody shore, whereon at some points a sort of squat small trees grew quite down to the sea, their branches so low as to touch the water. Hugely contrasting with these, were palm trees, being exceeding tall (160 feet at the least) and wholly destitute of branches to the very tops, where grew prodigious great leaves. The trunks were of a huge thickness and were covered with prickles.

Near the bottom of the bay a river flowed into the sea, on the marshy banks whereof those great trees did chiefly grow. In the background the woods grew very thick and high. I saw therein many brave cedar trees. At the farther extremity of the bay, where the woods were much thinner, there was a clear ground, and in the midst a wooden hut, the roof whereof was covered with the great leaves I have told you of. A smoke went up from a heap near the entry.

Even as I spied this hut, a man stepped forth from within, and was followed by another. On spying the ship, they immediately turned and hid themselves within the woods. They appeared to be white men, very slovenly dressed. I took them for hunters. I observed by the stirring of the undergrowth (albeit 'twas but slight) that they worked their way in the coverts of the woods alongst the shore towards the ship. Being come over against us, they stood concealed amongst the little thick trees beside the sea; and there they were, when, on my brother coming to me on the poop, I told him what I had seen.

He immediately ordered the jolly-boat to be launched and manned; and, this done, he put himself into the boat, and so did I.

We pulled to the shore, making to a point near the place where those two men lurked amongst the trees, and where there was ground fit to light upon. Having jumped ashore, the Captain hallooed to these people, telling them that he came in peace, and would by no means harm them; only he desired some discourse with them, and to trade with them.

Hereupon one of them made answer, in very poor English, that 'twas well; they would trade with him, and invited him to come and drink with them in their hut. They desired, however, that he would come alone; by reason, as they said, their little mean hut was not fit to entertain more. He thanked them, and told them he would go with them.

Then came they out of their hiding towards us into the open. They were a French buccaneer (or hunter of wild bulls and cows), and his slave. They were very slovenly dressed, and beastly dirty. The buccaneer wore a dirty linen shirt tucked into his breeches, which were dyed in the blood of the beasts he killed. He had round his middle a sailor's belt; a long sheath-knife hung from the belt at the back thereof: leggings he had of hairy boar-hide, shoes of dressed bull-hide, and a big wide-brimmed hat upon his head. The habit of the slave was likewise; only without belt or shoes, and on his head an old cloth montero-cap. Their faces were anointed with hog's grease to defend them from the stings of insects.

My brother went with them to the hut; and I, with Surgeon Burke, into the woods. For Burke took the opportunity of gathering divers medicinal herbs and woods that the place afforded.

Before he left the seamen, however, he warned them that they should by no means touch the fruit of any tree which was not pecked by birds; for, said he, 'twas an infallible sign that they were not good, and evinced those little squat trees that I had observed from the ship, which had apples on them that did smell very sweet. These were manchineel, or dwarf-apple trees, the fruit whereof no bird doth eat: and, indeed, it is so venomous that the very crabs that eat of it are poisonous. He that eats thereof is presently raving mad, and dead within a little while after. Moreover, the sap of this tree doth raise on the skin terrible red blisters, as it were scalding water.

We roved up and down in the woods, gathering Burke's medicants; but, as the sun climbed, we began to be tormented with those big venomous gnats called mosquitoes, as with other flying and creeping pests also. And, though the Surgeon seemed not much to mind them, for me the incessant attacks and inroads of the creatures became well-nigh insupportable; but I endured them for the sake of the novelty of the way.

Care was ever had of us, as we drew farther from the seaside, not to lose touch of the river, though we saw little of it for the dense undergrowth.

At length the wood became pathless, which forced us to return. A little after, through a rift in the undergrowth towards the river, I spied a marvellous strange thing—or so I thought it. For, as it should seem, a great tree-log that floated in the river, did turn about and raise itself as if it were a living creature. And a living creature it really was, being nothing else but a prodigious great cayman, or crocodile, that, thus in semblance of a floating log, lay lurking for its prey, waiting until some wild boar or other came to drink thereby. This horrible beast could have had no less than threescore foot in length, and ten in breadth.

Another horrid creature I beheld before we returned to the sea-shore. This was a sort of huge hairy spider, very hideous. Its body was as big as an egg; its legs were like a crab's; four black teeth it had, with which it snapped at me as it ran scuttling away along a bough of a tree. I must confess it gave me a scare, and the more so because I thought it might be the dreadful tarantula whose bite doth make men mad. But Burke told me it was not venomous, and, moreover, that I needed not be afraid of being envenomed by anything in that place; for no creature in the whole Island of Hispaniola was venomous—no, not even snakes.

When we got to the boat, we found my brother was not yet returned, and the seamen much out of humour for the waiting. They sat on the shore, smoking their pipes, cursing the Captain and the mosquitoes, and viciously casting stones at the land crabs.

"I ain't going for to bide on this hell-shore much longer," said one, "Cap'n or no Cap'n! Oh, to hell with them mosquiters!"

But Burke essayed to turn their minds, and "Why, what's amiss with 'em?" says he merrily, "They need their victuals, like the rest of us. I've been feeding a score of 'em since I came ashore."

"Well, you may say so, too!" returned the seaman. "You have enough and to spare on your bones, old sawbones!"

Burke laughed, and slapped him on the shoulder. With such jolly talk did he physic their minds, and had soon restored them to good health. But, on a sudden, came a sound of another sort of jollity: drunken shout and revelry in the buccaneer's hut; and, as he hearkened, I saw the merriment quite go out of Burke: while one of the seamen said harshly:

"Hark to 'em, boys, roystering yonder! lying snug an' easy on their liquor, like fine gentlemen, whilst we be sweltering here!"

So the ill-temper of the seamen returned, nor was Surgeon Burke able to mollify them.

And now the sun began to shine very hot, and the hunger and thirst of the mosquitoes appeared even to increase. After a further spell of waiting (the clamour in the hut continuing), those belated and miserable seamen did conclude that they had endured enough, and would have put themselves into the boat and launched forth for the ship.

However, Burke proffered to go to the hut and bring them word again, and persuaded them to wait his return. So he went, and I with him.

We forced our way in haste alongst the woody shore, whilst behind us the curses of the seamen, in front the shouts and laughter of the revellers, sounded in our ears; whilst the sun scorched us like a furnace, and the humming mosquitoes stung our bare faces. Many discomforts and hardships of body I have suffered, but never a one of them comparable to that shore-passage at Hispaniola!

At last we came to the hut, and straightway entered in. The drinkers sat on a couple of chests and a stool, which were disposed about a table on which were canakins and an earthen jar, or bottle.

They had their load: the buccaneer and his slave looked blankly up at us as we entered, and the buccaneer broke off in singing a drunken song; but my brother stirred not hand or foot. He sat fallen forward upon the board, being completely conquered with the drink. 'Twas veycou, as they call it, the beer of the buccaneers. (It is made from Cassava root, from which, also, they make their meal or flour.)

Surgeon Burke worked his way round the cabin towards my brother, and, taking him smartly by the shoulder, endeavoured to rouse him up; but he could not.

Meanwhile the buccaneer began to be contrary and truculent, and tipsily abused us in the French tongue. But we minded him not, so long as he contented himself with words. When, however, he pulled out a pistol and began to threaten us with it, Burke leant swiftly over and snatched it from him. On that, the buccaneer rose up to have grappled with him, but Burke poked him smartly in the wind, which doubled him up; and he rolled over upon the floor, and lay there muttering, swearing, and singing this catch:

Lolonois! Lolonois!
On doit suivre Lolonois!
Un si brave Capitaine!

As for the slave, he meddled not with us, but sat still, drinking down a last panakin of the veycou; whereupon he settled also, and presently slept.

They being all three thus disposed and settled on their lees, as the saying is, Surgeon Burke desired me to return alone to the mariners, and to bid them launch forth and bring the boat towards a little landing-place which was over against the hut.

Before I went, he anointed my face and hands with hog's grease (a vessel whereof he found in a corner), to solace my mosquito bites, which now began to be very grievous to me.

So I went. When I came to the seamen, I found that they had been joined by several others, who had come ashore in the launch, or longboat, and Thalass, the Mosquito Indian, with them. This was told me by two of them who stood by the boats, and that the rest were gone away straggling into the woods to shoot wild fowl, some of those who had come in the longboat having muskets.

This put me to my trumps for men to manage the boat, and I started off to see for them. Suddenly a musket-shot rang out in the woods, and was succeeded by a great hoarse croaking of crows, or ravens, that rose flocking above the tree-tops in a black multitude; and then, on a sudden, arose a great outcry of men.

I set off running that way, and soon perceived what the matter was. Two of the seamen were locked in fierce fight. Now, this was a dreadful thing to see; for one of the fighters was a one-armed man—I mean, his left arm had been amputated below the elbow, and, in lieu of an arm, he had an iron rod with a hook to it. With this hook had he grappled hold of the other, and with his sailor's knife he made fierce clawing cuts at his face. The rest stood by, viewing the fight.

However, all was over in a moment, the one-armed man having murdered the other. When I came up, he was rummaging in the pockets of the dead man's coat. He seemed to have a huge impatience about something he sought after, digging amongst the cloth stuff, his face red like fire.

At last he grimped out a flask of water, which immediately he uncorked, and drank off the contents.

The man was stark mad. Being one of those who had come ashore in the second boat, he had neither heard the Surgeon's warning against eating of the fruit of the manchineel, nor knew any-

670 • THE GIGANTIC BOOK OF PIRATE STORIES

thing at all of the danger; arid, being attracted, I suppose, by the pleasant appearance and sweet smell of those deadly apples, he had tasted and eaten of them. Whereupon such huge drought and uncontrollable thirst seized on the poor maddened wretch, as inflamed him to that dreadful act of ferocity I have told you of. Now madness seized hold on him indeed, insomuch that he ran up and down, roaring and cutting the air and the trees with his knife. But the boatswain, who stood by, quickly put a period to his misery by running him through with his hanger.

After this I told the boatswain what Burke desired, and he mustered half a dozen of that company, and brought them with me to the boats. We put ourselves into the longboat, launched forth, and pulled towards the farther point of the bay, where we found Burke without the hut, stirring the heap of tobacco-leaves that was laid up before the entry for a protection against the mosquitoes. We went ashore to him, and with him into the hut.

The jolly company lay in the same posture, all three slumbering. Burke bid our men to remove the Captain into the boat, and they began to set about it. But, while this was doing, the buccaneer stirred, and presently woke up; and, having looked stupidly round, he enquired who we were and what we did in his habitation.

He was answered pleasantly by Burke, who said:

"Bon jour, monsieur, j'espère que vous avez bien dormi. Il faut que nous vous quittions. Mais je suis vraiment très fâché de ne plus voir votre beau visage!"

But this was taken very ill by the buccaneer, who started up, crying:

"Insolent! maraud d'Anglais! petit gros homme! Mort Dieu! vous me le paierez."

And he felt for his knife.

The Surgeon, however, had removed it whilst he slept; and, when he understood this, he would have fallen upon Burke with his fist. But one of the seamen who stood near, knocked him on the head with the butt of his pistol, which felled him senseless.

Hereupon, waked by the scuffle, the slave began to cry out, and then roared for quarter, as a seaman lifted his pistol to have served him after the same manner as his master. But Burke made the man desist.

Burke's care now was to get the Captain (who continued to slumber) into the boat, and thence all back into the ship again; and this he did effect, mainly by reason of his foresight in absconding amongst the bushes the buccaneer's store of veycou before our men came to the hut.

*   *   *   *   *

That night I took an opportunity of questioning Thalass about his knowledge of the Haunted Island and acquaintance with those pirates. But, though he answered me very frankly and told me what possibly he could, I learnt not much; for the eyes of a poor Indian are not as an European's, and here were strange and unfamiliar things.

It appeared, also, that Thalass had never stayed on the island for any considerable space of time, but used to go out on one pirate vessel or another (for, it seems, there were two or three), and, even at such times as he was on the island, he kept himself aloof from the rest, living in the woods.

Thalass told, indeed, of great pieces of ordnance and fortifications; and of that subterraneous place spoken of by the Englishman. Of the terrible old man the Englishman had called the Doctor, he could tell me nothing but what I knew. He had heard of the ghost, but had never seen it.

For the rest, he had consorted with the Englishman and made great friends with him; and at last (being taken out together on the same ship), they had contrived to escape in the cock-boat, and (after many days, and when such provisions as they had were long spent) had fallen in with our ship in manner related.

I asked him how first he came to consort with those pirates; he answered, that, being "many sleeps ago at Quibo," there came one of their ships, and he had gone away with them.

Next day I gave the Captain and Surgeon Burke an account of all that I had learnt of the Haunted Island, as well from the Englishman as from the Mosquito Indian.

The Old Buccaneer

ROBERT LOUIS STEVENSON

Squire Trelawney, Dr. Livesey, and the rest of these gentlemen having asked me to write down the whole particulars about Treasure Island, from the beginning to the end, keeping nothing back but the bearings of the island, and that only because there is still treasure not yet lifted, I take up my pen in the year of grace 17—, and go back to the time when my father kept the "Admiral Benbow" inn, and the brown old seaman, with the sabre cut, first took up his lodging under our roof.

I remember him as if it were yesterday, as he came plodding to the inn door, his sea-chest following behind him in a handbarrow; a tall, strong, heavy, nut-brown man; his tarry pigtail falling over the shoulders of his soiled blue coat; his hands ragged and scarred, with black, broken nails; and the sabre cut across one cheek, a dirty, livid white. I remember him looking round the cove and whistling to himself as he did so, and then breaking out in that old sea-song that he sang so often afterwards:

"Fifteen men on the dead man's chest—
Yo-ho-ho, and a bottle of rum!"

in the high, old tottering voice that seemed to have been tuned and broken at the capstan bars. Then he rapped on the door with a bit of stick like a handspike that he carried, and when my father appeared, called roughly for a glass of rum. This, when it was brought to him, he drank slowly, like a connoisseur, lingering on the taste, and still looking about him at the cliffs and up at our signboard.

"This is a handy cove," says he, at length; "and a pleasant sittyated grog-shop. Much company, mate?"

My father told him no, very little company, the more was the pity.

"Well then," said he, "this is the berth for me. Here you, matey," he cried to the man who trundled the barrow; "bring up alongside and help up my chest. I'll stay here a bit," he continued. "I'm a plain man; rum and bacon and eggs is what I want, and that head up there for to watch ships off. What you mought call me? You mought call me captain. Oh, I see what you're at—there"; and he threw down three or four gold pieces on the threshold. "You can tell me when I've worked through that," says he, looking as fierce as a commander.

And, indeed, bad as his clothes were, and coarsely as he spoke, he had none of the appearance of a man who sailed before the mast; but seemed like a mate or skipper, accustomed to be obeyed or to strike. The man who came with the barrow told us the mail had set him down the morning before at the "Royal George"; that he had inquired what inns there were along the coast, and hearing ours well spoken of, I suppose, and described as lonely, had chosen it from the others for his place of residence. And that was all we could learn of our guest.

He was a very silent man by custom. All day he hung round the cove, or upon the cliffs, with a brass telescope; all evening he sat in a corner of the parlour next the fire, and drank rum and water very strong. Mostly he would not speak when spoken to; only look up sudden and fierce, and blow through his nose like a fog-horn; and we and the people who came about our house soon learned to let him be. Every day, when he came back from his stroll, he would ask if any seafaring men had gone by along the road. At first we thought it was the want of company of his own kind that made him ask this question; but at last we began to see he was desirous to avoid them. When a seaman put up at the "Admiral Benbow" (as now and then some did, making by the coast road for Bristol), he would look in at him through the curtained door before he entered the parlour; and he was always sure to be as silent as a mouse when any such was present. For me, at least, there was no secret about the matter; for I was, in a way, a sharer in his alarms. He had taken me aside one day, and promised me a silver fourpenny on the first of every month if I would only keep my "weather-eye open for a seafaring man with one leg," and let him know the moment he appeared. Often enough, when the first of the month came round, and I applied to him for my wage, he would only blow through his nose at me, and stare me down; but before the week was out he was sure to think better of it, bring me my fourpenny piece, and repeat his orders to look out for "the seafaring man with one leg."

How that personage haunted my dreams, I need scarcely tell you. On stormy nights, when the wind shook the four corners of the house, and the surf roared along the cove and up the cliffs, I would see him in a thousand forms, and with a thousand diabolical expressions. Now the leg would be cut off at the knee, now at the hip; now he was a monstrous kind of a creature who had never had but the one leg, and that in the middle of his body. To see him leap and run and pursue me over hedge and ditch was the worst of nightmares. And altogether I paid pretty dear for my monthly fourpenny piece, in the shape of these abominable fancies.

But though I was so terrified by the idea of the seafaring man with one leg, I was far less afraid of the captain himself than anybody else who knew him. There were nights when he took a deal more rum and water than his head would carry; and then he would sometimes sit and sing his wicked, old wild sea-songs, minding nobody; but sometimes he would call for glasses round, and force all the trembling company to listen to his stories or bear a chorus to his singing. Often I have heard the house shaking with "Yo-ho-ho, and a bottle of rum"; all the neighbours joining in for dear life, with the fear of death upon them, and each singing louder than the other, to avoid remark. For in these fits he was the most over-riding companion ever known; he would slap his hand on the table for silence all round; he would fly up in a passion of anger at a question, or sometimes because none was put, and so he judged the company was not following his story. Nor would he allow anyone to leave the inn till he had drunk himself sleepy and reeled off to bed.

His stories were what frightened people worst of all. Dreadful stories they were; about hanging, and walking the plank, and storms at sea, and the Dry Tortugas, and wild deeds and places on the Spanish Main. By his own account he must have lived his life among some of the wickedest men that God ever allowed upon the sea; and the language in which he told these stories shocked our plain country people almost as much as the crimes that he described. My father was always saying the inn would be ruined, for people would soon cease coming there to be tyrannised over and put down, and sent shivering to their beds; but I really believe his presence did us good. People were frightened at the time, but on looking back they rather liked it; it was a fine excitement in a quiet country life; and there was even a party of the younger men who pretended to admire him, calling him a "true sea-dog," and a "real old salt," and such-like names, and saying there was the sort of man that made England terrible at sea.

In one way, indeed, he bade fair to ruin us; for he kept on staying week after week, and at last month after month, so that all the money had been long exhausted, and still my father never plucked up the heart to insist on having more. If ever he mentioned it, the captain blew through his nose so loudly, that you might say he roared, and stared my poor father out of the room. I have seen him wringing his hands after such a rebuff, and I am sure the annoyance and the terror he lived in must have greatly hastened his early and unhappy death.

All the time he lived with us the captain made no change whatever in his dress but to buy some stockings from a hawker. One of the cocks of his hat having fallen down, he let it hang from that day forth, though it was a great annoyance when it blew. I remember the appearance of his coat, which he patched himself upstairs in his room, and which, before the end, was nothing but patches. He never wrote or received a letter, and he never spoke with any but the neighbours, and with these, for the most part, only when drunk on rum. The great sea-chest none of us had ever seen open.

He was only once crossed, and that was towards the end, when my poor father was far gone in a decline that took him off. Dr. Livesey came late one afternoon to see the patient, took a bit of dinner from my mother, and went into the parlour to smoke a pipe until his horse should come down from the hamlet, for we had no stabling at the old "Benbow." I followed him in, and I remember observing the contrast the neat, bright doctor, with his powder as white as snow, and his bright, black eyes and pleasant manners, made with the coltish country folk, and above all, with that filthy, heavy, bleared scarecrow of a pirate of ours, sitting far gone in rum, with his arms on the table. Suddenly he—the captain, that is—began to pipe up his eternal song:

> *"Fifteen men on the dead man's chest—*
> *Yo-ho-ho, and a bottle of rum!*
> *Drink and the devil had done for the rest—*
> *Yo-ho-ho, and a bottle of rum!"*

At first I had supposed "the dead man's chest" to be that identical big box of his upstairs in the front room, and the thought had been mingled in my nightmares with that of the one-legged seafaring man. But by this time we had all long ceased to pay any particular notice to the song; it was new, that night, to nobody but Dr. Livesey, and on him I observed it did not produce an agreeable effect, for he looked up for a moment quite angrily before he went on with his talk to old Taylor, the gardener, on a new cure for the rheumatics. In the meantime, the captain gradually brightened up at his own music, and at last flapped his hand upon the table before him in a way we all knew to mean—silence. The voices stopped at once, all but Dr. Livesey's; he went on as before, speaking clear and kind, and drawing briskly at his pipe between every word or two. The captain glared at him for a while, flapped his hand again, glared still harder, and at last broke out with a villainous low oath: "Silence, there, between decks!"

"Were you addressing me, sir?" says the doctor; and when the ruffian had told him, with another oath, that this was so, "I have only one thing to say to you, sir," replies the doctor, "that if you keep on drinking rum, the world will soon be quit of a very dirty scoundrel!"

The old fellow's fury was awful. He sprang to his feet, drew and opened a sailor's clasp-knife, and, balancing it open on the palm of his hand, threatened to pin the doctor to the wall.

The doctor never so much as moved. He spoke to him, as before, over his shoulder, and in the same tone of voice; rather high, so that all the room might hear, but perfectly calm and steady:

"If you do not put that knife this instant in your pocket, I promise, upon my honour, you shall hang at next assizes."

Then followed a battle of looks between them; but the captain soon knuckled under, put up his weapon, and resumed his seat, grumbling like a beaten dog.

"And now, sir," continued the doctor, "since I now know there's such a fellow in my district, you may count I'll have an eye upon you day and night. I'm not a doctor only; I'm a magistrate; and if I catch a breath of complaint against you, if it's only for a piece of incivility like to-night's, I'll take effectual means to have you hunted down and routed out of this. Let that suffice."

Soon after Dr. Livesey's horse came to the door, and he rode away; but the captain held his peace that evening, and for many evenings to come.

*   *   *   *   *

It was not very long after this that there occurred the first of the mysterious events that rid us at last of the captain, though not, as you will see, of his affairs. It was a bitter cold winter, with long, hard frosts and heavy gales; and it was plain from the first that my poor father was little likely to see the spring. He sank daily, and my mother and I had all the inn upon our hands; and were kept busy enough, without paying much regard to our unpleasant guest.

It was one January morning, very early—a pinching, frosty morning—the cove all grey with hoar-frost, the ripple lapping softly on the stones, the sun still low and only touching the hilltops and shining far to seaward. The captain had risen earlier than usual, and set down to the beach, his cutlass swinging under the broad skirts of the old blue coat, his brass telescope under his arm, his hat tilted back upon his head. I remember his breath hanging like smoke in his wake as he strode off, and the last sound I heard of him, as he turned the big rock, was a loud snort of indignation, as though his mind was still running upon Dr. Livesey.

Well, mother was upstairs with father; and I was laying the breakfast table against the captain's return, when the parlour door opened, and a man stepped in on whom I had never set my eyes before. He was a pale, tallowy creature, wanting two fingers of the left hand; and, though he wore a cutlass, he did not look much like a fighter. I had always my eye open for seafaring men, with one leg or two, and I remember this one puzzled me. He was not sailorly, and yet he had a smack of the sea about him too.

I asked him what was for his service, and he said he would take rum; but as I was going out of the room to fetch it he sat down upon a table and motioned me to draw near. I paused where I was with my napkin in my hand.

"Come here, sonny," says he. "Come nearer here."

I took a step nearer.

"Is this here table for my mate Bill?" he asked, with a kind of leer.

I told him I did not know his mate Bill; and this was for a person who stayed in our house, whom we called the captain.

"Well," said he, "my mate Bill would be called the captain, as like as not. He has a cut on one cheek, and a mighty pleasant way with him, particularly in drink, has my mate Bill. We'll put it, for argument like, that your captain has a cut on one cheek—and we'll put it, if you like, that that cheek's the right one. Ah, well! I told you. Now, is my mate Bill in this here house?"

I told him he was out walking.

"Which way, sonny? Which way is he gone?"

And when I had pointed out the rock and told him how the captain was likely to return, and how soon, and answered a few other questions, "Ah," said he, "this'll be as good as drink to my mate Bill."

The expression on his face as he said these words was me stranger was mistaken, even supposing he meant what he said. But it was no affair of mine, I thought; and, besides, it was difficult to know what to do. The stranger kept hanging about just inside the inn door, peering round the corner like a cat waiting for a mouse. Once I stepped out myself into the road, but he immediately called me back, and, as I did not obey quick enough for his fancy, a most horrible change came over his tallowy face, and he ordered me in, with an oath that made me jump. As soon as I was back again he returned to his former manner, half fawning, half sneering, patted me on the shoulder, told me I was a good boy, and he had taken quite a fancy to me. "I have a son of my own," said he, "as like you as two blocks, and he's all the pride of my 'art. But the great thing for boys is discipline, sonny—discipline. Now, if you had sailed along of Bill, you wouldn't have stood there to be spoke to twice—not you. That was never Bill's way, nor the way of sich as sailed with him. And here, sure enough, is my mate Bill, with a spyglass under his arm, bless his old 'art to be sure. You and me'll just go back into the parlour, sonny, and get behind the door, and we'll give Bill a little surprise—bless his 'art, I say again."

So saying, the stranger backed along with me into the parlour, and put me behind him in the corner, so that we were both hidden by the open door. I was very uneasy and alarmed, as you may fancy, and it rather added to my fears to observe that the stranger was certainly frightened himself. He cleared the hilt of his cutlass and loosened the blade in the sheath; and all the time we were waiting there he kept swallowing as if he felt what we used to call a lump in the throat.

At last in strode the captain, slammed the door behind him, without looking to the right or left, and marched straight across the room to where his breakfast awaited him.

"Bill," said the stranger, in a voice that I thought he had tried to make bold and big.

The captain spun round on his heel and fronted us; all the brown had gone out of his face, and even his nose was blue; he had the look of a man who sees a ghost, or the evil one, or something worse, if anything can be; and, upon my word, I felt sorry to see him, all in a moment, turn so old and sick.

"Bill, surely," said the stranger.

The captain made a sort of gasp.

"Black Dog!" said he.

"And who else?" returned the other, getting more at his ease. "Black Dog as ever was, come for to see his old shipmate Billy, at the 'Admiral Benbow' inn. Ah, Bill, Bill, we have seen a sight of times, us two, since I lost them two talons," holding up his mutilated hand.

"Now, look here," said the captain; "you've run me down; here I am; well, then, speak up: what is it?"

"That's you, Bill," returned Black Dog, "you're in the right of it, Billy. I'll have a glass of rum from this dear child here, as I've took such a liking to; and we'll sit down, if you please, and talk square, like old shipmates."

When I returned with the rum, they were already seated on either side of the captain's breakfast table—Black Dog next to the door, and sitting sideways, so as to have one eye on his old shipmate, and one, as I thought, on his retreat.

He bade me go, and leave the door wide open. "None of your keyholes for me, sonny," he said; and I left them together, and retired into the bar.

For a long time, though I certainly did my best to listen, I could hear nothing but a low gabbling; but at last the voices began to grow higher, and I could pick up a word or two, mostly oaths, from the captain.

"No, no, no, no; and an end of it!" he cried once. And again, "If it comes to swinging, swing all, say I."

Then all of a sudden there was a tremendous explosion of oaths and other noises—the chair and table went over in a lump, a clash of steel followed, and then a cry of pain, and the next instant I saw Black Dog in full flight, and the captain hotly pursuing, both with drawn cutlasses, and the former streaming blood from the left shoulder. Just at the door, the captain aimed at the fugitive one last tremendous cut, which would certainly have split him to the chine had it not been intercepted by our big signboard of Admiral Benbow. You may see the notch on the lower side of the frame to this day.

The blow was the last of the battle. Once out upon the road, Black Dog, in spite of his wound, showed a wonderful clean pair of heels, and disappeared over the edge of the hill in half a minute. The captain, for his part, stood staring at the over his eyes several times, and at last turned back into the house.

"Jim," says he, "rum"; and as he spoke, he reeled a little, and caught himself with one hand against the wall.

"Are you hurt?" cried I.

"Rum," he repeated. "I must get away from here. Rum! rum!"

I ran to fetch it; but I was quite unsteadied by all that had fallen out, and I broke one glass and fouled the tap, and while I was still getting in my own way, I heard a loud fall in the parlour, and, running in, beheld the captain lying full length upon the floor. At the same instant my mother, alarmed by the cries and fighting, came running downstairs to help me. Between us we raised his head. He was breathing very loud and hard; but his eyes were closed, and his face a horrible colour.

"Dear, deary me," cried my mother, "what a disgrace upon the house! And your poor father sick!"

In the meantime, we had no idea what to do to help the captain, nor any other thought but that he had got his death-hurt in the scuffle with the stranger. I got the rum, to be sure, and tried to put it down his throat; but his teeth were tightly shut, and his jaws as strong as iron. It was a happy relief for us when the door opened and Doctor Livesey came in, on his visit to my father.

"Oh, doctor," we cried, "what shall we do? Where is he wounded?"

"Wounded? A fiddle-stick's end!" said the doctor. "No more wounded than you or I. The man has had a stroke, as I warned him. Now, Mrs. Hawkins, just you run upstairs to your husband, and tell him, if possible, nothing about it. For my part, I must do my best to save this fellow's trebly worthless life; and Jim here will get me a basin."

When I got back with the basin, the doctor had already ripped up the captain's sleeve, and exposed his great sinewy arm. It was tattooed in several places. "Here's luck," "A fair wind," and "Billy Bones his fancy," were very neatly and clearly executed on the forearm; and up near the shoulder there was a sketch of a gallows and a man hanging from it—done, as I thought, with great spirit.

"Prophetic," said the doctor, touching this picture with name, we'll have a look at the colour of your blood. Jim," he said, "are you afraid of blood?"

"No, sir," said I.

"Well, then," said he, "you hold the basin"; and with that he took his lancet and opened a vein.

A great deal of blood was taken before the captain opened his eyes and looked mistily about him. First he recognised the doctor with an unmistakable frown; then his glance fell upon me, and he looked relieved. But suddenly his colour changed, and he tried to raise himself, crying:

"Where's Black Dog?"

"There is no Black Dog here," said the doctor, "except what you have on your own back. You have been drinking rum; you have had a stroke, precisely as I told you; and I have just, very much against my own will, dragged you head-foremost out of the grave. Now, Mr. Bones——"

"That's not my name," he interrupted.

"Much I care," returned the doctor. "It's the name of a buccaneer of my acquaintance; and I call you by it for the sake of shortness, and what I have to say to you is this: one glass of rum won't kill you, but if you take one you'll take another and another, and I stake my wig if you don't break off short, you'll die—do you understand that?—die, and go to your own place, like the man in the Bible. Come, now, make an effort. I'll help you to your bed for once."

Between us, with much trouble, we managed to hoist him upstairs, and laid him on his bed, where his head fell back on the pillow, as if he were almost fainting.

"Now, mind you," said the doctor, "I clear my conscience—the name of rum for you is death."

And with that he went off to see my father, taking me with him by the arm.

"This is nothing," he said, as soon as he had closed the door. "I have drawn blood enough to keep him quiet a while; he should lie for a week where he is—that is the best thing for him and you; but another stroke would settle him."

*   *   *   *   *

About noon I stopped at the captain's door with some cooling drinks and medicines. He was lying very much as we had left him, only a little higher, and he seemed both weak and excited.

"Jim," he said, "you're the only one here that's worth anything; and you know I've been always good to you. Never a month but I've given you a silver fourpenny for yourself. And now you see, mate, I'm pretty low, and deserted by all; and, Jim, you'll bring me one noggin of rum, now, won't you, matey?"

"The doctor——" I began.

But he broke in cursing the doctor, in a feeble voice, but heartily. "Doctors is all swabs," he said; "and that doctor there, why, what do he know about seafaring men? I been in places hot as pitch, and mates dropping round with Yellow Jack, and the blessed land a-heaving like the sea with earthquakes—what do the doctor know of lands like that?—and I lived on rum, I tell you. It's been meat and drink, and man and wife, to me; and if I'm not to have my rum now I'm a poor old hulk on a lee shore, my blood'll be on you, Jim, and that doctor swab"; and he ran on again for a while with curses. "Look, Jim, how my fingers fidget," he continued, in the pleading tone. "I can't keep 'em still, not I. I haven't had a drop this blessed day. That doctor's a fool, I tell you. If I don't have a drain o' rum, Jim, I'll have the horrors; I seen some on 'em already. I seen old Flint there in the corner, behind you; as plain as print, I seen him; and if I get the horrors, I'm a man that has lived rough, and I'll raise Cain. Your doctor hisself said one glass wouldn't hurt me. I'll give you a golden guinea for a noggin, Jim."

He was growing more and more excited, and this alarmed me for my father, who was very low that day, and needed quiet; besides, I was reassured by the doctor's words, now quoted to me, and rather offended by the offer of a bribe.

"I want none of your money," said I, "but what you owe my father. I'll get you one glass, and no more."

When I brought it to him, he seized it greedily, and drank it out.

"Ay, ay," said he, "that's some better, sure enough. And now, matey, did that doctor say how long I was to lie here in this old berth?"

"A week at least," said I.

"Thunder!" he cried. "A week! I can't do that: they'd have the black spot on me by then. The lubbers is going about to get the wind of me this blessed moment; lubbers as couldn't keep what they got, and want to nail what is another's. Is that seamanly behaviour, now, I want to know? But I'm a saving soul. I never wasted good money of mine, nor lost it neither; and I'll trick 'em again. I'm not afraid on 'em. I'll shake out another reef, matey, and daddle 'em again."

As he was thus speaking, he had risen from bed with great difficulty, holding to my shoulder with a grip that almost made me cry out, and moving his legs like so much dead weight: His words, spirited as they were in meaning, contrasted sadly with the weakness of the voice in which they were uttered. He paused when he had got into a sitting position on the edge.

"That doctor's done me," he murmured. "My ears is singing. Lay me back."

Before I could do much to help him he had fallen back again to his former place, where he lay for a while silent.

"Jim," he said, at length, "you saw that seafaring man to-day?"

"Black Dog?" I asked.

"Ah! Black Dog," said he. "*He's* a bad 'un; but there's worse that put him on. Now, if I can't get away nohow, and they tip me the black spot, mind you, it's my old sea-chest they're after; you get on a horse—you can, can't you? Well, then, you get on a horse, and go to—well, yes, I will!—to that eternal doctor swab, and tell him to pipe all hands—magistrates and sich—and he'll lay 'em aboard at the 'Admiral Benbow'—all old Flint's crew, man and boy, all on 'em that's left. I was first mate, I was, old Flint's first mate, and I'm the on'y one as knows the place. He gave it me to Savannah, when he lay a-dying, like as if I was to now, you see. But you won't peach unless they get the black spot on me, or unless you see that Black Dog again, or a seafaring man with one leg, Jim—him above all."

"But what is the black spot, Captain?" I asked.

"That's a summons, mate. I'll tell you if they get that. But you keep your weather-eye open, Jim, and I'll share with you equals, upon my honour."

He wandered a little longer, his voice growing weaker; but soon after I had given him his medicine, which he took like a child, with the remark, "If ever a seaman wanted drugs, it's me," he fell at last into a heavy, swoon-like sleep, in which I left him. What I should have done had all gone well I do not know. Probably I should have told the whole story to the doctor; for I was in mortal fear lest the captain should repent of his confessions and make an end of me. But as things fell out, my poor father died quite suddenly that evening, which put all other matters on one side. Our natural distress, the visits of the neighbours, the arranging of the funeral, and all the work of the inn to be carried on in the meanwhile, kept me so busy that I had scarcely time to think of the captain, far less to be afraid of him.

He got downstairs next morning, to be sure, and had his meals as usual, though he ate little, and had more, I am afraid, than his usual supply of rum, for he helped himself out of the bar, scowling and blowing through his nose, and no one dared to cross him. On the night before the funeral he was as drunk as ever; and it was shocking, in that house of mourning, to hear him singing away at his ugly old sea-song; but, weak as he was, we were all in the fear of death for him, and the doctor was suddenly taken up with a case many miles away, and was never near the house after my father's death. I have said the captain was weak; and indeed he seemed rather to grow weaker than regain his strength. He clambered up and down stairs, and went from the parlour to the bar and back again, and sometimes put his nose out of doors to smell the sea, holding on to the walls as he went for suport, and breathing hard and fast like a man on a steep mountain. He never particularly addressed me, and it is my belief he had as good as forgotten his confidences; but his temper was more flighty, and, allowing for his bodily weakness, more violent than ever. He had an alarming way now when he was drunk of drawing his cutlass and laying it bare before him on the table. But, with all that, he minded people less, and seemed shut up in his own thoughts and rather wandering. Once, for instance, to our extreme wonder, he piped up to a different air, a kind of country love-song, that he must have learned in his youth before he had begun to follow the sea.

So things passed until, the day after the funeral, and about three o'clock of a bitter, foggy, frosty afternoon, I was standing at the door for a moment, full of sad thoughts about my father, when I saw someone drawing slowly near along the road. He was plainly blind, for he tapped before him with a stick, and wore a great green shade over his eyes and nose; and he was hunched, as if with age or weakness, and wore a huge old tattered sea-cloak with a hood, that made him appear positively deformed. I never saw in my life a more dreadful-looking figure. He stopped a little from the inn, and, raising his voice in an odd sing-song, addressed the air in front of him:

"Will any kind friend inform a poor blind man, who has lost the precious sight of his eyes in the gracious defence of his native country, England, and God bless King George!—where or in what part of this country he may now be?"

"You are at the 'Admiral Benbow,' Black Hill Cove, my good man," said I.

"I hear a voice," said he—"a young voice. Will you give me your hand, my kind young friend, and lead me in?"

I held out my hand, and the horrible, soft-spoken, eyeless creature gripped it in a moment like a vice. I was so much startled that I struggled to withdraw; but the blind man pulled me close up to him with a single action of his arm.

"Now, boy," he said, "take me in to the captain."

"Sir," said I, "upon my word I dare not."

"Oh," he sneered, "that's it! Take me in straight, or I'll break your arm."

And he gave it, as he spoke, a wrench that made me cry out.

"Sir," I said, "it is for yourself I mean. The captain is not what he used to be. He sits with a drawn cutlass. Another gentleman——"

"Come, now, march," interrupted he; and I never heard a voice so cruel, and cold, and ugly as that blind man's. It cowed me more than the pain; and I began to obey him at once, walking straight in at the door and towards the parlour, where our sick old buccaneer was sitting, dazed with rum. The blind man clung close to me, holding me in one iron fist, and leaning almost more of his weight on me than I could carry. "Lead me straight up to him, and when I'm in view, cry out, 'Here's a friend for you, Bill.' If you don't, I'll do this"; and with that he gave me a twitch that I thought would have made me faint. Between this and that, I was so utterly terrified of the blind beggar that I forgot my terror of the captain, and as I opened the parlour door, cried out the words he had ordered in a trembling voice.

The poor captain raised his eyes, and at one look the rum went out of him, and left him staring sober. The expression of his face was not so much of terror as of mortal sickness. He made a movement to rise, but I do not believe he had enough force left in his body.

"Now, Bill, sit where you are," said the beggar. "If I can't see, I can hear a finger stirring. Business is business. Hold out your right hand. Boy, take his right hand by the wrist, and bring it near to my right."

We both obeyed him to the letter, and I saw him pass something from the hollow of the hand that held his stick into the palm of the captain's, which closed upon it instantly.

"And now that's done," said the blind man; and at the words he suddenly left hold of me, and, with incredible accuracy and nimbleness, skipped out of the parlour and into the road, where as I still stood motionless, I could hear his stick go tap-tap-tapping into the distance.

It was some time before either I or the captain seemed to gather our senses; but at length, and about at the same moment, I released his wrist, which I was still holding, and he drew in his hand and looked sharply into the palm.

"Ten o'clock!" he cried. "Six hours. We'll do them yet"; and he sprang to his feet.

Even as he did so, he reeled, put his hand to his throat, stood swaying for a moment, and then, with a peculiar sound, fell from his whole height face foremost to the floor.

I ran to him at once, calling to my mother. But haste was all in vain. The captain had been struck dead by thundering apoplexy. It is a curious thing to understand, for I had certainly never liked the man, though of late I had begun to pity him, but as soon as I saw that he was dead, I burst into a flood of tears. It was the second death I had known, and the sorrow of the first was still fresh in my heart.

*　　　　*　　　　*　　　　*　　　　*

I lost no time, of course, in telling my mother all that I knew, and perhaps should have told her long before, and we saw ourselves at once in a difficult and dangerous position. Some of the man's money—if he had any—was certainly due to us; but it was not likely that our captain's shipmates, above all the two specimens seen by me, Black Dog and the blind beggar, would be inclined to give up their booty in payment of the dead man's debts. The captain's order to mount at once and ride for Doctor Livesey would have left my mother alone and unprotected, which was not to be thought of. Indeed, it seemed impossible for either of us to remain much longer in the house: the fall of coals in the kitchen grate, the very ticking of the clock, filled us with alarms. The neighbourhood, to our ears, seemed haunted by approaching footsteps; and what between the dead body of the captain on the parlour floor, and the thought of that detestable blind beggar hovering near at hand, and ready to return, there were moments when, as the saying goes, I jumped in my skin for terror. Something must speedily be resolved upon; and it occurred to us at last to go forth together and seek help in the neighbouring hamlet.

The hamlet lay not many hundred yards away though out of view, on the other side of the next cove; and what greatly encouraged me, it was in an opposite direction from that whence the blind man had made his appearance, and whither he had presumably returned. We were not many minutes on the road, though we sometimes stopped to lay hold of each other and hearken. But there was no unusual sound—nothing but the low wash of the ripple and the croaking of the crows in the wood.

It was already candle-light when we reached the hamlet, and I shall never forget how much I was cheered to see the yellow shine in doors and windows; but that, as it proved, was the best of the help we were likely to get in that quarter. For—you would have thought men would have been ashamed of themselves—no soul would consent to return with us to the "Admiral Benbow." The more we told of our troubles, the more—man, woman, and child—they clung to the shelter of their houses. The name of Captain Flint, though it was strange to me, was well enough known to some there, and carried a great weight of terror. Some of the men who had been to field-work on the far side of the "Admiral Benbow" remembered, besides, to have seen several strangers on the road, and, taking them to be smugglers, to have bolted away; and one at least had seen a little lugger in what we called Kitt's Hole. For that matter, anyone who was a comrade of the captain's was enough to frighten them to death. And the short and the long of the matter was, that while we could get several who were willing enough to ride to Dr. Livesey's, which lay in another direction, not one would help us to defend the inn.

They say cowardice is infectious; but then argument is, on the other hand, a great embold-ener; and so when each had said his say, my mother made them a speech. She would not, she declared, lose money that belonged to her fatherless boy; "if none of the rest of you dare," she said, "Jim and I dare. Back we will go, the way we came, and small thanks to you big, hulking, chicken-hearted men. We'll have that chest open, if we die for it. And I'll thank you for that bag, Mrs. Crossley, to bring back our lawful money in."

Of course, I said I would go with my mother; and of course they all cried out at our fool-hardiness; but even then not a man would go along with us. All they would do was to give me a loaded pistol, lest we were attacked; and to promise to have horses ready saddled, in case we were pursued on our return; while one lad was to ride forward to the doctor's in search of armed assistance.

My heart was beating finely when we two set forth in the cold night upon this dangerous venture. A full moon was beginning to rise and peered redly through the upper edges of the fog, and this increased our haste, for it was plain, before we came forth again, that all would be as bright as day, and our departure exposed to the eyes of any watchers. We slipped along the hedges, noiseless and swift, nor did we see or hear anything to increase our terrors, till, to our huge relief, the door of the "Admiral Benbow" had closed behind us.

I slipped the bolt at once, and we stood and panted for a moment in the dark, alone in the house with the dead captain's body. Then my mother got a candle in the bar, and, holding each other's hands, we advanced into the parlour. He lay as we had left him, on his back, with his eyes open, and one arm stretched out.

"Draw down the blind, Jim," whispered my mother; "they might come and watch outside. And now," said she, when I had done so, "we have to get the key off *that*; and who's to touch it, I should like to know!" and she gave a kind of sob as she said the words.

I went down on my knees at once. On the floor close to his hand there was a little round of paper, blackened on the one side. I could not doubt that this was the *black spot*; and taking it up, I found written on the other side, in a very good, clear hand, this short message: "You have till ten to-night."

"He had till ten, mother," said I; and just as I said it, our old clock began striking. This sudden noise startled us shockingly; but the news was good, for it was only six.

"Now, Jim," she said, "that key."

I felt in his pockets, one after another. A few small coins, a thimble, and some thread and big needles, a piece of pigtail tobacco bitten away at the end, his gully with a crooked handle, a pocket compass, and a tinder box, were all that they contained, and I began to despair.

"Perhaps it's round his neck," suggested my mother.

Overcoming a strong repugnance, I tore open his shirt at the neck, and there, sure enough, hanging to a bit of tarry string, which I cut with his own gully, we found the key. At this triumph we were filled with hope, and hurried upstairs, without delay, to the little room where he had slept so long and where his box had stood since the day of his arrival.

It was like any other seaman's chest on the outside, the initial "B." burned on the top of it with a hot iron, and the corners somewhat smashed and broken as by long, rough usage.

"Give me the key," said my mother; and though the lock was very stiff, she had turned it and thrown back the lid in a twinkling.

A strong smell of tobacco and tar rose from the interior, but nothing was to be seen on the top except a suit of very good clothes, carefully brushed and folded. They had never been worn, my mother said. Under that, the miscellany began—a quadrant, a tin cannikin, several sticks of tobacco, two brace of very handsome pistols, a piece of bar silver, an old Spanish watch and some other trinkets of little value and mostly of foreign make, a pair of compasses mounted with brass, and five or six curious West Indian shells. It has often set me thinking since that he should have carried about these shells with him in his wandering, guilty, and hunted life.

In the meantime, we had found nothing of any value but the silver and the trinkets, and neither of these were in our way. Underneath there was an old boat-cloak, whitened with sea-salt on many a harbour-bar. My mother pulled it up with impatience, and there lay before us, the last things in the chest, a bundle tied up in oilcloth, and looking like papers, and a canvas bag, that gave forth, at a touch, the jingle of gold.

"I'll show these rogues that I'm an honest woman," said my mother. "I'll have my dues, and not a farthing over. Hold Mrs. Crossley's bag." And she began to count over the amount of the captain's score from the sailor's bag into the one that I was holding.

It was a long, difficult business, for the coins were of all countries and sizes—doubloons, and louis-d'ors, and guineas, and pieces of eight, and I know not what besides, all shaken together at random. The guineas, too, were about the scarcest, and it was with these only that my mother knew how to make her count.

When we were about half-way through, I suddenly put my hand upon her arm; for I had heard in the silent, frosty air a sound that brought my heart into my mouth—the tap-tapping of the blind man's stick upon the frozen road. It drew nearer and nearer, while we sat holding our breath. Then it struck sharp on the inn door, and then we could hear the handle being turned, and the bolt rattling as the wretched being tried to enter; and then there was a long time of silence both within and without. At last the tapping recommenced, and, to our indescribable joy and gratitude, died slowly away again until it ceased to be heard.

"Mother," said I, "take the whole and let's be going"; for I was sure the bolted door must have seemed suspicious, and would bring the whole hornet's nest about our ears; though how thankful I was that I had bolted it, none could tell who had never met that terrible blind man.

But my mother, frightened as she was, would not consent to take a fraction more than was due to her, and was obstinately unwilling to be content with less. It was not yet seven, she said, by a long way; she knew her rights and she would have them; and she was still arguing with me, when a low whistle sounded a good way off upon the hill. That was enough, and more than enough, for both of us.

"I'll take what I have," she said, jumping to her feet.

"And I'll take this to square the count," said I, picking up the oilskin packet.

Next moment we were both groping downstairs, leaving the candle by the empty chest, and the next we had opened the door and were in full retreat. We had not started a moment too soon. The fog was rapidly dispersing; already the moon shone quite clear on the high ground on either side; and it was only in the exact bottom of the dell and round the tavern door that a thin veil still hung unbroken to conceal the first steps of our escape. Far less than half-way to the hamlet, very little beyond the bottom of the hill, we must come forth into the moonlight. Nor was this all; for the sound of several footsteps running came already to our ears, and as we looked back in their direction, a light tossing to and fro and still rapidly advancing, showed that one of the new-comers carried a lantern.

"My dear," said my mother suddenly, "take the money and run on. I am going to faint."

This was certainly the end for both of us, I thought. How I cursed the cowardice of the neighbours; how I blamed my poor mother for her honesty and her greed, for her past foolhardiness and present weakness! We were just at the little bridge, by good fortune; and I helped her tottering as she was, to the edge of the bank, where sure enough, she gave a sigh and fell on my shoulder. I do not know how I found the strength to do it at all, and I am afraid it was roughly done; but I managed to drag her down the bank and a little way under the arch. Farther I could not move her, for the bridge was too low to let me do more than crawl below it. So there we had to stay—my mother almost entirely exposed, and both of us within earshot of the inn.

*   *   *   *   *

My curiosity, in a sense, was stronger than my fear; for I could not remain where I was, but crept back to the bank again, whence, sheltering my head behind a bush of broom, I might command the road before our door. I was scarcely in position ere my enemies began to arrive, seven or eight of them, running hard, their feet beating out of time along the road, and the man with the lantern some paces in front. Three men ran together, hand in hand; and I made out, even through the mist, that the middle man of this trio was the blind beggar. The next moment his voice showed me that I was right.

"Down with the door!" he criedy.

"Ay, ay, sir!" answered two or three; and a rush was made upon the "Admiral Benbow," the lantern-bearer following; and then I could see them pause, and hear speeches passed in a lower key, as if they were surprised to find the door open. But the pause was brief, for the blind man again issued his commands. His voice sounded louder and higher, as if he were afire with eagerness and rage.

"In, in, in!" he shouted, and cursed them for their delay.

Four or five of them obeyed at once, two remaining on the road with the formidable beggar. There was a pause, then a cry of surprise, and then a voice shouting from the house:

"Bill's dead!"

But the blind man swore at them again for their delay.

"Search him, some of you shirking lubbers, and the rest of you aloft and get the chest," he cried.

I could hear their feet rattling up our old stairs, so that the house must have shook with it. Promptly afterwards, fresh sounds of astonishment arose; the window of the captain's room was thrown open with a slam and a jingle of broken glass; and a man leaned out into the moonlight, head and shoulders, and addressed the blind beggar on the road below him.

"Pew," he cried, "they've been before us. Someone's turned the chest out alow and aloft."

"Is it there?" roared Pew.

"The money's there."

The blind man cursed the money.

"Flint's fist, I mean," he cried.

"We don't see it here nohow," returned the man.

"Here, you below there, is it on Bill?" cried the blind man again.

At that, another fellow, probably him who had remained below to search the captain's body, came to the door of the inn. "Bill's been overhauled a'ready," said he, "nothin' left."

"It's these people of the inn—it's that boy. I wish I had put his eyes out!" cried the blind man, Pew. "They were here no time ago—they had the door bolted when I tried it. Scatter, lads, and find 'em."

"Sure enough, they left their glim here," said the fellow from the window.

"Scatter and find 'em! Rout the house out!" reiterated Pew, striking with his stick upon the road.

Then there followed a great to-do through all our old heavy feet pounding to and fro, furniture thrown over, doors kicked in, until the very rocks re-echoed, and the men came out again, one after another, on the road, and declared that we were nowhere to be found. And just then the same whistle that had alarmed my mother and myself over the dead captain's money was once more clearly audible through the night, but this time twice repeated. I had thought it to be the blind man's trumpet, so to speak, summoning his crew to the assault; but I now found that it was a signal from the hillside towards the hamlet, and, from its effect upon the buccaneers, a signal to warn them of approaching danger.

"There's Dirk again," said one. "Twice! We'll have to budge, mates."

"Budge, you skulk!" cried Pew. "Dirk was a fool and a coward from the first—you wouldn't mind him. They must be close by; they can't be far; you have your hands on it. Scatter and look for them, dogs! Oh, shiver my soul," he cried, "if I had eyes!"

This appeal seemed to produce some effect, for two of the fellows began to look here and there among the lumber, but half-heartedly, I thought, and with half an eye to their own danger all the time, while the rest stood irresolute on the road.

"You have your hands on thousands, you fools, and you hang a leg! You'd be as rich as kings if you could find it, and you know it's here, and you stand there malingering. There wasn't one of you dared face Bill, and I did it—a blind man! And I'm to lose my chance through you! I'm to be a poor, crawling beggar, sponging for rum, when I might be rolling in a coach! If you had the pluck of a weevil in a biscuit you would catch them still."

"Hang it, Pew, we've got the doubloons!" grumbled one.

"They might have hid the blessed thing," said another. "Take the Georges, Pew, and don't stand here squalling."

Squalling was the word for it, Pew's anger rose so high at these objections; till at last, his passion completely taking the upper hand, he struck at them right and left in his blindness, and his stick sounded heavily on more than one.

These, in their turn, cursed back at the blind miscreant, threatened him in horrid terms, and tried in vain to catch the stick and wrest it from his grasp.

This quarrel was the saving of us; for while it was still raging, another sound came from the top of the hill on the side of the hamlet—the tramp of horses galloping. Almost at the same time, a pistol-shot, flash and report, came from the hedge-side. And that was plainly the last signal of danger; for the buccaneers turned at once and ran, separating in every direction, one seaward along the cove, one slant across the hill, and so on, so that in half a minute not a sign of them remained but Pew. Him they had deserted, whether in sheer panic or out of revenge for his ill words and blows, I know not; but there he remained behind, tapping up and down the road in a frenzy, and groping and calling for his comrades. Finally he took the wrong turn, and ran a few steps past me, towards the hamlet, crying:

"Johnny, Black Dog, Dirk," and other names, "you won't leave old Pew, mates—not old Pew!"

Just then the noise of horses topped the rise, and four or five riders came in sight in the moonlight, and swept at full gallop down the slope.

At this Pew saw his error, turned with a scream, and ran straight for the ditch, into which he rolled. But he was on his feet again in a second, and made another dash, now utterly bewildered, right under the nearest of the coming horses.

The rider tried to save him, but in vain. Down went Pew with a cry that rang high into the night; and the four hoofs trampled and spurned him and passed by. He fell on his side, then gently collapsed upon his face, and moved no more.

I leaped to my feet and hailed the riders. They were pulling up, at any rate, horrified at the accident; and I soon saw what they were. One, tailing out behind the rest, was a lad that had gone from the hamlet to Dr. Livesey's; the rest were revenue officers, whom he had met by the way and with whom he had had the intelligence to return at once. Some news of the lugger in Kitt's Hole had found its way to Supervisor Dance, and set him forth that night in our direction, and to that circumstance my mother and I owed our preservation from death.

Pew was dead, stone dead. As for my mother, when we had carried her up to the hamlet, a little cold water and salts and that soon brought her back again, and she was none the balance of the money. In the meantime the supervisor rode on, as fast as he could, to Kitt's Hole; but his men had to dismount and grope down the dingle, leading, and sometimes supporting, their horses, and in continual fear of ambushes; so it was no great matter for surprise that when they got down to the Hole the lugger was already under way, though still close in. He hailed her. A voice replied, telling him to keep out of the moonlight, or he would get some lead in him, and at the same time a bullet whistled close by his arm. Soon after, the lugger doubled the point and disappeared. Mr. Dance stood there, as he said, "like a fish out of water," and all he could do was to despatch a man to B— to warn the cutter. "And that," said he, "is just about as good as nothing. They've got off clean, and there's an end. Only," he added, "I'm glad I trod on Master Pew's corns"; for by this time he had heard my story.

I went back with him to the "Admiral Benbow," and you cannot imagine a house in such a state of smash; the very clock had been thrown down by these fellows in their furious hunt after my mother and myself; and though nothing had actually been taken away except the captain's money-bag and a little silver from the till, I could see at once that we were ruined. Mr. Dance could make nothing of the scene.

"They got the money, you say? Well, then, Hawkins, what in fortune were they after? More money, I suppose?"

"No, sir; not money, I think," replied I. "In fact, sir, I believe I have the thing in my breast-pocket; and, to tell you the truth, I should like to get it put in safety."

"To be sure, boy; quite right," said he. "I'll take it, if you like."

"I thought, perhaps, Dr. Livesey——" I began.

"Perfectly right," he interrupted, very cheerily, "perfectly right—a gentleman and a magistrate. And, now I come to think of it, I might as well ride round there myself and report to him or the squire. Master Pew's dead, when all's done; not that I regret it, but he's dead, you see, and people will make it out against an officer of his Majesty's revenue, if make it out they can. Now, I tell you, Hawkins: if you like, I'll take you along."

I thanked him heartily for the offer, and we walked back mother of my purpose they were all in the saddle.

Captain Brown

JOSEPH CONRAD

"It all begins, as I've told you, with the man called Brown," ran the opening sentence of Marlow's narrative. "You who have knocked about the Western Pacific must have heard of him. He was the show ruffian on the Australian coast—not that he was often to be seen there, but because he was always trotted out in the stories of lawless life a visitor from home is treated to; and the mildest of these stories which were told about him from Cape York to Eden Bay was more than enough to hang a man if told in the right place. They never failed to let you know, too, that he was supposed to be the son of a baronet. Be it as it may, it is certain he had deserted from a home ship in the early gold-digging days, and in a few years became talked about as the terror of this or that group of islands in Polynesia. He would kidnap natives, he would strip some lonely white trader to the very pyjamas he stood in, and after he had robbed the poor devil, he would as likely as not invite him to fight a duel with shot-guns on the beach—which would have been fair enough as these things go, if the other man hadn't been by that time already half-dead with fright. Brown was a latter-day buccaneer, sorry enough, like his more celebrated prototypes; but what distinguished him from his contemporary brother ruffians, like Bully Hayes or the mellifluous Pease, or that perfumed, Dundreary-whiskered, dandified scoundrel known as Dirty Dick, was the arrogant temper of his misdeeds and a vehement scorn for mankind at large and for his victims in particular. The others were merely vulgar and greedy brutes, but he seemed moved by some complex intention. He would rob a man as if only to demonstrate his poor opinion of the creature, and he would bring to the shooting or maiming of some quiet, unoffending stranger a savage and vengeful earnestness fit to terrify the most reckless of desperadoes. In the days of his greatest glory he owned an armed barque, manned by a mixed crew of Kanakas and runaway whalers, and boasted, I don't know with what truth, of being financed on the quiet by a most respectable firm of copra merchants. Later on he ran off—it was reported—with the wife of a missionary, a very young girl from Clapham way, who had married the mild, flat-footed fellow in a moment of enthusiasm, and suddenly transplanted to Melanesia, lost her bearings somehow. It was a dark story. She was ill at the time he carried her off, and died on board his ship. It is said—as the most wonderful part of the tale—that over her body he gave way to an outburst of sombre and violent grief. His luck left him, too, very soon after. He lost his ship on some rocks off Malaita, and disappeared for a time as though he had gone down with her. He is heard of next at Nuka-Hiva, where he bought an old French schooner out of Government service. What creditable enterprise he might have had in view when he made that purchase I can't say, but it is evident that what with High Commissioners, consuls, men-of-war, and international control, the South Seas were getting too hot to hold gentlemen of his kidney. Clearly he must have shifted the scene of his operations farther west, because a year later he plays an incredibly audacious, but not a very profitable part, in a serio-comic business in Manila Bay, in which a peculating governor and an absconding treasurer are the principal figures; thereafter he seems to have hung around the Philippines in his rotten schooner, battling with an adverse fortune, till at last, running his appointed course, he sails into Jim's history, a blind accomplice of the Dark Powers.

"His tale goes that when a Spanish patrol cutter captured him he was simply trying to run a few guns for the insurgents. If so, then I can't understand what he was doing off the south coast of Mindanao. My belief, however, is that he was blackmailing the native villages along the coast. The principal thing is that the cutter, throwing a guard on board, made him sail in company towards Zamboanga. On the way, for some reason or other, both vessels had to call at one of these new Spanish settlements—which never came to anything in the end—where there was not only a civil official in charge on shore, but a good stout coasting schooner lying at anchor in the little bay; and this craft, in every way much better than his own, Brown made up his mind to steal.

"He was down on his luck—as he told me himself. The world he had bullied for twenty years with fierce, aggressive disdain, had yielded him nothing in the way of material advantage except a small bag of silver dollars, which was concealed in his cabin so that 'the devil himself couldn't smell it out.' And that was all—absolutely all. He was tired of his life, and not afraid of death. But this man, who would stake his existence on a whim with a bitter and jeering reckless-ness, stood in mortal fear of imprisonment. He had an unreasoning cold-sweat, nerve-shaking, blood-to-water-turning sort of horror at the bare possibility of being locked up—the sort of ter-ror a superstitious man would feel at the thought of being embraced by a spectre. Therefore the civil official who came on board to make a preliminary investigation into the capture, investigated arduously all day long, and only went ashore after dark, muffled up, in a cloak, and taking great care not to let Brown's little all clink in its bag. Afterwards, being a man of his word, he contrived (the very next evening, I believe) to send off the Government cutter on some urgent bit of special service. As her commander could not spare a prize crew, he contented himself by taking away before he left all the sails of Brown's schooner to the very last rag, and took good care to tow his two boats on to the beach a couple of miles off.

"But in Brown's crew there was a Solomon Islander, kidnapped in his youth and devoted to Brown, who was the best man of the whole gang. That fellow swam off to the coaster—five hundred yards or so—with the end of a warp made up of all the running gear unrove for the purpose. The water was smooth, and the bay dark, 'like the inside of a cow,' as Brown described it. The Solomon Islander clambered over the bulwarks with the end of the rope in his teeth. The crew of the coaster—all Tagals—were ashore having a jollification in the native village. The two shipkeepers left on board woke up suddenly and saw the devil. It had glittering eyes and leaped quick as lightning about the deck. They fell on their knees, paralysed with fear, crossing them-selves and mumbling prayers. With a long knife he found in the caboose the Solomon Islander, without interrupting their orisons, stabbed first one, then the other; with the same knife he set to sawing patiently at the coir cable till suddenly it parted under the blade with a splash. Then in the silence of the bay he let out a cautious shout, and Brown's gang, who meantime had been peering and straining their hopeful ears in the darkness, began to pull gently at their end of the warp. In less than five minutes the two schooners came together with a slight shock and a creak of spars.

"Brown's crowd transferred themselves without losing an instant, taking with them their firearms and a large supply of ammunition. They were sixteen in all: two runaway blue-jackets, a lanky deserter from a Yankee man-of-war, a couple of simple, blond Scandinavians, a mulatto of sorts, one bland Chinaman who cooked—and the rest of the nondescript spawn of the South Seas. None of them cared; Brown bent them to his will, and Brown, indifferent to gallows, was running away from the spectre of a Spanish prison. He didn't give them the time to trans-ship enough provisions; the weather was calm, the air was charged with dew, and when they cast off the ropes and set sail to a faint offshore draught there was no flutter in the damp canvas; their old schooner seemed to detach itself gently from the stolen craft and slip away silently, together with the black mass of the coast, into the night.

"They got clear away. Brown related to me in detail their passage down the Straits of Macassar. It is a harrowing and desperate story. They were short of food and water; they boarded several native craft and got a little from each. With a stolen ship Brown did not dare to put into any port, of course. He had no money to buy anything, no papers to show, and no lie plausible enough to get him out again. An Arab barque, under the Dutch flag, surprised one night at anchor off Poulo Laut, yielded a little dirty rice, a bunch of bananas, and a cask of water; three days of squally misty weather from the north-east shot the schooner across the Java Sea. The yellow muddy waves drenched that collection of hungry ruffians. They sighted mailboats moving on their appointed routes; passed wellfound home ships with rusty iron sides anchored in the shallow sea waiting for a change of weather or the turn of the tide; an English gunboat, white and trim, with two slim masts, crossed their bows one day in the distance; and on another occasion a Dutch corvette, black and heavily sparred, loomed upon their quarter, steaming dead slow in the mist. They slipped through unseen or disregarded, a wan, sallow-faced band of utter outcasts, enraged with hunger and hunted by fear. Brown's idea was to make for Madagascar, where he expected, on grounds not altogether illusory, to sell the schooner in Tamatave, and no questions asked, or perhaps obtain some more or less forged papers for her. Yet before he could face the long passage across the Indian Ocean food was wanted—water, too.

"Perhaps he had heard of Patusan—or perhaps he just only happened to see the name written in small letters on the chart—probably that of a largish village up a river in a native state, perfectly defenceless, far from the beaten tracks of the sea and from the ends of submarine cables. He had done that kind of thing before—in the way of business; and this now was an absolute necessity, a question of life and death—or rather of liberty. Of liberty! He was sure to get provisions—bullocks—rice—sweet-potatoes. The sorry gang licked their chops. A cargo of produce for the schooner perhaps could be extorted—and, who knows?—some real ringing coined money! Some of these chiefs and village headmen can be made to part freely. He told me he would have roasted their toes rather than be baulked. I believe him. His men believed him too. They didn't cheer aloud, being a dumb pack, but made ready wolfishly.

"Luck served him as to weather. A few days of calm would have brought unmentionable horrors on board that schooner, but with the help of land and sea breezes, in less than a week after clearing the Sunda Straits, he anchored off the Batu Kring mouth within a pistol-shot of the fishing village.

"Fourteen of them packed into the schooner's longboat (which was big, having been used for cargo-work) and started up the river, while two remained in charge of the schooner with food enough to keep starvation off for ten days. The tide and wind helped, and early one afternoon the big white boat under a ragged sail shouldered its way before the sea breeze into Patusan Reach, manned by fourteen assorted scarecrows glaring hungrily ahead, and fingering the breech-blocks of cheap rifles. Brown calculated upon the terrifying surprise of his appearance. They sailed in with the last of the flood; the Rajah's stockade gave no sign; the first houses on both sides of the stream seemed deserted. A few canoes were seen up the reach in full flight. Brown was astonished at the size of the place. A profound silence reigned. The wind dropped between the houses; two oars were got out and the boat held on upstream, the idea being to effect a lodgment in the centre of the town before the inhabitants could think of resistance.

"It seems, however, that the headman of the fishing village at Batu Kring had managed to send off a timely warning. When the long-boat came abreast of the mosque (which Doramin had built: a structure with gables and roof finials of carved coral) the open space before it was full of people. A shout went up, and was followed by a clash of gongs all up the river. From a point above two little brass six-pounders were discharged, and the round-shot came skipping down the empty reach, spirting glittering jets of water in the sunshine. In front of the mosque a shouting lot of men began firing in volleys that whipped athwart the current of the river; an irregular, rolling fusillade was opened on the boat from both banks, and Brown's men replied with a wild, rapid fire. The oars had been got in.

"The turn of the tide at high water comes on very quick in that river, and the boat in midstream, nearly hidden in smoke, began to drift back stern foremost. Along both shores the smoke thickened also, lying below the roofs in a level streak as you may see a long cloud cutting the slope of a mountain. A tumult of war-cries, the vibrating clang of gongs, the deep snoring of drums, yells of rage, crashes of volley-firing, made an awful din, in which Brown sat confounded but steady at the tiller, working himself into a fury of hate and rage against those people who dared to defend themselves. Two of his men had been wounded, and he saw his retreat cut off below the town by some boats that had put off from Tunku Allang's stockade. There were six of them full of men. While he was thus beset he perceived the entrance of the narrow creek (the same which Jim had jumped at low water). It was then brim full. Steering the long-boat in, they landed, and, to make a long story short, they established themselves on a little knoll about 900 yards from the stockade, which, in fact, they commanded from that position. The slopes of the knoll were bare, but there were a few trees on the summit. They went to work cutting these down for a breastwork, and were fairly intrenched before dark; meantime the Rajah's boats remained in the river with curious neutrality. When the sun set the glare of many brushwood blazes lighted on the river-front, and between the double line of houses on the land side threw into black relief the roofs, the groups of slender palms, the heavy clumps of fruit-trees. Brown ordered the grass round his position to be fired; a low ring of thin flames under the slow, ascending smoke wriggled rapidly down the slopes of the knoll; here and there a dry bush caught with a tall, vicious roar. The conflagration made a clear zone of fire for the rifles of the small party, and expired smouldering on the edge of the forests and along the muddy bank of the creek. A strip of jungle luxuriating in a damp hollow between the knoll and the Rajah's stockade stopped it on that side with a great crackling and detonations of bursting bamboo stems. The sky was sombre, velvety, and swarming with stars. The blackened ground smoked quietly with low creeping wisps, till a little breeze came on and blew everything away. Brown expected an attack to be delivered as soon as the tide had flowed enough again to enable the war-boats which had cut off his retreat to enter the creek. At any rate he was sure there would be an attempt to carry off his long-boat, which lay below the hill, a dark high lump on the feeble sheen of a wet mud-flat. But no move of any sort was made by the boats in the river. Over the stockade and the Rajah's buildings Brown saw their lights on the water. They seemed to be anchored across the stream. Other lights afloat were moving in the reach, crossing and recrossing from side to side. There were also lights twinkling motionless upon the long walls of houses up the reach, as far as the bend, and more still beyond, others isolated inland. The loom of the big fires disclosed buildings, roofs, black piles as far as he could see. It was an immense place. The fourteen desperate invaders lying flat behind the felled trees raised their chins to look over at the stir of that town that seemed to extend up-river for miles and swarm with thousands of angry men. They did not speak to each other. Now and then they would hear a loud yell, or a single shot rang out, fired very far somewhere. But round their position everything was still, dark, silent. They seemed to be forgotten, as if the excitement keeping awake all the population had nothing to do with them, as if they had been dead already."

◆◆◆

"All the events of that night have a great importance, since they brought about a situation which remained unchanged till Jim's return. Jim had been away in the interior for more than a week, and it was Dain Waris who had directed the first repulse. That brave and intelligent youth ('who knew how to fight after the manner of white men') wished to settle the business off-hand, but his people were too much for him. He had not Jim's racial prestige and the reputation of invincible, supernatural power. He was not the visible, tangible incarnation of unfailing truth and of unfailing victory. Beloved, trusted, and admired as he was, he was still one of *them*, while Jim was one of *us*. Moreover, the white man, a tower of strength in himself, was invulnerable, while Dain Waris could be killed. Those unexpressed thoughts guided the opinions of the chief men of the town, who elected to assemble in Jim's fort for deliberation upon the emergency, as if expecting to find wisdom and courage in the dwelling of the absent white man. The shooting of Brown's ruffians was so far good, or lucky, that there had been half-a-dozen casualties amongst the defenders. The wounded were lying on the verandah tended by their women-folk. The women and children from the lower part of the town had been sent into the fort at the first alarm. There Jewel was in command, very efficient and high-spirited, obeyed by Jim's 'own people,' who, quitting in a body their little settlement under the stockade, had gone in to form the garrison. The refugees crowded round her; and through the whole affair, to the very disastrous last, she showed an extraordinary martial ardour. It was to her that Dain Waris had gone at once at the first intelligence of danger, for you must know that Jim was the only one in Patusan who possessed a store of gunpowder. Stein, with whom he had kept up intimate relations by letters, had obtained from the Dutch Government a special authorisation to export five hundred kegs of it to Patusan. The powder-magazine was a small hut of rough logs covered entirely with earth, and in Jim's absence the girl had the key. In the council, held at eleven o'clock in the evening in Jim's dining-room, she backed up Waris's advice for immediate and vigorous action. I am told that she stood up by the side of Jim's empty chair at the head of the long table and made a warlike impassioned speech, which for the moment extorted murmurs of approbation from the assembled headmen. Old Doramin, who had not showed himself outside his own gate for more than a year, had been brought across with great difficulty. He was, of course, the chief man there. The temper of the council was very unforgiving, and the old man's word would have been decisive; but it is my opinion that, well aware of his son's fiery courage, he dared not pronounce the word. More dilatory counsels prevailed. A certain Haji Saman pointed out at great length that 'these tyrannical and ferocious men had delivered themselves to a certain death in any case. They would stand fast on their hill and starve, or they would try to regain their boat and be shot from ambushes across the creek, or they would break and fly into the forest and perish singly there.' He argued that by the use of proper stratagems these evil-minded strangers could be destroyed without the risk of a battle, and his words had a great weight, especially with the Patusan men proper. What unsettled the minds of the townsfolk was the failure of the Rajah's boats to act at the decisive moment. It was the diplomatic Kassim who represented the Rajah at the council. He spoke very little, listened smilingly, very friendly and impenetrable. During the sitting messengers kept arriving every few minutes almost, with reports of the invaders' proceedings. Wild and exaggerated rumours were flying: there was a large ship at the mouth of the river with big guns and many more men—some white, others with black skins and of bloodthirsty appearance. They were coming with many more boats to exterminate every living thing. A sense of near, incomprehensible danger affected the common people. At one moment there was a panic in the courtyard amongst the women; shrieking; a rush; children crying—Haji Saman went out to quiet them. Then a fort sentry fired at something moving on the river, and nearly killed a villager bringing in his women-folk in a canoe together with the best of his domestic utensils and a dozen fowls. This caused more confusion. Meantime the palaver inside Jim's house went on in the presence of the girl. Doramin sat fierce-faced, heavy, looking at the speakers in turn, and breathing slow like a bull. He didn't speak till the last, after Kassim had declared that the Rajah's boats would be called in because the men were required to defend his master's stockade. Dain Waris in his father's presence would offer no opinion, though the girl entreated him in Jim's name to speak out. She offered him Jim's own men in her anxiety to have these intruders driven out at once. He only shook his head, after a glance or two at Doramin. Finally, when the council broke up it had been decided, that the houses nearest the creek should be strongly occupied to obtain the command of the enemy's boat. The boat itself was not to be interfered with openly, so that the robbers on the hill should be tempted to embark, when a well directed fire would kill most of them, no doubt. To cut the escape of those who might survive, and to prevent more of them coming up, Dain Waris was ordered by Doramin to take an armed party of Bugis down the river to a certain spot ten miles below Patusan, and there form a camp on the shore and blockade the stream with the canoes. I don't believe for a moment that Doramin feared the arrival of fresh forces. My opinion is, that his conduct was guided solely by his wish to keep his son out of harm's way. To prevent a rush being made into the town the construction of a stockade was to be commenced at daylight at the end of the street on the left bank. The old *nakhoda* declared his intention to command there himself. A distribution of powder, bullets, and percussion caps was made immediately under the girl's supervision. Several messengers were to be despatched in different directions after Jim, whose exact whereabouts were unknown. These men started at dawn, but before that time Kassim had managed to open communications with the besieged Brown.

"That accomplished diplomatist and confidant of the Rajah, on leaving the fort to go back to his master, took into his boat Cornelius, whom he found slinking mutely amongst the people in the courtyard. Kassim had a little plan of his own and wanted him for an interpreter. Thus it came about that towards morning Brown, reflecting upon the desperate nature of his position, heard from the marshy overgrown hollow an amicable, quavering, strained voice crying—in English—for permission to come up, under a promise of personal safety and on a very important errand. He was overjoyed. If he was spoken to he was no longer a hunted wild beast. These friendly sounds took off at once the awful stress of vigilant watchfulness as of so many blind men not knowing whence the deathblow might come. He pretended a great reluctance. The voice declared itself 'a white man. A poor, ruined, old man who had been living here for years.' A mist, wet and chilly, lay on the slopes of the hill, and after some more shouting from one to the other, Brown called out, 'Come on, then, but alone, mind!' As a matter of fact—he told me, writhing with rage at the recollection of his helplessness—it made no difference. They couldn't see more than a few yards before them, and no treachery could make their position worse. By-and-by Cornelius, in his week-day attire of a ragged dirty shirt and pants, barefooted, with a broken-rimmed pith hat on his head, was made out vaguely, sidling up to the defences, hesitating, stopping to listen in a peering posture. 'Come along! You are safe,' yelled Brown, while his men stared. All their hopes of life became suddenly centred in that dilapidated, mean new-comer, who in profound silence clambered clumsily over a felled tree-trunk, and shivering, with his sour mistrustful face, looked about at the knot of bearded, anxious, sleepless desperadoes.

"Half an hour's confidential talk with Cornelius opened Brown's eyes as to the home affairs of Patusan. He was on the alert at once. There were possibilities, immense possibilities; but before he would talk over Cornelius's proposals he demanded that some food should be sent up as a guarantee of good faith. Cornelius went off, creeping sluggishly down the hill on the side of the Rajah's palace, and after some delay a few of Tunku Allang's men came up, bringing a scanty supply of rice, chillies, and dried fish. This was immeasurably better than nothing. Later on Cornelius returned accompanying Kassim, who stepped out with an air of perfect good-humoured trustfulness, in sandals, and muffled up from neck to ankles in dark-blue sheeting. He shook hands with Brown discreetly, and the three drew aside for a conference. Brown's men, recovering their confidence, were slapping each other on the back, and cast knowing glances at their captain while they busied themselves with preparations for cooking.

"Kassim disliked Doramin and his Bugis very much, but he hated the new order of things still more. It had occurred to him that these whites, together with the Rajah's followers, could attack and defeat the Bugis before Jim's return. Then, he reasoned, general defection of the townsfolk was sure to follow, and the reign of the white man who protected poor people would be over. Afterwards the new allies could be dealt with. They would have no friends. The fellow was perfectly able to perceive the difference of character, and had seen enough of white men to know that these new-comers were outcasts, men without country. Brown preserved a stern and inscrutable demeanour. When he first heard Cornelius's voice demanding admittance, it brought merely the hope of a loophole for escape. In less than an hour other thoughts were seething in his head. Urged by an extreme necessity, he had come there to steal food, a few tons of rubber or gum maybe, perhaps a handful of dollars, and had found himself enmeshed by deadly dangers. Now in consequence of these overtures from Kassim he began to think of stealing the whole country. Some confounded fellow had apparently accomplished something of the kind—single-handed at that. Couldn't have done it very well though. Perhaps they could work together— squeeze everything dry and then go out quietly. In the course of his negotiations with Kassim he became aware that he was supposed to have a big ship with plenty of men outside. Kassim begged him earnestly to have this big ship with his many guns and men brought up the river without delay for the Rajah's service. Brown professed himself willing, and on this basis the negotiation was carried on with mutual distrust. Three times in the course of the morning the courteous and active Kassim went down to consult the Rajah and came up busily with his long stride. Brown, while bargaining, had a sort of grim enjoyment in thinking of his wretched schooner, with nothing but a heap of dirt in her hold, that stood for an armed ship, and a Chinaman and a lame ex-beachcomber of Levuka on board, who represented all his many men. In the afternoon he obtained further doles of food, a promise of some money, and a supply of mats for his men to make shelters for themselves. They lay down and snored, protected from the burning sunshine; but Brown, sitting fully exposed on one of the felled trees, feasted his eyes upon the view of the town and the river. There was much loot here. Cornelius, who had made himself at home in the camp, talked at his elbow, pointing out the localities, imparting advice, giving his own version of Jim's character, and commenting in his own fashion upon the events of the last three years. Brown, who, apparently indifferent and gazing away, listened with attention to every word, could not make out clearly what sort of man this Jim could be. 'What's his name? Jim! Jim! That's not enough for a man's name.' 'They call him,' said Cornelius, scornfully, 'Tuan Jim here. As you may say Lord Jim.' 'What is he? Where does he come from?' inquired Brown. 'What sort of man is he? Is he an Englishman?' 'Yes, yes, he's an Englishman. I am an Englishman, too. From Malacca. He is a fool. All you have to do is to kill him and then you are king here. Everything belongs to him,' explained Cornelius. 'It strikes me he may be made to share with somebody before very long,' commented Brown half aloud. 'No, no. The proper way is to kill him the first chance you get, and then you can do what you like,' Cornelius would insist earnestly. 'I have lived for many years here, and I am giving you a friend's advice.'

"In such converse and in gloating over the view of Patusan, which he had determined in his mind should become his prey, Brown whiled away most of the afternoon, his men, meantime, resting. On that day Dain Waris's fleet of canoes stole one by one under the shore farthest from the creek, and went down to close the river against his retreat. Of this Brown was not aware, and Kassim, who came up the knoll an hour before sunset, took good care not to enlighten him. He wanted the white man's ship to come up the river, and this news, he feared, would be discouraging. He was very pressing with Brown to send the 'order,' offering at the same time a trusty messenger, who for greater secrecy (as he explained) would make his way by land to the mouth of the river and deliver the 'order' on board. After some reflection Brown judged it expedient to tear a page out of his pocket-book, on which he simply wrote, 'We are getting on. Big job. Detain the man.' The stolid youth selected by Kassim for that service performed it faithfully, and was rewarded by being suddenly tipped, head first, into the schooner's empty hold by the ex-beachcomber and the Chinaman, who thereupoh hastened to put on the hatches. What became of him afterwards Brown did not say."

"Brown's object was to gain time by fooling with Kassim's diplomacy. For doing a real stroke of business he could not help thinking the white man was the person to work with. He could not imagine such a chap (who must be confoundedly clever after all to get hold of the natives like that) refusing a help that would do away with the necessity for slow, cautious, risky cheating, that imposed itself as the only possible line of conduct for a single-handed man. He, Brown, would offer him the power. No man could hesitate. Everything was in coming to a clear understanding. Of course they would share. The idea of there being a fort—all ready to his hand—a real fort, with artillery (he knew this from Cornelius), excited him. Let him only once get in and … He would impose modest conditions. Not too low, though. The man was no fool, it seemed. They would work like brothers till … till the time came for a quarrel and a shot that would settle all accounts. With grim impatience of plunder he wished himself to be talking with the man now. The land already seemed to be his to tear to pieces, squeeze, and throw away. Meantime Kassim had to be fooled for the sake of food first—and for a second string. But the principal thing was to get something to eat from day to day. Besides, he was not averse to begin fighting on that Rajah's account, and teach a lesson to those people who had received him with shots. The lust of battle was upon him.

"I am sorry that I can't give you this part of the story, which of course I have mainly from Brown, in Brown's own words. There was in the broken, violent speech of that man, unveiling before me his thoughts with the very hand of Death upon his throat, an undisguised ruthlessness of purpose, a strange vengeful attitude towards his own past, and a blind belief in the righteousness of his will against all mankind, something of that feeling which could induce the leader of a horde of wandering cut-throats to call himself proudly the Scourge of God. No doubt the natural senseless ferocity which is the basis of such a character was exasperated by failure, ill-luck, and the recent privations, as well as by the desperate position in which he found himself; but what was most remarkable of all was this, that while he planned treacherous alliances, had already settled in his own mind the fate of the white man, and intrigued in an overbearing, offhand manner with Kassim, one could perceive that what he had really desired, almost in spite of himself, was to play havoc with that jungle town which had defied him, to see it strewn over with corpses and enveloped in flames. Listening to his pitiless, panting voice, I could imagine how he must have looked at it from the hillock, peopling it with images of murder and rapine. The part nearest to the creek wore an abandoned aspect, though as a matter of fact every house concealed a few armed men on the alert. Suddenly beyond the stretch of waste ground, interspersed with small patches of low dense bush, excavations, heaps of rubbish, with trodden paths between, a man, solitary and looking very small, strolled out into the deserted opening of the street between the shut-up, dark, lifeless buildings at the end. Perhaps one of the inhabitants, who had fled to the other bank of the river, coming back for some object of domestic use. Evidently he supposed himself quite safe at that distance from the hill on the other side of the creek. A light stockade, set up hastily, was just round the turn of the street, full of his friends. He moved leisurely. Brown saw him, and instantly called to his side the Yankee deserter, who acted as a sort of second in command. This lanky, loose-jointed fellow came forward, wooden-faced, trailing his rifle lazily. When he understood what was wanted from him a homicidal and conceited smile uncovered his teeth, making two deep folds down his sallow, leathery cheeks. He prided himself on being a dead shot. He dropped on one knee, and taking aim from a steady rest through the unlopped branches of a felled tree, fired, and at once stood up to look. The man, far away, turned his head to the report, made another step forward, seemed to hesitate, and abruptly got down on his hands and knees. In the silence that fell upon the sharp crack of the rifle, the dead shot, keeping his eyes fixed upon the quarry, guessed that 'this there coon's health would never be a source of anxiety to his friends any more.' The man's limbs were seen to move rapidly under his body in an endeavour to run on all-fours. In that empty space arose a multitudinous shout of dismay and surprise. The man sank flat, face down, and moved no more. 'That showed them what we could do,' said Brown to me. 'Struck the fear of sudden death into them. That was what we wanted. They were two hundred to one, and this gave them something to think over for the night. Not one of them had an idea of such a long shot before. That beggar belonging to the Rajah scouted down-hill with his eyes hanging out of his head.'

"As he was telling me this he tried with a shaking hand to wipe the thin foam on his blue lips. 'Two hundred to one. Two hundred to one … strike terror … terror, terror, I tell you. …'

His own eyes were starting out of their sockets. He fell back, clawing the air with skinny fingers, sat up again, bowed and hairy, glared at me sideways like some man-beast of folklore, with open mouth in his miserable and awful agony before he got his speech back after that fit. There are sights one never forgets.

"Furthermore, to draw the enemy's fire and locate such parties as might have been hiding in the bushes along the creek, Brown ordered the Solomon Islander to go down to the boat and bring an oar, as you send a spaniel after a stick into the water. This failed, and the fellow came back without a single shot having been fired at him from anywhere. 'There's nobody,' opined some of the men. It is 'onnatural,' remarked the Yankee. Kassim had gone, by that time, very much impressed, pleased, too, and also uneasy. Pursuing his tortuous policy, he had despatched a message to Dain Waris warning him to look out for the white men's ship, which, he had had information, was about to come up the river. He minimised its strength and exhorted him to oppose its passage. This double-dealing answered his purpose, which was to keep the Bugis forces divided and to weaken them by fighting. On the other hand, he had in the course of that day sent word to the assembled Bugis chiefs in town, assuring them that he was trying to induce the invaders to retire; his messages to the fort asked earnestly for powder for the Rajah's men. It was a long time since Tunku Allang had had ammunition for the score or so of old muskets rusting in their arm-racks in the audience-hall. The open intercourse between the hill and the palace unsettled all the minds. It was already time for men to take sides, it began to be said. There would soon be much bloodshed, and thereafter great trouble for many people. The social fabric of orderly, peaceful life, when every man was sure of to-morrow, the edifice raised by Jim's hands, seemed on that evening ready to collapse into a ruin reeking with blood. The poorer folk were already taking to the bush or flying up the river. A good many of the upper class judged it necessary to go and pay their court to the Rajah. The Rajah's youths jostled them rudely. Old Tunku Allang, almost out of his mind with fear and indecision, either kept a sullen silence or abused them violently for daring to come with empty hands: they departed very much frightened; only old Doramin kept his countrymen together and pursued his tactics inflexibly. Enthroned in a big chair behind the improvised stockade, he issued his orders in a deep veiled rumble, unmoved, like a deaf man, in the flying rumours.

"Dusk fell, hiding first the body of the dead man, which had been left lying with arms outstretched as if nailed to the ground, and then the revolving sphere of the night rolled smoothly over Patusan and came to a rest, showering the glitter of countless worlds upon the earth. Again, in the exposed part of the town big fires blazed along the only street, revealing from distance to distance upon their glares the falling straight lines of roofs, the fragments of wattled walls jumbled in confusion, here and there a whole hut elevated in the glow upon the vertical black stripes of a group of high piles; and all this line of dwellings, revealed in patches by the swaying flames, seemed to flicker tortuously away upriver into the gloom at the heart of the land. A great silence, in which the looms of successive fires played without noise, extended into the darkness at the foot of the hill; but the other bank of the river, all dark save for a solitary bonfire at the river-front before the fort, sent out into the air an increasing tremor that might have been the stamping of a multitude of feet, the hum of many voices, or the fall of an immensely distant waterfall. It was then, Brown confessed to me, while, turning his back on his men, he sat looking at it all, that not-withstanding his disdain, his ruthless faith in himself, a feeling came over him that at last he had run his head against a stone wall. Had his boat been afloat at the time, he believed he would have tried to steal away, taking his chances of a long chase down the river and of starvation at sea. It was very doubtful whether he would have succeeded in getting away. However, he didn't try this. For another moment he had a passing thought of trying to rush the town, but he perceived very well that in the end he would find himself in the lighted street, where they would be shot down like dogs from the houses. They were two hundred to one—he thought, while his men, huddling round two heaps of smouldering embers, munched the last of the bananas and roasted the few yams they owed to Kassim's diplomacy. Cornelius sat amongst them dozing sulkily.

"Then one of the whites remembered that some tobacco had been left in the boat, and, encouraged by the impunity of the Solomon Islander, said he would go to fetch it. At this all the others shook off their despondency. Brown applied to, said, 'Go, and be d—d to you,' scornfully. He didn't think there was any danger in going to the creek in the dark. The man threw a leg over the tree-trunk and disappeared. A moment later he was heard clambering into the boat and then clambering out. 'I've got it,' he cried. A flash and a report at the very foot of the hill followed. 'I am hit,' yelled the man. 'Look out, look out—I am hit,' and instantly all the rifles went off. The hill squirted fire and noise into the night like a little volcano, and when Brown and the Yankee with curses and cuffs stopped the panic-stricken firing, a profound, weary groan floated up from the creek, succeeded by a plaint whose heart-rending sadness was like some poison turning the blood cold in the veins. Then a strong voice pronounced several distinct incomprehensible words somewhere beyond the creek. 'Let no one fire,' shouted Brown. 'What does it mean?' … 'Do you hear on the hill? Do you hear? Do you hear?' repeated the voice three times. Cornelius translated, and then prompted the answer. 'Speak,' cried Brown, 'we hear.' Then the voice, declaiming in the sonorous inflated tone of a herald, and shifting continually on the edge of the vague waste-land, proclaimed that between the men of the Bugis nation living in Patusan and the white men on the hill and those with them, there would be no faith, no compassion, no speech, no peace. A bush rustled; a haphazard volley rang out. 'Dam' foolishness,' muttered the Yankee, vexedly grounding the butt. Cornelius translated. The wounded man below the hill, after crying out twice, 'Take me up! take me up!' went on complaining in moans. While he had kept on the blackened earth of the slope and afterwards crouching in the boat, he had been safe enough. It seems that in his joy at finding tobacco he forgot himself and jumped out on her off-side, as it were. The white boat, lying high and dry, showed him up; the creek was no more than seven yards wide in that place, and there happened to be a man crouching in the bush on the other bank.

"He was a Bugis of Tondano only lately come to Patusan, and a relation of the man shot in the afternoon. That famous long shot had indeed appalled the beholders. The man in utter security had been struck down, in full view of his friends, dropping with a joke on his lips, and they seemed to see in the act an atrocity which had stirred a bitter rage. That relation of his, Si-Lapa by name, was then with Doramin in the stockade only a few feet away. You who know these chaps must admit that the fellow showed an unusual pluck by volunteering to carry the message, alone, in the dark. Creeping across the open ground, he had deviated to the left and found himself opposite the boat. He was startled when Brown's man shouted. He came to a sitting position with his gun to his shoulder, and when the other jumped out, exposing himself, he pulled the trigger and lodged three jagged slugs point-blank into the poor wretch's stomach. Then, lying flat on his face, he gave himself up for dead, while a thin hail of lead chopped and swished the bushes close on his right hand; afterwards he delivered his speech shouting, bent double, dodging all the time in cover. With the last word he leaped sideways, lay close for a while, and afterwards got back to the houses unharmed, having achieved on that night such a renown as his children will not willingly allow to die.

"And on the hill the forlorn band let the two little heaps of embers go out under their bowed heads. They sat dejected on the ground with compressed lips and downcast eyes, listening to their comrade below. He was a strong man and died hard, with moans now loud, now sinking to a strange confidential note of pain. Sometimes he shrieked, and again, after a period of silence, he could be heard muttering deliriously a long and unintelligible complaint. Never for a moment did he cease.

" 'What's the good?' Brown had said unmoved once, seeing the Yankee, who had been swearing under his breath, prepare to go down. 'That's so,' assented the deserter, reluctantly desisting. 'There's no encouragement for wounded men here. Only his noise is calculated to make all the others think too much of the hereafter, cap'n.' 'Water!' cried the wounded man in an extraordinarily clear vigorous voice, and then went off moaning feebly. 'Ay, water. Water will do it,' muttered the other to himself, resignedly. 'Plenty by-and-by. The tide is flowing.'

"At last the tide flowed, silencing the plaint and the cries of pain, and the dawn was near when Brown, sitting with his chin in the palm of his hand before Patusan, as one might stare at the unscalable side of a mountain, heard the brief ringing bark of a brass six-pounder far away in town somewhere. 'What's this?' he asked of Cornelius, who bung about him. Cornelius listened. A muffled roaring shout rolled down-river over the town; a big drum began to throb, and others responded, pulsating and droning. Tiny scattered lights began to twinkle in the dark half of the town, while the part lighted by the loom of fires hummed with a deep and prolonged murmur. 'He has come,' said Cornelius. 'What? Already? Are you sure?' Brown asked. 'Yes! yes! Sure. Listen to the noise.' 'What are they making that row about?' pursued Brown. 'For joy,' snorted Cornelius; 'he is a very great man, but all the same, he knows no more than a child, and so they make a great noise to please him, because they know no better.' 'Look here,' said Brown, 'how is one to get at him?' 'He shall come to talk to you,' Cornelius declared. 'What do you mean? Come down here strolling as it were?' Cornelius nodded vigorously in the dark. 'Yes. He will come straight here and talk to you. He is just like a fool. You shall see what a fool he is.' Brown was incredulous. 'You shall see; you shall see,' repeated Cornelius. 'He is not afraid—not afraid of anything. He will come and order you to leave his people alone. Everybody must leave his people alone. He is like a little child. He will come to you straight.' Alas! he knew Jim well—that 'mean little skunk,' as Brown called him to me. 'Yes, certainly,' he pursued with ardour, 'and then, captain, you tell that tall man with a gun to shoot him. Just you kill him, and you shall frighten everybody so much that you can do anything you like with them afterwards—get what you like—go away when you like. Ha! ha! ha! Fine…' He almost danced with impatience and eagerness; and Brown, looking over his shoulder at him, could see, shown up by the pitiless dawn, his men drenched with dew, sitting amongst the cold ashes and the litter of the camp, haggard, cowed, and in rags."

◆◆◆

"To the very last moment, till the full day came upon them with a spring, the fires on the west bank blazed bright and clear; and then Brown saw in a knot of coloured figures motionless between the advanced houses a man in European clothes, in a helmet, all white. 'That's him; look! look!' Cornelius said excitedly. All Brown's men had sprung up and crowded at his back with lustreless eyes. The group of vivid colours and dark faces with the white figure in the midst were observing the knoll. Brown could see naked arms being raised to shade the eyes and other brown arms pointing. What should he do? He looked around, and the forests that faced him on all sides walled the cock-pit of an unequal contest. He looked once more at his men. A contempt, a weariness, the desire of life, the wish to try for one more chance—for some other grave—struggled in his breast. From the outline the figure presented it seemed to him that the white man there, backed up by all the power of the land, was examining his position through binoculars. Brown jumped up on the log, throwing his arms up, the palms outwards. The coloured group closed round the white man, and fell back twice before he got clear of them, walking slowly alone. Brown remained standing on the log till Jim, appearing and disappearing between the patches of thorny scrub, had nearly reached the creek; then Brown jumped off and went down to meet him on his side.

"They met, I should think, not very far from the place, perhaps on the very spot, where Jim took the second desperate leap of his life—the leap that landed him into the life of Patusan, into the trust, the love, the confidence of the people. They faced each other across the creek, and with steady eyes tried to understand each other before they opened their lips. Their antagonism must have been expressed in their glances; I know that Brown hated Jim at first sight. Whatever hopes he might have had vanished at once. This was not the man he had expected to see. He hated him for this—and in a checked flannel shirt with sleeves cut off at the elbows, grey bearded, with a sunken, sun-blackened face—he cursed in his heart the other's youth and assurance, his clear eyes and his untroubled bearing. That fellow had got in a long way before him! He did not look like a man who would be willing to give anything for assistance. He had all the advantages on his side—possession, security, power; he was on the side of an overwhelming force! He was not hungry and desperate, and he did not seem in the least afraid. And there was something in the very neatness of Jim's clothes, from the white helmet to the canvas leggings and the pipe-clayed shoes, which in Brown's sombre irritated eyes seemed to belong to things he had in the very shaping of his life contemned and flouted.

" 'Who are you?' asked Jim at last, speaking in his usual voice. 'My name's Brown,' answered the other, loudly; 'Captain Brown. What's yours?' and Jim after a little pause went on quietly, as if he had not heard: 'What made you come here?' 'You want to know,' said Brown, bitterly. 'It's easy to tell. Hunger. And what made you?'

" 'The fellow started at this,' said Brown, relating to me the opening of this strange conversation between those two men, separated only by the muddy bed of a creek, but standing on the opposite poles of that conception of life which includes all mankind—'The fellow started at this and got very red in the face. Too big to be questioned, I suppose. I told him that if he looked upon me as a dead man with whom you may take liberties, he himself was not a whit better off really. I had a fellow up there who had a bead drawn on him all the time, and only waited for a sign from me. There was nothing to be shocked at in this. He had come down of his own freewill. "Let us agree," said I, "that we are both dead men, and let us talk on that basis, as equals. We are all equal before death," I said. I admitted I was there like a rat in a trap, but we had been driven to it, and even a trapped rat can give a bite. He caught me up in a moment. "Not if you don't go near the trap till the rat is dead." I told him that sort of game was good enough for these native friends of his, but I would have thought him too white to serve even a rat so. Yes, I had wanted to talk with him. Not to beg for my life, though. My fellows were—well—what they were—men like himself, anyhow. All we wanted from him was to come on in the devil's name and have it out. "God d—n it," said I, while he stood there as still as a wooden post, "you don't want to come out here every day with your glasses to count how many of us are left on our feet. Come. Either bring your infernal crowd along or let us go out and starve in the open sea, by God! You have been white once, for all your tall talk of this being your own people and you being one with them. Are you? And what the devil do you get for it; what is it you've found here that is so d—d precious? Hey? You don't want us to come down here perhaps—do you? You are two hundred to one. You don't want us to come down into the open. Ah! I promise you we shall give you some sport before you've done. You talk about me making a cowardly set upon unoffending people. What's that to me that they are unoffending when I am starving for next to no offence? But I am not a coward. Don't you be one. Bring them along or, by all the fiends, we shall yet manage to send half your unoffending town to heaven with us in smoke!"

"He was terrible—relating this to me—this tortured skeleton of a man drawn up together with his face over his knees, upon a miserable bed in that wretched hovel, and lifting his head to look at me with malignant triumph.

" 'That's what I told him—I knew what to say,' he began again, feebly at first, but working himself up with incredible speed into a fiery utterance of his scorn. 'We aren't going into the forest to wander like a string of living skeletons dropping one after another for ants to go to work upon us before we are fairly dead Oh, no! … "You don't deserve a better fate," he said. "And what do you deserve," I shouted at him, "you that I find skulking here with your mouth full of your responsibility, of innocent lives, of your infernal duty? What do you know more of me than I know of you? I came here for food. D'ye hear?—food to fill our bellies. And what did *you* come for? What did you ask for when you came here? We don't ask you for anything but to give us a fight or a clear road to go back whence we came…" "I would fight with you now," says he, pulling at his little moustache. "And I would let you shoot me, and welcome," I said. "This is as good a jumping-off place for me as another. I am sick of my infernal luck. But it would be too easy. There are my men in the same boat—and, by God, I am not the sort to jump out of trouble and leave them in a d—d lurch," I said. He stood thinking for a while and then wanted to know what I had done ("out there," he says, tossing his head down-stream) to be hazed about so. "Have we met to tell each other the story of our lives?" I asked him. "Suppose you begin. No? Well, I am sure I don't want to hear. Keep it to yourself. I know it is no better than mine. I've lived—and so did you though you talk as if you were one of those people that should have wings so as to go about without touching the dirty earth. Well—it is dirty. I haven't got any wings. I am here because I was afraid once in my life. Want to know what of? Of a prison. That scares me, and you may know it—if it's any good to you. I won't ask you what scared you into this infernal hole, where you seem to have found pretty pickings. That's your luck and this is mine—the privilege to beg for the favour of being shot quickly, or else kicked out to go free and starve in my own way."…

"His debilitated body shook with an exultation so vehement, so assured, and so malicious that it seemed to have driven off the death waiting for him in that hut. The corpse of his mad self-love uprose from rags and destitution as from the dark horrors of a tomb. It is impossible to say how much he lied to Jim then, how much he lied to me now—and to himself always. Vanity plays lurid tricks with our memory, and the truth of every passion wants some pretence to make it live. Standing at the gate of the other world in the guise of a beggar, he had slapped this world's face, he had spat on it, he had thrown upon it an immensity of scorn and revolt at the bottom of his misdeeds. He had overcome them all—men, women, savages, traders, ruffians, missionaries—and Jim—that beefy-faced beggar. I did not begrudge him this triumph *in articulo mortis*, this almost posthumous illusion of having trampled all the earth under his feet. While he was boasting to me, in his sordid and repulsive agony, I couldn't help thinking of the chuckling talk relating to the time of his greatest splendour when, during a year or more, Gentleman Brown's ship was to be seen, for many days on end, hovering off an islet befringed with green upon azure, with the dark dot of the mission-house on a white beach; while Gentleman Brown, ashore, was casting his spells over a romantic girl for whom Melanesia had been too much, and giving hopes of a remarkable conversion to her husband. The poor man, some time or other, had been heard to express the intention of winning 'Captain Brown to a better way of life.' … 'Bag Gentleman Brown for Glory'—as a leery-eyed loafer expressed it once—'just to let them see up above what a Western Pacific trading skipper looks like.' And this was the man, too, who had run off with a dying woman, and had shed tears over her body. 'Carried on like a big baby,' his then mate was never tired of telling, 'and where the fun came in may I be kicked to death by diseased Kanakas if *I* know. Why, gents! She was too far gone when he brought her aboard to know him; she just lay there on her back in his bunk staring at the beam with awful shining eyes—and then she died. Dam' bad sort of fever, I guess… ' I remembered all these stories while, wiping his matted lump of a beard with a livid hand, he was telling me from his noisome couch how he got round, got in, got home, on that confounded, immaculate, don't-you-touch-me sort of fellow. He admitted that he couldn't be scared, but there was a way, 'as broad as a turnpike, to get in and shake his twopenny soul around and inside out and upside down—by God!' "

◆◆◆

"I don't think he could do more than perhaps look upon that straight path. He seemed to have been puzzled by what he saw, for he interrupted himself in his narrative more than once to exclaim, 'He nearly slipped from me there. I could not make him out. Who was he?' And after glaring at me wildly he would go on, jubilating and sneering. To me the conversation of these two across the creek appears now as the deadliest kind of duel on which Fate looked on with her cold-eyed knowledge of the end. No, he didn't turn Jim's soul inside out, but I am much mistaken if the spirit so utterly out of his reach had not been made to taste to the full the bitterness of that contest. These were the emissaries with whom the world he had renounced was pursuing him in his retreat. White men from 'out there' where he did not think himself good enough to live. This was all that came to him—a menace, a shock, a danger to his work. I suppose it is this sad, half-resentful, half-resigned feeling, piercing through the few words Jim said now and then, that puzzled Brown so much in the reading of his character. Some great men owe most of their great-ness to the ability of detecting in those they destine for their tools the exact quality of strength that matters for their work, and Brown, as though he had been really great, had a satanic gift of finding out the best and the weakest spot in his victims. He admitted to me that Jim wasn't of the sort that can be got over by truckling, and accordingly he took care to show himself as a man confronting without dismay ill-luck, censure, and disaster. The smuggling of a few guns was no great crime, he pointed out. As to coming to Patusan, who had the right to say he hadn't come to beg? The infernal people here let loose at him from both banks without staying to ask ques-tions. He made the point brazenly, for, in truth, Dain Waris's energetic action had prevented the greatest calamities; because Brown told me distinctly that, perceiving the size of the place, he had resolved instantly in his mind that as soon as he had gained a footing he would set fire right and left, and begin by shooting down everything living in sight, in order to cow and terrify the popu-lation. The disproportion of forces was so great that this was the only way giving him the slightest chance of attaining his ends—he argued in a fit of coughing. But he didn't tell Jim this. As to the hardships and starvation they had gone through, these had been very real; it was enough to look at his band. He made, at the sound of a shrill whistle, all his men appear standing in a row on the logs in full view, so that Jim could see them. For the killing of the man, it had been done—well, it had—but was not this war, bloody war—in a corner? and the fellow had been killed cleanly, shot through the chest, not like that poor devil of his lying now in the creek. They had to listen to him dying for six hours, with his entrails torn with slugs. At any rate this was a life for a life… And all this was said with the weariness, with the recklessness of a man spurred on and on by ill-luck till he cares not where he runs. When he asked Jim, with a sort of brusque despairing frankness, whether he himself—straight now—didn't understand that when 'it came to saving one's life in the dark, one didn't care who else went—three, thirty, three hundred people'—it was as if a demon had been whispering advice in his ear. 'I made him wince,' boasted Brown to me. 'He very soon left off coming the righteous over me. He just stood there with nothing to say, and looking as black as thunder—not at me—on the ground.' He asked Jim whether he had nothing fishy in his life to remember that he was so damnedly hard upon a man trying to get out of a deadly hole by the first means that came to hand—and so on, and so on. And there ran through the rough talk a vein of subtle reference to their common blood, an assumption of common experience; a sickening suggestion of common guilt, of secret knowledge that was like a bond of their minds and of their hearts.

"At last Brown threw himself down full length and watched Jim out of the corners of his eyes. Jim on his side of the creek stood thinking and switching his leg. The houses in view were silent, as if a pestilence had swept them clean of every breath of life; but many invisible eyes were turned, from within, upon the two men with the creek between them, a stranded white boat, and the body of the third man half sunk in the mud. On the river canoes were moving again, for Patusan was recovering its belief in the stability of earthly institutions since the return of the white lord. The right bank, the platforms of the houses, the rafts moored along the shores, even the roofs of bathing-huts, were covered with people that, far away out of earshot and almost out of sight, were straining their eyes towards the knoll beyond the Rajah's stockade. Within the wide irregular ring of forests broken in two places by the sheen of the river there was a silence. 'Will you promise to leave the coast?' Jim asked. Brown lifted and let fall his hand, giving everything up as it were—accepting the inevitable. 'And surrender your arms?' Jim went on. Brown sat up and glared across. 'Surrender our arms! Not till you come to take them out of our stiff hands. You think I am gone crazy with funk? Oh, no! That and the rags I stand in is all I have got in the world, besides a few more breechloaders on board; and I expect to sell the lot in Madagascar, if I ever get so far—begging my way from ship to ship.'

"Jim said nothing to this. At last, throwing away the switch he held in his hand, he said, as if speaking to himself, 'I don't know whether I have the power.' … 'You don't know! And you wanted me just now to give up my arms! That's good, too,' cried Brown. 'Suppose they say one thing to you, and do the other thing to me.' He calmed down markedly. 'I daresay you have the power, or what's the meaning of all this talk?' he continued. 'What did you come down here for? To pass the time of day?'

" 'Very well,' said Jim, lifting his head suddenly after a long silence. 'You shall have a clear road or else a clear fight.' He turned on his heel and walked away.

"Brown got up at once, but he did not go up the hill till he had seen Jim disappear between the first houses. He never set his eyes on him again. On his way back he met Cornelius slouching down with his head between his shoulders. He stopped before Brown. 'Why didn't you kill him?' he demanded in a sour, discontented voice. 'Because I could do better than that,' Brown said with an amused smile. 'Never! never!' protested Cornelius with energy. 'Couldn't. I have lived here for many years.' Brown looked up at him curiously. There were many sides to the life of that place in arms against him; things he would never find out. Cornelius slunk past dejectedly in the direction of the river. He was now leaving his new friends; he accepted the disappointing course of events with a sulky obstinacy which seemed to draw more together his little yellow old face; and as he went down he glanced askant here and there, never giving up his fixed idea.

"Henceforth events move fast without a check, flowing from the very hearts of men like a stream from a dark source, and we see Jim amongst them, mostly through Tamb' Itam's eyes. The girl's eyes had watched him, too, but her life is too much entwined with his: there is her passion, her wonder, her anger, and, above all, her fear and her unforgiving love. Of the faithful servant, uncomprehending as the rest of them, it is the fidelity alone that comes into play; a fidelity and a belief in his lord so strong that even amazement is subdued to a sort of saddened acceptance of a mysterious failure. He has eyes only for one figure, and through all the mazes of bewilderment he preserves his air of guardianship, of obedience, of care.

"His master came back from his talk with the white men, walking slowly towards the stockade in the street. Everybody was rejoiced to see him return, for while he was away every man had been afraid not only of him being killed, but also of what would come after. Jim went into one of the houses, where old Doramin had retired, and remained alone for a long time with the head of the Bugis settlers. No doubt he discussed the course to follow with him then, but no man was present at the conversation. Only Tamb' Itam, keeping as close to the door as he could, heard his master say, 'Yes. I shall let all the people know that such is my wish; but I spoke to you, O Doramin, before all the others, and alone; for you know my heart as well as I know yours and its greatest desire. And you know well also that I have no thought but for the people's good.' Then his master, lifting the sheeting in the doorway, went out, and he, Tamb' Itam, had a glimpse of old Doramin within, sitting in the chair with his hands on his knees, and looking between his feet. Afterwards he followed his master to the fort, where all the principal Bugis and Patusan inhabitants had been summoned for a talk. Tamb' Itam himself hoped there would be some fighting. 'What was it but the taking of another hill?' he exclaimed regretfully. However, in the town many hoped that the rapacious strangers would be induced, by the sight of so many brave men making ready to fight, to go away. It would be a good thing if they went away. Since Jim's arrival had been made known before daylight by the gun fired from the fort and the beating of the big drum there, the fear that had hung over Patusan had broken and subsided like a wave on a rock, leaving the seething foam of excitement, curiosity, and endless speculation. Half of the population had been ousted out of their homes for purposes of defence, and were living in the street on the left side of the river, crowding round the fort, and in momentary expectation of seeing their abandoned dwellings on the threatened bank burst into flames. The general anxiety was to see the matter settled quickly. Food, through Jewel's care, had been served out to the refugees. Nobody knew what their white man would do. Some remarked that it was worse than in Sherif Ali's war. Then many people did not care; now everybody had something to lose. The movements of canoes passing to and fro between the two parts of the town were watched with interest. A couple of Bugis war-boats lay anchored in the middle of the stream to protect the river, and a thread of smoke stood at the bow of each; the men in them were cooking their midday rice when Jim, after his interviews with Brown and Doramin, crossed the river and entered by the water-gate of his fort. The people inside crowded round him so that he could hardly make his way to the house. They had not seen him before, because on his arrival during the night he had only exchanged a few words with the girl, who had come down to the landing-stage for the purpose, and had then gone on at once to join the chiefs and the fighting men on the other bank. People shouted greetings after him. One old woman raised a laugh by pushing her way to the front madly and enjoining him in a scolding voice to see to it that her two sons, who were with Doramin, did not come to harm at the hands of the robbers. Several of the bystanders tried to pull her away, but she struggled and cried, 'Let me go. What is this, O Muslims? This laughter is unseemly. Are they not cruel, bloodthirsty robbers bent on killing?' 'Let her be,' said Jim, and as a silence fell suddenly, he said slowly, 'Everybody shall be safe.' He entered the house before the great sigh, and the loud murmurs of satisfaction, had died out.

"There's no doubt his mind was made up that Brown should have his way clear back to the sea. His fate, revolted, was forcing his hand. He had for the first time to affirm his will in the face of out-spoken opposition. 'There was much talk, and at first my master was silent,' Tamb' Itam said. 'Darkness came, and then I lit the candles on the long table. The chiefs sat on each side, and the lady remained by my master's right hand.'

"When he began to speak the unaccustomed difficulty seemed only to fix his resolve more immovably. The white men were now waiting for his answer on the hill. Their chief had spoken to him in the language of his own people, making clear many things difficult to explain in any other speech. They were erring men whom suffering had made blind to right and wrong. It is true that lives had been lost already, but why lose more? He declared to his hearers, the assembled heads of the people, that their welfare was his welfare, their losses his losses, their mourning his mourning. He looked round at the grave listening faces and told them to remember that they had fought and worked side by side. They knew his courage … Here a murmur interrupted him … And that he had never deceived them. For many years they had dwelt together. He loved the land and the people living in it with a very great love. He was ready to answer with his life for any harm that should come to them if the white men with beards were allowed to retire. They were evil-doers, but their destiny had been evil, too. Had he ever advised them ill? Had his words ever brought suffering to the people? he asked. He believed that it would be best to let these whites and their followers go with their lives. It would be a small gift. 'I whom you have tried and found always true ask you to let them go.' He turned to Doramin. The old *nakoda* made no movement. 'Then,' said Jim, 'call in Dain Waris, your son, my friend, for in this business I shall not lead.' "

◆◆◆

"Tamb' Itam behind his chair was thunderstruck. The declaration produced an immense sensation. 'Let them go because this is best in my knowledge which has never deceived you,' Jim insisted. There was a silence. In the darkness of the courtyard could be heard the subdued whispering, shuffling noise of many people. Doramin raised his heavy head and said that there was no more reading of hearts than touching the sky with the hand, but—he consented. The others gave their opinion in turn. 'It is best,' 'Let them go,' and so on. But most of them simply said that they 'believed Tuan Jim.'

"In this simple form of assent to his will lies the whole gist of the situation; their creed, his truth; and the testimony to that faithfulness which made him in his own eyes the equal of the impeccable men who never fall out of the ranks. Stein's words, 'Romantic!—Romantic!' seem to ring over those distances that will never give him up now to a world indifferent to his failing and his virtues, and to that ardent and clinging affection that refuses him the dole of tears in the bewilderment of a great grief and of eternal separation. From the moment the sheer truthfulness of his last three years of life carries the day against the ignorance, the fear, and the anger of men, he appears no longer to me as I saw him last—a white speck catching all the dim light left upon a sombre coast and the darkened sea—but greater and more pitiful in the loneliness of his soul, that remains even for her who loved him best a cruel and insoluble mystery.

"It is evident that he did not mistrust Brown; there was no reason to doubt the story, whose truth seemed warranted by the rough frankness, by a sort of virile sincerity in accepting the morality and the consequences of his acts. But Jim did not know the almost inconceivable egotism of the man which made him, when resisted and foiled in his will, mad with the indignant and revengeful rage of a thwarted autocrat. But if Jim did not mistrust Brown, he was evidently anxious that some misunderstanding should not occur, ending perhaps in collision and blood-shed. It was for this reason that directly the Malay chiefs had gone he asked Jewel to get him something to eat, as he was going out of the fort to take command in the town. On her remon-strating against this on the score of his fatigue, he said that something might happen for which he would never forgive himself. 'I am responsible for every life in the land,' he said. He was moody at first; she served him with her own hands, taking the plates and dishes (of the dinner-service presented him by Stein) from Tamb' Itam. He brightened up after a while; told her she would be again in command of the fort for another night. 'There's no sleep for us, old girl,' he said, 'while our people are in danger.' Later on he said jokingly that she was the best man of them all. 'If you and Dain Waris had done what you wanted, not one of these poor devils would be alive to-day.' 'Are they very bad?' she asked, leaning over his chair. 'Men act badly sometimes without being much worse than others,' he said after some hesitation.

"Tamb' Itam followed his master to the landing-stage outside the fort. The night was clear, but without a moon, and the middle of the river was dark, while the water under each bank reflected the light of many fires 'as on a night of Ramadan,' Tamb' Itam said. War-boats drifted silently in the dark lane or, anchored, floated motionless with a loud ripple. That night there was much paddling in a canoe and walking at his master's heels for Tamb' Itam: up and down the street they tramped, where the fires were burning, inland on the outskirts of the town where small parties of men kept guard in the fields. Tuan Jim gave his orders and was obeyed. Last of all they went to the Rajah's stockade, which a detachment of Jim's people manned on that night. The old Rajah had fled early in the morning with most of his women to a small house he had near a jungle village on a tributary stream. Kassim, left behind, had attended the council with his air of diligent activity to explain away the diplomacy of the day before. He was considerably cold-shouldered, but managed to preserve his smiling, quiet alertness, and professed himself highly delighted when Jim told him sternly that he proposed to occupy the stockade on that night with his own men. After the council broke up he was heard outside accosting this and that departing chief, and speaking in a loud, gratified tone of the Rajah's property being protected in the Rajah's absence.

"About ten or so Jim's men marched in. The stockade commanded the mouth of the creek, and Jim meant to remain there till Brown had passed below. A small fire was lit on the flat, grassy point outside the wall of stakes, and Tamb' Itam placed a little folding-stool for his master. Jim told him to try and sleep, Tamb' Itam got a mat and lay down a little way off; but he could not sleep, though he knew he had to go on an important journey before the night was out. His master walked to and fro before the fire with bowed head and with his hands behind his back. His face was sad. Whenever his master approached him Tamb' Itam pretended to sleep, not wishing his master to know he had been watched. At last his master stood still, looking down on him as he lay, and said softly, 'It is time.'

"Tamb' Itam arose directly and made his preparations. His mission was to go down the river, preceding Brown's boat by an hour or more, to tell Dain Waris finally and formally that the whites were to be allowed to pass out unmolested. Jim would not trust anybody else with that service. Before starting Tamb' Itam, more as a matter of form (since his position about Jim made him perfectly known), asked for a token. 'Because, Tuan,' he said, 'the message is important, and these are thy very words I carry.' His master first put his hand into one pocket, then into another, and finally took off his forefinger Stein's silver ring, which he habitually wore, and gave it to Tamb' Itam. When Tamb' Itam left on his mission, Brown's camp on the knoll was dark but for a single small glow shining through the branches of one of the trees the white men had cut down.

"Early in the evening Brown had received from Jim a folded piece of paper on which was written, 'You get the clear road. Start as soon as your boat floats on the morning tide. Let your men be careful. The bushes on both sides of the creek and the stockade at the mouth are full of well-armed men. You would have no chance, but I don't believe you want bloodshed.' Brown read it, tore the paper into small pieces, and, turning to Cornelius, who had brought it, said jeeringly, 'Goodbye, my excellent friend.' Cornelius had been in the fort, and had been sneaking around Jim's house during the afternoon. Jim chose him to carry the note because he could speak English, was known to Brown, and was not likely to be shot by some nervous mistake of one of the men as a Malay, approaching in the dusk, perhaps might have been.

"Cornelius didn't go away after delivering the paper. Brown was sitting up over a tiny fire; all the others were lying down. 'I could tell you something you would like to know,' Cornelius mumbled crossly. Brown paid no attention. 'You did not kill him,' went on the other, 'and what do you get for it? You might have had money from the Rajah, besides the loot of all the Bugis houses, and now you get nothing.' 'You had better clear out from here,' growled Brown, without even looking at him. But Cornelius let himself drop by his side and began to whisper very fast, touching his elbow from time to time. What he had to say made Brown sit up at first, with a curse. He had simply informed him of Dain Waris's armed party down the river. At first Brown saw himself completely sold and betrayed, but a moment's reflection convinced him that there could be no treachery intended. He said nothing, and after a while Cornelius remarked, in a tone of complete indifference, that there was another way out of the river which he knew very well. 'A good thing to know, too,' said Brown, pricking up his ears; and Cornelius began to talk of what went on in town and repeated all that had been said in council, gossiping in an even undertone at Brown's ear as you talk amongst sleeping men you do not wish to wake. 'He thinks he has made me harmless, does he?' mumbled Brown very low… 'Yes. He is a fool. A little child. He came here and robbed me,' droned on Cornelius, 'and he made all the people believe him. But if something happened that they did not believe him any more, where would he be? And the Bugis Dain who is waiting for you down the river there, captain, is the very man who chased you up here when you first came.' Brown observed nonchalantly that it would be just as well to avoid him, and with the same detached, musing air Cornelius declared himself acquainted with a backwater broad enough to take Brown's boat past Waris's camp. 'You will have to be quiet,' he said as an after-thought, 'for in one place we pass close behind his camp. Very close. They are camped ashore with their boat hauled up.' 'Oh, we know how to be as quiet as mice; never fear,' said Brown. Cornelius stipulated that in case he were to pilot Brown out, his canoe should be towed. 'I'll have to get back quick,' he explained.

"It was two hours before the dawn when word was passed to the stockade from outlying watchers that the white robbers were coming down to their boat. In a very short time every armed man from one end of Patusan to the other was on the alert, yet the banks of the river remained so silent that but for the fires burning with sudden blurred flares the town might have been asleep as if in peace-time. A heavy mist lay very low on the water, making a sort of illusive grey light that showed nothing. When Brown's long-boat glided out of the creek into the river, Jim was standing on the low point of land before the Rajah's stockade—on the very spot where for the first time he put his foot on Patusan shore. A shadow loomed up, moving in the greyness, solitary, very bulky, and yet constantly eluding the eye. A murmur of low talking came out of it. Brown at the tiller heard Jim speak calmly: 'A clear road. You had better trust to the current while the fog lasts; but this will lift presently.' 'Yes, presently we shall see clear,' replied Brown.

"The thirty or forty men standing with muskets at ready outside the stockade held their breath. The Bugis owner of the prau, whom I saw on Stein's verandah, and who was amongst them, told me that the boat, shaving the low point close, seemed for a moment to grow big and hang over it like a mountain. 'If you think it worth your while to wait a day outside,' called out Jim, 'I'll try to send you down something—bullock, some yams—what I can.' The shadow went on moving. 'Yes. Do,' said a voice, blank and muffled out of the fog. Not one of the many attentive listeners understood what the words meant; and then Brown and his men in their boat floated away, fading spectrally without the slightest sound.

"Thus Brown, invisible in the mist, goes out of Patusan elbow to elbow with Cornelius in the stern-sheets of the long-boat. 'Perhaps you shall get a small bullock,' said Cornelius. 'Oh, yes.

Bullock. Yam. You'll get it if *he* said so. He always speaks the truth. He stole everything I had. I suppose you like a small bullock better than the loot of many houses.' 'I would advise you to hold your tongue, or somebody here may fling you overboard into this damned fog,' said Brown. The boat seemed to be standing still; nothing could be seen, not even the river alongside, only the water-dust flew and trickled, condensed, down their beards and faces. It was weird, Brown told me. Every individual man of them felt as though he were adrift alone in a boat, haunted by an almost imperceptible suspicion of sighing, muttering ghosts. 'Throw me out, would you? But I would know where I was,' mumbled Cornelius, surlily. 'I've lived many years here.' 'Not long enough to see through a fog like this,' Brown said, lolling back with his arm swinging to and fro on the useless tiller. 'Yes. Long enough for that,' snarled Cornelius. 'That's very useful,' commented Brown. 'Am I to believe you could find that backway you spoke of blindfold, like this?' Cornelius grunted. 'Are you too tired to row?' he asked after a silence. 'No, by God!' shouted Brown suddenly. 'Out with your oars there.' There was a great knocking in the fog, which after a while settled into a regular grind of invisible sweeps against invisible thole-pins. Otherwise nothing was changed, and but for the slight splash of a dipped blade it was like rowing a balloon car in a cloud, said Brown. Thereafter Cornelius did not open his lips except to ask querulously for somebody to bale out his canoe, which was towing behind the long-boat. Gradually the fog whitened and became luminous ahead. To the left Brown saw a darkness as though he had been looking at the back of the departing night. All at once a big bough covered with leaves appeared above his head, and ends of twigs, dripping and still, curved slenderly close alongside. Cornelius, without a word, took the tiller from his hand."

◆◆◆

"I don't think they spoke together again. The boat entered a narrow by-channel, where it was pushed by the oar-blades set into crumbling banks, and there was a gloom as if enormous black wings had been outspread above the mist that filled its depth to the summits of the trees. The branches overhead showered big drops through the gloomy fog. At a mutter from Cornelius, Brown ordered his men to load. 'I'll give you a chance to get even with them before we're done, you dismal cripples, you,' he said to his gang. 'Mind you don't throw it away—you hounds.' Low growls answered that speech. Cornelius showed much fussy concern for the safety of his canoe.

"Meantime Tamb' Itam had reached the end of his journey. The fog had delayed him a little, but he had paddled steadily, keeping in touch with the south bank. By-and-by daylight came like a glow in a ground glass globe. The shores made on each side of the river a dark smudge, in which one could detect hints of columnar forms and shadows of twisted branches high up. The mist was still thick on the water, but a good watch was being kept, for as Tamb' Itam approached the camp the figures of two men emerged out of the white vapour, and voices spoke to him boisterously. He answered, and presently a canoe lay alongside, and he exchanged news with the paddlers. All was well. The trouble was over. Then the men in the canoe let go their grip on the side of his dug-out and incontinently fell out of sight. He pursued his way till he heard voices coming to him quietly over the water, and saw, under the now lifting, swirling mist, the glow of many little fires burning on a sandy stretch, backed by lofty thin timber and bushes. There again a look-out was kept, for he was challenged. He shouted his name as the two last sweeps of his paddle ran his canoe up on the strand. It was a big camp. Men crouched in many knots under a subdued murmur of early morning talk. Many thin threads of smoke curled slowly on the white mist. Little shelters, elevated above the ground, had been built for the chiefs. Muskets were, stacked in small pyramids, and long spears were stuck singly into the sand near the fires.

"Tamb' Itam, assuming an air of importance, demanded to be led to Dain Waris. He found the friend of his white lord lying on a raised couch made of bamboo, and sheltered by a sort of shed of sticks covered with mats. Dain Waris was awake, and a bright fire was burning before his sleeping-place, which resembled a rude shrine. The only son of Nakhoda Doramin answered his greeting kindly. Tamb' Itam began by handing him the ring which vouched for the truth of the messenger's words. Dain Waris, reclining on his elbow, bade him speak and tell all the news. Beginning with the consecrated formula, 'The news is good,' Tamb' Itam delivered Jim's own words. The white men, departing with the consent of all the chiefs, were to be allowed to pass down the river. In answer to a question or two Tamb' Itam then reported the proceedings of the last council. Dain Waris listened attentively to the end, toying with the ring which ultimately he slipped on the forefinger of his right hand. After hearing all he had to say he dismissed Tamb' Itam to have food and rest. Orders for the return in the afternoon were given immediately. Afterwards Dain Waris lay down again, open-eyed, while his personal attendants were preparing his food at the fire, by which Tamb' Itam also sat talking to the men who lounged up to hear the latest intelligence from the town. The sun was eating up the mist. A good watch was kept upon the reach of the main stream where the boat of the whites was expected to appear every moment.

"It was then that Brown took his revenge upon the world which, after twenty years of contemptuous and reckless bullying, refused him the tribute of a common robber's success. It was an act of cold-blooded ferocity, and it consoled him on his deathbed like a memory of an indomitable defiance. Stealthily he landed his men on the other side of the island opposite to the Bugis camp, and led them across. After a short but quite silent scuffle, Cornelius, who had tried to slink away at the moment of landing, resigned himself to show the way where the undergrowth was most sparse. Brown held both his skinny hands together behind his back in the grip of one vast fist, and now and then impelled him forward with a fierce push. Cornelius remained as mute as a fish, abject but faithful to his purpose, whose accomplishment loomed before him dimly. At the edge of the patch of forest Brown's men spread themselves out in cover and waited. The camp was plain from end to end before their eyes, and no one looked their way. Nobody even dreamed that the white men could have any knowledge of the narrow channel at the back of the island. When he judged the moment come, Brown yelled, 'Let them have it,' and fourteen shots rang out like one.

"Tamb' Itam told me the surprise was so great that, except for those who fell dead or wounded, not a soul of them moved for quite an appreciable time after the first discharge. Then a man screamed, and after that scream a great yell of amazement and fear went up from all the throats. A blind panic drove these men in a surging swaying mob to and fro along the shore like a herd of cattle afraid of the water. Some few jumped into the river then, but most of them did so only after the last discharge. Three times Brown's men fired into the ruck, Brown, the only one in view, cursing and yelling, 'Aim low! aim low!'

"Tamb' Itam says that, as for him, he understood at the first volley what had happened. Though untouched he fell down and lay as if dead, but with his eyes open. At the sound of the first shots Dain Waris, reclining on the couch, jumped up and ran out upon the open shore, just in time to receive a bullet in his forehead at the second discharge. Tamb' Itam saw him fling his arms wide open before he fell. Then, he says, a great fear came upon him—not before. The white men retired as they had come—unseen.

"Thus Brown balanced his account with the evil fortune. Notice that even in this awful outbreak there is a superiority as of a man who carries right—the abstract thing—within the envelope of his common desires. It was not a vulgar and treacherous massacre; it was a lesson, a retribution—a demonstration of some obscure and awful attribute of our nature which, I am afraid, is not so very far under the surface as we like to think.

"Afterwards the whites depart unseen by Tamb Itam, and seem to vanish from before men's eyes altogether; and the schooner, too, vanishes after the manner of stolen goods. But a story is told of a white long-boat picked up a month later in the Indian Ocean by a cargo-steamer. Two parched, yellow, glassy-eyed, whispering skeletons in her recognised the authority of a third, who declared that his name was Brown. His Schooner, he reported, bound south with a cargo of Java sugar, had sprung a bad leak and sank under his feet. He and his companions were the survivors of a crew of six. The two died on board the steamer which rescued them. Brown lived to be seen by me, and I can testify that he had played his part to the last."

The Ghost of Captain Brand

HOWARD PYLE

It is not so easy to tell why discredit should be cast upon a man because of something that his grandfather may have done amiss, but the world, which is never overnice in its discrimination as to where to lay the blame, is often pleased to make the innocent suffer in the place of the guilty.

Barnaby True was a good, honest, biddable lad, as boys go, but yet he was not ever allowed altogether to forget that his grandfather had been that very famous pirate, Capt. William Brand, who, after so many marvelous adventures (if one may believe the catchpenny stories and ballads that were written about him), was murdered in Jamaica by Capt. John Malyoe, the commander of his own consort, the *Adventure* galley.

It has never been denied, that ever I heard, that up to the time of Captain Brand's being commissioned against the South Sea pirates he had always been esteemed as honest, reputable a sea captain as could be.

When he started out upon that adventure it was with a ship, the *Royal Sovereign*, fitted out by some of the most decent merchants of New York. The governor himself had subscribed to the adventure, and had himself signed Captain Brand's commission. So, if the unfortunate man went astray, he must have had great temptation to do so, many others behaving no better when the opportunity offered in those far-away seas where so many rich purchases might very easily be taken and no one the wiser.

To be sure, those stories and ballads made our captain to be a most wicked, profane wretch; and if he were, why, God knows he suffered and paid for it, for he laid his bones in Jamaica, and never saw his home or his wife and daughter again after he had sailed away on the *Royal Sovereign* on that long misfortunate voyage, leaving them in New York to the care of strangers.

At the time when he met his fate in Port Royal Harbor he had obtained two vessels under his command—the *Royal Sovereign*, which was the boat fitted out for him in New York, and the *Adventure* galley, which he was said to have taken somewhere in the South Seas. With these he lay in those waters of Jamaica for over a month after his return from the coasts of Africa, waiting for news from home, which, when it came, was of the very blackest; for the colonial authorities were at that time stirred up very hot against him to take him and hang him for a pirate, so as to clear their own skirts for having to do with such a fellow. So maybe it seemed better to our captain to hide his ill-gotten treasure there in those far-away parts, and afterward to try and bargain with it for his life when he should reach New York, rather than to sail straight for the Americas with what he had earned by his piracies, and so risk losing life and money both.

However that might be, the story was that Captain Brand and his gunner, and Captain Malyoe of the *Adventure* and the sailing master of the *Adventure* all went ashore together with a chest of money (no one of them choosing to trust the other three in so nice an affair), and buried the treasure somewhere on the beach of Port Royal Harbor. The story then has it that they fell a-quarreling about a future division of the money, and that, as a wind-up to the affair, Captain Malyoe shot Captain Brand through the head, while the sailing master of the *Adventure* served the gunner of the *Royal Sovereign* after the same fashion through the body, and that the murderers then went away, leaving the two stretched out in their own blood on the sand in the staring sun, with no one to know where the money was hid but they two who had served their comrades so.

It is a mighty great pity that anyone should have a grandfather who ended his days in such a sort as this, but it was no fault of Barnaby True's, nor could he have done anything to prevent it, seeing that he was not even born into the world at the time that his grandfather turned pirate, and was only one year old when he so met his tragical end. Nevertheless, the boys with whom he went to school never tired of calling him "Pirate," and would sometimes sing for his benefit that famous catchpenny song beginning thus:

> Oh, my name was Captain Brand,
>> A-sailing,
>> And a-sailing;
> Oh, my name was Captain Brand,
>> A-sailing free.
> Oh, my name was Captain Brand,
> And I sinned by sea and land,
> For I broke God's just command,
>> A-sailing free.

'Twas a vile thing to sing at the grandson of so misfortunate a man, and oftentimes little Barnaby True would double up his fists and would fight his tormentors at great odds, and would sometimes go back home with a bloody nose to have his poor mother cry over him and grieve for him.

Not that his days were all of teasing and torment, neither; for if his comrades did treat him so, why, then, there were other times when he and they were as great friends as could be, and would go in swimming together where there was a bit of sandy strand along the East River above Fort George, and that in the most amicable fashion. Or, maybe the very next day after he had fought so with his fellows, he would go a-rambling with them up the Bowerie Road, perhaps to help them steal cherries from some old Dutch farmer, forgetting in such adventure what a thief his own grandfather had been.

Well, when Barnaby True was between sixteen and seventeen years old he was taken into employment in the countinghouse of Mr. Roger Hartright, the well-known West India merchant, and Barnaby's own stepfather.

It was the kindness of this good man that not only found a place for Barnaby in the counting-house, but advanced him so fast that against our hero was twenty-one years old he had made four voyages as supercargo to the West Indies in Mr. Hartright's ship, the *Belle Helen*, and soon after he was twenty-one undertook a fifth. Nor was it in any such subordinate position as mere supercargo that he acted, but rather as the confidential agent of Mr. Hartright, who, having no children of his own, was very jealous to advance our hero into a position of trust and responsibility in the countinghouse, as though he were indeed a son, so that even the captain of the ship had scarcely more consideration aboard than he, young as he was in years.

As for the agents and correspondents of Mr. Hartright throughout these parts, they also, knowing how the good man had adopted his interests, were very polite and obliging to Master Barnaby—especially, be it mentioned, Mr. Ambrose Greenfield, of Kingston, Jamaica, who, upon the occasions of his visits to those parts, did all that he could to make Barnaby's stay in that town agreeable and pleasant to him.

So much for the history of our hero to the time of the beginning of this story, without which you shall hardly be able to understand the purport of those most extraordinary adventures that befell him shortly after he came of age, nor the logic of their consequence after they had occurred.

For it was during his fifth voyage to the West Indies that the first of those extraordinary adventures happened of which I shall have presently to tell.

At that time he had been in Kingston for the best part of four weeks, lodging at the house of a very decent, respectable widow, by name Mrs. Anne Bolles, who, with three pleasant and agreeable daughters, kept a very clean and well-served lodging house in the outskirts of the town.

One morning, as our hero sat sipping his coffee, clad only in loose cotton drawers, a shirt, and a jacket, and with slippers upon his feet, as is the custom in that country, where everyone endeavors to keep as cool as may be—while he sat thus sipping his coffee Miss Eliza, the youngest of the three daughters, came and gave him a note, which, she said, a stranger had just handed in at the door, going away again without waiting for a reply. You may judge of Barnaby's surprise when he opened the note and read as follows:

Mr. Barnaby True.

Sir,—Though you don't know me, I know you, and I tell you this: if you will be at Pratt's Ordinary on Harbor Street on Friday next at eight o'clock of the evening, and will accompany the man who shall say to you, "The *Royal Sovereign* is come in," you shall learn something the most to your advantage that ever befell you. Sir, keep this note, and show it to him who shall address these words to you, so to certify that you are the man he seeks.

Such was the wording of the note, which was without address, and without any superscription whatever.

The first emotion that stirred Barnaby was one of extreme and profound amazement. Then the thought came into his mind that some witty fellow, of whom he knew a good many in that town—and wild, waggish pranks they were—was attempting to play off some smart jest upon him. But all that Miss Eliza could tell him when he questioned her concerning the messenger was that the bearer of the note was a tall, stout man, with a red neckerchief around his neck and copper buckles to his shoes, and that he had the appearance of a sailorman, having a great big queue hanging down his back. But, Lord! what was such a description as that in a busy seaport town, full of scores of men to fit such a likeness? Accordingly, our hero put away the note into his wallet, determining to show it to his good friend Mr. Greenfield that evening, and to ask his advice upon it. So he did show it, and that gentleman's opinion was the same as his—that some wag was minded to play off a hoax upon him, and that the matter of the letter was all nothing but smoke.

Nevertheless, though Barnaby was thus confirmed in his opinion as to the nature of the communication he had received, he yet determined in his own mind that he would see the business through to the end, and would be at Pratt's Ordinary, as the note demanded, upon the day and at the time specified therein.

Pratt's Ordinary was at that time a very fine and well-known place of its sort, with good tobacco and the best rum that ever I tasted, and had a garden behind it that, sloping down to the harbor front, was planted pretty thick with palms and ferns grouped into clusters with flowers and plants. Here were a number of little tables, some in little grottoes, like our Vauxhall in New York, and with red and blue and white paper lanterns hung among the foliage, whither gentlemen and ladies used sometimes to go of an evening to sit and drink lime juice and sugar and water (and sometimes a taste of something stronger), and to look out across the water at the shipping in the cool of the night.

Thither, accordingly, our hero went, a little before the time appointed in the note, and passing directly through the Ordinary and the garden beyond, chose a table at the lower end of the garden and close to the water's edge, where he would not be easily seen by anyone coming into the place. Then, ordering some rum and water and a pipe of tobacco, he composed himself to watch for the appearance of those witty fellows whom he suspected would presently come thither to see the end of their prank and to enjoy his confusion.

The spot was pleasant enough; for the land breeze, blowing strong and full, set the leaves of the palm tree above his head to rattling and clattering continually against the sky, where, the moon then being about full, they shone every now and then like blades of steel. The waves also were splashing up against the little landing place at the foot of the garden, sounding very cool in the night, and sparkling all over the harbor where the moon caught the edges of the water.

A great many vessels were lying at anchor in their ridings, with the dark, prodigious form of a man-of-war looming up above them in the moonlight.

There our hero sat for the best part of an hour, smoking his pipe of tobacco and sipping his grog, and seeing not so much as a single thing that might concern the note he had received.

It was not far from half an hour after the time appointed in the note, when a rowboat came suddenly out of the night and pulled up to the landing place at the foot of the garden above mentioned, and three or four men came ashore in the darkness. Without saying a word among themselves they chose a near-by table and, sitting down, ordered rum and water, and began drinking their grog in silence. They might have sat there about five minutes, when, by and by, Barnaby True became aware that they were observing him very curiously; and then almost immediately one, who was plainly the leader of the party, called out to him:

"How now, messmate! Won't you come and drink a dram of rum with us?"

"Why, no," says Barnaby, answering very civilly; "I have drunk enough already, and more would only heat my blood."

"All the same," quoth the stranger, "I think you will come and drink with us; for, unless I am mistook, you are Mr. Barnaby True, and I am come here to tell you that the *Royal Sovereign* is come in."

Now I may honestly say that Barnaby True was never more struck aback in all his life than he was at hearing these words uttered in so unexpected a manner. He had been looking to hear them under such different circumstances that, now that his ears heard them addressed to him, and that so seriously, by a perfect stranger, who, with others, had thus mysteriously come ashore out of the darkness, he could scarce believe that his ears heard aright. His heart suddenly began beating at a tremendous rate, and had he been an older and wiser man, I do believe he would have declined the adventure, instead of leaping blindly, as he did, into that of which he could see neither the beginning nor the ending. But being barely one-and-twenty years of age, and having an adventurous disposition that would have carried him into almost anything that possessed a smack of uncertainty or danger about it, he contrived to say, in a pretty easy tone (though God knows how it was put on for the occasion):

"Well, then, if that be so, and if the *Royal Sovereign* is indeed come in, why, I'll join you, since you are so kind as to ask me." And therewith he went across to the other table, carrying his pipe with him, and sat down and began smoking, with all the appearance of ease he could assume upon the occasion.

"Well, Mr. Barnaby True," said the man who had before addressed him, so soon as Barnaby had settled himself, speaking in a low tone of voice, so there would be no danger of any others hearing the words—"Well, Mr. Barnaby True—for I shall call you by your name, to show you that though I know you, you don't know me—I am glad to see that you are man enough to enter thus into an affair, though you can't see to the bottom of it. For it shows me that you are a man of mettle, and are deserving of the fortune that is to befall you to-night. Nevertheless, first of all, I am bid to say that you must show me a piece of paper that you have about you before we go a step farther."

"Very well," said Barnaby; "I have it here safe and sound, and see it you shall." And thereupon and without more ado he fetched out his wallet, opened it, and handed his interlocutor the mysterious note he had received the day or two before. Whereupon the other, drawing to him the candle, burning there for the convenience of those who would smoke tobacco, began immediately reading it.

This gave Barnaby True a moment or two to look at him. He was a tall, stout man, with a red handkerchief tied around his neck, and with copper buckles on his shoes, so that Barnaby True could not but wonder whether he was not the very same man who had given the note to Miss Eliza Bolles at the door of his lodging house.

" 'Tis all right and straight as it should be," the other said, after he had so glanced his eyes over the note. "And now that the paper is read" (suiting his action to his words), "I'll just burn it, for safety's sake."

And so he did, twisting it up and setting it to the flame of the candle.

"And now," he said, continuing his address, "I'll tell you what I am here for. I was sent to ask you if you're man enough to take your life in your own hands and to go with me in that boat down there? Say 'Yes,' and we'll start away without wasting more time, for the devil is ashore here at Jamaica—though you don't know what that means—and if he gets ahead of us, why, then we may whistle for what we are after. Say 'No,' and I go away again, and I promise you you shall never be troubled again in this sort. So now speak up plain, young gentleman, and tell us what is your mind in this business, and whether you will adventure any farther or not."

If our hero hesitated it was not for long. I cannot say that his courage did not waver for a moment; but if it did, it was, I say, not for long, and when he spoke up it was with a voice as steady as could be.

"To be sure I'm man enough to go with you," he said; "and if you mean me any harm I can look out for myself; and if I can't, why, here is something can look out for me," and therewith he lifted up the flap of his coat pocket and showed the butt of a pistol he had fetched with him when he had set out from his lodging house that evening.

At this the other burst out a-laughing. "Come," says he, "you are indeed of right mettle, and I like your spirit. All the same, no one in all the world means you less ill than I, and so, if you have to use that barker, 'twill not be upon us who are your friends, but only upon one who is more wicked than the devil himself. So come, and let us get away."

Thereupon he and the others, who had not spoken a single word for all this time, rose from the table, and he having paid the scores of all, they all went down together to the boat that still lay at the landing place at the bottom of the garden.

Thus coming to it, our hero could see that it was a large yawl boat manned with half a score of black men for rowers, and there were two lanterns in the stern sheets, and three or four iron shovels.

The man who had conducted the conversation with Barnaby True for all this time, and who was, as has been said, plainly the captain of the party, stepped immediately down into the boat; our hero followed, and the others followed after him; and instantly they were seated the boat was shoved off and the black men began pulling straight out into the harbor, and so, at some distance away, around under the stern of the man-of-war.

Not a word was spoken after they had thus left the shore, and presently they might all have been ghosts, for the silence of the party. Barnaby True was too full of his own thoughts to talk—and serious enough thoughts they were by this time, with crimps to trepan a man at every turn, and press gangs to carry a man off so that he might never be heard of again. As for the others, they did not seem to choose to say anything now that they had him fairly embarked upon their enterprise.

And so the crew pulled on in perfect silence for the best part of an hour, the leader of the expedition directing the course of the boat straight across the harbor, as though toward the mouth of the Rio Cobra River. Indeed, this was their destination, as Barnaby could after a while see, by the low point of land with a great long row of coconut palms upon it (the appearance of which he knew very well), which by and by began to loom up out of the milky dimness of the moonlight. As they approached the river they found the tide was running strong out of it, so that some distance away from the stream it gurgled and rippled alongside the boat as the crew of black men pulled strongly against it. Thus they came up under what was either a point of land or an islet covered with a thick growth of mangrove trees. But still no one spoke a single word as to their destination, or what was the business they had in hand.

The night, now that they were close to the shore, was loud with the noise of running tide-water, and the air was heavy with the smell of mud and marsh, and over all the whiteness of the moonlight, with a few stars pricking out here and there in the sky; and all so strange and silent and mysterious that Barnaby could not divest himself of the feeling that it was all a dream.

So, the rowers bending to the oars, the boat came slowly around from under the clump of mangrove bushes and out into the open water again.

Instantly it did so the leader of the expedition called out in a sharp voice, and the black men instantly lay on their oars.

Almost at the same instant Barnaby True became aware that there was another boat coming down the river toward where they lay, now drifting with the strong tide out into the harbor again, and he knew that it was because of the approach of that boat that the other had called upon his men to cease rowing.

The other boat, as well as he could see in the distance, was full of men, some of whom appeared to be armed, for even in the dusk of the darkness the shine of the moonlight glimmered sharply now and then on the barrels of muskets or pistols, and in the silence that followed after their own rowing had ceased Barnaby True could hear the chug! chug! of the oars sounding louder and louder through the watery stillness of the night as the boat drew nearer and nearer. But he knew nothing of what it all meant, nor whether these others were friends or enemies, or what was to happen next.

The oarsmen of the approaching boat did not for a moment cease their rowing, not till they had come pretty close to Barnaby and his companions. Then a man who sat in the stern ordered them to cease rowing, and as they lay on their oars he stood up. As they passed by, Barnaby True could see him very plain, the moonlight shining full upon him—a large, stout gentleman with a round red face, and clad in a fine laced coat of red cloth. Amidship of the boat was a box or chest about the bigness of a middle-sized traveling trunk, but covered all over with cakes of sand and dirt. In the act of passing, the gentleman, still standing, pointed at it with an elegant gold-headed cane which he held in his hand. "Are you come after this, Abraham Dawling?" says he, and thereat his countenance broke into as evil, malignant a grin as ever Barnaby True saw in all of his life.

The other did not immediately reply so much as a single word, but sat as still as any stone. Then, at last, the other boat having gone by, he suddenly appeared to regain his wits, for he bawled out after it, "Very well, Jack Malyoe! very well, Jack Malyoe! you've got ahead of us this time again, but next time is the third, and then it shall be our turn, even if William Brand must come back from hell to settle with you."

This he shouted out as the other boat passed farther and farther away, but to it my fine gentleman made no reply except to burst out into a great roaring fit of laughter.

There was another man among the armed men in the stern of the passing boat—a villainous, lean man with lantern jaws, and the top of his head as bald as the palm of my hand. As the boat went away into the night with the tide and the headway the oars had given it, he grinned so that the moonlight shone white on his big teeth. Then, flourishing a great big pistol, he said, and

Barnaby could hear every word he spoke, "Do but give me the word, Your Honor, and I'll put another bullet through the son of a sea cook."

But the gentleman said some words to forbid him, and therewith the boat was gone away into the night, and presently Barnaby could hear that the men at the oars had begun rowing again, leaving them lying there, without a single word being said for a long time.

By and by one of those in Barnaby's boat spoke up. "Where shall you go now?" he said.

At this the leader of the expedition appeared suddenly to come back to himself, and to find his voice again. "Go?" he roared out. "Go to the devil! Go? Go where you choose! Go? Go back again—that's where we'll go!" and therewith he fell a-cursing and swearing until he foamed at the lips, as though he had gone clean crazy, while the black men began rowing back again across the harbor as fast as ever they could lay oars into the water.

They put Barnaby True ashore below the old custom house; but so bewildered and shaken was he by all that had happened, and by what he had seen, and by the names that he heard spoken, that he was scarcely conscious of any of the familiar things among which he found himself thus standing. And so he walked up the moonlit street toward his lodging like one drunk or bewildered; for "John Malyoe" was the name of the captain of the *Adventure* galley—he who had shot Barnaby's own grandfather—and "Abraham Dawling" was the name of the gunner of the *Royal Sovereign* who had been shot at the same time with the pirate captain, and who, with him, had been left stretched out in the staring sun by the murderers.

The whole business had occupied hardly two hours, but it was as though that time was no part of Barnaby's life, but all a part of some other life, so dark and strange and mysterious that it in no wise belonged to him.

As for that box covered all over with mud, he could only guess at that time what it contained and what the finding of it signified.

But of this our hero said nothing to anyone, nor did he tell a single living soul what he had seen that night, but nursed it in his own mind, where it lay so big for a while that he could think of little or nothing else for days after.

Mr. Greenfield, Mr. Hartright's correspondent and agent in these parts, lived in a fine brick house just out of the town, on the Mona Road, his family consisting of a wife and two daughters—brisk, lively young ladies with black hair and eyes, and very fine bright teeth that shone whenever they laughed, and with a plenty to say for themselves. Thither Barnaby True was often asked to a family dinner; and, indeed, it was a pleasant home to visit, and to sit upon the veranda and smoke a cigarro with the good old gentleman and look out toward the mountains, while the young ladies laughed and talked, or played upon the guitar and sang. And oftentimes so it was strongly upon Barnaby's mind to speak to the good gentleman and tell him what he had beheld that, night out in the harbor; but always he would think better of it and hold his peace, falling to thinking, and smoking away upon his cigarro at a great rate.

A day or two before the *Belle Helen* sailed from Kingston Mr. Greenfield stopped Barnaby True as he was going through the office to bid him to come to dinner that night (for there within the tropics they breakfast at eleven o'clock and take dinner in the cool of the evening, because of the heat, and not at midday, as we do in more temperate latitudes). "I would have you meet," says Mr. Greenfield, "your chief passenger for New York, and his granddaughter, for whom the state cabin and the two staterooms are to be fitted as here ordered [showing a letter]—Sir John Malyoe and Miss Marjorie Malyoe. Did you ever hear tell of Capt. Jack Malyoe, Master Barnaby?"

Now I do believe that Mr. Greenfield had no notion at all that old Captain Brand was Barnaby True's own grandfather and Capt. John Malyoe his murderer, but when he so thrust at him the name of that man, what with that in itself and the late adventure through which he himself had just passed, and with his brooding upon it until it was so prodigiously big in his mind, it was like hitting him a blow to so fling the questions at him. Nevertheless, he was able to reply, with a pretty straight face, that he had heard of Captain Malyoe and who he was.

"Well," says Mr. Greenfield, "if Jack Malyoe was a desperate pirate and a wild, reckless blade twenty years ago, why, he is Sir John Malyoe now and the owner of a fine estate in Devonshire. Well, Master Barnaby, when one is a baronet and come into the inheritance of a fine estate (though I do hear it is vastly cumbered with debts), the world will wink its eye to much that he may have done twenty years ago. I do hear say, though, that his own kin still turn the cold shoulder to him."

To this address Barnaby answered nothing, but sat smoking away at his cigarro at a great rate.

And so that night Barnaby True came face to face for the first time with the man who murdered his own grandfather—the greatest beast of a man that ever he met in all of his life.

That time in the harbor he had seen Sir John Malyoe at a distance and in the darkness; now that he beheld him near by it seemed to him that he had never looked at a more evil face in all his life. Not that the man was altogether ugly, for he had a good nose and a fine double chin; but his eyes stood out like balls and were red and watery, and he winked them continually, as though they were always smarting; and his lips were thick and purple-red, and his fat, red cheeks were mottled here and there with little clots of purple veins; and when he spoke his voice rattled so in his throat that it made one wish to clear one's own throat to listen to him. So, what with a pair of fat, white hands, and that hoarse voice, and his swollen face, and his thick lips sticking out, it seemed to Barnaby True he had never seen a countenance so distasteful to him as that one into which he then looked.

But if Sir John Malyoe was so displeasing to our hero's taste, why, the granddaughter, even this first time he beheld her, seemed to him to be the most beautiful, lovely young lady that ever he saw. She had a thin, fair skin, red lips, and yellow hair—though it was then powdered pretty white for the occasion—and the bluest eyes that Barnaby beheld in all of his life. A sweet, timid creature, who seemed not to dare so much as to speak a word for herself without looking to Sir John for leave to do so, and would shrink and shudder whenever he would speak of a sudden to her or direct a sudden glance upon her. When she did speak, it was in so low a voice that one had to bend his head to hear her, and even if she smiled would catch herself and look up as though to see if she had leave to be cheerful.

As for Sir John, he sat at dinner like a pig, and gobbled and ate and drank, smacking his lips all the while, but with hardly a word to either her or Mrs. Greenfield or to Barnaby True; but with a sour, sullen air, as though he would say, "Your damned victuals and drink are no better than they should be, but I must eat 'em or nothing." A great bloated beast of a man!

Only after dinner was over and the young lady and the two misses sat off in a corner together did Barnaby hear her talk with any ease. Then, to be sure, her tongue became loose, and she prattled away at a great rate, though hardly above her breath, until of a sudden her grandfather called out, in his hoarse, rattling voice, that it was time to go. Whereupon she stopped short in what she was saying and jumped up from her chair, looking as frightened as though she had been caught in something amiss, and was to be punished for it.

Barnaby True and Mr. Greenfield both went out to see the two into their coach, where Sir John's man stood holding the lantern. And who should he be, to be sure, but that same lean villain with bald head who had offered to shoot the leader of our hero's expedition out on the harbor that night! For, one of the circles of light from the lantern shining up into his face, Barnaby True knew him the moment he clapped eyes upon him. Though he could not have recognized our hero, he grinned at him in the most impudent, familiar fashion, and never so much as touched his hat either to him or to Mr. Greenfield; but as soon as his master and his young mistress had entered the coach, banged to the door and scrambled up on the seat alongside the driver, and so away without a word, but with another, impudent grin, this time favoring both Barnaby and the old gentleman.

Such were these two, master and man, and what Barnaby saw of them then was only confirmed by further observation—the most hateful couple he ever knew; though, God knows, what they afterward suffered should wipe out all complaint against them.

The next day Sir John Malyoe's belongings began to come aboard the *Belle Helen*, and in the afternoon that same lean, villainous manservant comes skipping across the gangplank as nimble as a goat, with two black men behind him lugging a great sea chest. "What!" he cried out, "and so you is the supercargo, is you? Why, I thought you was more account when I saw you last night a-sitting talking with His Honor like his equal. Well, no matter; 'tis something to have a brisk, genteel young fellow for a supercargo. So come, my hearty, lend a hand, will you, and help me set His Honor's cabin to rights."

What a speech was this to endure from such a fellow, to be sure! and Barnaby so high in his own esteem, and holding himself a gentleman! Well, what with his distaste for the villain, and what with such odious familiarity, you can guess into what temper so impudent an address must have cast him. "You'll find the steward in yonder," he said, "and he'll show you the cabin," and therewith turned and walked away with prodigious dignity, leaving the other standing where he was.

As he entered his own cabin he could not but see, out of the tail of his eye, that the fellow was still standing where he had left him, regarding him with a most evil, malevolent countenance, so that he had the satisfaction of knowing that he had made one enemy during that voyage who was not very likely to forgive or forget what he must regard as a slight put upon him.

The next day Sir John Malyoe himself came aboard, accompanied by his granddaughter, and followed by this man, and he followed again by four black men, who carried among them two trunks, not large in size, but prodigious heavy in weight, and toward which Sir John and his follower devoted the utmost solicitude and care to see that they were properly carried into the state cabin he was to occupy. Barnaby True was standing in the great cabin as they passed close by him; but though Sir John Malyoe looked hard at him and straight in the face, he never so much as spoke a single word, or showed by a look or a sign that he knew who our hero was. At this the serving man, who saw it all with eyes as quick as a cat's, fell to grinning and chuckling to see Barnaby in his turn so slighted.

The young lady, who also saw it all, flushed up red, then in the instant of passing looked straight at our hero, and bowed and smiled at him with a most sweet and gracious affability, then the next moment recovering herself, as though mightily frightened at what she had done.

The same day the *Belle Helen* sailed, with as beautiful, sweet weather as ever a body could wish for.

There were only two other passengers aboard, the Rev. Simon Styles, the master of a flourishing academy in Spanish Town, and his wife, a good, worthy old couple, but very quiet, and would sit in the great cabin by the hour together reading, so that, what with Sir John Malyoe staying all the time in his own cabin with those two trunks he held so precious, it fell upon Barnaby True in great part to show attention to the young lady; and glad enough he was of the opportunity, as anyone may guess. For when you consider a brisk, lively young man of one-and-twenty and a sweet, beautiful miss of seventeen so thrown together day after day for two weeks, the weather being very fair, as I have said, and the ship tossing and bowling along before a fine humming breeze that sent white caps all over the sea, and with nothing to do but sit and look at that blue sea and the bright sky overhead, it is not hard to suppose what was to befall, and what pleasure it was to Barnaby True to show attention to her.

But, oh! those days when a man is young, and, whether wisely or no, fallen in love! How often during that voyage did our hero lie awake in his berth at night, tossing this way and that without sleep—not that he wanted to sleep if he could, but would rather lie so awake thinking about her and staring into the darkness!

Poor fool! He might have known that the end must come to such a fool's paradise before very long. For who was he to look up to Sir John Malyoe's granddaughter, he, the supercargo of a merchant ship, and she the granddaughter of a baronet.

Nevertheless, things went along very smooth and pleasant, until one evening, when all came of a sudden to an end. At that time he and the young lady had been standing for a long while together, leaning over the rail and looking out across the water through the dusk toward the westward, where the sky was still of a lingering brightness. She had been mightily quiet and dull all that evening, but now of a sudden she began, without any preface whatever, to tell Barnaby about herself and her affairs. She said that she and her grandfather were going to New York that they might take passage thence to Boston town, there to meet her cousin Captain Malyoe, who was stationed in garrison at that place. Then she went on to say that Captain Malyoe was the next heir to the Devonshire estate, and that she and he were to be married in the fall.

But, poor Barnaby! what a fool was he, to be sure! Methinks when she first began to speak about Captain Malyoe he knew what was coming. But now that she had told him, he could say nothing, but stood there staring across the ocean, his breath coming hot and dry as ashes in his throat. She, poor thing, went on to say, in a very low voice, that she had liked him from the very first moment she had seen him, and had been very happy for these days, and would always think of him as a dear friend who had been very kind to her, who had so little pleasure in life, and so would always remember him.

Then they were both silent, until at last Barnaby made shift to say, though in a hoarse and croaking voice, that Captain Malyoe must be a very happy man, and that if he were in Captain Malyoe's place he would be the happiest man in the world. Thus, having spoken, and so found his tongue, he went on to tell her, with his head all in a whirl, that he, too, loved her, and that what she had told him struck him to the heart, and made him the most miserable, unhappy wretch in the whole world.

She was not angry at what he said, nor did she turn to look at him, but only said, in a low voice, he should not talk so, for that it could only be a pain to them both to speak of such things, and that whether she would or no, she must do everything as her grandfather bade her, for that he was indeed a terrible man.

To this poor Barnaby could only repeat that he loved her with all his heart, that he had hoped for nothing in his love, but that he was now the most miserable man in the world.

It was at this moment, so tragic for him, that some one who had been hiding nigh them all the while suddenly moved away, and Barnaby True could see in the gathering darkness that it was that villain manservant of Sir John Malyoe's and knew that he must have overheard all that had been said.

The man went straight to the great cabin, and poor Barnaby, his brain all atingle, stood looking after him, feeling that now indeed the last drop of bitterness had been added to his trouble to have such a wretch overhear what he had said.

The young lady could not have seen the fellow, for she continued leaning over the rail, and Barnaby True, standing at her side, not moving, but in such a tumult of many passions that he was like one bewildered, and his heart beating as though to smother him.

So they stood for I know not how long when, of a sudden, Sir John Malyoe comes running out of the cabin, without his hat, but carrying his gold-headed cane, and so straight across the deck to where Barnaby and the young lady stood, that spying wretch close at his heels, grinning like an imp.

"You hussy!" bawled out Sir John, so soon as he had come pretty near them, and in so loud a voice that all on deck might have heard the words; and as he spoke he waved his cane back and forth as though he would have struck the young lady, who, shrinking back almost upon the deck, crouched as though to escape such a blow. "You hussy!" he bawled out with vile oaths, too horrible here to be set down. "What do you do here with this Yankee supercargo, not fit for a gentlewoman to wipe her feet upon? Get to your cabin, you hussy" (only it was something worse he called her this time), "before I lay this cane across your shoulders!"

What with the whirling of Barnaby's brains and the passion into which he was already melted, what with his despair and his love, and his anger at this address, a man gone mad could scarcely be less accountable for his actions than was he at that moment. Hardly knowing what he did, he put his hand against Sir John Malyoe's breast and thrust him violently back, crying out upon him in a great, loud, hoarse voice for threatening a young lady, and saying that for a farthing he would wrench the stick out of his hand and throw it overboard.

Sir John went staggering back with the push Barnaby gave him, and then caught himself up again. Then, with a great bellow, ran roaring at our hero, whirling his cane about, and I do believe would have struck him (and God knows then what might have happened) had not his manservant caught him and held him back.

"Keep back!" cried out our hero, still mighty hoarse. "Keep back! If you strike me with that stick I'll fling you overboard!"

By this time, what with the sound of loud voices and the stamping of feet, some of the crew and others aboard were hurrying up, and the next moment Captain Manly and the first mate, Mr. Freesden, came running out of the cabin. But Barnaby, who was by this fairly set agoing, could not now stop himself.

"And who are you, anyhow," he cried out, "to threaten to strike me and to insult me, who am as good as you? You dare not strike me! You may shoot a man from behind, as you shot poor Captain Brand on the Rio Cobra River, but you won't dare strike me face to face. I know who you are and what you are!"

By this time Sir John Malyoe had ceased to endeavor to strike him, but stood stock-still, his great bulging eyes staring as though they would pop out of his head.

"What's all this?" cries Captain Manly, bustling up to them with Mr. Freesden. "What does all this mean?"

But, as I have said, our hero was too far gone now to contain himself until all that he had to say was out.

"The damned villain insulted me and insulted the young lady," he cried out, panting in the extremity of his passion, "and then he threatened to strike me with his cane. But I know who he is and what he is. I know what he's got in his cabin in those two trunks, and where he found it, and whom it belongs to. He found it on the shores of the Rio Cobra River, and I have only to open my mouth and tell what I know about it."

At this Captain Manly clapped his hand upon our hero's shoulder and fell to shaking him so that he could scarcely stand, calling out to him the while to be silent. "What do you mean?" he cried. " An officer of this ship to quarrel with a passenger of mine! Go straight to your cabin, and stay there till I give you leave to come out again."

At this Master Barnaby came somewhat back to himself and into his wits again with a jump. "But he threatened to strike me with his cane, Captain," he cried out, "and that I won't stand from any man!"

"No matter what he did," said Captain Manly, very sternly. "Go to your cabin, as I bid you, and stay there till I tell you to come out again, and when we get to New York I'll take pains to tell your stepfather of how you have behaved. I'll have no such rioting as this aboard my ship."

Barnaby True looked around him, but the young lady was gone. Nor, in the blindness of his frenzy, had he seen when she had gone nor whither she went. As for Sir John Malyoe, he stood in the light of a lantern, his face gone as white as ashes, and I do believe if a look could kill, the dreadful malevolent stare he fixed upon Barnaby True would have slain him where he stood.

After Captain Manly had so shaken some wits into poor Barnaby he, unhappy wretch, went to his cabin, as he was bidden to do, and there, shutting the door upon himself, and flinging himself down, all dressed as he was, upon his berth, yielded himself over to the profoundest passion of humiliation and despair.

There he lay for I know not how long, staring into the darkness, until by and by, in spite of his suffering and his despair, he dozed off into a loose sleep, that was more like waking than sleep, being possessed continually by the most vivid and distasteful dreams, from which he would awaken only to doze off and to dream again.

It was from the midst of one of these extravagant dreams that he was suddenly aroused by the noise of a pistol shot, and then the noise of another and another, and then a great bump and a grinding jar, and then the sound of many footsteps running across the deck and down into the great cabin. Then came a tremendous uproar of voices in the great cabin, the struggling as of men's bodies being tossed about, striking violently against the partitions and bulkheads. At the same instant arose a screaming of women's voices, and one voice, and that Sir John Malyoe's, crying out as in the greatest extremity: "You villains! You damned villains!" and with the sudden detonation of a pistol fired into the close space of the great cabin.

Barnaby was out in the middle of his cabin in a moment, and taking only time enough to snatch down one of the pistols that hung at the head of his berth, flung out into the great cabin, to find it as black as night, the lantern slung there having been either blown out or dashed out into darkness. The prodigiously dark space was full of uproar, the hubbub and confusion pierced through and through by that keen sound of women's voices screaming, one in the cabin and the other in the stateroom beyond. Almost immediately Barnaby pitched headlong over two or three struggling men scuffling together upon the deck, falling with a great clatter and the loss of his pistol, which, however, he regained almost immediately.

What all the uproar meant he could not tell, but he presently heard Captain Manly's voice from somewhere suddenly calling out, "You bloody pirate, would you choke me to death?"

wherewith some notion of what had happened came to him like a flash, and that they had been attacked in the night by pirates.

Looking toward the companionway, he saw, outlined against the darkness of the night without, the blacker form of a man's figure, standing still and motionless as a statue in the midst of all this hubbub, and so by some instinct he knew in a moment that that must be the master maker of all this devil's brew. Therewith, still kneeling upon the deck, he covered the bosom of that shadowy figure pointblank, as he thought, with his pistol, and instantly pulled the trigger.

In the flash of red light, and in the instant stunning report of the pistol shot, Barnaby saw, as stamped upon the blackness, a broad, flat face with fishy eyes, a lean, bony forehead with what appeared to be a great blotch of blood upon the side, a cocked hat trimmed with gold lace, a red scarf across the breast, and the gleam of brass buttons. Then the darkness, very thick and black, swallowed everything again.

But in the instant Sir John Malyoe called out, in a great loud voice: "My God! 'Tis William Brand!" Therewith came the sound of some one falling heavily down.

The next moment, Barnaby's sight coming back to him again in the darkness, he beheld that dark and motionless figure still standing exactly where it had stood before, and so knew either that he had missed it or else that it was of so supernatural a sort that a leaden bullet might do it no harm. Though if it was indeed an apparition that Barnaby beheld in that moment, there is this to say, that he saw it as plain as ever he saw a living man in all of his life.

This was the last our hero knew, for the next moment somebody—whether by accident or design he never knew—struck him such a terrible violent blow upon the side of the head that he saw forty thousand stars flash before his eyeballs, and then, with a great humming in his head, swooned dead away.

When Barnaby True came back to his senses again it was to find himself being cared for with great skill and nicety, his head bathed with cold water, and a bandage being bound about it as carefully as though a chirurgeon was attending to him.

He could not immediately recall what had happened to him, nor until he had opened his eyes to find himself in a strange cabin, extremely well fitted and painted with white and gold, the light of a lantern shining in his eyes, together with the gray of the early daylight through the dead-eye. Two men were bending over him—one, a negro in a striped shirt, with a yellow handkerchief around his head and silver earrings in his ears; the other, a white man, clad in a strange outlandish dress of a foreign make, and with great mustachios hanging down, and with gold earrings in his ears.

It was the latter who was attending to Barnaby's hurt with such extreme care and gentleness.

All this Barnaby saw with his first clear consciousness after his swoon. Then remembering what had befallen him, and his head beating as though it would split asunder, he shut his eyes again, contriving with great effort to keep himself from groaning aloud, and wondering as to what sort of pirates these could be who would first knock a man in the head so terrible a blow as that which he had suffered, and then take such care to fetch him back to life again, and to make him easy and comfortable.

Nor did he open his eyes again, but lay there gathering his wits together and wondering thus until the bandage was properly tied about his head and sewed together. Then once more he opened his eyes, and looked up to ask where he was.

Either they who were attending to him did not choose to reply, or else they could not speak English, for they made no answer, excepting by signs; for the white man, seeing that he was now able to speak, and so was come back into his senses again, nodded his head three or four times, and smiled with a grin of his white teeth, and then pointed, as though toward a saloon beyond. At the same time the negro held up our hero's coat and beckoned for him to put it on, so that Barnaby, seeing that it was required of him to meet some one without, arose, though with a good deal of effort, and permitted the negro to help him on with his coat, still feeling mightily dizzy and uncertain upon his legs, his head beating fit to split, and the vessel rolling and pitching at a great rate, as though upon a heavy ground swell.

So, still sick and dizzy, he went out into what was indeed a fine saloon beyond, painted in white and gilt like the cabin he had just quitted, and fitted in the nicest fashion, a mahogany table, polished very bright, extending the length of the room, and a quantity of bottles, together with glasses of clear crystal, arranged in a hanging rack above.

Here at the table a man was sitting with his back to our hero, clad in a rough pea-jacket, and with a red handkerchief tied around his throat, his feet stretched out before him, and he smoking a pipe of tobacco with all the ease and comfort in the world.

As Barnaby came in he turned round, and, to the profound astonishment of our hero, presented toward him in the light of the lantern, the dawn shining pretty strong through the sky-light, the face of that very man who had conducted the mysterious expedition that night across Kingston Harbor to the Rio Cobra River.

This man looked steadily at Barnaby True for a moment or two, and then burst out laughing; and, indeed, Barnaby, standing there with the bandage about his head, must have looked a very droll picture of that astonishment he felt so profoundly at finding who was this pirate into whose hands he had fallen.

"Well," says the other, "and so you be up at last, and no great harm done, I'll be bound. And how does your head feel by now, my young master?"

To this Barnaby made no reply, but, what with wonder and the dizziness of his head, seated himself at the table over against the speaker, who pushed a bottle of rum toward him, together with a glass from the swinging shelf above.

He watched Barnaby fill his glass, and so soon as he had done so began immediately by saying: "I do suppose you think you were treated mightily ill to be so handled last night. Well, so you were treated ill enough—though who hit you that crack upon the head I know no more than a child unborn. Well, I am sorry for the way you were handled, but there is this much to say, and of that you may believe me, that nothing was meant to you but kindness, and before you are through with us all you will believe that well enough."

Here he helped himself to a taste of grog, and sucking in his lips, went on again with what he had to say. "Do you remember," said he, "that expedition of ours in Kingston Harbor, and how we were all of us balked that night?"

"Why, yes," said Barnaby True, "nor am I likely to forget it."

"And do you remember what I said to that villain, Jack Malyoe, that night as his boat went by us?"

"As to that," said Barnaby True, "I do not know that I can say yes or no, but if you will tell me, I will maybe answer you in kind."

"Why, I mean this," said the other. "I said that the villain had got the better of us once again, but that next time it would be our turn, even if William Brand himself had to come back from hell to put the business through."

"I remember something of the sort," said Barnaby, "now that you speak of it, but still I am all in the dark as to what you are driving at."

The other looked at him very cunningly for a little while, his head on one side, and his eyes half shut. Then, as if satisfied, he suddenly burst out laughing. "Look hither," said he, "and I'll show you something," and therewith, moving to one side, disclosed a couple of traveling cases or small trunks with brass studs, so exactly like those that Sir John Malyoe had fetched aboard at Jamaica that Barnaby, putting this and that together, knew that they must be the same.

Our hero had a strong enough suspicion as to what those two cases contained, and his suspicions had become a certainty when he saw Sir John Malyoe struck all white at being threatened about them, and his face lowering so malevolently as to look murder had he dared do it. But, Lord! what were suspicions or even certainty to what Barnaby True's two eyes beheld when that man lifted the lids of the two cases—the locks thereof having already been forced—and, flinging back first one lid and then the other, displayed to Barnaby's astonished sight a great treasure of gold and silver! Most of it tied up in leathern bags, to be sure, but many of the coins, big and little, yellow and white, lying loose and scattered about like so many beans, brimming the cases to the very top.

Barnaby sat dumb-struck at what he beheld; as to whether he breathed or no, I cannot tell; but this I know, that he sat staring at that marvelous treasure like a man in a trance, until, after a few seconds of this golden display, the other banged down the lids again and burst out laughing, whereupon he came back to himself with a jump.

"Well, and what do you think of that?" said the other. "Is it not enough for a man to turn pirate for? But," he continued, "it is not for the sake of showing you this that I have been waiting for you here so long a while, but to tell you that you are not the only passenger aboard, but that there is another, whom I am to confide to your care and attention, according to orders I have received; so, if you are ready, Master Barnaby, I'll fetch her in directly." He waited for a moment, as though for Barnaby to speak, but our hero not replying, he arose and, putting away the bottle of rum and the glasses, crossed the saloon to a door like that from which Barnaby had come a little while before. This he opened, and after a moment's delay and a few words spoken to some one within, ushered thence a young lady, who came out very slowly into the saloon where Barnaby still sat at the table.

It was Miss Marjorie Malyoe, very white, and looking as though stunned or bewildered by all that had befallen her.

Barnaby True could never tell whether the amazing strange voyage that followed was of long or of short duration; whether it occupied three days or ten days. For conceive, if you choose, two people of flesh and blood moving and living continually in all the circumstances and surroundings as of a nightmare dream, yet they two so happy together that all the universe beside was of no moment to them! How was anyone to tell whether in such circumstances any time appeared to be long or short? Does a dream appear to be long or to be short?

The vessel in which they sailed was a brigantine of good size and build, but manned by a considerable crew, the most strange and outlandish in their appearance that Barnaby had ever beheld—some white, some yellow, some black, and all tricked out with gay colors, and gold earrings in their ears, and some with great long mustachios, and others with handkerchiefs tied around their heads, and all talking a language together of which Barnaby True could understand not a single word, but which might have been Portuguese from one or two phrases he caught.

Nor did this strange, mysterious crew, of God knows what sort of men, seem to pay any attention whatever to Barnaby or to the young lady. They might now and then have looked at him and her out of the corners of their yellow eyes, but that was all; otherwise they were indeed like the creatures of a nightmare dream. Only he who was the captain of this outlandish crew would maybe speak to Barnaby a few words as to the weather or what not when he would come down into the saloon to mix a glass of grog or to light a pipe of tobacco, and then to go on deck again about his business. Otherwise our hero and the young lady were left to themselves, to do as they pleased, with no one to interfere with them.

As for her, she at no time showed any great sign of terror or of fear, only for a little while was singularly numb and quiet, as though dazed with what had happened to her. Indeed, methinks that wild beast, her grandfather, had so crushed her spirit by his tyranny and his violence that nothing that happened to her might seem sharp and keen, as it does to others of an ordinary sort.

But this was only at first, for afterward her face began to grow singularly clear, as with a white light, and she would sit quite still, permitting Barnaby to gaze, I know not how long, into her eyes, her face so transfigured and her lips smiling, and they, as it were, neither of them breathing, but hearing, as in another far-distant place, the outlandish jargon of the crew talking together in the warm, bright sunlight, or the sound of creaking block and tackle as they hauled upon the sheets.

Is it, then, any wonder that Barnaby True could never remember whether such a voyage as this was long or short?

It was as though they might have sailed so upon that wonderful voyage forever. You may guess how amazed was Barnaby True when, coming upon deck one morning, he found the brigantine riding upon an even keel, at anchor off Staten Island, a small village on the shore, and the well-known roofs and chimneys of New York town in plain sight across the water.

'Twas the last place in the world he had expected to see.

And, indeed, it did seem strange to lie there alongside Staten Island all that day, with New York town so nigh at hand and yet so impossible to reach. For whether he desired to escape or no, Barnaby True could not but observe that both he and the young lady were so closely watched that they might as well have been prisoners, tied hand and foot and laid in the hold, so far as any hope of getting away was concerned.

All that day there was a deal of mysterious coming and going aboard the brigantine, and in the afternoon a sailboat went up to the town, carrying the captain, and a great load covered over with a tarpaulin in the stern. What was so taken up to the town Barnaby did not then guess, but the boat did not return again till about sundown.

For the sun was just dropping below the water when the captain came aboard once more and, finding Barnaby on deck, bade him come down into the saloon, where they found the young lady sitting, the broad light of the evening shining in through the skylight, and making it all pretty bright within.

The captain commanded Barnaby to be seated, for he had something of moment to say to him; whereupon, as soon as Barnaby had taken his place alongside the young lady, he began very seriously, with a preface somewhat thus: "Though you may think me the captain of this brigantine, young gentleman, I am not really so, but am under orders, and so have only carried out those orders of a superior in all these things that I have done." Having so begun, he went on to say that there was one thing yet remaining for him to do, and that the greatest thing of all. He said that Barnaby and the young lady had not been fetched away from the *Belle Helen* as they were by any mere chance of accident, but that 'twas all a plan laid by a head wiser than his, and carried out by one whom he must obey in all things. He said that he hoped that both Barnaby and the young lady would perform willingly what they would be now called upon to do, but that whether they did it willingly, or no, they must, for that those were the orders of one who was not to be disobeyed.

You may guess how our hero held his breath at all this; but whatever might have been his expectations, the very wildest of them all did not reach to that which was demanded of him. "My orders are these," said the other, continuing: "I am to take you and the young lady ashore, and to see that you are married before I quit you; and to that end a very good, decent, honest minister who lives ashore yonder in the village was chosen and hath been spoken to and is now, no doubt, waiting for you to come. Such are my orders, and this is the last thing I am set to do; so now I will leave you alone together for five minutes to talk it over, but be quick about it, for whether willing or not, this thing must be done."

Thereupon he went away, as he had promised, leaving those two alone together, Barnaby like one turned into stone, and the young lady, her face turned away, flaming as red as fire in the fading light.

Nor can I tell what Barnaby said to her, nor what words he used, but only, all in a tumult, with neither beginning nor end he told her that God knew he loved her, and that with all his heart and soul, and that, there was nothing in all the world for him but her; but, nevertheless, if she would not have it as had been ordered, and if she were not willing to marry him as she was bidden to do, he would rather die than lend himself to forcing her to do such a thing against her will. Nevertheless, he told her she must speak up and tell him yes or no, and that God knew he would give all the world if she would say "yes."

All this and more he said in such a tumult of words that there was no order in their speaking, and she sitting there, her bosom rising and falling as though her breath stifled her. Nor may I tell what she replied to him, only this, that she said she would marry him. At this he took her into his arms and set his lips to hers, his heart all melting away in his bosom.

So presently came the captain back into the saloon again, to find Barnaby sitting there holding her hand, she with her face turned away, and his heart beating like a trip hammer, and so saw that all was settled as he would have it. Wherewith he wished them both joy, and gave Barnaby his hand.

The yawlboat belonging to the brigantine was ready and waiting alongside when they came upon deck, and immediately they descended to it and took their seats. So they landed, and in a little while were walking up the village street in the darkness, she clinging to his arm as though she would swoon, and the captain of the brigantine and two other men from aboard following after them. And so to the minister's house, finding him waiting for them, smoking his pipe in the warm evening, and walking up and down in front of his own door. He immediately conducted them into the house, where, his wife having fetched a candle, and two others of the village folk being present, the good man having asked several questions as to their names and their age and where they were from, the ceremony was performed, and the certificate duly signed by those present—excepting the men who had come ashore from the brigantine, and who refused to set their hands to any paper.

The same sailboat that had taken the captain up to the town in the afternoon was waiting for them at the landing place, whence, the captain, having wished them Godspeed, and having shaken Barnaby very heartily by the hand, they pushed off, and, coming about, ran away with the slant of the wind, dropping the shore and those strange beings alike behind them into the night.

As they sped away through the darkness they could hear the creaking of the sails being hoisted aboard of the brigantine, and so knew that she was about to put to sea once more. Nor did Barnaby True ever set eyes upon those beings again, nor did anyone else that I ever heard tell of.

It was nigh midnight when they made Mr. Hartright's wharf at the foot of Wall Street, and so the streets were all dark and silent and deserted as they walked up to Barnaby's home.

You may conceive of the wonder and amazement of Barnaby's dear stepfather when, clad in a dressing gown and carrying a lighted candle in his hand, he unlocked and unbarred the door, and so saw who it was had aroused him at such an hour of the night, and the young and beautiful lady whom Barnaby had fetched with him.

The first thought of the good man was that the *Belle Helen* had come into port; nor did Barnaby undeceive him as he led the way into the house, but waited until they were all safe and sound in privity together before he should unfold his strange and wonderful story.

"This was left for you by two foreign sailors this afternoon, Barnaby," the good old man said, as he led the way through the hall, holding up the candle at the same time, so that Barnaby might see an object that stood against the wainscoting by the door of the dining room.

Nor could Barnaby refrain from crying out with amazement when he saw that it was one of the two chests of treasure that Sir John Malyoe had fetched from Jamaica, and which the pirates had taken from the *Belle Helen.* As for Mr. Hartright, he guessed no more what was in it than the man in the moon.

The next day but one brought the *Belle Helen* herself into port, with the terrible news not only of having been attacked at night by pirates, but also that Sir John Malyoe was dead. For whether it was the sudden shock of the sight of his old captain's face—whom he himself had murdered and thought dead and buried—flashing so out against the darkness, or whether it was the strain of passion that overset his brains, certain it is that when the pirates left the *Belle Helen*, carrying with them the young lady and Barnaby and the traveling trunks, those left aboard the *Belle Helen* found Sir John Malyoe lying in a fit upon the floor, frothing at the mouth and black in the face, as though he had been choked, and so took him away to his berth, where, the next morning about ten o'clock, he died, without once having opened his eyes or spoken a single word.

As for the villain manservant, no one ever saw him afterward; though whether he jumped overboard, or whether the pirates who so attacked the ship had carried him away bodily, who shall say?

Mr. Hartright, after he had heard Barnaby's story, had been very uncertain as to the ownership of the chest of treasure that had been left by those men for Barnaby, but the news of the death of Sir John Malyoe made the matter very easy for him to decide. For surely if that treasure did not belong to Barnaby, there could be no doubt that it must belong to his wife, she being Sir John Malyoe's legal heir. And so it was that that great fortune (in actual computation amounting to upward of sixty-three thousand pounds) came to Barnaby True, the grandson of that famous pirate, William Brand; the English estate in Devonshire, in default of male issue of Sir John Malyoe, descended to Captain Malyoe, whom the young lady was to have married.

As for the other case of treasure, it was never heard of again, nor could Barnaby ever guess whether it was divided as booty among the pirates, or whether they had carried it away with them to some strange and foreign and, there to share it among themselves.

And so the ending of the story, with only this to observe, that whether that strange appearance of Captain Brand's face by the light of the pistol was a ghostly and spiritual appearance, or whether he was present in flesh and blood, there is only to say that he was never heard of again; nor had he ever been heard of till that time since the day he was so shot from behind by Capt. John Malyoe on the banks of the Rio Cobra River in the year 1733.

Captain Blood

RAFAEL SABATINI

The Trap

That affair of Mademoiselle d'Ogeron bore as its natural fruit an improvement in the already cordial relations between Captain Blood and the Governor of Tortuga. At the fine stone house, with its green-jalousied windows, which M. d'Ogeron had built himself in a spacious and luxuriant garden to the east of Cayona, the Captain became a very welcome guest. M. d'Ogeron was in the Captain's debt for more than the twenty thousand pieces of eight which he had provided for mademoiselle's ransom; and shrewd, hard bargain-driver though he might be, the Frenchman could be generous and understood the sentiment of gratitude. This he now proved in every possible way, and under his powerful protection the credit of Captain Blood among the buccaneers very rapidly reached its zenith.

So when it came to fitting out his fleet for that enterprise against Maracaybo, which had originally been Levasseur's project, he did not want for either ships or men to follow him. He recruited five hundred adventurers in all, and he might have had as many thousands if he could have offered them accommodation. Similarly without difficulty he might have increased his fleet to twice its strength of ships but that he preferred to keep it what it was. The three vessels to which he confined it were the *Arabella*, the *La Foudre*, which Cahusac now commanded with a contingent of some sixscore Frenchmen, and the *Santiago*, which had been refitted and rechristened the *Elizabeth*, after that Queen of England whose seamen had humbled Spain as Captain Blood now hoped to humble it again. Hagthorpe, in virtue of his service in the navy, was appointed by Blood to command her, and the appointment was confirmed by the men.

It was some months after the rescue of Mademoiselle d'Ogeron—in August of that year 1687—that this little fleet, after some minor adventures which I pass over in silence, sailed into the great lake of Maracaybo and effected its raid upon that opulent city of the Main.

The affair did not proceed exactly as was hoped, and Blood's force came to find itself in a precarious position. This is best explained in the words employed by Cahusac—which Pitt has carefully recorded—in the course of an altercation that broke out on the steps of the Church of Nuestra Señora del Carmen, which Captain Blood had impiously appropriated for the purpose of a corps-de-garde. I have said already that he was a papist only when it suited him.

The dispute was being conducted by Hagthorpe, Wolverstone, and Pitt on the one side, and Cahusac, out of whose uneasiness it all arose, on the other. Behind them in the sun-scorched, dusty square, sparsely fringed by palms, whose fronds drooped listlessly in the quivering heat, surged a couple of hundred wild fellows belonging to both parties, their own excitement momentarily quelled so that they might listen to what passed among their leaders.

Cahusac appeared to be having it all his own way, and he raised his harsh, querulous voice so that all might hear his truculent denunciation. He spoke, Pitt tells us, a dreadful kind of English, which the shipmaster, however, makes little attempt to reproduce. His dress was as discordant as his speech. It was of a kind to advertise his trade, and ludicrously in contrast with the sober garb of Hagthorpe and the almost foppish daintiness of Jeremy Pitt. His soiled and blood-stained shirt of blue cotton was open in front, to cool his hairy breast, and the girdle about the waist of his leather breeches carried an arsenal of pistols and a knife, whilst a cutlass hung from a leather baldrick loosely slung about his body; above his countenance, broad and flat as a Mongolian's, a red scarf was swathed, turban-wise, about his head.

"Is it that I have not warned you from the beginning that all was too easy?" he demanded between plaintiveness and fury. "I am no fool, my friends. I have eyes, me. And I see. I see an abandoned fort at the entrance of the lake, and nobody there to fire a gun at us when we came in. Then I suspect the trap. Who would not that had eyes and brain? Bah! we come on. What do we find? A city, abandoned like the fort; a city out of which the people have taken all things of value. Again I warn Captain Blood. It is a trap, I say. We are to come on; always to come on, without opposition, until we find that it is too late to go to sea again, that we cannot go back at all. But no one will listen to me. You all know so much more. Name of God! Captain Blood, he will go on, and we go on. We go to Gibraltar. True that at last, after long time, we catch the Deputy-Governor; true, we make him pay big ransom for Gibraltar; true between that ransom and the loot we return here with some two thousand pieces of eight. But what is it, in reality, will you tell me? Or shall I tell you? It is a piece of cheese—a piece of cheese in a mousetrap, and we are the little mice. Goddam! And the cats—oh, the cats they wait for us! The cats are those four Spanish ships of war that have come meantime. And they wait for us outside the bottle-neck of this lagoon. Mort de Dieu! That is what comes of the damned obstinacy of your fine Captain Blood."

Wolverstone laughed. Cahusac exploded in fury.

"Ah, sangdieu! Tu ris, animal? You laugh! Tell me this: How do we get out again unless we accept the terms of Monsieur the Admiral of Spain?"

From the buccaneers at the foot of the steps came an angry rumble of approval. The single eye of the gigantic Wolverstone rolled terribly, and he clenched his great fists as if to strike the Frenchman, who was exposing them to mutiny. But Cahusac was not daunted. The mood of the men en-heartened him.

"You think, perhaps, this your Captain Blood is the good God. That he can make miracles, eh? He is ridiculous, you know, this Captain Blood; with his grand air and his …"

He checked. Out of the church at that moment, grand air and all, sauntered Peter Blood. With him came a tough, long-legged French sea-wolf named Yberville, who, though still young, had already won fame as a privateer commander before the loss of his own ship had driven him to take service under Blood. The Captain advanced towards that disputing group, leaning lightly upon his long ebony cane, his face shaded by a broad-plumed hat. There was in his appearance nothing of the buccaneer. He had much more the air of a lounger in the Mall or the Alameda—the latter rather, since his elegant suit of violet taffetas with gold-embroidered button-holes was in the Spanish fashion. But the long, stout, serviceable rapier, thrust up behind by the left hand resting lightly on the pummel, corrected the impression. That and those steely eyes of his announced the adventurer.

"You find me ridiculous, eh, Cahusac?" said he, as he came to a halt before the Breton, whose anger seemed already to have gone out of him. "What, then, must I find you?" He spoke quietly, almost wearily. "You will be telling them that we have delayed, and that it is the delay that has brought about our danger. But whose is the fault of that delay? We have been a month in doing what should have been done, and what but for your blundering would have been done, inside of a week."

"Ah ça! Nom de Dieu! Was it my fault that …"

"Was it any one else's fault that you ran your ship *La Foudre* aground on the shoal in the middle of the lake? You would not be piloted. You knew your way. You took no soundings even. The result was that we lost three precious days in getting canoes to bring off your men and your gear. Those three days gave the folk at Gibraltar not only time to hear of our coming, but time in which to get away. After that, and because of it, we had to follow the Governor to his infernal island fortress, and a fortnight and best part of a hundred lives were lost in reducing it. That's how we come to have delayed until this Spanish fleet is fetched round from La Guayra by a guarda-costa; and if ye hadn't lost *La Foudre*, and so reduced our fleet from three ships to two, we should even now be able to fight our way through with a reasonable hope of succeeding. Yet you think it is for you to come hectoring here, upbraiding us for a situation that is just the result of your own ineptitude."

He spoke with a restraint which I trust you will agree was admirable when I tell you that the Spanish fleet guarding the bottle-neck exit of the great Lake of Maracaybo, and awaiting there the coming forth of Captain Blood with a calm confidence based upon its overwhelming strength, was commanded by his implacable enemy, Don Miguel de Espinosa y Valdez, the Admiral of Spain. In addition to his duty to his country, the Admiral had, as you know, a further personal incentive arising out of that business aboard the *Encarnacion* a year ago, and the death of his brother Don Diego; and with him sailed his nephew Esteban, whose vindictive zeal exceeded the Admiral's own.

Yet, knowing all this, Captain Blood could preserve his calm in reproving the cowardly frenzy of one for whom the situation had not half the peril with which it was fraught for himself. He turned from Cahusac to address the mob of buccaneers, who had surged nearer to hear him, for he had not troubled to raise his voice. "I hope that will correct some of the misapprehension that appears to have been disturbing you," said he.

"There's no good can come of talking of what's past and done," cried Cahusac, more sullen now than truculent. Whereupon Wolverstone laughed, a laugh that was like the neighing of a horse. "The question is: what are we to do now?"

"Sure, now, there's no question at all," said Captain Blood.

"Indeed, but there is," Cahusac insisted. "Don Miguel, the Spanish Admiral, have offer' us safe passage to sea if we will depart at once, do no damage to the town, release our prisoners, and surrender all that we took at Gibraltar."

Captain Blood smiled quietly, knowing precisely how much Don Miguel's word was worth. It was Yberville who replied, in manifest scorn of his compatriot:

"Which argues that, even at this disadvantage as he has us, the Spanish Admiral is still afraid of us."

"That can be only because he not know our real weakness," was the fierce retort. "And, anyway, we must accept these terms. We have no choice. That is my opinion."

"Well, it's not mine, now," said Captain Blood. "So, I've refused them."

"Refuse!" Cahusac's broad face grew purple. A muttering from the men behind enheartened him. "You have refuse'? You have refuse' already—and without consulting me?"

"Your disagreement could have altered nothing. You'd have been outvoted, for Hagthorpe here was entirely of my own mind. Still," he went on, "if you and your own French followers wish to avail yourselves of the Spaniard's terms, we shall not hinder you. Send one of your prisoners to announce it to the Admiral. Don Miguel will welcome your decision, you may be sure."

Cahusac glowered at him in silence for a moment. Then, having controlled himself, he asked in a concentrated voice:

"Precisely what answer have you make to the Admiral?"

A smile irradiated the face and eyes of Captain Blood.

"I have answered him that unless within four-and-twenty hours we have his parole to stand out to sea, ceasing to dispute our passage or hinder our departure, and a ransom of fifty thousand pieces of eight for Maracaybo, we shall reduce this beautiful city to ashes, and thereafter go out and destroy his fleet."

The impudence of it left Cahusac speechless. But among the English buccaneers in the square there were many who savoured the audacious humour of the trapped dictating terms to the trappers. Laughter broke from them. It spread into a roar of acclamation; for bluff is a weapon dear to every adventurer. Presently, when they understood it, even Cahusac's French followers were carried off their feet by that wave of jocular enthusiasm, until in his truculent obstinacy Cahusac remained the only dissentient. He withdrew in mortification. Nor was he to be mollified until the following day brought him his revenge. This came in the shape of a messenger from Don Miguel with a letter in which the Spanish Admiral solemnly vowed to God that, since the pirates had refused his magnanimous offer to permit them to surrender with the honours of war, he would now await them at the mouth of the lake there to destroy them on their coming forth. He added that should they delay their departure, he would so soon as he was reënforced by a fifth ship, the *Santo Niño*, on its way to join him from La Guayra, himself come inside to seek them at Maracaybo.

This time Captain Blood was put out of temper.

"Trouble me no more," he snapped at Cahusac, who came growling to him again. "Send word to Don Miguel that you have seceded from me. He'll give you safe conduct, devil a doubt. Then take one of the sloops, order your men aboard and put to sea, and the devil go with you."

Cahusac would certainly have adopted that course if only his men had been unanimous in the matter. They, however, were torn between greed and apprehension. If they went they must abandon their share of the plunder, which was considerable, as well as the slaves and other prisoners they had taken. If they did this, and Captain Blood should afterwards contrive to get away unscathed—and from their knowledge of his resourcefulness, the thing, however unlikely, need not be impossible—he must profit by that which they now relinquished. This was a contingency too bitter for contemplation. And so, in the end, despite all that Cahusac could say, the surrender was not to Don Miguel, but to Peter Blood. They had come into the venture with him, they asserted, and they would go out of it with him or not at all. That was the message he received from them that same evening by the sullen mouth of Cahusac himself.

He welcomed it, and invited the Breton to sit down and join the council which was even then deliberating upon the means to be employed. This council occupied the spacious patio of the Governor's house—which Captain Blood had appropriated to his own uses—a cloistered stone quadrangle in the middle of which a fountain played coolly under a trellis of vine. Orange-trees grew on two sides of it, and the still, evening air was heavy with the scent of them. It was one of those pleasant exterior-interiors which Moorish architects had introduced to Spain and the Spaniards had carried with them to the New World.

Here that council of war, composed of six men in all, deliberated until late that night upon the plan of action which Captain Blood put forward.

The great freshwater lake of Maracaybo, nourished by a score of rivers from the snow-capped ranges that surround it on two sides, is some hundred and twenty miles in length and almost the same distance across at its widest. It is—as has been indicated—in the shape of a great bottle having its neck towards the sea at Maracaybo.

Beyond this neck it widens again, and then the two long, narrow strips of land known as the islands of Vigilias and Palomas block the channel, standing lengthwise across it. The only passage out to sea for vessels of any draught lies in the narrow strait between these islands. Palomas, which is some ten miles in length, is unapproachable for half a mile on either side by any but the shallowest craft save at its eastern end, where, completely commanding the narrow passage out to sea, stands the massive fort which the buccaneers had found deserted upon their coming. In the broader water between this passage and the bar, the four Spanish ships were at anchor in mid-channel. The Admiral's *Encarnacion*, which we already know, was a mighty galleon of forty-eight great guns and eight small. Next in importance was the *Salvador* with thirty-six guns; the other two, the *Infanta* and the *San Felipe*, though smaller vessels, were still formidable enough with their twenty guns and a hundred and fifty men apiece.

Such was the fleet of which the gauntlet was to be run by Captain Blood with his own *Arabella* of forty guns, the *Elizabeth* of twenty-six, and two sloops captured at Gibraltar, which they had indifferently armed with four culverins each. In men they had a bare four hundred survivors of the five hundred-odd that had left Tortuga, to oppose to fully a thousand Spaniards manning the galleons.

The plan of action submitted by Captain Blood to that council was a desperate one, as Cahusac uncompromisingly pronounced it.

"Why, so it is," said the Captain. "But I've done things more desperate." Complacently he pulled at a pipe that was loaded with that fragrant Sacerdotes tobacco for which Gibraltar was famous, and of which they had brought away some hogsheads. "And what is more, they've succeeded. Audaces fortuna juvat. Bedad, they knew their world, the old Romans."

He breathed into his companions and even into Cahusac some of his own spirit of confidence, and in confidence all went busily to work. For three days from sunrise to sunset, the buccaneers laboured and sweated to complete the preparations for the action that was to procure them their deliverance. Time pressed. They must strike before Don Miguel de Espinosa received the reënforcement of that fifth galleon, the *Santo Niño*, which was coming to join him from La Guayra.

Their principal operations were on the larger of the two sloops captured at Gibraltar; to which vessel was assigned the leading part in Captain Blood's scheme. They began by tearing down all bulkheads, until they had reduced her to the merest shell, and in her sides they broke open so many ports that her gunwale was converted into the semblance of a grating. Next they increased by a half-dozen the scuttles in her deck, whilst into her hull they packed all the tar and pitch and brimstone that they could find in the town, to which they added six barrels of gunpowder, placed on end like guns at the open ports on her larboard side.

On the evening of the fourth day, everything being now in readiness, all were got aboard, and the empty, pleasant city of Maracaybo was at last abandoned. But they did not weigh anchor until some two hours after midnight. Then, at last, on the first of the ebb, they drifted silently down towards the bar with all canvas furled save only their spritsails, which, so as to give them steering way, were spread to the faint breeze that stirred through the purple darkness of the tropical night.

The order of their going was as follows: Ahead went the improvised fire-ship in charge of Wolverstone, with a crew of six volunteers, each of whom was to have a hundred pieces of eight over and above his share of plunder as a special reward. Next came the *Arabella*. She was followed at a distance by the *Elizabeth*, commanded by Hagthorpe, with whom was the now shipless Cahusac and the bulk of his French followers. The rear was brought up by the second sloop and some eight canoes, aboard of which had been shipped the prisoners, the slaves, and most of the captured merchandise. The prisoners were all pinioned, and guarded by four buccaneers with musketoons who manned these boats in addition to the two fellows who were to sail them. Their place was to be in the rear and they were to take no part whatever in the coming fight.

As the first glimmerings of opalescent dawn dissolved the darkness, the straining eyes of the buccaneers were able to make out the tall rigging of the Spanish vessels, riding at anchor less than a quarter of a mile ahead. Entirely without suspicion as the Spaniards were, and rendered confident by their own overwhelming strength, it is unlikely that they used a vigilance keener than their careless habit. Certain it is that they did not sight Blood's fleet in that dim light until some time after Blood's fleet had sighted them. By the time that they had actively roused themselves, Wolverstone's sloop was almost upon them, speeding under canvas which had been crowded to her yards the moment the galleons had loomed into view.

Straight for the Admiral's great ship, the *Encarnacion*, did Wolverstone head the sloop; then, lashing down the helm, he kindled from a match that hung ready lighted beside him a great torch of thickly plaited straw that had been steeped in bitumen. First it glowed, then as he swung it round his head, it burst into flame, just as the slight vessel went crashing and bumping and scraping against the side of the flagship, whilst rigging became tangled with rigging, to the straining of yards and snapping of spars overhead. His six men stood at their posts on the larboard side, stark naked, each armed with a grapnel, four of them on the gunwale, two of them aloft. At the moment of impact these grapnels were slung to bind the Spaniard to them, those aloft being intended to complete and preserve the entanglement of the rigging.

Aboard the rudely awakened galleon all was confused hurrying, scurrying, trumpeting, and shouting. At first there had been a desperately hurried attempt to get up the anchor; but this was abandoned as being already too late; and conceiving themselves on the point of being boarded, the Spaniards stood to arms to ward off the onslaught. Its slowness in coming intrigued them, being so different from the usual tactics of the buccaneers. Further intrigued were they by the sight of the gigantic Wolverstone speeding naked along his deck with a great flaming torch held high. Not until he had completed his work did they begin to suspect the truth—that he was lighting slow-matches—and then one of their officers rendered reckless by panic ordered a boarding-party on to the sloop.

The order came too late. Wolverstone had seen his six fellows drop overboard after the grapnels were fixed, and then had sped, himself, to the starboard gunwale. Thence he flung his flaming torch down the nearest gaping scuttle into the hold, and thereupon dived overboard in his turn, to be picked up presently by the longboat from the *Arabella*. But before that happened the sloop was a thing of fire, from which explosions were hurling blazing combustibles aboard the *Encarnacion*, and long tongues of flame were licking out to consume the galleon, beating back those daring Spaniards who, too late, strove desperately to cut her adrift.

And whilst the most formidable vessel of the Spanish fleet was thus being put out of action at the outset, Blood had sailed in to open fire upon the *Salvador*. First athwart her hawse he had loosed a broadside that had swept her decks with terrific effect, then going on and about, he had put a second broadside into her hull at short range. Leaving her thus half-crippled, temporarily, at least, and keeping to his course, he had bewildered the crew of the *Infanta* by a couple of shots from the chasers on his beak-head, then crashed alongside to grapple and board her, whilst Hagthorpe was doing the like by the *San Felipe*.

And in all this time not a single shot had the Spaniards contrived to fire, so completely had they been taken by surprise, and so swift and paralyzing had been Blood's stroke.

Boarded now and faced by the cold steel of the buccaneers, neither the *San Felipe* nor the *Infanta* offered much resistance. The sight of their admiral in flames, and the *Salvador* drifting crippled from the action, had so utterly disheartened them that they accounted themselves vanquished, and laid down their arms.

If by a resolute stand the *Salvador* had encouraged the other two undamaged vessels to resistance, the Spaniards might well have retrieved the fortunes of the day. But it happened that the *Salvador* was handicapped in true Spanish fashion by being the treasure-ship of the fleet, with plate on board to the value of some fifty thousand pieces. Intent above all upon saving this from falling into the hands of the pirates, Don Miguel, who, with a remnant of his crew, had meanwhile transferred himself aboard her, headed her down towards Palomas and the fort that guarded the passage. This fort the Admiral, in those days of waiting, had taken the precaution secretly to garrison and rearm. For the purpose he had stripped the fort of Cojero, farther out on the gulf, of its entire armament, which included some cannon-royal of more than ordinary range and power.

With no suspicion of this, Captain Blood gave chase, accompanied by the *Infanta*, which was manned now by a prize-crew under the command of Yberville. The stern chasers of the *Salvador* desultorily returned the punishing fire of the pursuers; but such was the damage she, herself, sustained, that presently, coming under the guns of the fort, she began to sink, and finally settled down in the shallows with part of her hull above water. Thence, some in boats and some by swimming, the Admiral got his crew ashore on Palomas as best he could.

And then, just as Captain Blood accounted the victory won, and that his way out of that trap to the open sea beyond lay clear, the fort suddenly revealed its formidable and utterly unsuspected strength. With a roar the cannons-royal proclaimed themselves, and the *Arabella* staggered under a blow that smashed her bulwarks at the waist and scattered death and confusion among the seamen gathered there.

Had not Pitt, her master, himself seized the whipstaff and put the helm hard over to swing her sharply off to starboard, she must have suffered still worse from the second volley that followed fast upon the first.

Meanwhile it had fared even worse with the frailer *Infanta*. Although hit by one shot only, this had crushed her larboard timbers on the waterline, starting a leak that must presently have filled her, but for the prompt action of the experienced Yberville in ordering her larboard guns to be flung overboard. Thus lightened, and listing now to starboard, he fetched her about, and went staggering after the retreating *Arabella*, followed by the fire of the fort, which did them, however, little further damage.

Out of range, at last, they lay to, joined by the *Elizabeth* and the *San Felipe*, to consider their position.

The Dupes

It was a crestfallen Captain Blood who presided over that hastily summoned council held on the poop-deck of the *Arabella* in the brilliant morning sunshine. It was, he declared afterwards, one of the bitterest moments in his career. He was compelled to digest the fact that having conducted the engagement with a skill of which he might justly be proud, having destroyed a force so superior in ships and guns and men that Don Miguel de Espinosa had justifiably deemed it overwhelming, his victory was rendered barren by three lucky shots from an unsuspected battery by which they had been surprised. And barren must their victory remain until they could reduce the fort that still remained to defend the passage.

At first Captain Blood was for putting his ships in order and making the attempt there and then. But the others dissuaded him from betraying an impetuosity usually foreign to him, and born entirely of chagrin and mortification, emotions which will render unreasonable the most reasonable of men. With returning calm, he surveyed the situation. The *Arabella* was no longer in case to put to sea; the *Infanta* was merely kept afloat by artifice, and the *San Felipe* was almost as sorely damaged by the fire she had sustained from the buccaneers before surrendering.

Clearly, then, he was compelled to admit in the end that nothing remained but to return to Maracaybo, there to refit the ships before attempting to force the passage.

And so, back to Maracaybo came those defeated victors of that short, terrible fight. And if anything had been wanting further to exasperate their leader, he had it in the pessimism of which Cahusac did not economize expressions. Transported at first to heights of dizzy satisfaction by the swift and easy victory of their inferior force that morning, the Frenchman was now plunged back and more deeply than ever into the abyss of hopelessness. And his mood infected at least the main body of his own followers.

"It is the end," he told Captain Blood. "This time we are checkmated."

"I'll take the liberty of reminding you that you said the same before," Captain Blood answered him as patiently as he could. "Yet you've seen what you've seen, and you'll not deny that in ships and guns we are returning stronger than we went. Look at our present fleet, man."

"I am looking at it," said Cahusac.

"Pish! Ye're a white-livered cur when all is said."

"You call me a coward?"

"I'll take that liberty."

The Breton glared at him, breathing hard. But he had no mind to ask satisfaction for the insult. He knew too well the kind of satisfaction that Captain Blood was likely to afford him. He remembered the fate of Levasseur. So he confined himself to words.

"It is too much! You go too far!" he complained bitterly.

"Look you, Cahusac: it's sick and tired I am of your perpetual whining and complaining when things are not as smooth as a convent dining-table. If ye wanted things smooth and easy, ye shouldn't have taken to the sea, and ye should never ha' sailed with me, for with me things are never smooth and easy. And that, I think, is all I have to say to you this morning."

Cahusac flung away cursing, and went to take the feeling of his men.

Captain Blood went off to give his surgeon's skill to the wounded, among whom he remained engaged until late afternoon. Then, at last, he went ashore, his mind made up, and returned to the house of the Governor, to indite a truculent but very scholarly letter in purest Castilian to Don Miguel.

"I have shown your excellency this morning of what I am capable," he wrote. "Although outnumbered by more than two to one in men, in ships, and in guns, I have sunk or captured the vessels of the great fleet with which you were to come to Maracaybo to destroy us. So that you are no longer in case to carry out your boast, even when your reënforcements on the *Santo Niño*, reach you from La Guayra. From what has occurred, you may judge of what must occur. I should not trouble your excellency with this letter but that I am a humane man, abhorring bloodshed. Therefore before proceeding to deal with your fort, which you may deem invincible, as I have dealt already with your fleet, which you deemed invincible, I make you, purely out of humanitarian considerations, this last offer of terms. I will spare this city of Maracaybo and forthwith evacuate it, leaving behind me the forty prisoners I have taken, in consideration of your paying me the sum of fifty thousand pieces of eight and one hundred head of cattle as a ransom, thereafter granting me unmolested passage of the bar. My prisoners, most of whom are persons of consideration, I will retain as hostages until after my departure, sending them back in the canoes which we shall take with us for that purpose. If your excellency should be so ill-advised as to refuse these terms, and thereby impose upon me the necessity of reducing your fort at the cost of some lives, I warn you that you may expect no quarter from us, and that I shall begin by leaving a heap of ashes where this pleasant city of Maracaybo now stands."

The letter written, he bade them bring him from among the prisoners the Deputy-Governor of Maracaybo, who had been taken at Gibraltar. Disclosing its contents to him, he despatched him with it to Don Miguel.

His choice of a messenger was shrewd. The Deputy-Governor was of all men the most anxious for the deliverance of his city, the one man who on his own account would plead most fervently for its preservation at all costs from the fate with which Captain Blood was threatening it.

And as he reckoned so it befell. The Deputy-Governor added his own passionate pleading to the proposals of the letter.

But Don Miguel was of stouter heart. True, his fleet had been partly destroyed and partly captured. But then, he argued, he had been taken utterly by surprise. That should not happen again. There should be no surprising the fort, Let Captain Blood do his worst at Maracaybo, there should be a bitter reckoning for him when eventually he decided—as, sooner or later, decide he must—to come forth.

The Deputy-Governor was flung into panic. He lost his temper, and said some hard things to the Admiral. But they were not as hard as the thing the Admiral said to him in answer.

"Had you been as loyal to your King in hindering the entrance of these cursed pirates as I shall be in hindering their going forth again, we should not now find ourselves in our present straits. So weary me no more with your coward counsels. I make no terms with Captain Blood. I know my duty to my King, and I intend to perform it. I also know my duty to myself. I have a private score with this rascal, and I intend to settle it. Take you that message back."

So back to Maracaybo, back to his own handsome house in which Captain Blood had established his quarters, came the Deputy-Governor with the Admiral's answer. And because he had been shamed into a show of spirit by the Admiral's own stout courage in adversity, he delivered it as truculently as the Admiral could have desired.

"And is it like that?" said Captain Blood with a quiet smile, though the heart of him sank at this failure of his bluster. "Well, well, it's a pity now that the Admiral's so headstrong. It was that way he lost his fleet, which was his own to lose. This pleasant city of Maracaybo isn't. So no doubt he'll lose it with fewer misgivings. I am sorry. Waste, like bloodshed, is a thing abhorrent to me. But there ye are! I'll have the faggots to the place in the morning, and maybe when he sees the blaze to-morrow night he'll begin to believe that Peter Blood is a man of his word. Ye may go, Don Francisco."

The Deputy-Governor went out with dragging feet, followed by guards, his momentary truculence utterly spent.

But no sooner had he departed than up leapt Cahusac, who had been of the council assembled to receive the Admiral's answer. His face was white and his hands shook as he held them out in protest.

"Death of my life, what have you to say now?" he cried, his voice husky. And without waiting to hear what it might be, he raved on: "I knew you not frighten the Admiral so easy. He hold us entrap', and he knows it; yet you dream that he will yield himself to your impudent message. Your fool letter it have seal' the doom of us all."

"Have ye done?" quoth Blood quietly, as the Frenchman paused for breath.

"No, I have not."

"Then spare me the rest. It'll be of the same quality, devil a doubt, and it does n't help us to solve the riddle that's before us."

"But what are you going to do? Is it that you will tell me?" It was not a question, it was a demand.

"How the devil do I know? I was hoping you'd have some ideas yourself. But since ye're so desperately concerned to save your skin, you and those that think like you are welcome to leave us. I've no doubt at all the Spanish Admiral will welcome the abatement of our numbers even at this late date. Ye shall have the sloop as a parting gift from us, and ye can join Don Miguel in the fort for all I care, or for all the good ye're likely to be to us in this present pass."

"It is to my men to decide," Cahusac retorted, swallowing his fury, and on that stalked out to talk to them, leaving the others to deliberate in peace.

Next morning early he sought Captain Blood again. He found him alone in the patio, pacing to and fro, his head sunk on his breast. Cahusac mistook consideration for dejection. Each of us carries in himself a standard by which to measure his neighbour.

"We have take' you at your word, Captain," he announced, between sullenness and defiance. Captain Blood paused, shoulders hunched, hands behind his back, and mildly regarded the buccaneer in silence. Cahusac explained himself. "Last night I send one of my men to the Spanish Admiral with a letter. I make him offer to capitulate if he will accord us passage with the honours of war. This morning I receive his answer. He accord us this on the understanding that we carry nothing away with us. My men they are embarking them on the sloop. We sail at once."

"Bon voyage," said Captain Blood, and with a nod he turned on his heel again to resume his interrupted meditation.

"Is that all that you have to say to me?" cried Cahusac.

"There are other things," said Blood over his shoulder. "But I know ye would n't like them."

"Ha! Then it's adieu, my Captain." Venomously he added: "It is my belief that we shall not meet again."

"Your belief is my hope," said Captain Blood.

Cahusac flung away, obscenely vituperative. Before noon he was under way with his followers, some sixty dejected men who had allowed themselves to be persuaded by him into that empty-handed departure—in spite even of all that Yberville could do to prevent it. The Admiral kept faith with him, and allowed him free passage out to sea, which, from his knowledge of Spaniards, was more than Captain Blood had expected.

Meanwhile, no sooner had the deserters weighed anchor than Captain Blood received word that the Deputy-Governor begged to be allowed to see him again. Admitted, Don Francisco at once displayed the fact that a night's reflection had quickened his apprehensions for the city of Maracaybo and his condemnation of the Admiral's intransigence.

Captain Blood received him pleasantly.

"Good-morning to you, Don Francisco. I have postponed the bonfire until nightfall. It will make a better show in the dark."

Don Francisco, a slight, nervous, elderly man of high lineage and low vitality, came straight to business.

"I am here to tell you, Don Pedro, that if you will hold your hand for three days, I will undertake to raise the ransom you demand, which Don Miguel de Espinosa refuses."

Captain Blood confronted him, a frown contracting the dark brows above his light eyes:

"And where will you be raising it?" quoth he, faintly betraying his surprise.

Don Francisco shook his head. "That must remain my affair," he answered. "I know where it is to be found, and my compatriots must contribute. Give me leave for three days on parole, and I will see you fully satisfied. Meanwhile my son remains in your hands as a hostage for my return." And upon that he fell to pleading. But in this he was crisply interrupted.

"By the Saints! Ye're a bold man, Don Francisco, to come to me with such a tale—to tell me that ye know where the ransom's to be raised, and yet to refuse to say. D'ye think now that with a match between your fingers ye'd grow more communicative?"

If Don Francisco grew a shade paler, yet again he shook his head.

"That was the way of Morgan and L'Ollonais and other pirates. But it is not the way of Captain Blood. If I had doubted that I should not have disclosed so much."

The Captain laughed. "You old rogue," said he. "Ye play upon my vanity, do you?"

"Upon your honour, Captain."

"The honour of a pirate? Ye're surely crazed!"

"The honour of Captain Blood," Don Francisco insisted. "You have the repute of making war like a gentleman."

Captain Blood laughed again, on a bitter, sneering note that made Don Francisco fear the worst. He was not to guess that it was himself the Captain mocked.

"That's merely because it's more remunerative in the end. And that is why you are accorded the three days you ask for. So about it, Don Francisco. You shall have what mules you need. I'll see to it."

Away went Don Francisco on his errand, leaving Captain Blood to reflect, between bitterness and satisfaction, that a reputation for as much chivalry as is consistent with piracy is not without its uses.

Punctually on the third day the Deputy-Governor was back in Maracaybo with his mules laden with plate and money to the value demanded and a herd of a hundred head of cattle driven in by negro slaves.

These bullocks were handed over to those of the company who ordinarily were boucan-hunters, and therefore skilled in the curing of meats, and for best part of a week thereafter they were busy at the waterside with the quartering and salting of carcases.

While this was doing on the one hand and the ships were being refitted for sea on the other, Captain Blood was pondering the riddle on the solution of which his own fate depended. Indian spies whom he employed brought him word that the Spaniards, working at low tide, had salved the thirty guns of the *Salvador*, and thus had added yet another battery to their already overwhelming strength. In the end, and hoping for inspiration on the spot, Captain Blood made a reconnaissance in person. At the risk of his life, accompanied by two friendly Indians, he crossed to the island in a canoe under cover of dark. They concealed themselves and the canoe in the short thick scrub with which that side of the island was densely covered, and lay there until daybreak. Then Blood went forward alone, and with infinite precaution, to make his survey. He went to verify a suspicion that he had formed, and approached the fort as nearly as he dared and a deal nearer than was safe.

On all fours he crawled to the summit of an eminence a mile or so away, whence he found himself commanding a view of the interior dispositions of the stronghold. By the aid of a telescope with which he had equipped himself he was able to verify that, as he had suspected and hoped, the fort's artillery was all mounted on the seaward side.

Satisfied, he returned to Maracaybo, and laid before the six who composed his council—Pitt, Hagthorpe, Yberville, Wolverstone, Dyke, and Ogle—a proposal to storm the fort from the landward side. Crossing to the island under cover of night, they would take the Spaniards by surprise and attempt to overpower them before they could shift their guns to meet the onslaught.

With the exception of Wolverstone, who was by temperament the kind of man who favours desperate chances, those officers received the proposal coldly. Hagthorpe incontinently opposed it.

"It's a harebrained scheme, Peter," he said gravely, shaking his handsome head. "Consider now that we cannot depend upon approaching unperceived to a distance whence we might storm the fort before the cannon could be moved. But even if we could, we can take no cannon ourselves; we must depend entirely upon our small arms, and how shall we, a bare three hundred" (for this was the number to which Cahusac's defection had reduced them), "cross the open to attack more than twice that number under cover?"

The others—Dyke, Ogle, Yberville, and even Pitt, whom loyalty to Blood may have made reluctant—loudly approved him. When they had done, "I have considered all," said Captain Blood. "I have weighed the risks and studied how to lessen them. In these desperate straits ..."

He broke off abruptly. A moment he frowned, deep in thought; then his face was suddenly alight with inspiration. Slowly he drooped his head, and sat there considering, weighing, chin on breast. Then he nodded, muttering, "Yes," and again, "Yes." He looked up, to face them. "Listen," he cried. "You may be right. The risks may be too heavy. Whether or not, I have thought of a better way. That which should have been the real attack shall be no more than a feint. Here, then, is the plan I now propose."

He talked swiftly and clearly, and as he talked one by one his officers' faces became alight with eagerness. When he had done, they cried as with one voice that he had saved them.

"That is yet to be proved in action," said he.

Since for the last twenty-four hours all had been in readiness for departure, there was nothing now to delay them, and it was decided to move next morning.

Such was Captain Blood's assurance of success that he immediately freed the prisoners held as hostages, and even the negro slaves, who were regarded by the others as legitimate plunder. His only precaution against those released prisoners was to order them into the church and there lock them up, to await deliverance at the hands of those who should presently be coming into the city.

Then, all being aboard the three ships, with the treasure safely stowed in their holds and the slaves under hatches, the buccaneers weighed anchor and stood out for the bar, each vessel towing three piraguas astern.

The Admiral, beholding their stately advance in the full light of noon, their sails gleaming white in the glare of the sunlight, rubbed his long, lean hands in satisfaction, and laughed through his teeth.

"At last!" he cried. "God delivers him into my hands!" He turned to the group of staring officers behind him. "Sooner or later it had to be," he said. "Say now, gentlemen, whether I am justified of my patience. Here end to-day the troubles caused to the subjects of the Catholic King by this infamous Don Pedro Sangre, as he once called himself to me."

He turned to issue orders, and the fort became lively as a hive. The guns were manned, the gunners already kindling fuses, when the buccaneer fleet, whilst still heading for Palomas, was observed to bear away to the west. The Spaniards watched them, intrigued.

Within a mile and a half to westward of the fort, and within a half-mile of the shore—that is to say, on the very edge of the shoal water that makes Palomas unapproachable on either side by any but vessels of the shallowest draught—the four ships cast anchor well within the Spaniards' view, but just out of range of their heaviest cannon.

Sneeringly the Admiral laughed.

"Aha! They hesitate, these English dogs! Por Dios, and well they may."

"They will be waiting for night," suggested his nephew, who stood at his elbow quivering with excitement.

Don Miguel looked at him, smiling. "And what shall the night avail them in this narrow passage, under the very muzzles of my guns? Be sure, Esteban, that to-night your father will be paid for."

He raised his telescope to continue his observation of the buccaneers. He saw that the piraguas towed by each vessel were being warped alongside, and he wondered a little what this manœuvre might portend. Awhile those piraguas were hidden from view behind the hulls. Then one by one they reappeared, rowing round and away from the ships, and each boat, he observed, was crowded with armed men. Thus laden, they were headed for the shore, at a point where it was densely wooded to the water's edge. The eyes of the wondering Admiral followed them until the foliage screened them from his view.

Then he lowered his telescope and looked at his officers.

"What the devil does it mean?" he asked.

None answered him, all being as puzzled as he was himself.

After a little while, Esteban, who kept his eyes on the water, plucked at his uncle's sleeve. "There they go!" he cried, and pointed.

And there, indeed, went the piraguas on their way back to the ships. But now it was observed that they were empty, save for the men who rowed them. Their armed cargo had been left ashore.

Back to the ships they pulled, to return again presently with a fresh load of armed men, which similarly they conveyed to Palomas. And at last one of the Spanish officers ventured an explanation:

"They are going to attack us by land—to attempt to storm the fort."

"Of course." The Admiral smiled. "I had guessed it. Whom the gods would destroy they first make mad."

"Shall we make a sally?" urged Esteban, in his excitement.

"A sally? Through that scrub? That would be to play into their hands. No, no, we will wait here to receive this attack. Whenever it comes, it is themselves will be destroyed, and utterly. Have no doubt of that."

But by evening the Admiral's equanimity was not quite so perfect. By then the piraguas had made a half-dozen journeys with their loads of men, and they had landed also—as Don Miguel had clearly observed through his telescope—at least a dozen guns.

His countenance no longer smiled; it was a little wrathful and a little troubled now as he turned again to his officers.

"Who was the fool who told me that they number but three hundred men in all? They have put at least twice that number ashore already."

Amazed as he was, his amazement would have been deeper had he been told the truth: that there was not a single buccaneer or a single gun ashore on Palomas. The deception had been complete. Don Miguel could not guess that the men he had beheld in those piraguas were always the same; that on the journeys to the shore they sat and stood upright in full view; and that on the journeys back to the ships, they lay invisible at the bottom of the boats, which were thus made to appear empty.

The growing fears of the Spanish soldiery at the prospect of a night attack from the landward side by the entire buccaneer force—and a force twice as strong as they had suspected the pestilent Blood to command—began to be communicated to the Admiral.

In the last hours of fading daylight, the Spaniards did precisely what Captain Blood so confidently counted that they would do—precisely what they must do to meet the attack, preparations for which had been so thoroughly simulated. They set themselves to labour like the damned at those ponderous guns emplaced to command the narrow passage out to sea.

Groaning and sweating, urged on by the curses and even the whips of their officers, they toiled in a frenzy of panic-stricken haste to shift the greater number and the more powerful of their guns across to the landward side, there to emplace them anew, so that they might be ready to receive the attack which at any moment now might burst upon them from the woods not half a mile away.

Thus, when night fell, although in mortal anxiety of the onslaught of those wild devils whose reckless courage was a byword on the seas of the Main, at least the Spaniards were tolerably prepared for it. Waiting, they stood to their guns.

And whilst they waited thus, under cover of the darkness and as the tide began to ebb, Captain Blood's fleet weighed anchor quietly; and, as once before, with no more canvas spread than that which their sprits could carry, so as to give them steering way—and even these having been painted black—the four vessels, without a light showing, groped their way by soundings to the channel which led to that narrow passage out to sea.

The *Elizabeth* and the *Infanta*, leading side by side, were almost abreast of the fort before their shadowy bulks and the soft gurgle of water at their prows were detected by the Spaniards, whose attention until that moment had been all on the other side. And now there arose on the night air such a sound of human baffled fury as may have resounded about Babel at the confusion of tongues. To heighten that confusion, and to scatter disorder among the Spanish soldiery, the *Elizabeth* emptied her larboard guns into the fort as she was swept past on the swift ebb.

At once realizing—though not yet how—he had been duped, and that his prey was in the very act of escaping after all, the Admiral frantically ordered the guns that had been so laboriously moved to be dragged back to their former emplacements, and commanded his gunners meanwhile to the slender batteries that of all his powerful, but now unavailable, armament still remained trained upon the channel. With these, after the loss of some precious moments, the fort at last made fire.

It was answered by a terrific broadside from the *Arabella*, which had now drawn abreast, and was crowding canvas to her yards. The enraged and gibbering Spaniards had a brief vision of her as the line of flame spurted from her red flank, and the thunder of her broadside drowned the noise of the creaking halyards. After that they saw her no more. Assimilated by the friendly darkness which the lesser Spanish guns were speculatively stabbing, the escaping ships fired never another shot that might assist their baffled and bewildered enemies to locate them.

Some slight damage was sustained by Blood's fleet. But by the time the Spaniards had resolved their confusion into some order of dangerous offence, that fleet, well served by a southerly breeze, was through the narrows and standing out to sea.

Thus was Don Miguel de Espinosa left to chew the bitter cud of a lost opportunity, and to consider in what terms he would acquaint the Supreme Council of the Catholic King that Peter Blood had got away from Maracaybo, taking with him two twenty-gun frigates that were lately the property of Spain, to say nothing of two hundred and fifty thousand pieces of eight and other plunder. And all this in spite of Don Miguel's four galleons and his heavily armed fort that at one time had held the pirates so securely trapped.

Heavy, indeed, grew the account of Peter Blood, which Don Miguel swore passionately to Heaven should at all costs to himself be paid in full.

Nor were the losses already detailed the full total of those suffered on this occasion by the King of Spain. For on the following evening, off the coast of Oruba, at the mouth of the Gulf of Venezuela, Captain Blood's fleet came upon the belated *Santo Niño*, speeding under full sail to reënforce Don Miguel at Maracaybo.

At first the Spaniard had conceived that she was meeting the victorious fleet of Don Miguel, returning from the destruction of the pirates. When at comparatively close quarters the pennon of St. George soared to the *Arabella's* masthead to disillusion her, the *Santo Niño* chose the better part of valour, and struck her flag.

Captain Blood ordered her crew to take to the boats, and land themselves at Oruba or wherever else they pleased. So considerate was he that to assist them he presented them with several of the piraguas which he still had in tow.

"You will find," said he to her captain, "that Don Miguel is in an extremely bad temper. Commend me to him, and say that I venture to remind him that he must blame himself for all the ills that have befallen him. The evil has recoiled upon him which he loosed when he sent his brother unofficially to make a raid upon the island of Barbados. Bid him think twice before he lets his devils loose upon an English settlement again."

With that he dismissed the Captain, who went over the side of the *Santo Niño*, and Captain Blood proceeded to investigate the value of this further prize. When her hatches were removed, a human cargo was disclosed in her hold.

"Slaves," said Wolverstone, and persisted in that belief, cursing Spanish devilry until Cahusac crawled up out of the dark bowels of the ship, and stood blinking in the sunlight.

There was more than sunlight to make the Breton pirate blink. And those that crawled out after him—the remnants of his crew—cursed him horribly for the pusillanimity which had brought them into the ignominy of owing their deliverance to those whom they had deserted as lost beyond hope.

Their sloop had encountered and had been sunk three days ago by the *Santo Niño*, and Cahusac had narrowly escaped hanging merely that for some time he might be a mock among the Brethren of the Coast.

For many a month thereafter he was to hear in Tortuga the jeering taunt:

"Where do you spend the gold that you brought back from Maracaybo?"

The Pyrates Attack

GEORGE MACDONALD FRASER

Silence … as the *Twelve Apostles* glides on over the dark green sea bounded by distant banks of thin sea-mist. The moon is down, the sky a dark arch overhead, eastward there is still no shimmer of dawn. Upstairs the ship is deserted, save for the yawning lubber propped against the wheel, and the look-out in the crow's-nest who has finished *Moll Flanders* and is frowning over the cross-word in the *South Sea Waggoner*. One across, 'What ships usually sail on', three letters. Rum? Bog? He peeps down to see what the *Twelve Apostles* is floating on at the moment. Water? Too many letters. He sighs; another bloody anagram, probably … what kind of nut thinks these things up?

Below, the crew packed tight in their focsle hammocks have really got their heads down; even the rats and weevils are flat out. Aft, in the First Class, everyone is lapping it up except Captain Yardley, who pores over a chart in his great cabin, scratching grizzled pate and muttering

'Belike an' bedamned' as he plots his u-turn round the bottom of Africa. Vanity, beautifully made up even in slumber, sighs gently as the distant tinkle of eight bells is faintly heard. Of course she doesn't snore! It was Rooke all the time, sprawled in his cot across the passage, his stentorian rumblings bulging the ship's timbers and causing his dentures to rattle in their glass. Avery, in his cabin, is kipping away like an advertisement for Dunlopillo, eyes gently closed, hair neatly arranged, mouth perfectly shut and breathing through his nose. A smile plays about his mobile lips: he is dreaming of Vanity darning his socks in a rose-bowered summer-house, you'll be glad to know. Over the way Blood grunts and mutters in his sleep, one hand on the hilt of a dagger 'neath's pillow—if you've a conscience like his you keep your hardware handy. And deep in the foetid orlop Sheba writhes restlessly on her straw, her fetters clanking dismally.

Everybody bedded down, right? All serene? You know better.

As the last bell sounded, ending the middle watch, a stalwart figure in neatly-pressed white calico took over the wheel, and a massive untidy heap crouched by the side-rail clawing his red hair out of his eyes the better to scan the distant sea. Seeing nothing, he started striking matches, instinctively setting his beard on fire and having to put his head in a bucket of water to douse the blaze. But the brief conflagration had served its purpose; far off in the sea-mist a pale light blinked, and as he coughed and spluttered and threw away clumps of burned hair, Firebeard was able to cackle triumphantly:

" 'Ere they be, Calico! Good dogs! Brave boys! They'm dead on time, wi' a curse, say I, an' that! Unless," he added doubtfully, "it's some bloody fool as we don't know on, playin' about wi' lights unauthorised an' wanton! Eh?" Rage suffused his unwashed features. "I'll tear him, I'll kill him, I'll cast anchor in him!" he was starting to rave, until a curt word from Rackham sent him lumbering below, where he blundered about among the hammocks whispering: "We have lift-off! Rise an' shine! Rogues on deck, honest men stay where ye are! Get your cold feet on the warm floor! Up and at 'em!"

In a trice his accomplices among the crew had piled out, pulling on their socks, hunting for their combs and toothbrushes, adjusting their eye-patches, and scampering silently up the companion, while the honest sailors turned over drowsily muttering: "Shut that bloody door! Is that you up again, Agnes?" and the like, before resuming their unsuspecting slumbers. Up on deck the little knot of rascals received Rackham's urgent whispered orders, and scuttled away to seize the arms chest and guard the hatchways, the tardier spirits among them goofing off and tying knots in the rigging to make it look as though they were working. Firebeard blundered up last, to report "All villains roused an ready, by the powers, d'ye see, Calico camarado, aarrgh like!" and Rackham despatched him to the masthead to deal with the look-out. Firebeard panted busily upwards, taking several wrong turnings along yardarms and getting his leg stuck through futtock-shrouds, lubbers'-holes, and possibly even clew-lines, before he arrived at the crow's-nest to hear from within fevered mutters of "Pot? Tea? Gin? It's another flaming misprint, that's what is is!" Firebeard sandbagged the look-out smartly, snarling "Take that, ye bleedin' intellectual!" and hastened down again to join Calico Jack who, grimly smiling, was at the rail watching Black Bilbo keep their rendezvous.

Out of the mist they came just as the first glimmer of sun topped the eastern horizon—three fell shapes o' doom and dread, surging in on the hapless merchantman. First, the rakish corsair galley of Akbar the Damned, its great steel beak aglitter, the green banner of Islam aloft, its oars thrashing the water as the drivers flogged the naked slave-rowers and rounded up those who had nipped aft for a quiet smoke. Its deck crammed with swarthy, bearded rovers of Algiers and Tripoli, flashing their teeth, brandishing their scimitars and getting their spiked helmets caught in the rigging, the galley was a fearsome sight to Christian eyes, and hardly less disturbing to Buddhists or even atheists. And naught more fearsome than the dark, hawk-faced, hairy-chested figure of Akbar himself, lounging on his stern-castle in gold lamé pyjama trousers, his forked beard a-quiver as he munched rahat lakoum proffered by nubile dancing-girls, his fierce eyes glinting wildly as he practised cutting their gauzy veils in two with his razor-edged Damascus blade.

Secondly came that gaily-decked galleon of evil repute, the *Grenouille Frénétique*, or *Frantic Frog*, flagship of Happy Dan Pew, French filibuster, gallant, bon vivant and gourmet, who was given to dancing rigadoons and other foreign capers as his vessel sailed into action. Clouds of aftershave wafted about his ship, whose velvet sails were fringed with silk tassels in frightful taste, its crew of Continental sea-scum lining the rails crying "Remember Dien Bien Phu!" and "Vive le weekend!" as their graceful craft seemed to can-can over the billows with élan and espièglerie.

[In fact, Happy Dan Pew wasn't French at all. His real name was Trevor O'Grady from St Helens, but he had been hit on the head by a board-duster while reading a pirate story during a French lesson, and his mind had become unhinged. From that moment he suffered from the delusion that he was a Breton buccaneer, but since he spoke no French beyond Collins' Primer, his crew had a confusing time of it.]

Third and last came Black Bilbo's ghastly sable barque, the *Laughing Sandbag*—he was last on account o' he bein' barnacled, d'ye see? Or, in the rather coarse expression of the time, his bottom was foul. Consequently Bilbo was in a rare passion, stalking the poop, inhaling snuff and pistolling mutineers with murderous abandon. He couldn't bear being second to Happy Dan, who had pipped him for Best-dressed Cut-throat o' the Year.

As his fellow-rascals brought their ships in against the ill-fated *Twelve Apostles*, Calico Jack snapped to his small band of villains, "Down and take, 'em, bullies!" and with glad cries of 'Geronimo!' 'Carnival!' and 'After you!' they raced below to overpower anyone who happened to be around—crewmen who were still in the focsle ringing for their coffee, or had gone to the bathroom, or were doing their early morning press-ups. Having disposed of these, the pirates stormed howling to the stern of the ship, recklessly disregarding the 'First Class Passengers Only' notices, and bursting into the cabins without knocking. Thus:

Captain Yardley stared at his chart, in which a thrown knife was quivering beside his pencil point; ere he could so much as cry out a despairing "Belike!" pirates were jumping all over him, binding and gagging him, untying his shoe-laces, giving him a hot-foot, and playing with his set-square and compasses. His discomfiture was complete.

Admiral Rooke awoke to find an apple being stuck in his open mouth, and Firebeard's shaggy countenance leering down at him yelling: "Breakfast in bed, milord, har-har? Nay, then 'ee'll make a rare boar's head, wi' a curse! Haul him aloft, give him the message, do him the dirty, wi' a wannion, by the powers, har-har!" And as the unfortunate Admiral was secured, gasping and choking, Firebeard began to break up the furniture.

What of our two bright boys? Blood, seasoned in alarms, was rolling out of bed, sword in hand, even as the first pirates came ramping in yelling: "Surprise, surprise!" He blinded one with hair-powder, kicked a second in the stomach, crossed swords with a third, and then, having weighed up the odds, dropped his weapon and raised his hands, automatically reciting: "I'll-come-quietly-officer-but-devil-a-cheep-ye'll-get-out-o'-me-till-I've-talked-to-a-lawyer." Thus tamely did the rascal chuck up the sponge.

Not so across the passage, where a flashing-eyed Avery was holding crowds of desperadoes at bay with his whirling blade, jumping on tables, swinging from chandeliers, throwing chairs at their shins, knocking over candlesticks, and swathing his attackers in torn-down curtains. It couldn't last, of course; it never does. They bore him down, cursing foully (them, not him, he never cursed), and he struggled vainly in their brutal grasp, his hair becomingly rumpled, his shirt slightly torn, and the teeniest trickle of blood on his determined chin. But his eyes gleamed undaunted; by Jove, they'd better watch him.

Down i' the foetid orlop an exultant Sheba was being unchained by the little Welsh pirate, who had also brought her a fresh wardrobe so that she can be properly attired for the big confrontation scene on deck, which comes in a minute. She hurled aside her loathed fetters, gnashing with delight, and the little Welshman modestly looked away as she donned her scarlet silk breeches and shirt, buckled her diamanté rapier at her hip, drew on her long Gucci boots, exclaimed at the state of her coiffure, clapped on her plumed picture hat, dabbed a touch of Arpège behind her ear, and then spent ten minutes selecting one long earring and applying her lipstick. Finally, with a curt "Tidy up!" to the little Taffy, she strode lithely up the companion, pausing briefly at the full-length mirror in the gun-crews' recreation room, to adjust her hat fractionally and turn her voluptuous shape this way and that, wondering if she had lost weight during her captivity. A pound? Pound and a half? Mmh, maybe not … still …

She was brooding about this when she stepped into the cabin passage, to meet a bawling Firebeard, who had bagged Rooke's coat and wig, thrown on any old how, and was kicking in doors just for laughs. He swung her up in his hairy arms, yelling:

"She's all ours! Ho-Ho! We'm masters o' the ship, look'ee, and Bilbo an' t'others be layin' alongside, shiver me timbers! Har-har! Tear 'em up, bully boys! Sick 'em, pups!"

"Put me down, you walking tank of pigswill," hissed Sheba, "and if you've got spots on my new outfit I'll carbonado you! And get that drunken rabble on deck!" She pointed imperiously at Firebeard's mob who were looting and rampaging and writing graffiti on the walls and knocking the tops off bottles. They cowered before her flashing eyes, knuckling their foreheads and belching guiltily, and Sheba scorched them with a look before pirouetting neatly to the last unopened cabin door. She flung it wide, and—

Lady Vanity sat bolt upright in bed in a froth of lace, gold ringlets, and confusion, blue eyes wide, ruby lips parted, eye-lashes fluttering like net curtains in a high wind. She was distraught, astonished, and envious all in one at the brilliant spectacle of Sheba swaggering in, a hateful smile on her proud lips, one fist poised on a shapely hip as she gloatingly pondered the petrified English rose. What an absolutely stunning colour combination, thought Vanity—lipstick not *quite* the right shade, though, but what else could one expect? … and then she saw the monstrous Firebeard rolling and goggling in the doorway, and squealed with indignation.

"How dare you come in here without permission? Leave at once, you inferior persons! Underlings! Peasants! Savages!"

"Savage! That's me!" howled Firebeard gleefully, drumming his chest with his fists. "I'll show ye savage, me little honey-flower! Har-har!" And he rushed lustfully towards Vanity, great mottled hands outstretched, but Sheba, whose hips were not just for decoration, body-checked him elegantly as he galloped past, and he went flying in a tangle of shattered furniture and lay there roaring. Sheba stalked past him to a table where fruit and sweetmeats o' Peru were temptingly piled, and crammed handfuls into her mouth, for prison rations had left her with that between-meals feeling, and she wanted to restore that pound-and-a-half without delay. Vanity shrieked with outrage.

"Put that down this instant! Oh! How dare you, you insolent black wench! Those are my personal goodies! Put them—"

And she scrambled out of bed indignantly, only to be met by a well-aimed squashy fruit, and staggered back, tripping and falling into the embrace of Firebeard, who crowed with unholy joy, pinning her arms and pawing and nuzzling lasciviously. "Wriggle away, me plump little dove!" he chortled. "Split me, but ye'll coo soft enough presently!" And it might easily have been X-certificate stuff then and there (always assuming that Firebeard, not overbright at best and in a confused state after his fall, had been able to remember what to do next), had not Black Sheba, gulping a final avocado and wiping the juice on Vanity's costly coverlet, kicked him sharply in the groin.

"Drop it, thou whoreson randy old badger! She's not for thee—yet. Take her on deck!" And she turned her attention to Vanity's dressing-table knick-knacks while Firebeard, muttering "Coo-o-o!" and holding himself painfully, hauled his struggling captive to her feet as she beat dainty fists on his matted chest.

"Let me go! Ah, unhand me thy vile clutches, reeking knave! Oh, the indignity! That this should happen to me, Deb of the Year and daughter of an Admiral! Eek! My jewels—put them down, thief!"

This last was addressed to Sheba, who was proddling with her rapier in Vanity's jewel-box, sneering at the merchandise but privately thinking that these Society bitches did all right on Daddy's allowance. With one vicious sweep of her blade she sent box and all in a glittering cascade across the room, and stalking menacingly over to Vanity, thrust her dusky face to within an inch of that pale peach-blossom complexion.

"*Your* jewels, sister? Pah!" Sheba's voice was like oiled gravel. "You have no jewels, tender little lady—no perfumes o' price, no fine garments, no dainty kickshaws and furbelows—none!" Her sword swept Vanity's scent-flasks away in splinters, and slashed great rents in those hanging dresses which Sheba had decided were too short in the sleeve anyway. "And soon," the sepia nemesis chuckled evilly, "shalt have no body, neither ... and no soul! I see you use Helena Rubinstein's pasteurised special," she added, "but I'll find a home for that, since you won't be needing it. Take her away!"

For the first time Vanity's intrepid spirit quailed. "Not the Helena Rubinstein!" she quavered. "You can't get it these days ... ah, of your pity, dark and sinister woman, not that! The line's been discontinued ..."

"Don't I know it?" growled Sheba, scooping up the precious pots. "Haven't I scoured every boutique in Tortuga? Away with her, Firebeard!"

As Vanity, wailing piteously, was dragged out, and Sheba was sizing up a suede number by Balmain which might just do if it was let down a smidgin, the other passengers were likewise being rudely hustled aloft. Blood, an old hand at being apprehended and frog-marched, was murmuring: "Right, all right, fellows, I know the way," as they thrust him up the companion; Avery, tight-lipped and pinioned, came face to face with Rooke, who was still in his night-shirt, leering pirates grasping his elbows. The Admiral was in fine voice, though, damning them for pirate scum and promising to see them quartered and sun-dried; he cheesed it momentarily to inquire of Avery in a hoarse whisper: "Is *it* safe?", and Avery, inwardly cursing this indiscretion, nodded imperceptibly. Not imperceptibly enough, however, for a silky voice cut menacingly in:

"Is *what* safe?"

And there, on the ladder just above them, was the fearsome figure of Black Bilbo, who had come aboard and made straight for the quality's cabins in the hope of finding some Sea Island steenkirks or spray-on talc. He lounged wolfishly, hand on hilt, taking snuff delicately from the case proffered by Goliath the dwarf.

"Now, gentles," quo' he softly, his dark eyes gliding from one to t'other, "what precious item, what thing o' price, is this—that is 'safe', ha?" They remaining silent, Bilbo nodded, making play with a soiled lace kerchief from which, to his annoyance, he realised he had forgotten to remove the laundry tag. "So, so," he hissed, clipping Goliath over the ear for luck, "we shall discover anon. Keep me this bellowing bullock below—" he kicked Rooke savagely "—and hale the fighting cock on deck."

The scene which met Avery's eyes may be old stuff to you if you saw 'The Black Swan', but it was new to him—a helpless merchantman in the talons of the hawks of the sea. Chaps in hairy drawers and coloured hankies staggering about, draped in loot, letting off pistols, getting beastly drunk, singing 'Blow the man down', throwing bottles around, and manhandling hapless prisoners. Firebeard had thrust Vanity sprawling on the deck in her scanty night-rail, to the accompaniment of wolf-whistles and cries of "Hubba-hubba!"; she scrambled up, trying to look haughty, which isn't easy when there's nothing between you and the goggle-eyed rabble except a wisp of brushed nylon and a few ribbons. "Shake it, blondie!" they chorused, and Avery clenched his teeth in fury.

Looking down from the quarter-deck was the stalwart figure of Calico Jack, the barbaric splendour of Akbar, and the slender finery of Happy Dan, who viewed the scene through his quizzing-glasses and exclaimed Froggishly.

"What is what is this what? I am aboard. I look about myself. Zut alors donc! What a doll, that! What talent! Ah, ma chérie, mon coeur est toujours à toi! How about it, hein?" He minced and bowed and fluttered his fingers at Vanity, while Akbar's eyes glowed with strange fires, and Rackham threw up a hand to silence the motley mob swarming beneath—bearded white faces, coal-black Nubians, slant-eyed Chinese devils, swarthy Asiatics, squat and evil Malays—the usual lot on pirate ships in those days. Now among them glided Black Sheba, her glance dwelling darkly on the bound figure of Avery ere she took her place, lounging on a convenient capstan.

"Camarados, brothers!" cried Rackham. "We ha' ta'en this fine ship, and released our dear comrade and fellow-skipper Sheba from durance shameful and doom o' hellish slavery! (Cries of 'Hear, hear!', applause, breaking of bottles and an attempt by the little Welsh pirate to lead a chorus of 'We'll keep a welcome in the valleys'.) And we ha' ta'en also captives o' rank and quality—a Lord Admiral, no less—" Yells of hatred and blowing of raspberries, with Firebeard bawling: "Hang him up! Rip his guts out! He's an honest man—I hate him!" He rolled on the deck in a frenzy of rage, and the pirates cheered amain. Bilbo sauntered forward, sporting his shabby finery, his tight boots squeaking painfully.

"All in good time, lambkin," quotha. "But, by y'r leave, Brother Rackham, I ha' matter to impart to the company. (Cries of 'Order, order!' 'Chair, chair!'.) I learn that there is some precious 'thing' aboard this vessel, and that this—" he flicked a tiny poniard from his sleeve so that it quivered in the mast by Avery's ear; a shocking show-off, Bilbo was "—fortunate fellow is privy to its whereabouts. Shall we inquire, ha?"

"Aye, aye!" roared the pirates. "Go on, ask him; it can't do any harm."

"Well, bully?" said Bilbo silkily. "What is't, and where, eh? Discourse, friend, and discover. Don't be shy."

This was the chance that Avery had been waiting for. Jumping on tables, pinking adversaries, was all right in its way, but this is the kind of moment he is in the book for, really. His handsome head came up, his contemptuous glance swept from sinister Bilbo to frowning Rackham to swarthy Akbar to epicene Happy Dan, to the ring of hideous snarling ruffians, dwelt softly for an instant on Vanity, beauteously pale, got contemptuous again, and finally settled back on Bilbo with unfaltering disdain. Avery's lip curled, and his perfectly-modulated voice might have been addressing a careless servant as he spoke with the calm good-breeding of his kind.

"Up yours," he said crisply. He had no idea what it meant, but he had heard it hurled at the Moors by an officer refusing to surrender one of the Tangier bastions, and had rather liked the sound of it. Brief, punchy, and definite.

The pirates went bananas at his defiance. They howled round him, hurling vile threats and making lurid suggestions for his interrogation. A heated debate broke out, the nub being to decide which torture would best satisfy the twin requirements of getting the information and providing an interesting spectacle. Happy Dan Pew's proposal was finally carried, and a bucket of offal was hurled over the side to attract sharks, while Avery was lowered by one leg from the ship's rail until his head was just above the water racing past the ship's side.

This is a rotten position to be in, and it taxed even Avery's powers to keep up a dignified appearance. He preserved a poker-faced nonchalance, of course, but this was wasted since no one could see it. The spray lashed through his hair, the salt water stung his eyes, and the rope round his ankle burned like fire; up on deck Vanity was swooning on the planks, and the callous villains holding the rope were saying grace. A yell of delight greeted the sight of two hideous dorsal fins cutting the water towards the ship's side, at which point they lowered Avery so that his head and shoulders were immersed.

Our hero was now perturbed. Not on his own account—this, he told himself, as his keen eyes pierced the green murk and detected the great dark shapes homing in on him, was what he was paid three shillings a day for—nay, his concern was all for the fair and graceful figure which he had seen collapsing becomingly when they gave him the old heave-ho. What should become of her, when the sharks had retired burping gently to look for the sweet trolley, and all that remained of him was a sock and a buckled shoe? He must get out of this somehow, for her sake … and Captain Avery's eyes narrowed underwater, his lips parted in that grim fighting smile as he observed the horrible monsters rolling neatly to get under him and come zooming up, their enormous jaws parting to reveal serried rows of glittering fangs. That gave him an idea—he would bite the brutes; it was the last thing they would expect …

But even as he prepared to meet them, tooth to tooth, he felt himself suddenly whirled upwards, into the fresh air, just as the first shark leaped and snapped its great jaws close enough to clip his hair. He banged painfully against the ship's side, and then he was hauled brutally over the rail and dropped on the deck, opening his eyes to find a pair of Gucci boots bestriding him, and hear Black Sheba's voice scorching the pirates who yet clamoured for his blood.

"Unthinking dolts! He'll never talk! I know his kind!" And she flashed him a glance in which he seemed to read yearning admiration behind the feral glare of the amber eyes. "But he'll sing like a canary if you threaten his friends!" she added spitefully, and Avery groaned inwardly as the ruffians roared approval and seized on the swooning Vanity with cries of "Now you'm talking! Heave the doxy over! Har-har, here be plumptious titbit for the sharks, wi' a curse, an' that!"

"Belay that!" snapped Sheba, and drawled cruelly: "We'll find a better use for her mealy milksopishness, damn her! No … that one!" And she flung out a hand towards Colonel Blood.

You may have wondered what the Colonel was doing during all this excitement. Looking inconspicuous, that's what, and wondering how he could pass himself off as one of the pirate gang. Even now he tried to look puzzled, glancing over his shoulder to see whom Sheba meant, but it was no go. They whipped the rope round his ankle, bundled him protesting on to the rail, and were about to launch him when he found his breath and wits together.

"What's the hurry, now?" he wondered. "Let's talk it over, boys ... don't do something ye'll regret."

Firebeard, gripping the Colonel's shoulders, hesitated, growling and rolling his eyes. "What was it you were asking, now?" inquired the Colonel, and Avery, in sudden alarm, cried from the deck: "No! Blood, you cannot! You must not!"

"Och, be reasonable," said the Colonel, slightly exasperated. "D'ye expect me to be a fish's dinner for the sake of your bloody crown?"

Since the answer to that was 'Yes', but it isn't the sort of thing that any self-respecting hero can say, Avery was silent, but the glare he shot at Blood would have curdled minestrone. His first instinct had been right—why, the blighter *was* a blighter, after all; when any decent chap would have been spitting in their eyes with a dauntless smile, he was actually perspiring shiftily and demanding:

"If I tell ye, will ye spare our lives?"

The pirates growled, disappointed of their sport. There were cries of "Yes!" "No!" and "Toss for it, best out of three!", and then Rackham came shouldering through the press to confront the desperate Colonel.

"Speak," said he bluntly, "and the sharks can go hungry."

It wasn't total reassurance, exactly, but when you're perched on a ship's rail with Firebeard giving you the benefit of his halitosis and the jumbo-sized piranhas waiting underneath, it's worth stretching a point. "Under the bunk in his cabin," gasped Blood, nodding at Avery, and as the Captain's furious gaze took on a disgust so icy that it almost froze the sea-water in his hair, Blood added philosophically: "Ye see, Captain, where I come from there are no heroes' graves—just holes in the ground for fools."

You may imagine the indignant rage that boiled through Avery's manly thorax at this caddish cynicism, but it was nothing to the shame and anguish he felt when the Madagascar crown was exposed in all its brilliant effulgence on the deck, and the pirates, after a moment's stunned silence, stood around exclaiming "Hot tamales!" and "Jackpot!" and "You won't pick up one o' those at Woolies!" while their leaders regarded the unbelievable glittering prize with racing thoughts. For each realised that this was the Big Time, with a vengeance—to Akbar, grinding his molars and tugging his forked beard, it was the bankroll that should buy him his way to supremacy in Barbary, perhaps even to the throne of the Sublime Porte itself; to Bilbo, as he clenched his soiled kerchief in nervous fingers, it was that estate in Bucks, a seat in the Lords, and—oh, rapture!—membership of the Army and Navy Club; to Rackham, slightly pale under his tan, it was a fortune invested in Building Societies with enough over to start a modest pub; to Happy Dan Pew it was a villa at Antibes, his own permanent private suite at the Negresco, and a custom-built coach with tortoiseshell panels rolling him along the Croisette while starlets from the Comédie Française vied for his attention; to Black Sheba it was her own private desert island plantation where all the enemies and oppressors of her past should labour in misery and torment while she lived it up in Balenciaga creations (this was her fondest dream, and with a start she realised that it now included Captain Avery, in powdered wig and buckled shoes, taking her in to dinner and exchanging glances of adoration with her from the other end of their sumptuous table). To Firebeard, the sixth of those desperate commanders, it conjured up visions of unlimited booze, wrecked taverns, senseless constables, and shattered fruit machines—and the wherewithal to impress that snooty barmaid at the Bucket of Blood in Tortuga, the blonde one with the big knockers.

And then the fight started. With one accord the pirates flung themselves on the marvellous trophy, clawing and biting to be at it, and if Rackham had not kept his head and hurled them back with boot and fist, aided by Bilbo's flashing rapier and Firebeard's enormous strength, things might have degenerated into anarchy. Back the captains drove them, a snarling, loot-crazed mob, and Rackham set the great gleaming crown on the capstan and demanded of the captives what it might be.

Avery, of course, preserved a glacial silence, but Blood, at one growl from Firebeard, sang like a bird.

" 'Tis the crown for the new king of Madagascar. He was to deliver it—" this with a nod to Avery "—and if ye've any sense you'll offer it for a ransom to the British Government rather than try to flog it on the open market. I'd be willing to act as go-between myself, for a consideration," he went on smoothly. "After all, I've got contacts and that sort o' thing—"

But the pirate mob would have none of this. "Shares! Shares!" they roared. "Fair does among mates! Divvy out, we're all on the coupon!" and Rackham raised his hands to still the clamour.

"Brothers, hear me! We share, according to articles, but 'tis plain we cannot divide this great treasure among all at once. Now, there are six captains here, and six great crosses on this crown—so let each captain take one and be responsible for selling it and sharing among his followers. Agreed?"

The pirates whooped approval, and Avery watched in horror, writhing helpless in his bonds, as his precious charge was laid on the deck and a huge Chinese, wielding a massive axe, chopped it with six mighty strokes into as many glittering pieces, while the gleeful buccaneers chanted:

"One! Two! Three! ..." at each blow. Then, as Firebeard turned his back, the Chinese held up each cross in turn, and according to age-old custom Rackham cried out: "Who shall have this?" and Firebeard named the captains in any order that occurred to him, beginning with Sheba and ending with himself. So each captain received a cross, and their crews crowded round, wolf-eyed, to handle the pretty baubles and gloat on the prospect of their own shares.

Avery watched the scene appalled; it occurred to him that the recapture and eventual safe delivery of the crown—which had never been far from his active mind—was now going to be rather complicated. However, he would come to that; in the meantime, could he gnaw through his bonds, or cut them on a bit of the broken bottles which the pirates were strewing carelessly all over the place, seize the half-fainting Vanity in one arm and a sword in the other, fight his way aft, release the captured loyal seamen, and turn the tables on the villains? It seemed the obvious course—yes, and then they could hang the treacherous Blood, and no doubt a dab of Airfix would put the crown to rights, and Admiral Rooke would probably recommend him for a decoration, and Vanity would be wide-eyed and weak-kneed with gratitude, and the whole affair wouldn't do his promotion chances any damage, either. Yes, he was thinking along the right lines—but before he could put his plan into operation the pirates, having gloated their fill and finished off all the drink, forestalled him by remembering that there were prisoners to play with. With cries of "Let's sort out the helpless captives!" "Aye, aye, let's fall to merry torturin' an' that!" and "Who's for a gang-bang wi' the Admiral's daughter?" they advanced on the hapless trio.

Naturally, they concentrated on Vanity, who shrank back in terror from the bearded leering faces and lecherous paws while Avery struggled like a madman in his bonds, but before their sweaty hands could tear away her shortie nightdress and confront the censor with all sorts of problems, Black Sheba had slipped lissomely between, one hand outflung to restrain them, the other on her rapier hilt.

"Hold!" cried she, and before the command in those fiery amber eyes, the hardened ruffians paused. As Goliath the dwarf, with a chortle of "Bags I first!", made a grab at Vanity's thigh, Sheba kicked his wooden leg from under him and sent him sprawling on the deck. "Calico, I claim disposal o' this woman!"

At this there was hubbub and amaze, in which you may well be sharing. What is this? Has womanly pity touched the agate heart of the ruthless corsair queen? Is she moved by finer feelings to shield Vanity from shame and ravishment? Perchance has some memory from her own dark past—as when she was the star attraction of 'Strip, Strip, Hooray!' at the Port-o'-Spain Rotary stag night, and the patrons rushed the stage at the torrid climax of her bubble dance before she could escape to the wings—stirred her compassion for the defenceless English maid? Don't you believe it. Baser motives far were at work in Sheba's evil heart. She had remarked the distraught looks of anguish and concern that Avery had been shooting in Vanity's direction, and had thought: aha, so he's got the hots for Miss Cheltenham of 1670, has he? Right, we'll fix her wagon. And reasoning that the satisfaction of seeing her rival ravished by the crews of three pirate ships would be better foregone in the interests of getting the insipid pullet out of the way permanently, thus leaving Sheba a clear field with Avery, the sepia Medusa had hatched a diabolic plan.

She fronted the frustrated pirates imperiously, while the tremulous Vanity clutched her flimsy nylon about her and wished she'd gone in for sensible long flannelette.

"Back, blind besotted curs!" snarled Sheba. "You can't all have her—why, 'tis pampered, puling ninny would die o' the vapours wi' the first of you! But—" and her eyes narrowed in a cruel smile "—all can share in the price if we sell her!" She jerked Vanity brutally to her feet and held her in a steely grasp while she stroked a dark finger across the girl's soft cheek. "Think what the rich rajahs and fat degenerates will pay for such a plump white pigeon in the slave-marts of Basra or Goa! You know how they go for Bluebell Girls—she'll fetch enough to buy each of you a real wench, not some flabby reserve for the Upper Fifth tennis team. Let Akbar take her and sell her on behalf of us all!"

Prolonged applause greeted this monstrous proposal, and Sheba turned with a triumphant sneer to run mocking fingers through the ringlets of the horror-stricken prisoner.

"Try that on your clavichord, duchess!" she hissed spitefully. "Golden Vanity—pah! We'll see how you enjoy your slavery!"

If aught had been required to cement Avery's adoration for the Admiral's beauteous daughter (and frankly, not much was), it would have been her response to Sheba's gloating taunt. Her face pale but proud, her bosom heaving with hauteur in a manner which caused some of the pirates to wonder whether selling her was such a bright idea after all, Lady Vanity countered with a swift one-two. "Among slaves I shall still be a lady," she cried proudly. "Among ladies you will always be a slave!" Even the callous ruffians could not forbear to chant their approval of her dauntless spirit. "One in a row, boo-boom!" they cried, while Sheba sprang clawing to avenge the insult. But Akbar, with a hellish laugh, had already swung Vanity's struggling form up on his shoulder, and bore her swiftly to his galley while Avery went ape, alternately cursing his captors and demanding that they sell him in Vanity's place. They pointed out, reasonably enough, that he was down-market stuff by comparison.

"An' anyways, we got a better use for you, cully, an' ye may lay to that!" bawled Firebeard. "What say we keelhaul him, mates? It's ages since we had a good keel-haulin'—"

But again Sheba barred the way. "Avast there, blubber-guts!" She paced slowly to Avery, thoughtfully plucking her nether lip 'twixt shapely fingers. "This King's captain is too good a man to lose—'tis lad o' rare mettle has earned the right to join us as a free companion, if he so chooses. That—or slow death," she added, with a look of smouldering ardour at Avery that would have melted treacle. At which the pirates nudged each other and stifled discreet coughs, glancing innocently at the mast-heads and whistling airily. Happy Dan Pew sniggered and grimaced froggishly.

"Great round basins behind the house of Monsieur and Madame Desgranges!" exclaimed he, all roguish-like. "One addresses to oneself the question: what companionship does La Belle Noire have in mind for our prisoner so stalwart and gallant, hein? Is it to make the promenade au bicyclette in search of cabbages, jewels, small pebbles, and stained-glass windows? Not on votre vie, if you ask me!" And he minced and chuckled lewdly, while Rackham frowned 'neath knitted brows and glanced from Sheba to Avery.

"Well, bully, what say ye? Wilt join us on th'account, ha?"

Avery was on the point of replying coldly that he would rather be shot from a cannon, but it occurred to him that there was no point in putting ideas into people's heads, so he maintained a contemptuous silence. Not so Blood, who clamoured to join, inquiring eagerly about pension rights, sickness benefits, and overtime. They shushed him impatiently, crowding round Avery with menace in their looks, while Sheba gnawed her lip in anxiety and tensed herself to spit the first man who laid a finger on him. It was one of those explosive moments when eyeball rolls at eyeball and wills clash in ponderous confrontation and no one has much idea what the hell is going to happen next because they've forgotten what the question was in the first place. Rackham, that canny leader of men, read the situation in one shrewd glance, and moved to defuse it.

"Right," quo' he, "break it up. We'll give him a few hours to think it over. Not fair to rush the chap. Put 'em both in irons—and then let's get sail on this rust-bucket afore she grows barnacles! About it, ye dogs! Firebeard, man the larboard scuppers! Bilbo, have thy villains lay aft the focsle! Sheba, your mascara's running! Happy Dan, write out the verb être six times before lunch, and the rest of you for heaven's sake join in the chorus!"

These sailorly words acted on the fractious pirates like magic. In a trice they had hustled Avery and Blood below decks, swept up the broken glass, clewed up everything in sight, and repaired to the Merino Lounge for before-lunch cocktails while they discussed the exciting events of the day so far. Only Black Sheba brooded sombrely on her high stool at the bar, and many there were who remarked how she was moodily squeezing that pink pimento stuff out of her martini olives, and wondered what this might portend.